Women
in the New
Taiwan

Taiwan's rapid socioeconomic and political transformation has given rise to a gender-conscious middle class that is attempting to redefine the roles of women in society, to restructure relationship patterns, and to organize in groups outside the family unit. This volume focuses on the changing roles of women and men in the "Taiwan Miracle." It considers the internal psychological processes and external societal processes as the feminist movement in Taiwan expands and new gender roles are explored. The issues facing Taiwan's women's movement are placed in social, political, and economic contexts. The book examines gender relations, the role of women in Chinese society over time, the contemporary roles that women play in Taiwan's work force today, and how the sexes perceive each other in the workplace. The role of women in the island's industrial, commercial, and agricultural sectors is also discussed. Feminism and gender relations are viewed from the context of film and literature, while different facets of feminism and the women's movements in Taiwan and mainland China are compared. The chapter authors represent a cross section of different disciplines—history, anthropology, and sociology—and different generations of China/Taiwan scholars.

TAIWAN IN THE MODERN WORLD
Series Editor
Murray A. Rubinstein

Women in the New Taiwan

Gender Roles and Gender Consciousness in a Changing Society

Catherine Farris
Anru Lee
Murray Rubinstein
Editors

AN EAST GATE BOOK

M.E.Sharpe
Armonk, New York
London, England

An East Gate Book

Copyright © 2004 by M.E. Sharpe, Inc.

Library of Congress Cataloging-in-Publication Data

Women in the new Taiwan : gender roles and gender consciousness in a changing society /
edited by Catherine Farris, Anru Lee, Murray Rubinstein.
  p. cm. — (Taiwan in the modern world)
"An east gate book."
Includes bibliographical references and index.
ISBN 0-7656-0814-6 (alk. paper)
  1. Women—Taiwan—Social conditions. 2. Women—Taiwan—Economic conditions.
3. Sex role—Taiwan. 4. Sex role in the work environment—Taiwan. 5. Man-woman
relationships—Taiwan. 6. Middle class women—Taiwan—Attitudes. 7. Taiwan—Social
conditions. 8. Taiwan—Politics and government. 9. Feminism—Taiwan. I. Farris,
Catherine S.P. II. Lee, Anru. III. Rubinstein, Murray A., 1942– IV. Series.

HQ1777.W66 2003
305.42′095124′9—dc21

2003042444

MV (c) 10   9   8   7   6   5   4   3   2   1

Contents

Introduction

Catherine S.P. Farris, Anru Lee, and
Murray A. Rubinstein

Taiwan's women and men stand poised between past and future. Both sexes are heir to China's long and complex patterns of gender definitions and relationships. They are also heirs to the unique course of development that Taiwan has been forced to take in the past fifty years. Even as the Chinese mainland was being reshaped by revolutionary Marxists who were always trumpeting the message of gender equality, Taiwan, ruled since 1945 by the corporatist Nationalist Party (Kuomintang or KMT), was also transforming itself. Taiwan became, to the shock of many conservative hard-liners within the KMT, a democratizing state whose professional middle class pushed for a new consciousness of gender equality. Taiwan is a place where one can observe the transformation of attitudes and behaviors in an environment of rapid socioeconomic and political change. This book focuses on one aspect of that transformation: the place of women in the "Taiwan Miracle." This focuses on women's lives, their definitions of their roles, and their attempts to restructure the patterns of relationships with men and to organize themselves. Men's perspectives on the evolving gender relations are also examined in several essays.

Objectives and Contexts

Taiwan began to transform itself after the painful years of the early Retrocession—the restoration of Chinese rule. In 1949, the KMT retreated to Taiwan and then began to redesign the island in its own image. With a U.S. military protecting Taiwan and with U.S. aid rebuilding and backing up the state's military defense system, the KMT government then felt secure enough to push an ambitious domestic restructuring plan. First, under the then less-than-kind hand of Chiang Ching-kuo, the extremist elements within the KMT itself were purged. An ambitious and effective system of land reform was introduced and carried through successfully—something the government of the Republic of China (ROC) had not been able to do on the mainland during the Nanking Decade (1927–37). Next, a program of import substitution was introduced and a new industrial infrastructure was put in place. Finally, the Western-style, Japanese-introduced, educational system was expanded and refined, with Mandarin Chinese replacing Japanese as the medium of instruction. The education system then began to produce tens of thousands of well-educated—and Mandarinized—young men and women. By the early 1960s, as a result of these efforts, a new Taiwan, with a more Chinese than Japanese character, began to emerge. This Taiwan produced a new and more aggressive middle class, one now less willing than were previous generations to be cowed and controlled by the Nationalist Garrison Command and related security forces. It became, to the surprise of many, a democratizing state, some of whose professional middle class pushed for, among other things, a new consciousness of gender equality. Thus, Taiwan became a place where one could observe the transformation of human behavior in an environment of rapid socioeconomic change. Some male members of the emergent middle class, with pressure from feminist leaders who were the vanguard of an expanding and visible feminist movement, began to exhibit a willingness to examine traditional views of women's status and roles, and to redefine the nature of relations between men and women.

The "first wave" of an indigenous women's movement in Taiwan begun under the Japanese occupation, according to Hsin-yi Lu (this volume). Following the second wave in the 1970s, led by Annette Lu Hsiu-lien (discussed below in Chapters 12 and 16, by Rubinstein and Farris, respectively), academic activity to study women's lives and to promote juridical and social gender equality began in the 1980s. The first academic center, the Women's Research Program, was created at the nation's premier university, National Taiwan University (NTU), in Taipei, and a conference on "The Role of Women in the National Development Process in Taiwan" was held in 1985, resulting in conference proceedings published in two volumes (Chiang 1985). Although the proceedings were in Chinese, abstracts were published in English. Nora Chiang and Yenlin Ku (1985) also published an English monograph summarizing the "Past and Current Status of Women in Taiwan." Since the path-breaking work of the NTU center to legitimate gender studies as an object of academic inquiry in Taiwan, other centers of study have been established, such as the Research Program on Gender and Society at National Tsing-hua University and the Center for Gender and Sexuality at National Cheng-kung University. In the wake of this rising tide of feminism, feminist publications became part of the larger elite and popular discourses. Scholarship in Taiwan about women and gender studies has flourished since the mid-1980s; however, little of this literature has found its way into Western publications. Thus, one of the objectives of this book is to introduce this literature to a Western, English-speaking audience.

This effort also reflects on the composition of the editors and contributors. Not only do the three editors (Catherine S.P. Farris, Anru Lee, and Murray A. Rubinstein) have highly different personal and academic backgrounds, but the scholars who have contributed articles to this volume also represent different sexes, countries of origin, disciplines, and generations of scholarship. This inclusiveness is highly important, as it brings different sets of gender and ethnic consciousness to the discussion. Different continents and countries are represented as well. Some of the authors are from Taiwan, and most of these individuals have studied in the United States and in other Western nations. Others are from the West—notably the United States and Canada—and they have studied and done fieldwork both on Taiwan and in the People's Republic of China (PRC). Finally, some of the authors are trained historians; others are anthropologists or sociologists. However, over the course of recent years, through active cooperation in various scholarly venues, the editors and contributors have come to occupy intellectually a large common ground and to recognize the existence of a shared consciousness. Together, they challenge older ways of perceiving the nature of gender issues and older approaches to the study of gender on Taiwan.

Structure of the Book

This volume is divided into four parts. Part I deals with questions of context and continuity. Part II covers issues of gender in the workplace, and questions of female-male interaction in both urban and rural, as well as industrial and agricultural, settings. In Part III, different facets of feminism on KMT-run Taiwan are studied. The book concludes with a long essay that compares feminism and the women's movement on Taiwan with feminism and the struggle for women's liberation found in the PRC.

Part I: Gender in Historical Perspective

This book is one of many new collaborative volumes that examine the role of women in Chinese societies over time. The best model so far of a collaborative volume is Christina Gilmartin et al., eds., *Engendering China: Women, Culture, and the State* (1994), which deals with women in China over an extended period and focuses attention on issues of history and society as seen from a different perspective from that of the male-authored and male-centered narratives that have been the norm in Western scholarship. This breakthrough volume made the larger audience of Sinologists aware of the new direction of women's history and women's studies in the universe of Chinese studies. Another important collaborative work that also deals with women is Ellen Widmer and Kang-I Sun Chang's *Writing Women in Late Imperial China* (1997). This thoughtful volume of important essays again adds to our understanding of women and their place in this vital sphere of Chinese cultural life. Both books have helped this book and, in particular, this section, written by Rubinstein, take shape.

We are fortunate to begin with an essay by one of the major figures in Ch'ing history and one of the masters of the emerging field of Chinese women's history, Susan Mann. Her recent works, most notably her important essay, "Learned Women in the Eighteenth Century," in *Engendering China* (1994) and her new study, *Precious Records: Women in China's Long Eighteenth Century* (1997), attempt to show the roles that women played as figures within an emerging cosmopolitan and literary, late Ch'ing, print-oriented society. In this monograph and the essay that preceded it, Mann continued to develop and expand on themes first worked through by Dorothy Ko in her own path-breaking monograph, *Teachers of the Inner Chambers* (1994).

Professor Mann has also explored issues of the new historiography on women. Her article in this volume as Chapter 1, "What Can Feminist Theory Do for the Study of Chinese History? A Brief Review of Scholarship in the United States," is a clear and powerful introduction to feminist theory and shows us how feminist theory has begun to be used to create the new subfield—the history of women as well as gender relations in China—as feminist theoreticians begin to produce a new, and more radical, gender-conscious historiography. That this process has already started can be demonstrated by examining the work of Francesca Bray (1997) on women's roles in the development of specific technologies and in Gail Hershatter's (1997) controversial and important examination of prostitution in Shanghai. Dr. Mann's article, reprinted in the present volume, was originally published in the journal *Chin-tai Chung-kuo fu-nü yen-chiu* (Research on Women in Modern Chinese History) by the Institute of Modern History of the Academia Sinica in Taipei. This publication, at a key moment in time—in the midst of the maturation stage of Taiwan's educational and sociopolitical revolution—became an agent of the larger process of change itself with its author's clarion call for a careful rereading of and a deliberate rethinking of Chinese history in ways that take into account the often unvoiced message of 50 percent of China's—and Taiwan's—population.

Chapter 2 is by the Brown University–trained social historian Ping-chen Hsiung. Dr. Hsiung is a member of the Institute of Modern History of the Academia Sinica, where she has pioneered feminist history and the history of the Chinese family, and, in particular, childhood in late imperial China. Her essay in this volume, "Sons and Mothers: Demographic Realities and the Chinese Culture of *Hsiao*," lays out the general social and historical context of this set of relationships. Using a variety of historical texts, the essay provides a set of examples of each of these stages of the mother-son relationship as it unfolds, linking these stages and patterns to the underlying concept of *hsiao*—filial piety—and provides some fascinating case studies. This richly textured article provides much necessary background that enables us to better understand the types of changes in family relationships and in the specific dyadic relationships between gender and members of the family that the authors in Parts II and III of this book lay out in their articles.

Chapter 3, Emma Teng's elegant "An Island of Women: The Discourse on Gender in Ch'ing Travel Accounts of Taiwan," takes us to the island that is the geographic center of our volume. Her article uses Ch'ing travel literature of the seventeenth and eighteenth centuries to examine issues of ethnicity and gender. She argues that Ch'ing travelers were fascinated and yet repulsed by aborigine societies and the gender-role reversal that permeated major tribal societies, and that they studied and wrote about these societies and their practices in detail. Ch'ing travelers wrote these articles and books to feed the existing appetite for such accounts of exotic society but also as a subtle means of critiquing the social mores and patterns of their own society. Using the work of Edward Said and other postmodernist scholars, Teng presents a fascinating account of the way the Ch'ing literati saw the alien other and made use of these images for the purpose of reinforcing their own power base and control of society and family.

Chapter 4 also serves as an example of the new women-centered history that is discussed by Susan Mann. Susan Gronewold's chapter, "From Shanghai to Taipei: Exile and Identity," focuses on an organization that Western women, working under the umbrella of the Western missionary enterprise and supported by Chinese business and city leaders, set up to help Chinese women in Shanghai. Many of these women were prostitutes, and others were from the new working class of factory employees. As such, Gronewold's research fits into a subcategory of Chinese women's history—the evolving literature on women in the municipal giant that is Shanghai. She has already contributed much to the new subfield and her new work complements that of Emily Honig (1986), who dealt with women factory workers, and the previously mentioned work by Gail Hershatter. Gronewold's essay shows how this organization, the Door of Hope Refuge, operated in Shanghai and how it was able to transfer its activities to Taiwan in the years after the Communist revolution. It deals with a Western group that attempted to help the women of China, first in the major mainland metropolis of Shanghai and then in the KMT's provisional capital of Taipei. It is an interesting example of a Western benevolent institution that had succeeded in its original location but then failed to find a place for itself in its new urban setting on Taiwan.

In Chapter 5, "Imagining 'New Women,' Imagining Modernity: Gender Rhetoric in Colonial Taiwan," Hsin-yi Lu examines the emergence of feminist thought during the period in which Japan held Taiwan. In this article, Lu examines the origins of Taiwanese feminism within a larger discussion of the way Taiwanese intellectuals during this fifty-year period (1895–1945) dealt with Taiwan's status as a colony. It argues that feminism arose, in part, out of the intellectuals' discussion of how to see women and to understand their even more complex status within Han-Taiwanese society during a period of foreign domination by a modernizing and expansionistic East Asian state. It is a rich and multileveled analysis of a set of interlocking issues that opens the door to the discussion of the modern forms of Taiwanese feminist thought covered by other authors in this volume.

Part II: Gender and Social Interaction in Contemporary Taiwan

Part II shifts to problems of gender and sexuality in contemporary settings. The articles in this section focus upon the roles that women play in the island's industrial, commercial, and agricultural sectors and how the sexes relate to and perceive each other in work-centered environments. The articles also examine questions of the formation of "maleness" and "femaleness" in Taiwanese society.

Social scientists normally compare the lives of successive generations that are twenty years apart. However, given the fact that the socioeconomic conditions in Taiwan have been changing with astounding rapidity, a new generation with a refreshed worldview and life expectation emerges every ten years (cf. Salaff 1995). By the mid-1990s, Taiwan had lost its status as a manufacturing powerhouse of light consumer commodities to its neighboring countries in the Pacific Rim. The economy had become much more diverse, and industries had been upgraded and become more capital intensive. Young women largely shunned factory employment, leaving it to older married women with greater family responsibility yet less education or fewer skills needed in the contemporary service sector.

Within the context of Taiwan's recent economic restructuring as a way to reinvigorate capital accumulation, notably the relocation overseas of industrial production and the introduction of foreign labor, Anru Lee investigates the paradoxes facing young women in small family firms as they are caught between better opportunities for personal advancement and increasing labor needs in family businesses. To solve the problem of labor shortage and to keep the labor costs low, small-factory owners often call upon family loyalty to draw their daughters away from outside employment and back to work for family businesses. Yet Lee shows in Chapter 6, "Between Filial Daughter and Loyal Sister: Global Economy and Family Politics in Taiwan," that young women are keenly aware of the coercive nature of family loyalty even though they often answer the call faithfully. The family is a field of contention where members constantly compete for meanings, and definitions, of rights and obligations.

Whereas Anru Lee stresses the production aspect of Taiwan's recent economic restructuring, Fang-chih Irene Yang focuses on the internationalization of Taiwanese consumer culture as it intersects with global commercial capital within the same background. Using women's magazines as an example, in Chapter 7, "Internationalizing Women's Magazines in Taiwan," Yang discusses the process in which gender images are refashioned in Taiwan's cultural market as a result of the rapid penetration of global economic forces. International women's magazines—that is, Chinese editions of women's magazines owned by multinational corporations or as part of joint ventures between multinational and Taiwanese companies, such as *Cosmopolitan*—differ from traditional women's magazines in two major yet interconnected ways. First, whereas traditional women's magazines emphasize women's roles as wives and mothers, thereby featuring articles emphasizing the moral importance of and knowledge to enhance these roles, international women's magazines stress women as individuals with their own identities. New lifestyles are contrived as women are now to be urban, modern, and cosmopolitan. However, new commodities such as cosmetics and designer clothing are needed in order for one to achieve these new lifestyles. This leads to the second major difference between international women's magazines and traditional ones. As traditional women's magazines mostly rely on subscriptions for profit, international women's magazines are closely associated with multinational advertising agencies and thus derive their revenues primarily from advertising. The new images of women promoted by the latter thereby are a product of contemporary global commercial interests.

Although most of the literature on gender issues in Taiwan focuses on the women's perspective, the chapters by Robert Marsh, Avron Boretz, and Paul Festa provide a rare lens for examining gender consciousness from men's point of view. Robert Marsh's widely acclaimed book *The Great Transformation* (M.E. Sharpe, 1996) provides an extensive comparative study of Taiwan's social conditions in the early 1960s and early 1990s. In Chapter 8, "Should Women Get Equal Pay for Equal Work? Taiwanese Men's Attitudes in 1963 and 1991," he examines the ways men see women in the workplace in 1963 and 1991, two different moments in Taiwan's postwar history. Marsh's study shows a striking similar level of men's support of "equal pay for equal work" in spite of the rapid economic development and societal modernization that have occurred. Notwithstanding the different reasons elicited for the similar level of support, the data indicate a persistence of discriminatory attitudes toward women, which Marsh suggests may have contributed to women's poor performance on the job when compared with that of men. This raises questions to a neoclassical economic explanation that lower pay for women is a consequence of their "lower productivity" and "poor human capital," which could be in fact the results of patriarchal practices in the family and in the society at large.

Avron Boretz's article, Chapter 9, "Carousing and Masculinity: The Cultural Production of Gender in Taiwan," explores issues of the construction of male subjectivity, which is an area of research that has remained largely untouched in Taiwan studies. Boretz focuses here on karaoke culture, an occasion for male bonding and the competition and display of manliness and social status. In conjunction with Lee's discussion on power relations within the family and the economic functions they serve in Taiwan's economic history, the pattern of social interaction in karaoke bars demonstrates an extension of the process of production and articulation of gender domination in the public arena. It also reflects the gender-specific forms of recreation in contemporary Taiwan, continuing the theme of consumption and cultural production developed in Yang's article on women's magazines.

Chapter 10, "The Blue Whirlwind Strikes Below the Belt: Male Sexuality, Gender Politics, and the Viagra Craze in Taiwan," by Paul E. Festa, provides a fascinating description of the Viagra craze now sweeping Taiwan. The article shows how the use of this powerful anti-impotency drug is being accepted in Taiwan and how its mystique neatly fits into established patterns of male belief and behavior. It is a telling and instructive tale of the way gender relations may change even as they stay the same. It is also a cautionary tale of the ability of a society to adopt devices—in this case, medicines—from the outside and fit such devices or potions into an existing behavioral matrix.

Part III: Feminisms and Cultural Critique

Part III studies different facets of feminism and the women's movement on KMT-run Taiwan, which will then be compared with its counterpart in the Communist Party–

controlled mainland as discussed by Catherine Farris in the conclusion to this volume. The articles in this section are selected to show not only the various dimensions of concern among Taiwanese women but also the historical evolution of the issues raised by feminists and women activists. This is not to say that the development of the women's movement in Taiwan has occurred in a linear chronological fashion. We recognize the complexity and multiplicity of women's issues, and the many and often conflicting ways the issues are expressed and debated. While acknowledging a continued struggle of some of the issues over time, we also intend to show the shifting meanings and strategies of similar issues that can only be understood as interlocking with specific social, political, and economic contexts.

To begin with, Hwei-syin Lu's article, Chapter 11, "Transcribing Feminism: Taiwanese Women's Experiences," looks at the feminist movement on Taiwan as it was constituted in the 1980s and 1990s. Lu points out that the Chinese definitions of gender/sex do not imply an intrinsic opposition, which contrasts with the Western conception of male and female as two separate entities. The embedded nature of Chinese personhood in a web of social relationships enables Taiwanese women to strategize for their best interests by positioning themselves among different social roles. Therefore, even though many women in Lu's study lost their wifely identity (through divorce or widowhood), by emphasizing their maternal role or repositioning themselves as committed daughter to the affairs of their birth family, these women regained a culturally legitimate space to seek independence or even exercise influence.

In Chapter 12, "Lu Hsiu-lien and the Origins of Taiwanese Feminism, 1944–1977," Murray Rubinstein discusses the background of the early career of Annette Lu Hsiu-lien, one of the key figures in the Taiwanese feminist movement of the 1970s, and currently the vice-president of the Republic of China (ROC) on Taiwan. Although Lu Hsiu-lien has been widely acknowledged as one of the early figures who publicly raised gender inequality issues and introduced Western feminist thought to Taiwan, she does not devote her passion solely to women's issues. Coming of age at a time when the political atmosphere of Taiwan was extremely repressive, Lu's biography is closely related to the Taiwanese struggle against the KMT for civil rights and political freedom. Her experience in political participation makes her outlook on women's issues distinct from those who had been active in the late 1980s, when Taiwan's political circumstances were more relaxed (as evinced by the three women's self-growth groups studied by Hwei-syin Lu in this volume).

Yu-hsiu Liu is an influential figure on gender issues and grassroots-organization empowerment in Taiwan and has written Chapter 13, "The Story of Power and Desire: *A Brighter Summer Day.*" She examines the different images of father presented in the Taiwanese film *A Brighter Summer Day* (1991) directed by Edward Yang. Widely acknowledged by film critics as a cultural critique of patriarchy and social hierarchy in contemporary Taiwanese society, the film emphasizes positive father-son relationships based on mutual trust that are rarely seen in other films. However, Liu points out that the film falls into the fallacy of depicting women as the cause of conflicts among men, while trying to establish a "new morality" of brotherly love and equality. As such, the film falls short of being an acute critique of Chinese patriarchy.

Ping-chun Hsiung's article, in Chapter 14, "Between Bosses and Workers: The Dilemma of a Keen Observer and a Vocal Feminist," examines the problem of participant observation and the inner tensions derived from being a "native" researcher that have to be dealt with by a Western-trained Taiwanese feminist scholar. Hsiung began her career studying satellite factories in Taiwan, focusing on the exploitative nature of family enterprises with particular regard to married women's labor. Lately she has expanded her research to include women's struggles and women's movements in the PRC. Her own experience of doing fieldwork in Taiwan refutes a simple dichotomy between a powerful, intrusive researcher and her defenseless, exploited informants, which is often raised in the discussion of feminist methodology and epistemology. Her roles as "keen observer" and "vocal feminist"—and simultaneously being outsider and insider—often create contradictions, revealing the complex and multilayered power relations that not only feminist researchers but Taiwanese men and women have to encounter in daily context.

The concluding article in this section, Chapter 15, "Feminist Art in Taiwan: Textures of Reality and Dreams," is by Richard Kagan. Long a student of Taiwan's politics, society, and culture, Kagan explores here women's contribution to the world of modern art on Taiwan. He sets the work of these artists in context and then provides a useful and sophisticated introduction to the evolving body of art by feminists who are now painting and sculpting and having their works exhibited on Taiwan. That such art, decidedly feminist in nature, is being produced in a bastion of male domination and patriarchy is yet another example of how a new and decidedly modern consciousness of gender roles and gender relations has begun to find a place in modern Taiwan.

Concluding Section

In the final section, Chapter 16, Catherine Farris discusses the idea of women's liberation in "Women's Liberation under 'East Asian Modernity' in China and Taiwan: Historical, Social, and Comparative Perspectives." She questions whether the idea of "women's liberation" is a cross-culturally valid, universal category, or merely a concept derived from and embedded in Western political and philosophical discourse and tradition. The emancipation of women is usually considered as part of the larger historical process of "modernization." As China struggled to become a modern nation-state beginning in the nineteenth century, the liberation of women became a trope for and a signifier of modernity. In the twentieth century, the Chinese Communist Party (CCP) and the KMT developed sometimes radically different visions of China's search for modernity, but each touted the liberation of women as a necessary component of that transformation.

Farris notes that mainstream Western feminists have pointed to women's labor force participation and familial roles as particularly important sites for the struggle over gender equality. Socialist feminists in particular argue that economic independence through paid work, along with public childcare and an end to kinship structures which subordinate females to male descent groups, are necessary prerequisites for true liberation of women. In the context of the Chinese societies in the PRC and Taiwan, these assertions generate a number of questions to Farris. First, how have modernization processes of socialism versus capitalism affected progress toward women's liberation? Are there distinct models of modernization based on different modes of production, or different cultural contexts? Is there an East Asian model of modernity, and, if so, can women be liberated within it? Do Chinese feminists themselves see "liberation" in the same light as do those in the West? This concluding essay is an anthropologically informed commentary on processes of women's liberation in the PRC and in Taiwan, which the author hopes is sensitive to critiques of First World readings and allows voices of Chinese women and men to inform the discourse.

References

Bray, Francesca. 1997. *Technology and Gender: Fabrics of Power in Late Imperial China.* Berkeley: University of California Press.

Chiang, Nora. 1985. *The Role of Women in the National Development Process in Taiwan.* (In Chinese). Conference Proceedings. Taipei: Women Research Program, Population Studies Center, National Taiwan University.

Chiang, Nora, and Ku Yenlin. 1985. *Past and Current Status of Women in Taiwan.* Taipei: Women Research Program, Population Studies Center, National Taiwan University.

Gilmartin, Christina, Gail Hershatter, Lisa Rofel, and Tyrene White, eds. 1994. *Engendering China: Women, Culture, and the State.* Cambridge: Harvard University Press.

Gronewold, Sue. 1982. *Beautiful Merchandise: Prostitution in China, 1860–1936.* New York: Haworth Press.

Hershatter, Gail. 1997. *Dangerous Pleasures: Prostitution and Modernity in Twentieth-Century Shanghai.* Berkeley: University of California Press.

Honig, Emily. 1986. *Sisters and Strangers: Women in the Shanghai Cotton Mills, 1919–1949.* Stanford: Stanford University Press.

Ko, Dorothy. 1994. *Teachers of the Inner Chambers: Women and Culture in Seventeenth-Century China.* Stanford: Stanford University Press.

Mann, Susan. 1997. *Precious Records: Women in China's Long Eighteenth Century.* Stanford: Stanford University Press.

———. 1994. "Learned Women in the Eighteenth Century." In Gilmartin et al., eds., *Engendering China,* 27–46.

Marsh, Robert M. 1996. *The Great Transformation: Social Change in Taipei, Taiwan, Since the 1960s.* Armonk, NY: M.E. Sharpe.

Salaff, Janet. 1995. *Working Daughters of Hong Kong.* New York: Columbia University Press.

Widmer, Ellen, and Kang-I Sun Chang. 1997. *Writing Women in Late Imperial China.* Stanford: Stanford University Press.

Wolf, Margery. 1972. *Women and the Family in Rural Taiwan.* Stanford: Stanford University Press.

Part I

Gender in Historical Perspective

1

What Can Feminist Theory Do for the Study of Chinese History?

A Brief Review of Scholarship in the United States

Susan Mann

Defamiliarizing the Familiar

In the United States, feminist studies developed over the past two decades have presented new challenges and new opportunities for historians of Chinese women. One such challenge is the prospect of defamiliarizing familiar materials, dislodging them from conventional frameworks and turning them to new uses as texts. These familiar texts include biographies of exemplary women contained in official histories (*lieh-nü chuan*) and epitaphs (*mu-chih-ming*) or funeral odes (*chi-wen*) composed by men to honor the women they loved or admired.

The reason these familiar materials gain new historical meaning when subjected to feminist analysis is that feminist theory attempts explicitly to link structures of kinship, community, class, and state—structures where power is lodged—to the meaning or meanings of gender and sexuality at specific places and points in time. In particular, feminist theory argues that state-sponsored institutions—especially laws defining property relations, inheritance procedures, tax collection, corvée and military service, and criminal conduct—have a coherent historical relationship to the norms, ideologies, or values lodged in other social and cultural systems such as the family, religious organizations, and aesthetic or creative activities. These norms, ideologies, and values invariably include conceptions of what it means to be female or male, masculine or feminine (Ross and Rapp 1981).

Thus feminist theory has special promise for historians of China. We have reams of material about temporal change in China's imperial institutions and organizations, but we have tended to assume that "virtue" and other norms governing gen-

The author thanks Professor Yip Hon-ming of the Chinese University of Hong Kong for critical comments on an earlier draft.

Originally published in *Research on Women in Modern Chinese History* 1 (1993): 241–60. Used with permission.

der and sexuality are somehow timeless and transcendent, disembodied from other aspects of social and cultural change.

For historians of China working in the United States, the path-breaking work exploring the relationship between gender and power in Chinese society has come from outside the discipline of history. The first was anthropologist Margery Wolf's classic *Women and the Family in Rural Taiwan* (first published in 1972), in which her analysis of what she called the "uterine family" and the women's community in a Taiwan village permanently complicated and defamiliarized our male-centered view of the so-called patriarchal Chinese family system. The next major break-through was sociologist Judith Stacey's feminist analysis of the Chinese Revolution—*Patriarchy and Socialist Revolution in China*, published in 1983. Stacey's analysis of Mao Tse-tung's New Democracy policy showed, for example, that from a feminist perspective New Democracy actually meant, simply, "a wife for every peasant."

Both Wolf and Stacey chose subjects about which U.S. historians of China had published widely accepted, well-documented interpretations. But the two authors turned those interpretations upside down, simply by reanalyzing them from a feminist perspective. They simply defamiliarized the familiar.

Familiar Chinese historical materials have continued to yield new insights when gender as a category of analysis is used. One of the most striking areas of research has been female biography. Biographies of women fill the pages of every standard history, whether compiled by the central government or by a county magistrate. Already, numerous studies of female biographies have demonstrated that, far from being timeless, they display both temporal and regional variation. T'ien Ju-k'ang's (1988) study of women's suicide, based on biographies from three parts of China, calls attention to the specific cultural and economic conditions that encouraged women in Fukien to commit suicide in extraordinary numbers. Mark Elvin (1984) has analyzed the role of the Ming and Ch'ing Chinese state in promoting the chaste-widow cult as an example of state intrusion into a realm marked as "domestic" or "private" in Western societies. Ann Waltner (1981) and others (e.g., Mann 1987) have used female biography to examine changing attitudes toward women in late imperial times. A recent study by Katherine Carlitz (1991) has focused on readers and publishers of female biographies in Ming times.

Other new studies have dramatized shifts in Confucian values and attitudes affecting women and women's roles, once again by rereading familiar materials. Joanna Handlin's (1975) research on Lü K'un revealed changes in late-Ming attitudes toward women's education. Kang-I Sun Chang's (1991) recent study of Ch'en Tzu-lung and Liu Ju-shih shows how women came to serve as symbols of "love and loyalism" at a particular point in historical time, under the particular conditions of the late Ming collapse. Statecraft writings of the mid-Ch'ing period can be analyzed to show that promoting women's work was part of mid-Ch'ing programs to maintain a viable tax base while ensuring the continued prosperity and well-being of the farm population (Mann 1992).

Rediscovering Neglected Sources

Feminist theory produces not only startling new discoveries when applied to familiar sources. It also stimulates a quest for new or neglected sources. Studies of familiar works about women written by men have provoked interest in writings by women themselves. This in turn has inspired a search for lost or neglected women's writings, especially since the publication of Hu Wen-k'ai's (1985) survey of writings by women in Chinese history. In the United States, a new field of literary studies is exploring changes in women's writings and identifying the differences between the male and the female voice in Chinese literary works.[1] Dorothy Ko (1994) has just completed a new history of women in the late Ming and early Ch'ing that is based almost exclusively on writings by women themselves. Kang-I Sun Chang is compiling a mammoth three-volume set of translations of poetry by Chinese women.[2] In art history, interest in female painters and calligraphers is growing rapidly, together with related research on women's clothing, fashion, hairstyles, and the representation of the female body in art.[3] Charlotte Furth (1987, 1988) is completing a systematic study of medical practice and conceptions of the female body represented in medical texts. These new interests are increasingly evident in exhibits and conference papers.[4]

Still, as Patricia Ebrey commented at a recent academic meeting, gender as a category of analysis has yet to make a broad impact on historical studies of China, especially for earlier periods.[5] In the field of China studies in the United States, research placing women at the center has yet to realize its potential to reshape the historical record.

Reconceptualizing the Organization of Chinese Society in Historical Time

The first wave of historical research on Chinese women in both the United States and China was devoted to documenting and criticizing women's oppression by men. A major target of criticism was patriarchy. Feminist scholarship on Chinese women by historians in the United States, which exploded during the 1970s, followed leads established decades earlier by Chinese historians—Chinese historians in turn were influenced by China's own early feminist movement, especially by the May Fourth critique of Confucianism and the patriarchal family system. Ch'en Tung-yuan 1977 [1928] and others wrote the classic secondary works on which U.S. historians have relied to pursue their research on the place of women in Chinese history.

In the United States recent feminist research on Chinese women's history has now moved in different, although related, directions. The aim is not to document women's oppression but rather to illuminate the connections between gender relations and other larger structures of power lodged in economic organizations, political structures, and so forth. For example, the first English-language historical study of prostitution in China, Sue Gronewold's (1982) "Beautiful Merchandise:

Prostitution in China, 1860–1936," focused on the Chinese patriarchal system and the ways in which it facilitated a traffic in women's bodies. But her evidence may be pushed beyond a critique of oppression and toward a new understanding of the broad systems and structures that organize gender relations in Chinese history.

To do this, scholars might start by asking the same questions that have been asked about the history of prostitution in the West:

1. How do the structural conditions expressing and articulating certain conceptions of gender self-reproduce?
2. How are these conditions connected to larger structures of kinship, community, class, and state formation in history?
3. How do they change over time?

Asking those questions enables us to identify two complementary, but discrete, structures of female sexuality in late imperial China. The first was a structure of marriage and reproduction; the second, a structure of prostitution and procurement.

These two structures of traffic in women, to borrow a phrase from Gayle Rubin (1975), were separate. The first of these built family systems and reproductive systems through the exchange of brides. The second replicated itself through a cycle in which young girls were sold or forced into prostitution, then, compelled by aging to abandon their profession for the role of procuress, obtained other girls to serve as prostitutes, and so forth. With those two structures in mind, we could then divide all Chinese families with daughters in late imperial times into two groups: those who married their daughters into the structures of sexual reproduction within the family; and those who sold their daughters into the structures providing sexual gratification outside the family.

Of course, the two structures were not entirely discrete. In times of political upheaval, respectable married women could be forced into prostitution. Among certain classes and certain ethnic or subethnic groups, prostitution by female family members (including wives and marriageable daughters) served as a legitimate means of supporting the family or earning a dowry. Even respectable widows and divorcees, if impoverished, might turn to prostitution. By the same token, a prostitute or courtesan favored by a rich patron might be purchased to join his family as a concubine. In addition, some might argue that the line separating "sale" of daughters from "marriage" of daughters was not entirely clear because of the customary bride's price required in many parts of the empire. Finally, we know that a very few women seceded entirely from both of these systems, either as spiritual adepts devoted to solitary meditation or as members of sisterhoods or convents. Ann Waltner's studies of T'an Yang-tzu (1987) explore this side of women's spirituality. Marjorie Topley (1975), Janice Stockard (1989), Maria Jaschok (1988), and others have studied the sisterhoods and delayed-transfer marriage patterns unique to the Canton delta region.

For the sake of argument, however, suppose we treat these two structures as separate worlds, produced and reproduced in the everyday lives of women and their families. If we look to the systems that upheld, stabilized, and protected the binary structure of traffic in women in the late empire, we find three levels where crucial decisions were made or policies implemented to maintain them: the household, the community, and the state. At the household level the most basic decisions began the process that determined which structure a woman would enter. Poor families were the first to sell or pawn their women, though not necessarily with the intention of sending a daughter into prostitution. Poor families also lacked the resources and the networks to verify the credentials that distinguished prospective buyers from bona fide marriage partners. At the household level, then, the dividing line between the two structures was the line separating those families who could protect their women from sale, and everybody else. This definition of "class" in late imperial Chinese society becomes visible only through the lens of feminist analysis.

A second critical decision-making level was the community. Mores in some communities may have sanctioned the participation of member households in both structures of sexuality.[6] However, it seems likely that most local communities echoed the formal state sanctions demeaning prostitutes, by excluding former and present prostitutes from the ranks of young women eligible for marriage into respectable families.

This calls our attention to the fact that the state—through laws and normative sanctions—upheld these separate but curiously equal realms of female sexuality through a combination of policies that affirmed the importance of women's sexual purity, prohibited the sale of women by their husbands, and at the same time required hereditary registration for prostitutes, who were legally classified as members of the *chien-min*, or demeaned peoples, and whose descendants were barred from upward mobility for three successive generations even if they left their profession.

Gronewold tantalizingly suggests that the state, above all, held the determining interest in perpetuating two separate worlds of female sexuality. Why? To uphold a family system that cloistered wives for purposes of reproduction and child socialization; and to provide access to women for the otherwise restless and potentially rebellious (sometimes single) males unable to find sexual gratification within the confines of the cloistering family system, which was organized to minimize strong emotional and affective bonds between spouses. In other words, the carefully defined separate and distinct worlds of marriage and prostitution provide one measure of the impact of late imperial state authority on gender hierarchies and on conceptions of sexuality.

If these insights are then placed in historical perspective, we must ask the following: When were these two gender systems different, and how did they change? Here Patricia Ebrey's work on women in the Sung has provided important insights into the roots of the late imperial binary structure of sexuality. In an early essay published in 1981, Ebrey noted that women in the upper-class lineages of the emerging "gentry" society, unlike upper-class women in Ch'ing times, enjoyed property rights within their natal families and prolonged close contact with their natal families after marriage. The Sung family system, she argues, was both structurally and symbolically different from its Ch'ing counterpart. In her subsequent work, Ebrey (1990, for example) has continued to elaborate that view.

Clearly, as Ebrey's work has shown,[7] the T'ang-Sung-Yuan transition is a period on which feminist historians of China should train their lenses to clarify precisely the temporal and regional scope of changes in structures of sexuality and to explain how and why they occurred. If male-female relations in the Sung upper classes were more egalitarian and open than they were by the Ch'ing period, what of gender relations outside the elite? The Sung upper class was probably a much smaller percentage of the total population; females may have been confined within structures of indentured servitude, sequestered both from the commoner marriage market and from commercial sex markets. If that is the case, then the urbanization of the Sung period, with its new job markets for women, may be a portent of the more market-based traffic in women characteristic of late imperial times.

Such a view would shed new light on Sung neo-Confucian ideology stressing the importance of female virtue. This ideology may have been a profound outcry of rage and dismay *not* at the breakdown of female virtue per se, but at the erosion of the system of elite land tenure and labor management in the countryside, which was threatened by growing urban economies.

Critique of Western Feminist History

Promising though it may be, Western feminist theory has come under increasing criticism during the past two decades by feminist scholars themselves. Some of the most important criticism has come from feminist scholars writing about India and about Islamic societies who, because of colonial legacies, have long addressed a scholarly audience using English. In many cases, these scholars have reacted angrily to Western feminist judgments about their culture and women's place in it. They argue that Western feminists have imposed a universalistic framework of analysis on cultures where Western feminist theories have little or no explanatory power, and they charge that Western feminists are heirs to an insidious legacy of Orientalism[8] or what has come to be called colonial discourse (Mohanty 1991).

Some of the most articulate critiques of Western feminist scholarship come from Islamic cultures, where in Muslim fundamentalist movements the return of the veil has become an emblem of resistance to Western imperialism. In the United States, Leila Ahmed's writings have drawn the attention of feminist scholars to the relationship between feminism and the colonial legacy. As Ahmed (1992: 154–55) points out in her latest book:

> Whether in the hands of patriarchal men or feminists, the ideas of Western feminism essentially functioned to morally justify the attack on native societies and to support the notion of the comprehensive superiority of Europe. . . . [W]hatever

the disagreements of feminism with white male domination within Western societies, outside their borders feminism turned from being the critic of the system of white male dominance to being its docile servant.

Ahmed's studies have emphasized the particular contradictions that face non–Western feminist scholars critical of Western feminist theory. Reviewing a leading Egyptian feminist's attack on clitoridectomy and other abusive customs in Middle Eastern societies,[9] Ahmed took note of the book's paradoxical "anger at the West, its imperialism, its despoiling of the peoples of the Third World, and its civilizational arrogance resting, as it does, so squarely upon ignorance." Then she made the following comment:

> I think that there is not one of us who has not known the anger out of which she speaks and who has not known what it is to be slighted casually and constantly in one's racial or cultural identity. Such a slight, a belittlement, a degradation can be, as many feminists have made clear, even more unendurable than our oppression as women.[10]

Ahmed then offered some tentative advice to Western feminists:

> It would be well if Western women did not merely replicate Western men's view of the Third World, particularly in their assumption that technological and material backwardness denotes civilizational backwardness and it would be well if feminists at least made themselves more aware of the elaborate and rich traditions out of which "other" women speak.

Ahmed's point was echoed in an early exchange between Vina Mazumdar, a leading Indian feminist, and Dorothy Stein, who published a critique of the victimization of women resulting from the practice of Indian *sati* (widow-burning). Mazumdar described her own great-great grandmother's act as representing not victimization but defiance by casting herself on her husband's funeral pyre; she flouted the law of the land along with the concerns, the interests, and indeed the orders of the living male patriarchs of her family.[11]

Critiques like Mazumdar's and Ahmed's stimulated a search for less ethnocentric approaches to the study of women in non-Western cultures. One early example, again from Arab studies, appeared in Rosemary Sayigh's article criticizing Orientalist approaches to Arab women. Sayigh proposed an agenda to purge Western feminist scholarship of its Orientalist legacy:

> A new approach to Arab women would begin, not with Arab "difference," but with social formations and the political and economic forces that shape them. The focus would not be on unchangeability but on historical change, not on an ideal-typical "Arab woman," but on variations between regions, group, and castes.

She stressed that class and sect can dramatically reshape the role that powerful kinship organizations play in prescribing women's roles. She also argues that by focusing on "status," Western approaches to Arab women had ignored women's roles and activities, perpetuating the image of passivity so compatible with the Orientalist perspective.[12]

Martin King Whyte's (1978) important survey of the status of women in preindustrial societies pointed to other ways of analyzing women's status. Whyte demonstrated that no single variable or cluster of variables serves as an adequate measure of what one might call "women's status" in any society. In all preindustrial societies, women have more power in some spheres than in others, and women's spheres of power and influence vary across cultures. Whyte found, on the other hand, that the development of complex agrarian empires may have represented the historic nadir of women's status. His findings suggest that scholars interested in the status of women in Ming and Ch'ing China need to reexamine both the particular context of late imperial culture in all its varieties *and* the common history of preindustrial bureaucratic states.

In sharp contrast to Whyte's multivariate sociological analysis, but also in the spirit of Sayigh's critique, was Lila Abu-Lughod's (1986) anthropological study of women's communities and women's writing among the Awlad Ali Bedouins of the Egyptian Western Desert. Abu-Lughod portrays the women's community among the Bedouin as an autonomous sphere where women develop social responsibility, pride in their personalities and their bodies, and a realm of shared experience that provides them with lives that are rich in affect and intimacy. She challenges the feminist critique of veiling and female seclusions and forces a reexamination of the premises that conflate sex segregation with the subjugation of women.

The transnational critique of Western feminist theory and resistance to its colonial legacy is just beginning to have its impact on the China field in the United States.[13] However, as Sayigh pointed out and as studies of women in Chinese history have already begun to show, it is possible to deploy insights of feminist theory in cross-cultural or comparative studies while avoiding the Orientalist pitfalls of some Western feminism, especially by focusing on variation by class and region and through time.

Conclusion

Feminist theory has not only caused historians to reexamine familiar materials and query them for new insights, it has also inspired a quest to recover lost or neglected sources by and about women. Sources written by or about women have been ignored by China historians because these sources have not been readily available, or because they have seemed irrelevant to the "larger" enterprises of institutional or intellectual history that mainstream historians like to do. However, the social, political, and economic institutions that constitute the favored subjects of China historians and the intellectual traditions China historians like to study are all intimately connected to the cultural construction of gender. Feminist theory deployed to reveal sexual meanings in the Chinese cultural context will yield a more complex understanding of institutions and ideas in Chinese history. Such theory will advance us beyond the stage of criticizing a timeless patriarchy and the oppression of Chinese women. And it will reveal systems and structures erased by conventional historical methods that ignore gender and conceal women from the historian's gaze.

Notes

1. See the special issue on women's culture in *Late Imperial China* 13, no. 1 (June 1992), especially Robertson 1992. Path-breaking articles include Widmer 1989, Waltner 1987, 1989.

2. *Women Writers of Traditional China: An Anthology of Poetry and Criticism*, with Haun Saussy (Stanford: Stanford University Press, 1999).

3. See *Views from the Jade Terrace*, a catalogue from an exhibition of the same name, which includes articles by Marsha Wagner, Ellen Johnston Laing, and others. See also Laing 1990a and 1990b and Wagner 1990.

4. Proceedings of the conference "Family Process and Political Process in Modern Chinese History" (Institute of Modern History, Academia Sinica, Taipei, January 1992) have already been published (Institute of Modern History, Academia Sinica, ed., 1992). The proceedings include important new studies of gender and family carefully situated in historical context. A conference on "Engendering China: Women, Culture, and the State," attended by scholars from the United States, Taiwan, and mainland China, was held at Harvard University and Wellesley College, February 7–9, 1992; selected papers from that conference have been published in Christina Gilmartin et al., ed., *Engendering China: Women, Culture, and the State* (Cambridge: Harvard University Press, 1994). At the annual meeting of the Association for Asian Studies, Los Angeles, March 1993, panels and papers on Chinese women attracted enormous attention. These included a panel, chaired by Gail Hershatter and titled "Thinking about Chinese Women and Feminism," on which three scholars from the mainland presented papers for discussion; a panel on "Male Anxiety and the Representation of the Female in Ming-Ch'ing Fiction," chaired by Robert E. Hegel; a panel entitled "'Firsts' for Women in Han Times," on which Yü Ying-shih served as discussant; and a panel "Playing with Gender in Pre-Modern Chinese Drama," with Ann Waltner acting as discussant.

5. Patricia Ebrey, "Gendering Song History" (paper presented at the panel "Song Studies: The State of the Field, Part I," annual meeting of the Association for Asian Studies, Los Angeles, 28 March 1993).

6. See, for example, Wolf 1968, 1972, in which the author shows that under certain conditions, community mores sanctioned prostitution as a form of filial piety for the unmarried daughter supporting her parents. Eugene Cooper has also reported to me that prostitution was a common way for young women among the "boat people" households of Kwangtung to earn money for their dowries (personal communication, February 26, 1983).

7. See Ebrey 1990 and 1991 for broad statements of the issues.

8. See Said's (1978) critical analysis of what he called the "discourse" of Orientalism. Said charged that Western scholarly analyses of Asian societies had an implicit common goal: to "enlighten" the people called Orientals; to make change happen so that Orientals would become more like Westerners. Orientalists, he noted, spoke of "our Orient," "our people," "our dominions." In other words, according to Said, Western scholarship on Asia was rooted in a Western impulse to appropriate the Orient, to make Asia its own, to define and change it in the West's own image.

9. Nawal El Saadawi, *The Hidden Face of Eve: Women in the Arab World*, trans. Sherif Hetata (London: Zed Press, 1980).

10. *Signs* 6, no. 4 (1981): 750–51.

11. Dorothy K. Stein, "Women to Burn: Suttee as a Normative Institution," *Signs* 4, no. 2 (1978): 253–68; Vina Mazumdar, "Comment on Suttee," *Signs* 4, no. 2 (1978): 269–73. For recent critical views of *sati,* stressing the complexity of doing cross-cultural and transnational research, see Lata Mani, "Multiple Mediations: Feminist Scholarship in the Age of Multi-National Reception," *Feminist Review* 35 (1990): 24–41.

12. "Roles and Functions of Arab Women: A Reappraisal," *Arab Studies Quarterly* 3, no. 3 (1981): 258–74.

13. See, for example, critical essays on feminist approaches to the study of China in the first issues of the new cultural studies journal *Positions: East Asia Cultures Critique* 1, no. 1 (Spring 1993).

References

Abu-Lughod, Lila. 1986. *Veiled Sentiments: Honor and Poetry in a Bedouin Society.* Berkeley: University of California Press.

Ahmed, Leila. 1992. *Women and Gender in Islam: Historical Roots of a Modern Debate.* New Haven: Yale University Press.

Carlitz, Katherine. 1991. "The Social Uses of Female Virtue in Late Ming Editions of Lienü Zhuan." *Late Imperial China* 12, no. 1: 117–48.

Chang, Kang-I Sun. 1991. *The Late-Ming Poet Ch'en Tzu-lung: Crises of Love and Loyalism.* New Haven: Yale University Press.

Ch'en Tung-yuan. 1977 [1928]. *Chung-kuo fu-nü sheng-huo shih* (The Life Histories of Chinese Women). Taipei: Commercial Press.

Ebrey, Patricia Buckley. 1991. "Shifts in Marriage Finance from the Sixth to the Thirteenth Century." In *Marriage and Inequality in Chinese Society,* ed. Rubie S. Watson and Patricia Buckley Ebrey, 97–132. Berkeley: University of California Press.

———. 1990. "Women, Marriage, and the Family in Chinese History." In *Heritage of China: Contemporary Perspectives on Chinese Civilization,* ed. Paul S. Ropp, 197–223. Berkeley: University of California Press.

———. 1981. "Women in the Kinship System of the Southern Song Upper Class." In *Women in China: Current Directions in Historical Scholarship,* ed. Richard W. Guisso and Stanley Johannesen, 113–28. Historical Reflections, no. 3. Youngstown, NY: Philo Press.

Elvin, Mark. 1984. "Female Virtue and the State in China." *Past and Present* 104: 111–52.

Furth, Charlotte. 1988. "Androgenous Males and Deficient Females: Biology and Gender Boundaries in Sixteenth- and Seventeenth-Century China." *Late Imperial China* 9, no. 2: 1–31.

———. 1987. "Concepts of Pregnancy, Childbirth, and Infancy in Ch'ing Dynasty China." *Journal of Asian Studies* 46, no. 1: 7–35.

Gronewold, Sue. 1982. "Beautiful Merchandise: Prostitution in China, 1860–1936." *Women and History* 1, no. 1: 1–114.

Handlin, Joanna F. 1975. "Lü K'un's New Audience: The Influence of Women's Literacy on Sixteenth-Century Thought." In *Women in Chinese Society,* ed. Margery Wolf and Roxane Witke, 13–38. Stanford: Stanford University Press.

Hu Wen-k'ai. 1985. *Li-tai fu-nü chu-chuo k'ao* (A Survey of Women Writers Through the Ages). Shanghai: Shanghai ku-chi ch'u-pan-she.

Institute of Modern History, Academia Sinica, ed. 1992. *Family Process and Political Process in Modern Chinese History.* 2 vols. Nankang, Taipei: Institute of Modern History, Academic Sinica.

Jaschok, Maria. 1988. *Concubines and Bondservants: The Social History of a Chinese Custom.* London: Zed Books.

Ko, Dorothy. 1994. *Teachers of the Inner Chambers.* Stanford: Stanford University Press.

Laing, Ellen Johnston. 1990a. "Notes on *Ladies Wearing Flowers in their Hair.*" *Orientations* 21, no. 2: 32–39.

———. 1990b. "Chinese Palace-Style Poetry and the Depiction of *A Palace Beauty.*" *Art Bulletin* 72, no. 2: 284–95.

Mann, Susan. 1992. "Household Handicrafts and State Policy in Qing Times." In *To Achieve Security and Wealth: The Qing Imperial State and the Economy, 1644–1911,* ed. Jane Kate Leonard and John Watt, 75–96. Ithaca, NY: Cornell East Asia Series.

———. 1987. "Widows in the Kinship, Class, and Community Structures of Qing Dynasty China." *Journal of Asian Studies* 46, no. 1: 37–56.

Mohanty, Chandra Talpade. 1991. "Under Western Eyes: Feminist Scholarship and Colonial Discourses." In *Third World Women and the Politics of Feminism,* ed. Mohanty, Ann Russo, and Lourdes Torres, 51–80. Bloomington: Indiana University Press.

Ortner, Sherry B. 1978. "The Virgin and the State." *Feminist Studies* 14, no. 3: 19–35.

Robertson, Maureen. 1992. "Voicing the Feminine: Constructions of the Gendered Subject in Lyric Poetry by Women of Medieval and Late Imperial China." *Late Imperial China* 13, no. 1: 63–110.

Ross, Ellen, and Rayna Rapp. 1981. "Sex and Society: A Research Note from Social History and Anthropology." *Comparative Studies in Society and History* 23, no. 1: 51–72.

Rubin, Gayle. 1975. "The Traffic in Women: Notes on the 'Political Economy' of Sex." In *Toward an Anthropology of Women,* ed. Rayna R. Reiter, 157–210. New York: Monthly Review Press.

Said, Edward. 1978. *Orientalism.* New York: Pantheon Books.

Stacey, Judith. 1983. *Patriarchy and Socialist Revolution in China.* Berkeley: University of California Press.

Stockard, Janice. 1989. *Daughters of the Canton Delta: Marriage Patterns and Economic Strategies in South China, 1860–1930.* Stanford: Stanford University Press.

T'ien, Ju-k'ang. 1988. *Male Anxiety and Female Chastity: A Comparative Study of Chinese Ethical Values in Ming-Ch'ing Times.* Leiden: E. J. Brill.

Topley, Marjorie. 1975. "Marriage Resistance in Rural Kwangtung." In Wolf and Witke, eds., *Women in Chinese Society,* 67–88.

Views from the Jade Terrace: Chinese Women Artists, 1300–1912. 1988. Indianapolis: Indianapolis Museum of Art [catalogue of exhibit].

Wagner, Marsha, ed. 1990. *Flowering in the Shadows: Women in the History of Chinese and Japanese Painting.* Honolulu: University of Hawaii Press.

Waltner, Ann. 1989. "On Not Becoming a Heroine: Lin Daiyu and Cui Yingying." *Signs* 15, no. 1: 61–78.

———. 1987. "T'an Yang-tzu and Wang Shih-chen: Visionary and Bureaucrat in the Late Ming." *Late Imperial China* 8, no. 1: 105–33.

———. 1981. "Widows and Remarriage in Ming and Early Qing China." In Guisso and Johannesen, eds., *Women in China: Current Directions in Historical Scholarship,* 129–46.

Whyte, Martin King. 1978. *The Status of Women in Preindustrial Societies.* Princeton: Princeton University Press.

Widmer, Ellen. 1989. "The Epistolary World of Female Talent in Seventeenth-Century China." *Late Imperial China* 10, no. 2: 1–43.

Wolf, Margery. 1972. *Women and the Family in Rural Taiwan.* Stanford: Stanford University Press.

———. 1968. *The House of Lim: A Study of a Chinese Farm Family.* Englewood Cliffs, NJ: Prentice-Hall.

2

Sons and Mothers

Demographic Realities and the Chinese Culture of *Hsiao*

Ping-chen Hsiung

In the study of human relations, the mother-son bond is especially intriguing in the Chinese context for both its rich complexity and its ambivalence. Women and children were relatively powerless in the Chinese household, but the nurturing mother commanded resources enough for her children and brought family members together in the process.[1] The youthful, robust mother bears, feeds, raises, and disciplines her sons. In less than one generation's time dependent sons grew to be male heads of the family, and the mother became an old woman, needing care, filial devotion, and perhaps pity. Aware of what lies ahead, a mother invested greatly in the emotional bond for personal satisfaction as well as for securing practical needs.

This mutual dedication and deep affection were potentially subversive for both the family line, which stressed patriarchal descent, and for the horizontal gender relations that existed between husbands and wives, men and women, and so forth. There is much to learn from examining this mother-son bond within the context of the family life cycle,[2] delineating the various outcomes, personal and social, and measuring the potential for hurt, joy, or even alienation. The power relationships involving aging mothers and their adult sons evolved greatly; no sooner had the son acquired his own family than the former mother-son bond was subject to serious stress created by the new spousal relationship. The mother's daily needs expectedly became complicated and burdensome as the family grew in structural complexity and as time passed. We do not see the gender-generational interplay if we examine men only as sons (not yet husbands, fathers, adult brothers, or kinsmen) and women only as mothers (neglecting the roles of daughter, wife, sister, and in-law). Time, gender, and personal needs (both practical and emotional) ensure that there's much to be learned in this mother-son story.

The Phases

Two main factors are fundamental to our understanding of the mother-son relation: the death of the mother and the marriage of the son. Both are fundamental passages of life that produce obvious effects on family structure and familial relations. Yet the specific and intricate social and psychological implications these events bear, at various times and under variant circumstances within the traditional Chinese family, engender several different categories that deserve close examination and further consideration.

The death of a mother might occur at any point when a son is still a child, when a young adult, or middle-aged. In each of the three cases, the son's dependence (both practical and psychological) develops into self-reliance (especially concerning marriage and employment), and the shouldering of the family burdens. Typically, when a male child lost his mother, the most severe blow was to his emotions; the practical needs were usually taken care of either by close relatives or a stepmother (remarriage of fathers was customary in traditional China). But an abruptly terminated emotional bond left an emptiness in the child as he grew up. For example, Kuei Yu-kuang's (1506–71) mother passed away when he was eight. Here, as in many such cases, a warm bond existed between the young mother and her dependent children, thus the sense of loss was felt keenly. Kuei conveyed this loss in a memorial essay depicting his youthful mother—hardworking, devoted, and kind, yet suddenly taken away:

> Though free of any worry about such things as the daily supply of rice and salt, mother nonetheless worked hard, as if the household were to run out of food that very evening. In winter, she directed maids to make fuel balls out of coal crumbs (from the ashes burned the night before), drying out the ashes on the steps. Under her management, she let nothing go to waste, nor was there a single person unoccupied. As for her children, the older ones always clung to her skirts while the younger were either in her arms or at her breast.[3]

The traumatic experience comes out vividly in Kuei's reminiscence:

> Since losing mother at a young age, I often feel uncomfortable when left alone, brooding constantly over those who have passed on and wondering about things I never knew concerning them. It always worries me, too, that there may not be enough time to be fully acquainted with people who are still alive—all because of that tragic event, which still hurts me so very deeply.[4]

Her death at age twenty-six happened on a summer day in 1515 and left five surviving children (out of the seven born of a ten-year marriage). Sad memories came back to haunt Kuei. He tells of his habit of holding onto the gowns of the elders in the house and asking about every domestic detail. Well into adulthood, he was moved to tears by his mother's maid's reminiscences about his mother. The obsession with his mother did not diminish with the passing of time; as an old man close to sixty, Kuei became emotional about the childhood trauma on occasions such as the mere greeting of a relative. Or, happily married at the age of twenty-three and blessed with a daughter a year later, melancholy thoughts were stirred up when speaking of his mother to his wife.

Traditional Chinese culture contains a deep vein of filial piety (*hsiao*), a complex of rites and relations that calls for a lifelong indebtedness on the part of the children (primarily the sons) to their parents and ancestors. In this cultural complex the mother's place is important, yet not officially recognized. The ancient *Book of Odes* contains a lament in which an orphan wails for deceased parents. "Luxuriously growing in the garden appear the artemisia leaves, [upon closer glance, however] they are not artemisia but bugworts," part of it reads, "[the sense of loss strikes me as I think of] my sad parents who gave birth to me with such harsh labor and pain." The verses continue to allegorize, with ironic results, the loss of parental devotion in terms of a labored-over vegetable garden. At the end, the orphan, grief-ridden and filled with filial guilt, lets out a cry: "The debt to my father and my mother shall remain forever vast as the boundless sky."[5]

Such sentiment belonged not only to the elite class, but to ordinary people, whose daily mottoes warned: "When the trees wish to stand still yet the wind will not subside, just as a child wants [when finally allowed] to feed his parents, they no longer remain." These proverbs preyed upon the consciences of offspring.[6] Charts of Merit and Demerits, as well as the imperial legal codes, deemed the harming of one's parents as a crime subjected to the severest of punishment: a thousand demerits, or, in the case of the legal code, decapitation. All of this was a manifestation of a deep conviction and a popular ethic embedded in common beliefs and grounded in state institutions. History was dotted throughout with comments from nonbelievers, such as the third-century scholar-official K'ung Jung (153–208) who sniffed at filiality in his satirical remark that the birth of a child signaled but a momentary indulgence in carnal lust by a man and a woman.[7] But such comments were always presented as scandals and insults engendering general consternation.

The accepted norm held that to give birth and raise a child meant pain and exhausting devotion, thus creating a lifelong debt for the child to pay back in some way. By the late imperial period, printed texts and illustrations, paintings, folktales, and theatrical renditions of exemplary stories of filiality, as well as other didactic materials, continued to pour into the market to be consumed by ordinary people (for example, the *Hsiao-ching* [Book of Filial Piety] and *The Buddhist Sutra on the Heavy Debt to Parents*).[8] State policies and institutional forces joined in enhancing this culture of *hsiao*. There was not a single, agreed-upon practice of *hsiao,* the reality always being different from the ideal.

Demographic realities, however, gave shape to the ways that *hsiao* was practiced. This was, of course, with respect to varying social and economic conditions, or specific historical realities. Major life-course events (birth, marriage, death) occurred to family members at particular points in time. This generated different situations in which familial relations were to be played out in the ongoing life cycles of both the individual and the family. When mothers passed away while a son was still a boy, there was an abrupt deprivation in emotional terms. For the future, the son would live out the high expectations of both his deceased mother and the family with his own effort.[9] But as soon as the son came into his own, seeking his employment, entering into marriage, and building his family, the mother was no longer present.[10]

For sons whose mothers survived their childhood and youth, the contour of the relationship with their mothers depended to a large extent on when or how they were to discharge their filial duty of providing for their mothers, which in turn depended (other than the mother's remaining alive) upon the sons' marriage and career. Because Chinese women tended to marry young and bear children right away; sons who were early in the birth order more often than not grew into their twenties while their mothers were still alive. But statistically, given that a woman's average life-expectancy was in the late thirties, the majority of men tended to lose their mothers in their late teens or early twenties—a time when most males were struggling to enter the work force, to establish themselves, and to get married. In real terms, therefore, the situation in which a male in late imperial times would serve his mother in person was not at all frequent. It is not certain whether such sons in fact truly desired to aid their aging parents, as relatively few pairs existed. The grief for the missed, however, would have been similar to that felt at the loss at an early age of one's mother, even though the emotional impact and practical deprivation were different.

The scholar Liu Pao-nan (1791–1855) was born to a fifty-three-year-old father, but his mother, his father's second wife, was considerably younger. The father's death when Liu was four and his mother's long widowhood afterward were to be expected. These typical "widowed-mother and orphaned child" situations epitomized in moral tales could take different shapes, depending on the life-span of the mother. Liu was wed in 1811 when he was twenty-one, but Liu's mother passed away a mere two weeks after that.[11] To lose one's mother within months after a wedding strikes us as perhaps tragic, but it was more the norm than the rarity in China.[12]

For those men whose mothers lived on, the relationship could take either of two roads: a short relationship, roughly five to ten years (or less), or a very long one that would continue well into the son's late thirties or forties. In both situations, duration is the key issue, in terms of both his life and his career, as well as his marriage. With a short period of filial service, the son would only begin to obtain a foothold economically and may have produced grandchildren. Material provisions and successful procreation both realized, a son thus proved his worth. The wife's service, however, was crucial to discharging both duties properly. While childbearing, to serve an aging matron concurrently was not always easy. But the demands were put upon the young couple when they were endowed with more energy; and a mother's not reaching an extreme age meant that the task of nursing care and the risk of familial friction thus created would not be great.

Wang Hui-tsu (1730–1807) married at twenty, while still a student preparing for the civil examinations. At twenty-two, he began tutoring youngsters while continuing his studies. Whatever filial obligations he had at this time were met in practical terms with the three taels of silver he earned for teaching. Later on, he began to hire himself out on secretarial jobs with merchants and officials; however, the financial needs of a household began to show its pressure. Another two years passed, and his marriage produced a daughter. When Wang was thirty-two, his mother passed away, along with her worry about his neglected study and the prospect of his begetting a male heir. After ten years of marriage without a son, Wang at twenty-nine had become involved with a concubine, who traveled with him on distant employment trips. A little over one month after the mother's death, Wang was blessed with a son, and he became an accomplished man at thirty-three.[13]

The eighteenth-century social critic Hung Liang-chi (1746–1809) married his maternal cousin in an uxorilocal marriage at age twenty-three. His wife soon produced two daughters; the first died shortly after birth and the second was lost to smallpox the following year. Because his mother passed away when he was thirty-one, eight years into his marriage, he thus failed in the essential filial act of giving the family a male heir. Being a poor intellectual in his early thirties, moreover, Hung also felt he had little means in the way of providing for his mother's material welfare. He was unable even to look after her funeral in person, a pain that he said he carried with him for as long as he lived. To atone for this inadequacy and in memory of his mother, Hung decided to pursue the strict mourning ritual of taking no meat and having no sex on her memorial day every year for his remaining thirty-some years.[14]

The philosophical writer Kung Tzu-chen's (1792–1841) mother was the daughter of the eminent philologist Tuan Yü-ts'ai (1735–1815). Their chanting of poems together at night and her affection were not atypical of well-bred elite children. Kung's mother said that as a young man of sixteen or seventeen, Kung still looked like a baby. Kung himself revealed that as he grew up and sought employment away from home, whenever reciting the poems taught by his mother, the same tender attachment at her came back to him. Kung married his cousin at twenty-one, but their companionship lasted only a year, when his wife died. He married again at twenty-four. His mother passed away eight years later when he was thirty-two. So, even in the best of conditions, lives were short, and more often than not the mother-son bond was cut off early.

The rarer case was that of a mother living to an older-than-usual age. This is the kind of happiness, longevity, and veneration that people hoped and prayed for. As the entire community and society observed and swayed toward moral behavior, the burden of Confucianism's faith in the "naturalness" of familial ethics and filiality was indeed vested in but a few good sons.

The atypical instances carried enormous social and cultural implications, to the point of forming a religion or creating a mythology in late imperial China. Fang Pao (1668–1749), a scholar from the heavily neo-Confucian town of T'ung-ch'eng in Anhuei province, lost his mother when he was forty-eight. His father had passed away eight years earlier in 1708, the same year he remarried. His first marriage lasted sixteen years (1691–1707), producing no son; his first son was born in 1703 to a concubine taken shortly beforehand. In the twenty-some years in between his marriage at age twenty-three and her death two and half decades later, Fang had considered it his first duty to fulfill his mother's needs, or so he liked to profess. He moved his residence to places of her choice; he took her for walks after meals; together they looked at the moon at night, musing over daily household events. He rushed home whenever she fell ill, even thousands of miles from the capital when, at the age of thirty-nine, he had just received the highest degree (*chin-shih*) and forfeiting the final court orals, which, people said, would have put him in first place. He moved her with him when he was assigned to teach the heir-apparent when he was forty-six, wearing her frailty as a badge of his own virtue. Less than two years later she passed away, after a serious illness that involved the emperor providing his own physician.[15]

The anti-T'ai-p'ing leader Hu Lin-yi (1812–1861) was the first son born to his father's primary wife (his father later took in two concubines, even though he had a male heir). Hu's mother lived until he was forty-seven—a rare blessing. She died of old age at eighty-four, in 1859, and Hu himself died two years later. In Hu's view, providing for and serving his aging mother was always his top priority. From time to time, he claimed filial duty in order to decline public invitations and official engagements—not an unusual pretext for men with aged parents, albeit sometimes employed deceptively. With three marital partners, Hu's father produced seven children, six of whom were females. The two oldest daughters died early, and one was born just after the father died, when Hu was already thirty. Hu was the eldest and the only male child; and thus it was imperative that he be given filial responsibility. For a son born in his parents' middle years (his mother was thirty-seven and his father thirty-four), the mother probably always seemed old. He brought his *lao-mu* (old mother) along wherever his civil or military posts took him. She often complained about the inconveniences of life away from home and asked to return. He promptly complied whenever possible. When she was at his campaign headquarters, however, he personally watched her eat and sleep. He was said to have rushed to his staff with joyful reports whenever the old lady had taken an additional serving of rice at meal time. But it is unclear what is meant by such stock remarks as "he was famous for his filial deeds" or "he always took great pleasure in his morning greetings and close attendance." As to the more tangible of a son's duties, it is, however, rather certain that Hu was completely impotent. Other than his first wife, whom he married at nineteen, he married at least two secondary wives, at twenty-four and twenty-nine, respectively. Yet not only had he disappointed his parents' wish for a grandchild before they died, but he must have also disappointed himself, when, approaching his end, he realized that his funeral would be conducted by a mere adopted son. One's filiality thus could be fraught with problems.[16]

When a man such as minor official Hsu Ts'ai (1810–1869) revealed that in order to "serve [his] mother" he had resolved to quit "drinking at night," it pointed to what he perceived as a heavy duty. Hsu had positioned himself dutifully vis-à-vis his mother, bringing her medicine and watching her eat while working, editing and compiling alongside her. A mere five months after Hsu gave up drinking, his mother passed away when she was in her eighties.[17]

To have one's mother alive beyond one's middle age was unusual, and a mixed blessing as well. The behavior of sons in their fifties or sixties, whose mothers were still living, warrants more than a cursory examination. The court scholar Li Hung-ts'ao (1820–1898) served his mother until her death, when he was forty-seven. Imperial commendation named him as a son who had "attended his mother with utmost filiality." There is a surviving document of his request for a ten-day leave in the summer of that year, when his "heir-mother" (ssu-mu) succumbed to an epidemic. She was really his great-aunt (wife of his great-uncle), whose family line he was assigned to revive as well as that of his natal parents. At seventy-four, his mother became seriously ill and had severe symptoms; Li obtained physicians and medicines. However, after only two days of care she fell unconscious, dying a day later. Yet, all along, Li also had to provide for and pay service to his biological mother (pen-sheng-mu). This mother was with him for another eleven years, before she died at the age of eighty-five, when Li was fifty-eight. Once more he provided care and nursing, and mourned, as he did for his heir-mother. By then, however, his wife and son had long been dead, victims of a diphtheria epidemic in Peking in 1871, when he was fifty-one. Li was alone and old.[18] Before then, the daily provision and care for the mother was hardly a problem, even for his wife, who had maids and servants at her disposal. This was, no doubt, partly a benefit of their high standing. But in the conspicuous position as imperial tutor, and with the unlikely burden of answering to the two regent empresses (the infamous Empress Dowager Tz'u-hsi and, later, the Kuang-hsü emperor's formal mother, the Empress Dowager Tz'u-an), there was probably little room for Li to have behaved otherwise.[19]

For a man past fifty to have a surviving mother was extraordinary by premodern standards. The philologist Wang I-jung's (1815–1900) mother died when he was fifty-two (in 1867). He was the eldest son. His father had died ten years previously, his first wife nineteen years before that, and his eldest son died three years before his first wife. His mother outlived not only her spouse, but her children, children-in-law, and even grandchildren. For the survivor, like Wang, the family's support network was running thin. Wang's mother had watched, as had he, her grand-daughter's death from smallpox at the age of three and his brother's death at six-teen. Wang himself almost died of malaria when he was thirty; and his first wife lost her life to a serious hemorrhage after childbirth in 1878 at the age of thirty-seven (she had been ill for a number of years before then).[20] So who could have been capable and energetic enough, with good spirits and health, to serve the needs of the old mother, as prescribed by the hsiao ideal?

Yü Yüeh's (1821–1906) mother lived until he was fifty-eight. His brothers had divided the household thirty-one years earlier; and Yü, not being the eldest, was not the primary caretaker of their mother—his elder brother was. In his poems, Yü, in his old age, depicted scenes peopled with "an old mother who no longer strolled about the moon, and a sick wife who got mindlessly drunk amidst flowers." Dividing the family before the death of the parents could suggest the existence of discord. An immobile old mother and a feeble-minded sick wife certainly do not conjure up a picture of senior years spent contentedly.[21]

Then there are the remarkable instances of living mothers of sixty-year-old men. Li Kung's (1659–1733) mother did not pass away until he reached sixty-three; and Huang Shu-lin's (1672–1756) mother lived with him until he was sixty-eight (she ninety-two). These two instances occurred in what seems to have been the socioeconomically less advantaged north (Hopeh province) during chaotic times. Reading more closely into the details, however, one quickly realizes what China's culture of filiality meant in real terms. As previously mentioned, in such lengthy relationships even the most resourceful of families might become low on human support. By the time Huang's mother died, all three of his successive wives had long passed away. (The marriages lasted two, seven, and twenty years, when he was aged nineteen to twenty-one, twenty-two to twenty-nine, and thirty-three to fifty-three, respectively.) He also served his grandfather and father in their waning days, but that was when he was in his late twenties and early thirties. (His adoptive grandfather died when he was twenty-nine, and his father died at sixty-one, when Huang was thirty-four). When his mother needed assistance, he had become an old man deprived of the helping hands of wives and daughters. But *hsiao* was a duty that took precedence over everything else, even for this high-ranking official who had won third place in the imperial examinations. So Huang obliged. He took care of his mother in ways expected of him. He followed her will in various matters, preparing a dowry for his half-sister, for example, which he had no inclination to do at first. While conducting these duties, he also sponsored the reprinting and distribution of the *Yen Family Instructions,* to promote family ethics and, perhaps, as a personal reminder as well.[22]

Li Kung was burdened by duty to more than one mother—before the age of thirty-three he had two. Besides his natural mother, he took care of his formal mother (his father's first, and official, wife). In his twenties, while a student, he also learned medicine and sold herbs and drugs "to help support (his) parents." The strain of his double duty visibly wore on him. As a neo-Confucianist strict about rituals, on every first and sixteenth dates of the lunar month he paid special respects to the parents by walking about eight miles to ask about his formal mother's health, then back the same distance from town the next day, to throw himself at the knees of his own mother. His formal mother died at seventy-nine, leaving one daughter. His natal mother bore four sons other than himself. Being the eldest, though, he was required to "practice filiality diligently" in her remaining years. He was said to have performed his duty in model fashion. In providing for her for more than a half-century, he always acted with respect; he "talked to her in a humble voice and with pleasant gestures." In her advanced years, he fed her, fanned her during the heat, and rubbed her back for comfort. And he asked both his wife and his concubine to do needlework with the old woman to keep her company and entertain her. Not that any of this was a novelty in a gentleman's home, but he did judge his spouses according to how well they served their mothers-in-law.

Li's first wife died of consumption, only one year after the wedding. He spoke highly of her virtue of "bending her own will to serve our formal mother." His second wife (he remarried two years later) probably did not fare so well at the task, as she was dismissed (divorced), though she was never sent away. When she died, he told his sons that, though they might choose to bury her as a mother, they were not required to do so. The concubine that his friend purchased for him when he was forty (he had asked for proof that this sixteen-year-old was a virgin) also performed well at her spousal duties. In his words, she was hardworking, thrifty, and accommodating—one who agreed to sew in her mother-in-law's chamber even if unappreciated. But their relationship lasted for only eight short years; she passed away at twenty-four, leaving two sons. As far as we can tell, he did not remarry. So for the last fifteen years of his mother's life, he alone served her needs. And she was difficult to please. He had already given orders that tedious affairs of the house be kept from her. Still, the old lady often appeared despondent, saying that she missed her two grandsons by her youngest son (Li's youngest brother, Yen). And she wanted to be in direct control of the house—"personally in control of the rice and salt," as she put it. Li granted this to her. His first action, whenever he returned home, was to pay his respects, and he commented that her health, her eye problems, and so on, "caused pains like those of a knife wound."[23]

Thus only a few such mother-son pairs were given the task of upholding the ideal and performing the myth. The statistical majority, those without mothers, had no choice but to live out their lives in her honor and to remain emotionally involved through reminiscences. Both categories were important to the continuation of the culture of *hsiao,* and both involved tasks and duties. In any case, it is only when modern civilization lengthened the lives of both men and women that things became complicated, and that, arguably, the Chinese ethics of *hsiao* was put to a genuine, full-scale test, albeit under different conditions.

The Faces

As families progress through stages, and as individual members move through their life cycles, not only do specific family relationships—such as the one between mothers and sons—enter into different phases, but also they respond to changes in the family's power structure. Extended families with adult sons and surviving parents, at some point, had to make the transition from "parent-in-command" to that of "son-in-command." In the latter situation the adult son (with his marriage and a gainful income) was clearly in control; he made major family decisions, played the dominant role over his parents in most respects and activities, and lived in his house along with his aging parents (mother included) as dependents who were mostly given a subordinated status. This situation appears to be blasphemy in the Chinese high ideal of *hsiao.* But looking at the reality, it

represented a much larger part of family experience, more so than people generally admit. Anthropological observations of rural Chinese families in the early
twentieth century reported that obligations to support the parents and of allegiance
to them by no means implied that elders continued to hold authority in the house.
Older men or widows living with their married sons did not normally continue to
be household heads. "The leadership passes to the next generation and the elders
become subordinates."[24] The shifting of power and authority from the older to the
younger generation accelerated as the son gained in age and success (measured
mostly by social status and increase in income), and depending on her health and
vigor, the mother's influence declined.

The picture of a son dominating or ordering his mother about, or an old parent's
dependence upon, or even intimidation by, the son was not something Confucianism allowed. Confucius once compared support of one's parent without the proper
esteem to the feeding of dogs and horses. Small wonder that such situations were
hard to find, their traces most likely suppressed or concealed. Legal records and
literary depictions provide a relatively detailed picture, in comparison with standard-
history sources, but biographical materials, when read and relived with enough
patience and judicious care, offer much in their own right.

Biographies hold frequent mention of *fen-chia* (dividing of the household). As
the sons grew up, the assumption was that at some point they would be in charge of
their separate households. In most situations, the second generation had already
manifested enough independence and power to precipitate the separation. As mentioned above, Yü Yüeh divided the household with his elder brother when he was
twenty-seven. From then on the mother alternated living with, and being supported
by, her two adult sons. The principle whereby the eldest son bore a large responsibility for parental support might have been the convention, but in reality convenience, ability, personal inclination, and social prestige all came into play in
formulating the arrangement. In Yü's case, when *fen-chia* took place in 1847, the
mother began by living with her elder son, as convention would have it. The next
year, she moved to the house of her younger son, to benefit allegedly from the
daughter-in-law's exceptional competence in household management while free-
ing up both sons to travel in order to find better employment. When the older son
received a post as district magistrate, however, she moved (or was moved) back to
his place again to enjoy the status that was properly hers. Decades later, when her
grandson by the younger son (the eldest son of Yü Yüeh) was appointed as a waterways transport official, she was pleased to accept the homage with her son and
daughter-in-law attired in imperially granted, honorific gowns.[25] Thus the work of
parental support, whether practical or ritual, was often shared, negotiated, or exchanged, as the parties chose. But as parents (here, mothers) moved back and forth
between sons and households, better to accord with their earnings and statuses,
there is little doubt as to who was really in charge: It was the elderly parent who
became a dependent. The case of Yü Yüeh was only one such example.

Other examples must be weighed as showing that power and authority were contested in the family. For example, the parent might complain of losing control, or ask to be given back her "old roles." Li Kung's mother provided us with an example of this, as seen above. For a gentried family with means, to turn over various household supplies to the mother and to have entertainment for her provided for her were not difficult arrangements. But the fact remained that Li Kung's aging mother was unhappy about having been withdrawn as manager. All considered, nothing worked as the ultimate pacifier for an embittered mother, the not-yet-so-frail (she was sixty-two) woman seeing her own regime toppled and taken over by her rightfully energetic replacements, the middle-aged son (he was forty-four) and the daughters-in-law.

To assuage and entertain one's aging parents was traditionally an essential of the culture of *hsiao*. "Lao-lai-tzu's playing the clown to please his parents" was a model story of filiality.[26] No one mentioned, or was willing to acknowledge, that power loss and its frustration was at the core of a senior's sadness, something only partially ameliorated by appeasement. The mother of the seventeenth-century novelist P'u Sung-ling (1640–1715) was said to have remembered the details of his birth (some forty years earlier) and often retold the story at family celebrations, while apologizing for the recent burden she had been to him.[27] To instill the sense of indebtedness was the strongest leverage some mothers could muster in order to restore or retain a position of power within the family.

Some mothers retired to a secondary and auxiliary position as soon as a son showed himself to be an adult or when a daughter-in-law moved in to be the housekeeper. There are many accounts of grandmothers "helping out" with childrearing and chores (grandfathers, too, for some activities). Yang Tao-lin's (1837–1911) widowed grandmother in hard times made vegetable pancakes for her grandchildren to take to school.

Then there were cases where mothers seemed to remain very much on top of things for quite some period after the sons had grown. The mothers demonstrated authority in more than one way; they continued to hold the family's purse and rice bucket; they quibbled; they acted mercilessly and ruthlessly; they sometimes even beat up their adult sons. Tao-lin had a great-grand-aunt who was known for having scratched her son's face to bloody scars for his imprudence in entering his bride's room without first paying tribute to his mother.[28] Yang Tao-lin also remembered that up until age five or six his grandmother "was *still* in charge of family affairs."[29] This was stated as fact, without a grudge, but it was a condition far from normal. Numerous accounts mention grandparents making decisions about selling and buying estates, the education of a grandson, tutors, career decisions of family members, the marriage matches for their children and grandchildren, even where to live. The old women did not universally or easily yield power to their sons.

Then there were the moody and oppressive women, like Chao Yü-ching's (1652–1707) grandmother, who were frequently enraged for no obvious reason. The entire family—men, women, and children—fell to their knees until her forgiveness came.[30] Chinese dramas and novels have no shortage of abhorrent matriarchs and submissive sons. Legal documents abound with mothers wounding or killing their sons or daughters-in-law for such offenses as spilling tea on garments or offering cold rice. The opposite case, of neglected and abused mothers, existed as well.

The physical violence that a mother could use against her grown son seems especially novel from a modern perspective. Wang Hui-tsu, for example, was severely beaten by his mother when he was a young man of seventeen.[31] If this is not alarming, recall the complexity depicted in the novel *Hung lou meng* (Dream of the Red Chamber), when Chia Cheng submitted his own teenage son, Pao Yü, to heavy scolding and painful "family punishment" when his autocratic grandmother and his distressed mother intervened. This occurred when Chia Cheng himself was an official in his fifties.[32] Such things took place usually when the "old" woman was still, relatively speaking, an energetic "young" grandmother (perhaps in her late fifties or early sixties), before the household was divided, and when she still had a lot working in her favor and was contributing a large share to the family's welfare. Such tugs-of-war often stopped only at the death of one of the parties.

Motherly Devotion and Womanly Needs

Sociologists, anthropologists, demographers, and historians have long thought that mothers went about the task of reproduction due to not simply their biological inclinations, but also out of self-preservation. The bearing and raising of children were theorized as being a woman's "investment," a form of insurance for a parent's senior years before the existence of the modern state. Thus, many efforts were made to examine the "productive" side of things: to analyze the number of hoped-for children; the way children were reared and socialized; and the cultural values and religious beliefs that might have made reproduction rational in economic terms. The Chinese tradition of *hsiao* might thus be explained away as an example of a cultural component of "reproductive strategy." Over the years, however, few have inquired about the "harvesting" end of the process. In this business of social reproduction, how many parents did live long enough to reap the fruits of their labor? Did mothers, in other words, receive support when needed, and in ways agreeable to them? Furthermore, if the provision and protection that the senior generation received was less than expected or far from adequate, could complaints or gossip actually mend or undermine people's attitudes and behaviors?

When people speak of parental investment and return, they are usually considering matters from an economic or practical perspective. For example, when parents give birth they are seen as allocating the resources at their disposal in their productive and capable years to plan for valuable yields in later years. Such gains can be understood in terms of ordinary material provision, or protection and assistance (physical as well as emotional) in crisis or disaster. In either case, the benefits are assumed to be real and for actual use. When, historically, the average life-expectancy for both men and women barely exceeded the fortieth birthday, such assumptions, however, seem odd. Why should provision and protection be important when nobody lived much past forty? Moreover, children younger than the teen years could hardly render much help during a calamity. Thus, other than ordinary assistance, what use were children to their parents as protection in their senior years? The historical experience of Chinese landed-gentry families in the late imperial period can be of particular interest in this regard, for, in addition to abundant source materials, with nuanced details of an unusually private nature, this was a group of people who were both well off and inculcated in the ancient culture of *hsiao*.

What is uncovered, nevertheless, is a mixed picture regarding sons' provision for their mothers. First, even this socioeconomically privileged group had no escape from the high mortality rate. Thus, in the great majority of cases, if the son did not fall victim to infant or youth mortality himself, rarely did he have the chance to live to an age of financial solidity before his mother succumbed. Even in earlier times, for which numerous statistics and data are not extant, people must have been aware of what was taking place. So if motherly devotion to childbearing and procreation are still approached in terms of necessity and strategy, we are forced to consider other angles. Failed cases, in which mothers did not live long enough to enjoy their sons' support, may prove to hold part of the answer.

Weng Shu-yuan (1633–1701) grew up in an impoverished scholar's family. His father died when he was five, after which his mother kept the family together and brought up the young by herself. The widow and her three children then pulled their resources together. Weng was not the oldest among the boys, but, as he related, in times of crisis, his suggestion for "advancing or retreating" were often heeded by his mother and his elder brother. Although Weng was a strong force, the mother's strength, or at times the lack of it, was felt by all family members. Once, when he was eleven, his mother was seized by her chronic illness, which "gave her problems in her back." In distress, Weng threw himself upon her and "sucked her back with his mouth, breathing in and out hard with warm air for seven days and nights," before her condition improved. Weng carried this nightmarish experience with him for the rest of his life. He noted, as he was putting his autobiography together, that he still had bad dreams in which he was curled up, ready to seal his mouth onto someone's back. He would then break out crying and wake up in horror. The childhood pain lasted to haunt an old man (a son) at sixty-five.

As an indigent student, he engaged in an uxorilocal marriage at seventeen, and went to the bride's house. His family's failure in supplying the new couple with at least sheets and quilts earned them scorn and laughter. In the first years into the marriage Weng admitted having often to borrow from his wife to help with the subsistence of his natal family. Just around this time, though, his studying began to bring recognition and rewards. He became an "official student," and was given a modest allowance. Weng and his wife continued to "lend" money to his own mother and brother.

At nineteen, Weng was able to rent a place and move his wife and his natal family into it, the first sign of self-establishment. That same year his mother passed away, leaving him in remorse and regret. In Weng's long and eventually successful life, he ascended to high offices, passing the exams with high marks and serving at the Imperial Board of Justice. No one could compensate, Weng conceded, for the youthful years spent in humiliation, unable to rectify his mother's suffering. He set about compiling a family genealogy during the time that he was marrying off members of the next generation. He was sixty-four.[33]

The harsh demographic realities of premodern times were such that people like Weng, who lost his mother while in his late teens, or Kuei Yu-kuang, who lost his mother when he was a child of eight, represented the norm rather than the exception. These two types of experience constituted the majority of historical populations everywhere, China included. Thus, a mother who inculcated *hsiao*, or established a bond with a son, was unlikely to reap the benefits in her lifetime. We are compelled, therefore, to examine reproduction in social and ritual terms in addition to the biological sense. What then are the possible implications of *hsiao* beyond physical provision? As the ancient motto goes, "At the highest level, *hsiao* requires one to honor parents with fame and success, second, not to invite humiliation [upon them], and the very least, to support them with their needs."[34] So China's filial culture does not necessarily involve the material. Even the much-quoted Confucian dictum that "among the three offenses of *hsiao*, the failure in producing a male heir is the gravest," does not imply that the task had to be completed within the parent's lifetime, although it was preferred that it was. Examples, like those of Kuei and Weng, as well as countless others, show clearly that such devotion to one's mother could help urge one on toward success in life and to fortify the family and clan (or, in some cases, unhappily lead to violence and resentment).[35]

Biographies of monks and nuns provide another angle on the question of reproduction and the culture of *hsiao*. Master Hsü-yun (1840–1959; yes, he lived to the age of 119!) came from a clerk's family in Hunan. Fascinated with Buddhism at a very early age, he ran away from home and entered the priesthood. He failed in this first attempt, however, resulting in a forced, purportedly unconsummated marriage at seventeen. For decades, he was ignorant of any information about his birth family, claiming unawareness of his father's death six years later when he himself was twenty-five, and the monastic vows that his stepmother and his father's wives took shortly thereafter. At one point, though, he undertook at age forty-three to perform a three-year pilgrimage of holy mountain sites, "as a tribute to the gratitude of [my] parents." After so many years, and as he was just beginning to establish himself in the Buddhist order, he was seized by the thought of filial duty. Deeply remorseful, he confided that he had turned his back against the man and woman who gave him life—a mother who had lost her own life after giving birth to him. He now deeply missed his mother, whom he had never met, he said, and felt unable to repay his debt toward his parents and assuage his guilt. He chanted as he walked his miles, praying so that his dedication would move the merciful bodhisattva to bestow salvation on the souls of his mother and father, to relieve them of the sea of suffering and deliver them to the pure land.[36]

Hsiao encompassed ritual as well as practical and moral rewards. Remember that for mothers, who led their lives as people of secondary and submissive status, to be a recipient of a son's *hsiao* devotion could mean a long-term communal improvement for the family as a group. And, in addition to spiritual fulfillment, honors could be translated into tangible resources as well. This whole hypothesis that Chinese women lived out their lives as wives and mothers primarily with concerns for benefit in their declining years, while a useful mental exercise, is nonetheless more abstract than real. Women were socially molded with a deep sense of themselves as family members whose needs were no longer solely or personally theirs. A mother's desires did exist, but such desires were also firmly grounded in the family context and should not be measured or understood in material, biological, or strictly utilitarian terms.

For instance, a married woman who failed to bear any children (sons especially), thus elevating her status from that of a woman and wife to that of a mother, was not permitted to enter the family shrine after death—she was a lost ghost in the realm of the spirit and the afterlife. Therefore, even if a son born to her did not live long, she could always be grateful for her salvation and vindication, heavenly sent, for this life and the next.

It is interesting to take things yet a bit further and to ponder the idea of "mother's authority" versus "women's rights." Can motherly power be the equivalent to, or translated as, a kind of women's rights? The data on instances where mothers survived to an exceptionally advanced age along with their sons may be illuminating. A thoughtful review of these cases prompts a reply of "no." In instances when despotic mothers ruled, what they possessed was anything but womanly and had a minimum to do with their identity as females. This was so for two reasons. One, the authority that empowered mothers was designated by generation and seniority, not by gender. Therefore, when Yü Yüeh served his mother humbly,[37] when Li Kung exchanged words with his mother softly,[38] or when Hsü Ts'ai served medicine for his mother,[39] they were revering a parent, not a woman. The antagonisms that often existed between mothers and their daughters-in-law also can remind us that gains in motherly influence were not the same as gains in a woman's standing. And, second, whatever the mothers acquired in status and control fell squarely within the domestic sphere, bearing no significance outside her house. A domineering matron had no say and no role in the matters of society or the state. Anything she aspired to in the public domain, whether as a mother or as a woman, would have to be instilled discreetly and directly through the men in her life—most likely her sons.

Sonly Duty and Manly Life

A son's relationship with his mother in his childhood years grew increasingly complex as he matured, especially by his becoming wedded and an important breadwinner. Then, the past connections with his mother, his memories of her toil or compassion, were transformed pertaining to duties and indebtedness toward a virtually infinite parental grace. The mother's grace consisted of primarily two elements: one, her selfless act of giving birth; and two, her good works in nursing and socially molding the child. Both aspects were enthroned in the codes of *hsiao*. One's homage and duty to the biological mother was equal to that regarding the formal mother, secondary mother, stepmother, and adoptive or foster mother. The honor due to the biological mother could be neither overlooked nor trivialized. The well-known dispute over the Wan-li emperor's proper obligation to his natal mother as opposed to the reigning empress (his formal mother) indicates the seriousness of *hsaio*.[40] The debt owed to the women who personally toiled to nurture and educate a child born by someone else, on the other hand, could hardly be belittled. More than a few men in history described bearing the imprint not of the woman who bore them, but of the one (or ones) who nurtured them.[41]

The scholar Liang Chi (1859–1918) was born of his father's secondary wife. While young, however, it was always his formal mother (née Liu) who had the responsibility for his education. She was the one who initiated him in his lessons, who hand-copied and bound his primers, who supervised the daily learning and nightly homework, and who enforced the rigid discipline and severe punishments (which raised critical eyebrows in the community). In a word, she made up his entire mental and social environment, while his biological mother merely labored over household chores. The pattern we witness here is by no means exceptional or individual. In families where there were several categories of mother, the first was always the one in command, while secondary wives or concubines took on the small duties, even regarding their own children. This was so partly because of the system of polygamy itself. A man's first, and formal, wife was chosen to match the family's socioeconomic standing, while the second and subsequent ones were chosen out of passion or out of domestic need. In her cultural and social roles then, a child's formal mother assumed authority almost akin to that of the father (in Liang's case, his father was serving away from home). Soon enough, Liang's formal mother even began to take in small children in order to earn money for her son's schooling. Thus the high esteem and indebtedness Liang showed to her as he grew old ought not to be a surprise. He composed poems and essays remembering her deeds, personally served her in her senility, and left behind a diary, called *Diary in Service by the Sickbed.* Mentions of his biological mother are scarce and cannot be compared. Her seventieth birthday celebration supplies us the only trace of her existence in his adult activities. She passed away at the age of seventy-three when he was forty-nine.[42]

The practice of *hsiao* on the part of the son was complicated by the fact that for most men, under most circumstances, the mundane obligation of providing for their mothers was not carried out in person but by his domestic other—the female spouse(s). When the scholar Wang K'ai-yun's (1832–1916) son wrote in the years when both his mother and grandmother were alive, he always described his mother as toiling over the needs of the grandmother. In Wang's case, his wife's service lasted for seven years: he married at twenty-two and his mother died when he was twenty-nine, rendering the service to the mother (-in-law) a small portion of their conjugal relationship. The marriage lasted for another three decades before his wife passed on. Twenty-six years later, Wang died at age eighty-five.[43]

Even so, some of the men realized what a demanding job it was to serve their mothers daily. The loyalist-martyr Shih K'o-fa (1602–45), in letters he sent from his headquarters while battling the Manchus, consoled his wife time and again for her having such tasks. He comforted her, recognizing how tough it must have been for her to be at the service of his parents (including his father, his own mother, and his father's secondary wife). He once even confided that he thought his secondary mother (née Yang) was narrow-minded and bigoted. But, he continued, he had always considered her, his wife, to be kindhearted. Plus, he had hoped that she would aspire to be a character of great ability and great filiality. Shih told her once that he had long accepted the fact that hers was a life fated to bitterness; and she in her letters used the same term—bitter fate—to describe the harshness. He pleaded for understanding: "I am a man without any other choices." He regretted that he was a middle-aged man, without a son, separated from his family and unable to aid his parents or her in person. "If you, madame, would not carry out the filial duty and humble obedience for me, upon whom may I rely instead?" He often closed these epistles by praying and reaffirming their faith, that "Heaven up high shall not be unfair to people with good hearts"; that she should "try to be accommodating in all things," knowing that "Heaven will naturally examine and be clear of every-thing." Another irony lay in the fact that Shih also wrote (not to her) that his wife, the woman of whom he spoke so intimately and expected so much, was narrow-minded as well. And he missed his mother so much that he often woke up in tears after dreaming of her during his campaigns. He left us seven letters to his wife and four to his parents, a few to his brother and other relatives, before he paid with his life for the defense of the waning empire. Subsequently, his wife met a heroic and violent death.[44] Even ordinary men hardly ever had to act upon their duty of filial piety but delegated the mechanics to their spouses, as did Shih K'o-fa. The domes-tic domain was not their place, and their performances were always judged by what they did outside their home.

For the wife, on the other hand, serving the mother(s)-in-law constituted an indispensable part of her role, despite the ambivalence and difficulties in practice. The issues of gender relations, same-sex conflict (mothers and wives), and sexual attraction were also powerful forces. For instance, there were adult sons who clung to their mothers (partly out of the mother's successful cultivation and partly from the social ideology), and also there were aging mothers who controlled their sons. With the former, affective ties and intimacy at an early stage were the primary cause, more than power plays between generations and across gender lines. Huang P'eng-nien's (1823–1890) mother had always been compassionate toward her son, not unrelated to the fact that she had lost all children born before him and after. (As far as can be determined, at least six of his siblings perished during infancy and early childhood.) As a matter of fact, Huang was probably her only surviving child.

She had good reasons to "love him dearly." And he grew up visibly attached to her, "usually not ever leaving her side."[45] After marriage at eighteen and establishing himself beginning in his twenties as a scholar-lecturer and adviser, he declined invitations to travel or to serve in high offices because, he said, he did not want to leave his family behind, his mother in particular. She died when he was thirty-eight, and he composed not only a vivid biography of her but also poems and other writings recounting the bittersweet days when she made porridge and bran pancakes for her little boy, surprising him with peaches, while she contented herself with the mere pits.

Another example is that of Kung Tzu-chen, who missed the tender poem lessons his mother had taught, and he missed her deeply (his mother died in 1823 when he was thirty-two; she was probably fifty). Her understanding was evoked every time he immersed himself in a poem that she had made alive with her instructions. He stated that as he chanted these verses that the world of innocence, surrounded and protected by her passionate interests, "came right to life here with me in exactly the way as it had been when I threw myself cozily between her knees." Kung entered into two marriages in three years in his early twenties (the cousin he married at twenty-one immediately died). Both women were sophisticated, educated, and good companions, like his mother. His wives traveled with him to scenic spots, like West Lake, and they were said to have been fond also of lyrics. But he still missed motherly love. He rushed back to his mother's grave to plant fifty plum flowers, and stayed home for a year in filial remembrance, studying Buddhism.

In these instances of affection between sons and mothers, the devotion and warmth that the mothers showed were obviously decisive factors, but there also was a genuine, altruistic respect for their boys as they matured, thus allowing adequate emotional space for a reciprocal affinal tie. The tender care Huang P'eng-nien's mother had for her son and the endearing affection Kung Tzu-chen's mother had for her boy as an intellectual companion were genuine, radiating from admiration and dignity. The case of Pao Shih-ch'en (1775–1855) serves as another example. Pao came from a lower-gentry-scholar family, but his mother was illiterate. She relied on dictation and others' help in communicating with her grown son while he made his living as an itinerant secretary at various provincial governors' offices. He noted, however, her valuable advice at key junctures of his career: regarding a decision to take a post in Szechuan province at age twenty-five; deciding to enter the civil-service exams again; or protecting himself in various situations that would not compromise his integrity. Her words cautioned him "to advance when useful and to retreat while not," and that the most precious thing for a man was independence. These words had discernible effects on him. When she spoke, she expected her views to be taken seriously, but her knowledge of him and her interest in his welfare were essential to the development of those views. When a real crisis occurred, she was more than an analyst—she confronted the messengers in treachery and scolded them away while preventing her son from burning his notes and papers in a frightening bureaucratic purge. That year he was thirty-eight.

It is little wonder that she was the only family figure found, repeatedly, in his public biography documenting only his official acts and statecraft ideas. In Pao's mostly unsuccessful life, her presence was a valuable comfort. At the age of sixty-one, he felt compelled to make one last failed attempt at the official examinations, but she passed away before the result was known.[46]

Another intriguing aspect of mother-son relations is that sons could transfer their affections for their mothers through their spouses and daughters. Kuei Yu-kuang not only talked with his wives about his mother and thought of his mother in domestic and intimate moments, but he saw images of his mother in the characters and daily acts of his wives. In the biographies he wrote for his two spouses (sequential, not coexistent), he depicted them with the virtues of beauty and of competence in their feminine charm—qualities most evident first and foremost in his long-deceased mother.[47] Wang K'ai-yun, too, had a way of transferring the reverence he had for his mother to his wife, and even to his daughter. His was a scholarly household. During his mother's lifetime he did not touch the pages of *Li-chi* (Book of Rites) because he was superstitious about reading the book's content on funeral rituals. He also thought highly of his wife, who came from a good family. As he worked on his philological study on the ancient classics, she was the reader he had in mind, and in whose valuable company he labored for twenty-two years. The women in Wang's house lived cordially together, buoyed by his admiration of his mother.[48] He took his daughter along on boating and on journeys, and looked for the best doctors for her when she was ill.

With the political activist T'an Ssu-t'ung (1865–1898), we get something rather more Oedipal. In early childhood T'an's affective ties with his mother were heightened by her having fallen out of his father's favor. She ended up leaving their residence in the capital to her husband and his concubine and went back to the old home in the Hunan countryside. Tearfully and under stress, T'an never stopped longing for her. In time, he came to cherish a loving relation with his wife. They corresponded often as he himself became a minor official. When he later turned into a "radical" reformer, he dedicated the new-style schools with personal money, and named them after his wife. He established girls' education in her honor. He wanted to emphasize that his act had nothing to do with the resources of his father or the family that he abandoned. As the years went on, his martyrdom appeared inevitable and he consoled his wife with their mutual devotion to Buddhism. He left his estate to her, with no words for his father, and nothing went to his parental family. His disheartened mother had died of illness long before.[49]

Not all the stories are happy ones. But more important, not all unhappy cases were unhappy for the same reasons. The most frequent tragedies were not untimely death, as with Kuei Yu-kuang's mother, nor affectionate ties spoiled by oppressive acts, like those suffered by T'an Ssu-t'ung and his mother. They were usually domestic situations gone awry, such as a mother increasingly impossible to please. Sons "blessed" with long-lived parents understood this. Some endured it more tacitly or tactfully than others. This difficult type of mother-son bond appeared, on the surface, not unlike the affective mode just discussed. The mothers had strong wills and the sons behaved dutifully. But from the start, the mothers appeared possessive and authoritative, and the sons grew used to accepting this one relationship over and above his others. Wei Hsiang-shu's (1617–87) mother was so attached to her boy that she delayed in sending him out to tutors. As she aged, he asked for early retirement in order to be by her side, administering medicines when she was ill and personally directing the construction of dainty pavilions for her amusement. Later he wrote that he had vowed never to venture more than 100 *li* (about thirty miles) from her when she was old as his filial tribute. His autobiographic chronicle shows clear marks of a willful clinging to maternal ties.[50] P'u Sung-ling, too, had a mother who expected his personal attendance when she was sick. When outside employment demanded distance and long separations, to invoke a sense of obligation she used to tell and retell stories of her giving birth to him—of the auspicious dream his father had that night and of the family excitement.[51]

Maternal strategies and filial submissions have to be understood against the background of the Chinese patriarchy, which presupposed blood ties over marital relations and vertical ancestral loyalties over lateral domestic ties. With such priorities, multiple roles emerged. In traditional China, all men should think of themselves as sons foremost, not simply of their parents, but of the family, and of the ancestral shrine. And in that same line of thinking, women prepared for their performance as mothers. Some were more successful at it than others. As an adult son, for instance, Lao Nai-hsüan (1843–1921) had always made important decisions (regarding employment, family moves, traveling) according to the mind of his mother. He tried to appraise her feelings, her health, her mood before making a decision.[52] She was the reason behind the right choices, the best places to be, the correct transportation for getting around (cart, boat, mule, or horse), in the appropriate season, and on the auspicious date. Things became more complicated for Liu Pao-chen, whose widowed mother never developed trust or confidence in him. She continued to scold, to lecture, and to guide every move he made as an adult. He was spared by her relatively early death.

Even in a case where the mother-son pair enjoyed a long experience of mutual dedication and cooperation, the goal of rewarding one's parent could be wrenching. The classical scholar Lo Chen-yü (1866–1940) was used to helping out his mother with all kinds of housekeeping. He was sent out collecting rents and to the pawnshop to take out loans. His elder brother's premature death affected him deeply, and there was an immediate need to provide for the funeral and, eventually, a male heir. Lo had difficulty selling either his skills or the family estate. He gave his brother his eldest son to raise, and his own second son who was born four years later lived for only eight days. Lo's mother became anxious, and Lo's chronic insomnia came back to plague him. Next, his wife died, forcing him to send all the surviving children to the maternal grandparents. When his mother fell ill again, he cut his own flesh in the hope of her recovery, something that filiality might demand.

Such borderline masochism raises various issues. In the less pleasant as well as the more positive cases of the mother-son relationship, we must examine the effects upon the man's relationship with his spouse and on his attitude toward females in general. Under a roof where old matrons ruled men, knowingly or unwittingly, the latter sought asylum in intimate ties with women and struggled, or completely intimidated and turned off by women, found them frightening. At the very least, we recognize that conflicts occurred, not only between mothers and daughters-in-law, but also between husbands and wives. But Confucianism frowned upon strife between mothers and sons. Sweetness or bitterness in later years was rooted in what had transpired in an earlier phase.

The way a man's sonly duty affected his manly life had most to do with his sensibility toward vertical or patriarchal relations, as opposed to lateral or affinal associations. Fang Pao's (1668–1749) case is a good example. As previously mentioned, he was from a province heavily imbued with a wave of neo-Confucian revivalism in the eighteenth century—where priority of familial matters over personal needs and of patriarchal interests over affinal relations had deep roots. At twenty-three, he was married as arranged. Months before the wedding, however, his younger brother died (at twenty-one). Fang wanted to undertake mourning. For an older brother to take on a formal mourning ritual (in solemn mood, plain clothes, with no meat, celebration, or sexual activities) for a younger was unheard of, if not improper. Fang, however, insisted and declined to consummate the new marriage. As his quaint behavior entered its seventh month, clansmen and relations could no longer contain their repugnance. Under their pressure Fang was forced to "complete his marital duty," for which, however, he pronounced "a life-long resentment." In his mid-thirties he had clearly established his own family branch with a son (born by his secondary wife) and with many household responsibilities. There was probably little choice as far as household responsibilities were concerned, because by then he was the only surviving male among siblings (their mother, the father's secondary wife, bore three boys, and Fang's elder brother had also passed away when Fang was thirty-seven). The filial duty, however, does not alone account for all his actions, for he was to move with his mother to a special residence—Prospect Garden, specially constructed to her taste—and to devote himself to little else but to please her. He walked with her after meals, accompanied her to the maids, and they were known to have admired the moon together. In terms of public performances, Fang passed the highest level of the imperial examination and achieved the *chin-shih* title in 1707, at thirty-nine. But before the final court sessions to decide on the overall winner, he received news of his mother's illness and rushed home. People said that he had high hopes of winning first place, but he exhibited no regret. His sonly devotion, on the other hand, did not extend equally to his father, who died a year after Fang was awarded the degree. Fang cited his living mother as the reason for not staging an elaborate funerary or mourning ritual—this was a feeble excuse. His attitude toward women and spouses compared badly to the humility he showed to his mother. Later that same year, when he raced home from the capital because of his mother's poor health (and losing good career opportunities), his wife passed away as well. He composed mourning verses in her memory but when people sent him proposals of remarriage, he shot back with stern lectures. He did take a woman one year later, with no reason of propriety given. Biographical and personal notes were rich, however, with thoughts and deeds about only his mother, with scanty information on male relations, and even less on other womenfolk. It was recorded that he proudly brought his mother along when asked to serve as the councilor of the imperial study, and she spent her last two years of life with him. She died at an unknown advanced age; he was forty-eight at the time.

So even with commitments to one's filial duty as deeply placed and constantly involved as Fang Pao's, there could be no guarantee for a smooth sail. In fact, with the many built-in entanglements of power alignments constructed across both gender and generation, a theater of human struggle can be seen. Mothers who used to nurture came to depend on sons, and sons who used to be provided for became leaders who were supposed to submit formally but not substantially to their mothers. The ambivalence and pain experienced by Shih K'o-fa and the hard work and frustrations of Li K'ung, of Fang Pao, or of Pao Shih-ch'en, or of the many nameless sons, all present variations on a leitmotiv. The difficulties, or the schism, moreover, may not be understood simply as that doomed to occur between ideal and practice, or, as some phrase it, between people's "ultimate aspiration" and "life management." Ideals were shifting all the time, and had the capacity to adapt to different circumstances, during different life-phases. Some mothers and sons established a goal for themselves in the beginning, which, as life proceeded, was denied them, and thus they formulated a different scheme. In any event, ideals and practicality both could be more fluid than people (historical characters as well as their observers) assumed. The bond between mothers and sons in general may be perceived as socioculturally constructed and collectively formed, but it has always been individually arranged, privately manipulated, and personally endured.

The Questions of Time, Region, and Class

In a study already loaded with tales, it may appear excessive to add any further consideration. Yet it is odd to speak of Chinese families with no reference to time, space, or social class. Here I present briefly some preliminary thoughts in these categories, merely to invite future investigation. First of all, the late imperial era, or the Ming–Ch'ing period, appears to have been one in which Chinese family relations underwent intensified pressure, yet discovered fresh possibilities. Regarding the mother-son bond in particular, increasing opportunities for upward social mobility created by the institutionalized civil-service examination and the opening up of domestic and long-distance trade for merchant, artisan, and peasant families meant that almost every family was presented with opportunities, and thus they pressed their boys to strive for betterment. Most often, it was the mother upon whose shoulders lay the duty of preparing men and goading them toward this competitive race. The general trend was to inculcate intimacy, intensity, and comrade-ship on top of the old bonds. It could also breed a higher degree of bitterness caused by intensified pressure and disappointed anticipation. Some of the biographical data and family letters bear witness to such dependence and residual resentment. Second, the neo-Confucian revival in the seventeenth and eighteenth centuries, both in the southeast and in some corners of the north, generated a more rigid social atmosphere and created a more oppressive family ethic. Where intellectual and cultural movements held sway, motherly devotion and sonly duty, like female chas-tity and monarchical loyalty, were visibly solidified. By contrast, during this same period, a lively mercantile culture, along with a booming printing industry and bustling town life, loosened up old ethical ties, the effect of which was felt at the family and individual levels. After the beginning of the eighteenth century, more-over, the numbers of student-candidates who failed the examinations increased; these were young to middle-aged men with no fixed employment but with a fair amount of education and free time. These factors formed the social basis for a Chinese family life of greater intimacy, pushing toward generational closeness and gender fluidity and equality. Relations between husbands and wives as well as be-tween men and women were warming up, while the mother-son bond was simulta-neously tightening up and becoming a burden. The social ferment of the late nineteenth and early twentieth centuries had its seeds in this earlier development.

Regional culture and class differentiation may be viewed in a similar vein. From the sixteenth to the nineteenth centuries, China's southeastern provinces contained, on one hand, a rigid, authoritative clan culture or the genteel culture of towns, or else, on the other hand, the peasant mentality of rural areas. This contrast between strict neo-Confucian ethics and looser human relations spoke well for people liv-ing at the two ends of the spectrum. Families in the north tended to be more tradi-tional in the sense that neither the enthusiasm for neo-Confucian morality nor the flexible merchant–town life had as much influence on them. Here again, particular families (such as Li Kung's in Hopeh) and special cities (such as Peking, the capi-tal) reveal exceptions.

For this period, because of the factors mentioned above, the experiences of China's educated elite merited the most attention, more so than before, and not entirely for their leading position in society or the accessibility of source materi-als. For during this time when old family rules were yielding fresh meanings, when new modes of behavior were being attempted, when added demands strained people's endurance of the old ways, and when novel experiences were sought, by the bold, the curious, and the bored, it was this group of gentlemen and women and children whose struggle was enlisted, whose patience was tested, whose imagi-nation fruitfully explored, and whose feelings suggestively experimented. Statisti-cally and sociologically speaking, moreover, the number of China's educated was rapidly increasing. Socioeconomic status varied to such a great degree that in their ranks were included not only the noble but also the mean, the rich along with the poor, and the landed together with the penniless. It was on such grounds that their life stories should be counted—not in the old sense of a selected and privileged few—and which we are here to contextualize.

Conclusion

Time reveals all for people and for history. Individual lives unfolded, families evolved, emotions constructed, shattered, reconstructed, all within one generation's time. The particular Chinese tradition of filiality (*hsiao*), however, placed these in specific patterns. Respect or provision for one's aging parents was not unique. Historical Europe, contemporary Muslim societies, even populations in modern times have practiced these. But in late imperial China coresidence narrowed down choices and twisted feelings between aging parents and their grown children. The burdens and demands on mothers and sons proved especially trying because of both the power and the vulnerability upon which their relations were built, and the stark reverse course affected them both intensely, sparing little room for forgetting or ignorance. The mother had no official authority and resource, as did the father, thus hardly allowing her son(s) less concern morally later on. And a grown son did not have the distance afforded by physical separation, as the adult daughters did once they were married off. Death was ironically the only solution to end the bond, although with some, even that was not so complete a deliverance.

There was more than one way, it is true, that a mother and her son(s) might relate to each other. But in the end, motherly devotion was not entirely the same as womanly needs, and a son's duty certainly did not provide the answers to the many questions of a man's existence. It is hard enough to achieve satisfaction in gender and generational relations, not to mention when compounded and lived out within the realm of ancestral beliefs. In historical China, for all its roles, it might be that men only had to be good sons and women ultimately fine mothers (even the emperor, one may add, who was the Son of Heaven, and all the ministers and subjects who as his lawful children were always asked to yield loyalty as a form of filiality). And the majority of the Chinese female deities were motherly figures, material mercy and protection being their main attraction. The bond that both so carefully constructed provided hope and sustained them. Yet it was obviously a bondage even with the best intentions and under the better conditions, which tells us much about how or why, in the New Culture movement of the twentieth century, filiality was the first among the thousands of feudalistic evils to be dismantled, along with licentiousness at the top among the hundreds of virtues being pursued.

Notes

1. In an earlier study, entitled "Constructed Emotions: The Bond Between Mothers and Sons in Late Imperial China" (*Late Imperial China* 15, no. 1 [1994]: 87–117), I showed how a strong and intimate bond was formed between struggling young mothers and their vulnerable dependent sons in the childhood stage of the boys. The present chapter

intends to extend that observation to explore how that relation unfolds in the later phases of a family's life cycle in the adulthood of the sons and the old age of the mothers.

2. The family life cycle as a subject has not been attracting enough scholarly attention in the China field. Recently, Arthur Wolf and Chuang Ying-chang produced an interesting study on the topic, focusing particularly on the division of the household (*feng-chia*). See Arthur P. Wolf and Ying-chang Chuang, "Fraternal Fission, Parental Power, and the Life Cycle of the Chinese Family" (paper presented at the Conference on Asian Population History, Institute of Economics, Academia Sinica, January 1996).

3. Kuei Yu-kuang, "Hsien-p'i shih-lueh," in *Kuei Chen-ch'uan chi* (Taipei: Shih-chieh, 1960), 312–13.

4. Ibid.

5. *Shih-ching* (Cheng-chou: Chung-chou ku-chi, 1991), 360–62.

6. Han Ying, *Shih-wai-chuan* (Shanghai: Shanghai, 1993), *chuan* 7, 5.

7. Fan Yeh, *Hou-han-shu, K'ung Jung chuan* (Taipei: Ting-wen, 1981), *chuan* 7, 2278.

8. "T'ang hsuan-tzung yu-chu," in *Hsiao ching* (Taipei: Chung-hua, 1965); An Shih-kao, *Fu-mu-en-nan-pao-ching*, in *Wu-ching-t'ung-chuan*, 3.

9. In my earlier essay, "Constructed Emotions: The Bond Between Mothers and Sons in Late Imperial China," I had used subtitles such as "The Voice of the Mother," "The Mother Within the Son," and "In Memory of the Mother" to discuss such inheritance of the human emotions and its implication in late imperial Chinese history.

10. Many children share a fate like that of Shao T'ing-ts'ai (1648–1711), who was only eleven when his stepmother passed away. If anything, she may only wield her influence (whatever that could have been) posthumously, which incidentally is taken very seriously in China, as we shall see. See Yao Ming-ta, *Shao Nien-lu hsien-sheng nien-p'u* (Taipei: Shang-wu, 1982), 18–30.

11. See "Hsing-chuan" (Biography) and "Ti-chiu fu-chun hsing-chuan" (Biography of my father *ti-chiu*) as quoted in Liu Wen-hsin, *Ching liu chu-chen pao-nan nien-p'u* (Taipei: Kuang-wen, 1971), 3–4, 12–13.

12. My reading and analysis of Ming–Ch'ing biographical data have provided dozens of example of the loss of a mother by a newly married son. Chang Lü-hsiang (1611–74) married at eighteen and his mother passed away three years later. Liu's and Chang's experiences were hardly exceptions to the old family system and demographic reality. A small human anecdote to this general pattern was that in some instances, the proximity between the dates of a son's wedding and the mother's death was not purely coincidental. Li Pei-ching's (1826–1882) mother passed away a half-month or so after his wedding. That year he was nineteen, a prime age for marriage; yet, it is true that the ceremony took place at the insistence of the ailing mother, who was anxious to see the family line moved on in the twilight hours of her own life. Szu Tun-yuan, *Chang yang-yuan hsien-sheng nien-p'u* (Taipei: Kuang-wen, 1971), 3–4. Li Ch'eng-li, *Chu-chien-tao-jen tzu-shu nien-p'u* (Taipei: Kuang-wen, 1971), 4.

13. Wang Hui-tzu, *Ping-t'a meng-hen lu* (Taipei: Kuang-wen, 1971), 17–47.

14. Lu P'ei, *Kung Pei-chiang hsien-sheng nien-p'u* (Taipei: Kuang-wen, 1971), 17–28.

15. Szu Tun-yuan, *Fang Wang-hsi hsien-sheng nien-p'u* (Taipei: Kuang-wen, 1971), 45–63. Fang Pao's mother was his father's second wife. The age difference between the two is unclear, but Fang was the second son (of three), and the only surviving one in his mother's old age (his older brother died when Fang was thirty-seven and his younger brother died when Fang was twenty-one).

16. Fertility problems, incidentally, ran in the family. When Hu was in his twenties,

while he was struggling to procreate, his father was still struggling with his part of the task well into his own late fifties and early sixties. Mei Ying-chieh, *Hu Wen-chung kung nien-p'u* (Taipei: Kuang-wen, 1971), 5–47.

17. Hsu Ts'ai, *Pi-chou-chai chu-jen nien-p'u* (Taipei: Kuang-wen, 1971), 63.

18. Li Tsung-t'ung, *Li Hung-ts'ao hsien-sheng nien-p'u* (Taipei: Sheng-wu, 1971), 26–241. Li married exceedingly late at age twenty-nine, with his maternal cousin whom he had met while a child.

19. Ibid., 145–243.

20. Wang Ch'ung-huan, *Wang Wen-min kung nien-p'u* (Taipei: Kuang-wen, 1971), 17–41.

21. Cheng Chen-mo, *Yu Ch'iu-yuan hsien-sheng nien-p'u* (Taipei: Shang-wu, 1982), 16–51, 25.

22. Ku Chen, *Huang K'un-p'u hsien-sheng nien-p'u* (Taipei: Kuang-wen, 1971), 3–77.

23. Feng Ch'eng, *Li Shu-ku hsien-sheng nien-p'u* (Taipei: Kuang-wen, 1971), 1–435.

24. Norman Diamond, "K'un Shen: A Taiwan Village," 64, as quoted in John C. Caldwell, *Theory of Fertility Decline* (San Diego: Academic Press, 1982) , 225.

25. Cheng Chen-mo, *Yu Ch'iu-yuan hsien-sheng nien-p'u*, 19–52.

26. *Sung ko hsiao-ching* (T'ien-chin: Ku-chi, 1987), 62.

27. P'u Juo, *Liu Ch'uan P'i-kung hsing-lueh*; P'u Sung-ling, *Chiang-ch'en k'u-mu*, in Chang Ching-ch'iao, *P'u Sung-ling nien-p'u* (Taipei: Sheng-wu, 1970), 40–41.

28. Chao Yang Pu-we, "Wo-te-tzu-fu," *Chuan-chi-wen-hsueh* 3, no. 3: 3–4. See also Hsiung Ping-chen, "Constructed Emotions: The Bond Between Mothers and Sons in Late Imperial China," *Late Imperial China* 15, no. 1 (1994): 98.

29. Ibid.

30. Lu Yuan-liang, *Chao K'o-t'ing nien-p'u chi-lueh* (Taipei: Kuang-wen, 1971).

31. Wang Hui-tzu, *Ping-t'a meng-hen lu*.

32. Tz'ao Hsueh-ch'in, *Hung lou meng, chuan* 33.

33. Wong Shu-yuan, *Wong T'ieh-an nien-p'u* (Taipei: Kuang-wen, 1971), 2–92.

34. "T'ang hsuan-tzung yu-chu," in *Hsiao ching* (Taipei: Chung-hua, 1965), *chuan* 1, p. 2.

35. For the extended effects of the mother-son bond, see my discussion on "The Mother Within the Son" and "In Memory of the Mother" in "Constructed Emotions."

36. Tz'en Hsueh, *Hsu Yun ho-shang nien p'u*, 1–16.

37. Cheng Cheng-mo, *Yu Ch'iu-yuan hsien-sheng nien-p'u*.

38. Feng Ch'eng, *Li Shu-ku hsien-sheng nien-p'u*.

39. Hsu Ts'ai, *Pi-chou-chai chu-jen nien-p'u*.

40. Ann Waltner, *Getting an Heir: Adoption and the Construction of Kinship in Late Imperial China* (Honolulu: University of Hawaii Press, 1990).

41. In an earlier article I had discussed how the teachings and influences from their formal mothers had decisively set the life courses of important historical figures such as Ku Yen-wu (1613–1682), Wang Hui-tzu, and others, while admitted by these protagonists as such. See Hsiung Ping-chen, "Constructed Emotions," 88.

42. Liang Huan-ting, *Kuei-lin Liang hsien-sheng nien-p'u* (Taipei: Kuang-wen, 1971), 4–43.

43. Wang Tai-kung, *Hsiang-chi fu-chun nien-p'u* (Taipei: Kuang-wen, 1971), 20–338.

44. Chang Ch'un-hsiu, *Shih K'o-fa chi* (Shanghai: Ku-chi, 1984), 96–126.

45. Chen Ting-hsiang, *Huang T'ao-lou nien-p'u* (Taipei: Shang-wu, 1978), 2–19. The six deceased siblings were his elder brother, three younger brothers, and two younger sisters who died at ages nine, three, five, four, less than one month, and less than one month, respectively.

46. Hu Yun-yu, *Pao Shen-po hsien-sheng nien-p'u* (Taipei: Kuang-wen, 1971), 2–49.

47. Kuei Yu-kuang, "Chi Wang chen-jen wen, chi nien erh ch'i," in *Kuei Chen-ch'uan ch'un-chi.*

48. Wang Tai-kung, *Hsiang-chi fu-chun nien-p'u.*

49. T'an Ssu-t'ung, *Jen hsueh* (Shanghai: Chung-hua, 1958), 14–17, 51, 58, 60; Shen Ch'u-t'ang, *Liu-yang T'an hsien-sheng nien-p'u* (Taipei: Kuang-wen, 1971), 3–31.

50. Wei Hsueh-mi, *Wei Min-kuo kung nien-p'u* (Taipei: Kuang-wen, 1971), 2–55.

51. Chang Ching-ch'iao, *P'u Sung-ling nien-p'u,* 3–102.

52. Szu Tun-yuan, *Fang Wang-hsi hsien-sheng nien-p'u* (Taipei: Kuang-wen, 1971), 45–63.

3

An Island of Beautiful Women

The Discourse on Gender in Ch'ing Travel Accounts of Taiwan

Emma Teng

Seventeenth- and eighteenth-century Chinese travelers to the island colony of Taiwan almost invariably remarked that native custom gave precedence to the female sex. "The savages value woman and undervalue man" became a commonplace of Ch'ing (1644–1911) ethnographic writing on the indigenous peoples of the island, known to the Chinese as *fan* (savages). As a direct inversion of the Confucian patriarchal maxim "value man and undervalue woman," this pithy expression indexed the utter alterity of Taiwan to the Chinese who colonized the island in 1683. Encountering a land with female tribal heads, uxorilocal-residence marriage, and matrilineal inheritance, Chinese travelers perhaps thought that they had stumbled upon the mythical Kingdom of Women—the Chinese equivalent of Amazon. As in the Kingdom of Women, it seemed, here it was the women who took the lead and the men who followed. The anomalous gender roles of the indigenous peoples became one of the most popular topics in Ch'ing travel writing on Taiwan. Writers exhibited a particular fascination with the habits of "the savage woman." Women, and their daily activities, were also a favorite subject for illustrated ethnographic albums. Female sex roles attracted this intense interest not only because they appeared strange in and of themselves, but also because they served as a marker of the strangeness of Taiwan as a whole. The discourse of gender was thus central to Ch'ing colonial representations of Taiwan's "savagery."

Indeed, gender and ethnicity are closely intertwined in premodern Chinese ethnographic discourse. At least as far back as the Six Dynasties (222–589), the trope of gender inversion (the reversal of normative sex roles) was frequently used to represent foreignness in both historical and literary texts. Kingdoms of women were widely recorded in geographical texts such as the ancient *Shan-hai ching* (Classic of Mountains and Seas), as well as in the dynastic histories and travel accounts. Such lands also became a favorite subject of fiction, the most famous Ch'ing example being the nineteenth-century satiric novel, *Ching-hua yuan* (Flowers in the Mirror). The trope of gender inversion was particularly popular in accounts of the region now known as Southeast Asia, and (in the late Ch'ing) of

Originally published in *International Historical Review* 20, no. 2 (1998): 353–70. Used with permission.

America and Europe. In such writings, the discourse of gender became a means of demarcating the "civilized" from the "barbarian" or "savage." The rigidity of sex roles in Confucian ideology meant that deviations from normative definitions of femininity and masculinity were readily interpreted as signs of barbarism. Other gendered tropes, such as hypermasculinization and hyperfeminization, were also employed to establish the alterity of non-Chinese groups. Such tropes were particularly popular in literary forms such as frontier poetry.

In Ch'ing colonial discourse, gendered, or sexualized tropes are not only employed as a means of signifying the "otherness" of the colonial subject, but also quite often as a form of denigration. Thus, gender functions much as it does in the European discourse of discovery and colonialism—to express relations of domination and subordination. A critical point of difference, however, is that Ch'ing colonial discourse does not represent the colonized land itself as metaphorically feminine, or as virgin. Exploration and conquest, in turn, are not figured as sexualized acts of penetration and possession. Ch'ing travel writers did, however, represent colonial expansion as a masculine quest for sexual experience, a trope which postcolonial scholars have identified as a major theme of Western imperialist writings. Colonial relations, too, are sexualized in their textual representations, colonial power and ethnic prestige being symbolized by Chinese sexual license with the native women. Thus, in terms of gender, Ch'ing colonial discourse exhibits considerable overlap with European colonial discourses, but is yet not entirely parallel. An examination of gender dynamics in Taiwan travel literature reveals that insights from Western colonial theory can provide useful tools of analysis, but also that the particular gendered tropes of this literature are derived from within the Chinese literary tradition.

The uses of gender as a metaphor for conceptualizing inequality, or as a means of signifying relationships of power, have been extensively theorized by anthropologists, postcolonial studies, and feminist scholars. Gender appears to be a particularly apt metaphor for colonial discourse because it expresses both difference and hierarchy. The link between gender and the construction of the "other" has been widely noted since the publication of Edward Said's *Orientalism* in 1968. Said posited that in European representations of the "Orient" from the late eighteenth century onward, the Oriental subject is gendered "feminine" (weak, subordinated, irrational, lascivious), in contrast to the normative Western self, which is gendered "masculine" (strong, dominant, rational, continent). As such, there is a structural equivalence between male and female, major and minor. In the China field, anthropologists such as Dru Gladney and Stevan Harrell have found parallels to Western "Orientalism" in Chinese representations of non-Han "minority" peoples as a feminized and subordinated "other" to the Han majority. Other recent scholarship, such as that of Ann Stoler, Ann McClintock, and Susan Morgan, challenges the oversimplification of Said's paradigm and calls attention to colonial women's differential experiences of gender politics. Much of the newer scholarship adopts an intersectional approach, examining the connections of race, gender, class, and sexuality. Further elaborating the intersections between gender and ethnicity, Sau-ling Wong has written of the "ethnicizing of gender"—essentially the reverse phenomenon of Orientalism's "gendering" of ethnicity. Wong describes the "ethnicizing of gender" as the "attribution of allegedly natural ethnic essences such as 'Chineseness' or 'Americanness' to 'masculine' and 'feminine' behavior."[1] In the case of Ch'ing travel literature we see a similar attribution of "civility" and "barbarism" to "masculine" and "feminine" behaviors. The intersections of gender and ethnicity (or race) thus can be seen to be varied and multidimensional.

This article examines the representation of the "savage woman" in Ch'ing travel accounts of Taiwan, and the linkages between gender and ethnicity in Ch'ing colonial discourse. My central argument is that gender inversion is fundamental to the construction of the ethnic difference of the Taiwan indigenes. One aspect of this inversion, the feminization of the indigenous men, may be regarded as a means of expressing the subordinate status of the colonized subject. However, it is less the feminization of the men than the anomalous roles of women that preoccupy the Chinese travel writers. This fascination stems in large part from their desire to imagine "another world." Taiwan frequently served as a projection of this desire in the travel literature, whether as a world of the past, a world of marvels, or a "kingdom of women."

The savage woman not only symbolized difference to Chinese observers; she was also a pivotal figure in the representation of colonial relations: Colonial dominance was frequently represented in terms of Chinese access to indigenous women. Chinese writings thus typically hypersexualized the "savage woman," depicting her as more erotic, more promiscuous than the Chinese woman. Intermarriage between Han Chinese settlers and indigenous Taiwanese eventually became a source of contention in the local society, with women serving as a kind of contested terrain for the colonizers and colonized. At the same time, intermarriage between Han settlers and indigenous women was an important vehicle for transcultural exchange in colonial Taiwan: a two-way process of acculturation.

At other times, the discourse of gender in the travel literature was less about Taiwan itself than about the internal concerns of Ch'ing society, in particular, the changing roles of women. The idealization of the foreign woman became a common trope for a self-reflexive critique of Chinese society, in both travel literature and fiction. In this mode, the foreign woman serves as a projection for Confucian ideals perceived to be losing their hold in China. The figure of the savage woman, then, could serve a variety of rhetorical purposes, often opposing, to suit the needs of the travel writer.

The Ch'ing Travel Accounts

Ch'ing travel accounts of Taiwan were produced by colonial officials, military men, and others who traveled in the capacity of the Ch'ing colonial enterprise. Very few Chinese eyewitness accounts of the island exist from the period before the Ch'ing, when Taiwan was a Dutch colony and later an outpost of the Ming loyalist rebel Koxinga (Cheng Ch'eng-kung). The sole firsthand account of Taiwan from the Ming is Ch'en Ti's *Tung-fan chi* (Record of the Eastern Savages), written in 1603. This account was regarded as highly authoritative and was widely quoted by Ch'ing writers. As such, *Record of the Eastern Savages* established many of the major tropes of Taiwan travel writing in the Ch'ing dynasty. The number of accounts produced by Chinese increased dramatically after the Ch'ing colonization of Taiwan in 1683. These accounts were written in a variety of genres— the travel diary, the travel essay, the topically organized account, or the "random jottings" (*pi-chi*) style popular in the Ch'ing—and most included poetry in addition to prose. Travel accounts were an important source of information for the colonial administration, and were widely read by officials serving in Taiwan. The accounts served as source materials for geographical works, histories, and local gazetteers. Travel literature was also read for entertainment by urban audiences seeking "vicarious travel." The most famous accounts were anthologized in the literary *collectanea* that became so popular in nineteenth-century China.

The most well-known Ch'ing accounts include Lin Ch'ien-kuang's *Taiwan chi-lüeh* (Brief Record of Taiwan, ca. 1685), the first eyewitness account of Taiwan produced after the Ch'ing conquest, Yü Yung-ho's *P'i-hai chi-yu* (Small Sea Travelogue, 1697), a diary of a sulphur expedition; Huang Shu-ching's *T'ai-hai shih-ch'a lü* (Record of a Tour of Duty in the Taiwan Strait, 1736), a record of an official's tour of inspection of the island; and Wu Tzu-kuang's *Tai-wan chi-shih* (Taiwan Memoranda, ca. 1875), a series of essays about the island written by a Chinese settler. These accounts, among others, were chosen for this study because of their representative status and because they are widely quoted by later writers. The high degree of intertextuality in Taiwan travel accounts means that the conclusions I draw here hold true for Taiwan travel literature in general.

Certain practices emerged as indices of gender inversion in the literature: uxorilocal marriage; the "preference" for female children; matrilineal inheritance; the sexual assertiveness of women; the sexual division of labor; the absence of postpartum seclusion; and the fact that women were not sequestered. Although the existence of female tribal heads among certain groups represented an obvious inversion of the Chinese norm of male rule, it was the domestic roles of native women that became the focus of attention in the travel accounts. Chinese writers theorized that it was the savage woman's position in the family that accounted for her social dominance. There is very little discussion of women's roles in indigenous political life, or in religious life, aside from occasional references to "female local chiefs."

According to modern anthropologists, the indigenous groups of Taiwan employed a variety of marriage and inheritance systems before Chinese colonization. The Siraya of the southwest region, the core of Dutch and Chinese settlement, practiced uxorilocal marriage and matrilineal inheritance. The rest of the groups on the west coast practiced virilocal and ambilocal residence marriage and a variety of inheritance patterns (patrilineal, ambilineal, and bilateral).[2] Groups on the east coast practiced matrilineal inheritance. The majority of Ch'ing writers, however, tended to lump the various indigenous groups together as "savages." They generally characterized these "savages" as a gynocentric people who "valued woman and undervalued man." This generalization may have been due in part to the greater Chinese familiarity with the Siraya. Chinese sensationalism may have been another factor accounting for this stereotyping in the literature. Moreover, the tendency of Ch'ing ethnographic representation is to establish the identity of a group by fixing on its "unique," or "strange" features. My task here is not to establish the accuracy of Ch'ing descriptions of indigenous Taiwanese society, but rather to analyze their representational strategies.

Chinese travel writers may have been predisposed to view Taiwan as a gynocentric society due in part to the familiarity of tales of Kingdoms of Women (much as Ralegh was predisposed to find the Amazons in South America). Various Chinese geographical works, for example, Sung dynasty (960–1279) author Chao Ju-kua's *Chu-fan-chih* (Record of the Various Barbarians), located Kingdoms of Women in the general region near Taiwan, Japan, or the Malay archipelago. There may have been, then, some possible connections between Taiwan and a Kingdom of Women in the minds of Chinese travelers. Certainly these legends of "matriarchal lands" must have colored their perceptions of indigenous Taiwanese gender roles.

Ch'ing representations of the Taiwan indigenes were also influenced by a pattern of regional stereotyping in both literary and historical materials. By the T'ang dynasty (618–907) a pattern of feminizing the southern borderlands and masculinizing the northern frontiers had been firmly established in the Chinese literary tradition. The south was associated with sensuality, languor, literary refinement, femininity, and female promiscuity; the north was associated with barrenness, ruggedness, martial valor, and machismo. This divide between hyperfeminized southerners (peoples such as the Miao and the Tai), on the one hand, and hypermasculinized northerners (peoples such as the Mongols and Jurchens), on the other hand, means that the simple structural equation male:female::major:minor is untenable. Rather, the Han Chinese configured the "other" in terms of polarized opposites of sexual excess, centering the Han self as the norm. Newly incorporated into the Chinese imperial domain in the seventeenth century, Taiwan seemed to fit neatly into preexisting images of "southern barbarians" as matriarchal types. Writers often borrowed tropes from earlier accounts of the Miao, the Lao, and even the natives of Siam to describe the indigenous peoples of Taiwan. The hypersexualization of Taiwan's indigenous women could also be fit into this larger pattern of stereotypes about the south. This gendering of the south as feminine thus forms an important context within which to read Ch'ing representations of the "savage woman" of Taiwan.

"Value Woman and Undervalue Man": Uxorilocal Marriage and Matrilineal Descent Among the Savages

Descriptions of uxorilocal marriage and matrilineal descent among the Taiwan indigenes commonly invoked the notion of inversion. The earliest Chinese account of native marriage practices can be found in Ch'en Ti's *Record of the Eastern Savages:*

> The girl hears [the suitor's music] and admits him to stay the night. Before daylight he straightaway departs without seeing the girl's parents. From this time on he must come in the dark and leave with the dawn when the stars are out, for years and months without any change. When a child is born, she for the first time goes to the man's home and [brings him back to her home] to be welcomed as the son-in-law, as [the Chinese] welcome a new bride, and the son-in-law for the first time sees the girl's parents. He then lives in her home and supports her parents for the rest of their lives, while his own parents can no longer regard him as their son. Therefore they are much happier at the birth of a girl than of a boy, in view of the fact that a girl will continue the family line, while a boy is not sufficient to establish the family succession.[3]

This passage clearly represents an interpretation of native customs through the lens of Chinese gender ideology. Ch'en Ti employs the discourse of inversion in likening the savage bridegroom to the Chinese bride. The phrase "to be welcomed as the son-in-law, as [the Chinese] welcome a new bride" sets up the equation: savage man = Chinese woman. At the end of Ch'en's description, he delivers what would become one of the quintessential formulations of gender inversion among the Taiwan savages: "they are much happier at the birth of a girl than of a boy." This inversion of normative Chinese values serves as a basic index of the difference between Chinese and savage. Rather than simply marveling at the strange nature of this inversion in savage society, however, Ch'en provides a rationale for this reversal of values. Because it is the savage women who assume the function of continuing the family succession (an all-important role in Chinese culture), an inversion of value results: Daughters, and not sons, become the privileged progeny. In identifying the inheritance system as the root of this gender hierarchy, Ch'en represents gender inversion as a product of social convention and economic relations. Such an explanation serves at once to distance the savages (they are matrilineal and we are patrilineal), and to normalize them (they, like us, value the sex that assures the succession of the family line).

Following Ch'en Ti, discussions of marital customs and their effects on the gender hierarchy became a standard element of descriptions of indigenous customs. Yü Yung-ho, author of perhaps the most well-known Chinese travelogue of Taiwan, provides this account of native courtship:

> In marriage they have no go-betweens; when the girls are grown, their parents have them live separately in a hut. The youths who wish to find a mate all come along, playing their nose-flutes and mouth-organs. When a youth gets the girl to harmonize with him, he goes in and fornicates with her. After they fornicate, he goes home of his own accord. After a long time, the girl picks the one she loves and "holds hands" with him. The "hand-holding" is to make public the private commitment. The next day, the girl tells her family, and invites the "hand-holding"

youth to come to her home. He knocks out the two top bicuspids to give to the girl and she also knocks out two teeth to give to the boy. They set a date to go to the wife's house to marry, and for the rest of his life he lives at the wife's residence. . . . The parents are not able to keep their son. Therefore, after one or two generations the grandchild does not know his ancestors; the savages have no family names.[4]

Highlighting female agency in mate selection, Yü paints a vivid picture here of the "sexual assertiveness" of the savage woman, an image that would have been shocking to Chinese audiences for whom arranged marriage was the norm. For Yü, gender inversion signaled the disruption of the entire kinship system, leading the savages to forget their own ancestors. The notion that the indigenes did not recognize their ancestors was another indication of their savagery, of their animal-like existence, since for Chinese, ancestor-worship was one of the cornerstones of civilization.

Other writers decried the "subordination" of the savage male by uxorilocal marriage practices. The nineteenth-century writer, Teng Ch'uan-an, for example, posited: "according to savage custom, the men who marry uxorilocally are just like women who marry virilocally [in China]. Obedient and dutiful, they do not dare to take their own initiative; they are debased to such a degree."[5] To such writers, uxorilocal marriage was not simply different and strange, but contemptible. The equivalence drawn in Chinese eyes between the savage groom and the Chinese bride provided an impetus for this interpretation of gender relations. That is, the notion of inversion, of a "mirror world," conditioned Chinese understandings of gender relations that differed from the Confucian norm.

The feminization of the indigenous male in Chinese sources may have initially been based on a structural similarity between their roles and the role of the Chinese wife; however, this feminization went beyond external metaphor to include the idea that there were shared features between the savage male and the female gender. The lack of facial hair among indigenous men was one characteristic that led Chinese observers to comment that the savage male was womanlike in his cosmetic habits. Others remarked that the beardless savage male was perhaps a natural eunuch. In either case, the absence of facial hair signified his minor status.

Industrious Women and Idle Men: The Sexual Division of Labor in Savage Society

The inversion of gender was also represented in the travel literature by descriptions of the sexual division of labor. Numerous Chinese observers expressed surprise at the fact that it was the indigenous women, and not the men, who were engaged in agricultural production. This perceived reversal of sex roles was interpreted by the Chinese as female "industriousness" and male "idleness." The indigenous male occupation of hunting was not recognized by the Chinese as "productive" activity. Ch'en Ti remarked on the superior work capacity of the native women in his *Record of the Eastern Savages:* ". . . the women are sturdy and active; they work constantly while the men are usually idle."[6] Lin Ch'ien-kuang painted an even more extreme picture of male sloth: "All of the tilling is done by the wife; the husband on the other hand stays at home waiting to be fed."[7] This image of the man's childlike dependence on his wife's labor recurred frequently in the literature, providing yet another rationale in Chinese eyes for female dominance in savage society.

This traditional sexual division of labor proved to be an obstacle for both the Dutch and the Chinese colonizers of Taiwan in their efforts to convert the island into a commercial agricultural economy. In his study of statecraft on the Taiwan frontier, John Shepherd describes the difficulties the Dutch and Chinese faced in convincing indigenous men to give up hunting and take up sedentary agriculture as a primary occupation: ". . . for them, farming had two major drawbacks: first, according to the traditional sexual division of labor, it was women's work; second, it was labor-intensive drudgery."[8] Both the Dutch and the Chinese, therefore, were forced to turn to the importation of Chinese labor in order to sustain commercial agricultural development.

By the arrival of the nineteenth century, the dominance of the female gender had become so much a part of the popular imagery of Taiwan that certain writers even attributed the stereotype of the supremely capable wife to the presence of Han women on the island.

The South as a Realm of Women

The depiction of Taiwan as a matriarchal land can be regarded as part of a long tradition of southern exoticism in classical Chinese literature. The ancient poetic tradition of the *Ch'ü-ts'u* (Songs of the South) established an association among the south, female goddesses, and eroticism that was to be replayed throughout Chinese literary history. The legend of Hsi Shih, a beauty from the southern region of Yüeh who was used to seduce the king of the rival kingdom of Wu, further mythologized the south as a region of sensuality and female beauty. The stereotype of the sensuous south was perhaps most firmly established by the poetic tradition of the Six Dynasties. It was during this time that "lotus picking songs" (*ts'ai-lien ch'ü*) portraying young girls of the southern Chiang-nan region came to represent the sensual image of the south and its waterways.

Historical and pseudohistorical accounts of non-Han peoples of the southern regions were another source of this stereotype. Historical works such as the *Han-shu* (History of the Han Dynasty), for example, commonly noted that it was the custom in various southern regions for women to bathe openly in streams. The Tai became particularly famous for this custom, an image that remains popular among PRC tourists today.[9] Indeed, the hypersexualization of non-Han in southern China has maintained a certain consistency over the centuries.

Female dominance, or gender inversion, was another favorite motif of accounts about "southern barbarians," both in histories and anomaly accounts. An entry on "The Lao Women" from the *T'ai-p'ing kuang-chi* (Accounts Widely Gathered in the Taiping Era), for example, focuses on gender inversion as its central point of interest. The entry in its entirety reads:

> In the south there are Lao women. They give birth to children and then get up. Their husbands lie in bed. Their diets are exactly the same as a nursing mother. They do not protect their pregnant women in the least. When the women go into labor, they give birth on the spot. They do not suffer in the least. They prepare food and gather firewood as usual. It is also said that according to Yüeh custom, if a wife gives birth to a child, after three days, she bathes in the stream. When she returns, she prepares gruel to feed her husband. The husband bundles the infant in the bedclothes and sits up in bed. They call him the "parturient husband." Their inversion is to such a degree.[10]

Ming and Ch'ing gazetteer descriptions, of groups such as the Miao, for example, followed a similar pattern of emphasizing female dominance or sexual assertiveness. In her study of Ming and Ch'ing representations of the Miao, Norma Diamond found that:

> the Miao album pictures and gazetteer texts highlight wherever possible the occurrence of reversal of proper gender roles: among the Nong Miao men are expected to care for infants, among the Bafan Miao women do most of the agricultural work, and in several groups men and women join together in farming, raiding the fields of others (presumably Han settlers) or hunting.[11]

Travel accounts of foreign lands south of China's borders similarly employed the trope of gender inversion. Ma Huan's account of the naval expeditions of the eunuch admiral Cheng Ho, for example, makes note of anomalous gender roles in several Southeast Asian and South Asian countries. He writes of Thailand, for instance:

> It is their custom that all affairs are managed by their wives. From the king to the common people, whenever there are matters which require thought and deliberation—punishments light and heavy, trading transactions great and small—they all follow the decisions of their wives, [for] the mental capacity of the wives certainly exceeds that of the men.[12]

Ma Huan furthermore characterized Thai women as "promiscuous," a common stereotype of Southeast Asian women in Chinese travel accounts from at least the Yüan dynasty onward.

This feminization of the south was contrasted against the masculinization of the northern frontiers in both literary and historical sources. These gendered stereotypes were influenced by several factors: the existence of matrilineal customs among southern "barbarians," the association of northern "barbarians" with warfare; theories of environmental determinism of human character (the environment of the north being rugged and that of the south being wet and fertile); and the relative strength of the expansionist northern dynasties vis-à-vis the overrefined and declining southern dynasties during the Six Dynasties era. These stereotypes were further developed in T'ang literary treatments of the northern frontiers and the southern borderlands. The southern male was in effect emasculated not only by contrast to the empowerment of the southern female, but also as part of a general feminization of the region. The feminization of southern peoples and the masculinization of northern peoples served to center the ideal Han self of the "central plains" as a privileged norm.

The feminization of the Taiwan indigenes should thus not simply be understood as part of a general case of "feminizing the Other," but also as part of this particular economy of regional stereotypes within the Chinese literary tradition. In describing the Taiwan indigenes as matriarchal, travelers were likely to have been influenced by the familiarity of images of female dominance in the south. Indeed, travel writers frequently compared the "savages" of Taiwan to the Southern Man "barbarians" or to "the people of Wu and Yüeh" in southern China. This is not surprising given the fact that the various Chinese ethnonyms for southern peoples, such as "Miao," "Lao," and "Man," while perhaps originally referring to specific ethnic groups, came to be commonly used to refer to "southern barbarians" in general. Thus, characteristics attributed to any particular group could be mapped onto other groups as part of the general stereotype of the "southern barbarian." The idea that there were parallels between the customs of the Taiwan savages and other Southeast Asian peoples was also noted by a number of Ch'ing writers.

The image of Taiwan as part of the sensual southland was promoted by descriptions of female bathers, native sexual habits, and remarks on female beauty. Yü Yung-ho, for example, frequently includes notes in his travelogue about the physical appearance (and indeed sexual attractiveness) of the women he encounters. His diary entry for one day includes the note, "of the savage women that we saw, many were fair-skinned and beautiful."[13] On another day he observes: "There were also three young girls working with mortar and pestle. One of them was rather attractive. They appeared in front of outsiders naked, but their composure was dignified."[14] Although there is frequent reference in the literature to both male and female nudity (nakedness in general being a sign of impropriety and thus cultural inferiority), it is only the savage woman's lack of shame concerning nudity that receives comment from the travel writers. One of the chief markers of proper femininity in Chinese culture being the shrouding of the body, the savage woman's lack of shame regarding her body must have appeared to Chinese observers as particularly strange and offensive.

It is partly for this reason that travel writers expressed great interest in the bathing habits of indigene women, noting in particular the frequency and openness of this practice. The censor Lui-shih-ch'i, a Manchu official who traveled to Taiwan in the mid-eighteenth century, went so far as to devote an entire entry of his travel account to the topic "Bathing in the Stream." His description explicitly eroticizes the act of bathing by linking it with play, flirtation, and voyeurism. The objectification of women is particularly apparent in Ch'ing ethnographic illustrations where women are often depicted in festival dress or as bare-breasted.

The image of Taiwan as a land of exotic sensuality was perhaps most promoted by descriptions of native courtship and marriage practices. A standard favorite in the Taiwan literature was the anecdote about youths sealing partnerships with young girls based on their ability to harmonize with them on the mouth organ: "to harmonize" being a pun on "to couple." For a Chinese audience, such anecdotes were reminiscent of poetic motifs in the ancient *Shih-ching* (Classic of Songs), and thus conjured up images of a primitive past. At the same time, the notion that the savages lacked an understanding of sexual propriety signaled their uncivilized status.

The absence of the segregation of the sexes and proscriptions against physical contact—a taboo signified in Chinese society by the Confucian precept, "in giving and receiving men and women do not touch [hands]"—were again marks of a lack of sexual propriety in savage society. Travel writers frequently remarked that savage men and women would sit together "mixed" or "without order." Other Ch'ing travelers saw an opportunity to indulge in voyeurism and other behavior taboo in their own society. The censor Lui-shih-ch'i, for example, made this note under the heading of "Suckling the Child" in his travel account: "The savages have no taboos against contact between male and female. When the savage woman nurses her child, those who see will play and tease from the side. She will be very pleased, thinking that people adore her child. Even if one touches her breast she will not prevent it."[15] The savage woman's body thus formed a direct contrast to the proper Chinese female body, which ideally remained out of sight and beyond touch. Such details added a titillating element to ethnographic description, bolstering the image of Taiwan as a fantasy island where Chinese men had free license with the native women.

Intermarriage: The Role of Woman in Transculturation

The notion that Chinese men had easy access to savage women's bodies fed into the representation of Chinese colonial prestige in travel writing. Interethnic marriage or sexual relations served in numerous narratives as a means through which to represent the ethnic hierarchy of the colonial society, calling attention to the unequal balance of power between Chinese and indigene. As an object of Han Chinese sexual desire, then, the "savage woman" became a site for the contestation of power between colonizer and colonized. Yü Yung-ho, for example, observed of the Chinese on the island, "'they take the barbarian women as their wives and concubines. Whatever is demanded of them they must comply; if they make a mistake they must take a flogging. And yet the barbarians do not hate them greatly."[16] Yü furthermore represents the accessibility of native women to Chinese as a product of ethnic privilege:

Should the [Chinese] guests take liberties with them [the women], they do not get angry. A husband, seeing a guest becoming intimate with his wife, is very pleased, saying that his wife is really charming, and that therefore Chinese like her. . . . However, should one of their own people fornicate with [a savage's wife], then he will take his bow and arrows, search out the adulterer, and shoot him dead. But he will not hold it against his wife.[17]

Such anecdotes portray the indigenes as clearly subordinated to the Chinese, supplying women and labor without animosity. The cuckolded husband is even said to interpret Chinese intimacy with his wife as a compliment, as proof of her exceptional qualities. For a Ch'ing audience, such an anecdote could serve to confirm the superior status of the Chinese vis-à-vis the colonized natives. The notion that this anecdote is more a reflection of Chinese desires than of actual conditions in Taiwan colonial society is confirmed by the fact that this passage has been lifted by Yü Yung-ho from an account of Siam in the *Ming-shih* (Ming History).

Other travel writers contradicted Yü's claim regarding the liberties allowed Chinese men, recording conflicts between Han settlers and the local populace over such relations. Indeed, as rates of intermarriage increased during the Ch'ing, because of an unfavorable sex-ratio among the Han settlers, the Chinese demand for indigenous women became seen as a source of ethnic conflict by the administration.[18] After a local revolt, the Ch'ing administration prohibited intermarriage in 1737. Although it was deemed expedient to limit intermarriage during this period in order to stabilize Han-indigene relations, it seems that there were no social prohibitions against such couplings. Shepherd found that, "the Chinese perceived no racial divide between Han and aborigines that would impede the ability of aborigines to acquire Chinese status characteristics or deny legitimacy to mixed marriages and their offspring."[19] In fact, such intermarriage could even be perceived as beneficial by officials who advocated an assimilationist colonial policy. One local official, for example, viewed intermarriage between Chinese and indigenes as an expedient means of assimilation. He argued, "with marriage and social intercourse, there will be no separation between the savages and the people. If the officials do not segregate them as a different race (*chung*), then after some time they will naturally assimilate (*hua*)."[20] As wives, then, indigenous women could be regarded as key vehicles for transculturation.[21] Indeed, anthropologist Melissa Brown has argued that during the Ch'ing "intermarriage was the primary mechanism for introducing and spreading Chinese values and practices into Aborigine communities."[22] Intermarriage may also have been an important mechanism for introducing indigenous practices into Chinese communities.

The Lady Pao-chu: Crossing Between Genders and Ethnicities

Examples of Han women marrying indigene men were comparatively rare, at least until the late Ch'ing.[23] There are few mentions of such marriages in the Ch'ing travel literature other than the fascinating legend of Pao-chu, a Han Chinese courtesan who became the female chieftain of an indigenous tribe. One nineteenth-century traveler, Ting Shao-i, reconstructs the identity of this mysterious figure by relating two items from the local lore, one concerning a female chieftain and one concerning the Chinese consort of a local chief. He writes:

> Prefect Teng Ch'üan-an of Fu-liang says in his *Measuring the Sea with a Cala-bash:* "During the Chia-ch'ing period (1796–1821), the female chieftain (*t'u-kuan*) Pao-chu made herself up like an aristocratic lady of China. In her administration, she followed the law. Someone sent the officials a memorial [stating that her tribe] followed the law obediently and respectfully, not killing people, not rebelling. Even though this is beyond the pale, how is it different from the interior [China]?" Leg-end has it that during the Chu I-kui rebellion, the chief of the Pei-nan-mi, Wen-chi, decided to get a beauty for his consort. There was a courtesan in Taiwan city who heard of this with delight and volunteered to go. The savages value women to begin with, and since the chieftain got a courtesan, he doted on her to the extreme, doing whatever she commanded. Then they got rid of their old customs, and were civi-lized with the rites and laws of China. Therefore the seventy odd villages of the Pei-nan-mi are the most orderly, and their customs were long different from those of the other savages. "Pao-chu" is not like a savage woman's name. Perhaps this so-called female chieftain is after all a prostitute?[24]

The equivalence between these two figures, Pao-chu and the Han courtesan, is based on one central point of coincidence, the woman's role in initiating the as-similation of her tribe to Chinese culture. It is an equivalence which is also al-lowed for by the liminality of both women: one a savage who resembles a Chinese; one a Chinese who resembles a savage. Ting thus speculates that they must be one and the same person.

By crossing ethnic boundaries to live among the savages, this figure "Pao-chu" was able to take advantage of both the gender inversion in savage society and the superior status of her ethnicity to elevate her standing: in other words, she placed herself in a position in which both her femininity and her Chineseness were val-ued. The story thus nicely demonstrates how in certain cases it is ethnicity that brings privilege, while in other cases, it is gender that brings privilege. In dramati-cally rising from the station of a prostitute to a chieftain, Pao-chu crossed not only ethnic boundaries but also status lines, "dressing herself up like an aristocratic lady of China." Pao-chu's identity thus remained in a liminal state, between the savage and the civilized, between the lowly and the noble, between the matriarchal and the patriarchal. It is from this liminality, this ambiguous status, that Pao-chu derived her power. The figure of Pao-chu serves as a metaphor for the unique culture produced in the "contact zone" of the frontier; it is in "giving up" her Chineseness that Pao-chu induces the savages to "give up" their savagery.[25] By straddling the insider/outsider opposition, by becoming a "hybrid," Pao-chu in effect obliterates this opposition. As Teng Ch'üan-an phrased it: "Even though this is beyond the pale, how is it different from the interior [China]?" In being placed at this point of cultural transference, on the cusp between different ethnicities and different gender ideologies, the figure of Pao-chu illustrates how ethnicity and gender combine variously in the constitution of power.

Gender Inversion and the Critique of Chinese Womanhood

While I have mainly examined the phenomenon of gender inversion as a means of signifying the "strangeness" of the Other, gender inversion could also be employed as a rhetorical device, often in a self-reflexive critique of Chinese mores. This device is generally linked to the mode of primitivism, in which the "less civilized" Other is seen as a repository of values associated with a more virtuous, simple past. The status of the foreign woman as Other made her a figure upon which not only undesirable, but also idealized traits could be projected. As an idealized Other, the foreign woman serves as a foil against which to contrast the flaws of Chinese womanhood.

This technique is employed in a Ch'ing vernacular story about a merchant's travels to Vietnam. The story entitled "On a Journey to Vietnam a Jade Horse Miniature is Exchanged for Crimson Velvet" (*Tzou Annan yü-ma huan hsing-jung,* ca. 1661) uses the exotic setting of Vietnam to demonstrate a moral lesson about the laxity of contemporary Chinese women. Two of the central devices employed to establish the foreignness of Vietnam are the familiar tropes of gender inversion and hypersexualization. In particular, it is the violation of Chinese norms of gender segregation that captures the attention of the narrator. However, a satirical twist in the story's rhetoric shifts the story into the mode of self-reflexive critique. While proclaiming Vietnamese women to be inferior in their customs and lax in their sense of public propriety, the narrator reveals his true object of criticism to be Chinese womanhood. A description of the public bathing habits of Vietnamese women becomes an opportunity to satirically deride Chinese women for their hypocrisy. He declares:

> [The Vietnamese women] are no comparison for our Chinese women, who close the door so tightly when they take a bath that no breeze gets through and yet still insist that the maid stand outside the window for fear that someone will peep on them. I think that these women's false pretenses are really just a big show. Just look at our women of the South. All day they go touring in the mountains or by the waters, visiting temples, leaning on gates and standing in doorways, going to plays or societies; they let the public see their powdered faces. And yet they want to criticize the shortcomings of men! Commenting and laughing at the looks of passersby, they don't know how to cherish the "face" of the family. But if the breeze so much as lifts up their skirts to reveal a bit of leg, or if they are feeding a baby and their breast is exposed, or if they are going to the toilet and their "thing" is exposed, they make a hundred gestures to cover this and conceal that, and put on airs of distress. They don't know that "face" and the body are one: if they want to cherish the body they should cherish "face"; if they want to conceal the body, they should cover the "face." The ancients said it well: "If the fence is secure, the dogs won't get in." If outsiders had not seen your face, how would they think of violating your body?[26]

Although the Vietnamese are portrayed as less civilized on account of their lack of gender segregation, the real critique in this passage is aimed at the moral degeneracy of Chinese women. Indeed, the narrator reveals at the conclusion that his dominant didactic concern is not the violation of gender norms by Vietnamese women, but rather the transgressions of Chinese women. The structure of the story allows the author to simultaneously indulge in exotic fantasy and advocate greater conservatism in gender roles.

In his *Taiwan Memoranda,* Wu Tzu-kuang employs a similar self-reflexive critique, idealizing the indigenous women of Taiwan as paragons of ancient simplicity and virtue. He writes:

> The rest of their clothing is all frugal and plain . . . and they have a profound understanding of the proprieties of antiquity. Moreover, they don't use cosmetics, just like the lady of Kuo [Yang Kuei-fei's sister] who feared being stained with color. They don't paint their eyebrows: even if they had the brush of Chang Ch'ang they wouldn't use it.[27] Their manners are far superior in virtue to those of Chinese women.[28]

Wu makes the claim here that it is the savages rather than the women of China who maintain the proprieties of Chinese antiquity. The women of China, he implies, have conversely become degenerate and frivolous. Rather than seeing an inversion of gender in the foreign culture, Wu projects a hyperrealization of Chinese gender ideals.

The idealization of the foreign woman as a foil to contemporary Chinese womanhood may have expressed an anxiety concerning the new social roles for women emerging during the late Ming and Ch'ing.[29] Confucian ideals that were no longer upheld by Chinese women were thus projected onto foreign women. A particularly poignant example of this move appears in the famous account of the Ch'ing massacre at Yang-chow, "A Record of Ten Days in Yang-chow" (*Yang-chou shih-jih chi*). At one point in this account a Manchu soldier derides the Chinese women for failing to demonstrate the chaste resolve of Korean women in the face of rape. The lesser commitment to Confucian strictures for female chastity is thus read as a symptom of the degeneration of Chinese society as a whole—an accusation that serves as an insinuated justification for the Manchu invasion. In all these examples, the association of particular sex roles with "civilization" and "barbarism" is turned on its head and used as a device to critique Chinese society, as "civilized" trades places with "barbaric."

The most famous Ch'ing example of this type of gender play is Li Ju-chen's novel, *Flowers in the Mirror.* In this work, Li creates a number of fantastically learned foreign female characters whose understanding of the Confucian classics far surpasses that of the average Chinese male. Throughout the novel, female literary talent is given an aura of glamour, and it is implied that China would be well served by the development of such talents among the female population. Li furthermore employs gender inversion in the Kingdom of Women episode of this novel to satirize, and thereby denaturalize, Chinese sex roles. In particular, he calls into question the humanity of practices such as footbinding. Through both satire and Utopian vision, Li Ju-chen presents an idealized model of accomplished (albeit still Confucian) femininity, embodied in the women of fabulous countries.

Whether through the idealization of the foreign woman, or through gender inversion, gender serves as a ready vehicle for the expression of ethnic alterity in Ch'ing travel accounts. The linkage between gender and ethnicity is particularly strong because the difference that is built into gender can be readily converted into the difference of the foreign, and vice versa. The particular objectification of women in Ch'ing ethnographic writing furthermore meant that Woman became a stand-in for the Other. Thus, the strangeness of the "savage" woman of Taiwan represented the strangeness of her culture as a whole. The native woman also served as a mediator between colonizer and colonized, and as such became a figure through which relations of desire, domination, and exchange were expressed. The multiplicity of gendered images, moreover, demonstrates that the linkages between gender and ethnicity are not simply based on a direct metaphoric equivalence, the analogy Chinese:savage as male:female. This is particularly true within the colonial or cross-cultural context, where gender itself is already racialized, or ethnicized, creating an instability around the terms of gender. Therefore, while feminization may be a form of denigration, not all women are denigrated. What is meant to be a Han woman in colonial Taiwan was vastly different from what it meant to be an indigene woman, as the legend of Pao-chu so nicely illustrates. Moreover, although the discourse of gender was central to the construction of ethnic difference in Ch'ing travel writing, this discourse could also be employed as a vehicle for comment on concerns internal to Chinese society. Ch'ing representations of "savage" gender relations thus in large measure reflected Chinese interests and cannot be read as reliable observations of indigenous life.

Epilogue

The figure of the indigenous "mountain woman" (*shan-ti fu-nü*) has continued to play a special role in modern Taiwan, being used to represent in many ways the "face" of indigenous culture to outside observers. The continuities between Ch'ing and modern discourse are aptly demonstrated in a media article from the 1960s entitled, "Aborigine Women of the Province [Taiwan] March toward the Realm of Civilization," which touts the achievements of the KMT in modernizing indigenous lifestyles.[30] The author, Yang Pai-yüan, not only employs many of the old tropes of gender inversion, but also argues that because of the vital role played by women in the matrilineal indigenous societies governmental efforts at "civilizing" the indigenes must be directed primarily at the women. Indigenous women are thus again expected to serve as vehicles for the transmission of Chinese culture.

The discourse of hypersexualization has also continued to be employed, with some very real consequences for indigenous women—namely their commodification in the tourism and sex industries. Photographs of indigenous women in traditional costume grace government tourist brochures. Costumed women are available for photo opportunities with Chinese and Western tourists at all the major sightseeing areas, and, of course, no tour of Wulai or Taroko Gorge would be complete without a show of dancing indigenous girls. Indigenous women also constitute a major part of the sex industry and sex tourism in Taiwan, and are disproportionately represented in illegal underage prostitution. Poverty is a driving force behind this phenomenon. Also at play, however, are stereotypes about the indigenes' propensity for heavy drinking, which are used to justify the "natural" suitability of indigenous women for bar-hostess and other nightclub work. Beginning in the 1980s, the feminist and indigenous rights movements in Taiwan have generated greater social awareness of discriminatory attitudes toward indigenous women, and we have seen a rejection of some of the older colonialist discourse. It remains to be seen what new images will emerge.

Notes

1. Sau-ling Wong, "Ethnicizing Gender: An Exploration of Sexuality as Sign in Chinese Immigrant Literature," in *Reading the Literatures of Asian America*, ed. S. Lim and A. Ling (Philadelphia: Temple University Press, 1992), 113.

2. See John Shepherd, *Statecraft and Political Economy on the Taiwan Frontier, 1600–1800* (Stanford: Stanford University Press, 1993), 44.

3. Translated in Laurence Thompson, "The Earliest Chinese Eyewitness Accounts of the Formosan Aborigines," *Monumenta Serica* 23 (1964): 173–74.

4. Yü Yung-ho, *P'i-hai chi-yu* (Small Sea Travelogue) (Taipei: Taiwan yin-hang, 1959), 35.

5. Teng Ch'uan-an, *Li-ts'u huei-ch'ao* (Measuring the Sea with a Calabash) (Taipei: Taiwan yin-hang, 1958), 10.

6. Thompson, "Earliest Accounts," 175.

7. Ibid., 181.

8. Shepherd, *Statecraft*, 366.

9. See Charles McKann, "The Naxi and the Nationalities Question," in *Cultural Encounters on China's Ethnic Frontiers*, ed. Stevan Harrell (Seattle: University of Washington Press, 1995), 45.

10. *T'ai-p'ing kuang-chi* (Accounts Widely Gathered in the Taiping Era) (Taipei, 1987), 3629.

11. Norma Diamond, "Defining the Miao: Ming, Ch'ing, and Contemporary Views," in Harrell, ed., *Cultural Encounters*, 103.

12. Ma Huan, *Ying-ya sheng-lan* (The Overall Survey of the Ocean's Shore), trans. J.V.G. Mills as *The Overall Survey of the Ocean's Shores* (Cambridge, UK: Cambridge University Press for the Hakluyt Society, 1970), 104.

13. Yü, *Small Sea*, 19.

14. Ibid., 18–19.

15. Liu-shih-ch'i, *Fan-she ts'ai-feng t'u-k'ao* (Illustrations of the Savage Villages) (Taipei: Taiwan yin-hang, 1961), 7.

16. Thompson, "Earliest Accounts," 196.

17. Ibid., 192–93.

18. Melissa Brown notes that specific rates of intermarriage cannot be estimated. Mel-

issa Brown, "On Becoming Chinese," in *Negotiating Ethnicities in China and Taiwan*, ed. M. Brown (Berkeley: Institute of East Asian Studies, University of California, 1996), 52.

19. Shepherd, *Statecraft*, 379.

20. Chiang Shih-ch'e, *T'ai-yu jih-chi* (Travelogue of Taiwan) (Taipei: Taiwan yin-hang, 1957), 46.

21. The term "transculturation" was coined by Fernando Oritz in the 1940s. Mary Louise Pratt defines it thus: "Ethnographers have used this term to describe how subordinated or marginal groups select and invent from materials transmitted to them by a dominant or metropolitan culture" (Mary Louise Pratt, *Imperial Eyes: Travel Writing and Transculturation* [New York: Routledge, 1992], 6).

22. Brown, "Becoming Chinese," 45.

23. Ibid., 52.

24. Ting Shao-i, *Tung-ying shih-lüeh* (Brief Record of Eastern Ying) (Taipei: Taiwan yin-hang, 1957), 78.

25. Pratt, *Imperial Eyes*, 6.

26. *Chuo-yuan-t'ing chu-jen* (The Master of Chuo-yuan Pavilion), "On a Journey to Vietnam a Jade Horse Miniature Is Exchanged for Crimson Velvet," in his *Chao-shih-pei* (The Cup That Reflects the World) (Shanghai, 1956; repr. Peking: Chung-hua shu-chu, 1991), 61–62.

27. Chang Ch'ang was a native of P'ing-yang during the Han dynasty who became governor of Ch'ang-an under the emperor Hsüan-ti. He was famous for having painted his wife's eyebrows.

28. Wu Tzu-kuang, *Taiwan chi-shih* (Taiwan Memoranda) (Taipei: Taiwan yin-hang, 1959), 31.

29. See Dorothy Ko, *Teachers of the Inner Chambers: Women and Culture in Seventeenth-Century China* (Stanford: Stanford University Press, 1994).

30. Yang Pai-yüan, "Chin-ju wen-ming ling-yü teh pen-sheng shan-ti fu-nü" (Aborigine Women of the Province [Taiwan] March Toward the Realm of Civilization), *Taiwan wen-hsien* 19, no. 4 (1968): 163–69.

4

From Shanghai to Taipei

Exile and Identity

Sue Gronewold

From 1945 until 1950, a slow trickle of exiles made their way across the straits that separate the Chinese mainland from the island of Taiwan. By 1949 that trickle had grown into a stream. No firm accounting of the number is available. Estimates range from 1 to 1.5 million people who made the journey by airplane, ship, or leaky boat. Most of the people who traveled were soldiers, either elite officers and military personnel closely associated with the leader of the Nationalist Party (Kuomintang, or KMT), Generalissimo Chiang Kai-shek, or ordinary foot soldiers in the Nationalist army who, probably rightly, believed their lives to be endangered if they stayed in China after the Communist victory. Perhaps half a million were the relatives these men were able to take with them—more intact families for the elite who had the resources and the foresightedness to make preparations to remove both their capital and their kin, but only partial families for the poor soldiers who were less resourceful and able only to get out a mother here, a wife and child there. These ragtag armies, fighting losing battle after losing battle, retreated with the Nationalist government that was pushed farther and farther into the interior, from Nanking to Wuhan, from Wuhan to Chungking, and then finally in 1949, conceding defeat and leaving the mainland altogether.[1]

These people were the most unusual of exiles, being both external and internal refugees. They left mainland China not for a foreign refuge but for an island that had long been considered part of China, and which had received migrants from southeastern provinces for centuries. Yet, they were also in the strange position of being losers of the civil war in China proper but victors and, increasingly, oppressors of the Taiwanese (the collective name given to diverse peoples who lived on the island before 1945, known in Chinese as the *pen-ti jen*). There were a little more than 6 million Taiwanese in 1945, most of them Hokkien speakers who had migrated over the centuries from southeastern Fukien province, plus a smaller number of ethnic Hakka migrants from southern Kwangtung province, and a tiny number of aboriginal peoples who had been pushed by succeeding waves of migrants into the hills. In 1945, all these peoples had expected that the war's end would liberate them from the overlordship of both the Japanese who had been ceded the island in 1895 after the

Chinese defeat in the Sino-Japanese War and the mainland Chinese government that had attempted, with varying degrees of success, to intensify its control over the island during the last dynasty. Instead of liberation, however, the Taiwanese were relegated once again to second-class citizenship, with control over every aspect of life, from government positions and housing, to language and school curricula, shifting in 1945 from the Japanese to the *wai-sheng jen* (mainlanders).

Yet, not all of the refugees who came to the island were in positions of strength, and this essay will focus on two quite different groups of people who made their way to Taiwan after 1945: western missionaries for whom China was "home" and who had been forced to leave the mainland when the Communists triumphed, and poor, needy mainland girls and young women generally absent from the stories and statistics that describe the mainland elite. These two groups met at institutions that had also been transplanted from the mainland, and we will examine one of them, the Door of Hope Refuge, a nondenominational institution that had been founded in 1900 in Shanghai and run by Anglo-American missionaries, eventually growing to be a huge complex serving thousands of girls and young Chinese women until forced to close in 1951.[2] Yet the presence of needy girls in Taiwan did not ensure that the Door of Hope would enjoy a success similar to that in Shanghai. When it closed in 1976, it had served only a few hundred girls in its twenty-two years on the island.[3] This essay attempts to explain why the institution, its workers, and poor, needy mainland girls all may have made the shift to Taiwan, but the winning formula of Shanghai's Door of Hope did not accompany them. What were the conditions in Taiwan and how did they compare with those in Shanghai? What adjustments did the missionaries make for any new circumstances? How did the Chinese imperialist structures of the KMT on Taiwan compare with the mixed Chinese and foreign presence and power in Shanghai? And, finally, does a gender analysis of the migration help us better understand the divergent experiences of these unwilling migrants and unusual exiles?

Who were the girls brought to the Door of Hope on Taiwan? What were their life stories? Let us look at the life stories of four girls brought to the Door of Hope Refuge in Taiwan, and then, in light of these stories and the old structures in new places that the Door of Hope represented, examine possible explanations for its inability to replicate its Shanghai success abroad, in exile in Taiwan.

> All [these girls] come from very desperate and difficult circumstances. Hsiao Ming, meaning "Little Brightness" . . . is the child of an insane mother, now in a mental hospital, and a very wicked father who taught her to steal. He would send her out to steal food and if she returned with nothing, she was beaten. Then the father disappeared and cannot be found. Little Hsiao Ming was left with a grandmother who went out to work each day and either locked the child in the house or left her on the street. We took her in and she was truly a naughty girl. But the Lord is working in her heart and she is learning a new way of life.

Do you think this is a real Door of Hope? Let me tell you about little Yu Kuei. Her name means "Precious Jewel" and that is just what she [was] . . . in that awfully crowded, evil smelling hut in which she, her father and mother, three brothers and one sister lived. Her father tried to make a living for the family by running a pedicab [a rickshaw propelled by a man on a bicycle instead of a man running and pulling it]. They were expecting another child which made life even more difficult, for the mother needed a doctor's care and had to go to the hospital. There was no money and so the father sold his pedicab to help pay the bills. A baby girl was born but the mother died. What could be done? His means of supporting his family of six children were gone! Someone told him of the Door of Hope. He brought his children to see us. What a sight! Yu Kuei was a girl and old enough to be accepted. But there were forms to be filled out and an X-ray to be taken which meant several trips. Each time she brought her bundle—all the clothes she possessed, [two ragged dresses] . . . she was given a bath, her hair was washed, and she was dressed in nice clean clothes. She forgot about her bundle and never asked for it again. . . . The Lord has undertaken for the rest of the family. The newborn baby was adopted by a friend; an aunt took the two-year-old girl; another orphanage took the four-year-old boy. The two older ones are at home with the father, but he is able to go out to work as they are in school. . . . There are many more just like Yu Kuei.

When Grandfather Chao brought Kun-ying to us, she was full of boils. She looked starved, with no desire but to go to sleep. She talked very little. Grandfather Chao is a garbage collector, selling the paper he picks up out of the trash cans. His son had died, and all he had left was his granddaughter, but he could not provide for her. Now she is a round-faced chubby little girl going to kindergarten. She is not only learning to play with the other children, but she is learning to read and sing about Jesus.

[L]ittle five and a half year old Pao Yu's, or "Precious Jewel's," mother had died. The father was very sick and very poor and was not able to take care of the child, so she was moved from house to house until a neighbor came to ask if we could add her to our family. When she came, how she needed Jesus![4]

It is clear from these examples that there were many needy girls from the mainland in Taiwan in the 1950s, yet the Door of Hope Refuge was able to reach out to only a few of them. In order to analyze the disappointing experience of the mission after it reopened in a different place, let us summarize several aspects of the institution developed over fifty years in Shanghai and compare them with those same features of the institution in its Taipei reincarnation. Perhaps then we might reach a better understanding of the institution's more limited success in its new environment.

Structure and Staff

In Shanghai, the Door of Hope was composed of two separate branches, each of which included several institutions: the Door of Hope Mission (Chi liang so), sometimes called the New Heart Home, and the Children's Refuge (Ai yu t'ang) or the

Love School. The mission served the goals of the institution that had been set up in 1900: to rescue prostitutes, later expanded to include other needy young women, with a Receiving Home in the heart of the brothel district that served as the initial refuge and sorting facility for the entire complex. Young women either were brought there or fled there on their own; their immediate needs were met and their stories were told. They were then sent to the most appropriate facility. If they were older, they were assigned to the First Home or, if ill, to the well-equipped, separate hospital. After the first year, women and older girls of promise were sent away for further education and training, others moved on to an "industrial home" for work and artisanal training. If the girls were young, they were assigned to the Children's Refuge located a short car or train ride away in the suburban countryside.

In addition to dormitories and hospitals, the complex also included chapels, preaching and teaching halls for lectures, revivals, services, and day schools for neighborhood children. The dormitories were meant to be like homes and as such were organized into families, with approximately ten girls under the care of servants and housemothers (Chinese), with matrons (also Chinese) overseeing them all. Working with the girls but not living with them, in the capacity of teachers and administrators, foreign missionaries taught elementary school classes, led the Bible study, instructed in sewing and knitting, needlework and later loom work, took care of correspondence, writing reports and responding to donors, and finally, dealt with the authorities in Shanghai, mostly with the court system that ruled on the best environment for the girls whose futures were contested: their homes and places of work with their real or fictive relatives or the Door of Hope with its alien but interested parties. Chinese women worked alongside these missionaries, but they always were referred to as "helpers" and were never accorded equal status. Nevertheless, their work as teachers, nurses, aides, cooks, servants, and occasional preachers (a category that frequently included the men affiliated with the institution) was invaluable to the mission and necessary to its functioning. The girls referred to them all by kinship terms, with "mothers" and "sisters" overseen by missionary "aunts."

Over this basic structure was a small administration. The resident missionaries had a great deal of freedom to develop policies and practices on the ground, but an administrative committee oversaw the connections between the institution and the communities it served in the hybrid environment of Shanghai's International Settlement. This committee was composed of a half-dozen women, primarily missionaries or the wives of important missionary officials, as nearly every Protestant denomination used Shanghai as its base. These women had status, continuity, access to resources, and usually a great deal of experience themselves in running homes, congregations, committees, and charities. Initially representing a wide variety of denominations in the early years of the mission, this group, as well as the majority of its supporters, volunteers, and missionaries, over the years became increasingly more evangelical and even Pentecostal.

In the 1930s, a further administrative level was added, with an all male, foreign board of trustees that included the British and American consuls as well as senior mission administrators. In the 1940s, however, this board changed, consisting from 1941 until 1951 of important Chinese Christians. The presence of this board, in both its foreign and its Chinese forms, underscores how embedded the institution was in the various worlds that made up the treaty port of Shanghai: the foreign mission community, the secular government of the treaty port, the Chinese Christians who worked and supported the institution, and the Chinese in the city who used the institution for their own purposes, as diverse as those might have been.

As a much smaller institution, the Door of Hope Refuge on Taiwan had a much simpler structure. Still divided into a children's refuge for younger girls and a home for older girls, the assignment in Taipei was determined by age, not morality, as it had been in Shanghai. Still divided into quasi-family groups with housemothers (again, Chinese), the refuge had a Chinese matron who watched over all the daily matters and Chinese servants, cooks, nurses, and support staff. But everything was on a diminutive scale, and except for a room used as a chapel and small building used as an infirmary, many of the ancillary features were absent from the institution in Taipei.

Besides the difference in scale, another major difference for the institution in Taiwan was that the Chinese staff, while sharing Chinese nationality with the girls, was in fact quite different from them. The staff seems to have been largely Taiwanese, not mainlander, and thus there were cultural barriers, from problems with language and religion, custom and cohesion. There was also friction between the two groups, with mainlanders viewing Taiwanese as inferior. The newsletters from the mission are filled with complaints about the resignations of yet more Chinese (that is, Taiwanese) staff and the inability to keep qualified and loving caretakers, like the one Freda Rempel hired in 1967 who "had a mother's heart."[5] This turnover suggests that work at a foreign refuge for poor mainlander children had neither sufficient status nor salary to attract and retain Taiwanese workers. As soon as better jobs were available, workers left the Door of Hope, which then faced the problem of inadequate staff. Worse yet, it also suggests that its already battered and beaten down children lacked the intimacy and emotional support that close, kin-like relationships with the staff could offer.

As in Shanghai, the structure at the Door of Hope Refuge in Taiwan concentrated power in the hands of the foreign missionaries. Never numbering more than five, and by 1958 only two or three, the foreign-resident missionaries had responsibility for the administration of the home and for the creation of a religious atmosphere, but their work was much more limited than in Shanghai. The education and the job training, which had occupied so much time and space in Shanghai, was done elsewhere in Taiwan. As a result, the Door of Hope was a much different institution in Taipei.

Emphasizing religious work was not a challenge for these missionaries, however, because they were all veterans of the Shanghai establishment who had dedicated their lives to the work of the mission. The mission had indeed been their lives; they had all worked in China since the 1910s and 1920s, with one woman in her eighties by the time she came to Taiwan and the others in their sixties and seventies. Yet after four years, even the familiarity of the work could not disguise the difficulties the older women were beginning to have. Age and the challenges of re-creating in Taipei what they had in Shanghai were beginning to take their toll.

In late 1958, the Door of Hope finally negotiated an agreement with another evangelical mission organization, TEAM (The Evangelical Alliance Mission) based in Wheaton, Illinois, which was increasing its social service work in Taiwan. By the time two TEAM missionaries joined the mission, only one elderly missionary remained from Shanghai. By 1963, even she had retired, and the refuge was then staffed by veteran TEAM missionaries, administered, in theory, from Wheaton, and supported by donations and mission assets taken over by TEAM.[6]

TEAM was a large organization, international in scope, with 800 missionaries worldwide and 40 in Taiwan, but it was an umbrella group, previously called the Scandinavian Alliance Mission, which included evangelical sects that had long been close to the mission. The best evidence for this connection was the assignment of Kathryn Merrill as a TEAM missionary to the refuge in 1960. Merrill, who retired in 1999 after nearly 40 years, came from a Santa Barbara, California, family that had supported and corresponded with the Shanghai mission since the 1930s. Working with the Door of Hope had been her dream since she was a small child.[7]

From 1941, during wartime, until TEAM took over the refuge in 1958, missionaries had shared its administration with others, including a Chinese committee in Shanghai and an "unofficial" foreign board established overseas to handle correspondence, reports, and donations, which continued even during hard times to flow into the institution. In fact, the tensions between the missionaries with their traditions and a board which took a broader view of the work is one of the unacknowledged but omnipresent issues in the mission after 1941. This "homelands" board was established by one of the stranded missionaries in the West after the internment of most of the missionaries in Japanese war camps. During the late 1940s and early 1950s, it consisted primarily of two longtime supporters of the mission, a Dr. Charles and Mrs. Anna Schuler. Their evangelical credentials were impeccable: Dr. Schuler had taught music at the evangelical Moody Bible Institute in Chicago, and they both had many personal ties to the mission, serving not only as board but as host and home to many of the missionaries when in the United States.[8]

The board of trustees, or actually, Charles and Anna Schuler, are such a presence in the records and reports from the mission from the 1950s and beyond that their presence obscures another important change. The Door of Hope after its move to Taiwan may have felt the need for administration first by a home board and then by an allied evangelical organization, but it did not establish a local management committee like the one in Shanghai. It did, however, form—and then drop—an advisory board composed of four missionaries and five foreign leaders in the religious community to assist in planning the new mission. One of the first actions TEAM took, in fact, was to establish a local committee in 1960, headed by Betty

Woodward of the China Sunday School Association who had done work with TEAM, to monitor the work of the mission, but this was within the TEAM network rather than any other church or political structure. The lack of a community board like the one that existed in Shanghai demonstrated the missionaries' unwillingness to have anyone else control them. What it did, however, was to deprive them of the kinds of community links and context with which they had operated in Shanghai. In reading the reports and letters from the mission after 1953, one is struck by this absence. Shanghai is present and vibrant in the world of the Door of Hope from 1900 to 1951; Taipei as a backdrop is nearly invisible. Yes, the missionaries had "come home," as they cried when they disembarked, echoing the assertions of mainlanders when they landed on the island, but the sights and sounds, the worlds and communities, are absent from the pages of the reports, and, one suspects, from the experience of the mission. The mission was less embedded in the worlds and lives of the city in Taipei than in Shanghai.

Taipei, after all, was not a treaty port. Although missionaries flocked there with the militarists, Taiwan was governed by Chinese, albeit with billions of dollars of U.S. foreign aid and the presence of many foreign advisers. In Taiwan, the missionary expatriate community was doubly exiled, not just from their homeland but also from their adopted land. As a result, they had less power and more limited legitimacy than they had claimed on the mainland. Taiwan was no longer a Western or even Eastern (Japanese) colony; the odd character of Taiwan after 1949 was that both the colonials and the colonized were Chinese. Institutions that were completely run by foreigners, then, like the Door of Hope, had no natural niche, particularly if they limited the population they served to a small segment of the privileged mainlander minority whose need for the mission decreased with time.

Support and Links to the State

A second feature of the two institutions, the Door of Hope Mission in Shanghai and the Door of Hope Refuge in Taipei, was their base of support, which includes both formal and informal links with the state and political structures. Again, one sees the difference in what I have termed the "embedded nature" of the institutions. From its inception, the Door of Hope Mission in Shanghai was linked to the government, in this case the Mixed Court and Municipal Council of the International Settlement, a semicolonial, treaty-port administration filled primarily by British and American men from the worlds of commerce and manufacturing. For almost fifty years, the mission received a fixed sum from the government, which, on the one hand, legitimized the mission and, on the other, allowed the authorities to use the institution for their own needs, depending upon the times. It must be noted that after 1927 this government became more and more Chinese (and Japanese) as extraterritoriality and the treaty-port system were gradually eliminated, yet it continued to support the Door of Hope and use it for its own ends. With this official link came all the powers and personnel of the state: the authorities from the municipal government; the lawyers and judges from the courts; and the minions of the legal and political system, the police and "detectives" who investigated allegations of abuse and rounded up young women and brought them to the mission.

For aid, the mission was able to call upon the other Shanghai worlds with which it had links: Westerners who gave both aid and needlework orders to the mission, from the missionaries (and male missionaries' wives) in Shanghai either temporarily on furlough or stationed there at mission headquarters, to the various social worlds of Westerners living in Shanghai, from those involved in banking and business to journalists and international tourists. Added to these Western supporters were Chinese elites, including those involved in municipal government and business, and Chinese Christians, who were involved in myriad social projects aimed at reducing poverty, illiteracy, child and wife abuse, and other social ills. Financially, donations and orders for work from the foreign community accounted for a sizable part of the yearly budget, which by 1938 was nearly $200,000 a year. For the first four decades of the Door of Hope in Shanghai, the largest donations came from abroad, from Bible schools, women's groups, church congregations, and individuals. Before 1941, the Chinese contributed a smaller amount, but their donations were important for the links they established to the Chinese worlds of Shanghai. After 1941, it was Chinese money that sustained the mission.

By the time the mission was reestablished on Taiwan in 1954, it could only count on an abbreviated number of supporters. Only foreign donations were accessible from Taiwan, and much of that money was tagged for particular missionaries, coming as it did from individuals and congregations that had been giving such earmarked aid for decades.[9] The amount given was not small, however; at least $1,000 on average was given each month, and the assets of the institution in 1958 were estimated at $125,000 (including its property holdings in Taiwan and the United States). The financial report in 1967–68 listed a budget of NT$810,000. Yet, because the institution was undenominational, it could not count upon any church or parachurch organization for either financial or administrative help. It had been informally allied with the China Inland Mission, for example, but its lack of formal ties meant that it could not depend upon the organization for financial support. In any event, with the expulsion of missionaries from China, the China Inland Mission was in the process of reinventing itself, transforming itself into the Overseas Mission Fellowship with a new structure and more diffuse international focus. The Door of Hope's major problems were not financial, however, but administrative. Therefore, when the possibility of merging (or what one missionary called "amalgamating") with TEAM arose, the missionaries were relieved to find a like-minded organization to run the institution for (and with) them.

It is not clear, however, why the Door of Hope on Taiwan received no support from the government. After 1949, it was restructured by the ruling Nationalist political-military elite to include both the national government of all China and the regional government of Taiwan, regarded as a province of China, with parallel national and provincial structures. Occasionally letters and reports from the refuge include references to police and "Chinese officials" bringing in girls,[10] but officials were not used systematically, and lists of contributions do not include any official donors. Most likely officials were aware of the institution as one of many that could be used in times of need to take in young girls. The Taiwan government depended on missionaries to set up services they were not able to provide, but there was no formal or informal connection between the Door of Hope and the state, as there had been in Shanghai. This absence of official sponsorship is doubly puzzling, though, because the supreme leader General Chiang Kai-shek and his wife were aware of the institution. Madame Chiang visited the Door of Hope in both Shanghai and Taipei, and there is some anecdotal evidence that she and her mother personally supported the work of the mission. In addition, the elderly missionary Gladys Dieterle had a lively Bible study group established among the KMT Officer Training Corps.[11]

We can only guess as to why the institution in Taiwan had no official support and seemed to be used only as an occasional social-service provider. The most likely reason was its small size, limited scope, and unimportant constituency. It was an organization devoted solely to the problems of girls from poor mainland families, probably the families of soldiers rather than officials, lower-rung officials rather than higher, poorer Chinese Christians rather than wealthier. The Nationalist government minimally provided for this population. A few soldiers' homes and later senior citizen homes were set up, but by and large, the government, which was in the business of asserting mainlander superiority, focused its resources on assisting the successful. It let the transplanted Western missionaries service this poorer population. After all, the foreigners were searching for a meaningful role in Taiwan and were most comfortable with mainlanders rather than with Taiwanese.[12] Moreover, even this population's need for the Door of Hope declined with time, as the girls reached adulthood and their families took advantage of their privileged mainlander status to secure a share of the growing economic opportunities of Taiwan.

The Door of Hope Refuge in Taipei, moreover, was even more limited. Run at first by a few elderly missionaries, even after their retirement, the mission continued to reflect their views and thus lacked the flexibility to change the patterns set in Shanghai. Missionaries with a wider vision, like those in TEAM, recognized that Taiwan was changing. Mainlanders had different concerns in 1958 than in 1949, and the role of missionaries therefore had to be defined differently. Reports from TEAM staff charged with monitoring the fieldwork, for example, stressed the need for arrangements for junior high school education (compulsory education ended with sixth grade and the girls usually left the mission). This would have entailed extended stays in the institution beyond age twelve or else arrangements with other missions, but veteran supporters insisted that the purpose of the mission was, in the words of one supporter, "not as much an educational institution but to give refuge to very needy children. . . . Far more important is that they become born-again Christians."[13] In the end, neither the missionaries nor the traditional donors of the Door of Hope could change. Thus the institution remained peripheral, serving merely as a stopgap measure at best and warehouse at worst for the most needy in the special population the mainlanders represented. By the mid-1970s, the need for a refuge of this type had ended, and it was closed. After 1976, it continued to service its "alums"—those women it had helped in its twenty-two years in Taiwan.

Residents and Exiles

The Door of Hope Refuge in Taiwan was also more limited in the scope of its work by the sorts of girls who were brought to its doors. In Shanghai, the supply of needy, homeless girls and young women was unlimited. During the initial decade of its existence, the institution opened up its doors first to prostitutes, then to the more ambiguous category of "prostitutes in training," and finally to any needy women. Increasingly it defined the women it served either as "sexual slaves" (prostitutes) or "social slaves" (abused girls and young women who were often either adopted daughters or concubines), categories that disguised as relatives women brought into households as servants. Once it had broadened its definition of the women it served and given its close ties to the authorities, it could be used for any population of needy women and girls. During times of extreme turmoil, "waifs and strays" was a residual category of girls brought to the home, especially with warlord depredations in the 1910s and 1920s, and with wartime refugees during the 1930s. Between two hundred and three hundred girls were brought in most years, with the number of residents approximately 500 women, on average. By the time of its closing in 1951, at least 5,000 girls had been brought to the Shanghai mission.

On Taiwan, by contrast, the official figure given by TEAM officials was 400 girls serviced by the refuge in its twenty-two active years. Because the refuge usually held around 100 girls (with a capacity for at least 200 after new dormitories were built in 1956 and 1957),[14] this low figure suggests that a large number of the girls at the refuge were long-term residents. In Shanghai, the long-term residents were the ones for whom no homes or jobs could be found: the invalid, the retarded, the handicapped. Perhaps this was also the case in Taipei. If so, it is further evidence of the difficulty of the mission to attract a sustainable population.

Another difference in Taipei was that many of the girls who came to the mission were either orphans or "semi-orphans," a new, larger category for the refuge. It appears that the majority of girls had relatives on Taiwan, but these family members were unable to care for them. Some were disabled mothers or elderly grandparents; others were fathers occupied with work or who were unavailable due to gambling, drugs, drink, or desertion. As many of these girls were related to lowly mainlander soldiers who were a world away from the help and support of extended families, it is not surprising that so many were unable to care for their daughters. Yet even those few family members in Taiwan stayed in contact with them. Links to families had not been completely severed in Shanghai, either, with many girls reabsorbed back into family structures after spending time at the mission, but the connections to families seems to have been even stronger in Taiwan. During Chinese New Year in 1959, for example, all but 9 of 77 girls left to celebrate with their families. Published regulations for the refuge constantly stressed limitations on family visits: once or twice a month was all that was allowed.[15] Rules were constantly reiterated, which suggests that families and girls preferred more time together. The struggle over home visits probably represented the greater role that Door of Hope girls' families played in their lives. TEAM seemed to be aware of this changed relationship. Their reports throughout the years commented that the Door of Hope did not prepare girls well enough to reenter Chinese family life and society.[16] The implicit message was that girls would have been better prepared and that more parents would have chosen to bring their daughters to the mission if it had been more congruent with Chinese realities.

But the most important characteristic of the girls at the mission in Taipei was their mainlander identity. Exiles on the island, separated from the grandmothers and aunts, neighbors, and clans who would have cared for them in China, girls were put into the refuge for a time by relatives temporarily unable to care for them. Yet, with the extreme sexual imbalance of mainlanders in a Taiwan where mainlanders were viewed as superior, their future, in their families' eyes, was secure. Marriage would not be difficult with so many males unable to secure mainlander mates,[17] and families saw the Door of Hope as a place to put the girls for a few years until they reached marriageable age. This was in stark contrast to the mission in Shanghai which controlled its residents more, separating them from the world outside while preparing them to marry Chinese Christian husbands or for lives as Bible women, domestic servants, or factory workers.

Roles and Religion

The changed nature of the institution and its different population meant that the function of the Door of Hope Refuge in Taipei was different from the role of the mission in the International Settlement of Shanghai. The Door of Hope Mission in Shanghai had initially been established as a rescue mission, like so many at the time in Western urban centers, from Portsmouth to Peoria, and it kept that identity long after other institutions had evolved into schools, homes for unwed mothers, or battered women's shelters.[18] Its focus, once girls were brought by police, remanded by the courts, or escaped on their own, was to get to work immediately on securing their souls. Yet, along with conversion, girls were immediately given education and training in preparation for their new lives: religious education for the Bible women who would "itinerate" in the villages and towns of rural China and higher education for the girls who would leave and later return to teach at the Door of Hope or a similar institution. Household skills were taught to the girls destined to be the wives of Chinese Christian men who would work along side their husbands in establishing Christian homes. "Industrial" training, especially needlework skills, was given to most of the other girls who would at least help their families by earning wages in the booming textile industries in Shanghai. The process in Shanghai was of rescuing, converting, reforming, and re-socializing through training and education, with a large number of the girls remade in the missionaries' own images. All this was possible given the very intense, relatively closed environment of the institution as it existed in Shanghai. The Door of Hope exercised control over all aspects of the girls' lives, from religion and social life, to job training and schooling. In addition, a large number of girls moved through the institution, with an alliance there between Chinese and Westerners, government officials and local elites, who supported the mission's efforts to reform and reconstruct Chinese women.

In Taipei, by contrast, the institution was never as closed but it served fewer worlds and enjoyed less local support. Families kept in contact with the mission residents in Taipei far more frequently than they did in Shanghai, and they apparently saw the refuge as a way station for their daughters while they struggled through hard times that they viewed as temporary. Apart from caring physically for the daughters, the role of the institution was apparently contested, with conversion still uppermost in the minds of the missionaries, but, it seems, frequently facing family resistance. Most of the families apparently were not Christian, and the "heathen" views of the parents and later, of the in-laws, plus the backsliding of the girls' own faith, are constant themes in the institution's letters and reports.[19] Moreover, missionaries at the Door of Hope Refuge were not even the sole religious teachers of its residents. Girls attended not a chapel on the institution's grounds but a nearby community church, Grace Church, and then later, the TEAM church, Joy (Hsi-lo) Church, for both worship services and Sunday school. Thus, while they were still given intense religious schooling, no longer was it administered within one institution, nor from the same staff who served their other needs. A common complaint in correspondence was, in fact, that the staff was usually neither Christian nor even mainland born, but instead consisted of "nationals" (that is, Taiwanese) who were neither Door of Hope graduates nor Christian.[20]

If religious instruction was not as intensely focused in Taiwan as in mainland China, secular education was almost completely given over to others. With compulsory elementary education in effect after 1946 and a network of public schools established, girls left the refuge by day and returned only in the evening for meals and homework, bedtime and evening devotions. The refuge's major function, apart from providing a religious atmosphere, was to act as support in other areas: in education and schooling, in social and emotional preparation for the worlds of work and marriage in Taiwan, including the girls' readjustment to the families that would take them back after age twelve (later, after age sixteen). In short, the institution's major function, from the missionaries' point of view, was to care and convert them. To the families' it was to care and prepare them for Taiwanese realities. After the acceptance of new residents ceased in 1976, the work was further abbreviated. A Door of Hope Center was set up first in a rented apartment and, after 1987, in a few rooms of the new TEAM Evangelical Building in downtown Taipei. There, the missionaries and alumnae "helpers" provided religious reinforcement—Bible study classes and holiday get-togethers—mixed with a great deal of social work and therapeutic support. Job searches, marital problems, child development, and language training, especially of English, seem to have been the major areas of concern for the "alums" in contact with Kathryn Merrill, the missionary who worked with them at the center.[21] In TEAM's view, Taiwan after 1976 was no longer the Taiwan of 1949 when a flood of refugees desperately needed help. The needs of the young women they had reached at the Door of Hope were not just "social" but were instead more "spiritual."[22]

Conclusion

Indeed, the Taiwan of 1976 was different from the island of 1949, and by the late 1980s it was even more transformed. By then, mainlanders had lost both their leadership and their prominence, symbolized by the census figures which indicate that intermarriage and population growth essentially overwhelmed the "mainlander" category over time. In 1950, 15 percent of the population of Taiwan, 1.1 million out of 7 million people, had been born on the mainland; by 1989, out of a population now of 20 million, some 2.8 million, or 14 percent, called themselves "mainlanders," but this number included Taiwanese women married to mainland men and children born in Taiwan to mainland parents. Of that number, roughly the same figure as before, or 1.2 million (6 percent), had been born on the mainland. By 1989, therefore, 94 percent of the population had been born on the island, versus 85 percent in 1950.[23] Because of the sexual imbalance, many mainland men had to marry Taiwanese women. The category "mainlander," then, was not only disappearing; the very meaning of the term had become ambiguous.[24] By restricting their work to mainlanders, the missionaries at the Door of Hope in Taipei committed themselves to closure. By not expanding to include needy Taiwanese, they essentially closed out the very category which could have continued their work.

Young Taiwanese women in the 1960s, 1970s and 1980s could have used the services of an institution aimed at helping girls and young women adrift in the city with problems that were both "social" and "spiritual," and, in fact, a few rescue missions were set up to serve them. The "economic miracle" of the 1960s was propelled by the labor and exploitation of young women first in textiles and then in electronics, especially assembly work. Young women moved in droves from hills and villages into the cities to look for work.[25] These Taiwanese women were not only easy prey for swindlers and thieves; they frequently discovered—or found themselves trapped into—work in brothels and dancehalls, bars and massage parlors.[26] In fact, the image of the poor, alienated village girl alone in the city, with no other choice than prostitution, came to symbolize life in modern Taiwan, particularly in popular culture such as in the nativist literature (*hsiang-t'u wen-hsueh*) of the 1970s and in the 1980s and 1990s films of young filmmakers like Hou Hsiao-hsien.[27]

Furthermore, these women, along with a goodly number of Taiwanese men, were spiritually adrift, living in a modern entrepreneurial environment that rewarded not honesty and persistence but manipulation and assertiveness. Scholars studying Taiwanese religion have noted the decline in mainstream religious systems, Buddhism as well as Christianity, and the rise instead of more popular religious sects such as fengshui (geomancy) and I-kuan-tao (the way of unity), which promise wealth and security, or syncretic religions such as the New Testament and the Assembly Churches that meld Pentecostal Christianity with Chinese popular religion.[28] It is not certain if a more flexible approach to their ministry would have enabled traditional religions to keep people who were facing the issues of modern Taiwan within the fold. But it is clear that maintaining their former style of mission work and refusing to minister to needy Taiwanese women meant at the very least the loss of an opportunity for the Door of Hope. In this behavior, the missionaries at the Door of Hope were not alone. As Murray Rubinstein has pointed out, the general tendency of transplanted missionaries on Taiwan was not to innovate but instead to continue their traditional tactics.[29]

The final image of the missionaries at the Door of Hope, as seen in the pages of the letters in their correspondence files at TEAM headquarters and in their monthly reports to the faithful, is a sad one. As soon as TEAM took over the sponsorship and administration of the work in 1958, the oldest missionaries, Gladys Dieterle and Winifred Watney, retired. A third, Inez Green, had died during the last year of negotiations, and a fourth, Clara Nelson, followed the other two into retirement in 1963. The letters deal primarily with the problems of the mission and the depredations of old age: illness, aberrant behavior, retirement. But they stress above all how difficult it was for any new, younger missionaries to fit into the outdated system that the Door of Hope as reconstituted on Taiwan represented.[30]

The Door of Hope Refuge on Taiwan was, in the end, a faint shadow of the institution in Shanghai. Shanghai's Door of Hope Mission was the model and the template; Taipei's Door of Hope Refuge was an exercise in nostalgia. For evangelical Christians, furthermore, the Door of Hope in Taipei was an opportunity lost. Its numbers are stark: of the thousands of young women who could have been reached in Taiwan, only four hundred girls lived at the Door of Hope Refuge in its twenty-two years of active mission work. By 1999, fewer than a hundred remained in contact with the Door of Hope Center in Taipei.[31]

Notes

1. For stories of this exodus, see Peng Ming-min, *A Taste of Freedom* (New York: Holt, Rinehart, and Winston, 1972); Ralph Clough, *Island China* (New York: New York University Press, 1978); George Kerr, *Formosa Betrayed* (Boston: Houghton Mifflin, 1965).

2. The story of the Door of Hope is found in its annual reports and pamphlets, with summaries of its work each year in missionary yearbooks. Information has been gathered from these sources, from missionary archives throughout the United States, England, Australia, and Taiwan, and from personal correspondence and interviews with people associ-

ated with the mission's fifty-year history in Shanghai. For descriptions of the mission, see standard guidebooks, like Mary Gamewell's *Gateway to China: Pictures of Shanghai* (New York: Fleming Revell, 1916), or my dissertation, "Encountering Hope: The Door of Hope Mission in Shanghai and Taipei, 1900–1976" (Columbia University, 1996).

3. The figure from Shanghai is my own calculation, based on spotty figures in the reports and periodic overviews and assessments of the institution's work, like Violet Matthews's "Escaped as a Bird: A Story of the Door of Hope in Shanghai" (Melbourne: Southland Press, n.d. but approximately 1950). The total for Taipei is from a letter written on September 24, 1976, from Carl Davis, assistant general director of TEAM (The Evangelical Alliance Mission), which took over the refuge in 1958 and whose archives are in Wheaton, Illinois, a western Chicago suburb and home of the evangelical Wheaton College with its Billy Graham Center Archives.

4. Hsiao Ming's story is from Clara Nelson's letter in the Door of Hope Mission Children's Refuge circular of February 1962, 3; Yu Kuei's story is told first in Clara Nelson's letter from the circular of September 1962, 4; Kun-ying's story is from Freda Rempel's letter in the newsletter of December 1963, 3; for Pao Yu's story see Clara Nelson's letter of November 1958, 2.

5. For example, see the letter written in March 1968 by Freda Rempel and especially her letter of March 9, 1971, to TEAM's director, Vernon Mortenson, in which she was quite explicit about the problems with young unmarried "national" women who came for a time and then were found inadequate, "incompatible," or left to get married or because they were "called" to another line of work. Mortenson had another concern with the quality of the Chinese staff. In comparing staff of the Door of Hope with successful orphanages in Korea, his comment in a September 19, 1960, confidential letter home was that in Korea, all seemed to work together for the children and all regarded it as their joint ministry; at the Door of Hope, by contrast, the staff were merely "employees." Clearly, trying to enforce the traditional tactics on the new staff was not good for either the children or for staff morale.

6. For a description of the agreement, see the letters from Anna Schuler to Winifred Watney, December 20, 1958; Anna Schuler's letter of March 1959, alerting supporters of the changes; and the TEAM files from this period, which include the applications for official TEAM missionary status from Dieterle, Watney, Green, and Schuler, as well as information on the disposition of Door of Hope property, both in Taiwan and in the United States.

7. From my interviews, correspondence, and photographs from Kathryn Merrill from 1991 until her untimely death in 2000.

8. From TEAM files, especially from Anna Schuler's application for TEAM missionary status.

9. TEAM files contain lists of donors, with names, addresses, and amounts of aid, especially for the years 1959 and 1964. The donations were rather substantial, as a matter of fact. For the year 1959, for example, approximately $1,000 a month was recorded as sent to the institution, with a great deal of it earmarked for particular missionaries. Although many of the donations appeared to symbolize the "widow's mite," being in the $5 to $15 range, there were many contributions over $100 and many were several hundreds of dollars. Among the contributors were former missionaries and volunteers at the mission; some were overseas Chinese who had had contact with the mission in Shanghai, many of them apparently related to women who had been at the mission and who now lived in the United States or Hong Kong.

10. For example, a "Chinese government official" brought little Hsiao Ch'in ("Little Musical Instrument") according to a letter of November 1958.

11. Interview with Kathryn Merrill in New York, July 1992.

12. See discussions about missionaries' search for meaningful work after leaving the People's Republic of China, as in Murray Rubinstein, *The Protestant Community of Modern Taiwan* (Armonk, NY: M.E. Sharpe, 1991), 33–36

13. See, for example, notes attached to Kathryn Merrill's letter of August 1966, suggesting that girls stay until age eighteen and help with the more advanced students; she also suggested a more rigorous home economics course for those not able to pass the exams at grade six, although she wasn't sure if Chinese parents would approve of such a skill-based education, preferring instead to have academic credentials. Another issue that TEAM materials discuss throughout its association with the mission was the issue of contact with alumnae. See reports and letters from Anna Schuler's report on her Asian trip of August 1961, when she wrote about the "most critical age" that girls left the mission to "return to the evil influence and heathen classmates." In the next few years, Door of Hope alumnae received a few pamphlets and invitations to an annual retreat, but few responded to these initial overtures, probably because they had not continued practicing Christianity.

14. See the newsletters from 1956 and 1957 and the TEAM report of November 19, 1958, by Oliver Olson to the director, Vernon Mortenson, who wrote of the "smooth-running, very efficient establishment" in a "wonderful new compound with several buildings and very suitable grounds for the care of about 100 children. The assets must be over $125,000," he surmised. Another report, written by Mr. Mortenson, after a number of visits to the home, suggests that the buildings could take as many as 200 and that the property "is far and away the best of any connected with TEAM's ministry in Formosa, and possibly anywhere in the world."

15. See regulations publicized in mission pamphlets, like the one sent out with no date, but probably in 1957.

16. See, for example, TEAM director Vernon Mortenson's letter of May 7, 1971, to Mrs. Schuler, in which he refers to the "concern of the Door of Hope Committee and the [TEAM] Field Council . . . that the girls be better prepared for life in Chinese homes. It is felt and with this Chinese advisors agree that the prolonged guidance by North Americans does tend to put these children under some disadvantage as compared to those who are guided in their training by Chinese." Kathryn Merrill's letter of August 1966, referred to above, also suggested that parents were reluctant to put their daughters in the refuge unless it could offer them the higher level of education and support that was needed in the new Taiwan.

17. Hill Gates, "Ethnicity and Social Class," in *The Anthropology of Taiwanese Society*, ed. Emily Ahern and Hill Gates (Stanford: Stanford University Press, 1981), 258, refers to the mainlander women who are "much in demand in the distorted marriage market . . . as long as they remain respectable." She goes on to say that "one hears of very few who are prostitutes or beggars, and few take menial jobs as domestics or as factory hands (though their mothers may have). . . . By contrast, among lower-class Taiwanese there are a substantial number of prostitutes, gangsters, beggars, opera players, and the merely poor."

18. For a picture of the evolution of many rescue homes over time, see Sherrill Cohen, *The Evolution of Women's Asylums Since 1500: From Refuges for Ex-Prostitutes to Shelters for Battered Women* (New York: Oxford University Press, 1994), chapter 7, or the histories of any of the rescue homes, like the Magdalene Asylums or Florence Crittendon Homes. I thank Dr. Gainey of the Grace Home in Poughkeepsie, New York, which now serves as a battered women's shelter, for pointing out that most of these institutions began in the early part of the century as rescue homes and then over time evolved with women's needs.

19. As early as September 1962, the Door of Hope monthly circular referred to the need for a "native evangelist" to work among the families of the girls and to keep in touch with the girls after they left to reinforce their faith. This theme is repeated in nearly all the letters and reports of the mission.

20. Freda Rempel's letters cited above about the difficulty of finding adequate staff include the lack of Christian candidates as one of the problems in finding suitable matrons and housemothers for the girls.

21. See her monthly reports, especially since the Door of Hope Center was established in 1987 as part of the TEAM Evangelical Building on former Door of Hope property, with very nice meeting rooms for the alumnae. She does remark on the apparent irony that whereas contact with North Americans had long been criticized, in the 1990s it was precisely this connection that helped alumnae search her out, with her language and U.S. connections avidly sought by the young women now hoping to go abroad. See her letter of November 1992, in which she suggests that "now it appears that we helped to prepare the girls for changes that would come to Taiwan."

22. See the letter from Carl Davis, assistant TEAM general director, to the supporters of the Door of Hope, of September 24, 1976, as TEAM prepared to phase out the active orphanage work and instead focus on reaching alumnae.

23. These figures are from Tien Hung-mao, "Transformation of an Authoritarian Party State," in *Political Change in Taiwan*, ed. Tun-jen Cheng and Stephan Haggard (Boulder, CO: Lynne Rienner, 1992), 36.

24. For a clear discussion of many of the ethnic issues of identity resulting from these ambiguities, see Alan Wachman, "Competing Identities in Taiwan," in *The Other Taiwan*, ed. Murray Rubinstein (Armonk, NY: M.E. Sharpe, 1994), 23.

25. There has been substantial work done on the feminization of the workplace and its importance in the Asian economic miracle. For Taiwan, see especially Rita Gallin, "Women, Family, and the Political Economy of Taiwan," *Journal of Peasant Studies* 12, no. 1 (1984): 76–92; Lydia Kung, "Perceptions of Workers Among Factory Women," in Ahern and Gates, eds., *The Anthropology of Taiwanese Society*; Susan Greenhalgh, "Sexual Stratification: The Other Side of 'Growth with Equity' in East Asia," *Population and Development Review* 11, no. 2 (1985): 265–314; Bih-er Chou, "Changing Patterns of Women's Employment in Taiwan, 1966–1986," in Rubinstein, ed., *The Other Taiwan*, 330–56.

26. The most compelling description of this phenomenon is Margery Wolf's study of women in a village, *The House of Lim: A Study of a Chinese Farm Family* (Stanford: Stanford University Press, 1968), and her more analytical *Women and the Family in Rural Taiwan* (Stanford: Stanford University Press, 1972).

27. See, for example, Thomas Gold's discussion about the quest for a unique Taiwanese identity of the 1970s and its expressions in popular culture in his "Civil Society and Taiwan's Quest for Identity," in *Cultural Change in Postwar Taiwan*, ed. Stevan Harrell and Huang Chun-chieh (Boulder: Westview Press, 1994), 61–62. See the discussion of feminist consciousness and sexuality expressed in Taiwanese literature in Sung Mei-hwa's "Feminist Consciousness as Expressed in the Contemporary Fiction of Taiwan," in ibid., 281–87.

28. The standard discussion of sectarian religion on Taiwan is David Jordan and Daniel Overmyer, *The Flying Phoenix: Aspects of Chinese Sectarianism in Taiwan* (Princeton: Princeton University Press, 1986). For discussions of Christianity, see Rubinstein, *The Protestant Community on Modern Taiwan*.

29. Rubinstein, ed., *The Other Taiwan*, 42.

30. See especially TEAM concerns about the mission in letters of September 29, 1960; May 31, 1962; and May 7, 1971.

31. Eighty-eight is my own count after carefully reading Merrill's last newsletters and correspondence from the Door of Hope Center. Of course, it needs to be emphasized that although the Door of Hope in Taiwan was small, for those 88 women it had served a crucial role and had indeed been a lifesaver. I was privileged to meet a number of the "alums" over the years that I knew Merrill, from 1991 until her death in 2000. Their gratitude and deep love for her was never more apparent than in her last days when a steady stream of Door of Hope alumnae from Taiwan and abroad filled her room. Her memorial service on April 6, 2000, was a loving testimonial to the importance of her mission.

5

Imagining "New Women," Imagining Modernity

Gender Rhetoric in Colonial Taiwan

Hsin-yi Lu

This essay was inspired by the recent debates of identity issues in Taiwan. Unlike in other Asian countries, in Taiwan, the evocation of nation-state formation—whose primary goal is to construct a separate identity from mainland China—is often articulated with the colonial experience and logic that came under the Japanese rule. This significant phenomenon has compelled me to explore the colonial roots of Taiwan's contemporary nationalist discourse in its earliest enunciations. In surfing through Taiwan's early enlightenment journals I found that "woman" is an encompassing sign that signifies the emergence of modernity, as well as the ambivalent colonial mentality, in colonial Taiwan.[1] Accordingly, this essay focuses on the manipulation of gender rhetoric in Taiwanese intellectual discourse during the 1920s and 1930s, when a modernist project was provoked. I then illustrate how the transition of identification was manifested in the transforming connotation of the sign "woman" after the mid-1930s. For the sake of clarity, I begin my essay with a recent political event—the Southern Advance Event—which best shows the interweaving relationships between nation-state formation and colonial memories in contemporary Taiwan.

In 1994, after a New Year's trip to Southeast Asia, Lee Teng-hui, president of Taiwan, announced his *Nanchin* (Southern Advance) policy. According to this policy, the government should encourage Taiwanese industries to expand their commerce and influence to Southeast Asia. By utilizing the natural resources and cheap labor forces in Southeast Asia, Taiwan's economic problems, resulting from increasing domestic labor costs and pressure from environmentalists, might be solved.[2] In addition to economic interests, the *Nanchin* policy was proposed to impede the increasing economic dependence of Taiwanese business on the Chinese market. Rather than being incorporated into the "Great Chinese Economic Sphere,"[3] Lee and his staff suggested another direction for Taiwan to explore overseas markets.

Interestingly, the notion of *Nanchin* was a replica of an earlier Japanese imperialist project—*Nanshin* (Southern Advance).[4] *Nanshin* refers to Japanese expansionist thought that Japan should extend its interests and influence south to Southeast Asia and the South Pacific (at that time European colonies), to pursue economic advantage and national security.[5] As the first colony of the Japanese colonial empire, Taiwan played an indispensable role in the *Nanshin* program. As early as the "Kodama Report of 1902," proposed by the second governor of colonial Taiwan, Taiwan was appraised as a "stone aiming at the southeast," a military base for the conquest of Southeast Asia.[6] After ninety years, these ideas became Taiwanese. Although Lee's policy was soon thrown out (which is not uncommon in Taiwan's political circuit), his suggestion and the accompanying discussions manifest a deferred identification with colonial logic in the postcolonial era.[7] The memory of colonial rule came back to haunt the cultural imagery of this former colonial intellectual.

Lee Teng-hui, like many of his colleagues who were educated under the Japanese system, spoke Japanese more fluently than Mandarin, and was more familiar with Japan than China.[8] As the historian Lai Tse-han (Lai et al. 1991) points out, Lee and his fellows belong to the "second generation of Taiwanese elite stratum," which emerged and matured by the 1940s. Their sense of identity and status derived from their success in top Japanese schools and universities and from access to a cosmopolitan culture that their Japanese education had provided for them. Accordingly, many of this generation shared a Japanese worldview to a great extent, although not all of them collaborated with the Japanese government.[9] A good example is Wu Chuo-liu. In his autobiography, Wu wrote that he was very critical of the colonial oppression in Taiwan before leaving for mainland China in 1941; however, the experience of going to China only disappointed him:

> After arriving [in Shanghai] I found that I could not understand a word [of Mandarin]. Although this was my ancestors' land, I felt like I was living in a foreign country. Shanghai was not the paradise that I once imagined it to be.[10]

Wu immediately found that his longing for individual freedom and dignity, which were lacking under Japanese colonial rule in Taiwan, could not be fulfilled in mainland China either. Worse than that, in wartime China Taiwanese people were viewed as "Japanese spies." Thus, Wu had to hide his Taiwanese identity for his own safety.[11]

In contrast to his experience of the hostility toward the Taiwanese by the mainland Chinese, Wu made some close Japanese friends while working in Nanking. He wrote: "My Japanese friends were all well-educated liberals. They did not have any racial prejudices."[12] He admired those Japanese intellectuals' open-minded viewpoints, while lamenting China's pitiful situation: "I felt that Chinese people were more contemptible than people in Taiwan. It was meaningless to stay in Nanking anymore."[13]

Wu's statements characterize the ambivalence Taiwanese intellectuals felt toward China and Japan during the period of the Japanese occupation. This aspect of the colonized mentality has been largely neglected in the two opposing nationalist discourses in Taiwan and the People's Republic of China (PRC) since the end of World

War II.[14] In Taiwan, along with the political situation, discussions about Taiwanese colonial literature have also been highly regulated. Themes involving anticolonial struggles and the oppressed colonized experience were highly praised and elaborated on, whereas portrayals of ambivalence toward the colonizers were simplified or ignored. In the rare cases that such ambivalence is mentioned, it is usually interpreted by the rhetoric of both sides of the Taiwan strait as escape from, or submission to, the harsh situation under the strict literary policy of the Japanese colonial government.[15] Although Lai Tse-han (along with his coauthors) did address this ambiguous identification in his book (1991), he still attributed Taiwan's identity issue to a simple choice between Japan and China, and ignores the complex process of appropriation and transformation through which this identity was formed.

In his classic study *The Intimate Enemy* (1983), social theorist Ashis Nandy proposes that "the first differentia of colonialism is a state of mind in the colonizers and the colonized, a colonial consciousness which included the sometimes unrealizable wish to make economic and political profits from the colonies."[16] He problematizes the conceptualization of colonial mentalities in terms of a binary division between the oppressor and the oppressed, and argues that the identification with the aggressor was crucial to the consolidation of "colonialism proper." This is evident in the case of British colonial rule in India, where the British and the Indians both ascribed cultural meanings to British domination, and the Indians internalized the colonial definition in sex roles and politics. Similarly, the colonial experience resulted in a divide between Taiwanese people and mainland Chinese, which has continued to affect the postwar nation-state–building process in Taiwan, as the "*Nanchin* Event" implies.

The recent debates about Taiwan's identity and national consciousness compel me to look at the past, using a genealogical method to sort out the traces of Japanese colonialism in the controversies about identity and nation-state–building in contemporary Taiwan. In this essay I shall focus on the discourse of modernity that emerged in the 1920s and 1930s among the Taiwanese intelligentsia, when the first confrontations with Japan and China caused a number of intellectual conflicts. These conflicts were often manifested in the contradictory images of the "new woman" and in discussions of *fu-nü chieh-fang* (women's liberation). Because of the promise brought by the colonizers, Taiwanese people incorporated the logic of modernity and utilized it to criticize the backwardness of *Toyo*, a Japanese term referring to China. I propose that there were at least two crucial factors enabling the emergence of the modern period: first, the chance for the intellectuals to become immersed in the modern atmosphere of Japanese education, and, second, the blurring of racial boundaries between the Japanese colonizers and the people they colonized.

Historical Background

Regarding the relationship between racial discourse and colonial power, many scholars agree that in comparison to Western colonial powers, the Japanese empire was a special case. For example, Ichiro Tomiyama (1995) suggests that "[Japanese] colonialist practice was not narrated as an opposition of races and cultures, but one of 'cooperativism' as exemplified by the 'Great East Asia Co-Prosperity Sphere,' a discourse connected with such reforms as medicine, hygiene and education."[17] In a footnote, Ashis Nandy also maintains that one of the main themes of Japanese imperialism was the "stress of Japan's greater modernization and on its 'responsibility' to modernize other Asian societies."[18] It would be oversimplifying the complex reality, however, to conclude that there was a consistent racial policy or notion within Japanese colonialism. The shifting in Japanese racial policies can best be illustrated by Taiwan's case.

The Japanese empire's first colony—Taiwan—was a particular case of "an imperial accessory; it was a laboratory where the newcomer among the colonial powers could show off its modernizing skills."[19] Beginning with the military pacification of Taiwan in 1895, the colonial process took several different steps. In the first few years, the colonial administration was most concerned with the liquidation of resistance. The creation of a rationalized central administrative system was the next crucial task to consolidate military and political power. Under the authoritarian regime, there was little if any interaction between the Japanese and Taiwanese. It was forbidden for Japanese women to settle in Taiwan before 1914. From 1914 to 1924, however, colonial rule was pushed forward by a more liberal administration, along with domestic political changes in Japan. Liberal currents in Japan encouraged an "assimilation" policy and granted the Taiwanese some basic rights enjoyed by Japanese citizens. The modern educational system was one of the few spheres reformed under this liberal trend. In 1922, educational segregation between Japanese and Taiwanese in Taiwan was lifted. The prestigious primary schools, previously the preserve of the children of Japanese colonials, were made available to Taiwanese children. This educational reform, accompanying the increasing number of Taiwanese students studying in Tokyo after the 1920s, helped narrow the differences between the Japanese and Taiwanese people. The racial boundary was questioned by Taiwanese and Japanese liberal intellectuals. For example, in the early 1920s, advocating the abolishment of the prohibition of marriage between Japanese and Taiwanese was often heard in liberal circles.

The status of Taiwan was constantly elevated as Japan expanded its imperial territory. In 1936, after the start of the Sino-Japanese War, the Japanese government endeavored to "Japanize" Taiwan through the *Kominka* (Japanization) policy which included the adoption of Japanese surnames, a ban on Chinese language, and military conscription for Taiwanese. The *Kominka* movement was driven by the fear that the Taiwanese people would seek an alliance with the Chinese with whom they shared a racial heritage. In the perspective of the Japanese government, it was essential to ensure the loyalty of the Taiwanese. Needless to say, the most effective way to achieve this loyalty was by diminishing the distinction between Japanese colonizers and Taiwanese colonized people. Therefore, in a sense, the Taiwanese did have the opportunity to "become" Japanese. Joining the army became one way for Taiwanese youth to prove their equality to Japanese. As Chou Wan-yao (1994) suggests, the experience of the *Kominka* movement, which gave rise to a new generation of colonial elites, was indispensable to the emergence of contemporary Taiwanese separatism.

Women, Nation, and Modernity

Gender issues and women's emancipation have seldom been mentioned in discussions regarding Taiwanese anticolonial thoughts.[20] This negligence is surprising given the fact that gender issues first appeared in Taiwan's first enlightenment journal—*Tai-oan chheng-lian* (Taiwan Youth). In this section, the various gender issues mentioned by Taiwan's intellectuals under Japanese rule are discussed. I contextualize their arguments and show how these arguments were inspired by similar discussions in earlier periods in Japan and China. In their focus on gender issues these colonial intellectuals demonstrated their aspirations for modernity—a project promised by the colonial government. I will use three major enlightenment journals—*Tai-oan chheng-lian*, *Tai-wan*, and *Tai-wan min-pao*—as my resources to document the aspirations for modernity in intellectual discourses during the 1920s. I then focus on "modernist" literature, a new genre appearing in the late 1930s, when a new Taiwanese intelligentsia, educated in Japan, matured and started to participate in the dreamscape of modernity.

Now, if any agreement were to occur in contemporary feminist thought, it would be the notion that "woman" is not a pre-given object. The significance of the category "woman" is historically constructed and implicated in various discursive formations and institutional practices (Adams and Cowie 1990). In a similar vein, Floya Anthias and Nira Yuval-Davis (1993) argue that the articulation of gender and other social categories, such as race, class, and ethnicity, is a historically contingent process. Therefore, the social efficacy of these categories must be theorized in terms of the ways such categories interrelate in different contexts. This perspective opens up the possibility for us to examine the articulation of various social forces at a particular historical moment when the notion of "gender" or "woman" was formulated.

Interestingly, once this liberating notion of gender was formed, it soon became a common trope exploited by other discourses, such as nationalism and colonialism. Frank Dikötter (1995) notes that sex or sexuality became a signifier for Chinese intellectuals in the Republican period to appropriate the modern; he also points out that the "discourses of modernity" in China were generated by a loose association of various disciplines instead of a state-directed project. In literary discourse the "new woman" is often used as an index of the identity crisis for the enunciating subject in a transitional period. Ching-kiu Stephen Chan (1993) indicates that the search for a new subjectivity in the May Fourth cultural movement was carried out frequently in terms of capturing the identity crisis of the "new woman." In investigating the male construct of urban women in Shanghai, literary scholar Zhang Henghao (1991a, 1991b) finds that the image of "new" elusive women is equivalent to a quintessential figure of the city. Lydia Liu (1993a) also notices that in the May Fourth discourse "women" were usually portrayed as an opposing signifier to modernity and tradition. She analyzes Yu Dafu's stories and concludes that in these stories male protagonists (intellectuals) often travel between modern woman and traditional woman, hoping to work out their own crisis of identity through their choice.

Regarding the interactions between nationalism and the notion of womanhood, Tani Barlow (1993) suggests that Chinese modernity had the potential to emancipate women. However, its dominant essence was still masculine due to its association with nationalism. All nations rely on the construction of gender, and women are typically constructed as the symbolic bearer of the nation. This trope of the nation-as-woman, however, depends on a particular image of woman as chaste and maternal, or as guardian of "tradition," for its representational efficacy (Parker et al. 1992). Accordingly, a disparity grew between the women's liberation and nationalist movements, and contestation developed in the quest of womanhood in nationalist discourse (Chatterjee 1989, 1990).

How are modernity and nationalism gendered (if they are gendered)? Many scholars have pointed out that the very definition of nationhood rests on the male recognition of identity (Gilmartin et al. 1994; Kandiyoti 1993). Barlow (1993) has focused on the masculine nature of Chinese modernity. In sorting out the polysemic meanings of the notion of modernity in Europe at the turn of the last century, Rita Felski (1995) contends that the narrative of modernity is shaped by gender symbolism and is ostensibly male, but that feminine phenomena were still given a central importance in the analysis of the culture of modernity. Sangari and Vaid (1990) then called for a "feminist historiography" to think of gender difference as structuring a wide set of social relations at a certain historical moment.

From the historical perspective, there is a striking similarity in the modern histories of China and Japan in that the emergence of women's liberation was tied to the nation-building process. In both cases, however, women's identity was also subsumed by the notion of nationhood. In the Japanese context, state attention to women's roles was inaugurated by the interest in strengthening that nation's power. Behind various reform policies toward women was the general notion of *ryosai kenbo* ("Good Wife, Wise Mother") popularized by the Education Ministry (Nolte and Hastings 1991). Women were expected to contribute to state building by devoting their labor to the industrial economy and taking care of the family. In order to improve women's productivity and capability to bring up the next generation, various compelling programs on women's education were practiced to articulate an ideal of womanhood. This guiding aphorism was, however, challenged by later female literati. The debates over "new woman" flourished in the liberal era of "Taisho Democracy," carried out by some liberal journalists and intellectuals who demanded a reexamination of women's roles and the Meiji state version of womanhood. The most radical challenge was the one made to the Japanese marriage system for yielding women to power. Women, in these arguments, should be granted the right to choose their spouses based on love, and gain autonomy in the home.

In the Chinese context, Liu (1993b) points out that a "totalistic" idea of woman had been invented. Barlow (1994a, 1994b) further argues that this totalizing notion of *fu-nü* became a state category for history and national politics. "Modern *funu*/women provided staging ground, offering the sexed bodies of peasant women as a space of modernization."

A parallel in women's liberation movements between Japan and China is further evident in the case of Ibsen's play *A Doll's House,* which was equally well received in both countries around 1910: "Dora's abandonment of the patriarchal household . . . announced the primacy of individual fulfillment over social restraints, [and] implied a wide-ranging rebellion against Confucian norms."[21] Although in China discussions about the meanings of the play were merely conducted by male intelligentsia, they did raise some important issues, such as the new awareness of the importance of financial independence for women.

Given these liberal precedents, Taiwanese intellectuals began noticing women's issues. In the 1920s, Taiwanese students studying in Tokyo established the journal *Tai-oan chheng-lian.* The mission statement of the opening volume expressed anxiety toward the global modernization inspired by the pan-European and India's nation-state movements after World War I:

> Such a world war is unprecedented and has perhaps never occurred in human history . . . It is from this absolute misfortune that the survivors were awakened from the past lazy sleep, for the purpose of embracing enlightenment and abandoning darkness. They were awakened from the selfish, xenophobic, solipsistic savage life to accomplish the cooperative, mutually tolerant cultural movement.[22]

The statement then maintains that after the global transformations—such as the establishment of the League of Nations, respect for the autonomy of nations, the realization of gender egalitarianism, and labor movements—the Taiwanese youth must wake up from their previous situation. Nonetheless, it laments that Taiwan's marginality in global politics and its limited environment have resulted in Taiwan becoming backward compared to the grand trend of the "cultural world." Therefore, the intellectuals should reflect on their negligence, and learn from foreign thought to alleviate the suffering of the three million Taiwanese people.

After the first volume of *Tai-oan chheng-lian,* articles relating to issues of women's education, marriage, and family often appeared in the journal. As I show below, the imagination of (and utterance from) the position of "new woman" was common in Taiwan's literature. This trope, the representation of new women, had multiple connotations. It represents the suffering of the Taiwanese nation, the yet-to-be-fulfilled reformist ideal, the narcissistic self-pity, and the confusing desire of male intelligentsia. In the following sections, I will weave discussions of these enlightenment journals with the tropes in fiction to illustrate how the image of "woman" was deployed in the intellectual discourse of modernity in Taiwan.

Emergence of Feminist Thought

What was specific to Taiwanese feminist thought was its concurrence with the encounter of colonial power and knowledge.[23] In *Tai-oan chheng-lian*, the status of uneducated women was often equated with the backward situation of Taiwan compared to other advanced nations. The first essay on women's issues appeared in the journal in 1920, written by Peng Hua-ying. The article "Do Women's Problems Exist in Taiwan?" began with the celebration of a new era after the end of World War I. In the article the author argues that a great reform had occurred, which radically challenged the old monarchy and feudal thought. In a new world where the spirit of freedom and equality prevailed, Peng believed that educated people should think about some new social issues to fit the trend of the new era, among them were the concerns of labor, race, and women. Women's problems and labor problems emerged as the most urgent issues. The author then compared women's situations in the West and the East. Although Western women had enjoyed the right to vote and participate in politics, women in most Eastern societies remained obedient to men's power. "This is against the trend of *social evolution*," Peng argued.[24] Furthermore, whereas the feminist movement in Tokyo was in accordance with the world wave of women's liberation, "Taiwan is just an isolated island on the ocean. But we should be concerned with these kinds of issues to avoid being deserted by world civilization."[25] He then suggests that the arranged marriage system should first be abolished. He believes that marriage should be based on the free love between prospective husband and wife, and that the oppressive marriage system is the primary evil force that restricted women's opportunities to develop according to their free will. In order to pursue the emancipating marriage system, the interaction between male and female should be opened. Women should have the equal right to a social life, just as men. In the end, since this is the "general trend of social evolution," those unreasonable restrictions to the development of women's personality should be abolished soon, and women needed education to liberate their own will.

It should be noted that ever since the beginning of Taiwan's enlightenment, there has been a wide range of differences regarding the notion of gender. Some notions accepted the radical view of left-wing feminists and proposed that the gendered division of labor in the domestic sphere should also be questioned. Other beliefs, however, were aligned with the notion in the Meiji Restoration that women's role in the family should be consolidated to constitute a strong nation. For example, another article written by Chen Ying in the same volume as Peng Hua-ying's article also alerts the readers to the necessity of women's education. However, Chen's viewpoint is different from Peng's. Whereas Peng believed that the domestic role is not women's innate obligation, Chen obviously adopted the notion of "Good Wife, Wise Mother" and argued that women are the basis of the family—the basic social unit:

> Today they are girls; tomorrow they will be wives and mothers, bearing an important duty. The prosperity and the wisdom of the offspring are both women's duty. Therefore, it is absolutely urgent to educate women.[26]

In a similar tone, Wang Min-chuan suggests that uneducated women could not pursue chastity. The inculcation of "virtue" was the primary issue in women's education, which would help elevate the level of cultural development and civilization of the nation.[27] In an address at the Taipei Girls' High School, the most prestigious girls' high school in northern Taiwan, Wang Chin-hai juxtaposed the backwardness of Taiwan's intellectuals to the primitive condition of women's education.[28] He lamented that most of the social mass still thought that women's education was unnecessary.

Another barrier was the segregation of the sexes. Wang Chin-hai then proposed that not only should more women's schools be established in the future, but that women should also take a break from their limited domestic sphere and go out and travel, to broaden their vision. Interestingly, one major reason for Wang to promote women's learning broad knowledge, including politics, arts, economics, and so on, and not just domestic skills, was because "talking with western women about literature and politics was very enjoyable, whereas it was no fun to talk with Asian women about similar topics."[29]

Women's Awareness as the Measurement of National Strength

The much-written-about powerless situation of Taiwanese women symbolized the weakness of the Taiwanese nation. For example, Chou Tao-yuan attacked the "bad situation" of Taiwanese women, arguing that the women's movement was an indispensable part of world progress. Because of the bad influence from the "Eastern hemisphere," Taiwan's women were denied autonomy, education, and political rights. He then critiqued the trade of women, prostitution, and the custom of adopting daughters in Taiwan, claiming that only education could diminish social diseases such as these.[30]

Tai-oan chheng-lian changed its name to *Tai-wan* in 1920,[31] and then to *Tai-wan min-pao* (*TWMP*) in 1923. The mission statement of *TWMP* said that the purpose of the journal was to "educate society . . . [and] enlighten Taiwan's culture . . . promoting peace in East Asia."[32] This project of enlightenment was inspired by the "new knowledge and transformation" that occurred worldwide after World War I ended. The content of *TWMP* consisted mostly of international news from Japan and China, but also included news of South Asia and Europe, in an effort from its editors to create a modern journal with a global perspective. Also, compared to its predecessors, *TWMP* was obviously more activist. After moving to Taipei in 1927, *TWMP*'s contributors gave speeches as well as published articles, and held study groups in every corner of Taiwan, thereby becoming crucial players in the various social movements, which emerged in Taiwan during the late

1920s. Accordingly, there were lots of reported speeches and short reports of study groups and summer camps published in *TWMP*. There was a clear trend during the period of *TWMP* that the women's movement was situated along with other social movements, such as labor, peasant, and nationalist movements.

Noteworthy in the first issue of *TWMP* was a special essay on women's political involvement. The author briefly introduced, and commented on, women's political movements in Japan and China, then lamented that there had been no such actions among Taiwan's women. "Is it not pitiful?" he inquired, "I hope the men of Taiwan would liberate our women, give them freedom. Meanwhile, women themselves should be awakened and start an emancipation movement!"[33]

Romantic Love, Marriage, and Sexuality

Many authors' propositions for women's liberation begin from the discussion of issues such as arranged marriage, polygamy, concubinage, and the dowry system. Writer Hsieh Chun-mu argues that "before reforming global society activists need to reform their families first."[34] He continues on to say that the problem of marriage is a specific problem among Asian countries such as Japan and China. In Western society there is no such problem because of the belief in free love. In order to solve this problem we should "enhance the education of women, and promote opportunities for social interaction between men and women."[35]

One report from Kwangtung was quoted to defend prostitutes. In the article the author argued that prostitution was the product of an evil patriarchal society, putting the blame on men, not women. Before women obtained equal opportunity in economics, prostitution was an unavoidable choice.

Writer Tsai Tun-yao argues that women's liberation was to be the liberation of sexuality: "I think that the women's problems are generated by the binding of their bodies for the past thousands of years. Women have to free themselves. First, social interaction between the sexes should be encouraged. Women should pursue free love. After that inequality in politics, the legal system, education, and economics will be abolished."[36] Writer Kuo Hua-chou contends that the emancipation of women should be the product of the epoch. Again, "the most urgent need for women right now is to destroy the rigid feudal family system and establish the egalitarian, mutually responsible family."[37]

It should be noted that the common assumption behind these articles was a strong belief in social Darwinism. For example, writer Chen Kun-shu outlines the evolution of the marriage system from forced to consensus marriage. In the past, marriage only served the functions of fulfilling sexual desire, reproduction, and securing economic need. However, in the modern era, marriage should be based on heterosexual love. Interestingly, he also suggests that biological inheritance should be taken into account in choosing a spouse: "The level of education and physical health is more important than income,"[38] because it will determine the quality of marriage and the next generation.

The Predicament of "Advanced Women"

The promotion of heterosexual interaction has been a major issue since the first discussions of women's issues. The Confucian teaching of gender segregation, that man and woman should not sit around the same table, was the most common target attacked by these liberal writers. Many authors writing for *TWMP* encouraged women to go out of the home, expose themselves to new knowledge, and interact with men.[39] Huang Pu-chun, the first female writer to participate in this discussion, suggested that women and men should go to the same schools: "The more chance men and women have to interact, the less they would have any 'dirty thoughts.'"[40]

The celebration of educated, "sociable" women caused some problems too. A female student in Canton wrote an essay in the journal on free-love marriage and new women. She argued that "the family should be the reflection of both man and woman; however, until now family has been controlled by male power. The family is a patriarchal system, women are only a domestic machine."[41] She then suggested the equal rights of both sexes in a marriage, and concluded that women should pursue a free-love marriage, which is an index of the autonomy of personhood. Similar to May Fourth feminists, arranged marriage was one of the most attacked systems by *TWMP* authors. In a reader's letter to the journal a Taiwanese female student in Tokyo wrote that her parents had selected her marriage partner and asked her to marry right after graduation. She refused in the beginning, yet her father threatened to discontinue paying her living expenses in Tokyo if she rejected this marriage. She wrote: "How could this kind of thing occur in this 'civilized society?'"[42] In response, the editor suggested that she adopt her parents' view that it "was for the good of your future" to go home and meet her fiancé: "If he fits your ideal, then comply with your parents' decision that you marry him. If not, ask your parents to cancel the arrangement. This is a legal act; your parents would not dare to enforce their choice."

The depiction of the dilemma of "new women" was a common theme in Taiwan's modern fiction as well. In the next section I will use Taiwan's earliest modern fiction to illustrate how male intellectuals expressed their dissatisfaction with their traditional system through appropriating women's voices and dilemmas.

The Emergence of Modern Fiction

The emergence of fiction as a literary form was motivated by the "New Cultural Movement," which took place in Tokyo in the 1920s, along with the establishment of *Tai-oan chheng-lian*. Before then the literary circles of Taiwan were dominated by traditional gentry who were educated under the Confucian system, and whose major writings were classical Chinese poetry and essays.[43]

Tai-oan chheng-lian was not a literary journal. Its primary goal was to promote the welfare of Taiwan in the domestic political context of Japan. Nonetheless, there were some discussions about literary theories and the function of literature.

For example, Chen Hsin proposes that "healthy literature" is a precondition for a glorious nation: "Literature is the foundation of culture. If literature deteriorates, the nation would deteriorate too. As such, the primary goal of literature is to enlighten the culture and strengthen the nation."[44] Chen then critiques Taiwan's elder literati for sticking with outdated concepts, not pursuing progressive knowledge, thus limiting their own intellectual progress. Moreover, the writing of the old literature was considered obtuse and incomprehensible for a mass readership: "Literature only functions when the readers can comprehend its thought and emotions." Chen thus argues that Taiwan's new literature should adopt a vernacular written language, as promoted by the May Fourth intellectuals in mainland China.

The attacks on the classical literature and the promotion of literary realism based on a vernacular written language were continued in two other articles in *Tai-oan chheng-lian*. Kan Wen-fang maintained that literature should evolve with the progress of society by focusing on socially significant topics, instead of the aestheticism that viewed "literature existing only for the purpose of literature."[45] He argued, "Literature should serve the purpose of social reform" to bridge the extremist materialism in the West and the spirituality of the East.[46] Chen Tuan-ming also argued that only a vernacular literature is useful for Taiwan. There were two advantages of vernacular literature, according to Chen: First, it facilitated the dissemination of culture, and inspired the intellectual level of the masses to achieve civilization. Second, it was easy to understand, which would save lots of time for developing the skills of science and technology in Taiwan. Interestingly, Chen also pointed out that Taiwan should situate itself as a bridge between Japan and China, to contribute to peace in East Asia. Based on a progressivist perspective that Taiwan has gone from being a base for pirates to becoming an island of agricultural resources, Chen predicted that the future of Taiwan is overseas. Therefore, developing a vernacular literature would also assist Taiwanese economic expansion to South China and Southeast Asia.[47]

Based on these premises, the first piece of "modern" fiction was published in 1922 in *Tai-wan*, written in Japanese by Hsueh Chun-mu, a male student in Tokyo Normal High School. This piece, "Where Should She Go—Dedicated to the Sisters Disturbed by a Similar Problem," was about a Taiwanese girl, Kui-hua, who was stuck in a love triangle. Kui-hua was a well-educated girl who fell in love with Ch'eng-feng—an intellectual studying in Tokyo. The story begins with Ch'eng-feng's return from Japan and his reunion with Kui-hua. Kui-hua's dream about marrying Ch'eng-feng was broken by the fact that Ch'eng-feng had been engaged to his cousin A-lien two years earlier. In a letter written by Ch'eng-feng to Kui-hua, he blamed the oppression of feudal society and the patriarchal family, which forbade his pursuit of free love (although the engagement with A-Lien was his choice). Although he was truly in love with Kui-hua, he had to obey his father's order to keep his commitment to A-lien. At the end of this story, Kui-hua decided to go to Japan to study, and escaped from her heartbreaking love affair. On the boat to Tokyo, she met another girl who attempted to escape from the arranged marriage by escaping to Tokyo to pursue a new world. In talking and crying with this girl, Kui-hua finally realized that a social disease was rooted in the marriage system:

> Kui-hua: "It would not help much to keep crying."
>
> The girl: "Exactly. That's why I decided to go to Tokyo."
>
> Kui-hua: "The same here. I really hate our social customs, mostly because of the marriage system. Men perhaps still have some sort of freedom, however, women have to be absolutely obedient. The society forces us to behave like slaves. Even if the marriage contract is broken by men, society still blames and doubts the woman's virtue. How many women have hanged themselves for this reason?"

Although this story may not have great literary value,[48] it deserves to be discussed in great detail. First, the topic was strikingly similar to the critical literature of the May Fourth period in which the marriage system was the most commonly criticized social tradition. Therefore, it might be suggested that the author, Hsieh Chun-mu, was influenced by the May Fourth tradition in Tokyo.[49] This also indicates the parallel between Taiwan and mainland China in their literary movements. Second, the story focused on a "new woman," Kui-hua. She was represented as doubly victimized by feudal society and male chauvinism.

The Displacement of "Modern Women" by "Japanese Women"

After 1927, the split within the New Cultural Association and the establishment of the Taiwan People's Party, the discourse around women's issues in *Tai-wan min-pao* was dominated by Marxist feminist thought. Class interests took precedence over gender issues. Women's oppression was viewed as a form of class conflict. Therefore, the major concern in *TWMP* was transformed from bourgeois educated women to female peasants and laborers. On the other hand, however, there also emerged a new genre—*hsien-tai-p'ai hsiao-shuo* (modernist literature)[50]—in another literary circle, which was developed by several Taiwanese intellectuals who had studied in Japan. These writers were mostly influenced by *shi-shosetsu*, Japanese pre–World War II "I-novels," which generally designates an autobiographical narrative.[51] Similarly, Taiwan's modernist literature includes works of fiction that focus on the main characters' psychological issues, either in first-person or third-person accounts. In these writings, interestingly, the vehicle for the modern was displaced onto Japanese women. Accordingly, the longing for the modern was also transferred from the West (or just a vague concept) to Tokyo, the metropole. I use several stories to elaborate this transition.

The protagonist Chun-sheng was portrayed as a restless and indecisive young man in Weng Nao's short story, "Tsan-hsueh" (The Residue of Snow, 1935). He went to Tokyo to fulfill his dream—creating a glorious future in this great new world—at the cost of his relationship with Yu-chih, a young woman from his home village. After three years in Tokyo he developed a crush on Kimiko, a pretty Japanese woman from Hokkaido. At the same time, he received a letter from Yu-chih in Taiwan, and was haunted by her memory. Chun-sheng was uncertain how to choose between these women. Both of them, as well as their homes, looked equally remote to him. The following is the final paragraph of the story:

> Suddenly a bizarre idea appeared in his mind: Which place is farther, Hokkaido or Taiwan? He remembered that geographically Hokkaido is closer (to Tokyo) than Taiwan; deep in his heart, however, these two places appeared equally remote. The two women, Kimiko in Hokkaido and Yu-chih in Taiwan, both seemed to be at a great distance as well.
>
> "Since it is so, I am not going back to Taiwan, nor will I go to Hokkaido either," he told himself.[52]

It is interesting that Chun-sheng, a Taiwanese intellectual, decided to stay in Tokyo instead of choosing Taiwan as his destiny. Tokyo, the metropole, was the symbol of modernity, in contrast to the backward and confining Taiwanese society. To some extent, Chun-sheng's decision represents the tension and inner conflict of Taiwanese elites in Tokyo during the period of Japanese occupation. They sensed their difference from the Japanese; however, their colonial education had alienated them from their native society. "Shou yu ti" (Head and Body), written by Wu Yung-fu in 1933, employed the Cartesian mind-body split as a metaphor to describe the dual identities of the main character. In this story the anonymous protagonist was disturbed by the discord between his will and the expectation of his parents: He wished to stay in Tokyo to enjoy its advanced cultural life; however, his parents wanted him to return to Taiwan for an arranged marriage. Thus, he was trapped: "[T]his is the opposition between head and body. His mind wanted to stay in Tokyo, however, his family wanted his 'body' back."[53]

Employing the mythical figure of the sphinx, with its human head and lion body, as an allegory, Wu implied that the self-identity of Taiwanese elites had become alienated from their nurturing soil; they could never really be complete human beings, but would always remain as culturally miscegenated hybrids.

The memory of Japan kept haunting these Taiwanese intellectuals after they returned to Taiwan. The narrator in Wang Chang-hsiung's "Pen liu" (Running River, 1942) had lived in Tokyo for ten years before returning to take over his deceased father's medical practice in rural Taiwan. Yet, once home, he constantly recalled Tokyo:

> Three years ago in the spring I left Tokyo, the familiar place where I had lived for ten years. The images of that night are still vivid in my heart. I cannot control my emotions whenever images of Tokyo appear. Not only parting made me sad, but also loneliness and uncertainty. I was not sure when I would return to this capital again.

After working in rural Taiwan for several years, the narrator was bored with its restricting and uneventful life, and longed to return to Tokyo and the excitement there. Then he met Ito, who assuaged his yearning for Japan. Ito was ethnically Taiwanese but taught Japanese in high school and had married a Japanese woman. Ito was striving to assimilate himself into Japanese culture by breaking with his Taiwanese roots, which included abandoning his parents. Ito's home life reminded the narrator of his old life in Tokyo. Whenever meeting Ito's Japanese wife, he also felt regret for his past relationship with a Japanese woman who had introduced him to a new world of literature and arts. In contrast, a third character, Po-nien, a passionate young man, harshly criticized Ito's traitorous behavior. Thus, "I," the narrator, constantly shifted between the two opposing figures.

For many Taiwanese intellectuals, adopting Japanese ways implied adopting an advanced culture and creating new opportunities for upward mobility. This attempt, however, did not always succeed. Lung Ying-tsung's story, "Chih yu mu-kua shu ti hsiao-chen" (The Town of Papaya Trees, 1937), portrayed the frustration, despair, and desires of Taiwan's intellectuals in the late 1930s. The protagonist fought against his impoverished environment by assimilating with Japanese culture. He despised his nationality: "Look at those mean, illiterate, noisy and dirty people. Are they his [my] compatriots?"[54] Nonetheless, his development was restricted by the discrimination against Taiwanese employees by his Japanese boss. He became frustrated, and finally lost all his courage.

Fanon has addressed this ambiguity of self-identity in Antilles Negroes under French rule (Fanon 1967). In discussing the function of language, he states that to speak a language is to take on a world, a culture. The Antilles Negro who wanted to be white would become "whiter" as he gained better skill in the adopted language as a cultural tool.[55] By the same token, in the stories quoted above, the characters often equated using Japanese language with adopting Japanese culture. Speaking Japanese, the colonizers' tongue, opened new doors for Taiwanese.

Yet, the division between Japanese colonizers and Taiwanese people was not so clear-cut as in the case of white versus black. In a sense, Taiwanese people did have the opportunity to "become" Japanese, in particular during the war.[56] In 1937, at the beginning of the Sino-Japanese War, the Japanese colonial government started to promote the *Kominka* policy, which included adoption of Japanese surnames, a ban on Chinese language, and military conscription. The basic motive of the *Kominka* policy was to remake the Taiwanese people into "imperial subjects." Joining the army became one way for Taiwanese youth to prove their equality to Japanese. A blood letter written in 1937 by the ex-leader of the Youth Association in Kaohsiung said "Long live your majesty! I possess the Japanese masculinity and have assimilated the Yamato spirit. No matter how agonizing the suffering is, as far as it contributes to your majesty and the whole country, I would never be afraid. Please take me as a soldier."[57] This type of volunteering for military service was not rare.

The desire to become Japanese, and the possibility of fulfillment, is usually represented in the trope of the romantic relationship between Taiwanese men and Japanese women. In Lung Ying-tsung's "Lien-wu chih-t'ing" (The Yard of Wax Apple, 1941), the narrator, Chen, had a quasi-romantic relationship with his best friend's sister, Mikako: "I like Mikako, actually. Sometimes I even fantasized of happy days being with her. For example, I imagined that we would make a beautiful home and talk with each other on the porch all through the night."[58] Because of his concern about his poor financial situation and his sense of inferiority, Chen did not pursue his desire to marry Mikako, and felt sadness and self-pity for a long time. In the end of this story, he said: "Some people like to talk about 'the nation.' What a great issue. Nonetheless, I think that the main point is love. Only love can bring us, people of different nationalities, together. Theory is boring, only love matters."[59]

Fanon (1967) has explored the interweaving of race and sexuality in the relationship between a black man and a white woman. The basic motivation of the black male character in his story was the desire to be white: "I wish to be acknowledged not as black but as white. By loving me, she [the white woman] proves that I am worthy of white love. I am loved like a white man. Her love takes me into the noble road that leads to total realization. When I marry a white woman, I marry white culture, white beauty, and white whiteness."[60] In a similar vein, the Japanese woman was portrayed as an object of both longing and lack. She was what Taiwan was not.

In addition to racial difference, the desire for Japanese woman also represented the male colonial intelligentsia's longing for modernity. A similar trope also occurred in mainland China's May Fourth literature. In analyzing the emergence of "modern selfhood" in May Fourth literature, literary scholar Lydia Liu notices that, by utilizing first-person narration, the self is often constituted as a privileged site for the contest over the meaning of modernity.[61] In May Fourth discourse, "women" were usually portrayed as the opposing signifier between modernity and tradition. The desiring male intellectual travels between modern woman and traditional woman, hoping to work out his own crisis of identity through his free choice. In a strikingly similar way, the fictional poet Ouwai in Ting Ling's satire confronted a choice between his "bound-footed, oriental-style lover . . . and Wendy, the so-called modern girl."[62] Ouwai represents the treaty-port elites who "shaped its peculiar national political position through a strategy of appropriating knowledge from the colonial powers."[63] Therefore, the dilemma of Ouwai—being caught between two women—is also the male intellectual's awkward decision between the "nativist longing-for" tradition and a new sense of selfhood in relation to modernity.[64] In Taiwan's colonial context, however, the imaginary "new woman" is displaced onto the colonizer's women. In some Taiwanese autobiographies, this kind of romantic sentiment toward Japanese women often occurs. As Wu Chuo-liu recalled, it was because of the encouragement of a young Japanese female teacher that he became interested in modern literature.[65] In these men's memories, educated Japanese women were either the instructors who led them to a new knowledge or the first persons of the opposite sex with whom they could engage in challenging dialogues.[66]

Conclusion: Was It Really a "Nationalist Movement"?

In December 1914, Itagaki Taishuke, a well-known Meiji reformer and major promoter of the Assimilation Society,[67] delivered a speech at Taihoku (Taipei) Railway Hotel to a crowd composed of Taiwanese and Japanese colonial officials. After pointing out "the conspiracy of the white race to dominate Asia," he stressed the need for forming a joint-defense bridge between China and Japan, and expected Taiwanese people to perform that duty. Itagaki's idea was applauded by many Taiwanese intellectuals[68] and followed by various political and cultural movements. For the purpose of this chapter, however, I would like to point out that Itagaki's speech manifests the first moment for Taiwan to participate in the global issues such as modernization, social evolution, and women's liberation. Clearly in these writings were the excitement, anxiety, and dreams of Taiwanese intellectuals at that moment.

From that historical junction is where I develop my conclusion. For most of the scholars interested in Taiwan's colonial history, the framework of "the nationalist movement" is unproblematically adopted to contextualize elite activities during the 1920s and 1930s.[69] In this regard, literary critiques of Japanese policies and the later proletarian movements were viewed as anticolonial resistance; the projects of enlightenment and mass education were viewed as nationalist strategies to consolidate a national consciousness. Nonetheless, as suggested earlier, the establishment of the enlightenment journal *Tai-oan chheng-lian* involved intellectual efforts from three places—Japan, China, and Taiwan. The awareness of regional differences was manifest in the use of the term "Taiwanese." Moreover, the major issues proposed by authors in the first few volumes of the journal were far from promoting a national autonomy.[70] Instead, these colonial elites were anxious to participate in the global wave of modernity, to absorb new modes of knowledge, and to examine their homeland with a new vision. Women's issues were one of the new ways of thinking that they felt compelled to deal with.

The embrace of modernity resulted in the tension of the colonized subject's split loyalties, which anticipated the conflicts between mainland Chinese and Taiwanese natives that occurred after China's "retrocession" of Taiwan, resulting in the tragic February 28 (2–28) Incident of 1947. To explain what happen in that incident, Lai Tse-han maintained that, after fifty years of Japanese occupation, "a number of Taiwanese resented their status as colonial subjects while simultaneously appreciating many Japanese ways . . . and feeling superior to Chinese [as being more progressive]."[71] In a similar vein, the Japanese experience was often used by the opposition party in Taiwan to counter official policy: The futile but brutal KMT polity was often described as the antithesis of the efficient Japanese bureaucracy. At the same time, Japanese colonial oppression is often used by the Taiwan-centered opposition party as historical evidence of Taiwan's unique sociocultural condition that separates it from China. What is often missed in these arguments, however, is the notion that "being Taiwanese" has never been fixed but is a constitutive and incomplete process. Examining the ambiguous features of the colonized experience is necessary in order to explore the complexity of Taiwanese identity, and it is necessary to examine the ambiguous features of its colonized history.

Notes

1. Barlow (1991) provides this framework to make links between the past and the present, and to search for the appropriation of some crucial signs, such as women and sexuality, in other intellectual discourse.

2. For an elaborated discussion on the *Nanchin* policy and its subsequent discussion, see Chen Kuang-hsing (1994).

3. This idea was first proposed by pro-unification activists as the precedence of the unification between Taiwan and mainland China.

4. The Chinese characters of *nanshin* are exactly the same as those of *nanchin*. Indeed, *nanchin* was a loanword from Japanese.

5. Myers and Peattie 1988, 179.

6. Ibid., 90.

7. On March 2–4, 1994, the *China Times*, a major newspaper in Taiwan, published a series of articles contributed by some scholars and journalists to elaborate on the concept of "Southern Advance." It is interesting that all the contributors unanimously appreciated Lee Teng-hui's idea. Some of them repeated the notion that Taiwan should resituate itself as the center of Southeast Asia, both in economic and academic senses. Some of them used archeological evidence to support the idea that Taiwan was originally a part of a South Pacific cultural circle. For a deliberate critique on these articles, see Chen 1994.

8. It's probably not unrelated that Lee has only accepted personal interviews by Japanese journalists and mass media up to now. In an interview by the *Yomiuri News* in 1993, which was the first time he granted an interview to any journalist, Lee lamented on the oppressed history of Taiwan, the frustration of being a Taiwanese, and the nostalgia toward the old times—the Japanese period.

9. Lai et al. 1991, 44.

10. Wu 1988, 122.

11. Ibid., 125.

12. Ibid., 130.

13. Ibid., 132.

14. The problem of Taiwanese identity has been a highly contested issue across mainland China and Taiwan. On the one hand, Taiwan has always been positioned as one part of China within Chinese nationalist discourse. On the other hand, the notion of an autonomous identity has been gradually formulated within the Taiwanese nationalist discourse since the 1950s, after the tragic February 28 Incident occurred.

15. The first collection of Taiwanese novels written in the Japanese period was published in 1979—near the end of the Nativist Literary Movement (*hsiang-t'u wen-hsueh lunchan*). At that time the notion of a distinctive Taiwan separate from China was still a political taboo. Nonetheless, the editors of this collection tactically incorporated "Taiwanese novels" into the genre of Nativist literature, for the concept that literature had to reflect reality and be earthy was widely promoted and gradually achieved legitimate status in Taiwan at that time. One decade later, *History of Taiwanese Novels*, the first publication on such a topic, was published in mainland China. It was proposed in this book that Taiwanese literature is one branch of Chinese literature. As an example, the first sentence in its introduction is: "Taiwanese novels were rooted in the great tradition of Chinese novels." Accordingly, the author largely celebrated the accomplishment of "anticolonial" writers, whom he viewed as Chinese nationalist heroes. In contrast, he undermined the modernist novels as "pale, uprooted, and westernized hybrids"; thus, they should be discounted as having any

serious value. Two years after the publication of *History of Taiwanese Novels*, the most inclusive selection of Taiwanese novels to date was published in Taiwan. The editor acknowledged that the various influences from China and Japan were indispensable to the growth of Taiwanese literature; nonetheless, the uniqueness and autonomy of Taiwanese literary history was asserted. The editor wrote: "Taiwanese literature is the document of the struggles of our nation." Furthermore, he argued that the oppressed experience of the Taiwanese people has been consistently represented in these novels under different political regimes through time. Therefore, he implied that the shared oppression and repressed memory could be treated as a basis for the formation of Taiwanese collectivity.

16. Nandy 1983, 1.

17. Tomiyama 1995, 387.

18. Nandy 1983, 11, 13.

19. Mark R. Peattie, "Introduction," in Myers and Peattie 1988, 16.

20. The only exception, and the heretofore best work, is Yang 1993.

21. Brown 1988, 56.

22. *Tai-oan chheng-lian* [hereinafter, *TOCL*] 1, no. 1 (1920), 1.

23. See also Gilmartin et al. 1994.

24. *TOCL* 1, no. 2 (1920), 62.

25. Ibid., 63.

26. Ibid., 20.

27. *TOCL* 1, no. 3 (1920), 42.

28. *TOCL* 2, no. 1 (1921), 56.

29. Ibid., 59.

30. *TOCL* 2, no. 4 (1922), 30.

31. It is not clear why *Tai-oan chheng-lian* changed its title. The reason seems to be related to inner conflicts among the editorial board.

32. *TWMP*, no. 2 (1923), 1.

33. Ibid., 11.

34. Ibid., 3.

35. Ibid., 4.

36. *TWMP*, no. 219 (1928), 10.

37. *TWMP*, no. 140 (1927), 9–11.

38. *TOCL* 3, no. 1 (1921), 38.

39. *TOCL* 1, no. 2 (1920), 66.

40. *TOCL* 2, no. 1 (1921), 36.

41. *TOCL* 3, no. 1 (1922), 14.

42. Ibid., 15.

43. Hsu Chun-ya, "Tai-wan wen-hsueh san lun," *TOCL* 1, no. 1 (1920).

44. Kan Wen-fang, "The Real Society and Literature," *TOCL* 2, no. 3 (1921).

45. Kan, "The Real Society and Literature."

46. It should be pointed out that Kan Wen-fang made the division between "Western" and "Eastern" civilizations, which is a cliché in Chinese modern discourse. At some points in his essay he also juxtaposed "Chinese culture" with "Western culture," which aligns him with the May Fourth discourse of the mainland. This, however, has never been noted in postwar Taiwanese literary studies. Scholars did not seem to notice that *Tai-oan chheng-lian* was not a purely nationalist journal. It mixed articles written by Japanese, Chinese, and Taiwanese scholars, which suggests an un-delineated identity of Taiwanese intellectuals during the early 1920s.

47. Chen Tuan-min, "Jih gung wen ku chui lun" (Advocacy for Vernacular Literature), *TOCL* 4, no. 1 (1922), 25–27.

48. It is interesting that this piece is mentioned by almost all of the literary critics in both Taiwan and mainland China as the marker of the emergence of modern Taiwan literature. It

is also criticized as immature in terms of literary value. For example, see Ku (1989) and Hsu (1995, 224–25).

49. Indeed, Hsieh fled to China in 1931, and then joined the anti-Japanese movement in the Communist Party. He stayed in mainland China until his death in 1969.

50. This term "modernist fiction" is quoted in Ku Chi-t'ang, Tai-wan hsiao-shuo fa-chan shih (The History of Taiwanese Fiction) (Taipei: Wen shih che chu pan she, 1989), and in Hsu Chun-ya, *Jih-chu shih-chi tai-wan hsiao-shuo yen-chiu* (A Study of Taiwanese Novels During the Japanese Occupation) (Taipei: Wen shih che chu pan she, 1995).

51. Suzuki 1996, 1.

52. Weng Nao, "Tsan-hsueh," in Zhang 1991a, 74–75.

53. Wu Yung-fu, "Shou yu ti," 180.

54. Lung, "Chih yu mu-kua ti hsiao-chen," in Zhang 1991b, 38.

55. Fanon 1967, 38.

56. This point—the different attitudes of Japanese and Western governments toward colonialism—has been proposed by Mark Peattie (Myers and Peattie 1988). In my view, however, there were several shifts through time in respect to Japanese racial policies. For example, the wide promotion of the *Kominka* policy was closely linked to the Pacific War, which pitted "East Asian nations" against "Western nations." My assumption surely needs more detailed historical research.

57. Cited from Chou 1991, 149.

58. Lung Ying-tsung, "Lien-wu chih-t'ing" (The Yard of Wax Apple), in Zhang Henghao, ed., Tai-wan tso chia chuan chi IX: Lung Ying-tsung (The Collection of Taiwanese Writers IX: Selected Works of Lung Ying-tsung) (Taipei: Chien-wei chu pan she, 1991), 143.

59. Ibid., 157.

60. Fanon, "Black Skin, White Mask," 63.

61. Liu 1993a.

62. Barlow 1991, 1.

63. Ibid.

64. Ibid., 2.

65. Wu 1988, 103–4.

66. Similar narratives occur in Peng 1972 and Chang Liang-tse 1986.

67. Established in 1914, the Assimilation Society was a joint effort between Japanese liberals and Taiwanese elite. Its main goal was to advocate that basic civil rights be granted to Taiwanese. The society was forced by the colonial government to disband in 1915.

68. For example, Chen Tuan-min applies Itagaki's notion that Taiwan should be the bridge between China and Japan to celebrate the global expansion of Taiwan (*TOCL* 4, no. 1, 25–27).

69. For a general overview of the studies on the Taiwanese nationalist movement, see Fix 1993.

70. Indeed, major concerns, alongside the political activism, of these intellectuals during the early 1920s were the "Home Rule Movement," or "Local Rule Movement" (I-hui ch'ing-yuan yun-tung). The major goal of this movement was to raise the citizenship status of the Taiwanese people, then called the "outer land," to the level of "inner land," namely Japan proper. In other words, this was more like a civil rights movement, demanding true "assimilation." Nearly half of the contributors to *Tai-oan chheng-lian* and *Tai-wan* were Japanese intellectuals or politicians. After *Tai-wan min-pao* was established and moved to Taipei, however, the nationalist sentiment of the journal seemed to get stronger, given the fact that an overwhelming proportion of articles were written in vernacular Chinese and the percentage of Japanese contributors dramatically decreased. There have been very few studies on the transition toward nationalist sentiment in Taiwan's colonial history. For a more detailed historical account on the "Home Rule Movement," see Chou (1994). Kerr (1974) also has a chapter on this movement, although from a highly problematic perspective.

71. Lai et al. 1991, 41.

References

Journals in Chinese

Tai-oan chheng-lian (Taiwan Youth). Original version published in Tokyo, 1920–22. Reprinted by the Oriental Cultural Service, Taipei, 1973.
Tai-wan (Formosa). Original version published in Tokyo, 1922–23. Reprinted by the Oriental Cultural Service, Taipei, 1973.
Tai-wan min-pao (Taiwan Magazine). Original version published in Tokyo and Taipei, 1923–32. Reprinted by the Oriental Cultural Service, Taipei, 1973.

Books and Articles in Chinese

Chang Liang-tse. 1986. *Ssu-shih-wu tsu-shu: wo ti wen-hsueh li-ch'eng* (An Autobiography at the Age of Forty-five: My Literary Journey). Irvine, CA: Taiwan Publishing Co.
Chen Kuang-hsing. 1994. "Ti-kuo chih yen" (The Imperialist Eye: The Cultural Imaginary of a Sub-Empire and a Nation-State). *Taiwan: A Radical Quarterly in Social Studies* 17: 21–78.
Chou Wan-yao. 1994. "A Comparative Study of the Kominka Movement in Taiwan and Korea, 1937–1945." *Hsin shih hsüeh* 5:117–58.
Chung Chao-cheng, ed. 1992. *Tai-wan tso-chia ch'uan-chi* (Collections of Taiwanese Writers). Taipei: Chien-wei chu-pan-she.
Hsu Chun-ya. 1995. *A Study of Taiwanese Novels During Japanese Occupation* (Jih-chu shih-chi tai-wan hsiao-shuo yen-chiu). Taipei: wen shih che chu pan she.
Ku Chi-tang. 1989. *The History of Taiwanese Fiction* (Tai-wan hsiao-shuo fa-chan shih). Taipei: wen shih che chu pan she.
Wu Chuo-liu. 1988. *Wu hua kuo* (Flowerless Fruit). Irvine, CA: Taiwan Publishing Co.
Yang Tsui. 1993. *Jih-chü shih-chi Tai-wan fu-nü chieh-fang yun-tung* (Women's Liberation Movement in Taiwan Under Japanese Occupation). Taipei: Shih pao.
Zhang Henghao, ed. 1991a. *Tai-wan tso chia chuan chi VI: Weng Nao, Wu Yung-fu, yu Wang Chang-shiung* (Collection of Taiwanese Writers VI: Selected Works of Weng Nao, Wu Yung-fu, and Wang Chang-shiung). Taipei: Chien-wei chu-pan-she.
———. 1991b. *Tai-wan tso chia chuan chi IX: Lung Ying-tsung* (Collection of Taiwanese Writers IX: Selected Works of Lung Ying-tsung). Taipei: Chien-wei chu-pan-she.

Books and Articles in English

Adams, Parveen, and Elizabeth Cowie. Eds. 1990. *The Woman in Question: M/f.* Cambridge, Mass.: MIT Press.
Anthias, Floya, and Nira Yuval-Davis. 1993. *Racialized Boundaries: Race, Nation, Gender, Colour and Class and the Anti-Racist Struggle.* London: Routledge.
Barlow, Tani. 1991. "*Zhishifenzi* (Chinese Intellectuals) and Power." *Dialectical Anthropology* 16: 209–32.
———. 1993. "Introduction." In *Gender Politics in Modern China: Writing and Feminism,* ed. Barlow, 1–18. Durham: Duke University Press.
———. 1994a. "Politics and Protocols of *Funu:* (Un) Making National Woman." In *Engendering China: Women, Culture, and the State,* ed. Christina K. Gilmartin, Gail Hershatter, Lisa Rofel, and Tyrene White, 339–59. Cambridge: Harvard University Press.

————. 1994b. "Theorizing Woman: Funu, Guojia, Jiating." In *Body, Subject and Power in China*, ed. Angela Zito and Tani Barlow, 253–89. Chicago: University of Chicago Press.

Brown, Carolyn T. 1988. "Woman as Trope: Gender and Power in Lu Xun's 'Soap'." *Modern Chinese Literature* 4, no. 1–2: 55–70.

Chan, Ching-kiu Stephen. 1993. "The Language of Despair: Ideological Representations of the 'New Woman' by May Fourth Writers." In *Gender and Politics in Modern China: Writing and Feminism*, ed. Tani Barlow, 13–32. Durham: Duke University Press.

Chatterjee, Partha. 1986. *Nationalist Thought and the Colonial World—A Derivative Discourse*. London: Zed Books.

————. 1989. "Colonialism, Nationalism, and Colonialized Women: The Contest in India." *American Ethnologist* 16: 622–33.

————. 1990. "The Nationalist Resolution of the Women's Question." In *Recasting Women: Essays in Indian Colonial History*, ed. Kumkum Sangari and Sudesh Vaid, 233–54. New Brunswick, NJ: Rutgers University Press.

————. 1993. *The Nation and Its Fragments: Colonial and Postcolonial Histories*. Princeton: Princeton University Press.

Chen, Ching-chih. 1994. "The Japanese Ideal and Ideas of Assimilation in Taiwan, 1895–1945." In *Unbound Taiwan: Closeups from a Distance: Select Papers from the International Symposium on Taiwan Studies, 1985–1989*, ed. Marshall Johnson and Fred Y.L. Chiu, 31–48. Chicago: Center for East Asian Studies, University of Chicago.

Chen, Edward I-te. 1972. "Formosan Political Movements Under Japanese Rule, 1914–1937." *Journal of Asian Studies* 31: 477–97.

Chou, Wan-yao. 1991. "The Kominka Movement: Taiwan Under Wartime Japan, 1937–1945." Ph.D. dissertation, Yale University.

Dikötter, Frank. 1995. *Sex, Culture and Modernity in China: Medical Science and the Construction of Sexual Identities in the Early Republican Period*. Honolulu: University of Hawaii Press.

Dower, John W. 1986. *War Without Mercy*. New York: Pantheon Books.

Fanon, Frantz. 1967. *Black Skin, White Masks*. New York: Grove Press.

Felski, Rita. 1995. *The Gender of Modernity*. Cambridge: Harvard University Press.

Fix, Douglas Lane. 1993. "Taiwanese Nationalism and Its Late Colonial Context." Ph.D. dissertation. University of California, Berkeley.

Gilmartin, Christina, Gail Hershatter, Lisa Rofel, and Tyrene White, eds. 1994. *Engendering China: Women, Culture, and the State*. Cambridge: Harvard University Press.

Iwamoto, Yoshio. 1974. "Aspects of the Proletarian Literary Movement in Japan." In *Japan in Crisis: Essays on Taisho Democracy*, ed. H.D. Harootunian and B. Silberman. Princeton: Princeton University Press.

Kandiyoti, Deniz. 1993. "Identity and Its Discontents: Woman and the Nation." In *Colonial Discourse and Post-colonial Theory: A Reader*, ed. P. Williams and L. Chrisman, 376–91. New York: Columbia University Press.

Kerr, George H. 1965. *Formosa Betrayed*. Boston: Houghton Mifflin.

————. 1974. *Formosa: Licensed Revolution and the Home Rule Movement, 1895–1945*. Honolulu: University of Hawaii Press.

Lai Tse-han, Ramon H. Myers, and Wei Wou. 1991. *A Tragic Beginning: The Taiwan Uprising of February 28, 1947*. Stanford: Stanford University Press.

Liu, Lydia. 1993a. "Narratives of Modern Selfhood: First-Person Fiction in May Fourth Literature." In *Politics, Ideology, and Literary Discourse in Modern China: Theoretical Interventions and Cultural Critique*, ed. Kang Liu and Xiaobing Tang, 102–23. Durham: Duke University Press.

————. 1993b. "The Female Body and Nationalist Discourse." In *Scattered Hegemonies: Postmodernity and Transnational Feminist Practices*, ed. Inderpal Grewal and Caren Kaplan, 37–62. Minneapolis: University of Minnesota Press.

Myers, Ramon H., and Mark R. Peattie, eds. 1988. *The Japanese Colonial Empire, 1895–1945*. New York: Cambridge University Press.

Nandy, Ashis. 1983. *The Intimate Enemy: Loss and Recovery of Self under Colonialism*. Delhi: Oxford University Press.

Nolte, Sharon H., and Sally A. Hastings. 1991. "The Meiji State's Policy Toward Women, 1890-1910." In *Recreating Japanese Women, 1600-1945*, ed. Gail Lee Bernstein, 151-174. Berkeley: University of California Press.

Ong, Aihwa. 1988. "Colonialism and Modernity: Feminist Re-Presentations of Women in Non-Western Societies." *Inscriptions* 3, no. 4: 79–93.

Parker, Andrew, Mary Russo, Doris Sommer, and Patricia Yaeger. 1992. "Introduction." In *Nationalisms and Sexualities*, ed. Parker et al., 1–18. New York: Routledge.

Peattie, Mark R. 1984. "Japanese Attitudes Toward Colonialism, 1895–1945." In Myers and Peattie, eds., *The Japanese Colonial Empire, 1895–1945*, 80–127.

Peng, Ming-min. 1972. *A Taste of Freedom: Memoirs of a Formosan Independence Leader*. New York: Holt, Rinehart and Winston.

Sangari, Kumkum, and Sudesh Vaid. 1990. "Recasting Women: An Introduction." In *Recasting Women: Essays in Indian Colonial History*, ed. Sangari and Vaid, 1–26. New Brunswick, NJ: Rutgers University Press.

Stoler, Ann, and Frederick Cooper. 1997. "Between Metropole and Colony: Rethinking a Research Agenda." In *Tensions of Empire: Colonial Cultures in a Bourgeois World*, ed. Frederick Cooper and Ann Laura Stoler, 1–56. Berkeley: University of California Press.

Sugimoto, T. 1971. "Japanese in Taiwan." *Current Trends in Linguistics* 8: 969–95.

Suzuki, Tomi. 1996. *Narrating the Self: Fictions of Japanese Modernity*. Stanford: Stanford University Press.

Tomiyama, Ichiro. 1995. "Colonialism and the Sciences of the Tropical Zone: The Academic Analysis of Difference in 'The Island Peoples.'" *Positions* 3: 367–91.

Tsurumi, E. Patricia. 1977. *Japanese Colonial Education in Taiwan 1895–1945*. Cambridge: Harvard University Press.

Young, Robert, J.C. 1995. *Colonial Desire: Hybridity in Theory, Culture and Race*. London: Routledge.

Part II

Gender and Social Interaction in
Contemporary Taiwan

6

Between Filial Daughter and Loyal Sister

Global Economy and Family Politics in Taiwan

Anru Lee

My brother-in-law didn't invest in his children's education.
He keeps his daughters working in his factory. That is why he can
still manage without downsizing. Our kids have higher education.
They won't be interested in running a textile factory in the future.
[Thus] we don't have any plan to upgrade or enlarge our
production. I think we will close our factory after our retirement
(fifty-ish mother/factory owner in Homei, 1994).

I am really grateful to my daughters. They have done so much! In those
days [when they were in elementary schools], on weekends I always
enjoined them repeatedly: "Don't go away. Don't go play. You have to
make the woof shuttles. You have to tie the threads." [laughter] They
were all overwhelmed by the work then! Now they complain to me that
they were unable to go to school because they had to help me. I tell
them our family didn't have money, it's enough for them to graduate
vocational schools. . . . It is exactly because they have worked so hard
in our textile factory that I don't want my daughters to marry into
textile families. I don't want them to have a harsh life anymore
(seventy-ish woman/factory owner in Homei, 1995).

Prelude

June 1994:
The following incident occurred immediately after I arrived in Homei, a small town
in central Taiwan, to study the local textile industry and its recent changes. I was
living with a Wang family that owned a small weaving firm, and had spent most of

my time with Mei-ling, the family's youngest daughter. Wang Mei-ling had already passed her thirtieth birthday, and was the only daughter still unmarried. She worked in her brother's firm from nine in the morning to 5:30 in the afternoon, and attended junior college at night. During my first few days there, I watched Mei-ling work during the day and then went to school with her in the evening.

It was the beginning of June, and the end of the spring semester was approaching. The school gave all students three days off so that they could study for final exams. On the first day of this "study vacation," Mei-ling worked in the firm as usual. In the late afternoon, one of her married sisters, Mei-hua, visited her parents and stayed for dinner. After dinner, she left, telling her parents that she had to leave to look after her computer shop. Right after Mei-hua's departure, Mei-ling packed her book bag in the back seat of her car and told me it was time to go. "To where?" I asked. Mei-ling did not answer but only jumped into her car. However, we did not take our usual route to school; instead, we drove in the opposite direction, toward the city. "Where are we going?" I asked again. "To my sister's shop." Noticing my confusion, Mei-ling explained that she had arranged to spend the night with her sister. She said,

> You asked me where we were going at the dinner table, well, I didn't want to answer you there, because I didn't want my parents to know that I have three days off. If they know that I didn't have to go to school today, they'll ask me to work more hours at night. They'll be upset to see me out of school but not working. To keep them from knowing, my sister and I had to whisper; we had arranged to leave the house a few minutes apart. But you know, I wonder whether they might have figured it out just by watching us whispering to each other.

We spent that evening in Mei-hua and her husband's computer shop, watching TV and chatting. A different Mei-ling emerged that evening. She was nothing like the filial daughter I had observed at home and in the factory, that woman who rarely talked to her parents and usually had a gloomy look on her face. This evening Mei-ling suddenly brightened up. She talked loudly with her sister, argued with her brother-in-law, and laughed heartily at his jokes and silly remarks. She also expressed her opinions. Watching her, I could not help but think that she must have felt free here. At the same time, however, the image of a daughter who considered herself unjustly treated and constrained by her family continued to occupy my mind.

Mei-ling and I first met two weeks before I began to live with the Wangs. As soon as Mei-ling knew that I was a "university"[1] graduate and currently studying in the United States, she started to ply me with questions about the universities in Taiwan: about the sorts of departments different schools had, about the test scores needed to get into particular departments, about strategies and tactics to study for university entrance exams, and about my experiences in college and abroad. "You have such a wonderful life! You always get to do what you want.

You are so free," Mei-ling said in an astonished yet distressed tone. She told me that she wished to study at a university someday, although she suspected that it was only a fading dream in reality. Mei-ling did manage to attend junior college, eight years after she graduated high school, but she still had to endure the disapproval of her family. She said,

> None of them [the family members] supported my decision to go to junior college. They don't see any value of my going back to school. They want me to get married—or at least work for the family. I have always worked for the family, first for my father, now for my brother. But why do I have to do so? Why do I have to sacrifice myself for the family? Why me? Is it fair? Do you think it's fair?

Wang Mei-ling's anguished voice has echoed through my research ever since. Her indignant questioning challenged the popular belief that the Chinese are invariably willing to sacrifice for the economic betterment of their families, a belief shared by both the Taiwanese people and scholars at home and abroad. This is not to say that Mei-ling was not hardworking or that she was unwilling to meet family needs. In reality, she had worked in her father's weaving firm since graduating from junior high school. The issue at stake is the gap between the expectations of those who are in charge and those who work under them.

Emphasis on the collective aspect of the family economy conceals the fact that different family members usually endure different strains and are often rewarded unevenly. Mei-ling's call for fairness raises the often overlooked issue of gender inequality in a modern industrial family, such as the Wangs, which bases its economic success on the labor of children, sons and daughters alike, yet perpetuates a patrilineal practice which only rewards the labor of sons.

Juxtaposing Mei-ling's life story with recent changes in Taiwan's economy, this chapter examines the gender aspects of family production and its meanings to men and women. Two temporal junctures are specifically stressed in the chapter: one in relation to the economic exigency, under which many manufacturing families seek intensive family-labor deployment as a means of reinvigorating capital accumulation; the other in relation to the cultural transition derived from a generational shift in power and management, such as when Mei-ling's brother—the heir of the family—took over the factory. Both junctures occurred around the same time, which placed Mei-ling in a web of tensions, dilemmas, and opportunities.

The Family Question

The "family" has long captured the imagination of scholars of Chinese societies. A common view sees the Chinese family as a corporate unit to which family members contribute labor and income, under the authority of the household head, usually the eldest male (Skinner 1957; Freedman 1966; Cohen 1976; Harrell 1982, 1985). Widely discussed in the literature is the careful economic calculation in household division of labor that maximizes family prosperity (Cohen 1976, 1978, 1992; Basu 1991;

Oxfeld 1993). The effects of such calculation on family organization and demographic profile in rural communities are also frequently noted (Pasternak 1972, 1983; Pasternak and Salaff 1993; Chuang 1994). Recent studies of Taiwan's industrialization highlight the continued importance of family in these regards. Family ties and kin relations are seen as still providing the security, motivation, and networks which have made Taiwan's industrialization possible since the end of World War II (B. Gallin 1966; Gallin and Gallin 1985; Greenhalgh 1990; Hu 1983, 1984; Stites 1982, 1985; Gates 1987; Niehoff 1987; Bosco 1990; Ka 1993).

Within this literature's focus on collaborative welfare, individual conflicts of interest are less discussed. The presumed family solidarity also affects the analysis of women and industrial work in the Chinese context. For instance, in their pioneering and seminal studies of Chinese working women, Lydia Kung (1994) and Janet Salaff (1995) stress the subordination of working daughters' personal desires to the needs of their families. Both authors state that young factory women in Taiwan and Hong Kong did not resent the fact that they had to sacrifice themselves to achieve a higher living standard for the family and to pay for the education of sons in the family. They contend that this situation was compatible with the Chinese value placed on the family as a joint venture for survival and continuity. Furthermore, Salaff (1990, 1992, 1995) suggests that the extent to which a daughter is allowed to enjoy the fruits of her labor depends on the ratio of dependents to wage earners in her family.

Nevertheless, several authors have challenged the corporate family ideology by highlighting the difference in comprehension and action that they observed among family members. Myron Cohen (1976) reports that adult sons' calculations of self-interests will affect the timing of family division, often instigated by their wives. The wives are then blamed for disrupting family unity. In doing so the family saves the disgrace brought about by greedy sons who are the true members of the family. Another example is the creation of the "uterine family" by married women, which Margery Wolf (1972) argues indicates these women's efforts to secure their own position in the families. However, this very behavior can also be argued as submissive to the patrilineal principle and thus reproduces a society in which males are highly privileged. Taiwanese anthropologist Tai-li Hu (1985) shows in her study of rural Taiwanese families that the authority of male household heads has been undermined by the employment of the younger generations, especially under the circumstances when sons and daughters-in-law manage to retain the income they earn. Recently, more direct and critical critiques of the corporate family ideology have emerged as a result of surging feminist scholarship. Yeueh-tuan Li and Chih-ming Ka's study (1994) of a garment district in Taipei City shows that the success of small-scale manufacturing heavily depends on the (sometimes unwilling) participation of unpaid or under-paid female family members. By the same token, several scholars state that the collusion of Taiwan's subcontracting firms and the Chinese family system proves to be crucial for the former to remain competitive in the global economy (R. Gallin 1984b; Cheng and Hsiung 1992; Hsiung 1996).

Furthermore, Susan Greenhalgh (1985, 1994) argues that "by valorizing family collectivism and obfuscating the gender inequality on which it is based, the ideology not only reproduces Orientalist constructions of Chinese culture, but it also discourages the discovery of subjugated knowledge and lends support to a new, flexible form of capitalist accumulation that is based on gender and other social inequalities" (Greenhalgh 1994: 746).

In spite of these efforts, the degree to which women's awareness of gender inequality affects the labor deployment and resource distribution is yet to be explored. Equally important is the historical evolution of Taiwan's industrialization, its connection with the global economy at each stage, and the social change—especially changes in family and gender dynamics—that occurred over the course of this industrial process. Previous literature has attempted to answer these questions by pointing out that the new job opportunities and wealth engendered by the recent industrialization facilitated changes in the family as well as between the two sexes, although the changes came slowly and frequently with serious cultural and political drawbacks (Arrigo 1980, 1984, 1985; Diamond 1979; R. Gallin 1984a, 1990; Kung 1981, 1994; Salaff, 1995). My research shows, however, the direction of change is far from linear. Revealed in Mei-ling's life story is the multifarious and often conflictual consequences brought about by this process. A close look at the Wang family dynamics over time illustrates a conflation of economic strategic planning and women's submission to traditional family values at the early stage of Taiwan's export-oriented industrialization. Nonetheless, it also discloses a later departure when the society becomes more affluent (along with a changing economic structure and rising wage scales) while the competition in the international market has intensified. As a result, on the one hand, young women have more opportunities to pursue a life of their own, but, on the other, they are burdened with the demand of family loyalty at a time of waning manufacturing industries.

From Agriculture to Industry: The Case of the Wang Family

A Historical Account

Textiles have a long history in Homei. Since the end of the Japanese colonization (1895–1945), Homei has been known for weaving production. While most of Taiwan was suffering from severe shortages of daily goods due to the destruction of World War II, many Homei people enjoyed lucrative earnings from weaving and the sale of scarce and highly valuable cloth. Those were glorious days no one could forget! The elderly in town remembered that, at the end of each day, clerks from cloth stores in nearby cities would rush in, cut cloth from the looms, and rush to sell it. Sometimes the cloth was only several inches long, that is, too short to be of any great use, but the demand was so pressing that dealers craved for material of any length. *Homei Fabric* became highly sought after not only in central Taiwan but also in Taipei's Ti-hua cloth market, the largest fabric wholesale and retail center on Taiwan. Despite the fact that the weaving industry in Homei was once impeded by a lack of cotton, the raw material, and by competition from the influx of textile capital from Shanghai after the defeat of the Nationalist Party (KMT) in the Chinese Civil War in 1949, textile producers in Homei were able to regain their momentum thanks to the cotton and yarn supplied by the United States as part of the U.S. aid (Lee 2004).

The development of Homei's textile industry fully reflects the path of economic development of Taiwan in the postwar era. The 1950s was a period of import-substitution industrialization (hereafter, ISI). Light industries were gradually re-built with the assistance of U.S. aid. Based on their past foundation, textile producers in Homei quickly formed the Taichung County Hand-loom Textile Business Association to take advantage of the highly subsidized cotton. In addition, some companies were assisted by the KMT government's Entrusted Spinning and Weaving Policy (*Tai fang tai chi chi*), which was specifically designed to accelerate capital accumulation in the textile industry.[2]

Even though only a small number of firm owners in Homei received subsidized allotments of cotton, a larger population benefited indirectly. The prosperity brought about by the textiles not only enriched firm runners/entrepreneurs, it also brought regular and substantial income to those farming families whose children were able to find work in textile factories. As the weaving industry rapidly developed, increasing numbers of young people found such work. Girls tended looms. Young men usually worked as apprentices first, doing heavy labor such as uploading yarn to, and downloading cloth from, machines, but they eventually learned to maintain, adjust, and repair looms and became skilled mechanics. The impact of this new wave of employment was far-reaching. With the regular income brought home by the young generation came an improved material life, the repayment of the debt owed from previous poor farming seasons, and, ultimately, a surplus for savings. Together, increased savings, the spread of technological knowledge, and the business networks developed over time prepared Homei's textile industry for further development.

The period of Taiwan's ISI was short. The domestic market was quickly saturated by the commodities produced under the banner of ISI. As such, in the late 1960s the Taiwan government launched its campaign to push forward an export-oriented industrialization (EOI). Taiwan's export expansion parallels recent changes in the global economy, namely "flexible accumulation," that is, "a fundamental transformation in the dominant form of capital accumulation from one based on mass production to one based on the quick turnover of capital" (Harvey 1991, in Skoggard 1996: 69–70). Economic restructuring in advanced capitalist countries, and the subsequent relocation of manufacturing production from those countries to other parts of the world, facilitated Taiwan's EOI. In the case of the textile industry, Taiwan first benefited from Japan which was itself undergoing an over-production of synthetic fiber and a rapid rise of production costs. The Japanese were therefore interested in exporting the industry overseas. They sold synthetic fiber to Taiwan in the late 1950s, and later brought in orders for garments made of these materials. Final products were intended for the U.S. market (Lin 1994). Taiwan's textile industry was further moved forward by U.S. retailers who were looking for cheap apparel to sell in their domestic market (Cheng and Gereffi 1994; Gereffi and Pan 1994). The relation between the garment and textile industries is evidence of backward linkage, that is, when a downstream industry (such as garments) grows, it stimulates upstream industries (such as textiles) to grow as well. As Taiwan's garment industry boomed, the demand for yarn and fabric increased, and this in turn stimulated domestic spinning and weaving.

At the local level, for producers in Homei, new economic opportunities emerged not only from Taiwan's fast growing garment industry, but also from a nearby village that specialized in manufacturing umbrellas. This neighboring village, once called "the Umbrella Empire," was said to have produced one-third of the world's umbrella exports at its zenith. Artificial fabric was in great demand as "the Empire" expanded, and to economize transportation costs, most of it came from Homei.

Many former mechanics and their wives in Homei set up small weaving workshops to take advantage of Taiwan's booming economy. The prosperity of the local textile industry often ensured their success, inspiring more people to join the trade, including landowners, like Mei-ling's father, who had no previous industrial experience but money to invest. Following his fellow villagers, Mei-ling's father established a weaving factory on his own land in 1978 and mobilized his family to produce.

Family Cooperation: New Forms and New Meanings

Although the Wangs had hired workers from the very beginning, their four children always composed an essential part of the textile workforce. Mei-ling's eldest sister, with the best "mathematics mind" in the family, became the factory accountant. She also cooked for workers and tended looms when labor was short. She did that until she became married at age twenty-five. Mei-ling's elder brother first worked as a mechanic but gradually took over his father's supervisory role on the shop floor. As the only son, he would eventually inherit the family business. As such, it was taken for granted by the family that he had to learn how to run the factory. Mei-hua and Mei-ling, the two younger daughters, were still going to evening vocational high school when their father started the firm. They normally worked four hours in the morning and took a nap in the afternoon before going to school. However, they would have to work for more hours after coming back from school in the case of absent workers.

Family members working together under the supervision of a patriarch is not a novel arrangement in Chinese culture. However, the introduction of industrial production provides new ways to accumulate wealth, thereby giving family cooperation new forms and new meanings. A major factor responsible for Taiwan's export expansion is the international subcontracting system. Most of the subcontracted work is labor-intensive; it requires little capital investment to start and mainly relies on continuous labor input to create higher output (Skoggard 1996). Also, unlike agriculture, whose productivity is limited by the availability of land and the length of growing seasons, there is virtually no limit in industrial production. Machines can operate day and night, as long as the market continues to absorb their products (ibid.). As Taiwan's industrialization rapidly proceeded, surplus agricultural labor, mainly young women, became an invaluable potential workforce. For the first time in Taiwan's history, far from being a burden, daughters became the backbone of the family's economy. Those from landless families worked for other factory owners, and brought home regular and urgently needed cash income. Daughters of factory-owning families were even more indispensable. They not only worked full-time side by side with hired laborers, but could work even more to make up for the absent hired labor.

The importance of family labor was further augmented by the unequal relationships between Taiwanese manufacturers and buyers from advanced capitalist countries. Foreign buyers are primarily looking for cheap commodities. However, as the competition in their domestic markets as well as the international market intensifies, foreign buyers also ask for increasingly shorter turnaround time from potential subcontractors. Taiwanese manufacturers have proved themselves highly effective in meeting these demands. They are efficient and flexible, and highly capable of maintaining quality at a given price, while ensuring reliable, on-time delivery (Gereffi and Pan 1994). To accomplish this, however, manufacturers need to have the cooperation of a workforce willing to work cheaply around the production cycle, that is, working overtime for days or even weeks to meet deadlines and taking unpaid time off when the market is slow. Who could be more likely to satisfy these needs than a manufacturer's own family?

Therefore, many new industrialists, like Mei-ling's father, heavily rely on family labor to assure a profit and a smooth flow of production. Family members provide a steady source of labor, and factory owners can always count on them to work overtime whenever necessary. Most important, the labor of family members is cheap. In many family factories, they are not paid but receive a "monthly stipend" with a value much less than the wages they could otherwise make in the labor market. In the case of the Wangs, children received NT$5,000 (US$185) per month when the factory just started, and only in the early 1990s had their "salary" been raised to NT$15,000 (US$555). In comparison, weavers in Homei usually made NT$27,000 (US$1,000) or more each month in the mid-1990s.[3]

It had become a tradition in the Wang family that children stayed home and worked after graduating from vocational high school. Given the fact that many young women of Mei-ling's age in Homei have only junior-high- or even elementary-school education, daughters in the Wang family are in fact in a prestigious position. Ironically, although they might enjoy a better material life, Mei-ling and her sisters were largely bound by family duty and had less free time than working daughters in less affluent families.

Mei-hua and Mei-ling both came of age at a time when Taiwanese society was gradually becoming prosperous and the job market was expanding beyond manufacturing. Accordingly, they had expressed their wish to continue with their education, so that they could have a better chance to enter other occupations than working in a textile factory. Yet, their parents discouraged them. Apart from the fact that the family firm needed their labor, their parents shared the popular notion that women did not need much education, as it was a widely shared view in Homei that higher education was of no use to women. As far as Mei-ling's parents were concerned, no matter how much a woman had accomplished while she was single, she would eventually marry into someone else's family, cook for the family, and bear children for the family, as Chinese women had always done before and would always do in the future. The life trajectory Mei-ling's parents assumed for their daughters was that they stay home, work, and become married. Their primary responsibility as parents was therefore to find a respectable family for their daughters to marry into, and there was no need for their daughters to expect otherwise.

Although this had been the practice of many generations of Chinese parents in the past, it has different implications now. In the past, Taiwanese society considered young daughters of no economic value other than wasting the rice owned by their natal families. As the logic went, a daughter could not help to increase the wealth of her natal family, nor could she bear grandsons to continue her father's family line. Naturally, she should not be entitled to inherit the property of her natal family. However, daughters nowadays are no longer idle family members but valuable workers. Their labor contributes to the accumulation of family wealth. Yet, even though by Taiwanese law both sons and daughters have equal rights in inheritance, it is still widely viewed in Homei and many parts of Taiwan that only sons are the rightful heirs. Daughters, on the other hand, are given a dowry as a form of inheritance when they marry out.

One may argue that this practice is based on a logic of "exchange." That is, although a daughter is not entitled to the fruit of her own labor, after marriage, she enjoys the fruit of her husband's sisters' labor, just as her brothers and their wives are enjoying the result of her labor. This may sound fair, but in reality, inequality runs along gender lines. Although young men and women in the family may work equally hard, local customs grant inheritance rights to males only. Sons therefore have a much clearer notion of what the future holds for them. They see their future materialized day after day as they work on the shop floor. If the family factory makes a profit, they have better future prospects; if the family business loses money, they know that they will have to work harder on their own. Daughters, in contrast, will not be able to foresee their futures when they work for their parents. Who knows what kind of family they will eventually marry into?

Mei-ling's eldest sister married out as expected. She married into a local family who also owned a weaving firm, and became a hardworking weaver, along with her sisters-in-law, under the supervision of her father-in-law. Mei-hua married a few years later, but only after a long struggle with her parents on the matter of her career (Lee 1996). Mei-ling was a problem for her parents. She was supposed to marry and join another family long before the age of thirty. But instead, she remained home, and worse, she insisted upon going back to school. In her parents' view, Mei-ling's destiny was with her husband, not with them. Her husband's family would ultimately provide for her. Who would take care of her if she didn't marry? Her parents would not give her a piece of their property, not even if she remained single all her life. Mei-ling's situation reveals the dilemma faced by young women if they choose a life trajectory deviant from the cultural expectation.

From Sunrise to Sunset: Current Predicaments of the Textile Industry

Despite their effort to satisfy their daughters with a high school diploma, the Wang parents had to change their minds and allow Mei-hua to attend junior college after years of Mei-hua's insistence. Mei-hua thus became the first child in her family who was permitted to go to college. She returned to school in 1984, three years after she graduated from vocational high school. She was twenty-one years old then, and Mei-ling was nineteen. Mei-ling expressed her wish to go to school with her sister, but her parents refused. They told Mei-ling that they could not afford to pay for two college tuitions at the same time. But this was only one of their reasons. They were also concerned about the issue of labor supply. They could not bear to lose two workers concomitantly; they could at best allow one daughter to go each time. Yet, Mei-ling's parents did not send her back to school even after Mei-hua graduated from junior college. This time they had a more serious concern. Mei-hua was about to get married, and because of that, the Wang family would lose her labor permanently. As a result, Mei-ling's labor became even more indispensable. Once again, the family could not afford to let her go.

After Mei-hua married, Mei-ling was the only daughter still working for her parents. Meanwhile, the Wang factory underwent many changes due to the economic restructuring that was affecting the larger society. Formerly the leading industry in Taiwan's export economy, after the late 1980s textiles rapidly declined to become a "sunset industry."[4] Several factors account for this change. The first blow came from the U.S. government which pressured Taiwan to appreciate its currency in order to reduce the U.S. foreign-trade deficit (Schive 1992). The exchange rate of the New Taiwan dollar vis-à-vis the U.S. dollar plunged from forty in 1985 to twenty-six in 1990, which severely impeded Taiwan's export capability, just when Taiwan was facing soaring competition from China and other industrializing countries in Southeast Asia.

The prospect for textile manufacturing was further shattered by a nationwide labor shortage. Cheap labor had always been a key to success for Taiwan's labor-intensive industries such as textiles. However, Taiwanese textile manufacturers began experiencing a labor shortage after the early 1980s, mainly resulting from a declining birthrate after the 1960s and recent changes in the economy. The textile industry is traditionally a woman's industry; female workers tend looms. In recent years, however, a large number of young women entering the wage labor market for the first time have chosen to work in the booming service sector instead of in manufacturing.[5] Also, more and more young women in rural areas have continued their education to senior high school or beyond to prepare themselves for white-collar jobs (Chou, Clark, and Clark 1990). They are no longer pressed by their families to take on factory work right after elementary or junior high school, as their counterparts in prior generations had to do.

As the in-coming labor force is drawn to white-collar jobs in the service sector, employers in manufacturing industries have rapidly lost their advantage in the hiring market. Recent government surveys identified garments and textiles as the two industries that have suffered the most from a labor shortage and further pointed out that small operations faced more difficulty finding workers than large enterprises (Wu and Chang 1991). Employment in factories like the Wang family's was apparently at the bottom of Taiwan's job preference.

Textile wages have rapidly risen as a result of this labor shortage. Given the appreciation of the New Taiwan dollar, the labor shortage, competition from other industrializing countries, and international protectionism, textile manufacturers in Homei, and island-wide, have responded in two ways: by relocating and downsizing.

By the late 1980s many textile producers had closed down their plants in Taiwan and relocated to China and Southeast Asia in order to take advantage of cheap labor and inexpensive raw materials available in these regions (Klein 1992; Chang and Chang 1992; Bonacich et al. 1994). In Homei, according to local observers, more than half the looms had been removed from production since the beginning of the 1990s. For those who remained in business in Homei, some had rearranged work assignments on the shop floor or upgraded their machinery to reduce the number of workers needed. Nevertheless, only a few wealthy industrialists in town could afford new machines. Many of the small factory owners just sold some of their looms and downsized production to the extent that family members alone could provide a sufficient workforce.

To alleviate labor shortages, in the early 1990s, the Taiwan government finally legalized employment of foreign workers for some industries including textiles. Yet the manufacturers have complained that the quotas are too low and the hiring procedures too cumbersome to meet their pressing needs.

For those families who could neither find Taiwanese workers nor get the government's permission to hire foreigners, once again and even more crucially than before, they had to rely on family labor. However, as the younger generations have attained—or are attaining—higher education, and have more alternatives in the job market, parents are losing control over their children. They might desperately need their children's labor, but they can no longer count on them.

Between Filial Daughter and Loyal Sister

Mei-ling's father retired in 1991, after he decided that he was too old to endure the pressure of overseeing factory production. The business was passed on to his son, the family heir. Upon taking control of the business, Mei-ling's brother decided to downsize the factory. He sold all the old looms, and then used the money he made from the sale to purchase six new machines that were more advanced than the ones they previously owned. With the support of his parents, he formalized a plan that would require only one worker per shift (the local textile industry has been in a three-shift, twenty-four-hour production cycle). Besides being the "sales manager" of his own factory, he would also be the mechanic. With Mei-ling on one shift, he would need only two additional weavers to work the other two shifts. Mei-ling's labor was obviously seen as a factory asset transferred from the father to the son as part of his inheritance. As long as Mei-ling was not married, she belonged to the family, and so did her labor.

Meanwhile, Mei-ling was going to junior college at night. After many years of waiting, she eventually managed to return to school in 1990. She did not ask for her parents' permission this time, but only told them the day before she was to register. Her father could not force her to quit but had to accept it as fact. After her brother took over the factory, and while she was attending evening school, Mei-ling continued to work the day shift in her brother's factory. Her brother paid her NT$15,000 each month (US$555), as in the past when her father was in charge of the family business. However, she had her own plan: to find a job and have a career of her own after graduating from junior college. To work for her brother was only a temporary arrangement.

Mei-ling's determination to go back to school at a relatively old age was perceived by her family as the cause of her delay of marriage, but Mei-ling told me that it resulted from her parents' need to keep the factory going and their biased attitude of seeing sons as more important than daughters. She told me that her parents worked hard, and pushed their daughters to work hard, to make as much money as possible for their son. "I have told [my parents] many times that I am not going to get married unless I graduate from college, but they just didn't listen," she said to me, becoming upset, and then went on,

> It's all their fault that I'm still in school now and haven't yet gotten married. I always wanted to study, and I have expressed myself very clearly to them ever since Mei-hua graduated from college. And they kept saying yes to me, but never really supported my decision in action. But even if they had been willing to let me go, with a constant problem of labor shortage, what could they have done otherwise? They had no choice but to keep me working in the factory!

Mei-ling explained to me why she insisted on schooling first and marriage second, saying,

> Eventually I will be married out. If I don't get my education now, I won't have any chance at all after I become married. My own parents don't even support me on such matters. Who else in the world do you think will support me? My husband's family? Ha! In your dream!

Yet, Mei-ling's brother was not able to find the two workers he had planned to hire. In a time of labor shortage, jobs of the "night" and "graveyard" shifts were the least attractive positions, even with higher wages, than any daytime jobs. In any case, Mei-ling became her brother's only weaver. Although he had to turn off the machines at night to accommodate Mei-ling's schedule, he also tried to keep Mei-ling at work except for the time he had to let her go to school.

It was a necessary strategy on the part of Mei-ling's brother to keep the factory going, under the current labor shortage. However, Mei-ling spoke bitterly to me about it. She was always pressed to work overtime whenever she was not in school. The fact that her brother became married (in the same year when he took over the family factory) seemed only to aggravate her bitterness. Mei-ling's sister-in-law did not come from a textile family. She knew nothing about weaving, and it seemed that she was not eager to learn. Mei-ling's brother rarely asked his wife to work in the factory. "He loves his wife very much," said Mei-ling. It had become painfully obvious that it was Mei-ling's responsibility to keep the factory running. If she did not do her "share," even on those occasions when she had to take time off for school or personal reasons, she would be blamed for the failure of the business. Mei-ling felt particularly angry that her labor was taken for granted by her family. They rarely expressed appreciation for her contribution, nor did they support her decisions. She once said,

> If I were a hired worker, I would just brush off the dust on my hips and leave after eight hours of work. I would not give a damn about the progress of the production; it would be the boss's problem. But I am [his] sister! My mom always presses me, saying: "If you don't help your brother, who else are you going to help?" It is taken for granted that I should work as much as possible to help my brother. It never occurred to them that I also have my own things to do. I need to have my own time.

Mei-ling's insistence upon returning to school had soured her relationship with her brother and her parents. It became even worse when she asked to have Sundays off in addition to her school time. Apart from expressing his discontent directly to her, Mei-ling's brother also complained to their parents, calling upon their authority and influence to dissuade her. They never agreed to give her her Sundays off. In the end it was Mei-ling's action of going out every Sunday that forced them to accept her decision.

However, Mei-ling also endured an emotional hardship for her persistence. She said,

> My mother was particularly upset. She was offended by my request. She felt that I was letting down the family by taking Sundays off. Without me there, my brother would either have to tend the looms himself or to shut down the production completely. Either way, it would require him to work more or cut back his profit. How could I do this to my brother, particularly in such a difficult time? He had refused to talk to me for a very long time.

But they [the parents] only care about their son! This is their son's factory, not mine. I won't be able to live under my brother's roof for all of my life, even if I want to. I will have to find something for myself.

For a Better Future, or Not?

[P]eople in different social positions have different "interests," and they act accordingly. This does not in itself imply either conflict or struggle, nor does it imply that people with different interests hold radically different views of the world. It does imply, however, that they will seek to enhance their respective positions when opportunities arise, although they will do so by means traditionally available to people in their positions. Change comes about when traditional strategies, which assume traditional patterns of relations . . . are deployed in relation to novel phenomena which do not respond to those strategies in a traditional way. (Ortner 1984: 155)

Although Chinese family norms defined the proper behaviors of family members, thus placing Mei-ling under her parents' authority that made her work in the family factory as a filial daughter, the same norms also granted her an opportunity to escape from her ordeal when the family business passed from her father to her brother. He, too, had authority over her, but his authority was never as powerful and absolute as that of her parents. The boundary of family was opened up for different interpretations when part of the family estate (that is, the factory but not the farmland) was transmitted from the older generation to the younger one. Mei-ling's "old" age in combination with her unmarried status further added to the cultural ambiguity. Thus, on the one hand, Mei-ling was considered part of the "family" by her parents and brother, particularly when they were desperately in need of her labor. Family loyalty appeared to be a powerful justification to appeal for her sacrifice. On the other hand, they also recognized the fact that Mei-ling was not, and never could be, a permanent member of the Wang family. Under the patrilineal principle, she was not to carry the family name; neither was she to inherit the family property. She would marry out. Given the fact that she was over thirty but still single, and that she had refused her mother's matchmaking efforts, it seemed that Mei-ling's prospect for marriage grew increasingly dim. Culturally she became a nuisance at home, particularly as her brother was about to build his own family. She had neither an obligation nor full rights to stay under his roof. It seemed to the parents that they had no other choice but to let her go, which was also her personal wish.

Mei-ling graduated junior college in June 1994. She was determined to leave her brother's factory and to find a life of her own. Her parents continued to push her to work for her brother or to be married, although their efforts usually went in vain. Mei-ling left home to stay with her friends several times during that summer after quarreling with her parents. This seemed to become her way of protest and resistance whenever her communication with her parents failed. She no longer worked for her brother, who continued to be haunted by the problem of labor shortage. Losing Mei-ling's labor put him in a difficult situation. He had tried to cover the day shift himself and find another weaver to work at night, but none of the workers he hired stayed long. When he was asked about his sister, he usually shrugged and muttered: "She doesn't want to do it. What more can I say to her?" He did not feel that he was in a position to demand her cooperation.

Mei-ling decided to take the civil service exam at the end of 1994, as the first step in search of her new life, and she was spending most of her time studying for it. However, she was also worried about her future. She was hoping to find a job related to her training in junior college so that she could start building her career. Nonetheless, she also feared that to work full-time would take time from study and diminish her chance of passing the civil service exam. Nevertheless, being a woman in her thirties, she was hardly favored in the wage labor market. She was too old for entry-level jobs, which were usually reserved for women in their early twenties. Conventionally, women of Mei-ling's age are either married or about to be married. Employers perceive them as fading out of the labor market, and thus often hesitate to hire them. Yet, Mei-ling was not qualified for advanced-level jobs, either. She had no previous working experience other than as a weaver in the Wang family factory. After a few unsuccessful attempts, she eventually worked for her sister Mei-hua, helping her and her husband run their computer shop.

Mei-ling obtained her "freedom" at a high price. She continued to live with her parents, but she came to work in the early morning and went home at nearly midnight. She avoided spending time at home. She seldom talked to her parents or brother. It seemed that she was "dividing" herself from the family. Her future was hardly promising at this particular moment. From time to time she was extremely demoralized about not being able to find a real job, and feared the possibility that she might have to go back to textiles. Nonetheless, for all the uncertainty she faced, Mei-ling was still glad for the choice she made. A few years after she left her brother's factory, I asked her whether she ever regretted her decision to leave home, a big smile immediately burst on her face. She said,

I am glad. As long as I do not need to work for them, I am glad!

In a Subjugated Voice

In the past two decades feminist scholarship has followed the premise of "[m]aking the invisible visible, bringing the margin to the center, rendering the trivial important, putting the spotlight on women as competent actors, [and] understanding women as subjects in their own right rather than objects for men" (Reinharz 1992: 248–49). This chapter follows this tradition. However, beyond revealing the conflictual dimension of the Chinese family, I would also argue that it is even more important to contextualize the emergence of a woman's voice and the particular message it conveys. Daughters of the generations prior to that of Mei-ling's might not have had the luxury of dreaming of a future other than making money for the family and marrying afterward. The poverty that pervaded the society and the scarcity of employment at the time largely prevented them from pursuing an alternative route. It was only when Taiwanese women became an integral part of the workforce did women begin to see alternatives in their lives. However, rather than inferring the "liberating" effects of a modern, industrializing economy on Taiwanese women, we also see, through Mei-ling's eyes, the complex and often contradictory forces that affect a young woman's life.

Mei-ling's future is far from certain. In search of her career, she has traded the security and bargaining power she might otherwise have had by remaining in the circumscribed yet protected home environment for her freedom and autonomy. The job market continues to be unfriendly. Her parents do not seem to have changed their minds regarding their daughter's destiny or her inheritance right. Nonetheless, there is no definite closure of Mei-ling's struggle. The conclusion is still pending.

Notes

This chapter emerged from my fieldwork in Taiwan between September 1993 and January 1996. I am grateful for the generous support of grants from the Wenner-Gren Foundation for Anthropological Research and the Institute of Ethnology at the Academia Sinica in Taipei, and from the Taiwan government's fund for returned overseas scholars. My deepest thanks to Lucie Cheng, Julia Butterfield, Leon Arredondo, June Nash, Joan Mencher, Michael Blim, Fang-chih Yang, Keith Markus, and Murray Rubinstein for conversations about, and comments on, issues raised in this chapter.

To preserve the confidentiality of my informants, pseudonyms are used for the names of the town and the town's inhabitants.

1. *Ta-hsueh*, or a university or four-year college, is different from *chuan-k'o*, or a junior college, which requires only two or three years of study.

2. Under this policy a selected number of textile producers signed a contract to spin for the government, and they were rewarded with excess amounts of cotton that they used to develop their own enterprises. The yarn processed under this program was resold to textile manufacturers, again, at a heavily subsidized price. Finally, the government guaranteed to buy back from the manufacturers, at a favorable rate, a certain percentage of the cloth made. Under this policy, the selected textile manufacturers not only obtained cotton (that is, the raw material) or processing fees (the capital) from the government, they were also guaranteed a market share for their final products. All that these fortunate manufacturers needed to begin this extremely profitable business was production equipment (looms) (Liu 1992: 206–24).

3. US$1 = NT$27.

4. The good old days of the textile industry have gone and will never return. The industry will only go downhill from now on.

5. After four decades of economic expansion, Taiwan in the 1990s is no longer a blue-collar society. Manufacturing peaked at 35 percent of the working population in 1987; since then its share of the labor force declined gradually. Meanwhile, the proportion of the populace in the service sector has increased substantially. By the end of 1995, half of the working population held jobs in the service sector (*Monthly Bulletin of Labor Statistics*, 1996, which is published by the Council of Labor Affairs, Administration Yuan).

References

Arrigo, Linda Gail. 1980. "The Industrial Work Force of Young Women in Taiwan." *Bulletin of Concerned Asian Scholars* 12, no. 2: 25–38.
———. 1984. "Taiwan Electronics Workers." In *Lives: Chinese Working Women*, ed. Mary Sheridan and Janet W. Salaff, 123–45. Bloomington: Indiana University Press.
———. 1985. "Control of Women Workers in Taiwan." *Contemporary Marxism*, no. 11: 77–95.
Basu, Ellen Oxfeld. 1991. "The Sexual Division of Labor and the Organization of Family Firm in an Overseas Chinese Community." *American Ethnologist* 18, no. 4: 700–718.
Bonacich, Edna, et al., eds. 1994. *Global Production: The Apparel Industry in the Pacific Rim.* Philadelphia: Temple University Press.
Bosco, Joseph. 1990. "Family and State in Taiwan's Rural Industrialization." Ph.D. dissertation, Columbia University.
Chang, Raymond J.M., and Pei-chen Chang. 1992. "Taiwan's Emerging Economic Relations with the PRC." In *Taiwan: Beyond the Economic Miracle*, ed. Denis Fred Simon and Michael Y.M. Kau, 275–98. Armonk, NY: M.E. Sharpe.
Cheng, Lucie, and Gary Gereffi. 1994. "U.S. Retailers and Asian Garment Production." In *Global Production: The Apparel Industry in the Pacific Rim*, ed. Edna Bonacich et al., 63–79. Philadelphia: Temple University Press.
Cheng, Lucie, and Ping-chun Hsiung. 1992. "Women, Export-Oriented Growth, and the State: The Case of Taiwan." In *States and Development in the Asian Pacific Rim*, ed. Richard P. Appelbaum and Jeffrey Henderson, 233–66. Beverly Hills, CA: Sage.
Chou, Bih-er; Cal Clark; and Janet Clark. 1990. *Women in Taiwan Politics: Overcoming Barriers to Women's Participation in a Modernizing Society.* Boulder: Lynne Rienner.
Chuang, Ying-chang. 1994. *Chia tsu yu hun yin* (Lineage and Marriage). Taipei: Institute of Ethnology, Academia Sinica.
Cohen, Myron. 1976. *House United, House Divided: The Chinese Family in Taiwan.* New York: Columbia University Press.
———. 1978. "Developmental Process in the Chinese Domestic Group." In *Studies in Chinese Society*, ed. Arthur P. Wolf, 183–99. Stanford: Stanford University Press.
———. 1992. "Family Management and Family Division in Contemporary Rural China." *China Quarterly*, no. 130: 357–77.
Diamond, Norma. 1979. "Women and Industry in Taiwan." *Modern China* 5, no. 3: 317–40.
Freedman, Maurice. 1966. *Chinese Lineage and Society: Fukien and Kwangtung.* London: Athlone Press.
Gallin, Bernard. 1966. *Hsin Hsing, Taiwan: A Chinese Village in Change.* Berkeley: University of California Press.
Gallin, Bernard, and Rita Gallin. 1985. "Matrilateral and Affinal Relationships in Changing Chinese Society." In *The Chinese Family and Its Ritual Behavior*, ed. Hsieh Jih-chang and Chuang Ying-chang, 101–27. Taipei: Institute of Ethnology, Academia Sinica.
Gallin, Rita. 1984a. "Rural Industrialization and Chinese Women: A Case Study from Taiwan." Michigan State University, Women in International Development, Working Paper, no. 47.
———. 1984b. "Women, Family and the Political Economy in Taiwan." *Journal of Peasant Studies* 12, no. 1: 76–92.
———. 1990. "Women and the Export Industry in Taiwan: The Muting of Class Consciousness." In *Women Workers and Global Restructuring*, ed. Katherine Ward, 179–92. Ithaca, NY: ILR Press.
Gates, Hill. 1987. *Chinese Working Lives: Getting By in Taiwan.* Ithaca, NY: Cornell University Press.

Gereffi, Gary, and Mei-lin Pan. 1994. "The Globalization of Taiwan's Garment Industry." In Bonacich, et al., eds., *Global Production: The Apparel Industry in the Pacific Rim*, 126–46.
Greenhalgh, Susan. 1985. "Sexual Stratification: The Other Side of 'Growth with Equity.'" *East Asia Population and Development Review* 11, no. 2: 265–314.
———. 1990. "Families and Networks in Taiwan's Economic Development." In *Contending Approaches to the Political Economy of Taiwan*, ed. Edwin Winckler and Susan Greenhalgh, 224–48. Armonk, NY: M.E. Sharpe.
———. 1994. "De-Orientalizing the Chinese Family Firm." *American Ethnologist* 21, no. 4: 746–75.
Harrell, Stevan. 1982. *Ploughshare Village: Culture and Context in Taiwan*. Seattle: University of Washington Press.
———. 1985. "Why Do the Chinese Work So Hard? Reflections on an Entrepreneurial Ethic." *Modern China* 11, no. 2: 203–26.
Harvey, David. 1991. *The Condition of Postmodernity*. London: Basil Blackwell.
Hsiung, Ping-chun. 1996. *Living Rooms as Factories: Class, Gender, and the Satellite Factory System in Taiwan*. Philadelphia: Temple University Press.
Hu, Tai-li. 1983. "The Emergence of Small-Scale Industry in a Taiwanese Rural Community." In *Women, Men, and the International Division of Labor*, ed. June Nash and M. Patricia Fernandez-Kelly, 387–406. Albany: State University of New York Press.
———. 1984. *My Mother-In-Law's Village: Rural Industrialization and Change in Taiwan*. Taipei: Institute of Ethnology, Academia Sinica.
———. 1985. "T'ai-wan nung ts'un kung yeh hua tui fu nu ti wei ti ying hsiang" (The Impact of Rural Industrialization on Women's Status in Taiwan). In *Proceedings of the Conference on the Role of Women in the National Development Process in Taiwan*, 337–56. Taipei: Population Studies Center, National Taiwan University.
Ka, Chih-ming. 1993. *T'ai-wan tu shih hsiao hsing chih tsao ye to ch'uang yeh, ching ying yu sheng ch'an tsu chih* (Market, Social Networks, and the Production Organization of Small-Scale Industry in Taiwan). Taipei: Institute of Ethnology, Academia Sinica.
Klein, Donald W. 1992. "The Political Economy of Taiwan's International Commercial Links." In Simon and Kau, eds., *Taiwan: Beyond the Economic Miracle*, 257–74.
Kung, Lydia. 1981. "Perceptions of Work among Factory Women." In *The Anthropology of Taiwanese Society*, ed. Emily Martin Ahern and Hill Gates, 184–211. Stanford: Stanford University Press.
———. 1994. *Factory Women in Taiwan*. New York: Columbia University Press.
Lee, Anru. 1996. "A Tale of Two Sisters: Gender in Taiwan's Small-Scale Industry." In *Anthropology for a Small Planet: Culture and Community in a Global Environment*, ed. Anthony Marcus, 67–79. St. James, NY: Brandywine Press.
———. 2004. *In the Name of Harmony and Prosperity: Labor and Gender Politics in Taiwan's Economic Restructuring*. Albany: State University of New York Press.
Li, Yeueh-tuan, and Chih-ming Ka. 1994. "Hsiao hsing chih yeh ti ching ying yu hsing pieh fen kung: Yi Wufenpu ch'eng yi yeh sho ch'u wei an li ti fen hsi" (Sexual Division of Labor and Production Organization in Wufenpu's Small-Scale Industries). *Taiwan she hui yen chiu chih kan* 17: 41–81.
Lin, Chung-cheng. 1994. "T'ai-wan fang chih kung ye fa chan cheng ts'o chih yen chiu" (Research on the Policies of Taiwan's Textile Industry).
Liu, Ching-ching. 1992. *T'ai-wan chan hou ching chih fen hsi* (Analysis of Taiwan's Postwar Economy). Taipei: Jenchan.
Niehoff, Justin D. 1987. "The Villager as Industrialist: Ideologies of Household Manufacturing in Rural Taiwan." *Modern China* 13, no. 3: 278–309.

Ortner, Sherry. 1984. "Theory in Anthropology Since the Sixties." *Comparative Studies in Society and History* 26, no. 1: 126–66.

Oxfeld, Ellen. 1993. *Blood, Sweat, and Mahjong: Family and Enterprises in an Overseas Chinese Community.* Ithaca: Cornell University Press.

Pasternak, Burton. 1972. *Kinship and Community in Two Chinese Villages.* Stanford: Stanford University Press.

———. 1983. *Guests in the Dragon: Social Demography of a Chinese District, 1895–1946.* New York: Columbia University Press.

Pasternak, Burton, and Janet Salaff. 1993. *Cowboys and Cultivators: The Chinese Inner Mongolia.* Boulder: Westview Press.

Reinharz, Shulamit. 1992. *Feminist Methods in Social Research.* New York and Oxford: Oxford University Press.

Salaff, Janet. 1990. "Women, the Family, and the State: Hong Kong, Taiwan, Singapore— Newly Industrialized Countries in Asia." In *Women, Employment and the Family in the International Division of Labor,* ed. Sharon Stichter and Jane L. Parpart, 98–136. Philadelphia: Temple University Press.

———. 1992. "Women, the Family, and the State in Hong Kong, Taiwan, and Singapore." In Henderson and Appelbaum, eds., *States and Development in the Asian Pacific Rim,* 267–88.

———. 1995. *Working Daughters of Hong Kong.* New York: Columbia University Press.

Schive, Chi. 1992. "Taiwan's Emerging Position in the International Division of Labor." In Simon and Kau, eds., *Taiwan: Beyond the Economic Miracle,* 101–22.

Skinner, G. William. 1957. "Livelihood in a New Land: The Chinese Position in the Thai Economy Through the Fifth Reign." In *Chinese Society in Thailand: An Analytical History,* ed. Skinner, 91–125. Ithaca: Cornell University Press.

Skoggard, Ian. 1996. *The Indigenous Dynamic in Taiwan's Postwar Development: The Religious and Historical Roots of Entrepreneurship.* Armonk, NY: M.E. Sharpe.

Stites, Richard W. 1982. "Small-Scale Industry in Yingge, Taiwan." *Modern China* 8, no. 2: 247–79.

———. 1985. "Industrial Work as an Entrepreneurial Strategy." *Modern China* 11, no. 2: 227–46.

Stone, Linda, and Caroline James. 1995. "Dowry, Bride-Burning, and Female Power in India." *Women's Studies International Forum* 18, no. 2: 125–35.

Wolf, Margery. 1972. *Women and Family in Rural Taiwan.* Stanford: Stanford University Press.

Wu, Hui Lin, and Ching Hsi Chang. 1991. *T'ai-wan ti ch'u to lao li tuan ch'ueh yu wai chih lao kung wen ti* (Labor Shortage and Foreign Workers in Taiwan). Taipei: Chung-hua Institute for Economic Research.

7

Internationalizing Women's Magazines in Taiwan

Fang-chih Irene Yang

It is hard to miss the numerous convenience stores on the streets of Taiwan these days. Inside these stores, one can't help but notice the various women's magazines displayed on the shelves, calling for the customers' attention. On closer inspection, one sees titles such as *Cosmopolitan, Marie Claire, Elle,* and *Harper's Bazaar* on the glossy covers of these magazines, accompanying the sometimes Caucasian and sometimes Asian, but always glamorous and sexy, models. These magazines are what we call "international women's magazines" in Taiwan. In contrast to the multinational corporations who own the "original" versions of these magazines, the Taiwanese publishers of these magazines obtain their patent rights and turn them into "international women's magazines." Though written in Chinese, their content is mostly translated from the Western women's magazines that also furnish fashion spreads. Sometimes a few "English" words will appear here and there, although they probably won't make much sense to a native speaker of English.

As recently as the 1980s, not only were these international magazines unknown to the Taiwanese public, but so were the convenience stores, which have become the largest retailers for women's magazines and newspapers. The internationalization of women's magazines in Taiwan is closely connected to the expansion of convenience stores, and both developments are constitutive of the rise of Taiwanese consumer culture. My chapter therefore uses women's magazines as an entry point to understand the relationships between the rise of Taiwanese consumer culture and the expansion of global capital. The magazine market in Taiwan marked its new era of internationalization, or, as most people would like to label it, globalization, since the late 1980s. However, one needs to note that the "internationalization" of Taiwanese women's magazines is not a new phenomenon. Since the 1950s the Kuomintang (KMT, Nationalist Party) had launched women's magazines, pirated and translated from Western women's magazines, for political mobilization. What is different at the current stage of internationalization is the *contractual* relationship between the Western magazine moguls and the Taiwanese magazine publishers. This contractual relationship is the product of particular political and economic configurations.

This chapter explores the historical conditions that made way for the new internationalization of women's magazines in the late 1980s and the effects that international women's magazines brought to the field of magazine production in Taiwan. The first part of this chapter considers the political and economic forces that created the conditions for an "international" market in Taiwan. It discusses the global economic restructuring in the 1980s that had forced Taiwan to adopt the policy of internationalization in order to be further incorporated into the global economy. The second part continues to investigate the conditions for the emergence of international women's magazines, such as the lifting of press censorship and the implementation of global intellectual property rights. In the third part, this chapter explains the institutional processes in which women's magazines are produced in Taiwan. The fourth and final part explores the effects that international magazines bring to Taiwan's cultural market, focusing particularly on the practice of market research in changing not only the industrial practices of women's magazines but also the whole field of cultural production.

The Internationalization of the Market

The emergence of international women's magazines required a market that allowed international goods to flow without inhibition across national borders, and in the 1980s this market was created as a result of Taiwan's adoption of liberalization policies. The major force for this change came from U.S. pressure on Taiwan to open its markets. American direct foreign investment in Taiwan began primarily in the mid-1960s when the U.S. government sought to use multinational corporations (MNCs) to replace U.S. aid, thereby ensuring the survival of a non–Communist Chinese model of development (Gold 1988). The Taiwanese government's basic strategy for local accumulation has always been to fit Taiwan into the capitalist system to ensure the constant flow of capital, thereby stimulating industrial development and increasing foreign-exchange earnings. Taiwan's main resource at the time was its abundant, low-cost, literate, trainable, and disciplined labor force. As rising production costs in the West and in Japan reduced their competitiveness, and as companies developed global production strategies and capabilities, Taiwan's comparative advantage in cheap labor plus a battery of other incentives became lures for MNCs. Because production technology was capital intensive, American MNCs came to Taiwan to take advantage of the low-cost labor. Although the actual products were developed at R&D facilities at headquarters in the West, local and expatriate engineers in Taiwan continued research to improve production efficiency (Gold 1988: 195). Taiwan's bargaining chip was its ability to provide labor, political and social stability, a responsive bureaucracy, and financial incentives (Gold 1988: 201).

As East Asian scholar Edwin Winckler (1988) observes, the main political development by the 1980s was the Soviet Union's advance to global parity with the United States, whereas the main economic development was Japan's rise to global parity with the United States. The increasing costs these two developments imposed on the United States increased American efforts to displace these costs onto its allies: As a result, American business resorted still more extensively to Far Eastern "sourcing" for its increasingly transnationalized network of production and sales (Winckler 1988).

Although intensified American-Japanese economic competition still meant more opportunities for skill-intensive industries elsewhere in East Asia, the global economic contraction and rising production elsewhere in the Third World intensified competition with Taiwan's declining labor-intensive industries (Winckler 1988). The recruitment of cheap labor from Malaysia, Indonesia, and China influenced Taiwan the most and reduced Taiwan's competitiveness within this global economic restructuring in the 1980s. Taiwan had to find a new niche beyond cheap labor to survive in the global economy and upgrading the economy was the first step. Rather than staying in low-end production, Taiwan's main effort was to develop the R&D capacity for high-tech industries. In 1981, Hsin-chu Science and Industrial Park was built as the first effort toward a technology-oriented industry. Instead of cheap laborers, Taiwan began to advertise cheap engineers. Foreign investment in traditional exports, such as the textile industry, was discouraged, whereas investment in new ones, such as microelectronics and machinery, was encouraged by the government. Taiwan simultaneously tried to improve the quality of suppliers and worked to develop the island into a place that could ship goods and services from the "core" to less-developed countries. Efforts were also made by the government in the mid-1980s to develop offshore banking as a way of luring financial houses from Hong Kong (Gold 1988: 202). These efforts to upgrade the economy had some impact. In 1986, the proportion of high-tech exports was 27.6 percent; in 1993, it was 41.6 percent. At the same time, the GDP in the service sector increased from 47.9 percent to 55.9 percent (Hsia 1995).

The negative side of Taiwan's economic restructuring was the "running away" of multinational businesses from the island to countries where labor is cheaper. The increased cost of labor in Taiwan, the intensifying environmental concerns, and the forced appreciation of Taiwanese dollars caused many of Taiwan's businesses to move their production sites to China, Malaysia, and Indonesia. The impact of this corporate runaway was twofold. First, it intensified social injustice by suppressing the development of democratic social movements. The big corporations complained about the "bad investment environment" created by all kinds of social movements and the government assumed the business side. To ensure that the corporations would stay and, in the process, create more job opportunities, the then Minister of the Executive Yuan, Po-chun Hao, declared in 1990 that he was devoted to creating an environment conducive to business investment. In addition, immigration law was implemented to make use of cheap labor from the Philippines and Thailand to solve the high-cost labor problem. Despite all the measures the government took to prevent businesses from running away, businesses still left for places with abundant cheap labor. Economists and the politicians, worrying about the "emptification" of production, proposed to build Taiwan as an "Asia-Pacific Regional Operations Center" (APROC) in 1995.

The APROC project aimed to reposition Taiwan in the new global economy by making the country the base for domestic enterprises and as a gateway for international businesses that targeted Asian markets, especially those in Southeast Asia and mainland China. To do so, the Taiwan government proposed developing operation centers in financial services, telecommunications, air transportation, shipping, manufacturing, and media. The concept of the APROC was to make alliances with other transnational businesses and use Taiwan's resources and experiences in a way that could make Taiwan the springboard for the transnational businesses operating in the Asia-Pacific region (Hsia 1995). Yet, in order to do so, it was necessary for Taiwan to follow the rules of a free market. Therefore, since the 1980s, liberalization and internationalization drove all economic policies, especially once Taiwan decided to become the APROC. Financial sectors, service sectors (including telecommunications), and cultural sectors were all liberalized as a result.[1]

A large part of the pressure to liberalize Taiwan came from the United States. In the early 1980s, the United States faced the pressure of Japan becoming an economic power, threatening U.S. global hegemony. Furthermore, the growing trade deficit became a pressing issue for the U.S. economy as signs of economic depression started to show. These factors, over-simplified here for brevity, drove the United States to use its foreign policies to protect its interests. The U.S. trade deficit with Taiwan, caused by the trade privileges given to Taiwan since the outbreak of the Korean War, immediately made Taiwan the target of a liberalization campaign. Taiwan responded to U.S. pressure in two ways: First, it dispersed its market by expanding commerce with Japan and Europe; second, it lowered tariffs and lifted unnecessary restrictions on U.S. imports,[2] thereby increasing them. Taiwan also opened its service industry to direct U.S. investment, which included entertainment, tourism, finance, and insurance (Winckler 1988: 300).[3] As a result of this, there was an influx of imported goods in the early 1980s.

Creating International Women's Magazines in Taiwan

So far, I have sketched the background in which Taiwan was forced to liberalize and internationalize its market. The liberalization of the economy, especially in the service sector, created the necessary conditions for the emergence of international women's magazines. However, other structural factors—such as the expansion of international advertising agencies, the easing of press restrictions, and the enforcement of intellectual property rights law—brought about international women's magazines' visibility in Taiwan. Below, I will elaborate on these more specific features of the political economy that produces international women's magazines in Taiwan.

The Expansion of Western Advertising Agencies to Taiwan

Following the inflow of innumerable imported goods were the Western advertising agencies, which, with the support of the multinationals, came to Taiwan to sell the imported goods. The emergence of the advertising agency in Taiwan was closely related to the export-oriented industrialization policy, which helped Taiwan become included in the world economic order.[4] Although Taiwan's advertising industry was greatly influenced by Japan in its formative years in the 1960s and 1970s, it remained closed to foreign investment.[5] Therefore, prior to 1985, local agencies profited enormously from advertising both domestic and imported goods. However, when the government lifted the import restrictions and lowered tariffs in 1984, thereby allowing foreign goods to flood into Taiwan within a short amount of time, the restrictions on establishing wholly foreign-owned and joint-venture advertising operations were also lifted. As a result, according to Ho, "from 1987 through 1989, total advertising market expenditure experienced approximately 40 percent growth each year. Most of that came from a dramatic increase in foreign products newly available on the market, about 400 to 500 every year, of which an average of 100 will be advertised. Local agencies did not have the capacities to deal with that growth. Foreign agencies didn't come in to serve local advertisers, they came in to serve their already existing multinational client relationships" (*Free China Review*, quoted in Freuan 1996: 32).

Between 1984 and 1987, virtually every multinational advertising agency had set up an office in Taiwan (Freuan 1996). The first agency to arrive was Ogilvy and Mather (O&M), then Leo Burnett, J. Walter Thompson, McCann-Ericson, Lintas, and Saatchi & Saatchi all followed to divide the market. When these giants descended on Taiwan, they immediately took over the market. According to Freuan (1996), in 1995 the annual billings for the top thirty-seven advertising agencies in Taiwan totaled US$1 billion. Wholly owned foreign agencies and those with foreign majority shareholding accounted for 58 percent of that total, while those with foreign minority shareholding accounted for another 12 percent. As Hiro J. Oshina, executive vice chairman of the Taiwan Advertising Company, a joint venture with Japan's Dentsu, remarks: "The local advertising market is now controlled by international companies" (quoted in Freuan 1996: 32).

The Lifting of Press Restrictions

Another factor that contributed to the internationalization of women's magazines was the easing of press restrictions in January 1988, after which a sudden boom in printing ensued. The most significant restrictions dropped by the government were the removal of newspaper registration and of the twelve-page limit for a daily newspaper. With the removal of these two restrictions, newspapers increased their numbers of pages and added consumer information pages and women's pages in the daily newspapers. These pages included entertainment news, lifestyle information, consumer reports, the Cosmos (international cultural and entertainment news), the cultural editions (information on cultural activities such as concerts), and tips for women consumers, and so forth. These changes in the dailies not only helped to accelerate the transmission of consumer information but also to expand the reach of such information, thereby facilitating Taiwanese society's transition to a consumer society. In the process daily newspapers crossed their boundaries to "take over" issues that were considered to be the domain of women's magazines. In turn, women's magazines that traditionally identified themselves as "general interest magazines" faced an identity crisis. To solve this crisis, magazines distinguished themselves from the "general-interest" newspapers by claiming that newspapers were now for quickly digesting information during breakfast time or coffee breaks and that the consumer information pages in newspapers generated a need for more in-depth information. As a result, magazines came to position themselves as providing in-depth information and claimed to serve special-interest groups. However, this special-interest magazines rhetoric was more conducive to the existence of international women's magazine than domestic ones. Although Western women's magazines have a long history of serving "special interests"—middle-class, white, women—many Taiwanese versions faced the difficulties of transforming their self-images.

In addition to shaping a more consumption-oriented society and creating the need for special-interest magazines, the easing of press restrictions also created favorable conditions for "sexual advertising" (that is, using scantily clad, attractive women to sell commodities) in international women's magazines. Taiwan's pre-1980s press had been under the strict regulation of state censorship, particularly in the area of sex and politics. Domestic women's magazines' appeal to the "general-interest" rhetoric was also a response to this censorship in that by claiming the magazines as family reading material, the magazines also announced their "purity," that is, their absence of sexual matters. However, even with such strict censorship on the publication of sexual materials, local magazines, in one way or another, still managed to publish some sexual material. For example, Kuo (1997) showed that, in Taiwan during the 1960s and 1970s, there were many underground publications which dealt with the topic of sex that were oriented to a male readership. Some women's magazines used sex as their selling point (although some of them were censored, such as *Life* magazine). In many cases, when these sexual materials were banned, the publisher would merely change the title of the material in question and republish it. In some cases, the authors of these materials claimed their medical authority and smuggled in magazine content on love-making technique in the guise of eugenics (Kuo 1997). The persistence in publishing sexual material despite state censorship indicated the existence of a market for sexual material. The lifting of press restrictions therefore legitimized this market. Because Western advertising agencies "specialized" in "sexual advertising," and they tended to use sex as their trademark, Western women's magazines were easily transported into the Taiwanese market with the easing of press restrictions.

In short, the lifting of press restrictions created a demand for more in-depth consumer information. At the same time, it also created a more "liberated" atmosphere which tolerated the explicit use of women's bodies as a sales strategy. International women's magazines, featuring scantily dressed pin-ups on the cover pages and sexy topics inside the covers, could be distributed with the lifting of the press restrictions. Moreover, the international advertising agencies could sell goods to women with disposable income.

Enforcing Intellectual Property Rights Law

In addition to the lifting of press restrictions, the enforcement of intellectual property rights law in the late 1980s also provided a necessary condition for creating an international women's magazine market. The issue of intellectual property rights in Taiwan can be traced to 1903 when the Treaty of Friendship, Commerce, and Navigation was signed between China and the United States. The treaty "granted Chinese subjects the privileges of printing and selling original translations in Chinese of any written works or maps produced by American citizens" (Yeung 1989: 22). The agreement originally aimed to "boost China's development" (Ibid.) while, at the same time, achieving U.S. hegemony over less-developed countries. The spirit of this treaty remained alive for more than half a century. In the 1960s and 1970s, the issue of intellectual property rights came up again, this time in competition with other discourses. Intellectual property rights exemplified "American interests," which were in tension with the "developing country's right to exist" (Yeung 1989). However, at that time, the United States was still a superpower, so pirating in developing countries did not really constitute a danger to the existence of American businesses. In addition, pirating U.S. cultural products actually helped the United States to maintain its cultural dominance. Therefore, even with the tension, pirating was passively tolerated, until the global economic restructuring in the 1980s changed the way intellectual property rights were conceived.

To guarantee that U.S. business benefited from the operation of a "free" market, the approach under the presidencies of both Reagan and Bush to intellectual property rights became predicated on the ethics of market exchange and, therefore, needed to be enforced. This changing attitude on the part of the United States, while reflecting the restructuring of the center-periphery relationship to the demands of the market and the changing international division of labor, forced the major import countries such as Taiwan, South Korea, and China to observe intellectual property laws. The enforcement of intellectual property laws in Taiwan in the late 1980s made it possible for local publishing companies to negotiate with Western ones.[6] With the advent of "cooperation" between local and Western publishing companies, it is possible to argue that the sudden trend of producing international women's magazines in the late 1980s and early 1990s was partly a result of the intellectual property laws.

To summarize, the global economic contraction in the 1980s forced Taiwan to liberalize its economy and, with U.S. pressure, Taiwan opened up its domestic market to foreign investment. This step accelerated the formation of Taiwan's consumer culture because it triggered the inflow of imported goods to Taiwan within a short period of time and the immediate establishment of the affiliated industries that came to sell the goods. Multinational advertising agencies that came to Taiwan to sell Western goods are part of the trend. Therefore, international women's magazines came to Taiwan to serve these international giants by providing them with outlets. In addition, the lifting of press restrictions created a more sexually liberalized environment; and the enforcement of intellectual property rights guaranteed enormous profits for Western magazine industries while at the same time enabling the rise of international women's magazines in Taiwan. Consequently, *Cosmopolitan* was the first international women's magazine to test Taiwan's market, featuring scantily dressed, sexy pin-ups. This was followed by *Elle*, *Harper's Bazaar*, and *Marie Claire*, all of which were laden with extravagant international brands of consumer goods, gaining the attention of affluent modern Taiwanese women.

The Internationalization of Women's Magazines

In "We Are Writing Women's History," the chief editor of *Cosmopolitan* in Taiwan, Wu Li-ping, stated that:

> The publication of *Non-no* (an international women's magazine) divided the history of Taiwanese women's magazines into two stages. Before *Non-no*, women's magazines were very conservative; after *Non-no*, it became a mainstream practice for women's magazines to attend primarily to fashion information and consumer information. Because the information provided was closely connected to women's everyday lives, women's magazines had tremendous impact on women. After the success of *Non-no*, many of its editors went on to work in other women's magazines. *Non-no* used to run an ad which is quite telling: "Without *Non-no*, the world of women's magazines will never be as prosperous." Because all the magazines published after *Non-no* imitated *Non-no*'s style, finding a unique women's magazine was quite difficult. It was not until the publication of *Cosmopolitan* in 1989 that a new phenomenon began to emerge. *Cosmopolitan* found a new perspective and a new place for women's magazines. It expanded women's life space, emphasized women's self-actualization, and brought women to an age that valued taste, style, and depth. (*Cosmopolitan* August 1990: 4)

Before the 1980s, "conservative" women's magazines (as *Cosmopolitan*'s chief editor labeled them) claimed to serve women and all the members of the society even though the issues the publications addressed concerned mainly middle- and upper-middle-class women. Such an ideological claim to serve the interests of all members of the society was part of the rules of game that one needed to observe in the field of cultural production. However, the rise of television as the most popular medium made it impossible for magazines to use such rhetoric to attract advertisements, especially when magazines in Taiwan have always been too costly for a general audience. By the early 1970s, the total advertisement revenue for TV had already surpassed that of print media. Magazines responded by making a functional claim to serve special-interest groups, with Commonwealth (T'ien hsia Tsa chih) being the first special-interest magazine. Commonwealth, first published in June 1981, specialized in economics and in-depth business reporting; it also set high standards in graphics, layout, and printing. Packaged as a commodity, its professional format and marketing strategy gave rise to its early market dominance.

Among the special-interest magazines, three categories stand out: political magazines, financial management magazines, and women's magazines. The first women's magazine that took on the trend of market segmentation was Non-no, first issued in 1984. Before the publication of Non-no, women's magazines were called "Family and Women's magazines." Because the role of the woman/mother was equated with the family, women's magazines were designed for both women and family members; therefore, issues of morality, ethics, justice, aesthetics, and propriety were the most-often-discussed topics in letters to the editors. Furthermore, the letters to the editors in The Woman, an early "Family and Women's magazine," in the 1970s and early 1980s were mostly written by men, and the contents of the letters were not gender-specific. In these magazines, single women and teenagers were invisible categories, as a woman's destiny was to be a family caretaker or a housewife. However, the publication of Non-no, initially published to capture a share of the emerging teen-aged market, became one of the forces in the early and mid-1980s that enticed teenagers into creating consumer identities.[7]

When first introduced, Non-no was the pirate of a highly popular Japanese teen-aged girls' magazine of the same name. The publisher of the Taiwanese Non-no, Kuo-Tai Corporation, failed to negotiate issues of copyright with the Japanese publisher and pirated the title as well as the content and format of the Japanese Non-no. The publication of Non-no was immediately successful and remained the best-seller among women's magazines in the late 1980s and throughout the 1990s despite the competition from Western international magazines. Non-no's publication indicates several significant trends in the history of women's magazines. First, Non-no was the first women's magazine to use niche marketing. After its success, market segmentation became a necessary strategy for any successful magazine in Taiwan. Second, Non-no foregrounded the notion of lifestyle, articulated through extravagant consumption of fashion goods. As already noted, Non-no was the first women's magazine that "attended primarily to fashion information and consumer information." It was also the first magazine that provided information that was "closely connected to women's everyday lives." Because Non-No claimed to provide guidelines for women to live their everyday lives as consumers, the prominence of fashion in the pages of the magazine indicated that fashion information was seen as constituting women's everyday experiences. Following Non-no, subsequent women's magazines published in the mid- to late 1980s, such as Diana and Yun, packaged themselves as "pursuing taste and fashion." Since then, lifestyles have become the selling point for women's magazines. Finally, Non-no also foreshadowed the later "internationalization" trend in the magazine business. It was not until the publication of *Cosmopolitan* in 1989 that Taiwan's magazine market began its process of "official" internationalization. Hence, the aforementioned chief editor of *Cosmopolitan* Wu claimed that her magazine "found a new perspective and a new place for women's magazines." Despite their short history in the local market, all four of these foreign magazines, *Cosmopolitan, Elle, Harper's Bazaar,* and *Marie Claire,* stayed on the top-ten list for best-selling women's magazines (according to *Brain,* a monthly marketing and communications publication). Each magazine claimed to sell between ten thousand and thirty thousand copies a month, although circulation figures were not audited and were often unreliable. As a comparison, among the twenty or so viable women's magazines in Taiwan, it is estimated that one-third of these magazines sell more than ten-thousand copies per issue, 40 percent sell five- to ten-thousand copies, and 20 percent sell two- to five-thousand copies. The rest sell fewer than two-thousand copies, the bottom line for survival ("An Estimate of the Numbers of Magazines Produced in the Taiwan Area" 1993).

The obvious advantage of foreign-based publications is their vast international resources. "*Cosmo* is one hundred years old and has twenty-six editions worldwide, and *Bazaar* has around twenty editions. We exchange information with other editions all the time," explains Chang Ming-Chun, chairman of Hua-Ker Publishing, which publishes the Taiwan editions of both magazines under licensing from the U.S.-based Hearst Corporation. One of the biggest magazine publishing houses in Taiwan, Hua-Ker also owns the Taiwan edition of *Esquire and Arch,* a local interior design magazine. In addition to their abundant resources, international magazines also have the advantage of advertisements from international advertising agencies. Local advertising agencies lost their international clients when the international advertising agencies entered the Taiwan market because the international advertising agencies are able to place their advertisements in international magazines rather than local ones. Therefore, one-third to one-half of most women's magazines are filled with advertisements for Christian Dior, Ralph Lauren, Pierre Cardin, Lancôme, and Estée Lauder. Yet, despite these two advantages, international women's magazines have to deal with the tension between localization on the one hand and internationalization on the other in order to attract local readers. Each magazine has adopted a different strategy for dealing with this tension.

Tsai Tung-chao, the publisher of *Cosmopolitan,* emphasizes that international women's magazines are not magazines that are directly translated from American magazines: "The Chinese *Cosmopolitan* is not a direct translation of the American *Cosmopolitan.* Our readers will feel distanced if it is a direct translation. Our Chinese edition emphasizes the 'energetic, active, individualistic, and independent' spirit of the American *Cosmopolitan.* Following this spirit, we try to refashion a new modern Chinese woman and encourage women to improve themselves and face more challenges" (October 1989: 2). Given this definition of internationalization, different women's magazines try different ways to catch the "spirit" of the Western magazines. For example, about one-half to two-thirds of the content of both *Cosmopolitan* and *Harper's Bazaar* are adapted from other international editions (and mostly from American editions), and both magazines use Western cover girls. Although the adapted stories are sometimes modified (for example, the articles on sex might be written in more reserved and euphemistic language), they are still basically translations. "We insist on maintaining the style and tradition of these magazines," Chang Ming-Chun of *Cosmopolitan* says. "We translate articles on sex and relationships, which is *Cosmopolitan's* forte, and we adapt fashion reports, which is *Bazaar's* strong point, and we also translate or adapt the regular columns on health, beauty, interior design, cooking, horoscope, etc." (Yun 1994: 32). Despite their strong international coverage, these magazines must still provide some articles and columns written from a Taiwanese perspective in order to attract readers. According to the chief editor of *Cosmopolitan*, Iris Chou, "To localize the content of the magazines, we sometimes choose the topics from the American edition and interview local people and then write down the result of the interview from local people's perspectives" (personal interview by author with Iris Chou, 1996). In addition, both magazines include regular profiles of Chinese singers, actors, and other personalities; columns introducing local movies, books, concerts, and art exhibitions; and information on boutiques and jewelry stores around Taipei. According to Chang Ming-Chun, "50–50 is a healthy combination, but we are still experimenting" (Yun 1994: 32).

The Taiwan edition of *Marie Claire*, produced by *China Times Weekly*, has taken an even more locally oriented approach. The editor in chief said, "Eighty percent of its content is written in Taipei. Like the original French edition, many of these articles are more in-depth and thought-provoking than the typical half-page sex and beauty features in most fashion magazines." The magazine claims to appeal not only to its readers' fashion tastes, but also to its readers' intellect. *Marie Claire* seeks to pursue "individual taste, liberty and humanitarian concerns" (Yun 1994: 33).

Perhaps the most localized of the international fashion magazines is *Elle*, published in Taipei by Hatchette International, a joint venture between France Editions and Publications and Intercultural Magazines Ltd. in Taipei. Like *Marie Claire*, *Elle* always uses Chinese models on its covers, and its locally produced fashion spreads often have a distinctly Chinese quality. The articles and columns adapted from its other editions, which make up about one-third of *Elle's* content, are also given a strong local flavor. For example, *Elle* often compares local fashion to fashion abroad or invites comments from local designers. The Chinese is also more fluent, rather than inflected with an English flavor. Nevertheless, although the establishment of a local angle is important, it is still the international appeal that gives these magazines an edge (Yun 1994).

Changing the Market of Women's Magazines

The fact that international women's magazines have claimed positions on the "best-seller list for magazines" since they first hit the market posed great challenges for local women's magazines. As a result, local women's magazines underwent many changes to survive the market liberalization. The first strategy that local women's magazines adopted was market research. Before examining the strategies of local magazines, I will first look at the relationships between international women's magazines and the use of market research.

As discussed earlier, the Western advertising agencies came to Taiwan to sell imported commodities that were suddenly available to the Taiwanese people as a result of the state's decision to open its domestic market. Under the pressure of local manufacturers to compete with foreign goods, local advertising agencies improved their sales and promotion strategies by adopting strategies used by foreign agencies. Therefore, all local agencies implemented market research to survive the brutal competition from transnational giants. As Hiro Oshima notes: "In the past, local manufacturers thought that as long as they made a product, priced it competitively, and advertised it, then it would sell. Since clients thought this way, advertising agencies did accordingly. Neither had any idea about market research or targeted campaigns. Foreign agencies, on the other hand, first considered market analysis, consumer research and product positioning. They then decided the ad campaign's approach'" (quoted in Freuan 1996: 33). As a consequence, market segmentation, the necessary result of market research, became the mandatory business practice.

Market research, a scientific method used to understand consumers' buying habits and buying power, created a new category of special-interest magazines. According to Ohmann, market research was used to control the sales of products. When market research was first used in the United States, it was historically intended to reduce risks and increase competitive power by integrating production and consumption. Through market research, companies could divide up customers into shares of the market and differentiate products by matching particular segment of consumers with particular products based on customers' loyalty (Ohmann 1996: 53). As Raymond So of the J. Walter Thompson advertising agency stated:

> Foreign agencies differ from the local counterparts in [that] they have a more scientific approach toward consumer marketing. A successful agency must understand how consumers think and behave, particularly with regard to how they interact with the media and a brand. And you must understand how to use that knowledge to communicate effectively with consumers, both in terms of what media to use to reach them, and in knowing what kind of ideas they will respond favorably to. (quoted in Freuan 1996: 33)

What do the rise of international advertising agencies and the adoption of market research have to do with international women's magazines? As mentioned earlier, when restrictions on imported goods were lifted, international advertising agencies came to serve international commercial giants by selling their goods to the Taiwanese people. International women's magazines, therefore, came to serve the multinational advertising agencies by providing a forum for them to sell their goods. As a result, women's magazines came to depend more on advertising revenues than on individual sales and subscription rates. As the survival of women's magazines came to depend on advertising income, certain readers became more valuable than others because they had more buying power.

Local women's magazines, faced with the challenges coming from international women's magazines, also adopted market research to attract "quality" readers in order to sell them as "elite" readers to the advertising agencies. For example, in a local trade journal, *Modern Management Monthly,* Lin discusses the importance of market research and the idea of "special interest" in marketing:

> There are three types of women: traditional, modern, and family-oriented....
> Women possess a variety of lifestyles; every group of women has its unique
> thinking patterns and its special needs. Even if the manufacturers produce goods
> that possess attractive traits, there is no guarantee that all women will like the
> goods. The way to improve this is through market segmentation. You need to
> divide women into subgroups according to their age, occupation, education, income, and their lifestyle. Then you need to assess each group's buying power, its
> special traits, and demands. After these steps, you can start to plan your sales
> strategy and get into the market. (Lin 1985: 38)

Consequently, market research helps magazine industries control their profits by creating new identities for these groups, and then tailoring their products to different groups of affluent consumers.

Who constitutes this "special-interest" group toward which women's magazines imagine themselves to offer services? In the first issue of Taiwanese *Cosmopolitan,* Helen Gurley Brown gave a clear picture of its readers:

> *Cosmopolitan* is different from other women's magazines. It doesn't emphasize
> how to mother your children, how to be a good housewife, or other traditional
> roles. Our readers are women who desire to actualize their potentials. . . . We
> emphasize that a woman needs to have a career and romantic love to be truly
> happy. . . . We offer you information and ideas on how to help single women to
> find ideal partners, how to help married wives to take care of their husbands,
> their children, and their work without feeling overstressed, how to negotiate your
> sex lives, how to find a good job, etc. (Brown 1989: 6)

Brown's view about their readers is not specific to *Cosmo,* but is shared by all international women's magazines as well as the local ones. In general, women's magazines are targeting a group of women who "love men, children, work, and themselves" and whose principle in life is to "keep their youth and beauty forever" (*Cosmopolitan* May 1992: 8). In general, this "special interest" group is made of women who live in metropolitan areas, who have an office job, and who range in age from twenty to thirty-five, in other words, the group of women who are considered as having the strongest buying power by the advertisers.

From Brown's statement, we also infer the birth of a new "species." If women were traditionally associated with the family, as earlier general-interest magazines assumed, then international women's magazines signaled a new type of women. Instead of investing herself in her husband and children, she now has an identity of her own. She desires to actualize herself through her work and her romances. Her place has shifted from the domestic home to the public world of the workplace and romantic consumption.

Hence, the invention of the "special-interest" group by market research helped facilitate some women, in the form of the modern woman, in dissociating their identities from the home and re-orienting them toward the workplace and the market. This new identity of women as individuals dissociated from the traditional role of mothers and wives also contributed to the success of international women's magazines whose interest in individual consumption tended to exclude women with a family. Therefore, by catering to the category of "special-interest" women, women's magazines served the advertising agencies by providing them forums to sell their goods to a group of modern, metropolitan, young (age ranging from twenty to thirty-five), and affluent women consumers.

Where do these women come from? As Taiwan continued its process of modernization in the 1970s, more and more women, usually from the new middle-class and traditional middle-class (petty bourgeois) backgrounds, received college educations. Therefore, they worked in the modern industrial and service sectors as secretaries, assistants, administrative staff, and even professionals. This group of women grew up with Western influence and aspired to the cosmopolitan aesthetic that the international women's magazines helped to construct. However, at the same time, factory girls, women from lower social strata, and women of old age became more marginalized in the society because they did not constitute a "special-interest" group in the marketplace; therefore, they no longer had access to representation.

In addition to changing the character of women's magazines from "general interest" to "special interest," market research also changed the relationship between readers and writers.

Ohmann (1996) points out that U.S. market research, emphasizing sales and consumption, changed the identity of a worker from a producer to include that of a consumer. In the world of Taiwanese women's magazines, the opposite has happened. The readers of women's magazines, traditionally seen as pure consumers, have now become producers (writers). According to the chief editor of *The Woman*, the relationships between the "Writers and Readers" should be construed as follows:

> Before, the relationship between an author and a reader is analogous to that of a cook and a customer. They have very different roles and different identities [the customers do not cook, they only consume]. But nowadays, a reader can also take on the identity of a writer. . . . For example, with the recent changes in news media, newspapers also invite their readers to write and publish their ideas in the newspapers....We the editors would like to... eliminate the distance between the reader and the writer. For example, we sponsor opinion surveys, publish letters

to the editors, support public lectures and conferences, and we also communicate with the readers. (editorial 1994: 6)

Driven by profit, magazines became more interactive. The more the consumers participated, the more the producers understood the concerns of the consumers. Hence, magazine publishers sponsored activities such as luncheon talks, fashion shows, concerts, movies, and make-up workshops, particularly for college seniors who would soon be "social freshwomen." These activities not only promoted the sales of the magazines but also gave the producers a sense of who the readers were and what they wanted (so that the publishers could sell the audience back to the advertising agencies). To promote more sales and to ensure that the advertisements in women's magazines would reach the optimal number of consumers, some magazines such as *Elle* even began to distribute unsold magazines to participants in their sponsored activities. By doing this, publishers also solved the problem of overstocking magazines. Coupons and free cosmetic samples were also given out to consumers to induce sales.

It was not only the use of market research which changed the way women's magazines were marketed; the post-liberalization transformations in magazine distribution also changed magazines' formats, layouts, and cover designs. In the 1960s and 1970s, bookstores were not the major outlets for magazines. In fact, periodicals were rarely found in bookstores. At this time, magazine income came mostly from subscriptions rather than individual sales and advertising. Magazines were distributed through a general or local consignee, who mailed the magazine to subscribers each month (Wang 1976). This situation changed when Kingstone, the first chain bookstore in Taiwan, established special in-store sections for selling magazines in the mid-1980s. The establishment of magazine sections forced local women's magazines to compete with international magazines for customers' immediate attention.

Kingstone launched two strategies in bookselling that were eventually taken up by all other chain bookstores: the establishment of a magazine section in the front part of bookstores and the institution of best-seller billboards. The former made magazines the most visible commodities in a bookstore, whereas the latter changed the types of books being produced. With Kingstone pioneering the bookstore business, Ho-Chia-Jen and Hsin-Shuei-Yo followed suit and established their chain bookstore businesses in the busiest parts of Taiwanese cities. The result was a rapid expansion of chain bookstores and a rapid disappearance of traditional bookstores from street corners.

Along with the expansion of chain bookstores was the expansion of "fast bookstores" at the convenience stores.[8] Convenience stores were small so there was room for only books or magazines that had high circulation. Books that were "new, fast, practical, and simple," or "light, thin, short, and small," were sought because they did not take much counter space and they could be easily carried and digested. In 1990, Yen-liu Publishing Company made a breakthrough by cooperating with the 7–11 convenience stores to launch a series of Monthly Good Books, which dramatically increased the publishing company's sales (Li 1991).

In addition to the rise of chain bookstores and convenience stores, the cooperation between bookstores and department stores that began in 1987 contributed to changes in the publishing industry.[9] The industry regards books sold in bookstores that are attached to department stores as "extra" consumption because, in general, consumers do not go to department stores for books. Therefore, the books and magazines that are sold there are mostly entertainment- and leisure-oriented. Foreign magazines and women's magazines (international editions) are also available there (Chang 1996). With these changes in magazine and book outlets, the publishers now raced to produce "individualized, spontaneous, entertainment-oriented cultural commodities" with an emphasis on the appearance of the commodities. The result of this is an overflow of small, delicate books dealing with topics such as astrology, romance, comics, and dream notebooks. Changes in magazine and book outlets also caused the death of "serious" magazines, such as Wen-Hsin, The Human World, and The New Earth Literature in 1990 (Wu 1992). Local women's magazines, under pressure to get immediate attention from buyers at the magazine counters in bookstores or convenience bookstores, changed their cover design to include more sexy women. They also used more high-quality printing, transformed their format to the current standard in the industry, and shifted their content to focus more on fashion, celebrities, and consumer information.

With the changes in magazine outlets, which resulted in the easy availability of women's magazines, the publications came to depend more on individual sales. However, even with the dramatic increase in the number of women's magazines during the 1990s, Chih-Li Evening Daily observes that "there is not much increase in the percentage of women's magazines consumed by female readers." How then could women's magazines flourish in the publishing market if not enough women were buying magazines? The answer is obvious: advertising. The editor of Cosmopolitan clearly explains the significance of advertising in women's magazines:

> In fact, given the high quality of women's magazines, the financial burden is very heavy for the publishers. The fierce competition among different women's magazines forces the publishers and editors to make more investments in bettering the quality of women's magazines. Readers enjoy all the benefits because we cannot raise the price of the magazines.... As a result, advertisements naturally become the life source of women's magazines. (Cosmopolitan February 1990: 2)

About two-thirds of the magazine's income comes from advertising sales. Since magazines are the major media for cosmetic ads, more than 50 percent of the cosmetic ads go to women's magazines. According to Brain, female consumers in Taiwan spend an average of NT$25,390 each year (approximately U.S.$950) on cosmetics; hence there is a rapid growth in cosmetic advertising in women's magazines. For example, in 1992, there was a 15 percent increase in the number of cosmetic ads in women's magazines; in 1993, there was a 22.7 percent increase ("Elle Magazine's Female Consumer Survey on the Booming Cosmetic Market" 1994: 87). This begs the question of how these magazine publishers persuade the advertisers that their magazines have enough readers when circulation and subscription sales remain low.

In Taiwan, the availability of women's magazines in coffee shops, beauty salons, restaurants, teahouses, and rental bookstores makes it easy and convincing for the publishers to claim that their magazines reach a much larger audience than the retail sales demonstrate. This is also the main reason why even the best publications have a hard time building sales to subscribers or to individuals. In addition to the free magazines in public entertainment places, the high cost of women's magazines also drives some women to go to book-rental stores where current magazines, books, and comics can be borrowed for only $2.50 (U.S.) for a copy, instead of spending $7.50 (U.S.) on a copy.

The fact that women's magazines are easily available in these public spaces and the fact that the advertisers believe that women read these magazines in such places indicate that women's magazines have changed from a "domestic entertainment" in the 1970s to a "public entertainment" in the 1990s. In the 1970s, women's magazines imagined their readers to be domestic mothers who stayed at home taking care of the house and children. As a result, women's magazines were considered "domestic entertainment" in the sense that they were about women's domestic duties and were delivered to the home (through subscription) so that a woman could stay home and read women's magazines.

In the 1990s, the "imagined" readers are assumed to be "quality" women who roam around public places of consumption. If, as previously discussed, these "imagined" readers are the twenty to thirty-five-year-old women who are affluent, (mostly) single, metropolitan, and who care about their beauty and youth, their identity as such is grounded in the industry's calculation of their readers' accessibility to women's magazines. Accessibility here is defined as the readers' economic resources to obtain the magazines and their cultural resources to understand the magazines' aesthetic and textual practices, as well as their spatial access to these magazines. The easy availability of women's magazines in cafes, convenience stores, salons, book-rental stores, and chain bookstores is predicated on the image of a female consumer who is college educated, affluent, and mobile. Furthermore, the advertisements and the content in women's magazines also support this idea of a "public" woman whose mobility is extended (or confined?) to these consumption spaces. For example, the ads usually show different fashion items on display at department stores, the information page tells readers where these department stores are, and the special reports encourage the readers to buy these items for a better look that will enable her to find romance in the public space, such as the workplace and restaurants.

Changes in the Rules of Cultural Production

The use of market research, the reliance on advertising as the magazines' main source of support, and the changes in the distribution systems have reconfigured the way cultural workers do their businesses. Previously, women's magazines emphasized the importance of social responsibility as a marketing strategy. In promoting women's magazines as a form of social service, the editors and publishers of women's magazines at this stage also claimed their "disinterestedness," that is, they were there to help women improve their lives, not to earn money for themselves. However, in the 1990s, the rhetoric of disinterestedness was refuted in women's magazines. Instead, it is the recognition of culture as a business that seeks profits that is emphasized. This changing rhetoric indicates that the dominant principle of hierarchizing the "field" of cultural/magazine production is now structured by commercial interests.

French sociologist Pierre Bourdieu's notion of cultural production as a "field" offers a productive way to analyze the power struggles that take place within the realm of cultural production. In Bourdieu's analysis, any social formation is structured by way of a hierarchically organized series of fields: the economic field, the educational field, the political field, the cultural field, and so forth. Each field is defined as a "structured space with its own laws of functioning and its own relations of force independent of those of politics and the economy, except, obviously, in the cases of the economic and the political fields. Each field is relatively autonomous but structurally homologous with the others" (Johnson 1993: 6). The structure of a field is determined by "the relations between the positions agents occupy in the field." Hence, a field is a dynamic concept because "a change in agents' positions necessarily entails a change in the field's structure" (Johnson 1993: 6). Bourdieu points out that each agent in the field will necessarily do things to advance his or her own interests, which will result in the change of the structure of the field. Hence, Bourdieu argues that the field of cultural production is a field of struggles.

As Bourdieu (1993: 35) points out, cultural criticisms offer one productive site to examine how the struggles for power take place because cultural critics "take part in a struggle for the monopoly of legitimate discourse about the work of art." Even though Bourdieu is specifically referring to the field of art production, the notion of power struggles as manifested in the realm of cultural criticism can also be applied to the field of cultural production in general. As Bourdieu says,

> The production of discourse (critical, historical, etc.) about the work of art [and culture] is one of the conditions of production of the work. Every critical affirmation contains, on the one hand, a recognition of the value of the work which occasions it, which is thus designated as a worthy object of legitimate discourse, and on the other hand, an affirmation of its own legitimacy. All critics declare not only their own judgment of the work but also their claim to the right to talk about it and judge it. In short, they take part in a struggle for the monopoly of legitimate discourse about the work of art [and culture]. (Bourdieu 1993: 35–36)

In Taiwan, the debate over the role of women's magazines and the role of cultural workers between the elite cultural critics and the magazine editors provides an entrance to investigate the power struggles in the field of cultural production. From this debate, one can argue that women's magazines have changed from a product of elite culture to that of mass culture and that the pursuit of commercial interests has become the dominant principle in the field of magazine production in the 1990s. To elaborate this argument, let me turn to the cultural battle over the definition of cultural worker in the field of Taiwanese magazine production.

As previously mentioned, with the changing pace of everyday life, changes in the distribution system, and the need for "light, thin, short, small" books, "serious" magazines such as *The Human World* went out of business. Faced with this situation, many elite cultural critics blamed women's magazines for "corrupting" culture and humanity. Wong's "Unmasking Women's Magazines" provides an example of how the elite cultural critics both embraced the rhetoric of anti-economy and excluded women's magazines editors from the category of serious writers. I quote the text at length because the article represented most cultural critics' view toward women's magazines. Published in *China Times* (one of the largest daily newspapers in Taiwan) on January 15, 1990, Wong wrote:

> Let's start by looking at the "mask" of women's magazines. Women's magazines use models, sexy actresses on their covers, making them the objects of women's envy and identification and men's object of desire. As a result, women's bodies are commodified. Inside women's magazines are ads for cosmetics, fashion, and so on. They give us the message that a woman's ultimate concern in life is to have a beautiful face and a slender body. If we look closely at the content of women's magazines, we find that the topics they deal with are all very similar; they only talk about love, marriage, sex, skin care, horoscopes, and food. If these topics really reflect modern women's needs, then we will have to believe that the feminist movements in Taiwan have seriously failed: women's thoughts, ideals, consciousness, and their ability to be independent are still at their "infantile" stage.
>
> Under the guidance of "market segmentation," it is easy for us to see that the editors of women's magazines define women's life as confined in their pursuit of extravagant material life in metropolitan cities. There is no care for suffering human beings, no reflection on the social reality....What this reflects is that women's magazines have now become commercial institutions because all we have there is exquisite advertisements. The overflow of ravishing ads in women's magazines indicates that the function of women's magazines is to stimulate extravagant consumption.
>
> Superficially, you can buy the brandname fashion to show off your social status and to use it as a tool to attract the opposite sex, but these are not women's real needs. The proliferation of women's magazines is a backlash against Taiwan's women's movements. When feminists fight patriarchal social structures for women's liberation and independence, women's magazines, with their numerous readers, only show those "model dolls" who know nothing about improving themselves and the society but who follow fashion. Women's magazines not only fail to instruct women on how to raise women's consciousness and how to establish an equal world for men and women; they also reinforce gender stereotypes and, hence, trap women in their small world.

Implicit in this quote is a dichotomous thinking which divides traditional cultural workers from women's magazines editors and invokes the traditional cultural workers as the exemplar of autonomy from economic interests. Wong simultaneously condemns the magazine editors as having been coopted by commercial interests. The traditional cultural workers enact the mission of bettering the society, care "for suffering human beings," and reflect "on the social reality." On the other hand, the editors of women's magazines accept commercial interests and have made women's magazines the tools of the commercial institutions whose sole purpose is to "stimulate extravagant consumption"; as a result, they contribute to the decline of humanity in general. From Wong's critique of women's magazines, we can see that it is the autonomy from commercial interests that characterizes the role of a traditional cultural worker and the "purity" of traditional culture.

Immediately following the publication of this article, the chief editor of *Cosmopolitan* Wu Li-ping responded by redefining the term of culture and the role of cultural workers. In the editorial in the February 1990 issue of *Cosmopolitan*, Wu retorted:

I felt very sad after reading the article ["Unmasking Women's Magazines"]. In fact, like the author of the article, there are many people who hold the same view toward women's magazines. We call these people "the cultural workers who embrace the spirit of humanities and social consciousness," but they are definitely not the "critics who understand the dynamics of the economy and the direction of cultural businesses."

The number of ads is used to measure the growth of a nation's economy. Our neighbor, Japan, had a growth rate of 13 percent in 1988 and 9 percent in 1989 in their advertisements, and magazines enjoyed the largest growth in advertising. . . . If you walk on the streets of Tokyo . . . you will also find that the pedestrians are all properly dressed and full of energy. Does their mode of dress not reflect their society's cultural and material standard? *The definition of "culture" should not be limited to concerns of human suffering. Culture is about people, it is about people's everyday experiences, human behavior and human relationships. Culture is rooted in the good habits people have in their everyday experiences.* Therefore, in addition to emphasizing "know-how" information, women's magazines should also cover women's everyday-life experiences: They start with caring about and loving themselves, and then they can love others. This is the responsibility of women's magazines.

But we cannot deny that women's magazines are commodities. Because they are commodities, they have to pursue commercial interests (otherwise, how can we survive?). Hence, women's magazines have to find their niche by deciding who their readers are and what content to offer. Women's magazines work with advertising agencies to arrange the best content that is in harmony with the advertisements so that advertisements are not seen as intrusions into the content of the magazines. In order to know the newest market trend, the editors are also constantly investigating what the readers want, so that they can tailor their articles to the readers' preferences. . . .

I want to emphasize again that women's magazines are life magazines and advertisements are the necessary information for living a modern life. . . . Commercials and everyday life experiences are inseparable. . . . Let us view women's magazines from another perspective: "She" is the product of our economy, "she" is closely related to our everyday life experiences, and "she" reflects the heartbeat of our society. Little by little, women's magazines make contributions to educating women about their consciousness for life. Let us reposition women's magazines; let the humanitarian issues go back to the humanities; let women's rights issues go back to women's movements, environmental issues go back to environmentalism, and everyday life issues go back to women's magazines. In this case, we will not confuse the different "natures" of different magazines. (1990: 2)

Wu Li-ping uses four strategies here to defend her magazine's commercial interests and to impose commercial interests as the dominant principle. First, instead of defining the role of the critic as one who carries the mission of moral responsibility and who cares about humanity in general, the *Cosmopolitan* editor "pluralizes" the role of the cultural critic. By using the market rhetoric of difference (market segmentation), she argues that there are different kinds of cultural critics, and "the cultural workers who embrace the spirit of humanities and social consciousness" is only one of them. The editors of women's magazines do not deal with these social issues; instead, they only deal with issues concerning everyday life. However, in another response to Wong's criticism published in March 1990, Wu agrees with Wong's position that the cultural workers' mission entails "social responsibilities." Yet, in this case, she redefines the notion of social responsibility: "Some critics usually condemn women's magazines for not shouldering social responsibilities. But what is the definition of social responsibility? Women's magazines offer women a cultural forum to expand their thoughts and ideas. Isn't this also a form of social responsibility? It's just that we do not talk about social responsibility in that jargon" (Wu 1990: 2). Hence, the readers are informed that there are different types of cultural workers and that no universal standard should be imposed on what the cultural worker should do. Furthermore, even if there is a standard, such as a mission of social responsibility, women's magazines do not fail this mission; rather, it is only that they speak a different language—a language of everyday life—that is distinct from that of the traditional, jargon-spewing cultural elite.

The second strategy that the *Cosmopolitan* editor uses is to redefine the meaning of culture. For Wong, an elite cultural critic, culture is about uplifting humanity. Culture is the domain of the serious. However, women's magazines argue for a kind of anthropological definition of culture: The definition of "culture" should not be limited to concerns on human sufferings. Culture is about people; it is about people's everyday experiences, human behavior, and human relationships. This definition of culture justifies the existence of women's magazines. In addition to redefining culture, in a follow-up article published in March 1990, the editor of *Cosmopolitan* also claims that modern women's magazines should "integrate women's life experiences into women's magazines." The fact that modern women's magazines are the target of scorn is because those "old and stubborn women's magazines cannot step forward and modernize themselves." In this manner, a new dichotomy along the line of modern and traditional is established. The cultural elite's notion of culture as "uplifting the humanity" is now pushed to the realm of tradition (the old and the backward) and the new definition of culture as "everyday life experiences" is now elevated to the realm of the new and the modern.

The third strategy that Wu deploys is to adopt the dominant principle of hierarchization from the field of power (the economy). Unlike the cultural elite who claim their disinterestedness through a rhetoric of social responsibility (a mission that is ostensibly independent of the elite's own material interests), Wu asks readers to recognize the nature of women's magazines as cultural commodities. As commodities, magazines need to follow the dominant principle in the field of the economy; hence, commercial interests are recognized as essential to the survival of the magazine. As Wu asks the readers to recognize commercial interests as the dominant principle of the field of production, she also claims that the pursuit of commercial interests does not necessarily contradict the ideal of "social responsibility" that is traditionally associated with "disinterestedness." The *Cosmopolitan* editor posits:

> We are angry that cultural enterprises have been forced to "give feedback to the society." Why is it that publishing businesses cannot be "interested and idealistic"? It should not be taken for granted that publishing businesses necessarily have to lose money and to "give feedback to the society." We the editors of women's magazines have given what we learn and what we know to the readers through women's magazines. Isn't this also a form of giving feedback to the society? (Wu 1990: 2)

Fourth and finally, the editor of *Cosmopolitan* uses Japan as an example to legitimize women's magazines. By treating the proliferation of women's magazines as a sign of Japan's prosperity, the editor argues that the prosperity of Taiwan depends upon the increase in women's magazines. The reference to Japan or America as a way of authorizing the speaker's position is not specific to the field of cultural production (of either the magazine editors or the elite critics) but is characteristic of other fields in general. It is an ideology deeply embedded in Taiwan's modernization discourses across the cultural, economic, and political fields. Hence, women's magazines also use American critics' comments on women's magazines to discredit the Taiwanese critics' derogatory comments:

> In the West when women's magazines began to thrive, some "well-read" intellectuals, while having nothing to do, found fault in women's magazines. . . . The Second Wave feminist, Betty Friedan, in her *The Feminine Mystique*, pointed out that "[i]n the world of women's magazines there are only marriage, housework, and childrearing. Women's magazines trap women into gender ideologies." However, even though these feminists can deny marriage, housework, and childrearing, they cannot deny their existence because, for most women, these are the sources of their happiness.

The criticisms that our traditional cultural elite made were already talked about [and refuted] in the 1960s America. In other words, those critics who don't read women's magazines but condemn them either plagiarize their ideas from American "intellectuals" or they are just twenty years behind those traditional cultural elite from America. (Wu 1990: 2)

In general, by appropriating the ideology of modernization, editors like Wu appealed to the West and Japan as their sources of power and used this power to undermine the authority of the elite critics. In this debate, women's magazines established commercial interests as the dominant principle of hierarchization in the field of cultural production. The fact that women's magazines' editors won this struggle is evidenced by the death of traditional women's magazines such as *The Woman,* which appealed to a rhetoric of disinterestedness. Since the late 1980s, traditional women's magazines faced many challenges from international women's magazines; as a result, they adopted market research methods, changed their cover girls, and, furthermore, focused more on topics regarding sexuality, fashion, and consumption. However, despite these changes, these magazines still made claims to social responsibility and disinterestedness. For example, in the October 1993 issue of *The Woman*, the editor states: "*The Woman* not only deals with issues that concern the family but also goes beyond the family to include the larger social environments. We present our in-depth analysis to the readers about issues that concern the society and women's life realities" (1993: 36).

However, this rhetoric of social responsibility did not fare well in an intensifying market milieu. A year later, *The Woman* went out of business. In the last issue of *The Woman*, its chief editor lamented the declining standard of women's magazines characterized by their pursuit of commercial interests. *The Woman*, he added, because of its unwillingness to lower its standard and to bend to commercial interests, was forced to go out of business:

Ten years ago, Mr. Chang [the founder of the magazine] died of cancer. However, his insistence on what should be done (to improve the magazine's service to the society) and what should not be done (to surrender to commercial interests) became a good model for all his colleagues . . . Mr. Chang not only taught us to write good articles and edit magazines but also to be a principled person. . . . There were a lot of changes during the past ten years, especially after the lifting of the martial law. Many women's magazines arose like the shooting bamboo after the spring rain. . . . Some packaged themselves with glossy pictures and quality papers, some worked with international women's magazines to get information from other countries while also saving production expenses. . . . It is very hard for us to make it in this competitive market. If we adopt business methods to run this magazine, then it goes against our goal to serve the society. Therefore, we have decided to stop issuing this magazine and to say good-bye, though reluctantly, to our readers. (November 1994: 6)

Contrary to the *Cosmo* editor who insisted on seeing women's magazines as a business, the editor of *The Woman* refused to run a woman's magazine like a business. However, this refusal only led to its own demise. The bankruptcy of *The Woman* seems to indicate, in Bourdieu's words, a change of the dominant principle of hierarchization from the autonomous pole in the 1970s to the heteronomous pole in the 1990s. When discussing the production of art in France, Bourdieu argues that the field of cultural production is a site of struggle between two principles of hierarchization: the heteronomous principle and the autonomous principle. The heteronomous principle favors "those who dominate the field economically and politically" and the autonomous principle favors those who see themselves as independent of the economy. The most heteronomous cultural producers, because of their lack of symbolic capital, are least resistant to the dominant fields of power. They tend to discredit the autonomous cultural workers by defending their own interests through the dominant principles outside the field of cultural production. As a result, by serving their own interests, they also serve the interests of the dominant class. On the other hand, the autonomous cultural workers, while struggling to impose the principle of autonomy through a rhetoric of disavowal of economic interests within the field of cultural production, tend to see the heteronomous cultural workers as "enemy agents." Consequently, they exclude them from the definition of writers or artists.

Despite the editor's espousal of anticommercialism and spiritual uplift, if we further situate *The Woman*'s rhetoric of anticommercialism within the realm of the political and economic fields, one finds that the term "autonomy" cannot be used to characterize Taiwan's magazine production or cultural production in general. The survival of women's magazines before the mid-1980s (especially for *The Woman*, which won several awards) depended in large measure on their promotion of the state's goals including their complicity with the state in building a Chinese nation on Taiwan. More specifically, in the domain of culture, this meant that women's magazines had to make anticommercialism and the uplifting of spirituality their goal because the building of a Chinese nation on Taiwan required the production of frugal subjects and the inculcation of subjects who would look to Chinese culture and tradition as their roots. Hence, while the rhetoric of anticommercialism at first might seem to indicate the magazine editors' "autonomy" from economic pressure in the field of cultural production, it is the product of a particular political (and economic) configuration that predated liberalization. In this sense, with respect to the political field, the field of cultural production in the 1990s is much more "autonomous" than that of the 1970s because the imperative for women's magazines to promote the Nationalist agenda no longer exists. Rather than a shift from autonomy to heteronomy, the production of women's magazines has been regulated by different power mechanisms at different historical periods; and in the 1990s, it is the pursuit of commercial interests that lies at the heart of magazine production.

Moreover, the Taiwanese magazine editors' changing rhetoric (from a repudiation to an espousal of commercial interests) indicates that the better-funded international women's magazines have established a new paradigm, enabled by the changing material basis for what comprises the elite and the middle classes. Bourdieu points out that the field of cultural production is a "universe of belief"; in other words, in the field of cultural production, the critics only preach to the converted. In this sense, the demise of *The Woman* illustrates that the readers of women's magazines no longer believe in the rhetoric of spiritual uplift and social responsibility. Instead, the majority of these readers now believe in the role of magazines as providers of commercial information for everyday life-experiences, as established by international women's magazines. This change in the readers' beliefs can be explained by the changing constitution of women's magazines' readers. Although these magazines have always targeted upper- and middle-class women as their ideal readers, the constitution of the middle class is highly different in the 1970s from in the 1990s. In the 1970s, upper- and middle-class women still constituted a tiny part of the population and women's magazines therefore used a discourse of moral superiority (expressed through the rhetoric of social responsibility) to help these few better-educated people of the society to construct a sense of (class) difference. However, as the middle class rapidly expanded during the late 1970s and 1980s and a consumer capitalism began to take root in Taiwan, taste/style consumption came to replace moral superiority as a defining feature of the middle-class identity in women's magazines. Women's magazines' use of moral superiority and taste consumption has to be situated within a particular logic of the economy of cultural production. Before the mid-1980s, magazines were largely sponsored by subscription sales; hence, a women's publication had to speak to these middle-class women's sense of moral superiority in order to gain their support. However, in the 1990s, it is advertising that constitutes the majority of the magazines' income. Editors are therefore forced to address the affluent "mass" readers in order to sell them to the advertisers. As a result, the editors have to recognize their sponsors' (the advertisers') commercial interests, while at the same time making the claim to offer "service" to the readers; and what they now have to offer to the readers is very different from the discourse of spiritual uplifting in the 1970s.

Conclusion

To conclude, in this essay I have used the internationalization of Taiwanese women's magazines as a way to talk about the changes, and the forces that brought about these changes, in Taiwan's consumer culture. I have identified the political and economic forces that forced Taiwan's internationalization, including the economic restructuring in the 1980s. Areas of liberalization have included the lifting of press restrictions and of restrictions on advertising agencies, and the enforcement of intellectual property rights. These changes made it possible for international women's magazines to emerge in the Taiwanese market. In turn, the advent of international women's magazines restructured the local magazine market. Local women's magazines adopted market-research methods, shifted their content from the spiritually uplifting to that of consumption, and caused the outlook of older magazines for women to be revamped. International women's magazines targeted the "modern" woman, and tended to focus their articles on "self-care," including the maintenance of a certain body image, thereby promoting the beauty products advertised in the magazines. The working woman emerged as an individual who cared mainly about her image, her work, her romances, and her sexuality. The middle-class moral superiority and domesticity dominating the narratives of women's magazines in the 1970s and 1980s were now absent. The family woman that had been the primary figure before is now also transformed into the individualistic, enthusiastic, young single woman who desires a good sexual partner and a good career. The women "designed" in these magazines, like their editors, are devoid of the moral mission to better society by devoting themselves to the family or the society; they now care only about their own pleasure and their personal growth. Thus, the international women's magazines feature mostly entertainment news, cultural activities, consumer information, fashion, and content on women's love and sex lives (which are largely detached from the traditional notion of a family). International women's magazines, as a result of their aim to sell international name-brands, partly construct Taiwan's consumer society by shaping a new cosmopolitan, individualistic female subject whose primary passion is to consume.

Moreover, the field of magazine production, though once conceived as offering social services, has been transformed to a business enterprise. This shift toward cultural production as a business legitimizes the use of marketing strategies such as sponsoring make-up workshops. It also indicates that magazines have changed their identity from a form of elite culture that embraces moral superiority to that of consumer culture, and seeks profit maximization. In addition, the changes in the magazines' systems of income (from subscription sales to advertising) and of distribution (from home subscription to availability in bookstores, convenience stores, and cafes) also reshape the identity of a women's magazine from a domestic entertainment to a "public" entertainment. However, the implications of this change on the redefinition of femininity remains to be explored.

Notes

The author thanks Carol Stabile, James Hay, and Larry Grossberg for their insightful comments on this essay.

1. The agricultural sector, the last frontier of Taiwan's virgin land, is only now opening itself up to global competition due to Taiwan's admission into the World Trade Organization.

2. Since the import substitution industrialization (ISI) period in the 1950s, Taiwan had established high import tariffs to protect local businesses. Even with the changes in economic policies and the opening up of certain sectors to foreign investment, tariffs for imports remained high.

3. McDonald's was the first foreign service industry to test Taiwan's market in 1982. McDonald's success had a tremendous impact on the formation of Taiwan's consumer culture. For example, it shaped the young generation's eating habits; it affected the design and

the nature of food businesses; and it also played an important role in manufacturing the first generation of youth consumers in Taiwan.

4. The precursors of Taiwan's advertising industry can be traced to the ISI period, 1951–60. During the ISI period, in order to promote imported goods, Japan, and, later, Hong Kong, set up offices in Taiwan to advertise their products in newspapers. In 1958, a group of people who specialized in writing advertisements gathered together and formed Eastern Advertising, the first professional advertising agency in postwar Taiwan; it was, however, an industry far different from the current one. Around the same time, Japan's largest advertising agency, Dentsu Advertising, held the first conference on advertising in Asia, aiming to "strengthen the connection among the advertising field in Asia in order to promote economic progress and prosperity of the Asia region" (Freuan 1996). One conference attendee was from Taiwan. The second conference, held in 1960, had five conference attendees from Taiwan. Three of these five attendees formed three advertising companies, the first agency system in Taiwan. In 1961, Japan's Dentsu Advertising set up a branch office in Taiwan. In 1966, the Fifth Annual Conference was held in Taiwan, making advertising a discernible industry. Also, around this time, the United Daily News Group first signed a contract with the advertising agency, making it possible for the advertising agency to exist as an autonomous trade. (Before the late 1960s, there was no separate agency responsible for newspaper ad production. Advertising belonged to the newspaper industry.) In that year, the market's total advertising volume was U.S.$5.35 million (Freuan 1996).

5. Even though cooperative alliances were established between foreign and local agencies, such as Japan's Dentsu with Taiwan's Kuo-Hau Advertising, direct foreign investment was not allowed.

6. Special Treaty 301 was imposed on Taiwan by the United States in the late 1980s, forcing Taiwan to take action to criminalize pirating.

7. Other forces that came to construct teenagers as a consumer category included the emergence of McDonald's, pachinko parlors (computer-video-game stores transplanted from Japan), and MTV parlors (private rooms that show movies on tape, first established in 1986). The establishment of McDonald's in 1984 was the first move to promote the notion of teenagers as a consumer category. The targeted teenagers then, as mentioned, were the first generation in Taiwan to grow up en masse with abundant material goods.

8. The first convenience store, 7–11, settled in Taiwan in the mid-1980s, and rapidly took over the traditional community grocery stores. In 1991 there were more than 1,500 convenience stores in Taiwan. Among these were 594 7–11 stores, 375 President stores, and 88 Circle K stores.

9. Most of Taiwan's department stores are wholly or partially owned by Japanese conglomerates; as a result, bookstores in department stores sell mainly Japanese books and magazines. However, most international magazines are also available.

References

Publications in English

Bourdieu, Pierre. 1993. *The Field of Cultural Production: Essays on Art and Literature*, ed. Randal Johnson. New York: Columbia University Press.

Freuan, Christopher. 1996. "Internationalizing the Pitch" *Free China Review,* Dec. 1996: 30–37.

Gold, Thomas. 1988. "Entrepreneurs, Multinationals, and the State." In *Contending Approaches to the Political Economy of Taiwan*, ed. Edwin Winckler and Susan Greenhalgh, 175–205. Armonk, NY: M.E. Sharpe.
Johnson, Randal. 1993. "Editor's Introduction: Pierre Bourdieu on Art, Literature and Culture." In *The Field of Cultural Production: Essays on Art and Literature*, ed. Johnson, 1–25. Cambridge, UK: Polity Press.
Ohmann, Richard. 1996. *Selling Culture*. London: Verso.
Winckler, Edwin. 1988. "Mass Political Incorporations." In *Contending Approaches to the Political Economy of Taiwan*, ed. Edwin Winckler and Susan Greenhalgh, 63–87. Armonk, NY: M.E. Sharpe.
Yeung, Irene. 1989. "Two That Make a Difference." *Free China Review* (February): 20–24.
Yun, Eugenia. 1994. "A Beauty Bazaar." *Free China Review* (October): 32–35.

Publications in Chinese

Chang, Wen-chun. 1996. "Books Increase the Value of Department Stores." *Central Daily News*. January 1.
"*Elle* Magazine's Female Consumer Survey on the Booming Cosmetic Market." 1994. *Brain* 9: 87.
"An Estimate of the Numbers of Magazines Produced in the Taiwan Area." 1993. *Brain* 210: 14–18.
Hsia, Chu-joe. 1995. "Taiwanese Cities and Society in the Global Economy." *Taiwan: A Radical Quarterly in Social Studies* 20: 57–102.
Kuo, Wen-hua. 1997. "Family Planning in Taiwan from 1950–1970: Medical Policies and Women's Histories." Master's thesis. National Ching-Hua University.
Li, Chuei-ying. 1991. "New Trends in Publishing." *China Times*. April 20.
Lin, Hsiu-hung. 1985. "Segregating the Market: Her Lifestyle."*Modern Management Monthly* (November): 38–49.
Sen, Yi. 1994. "From Intra-Uterine-Device to the Highest Caesarean Section Rate in the World: The Development of Women's Magazines in Taiwan." *FMP Highlight* 21: 7–9.
Wang, Kuo-hua. 1976. "Keep the Chinese Tradition: *The Woman* Magazine." *Publishers' Magazine* 45: 75.
Wu, Chi-wen. 1992. "Annual Publishing Trends." *China Times* January 10.

Taiwanese Women's Magazines (cited)

(*Author's note*: In Taiwanese women's magazines, authors are usually not identified. If they are, they are mostly pseudonyms and are printed in small fonts in marginal places where people cannot see them unless they look for them carefully. Therefore, I have listed the women's magazines under analysis by title.)

References from The Woman

"Readers and Writers." Editorial. 1994. *The Woman* (March): 6.
"Reluctantly Saying Good-Bye to Our Readers." Editorial. 1994. *The Woman* (November): 6.

References from Cosmopolitan, Marie Claire, Elle, Harper's Bazaar, *and* Citta Belle

"Be a Woman Who Loves Her Husband, Children, and Career." Editorial. 1992. *Cosmopolitan* (May): 8.

Brown, Helen Gurley. 1989. "Walking into the World of *Cosmo.*" *Cosmopolitan* (October): 6.

Tsai, Tung-chao. 1989. "Spring Breezes Flow into Metropolitan Taipei." *Cosmopolitan* (October): 2.

Wu, Li-ping. 1990. "The Explosion of Women's Magazines." Editorial. *Cosmopolitan* (March): 2.

———. 1990."We Are Writing Women's History." Editorial. *Cosmopolitan* (August): 4.

8

Should Women Get Equal Pay for Equal Work?

Taiwanese Men's Attitudes in 1963 and 1991

Robert M. Marsh

Some feminists argue that discrimination against women is a result of patriarchy (Hartmann 1976). To sustain this claim, it is necessary to identify the specific elements of "patriarchy" that lead to specific aspects of discrimination. While many feminist studies focus exclusively on women, this essay will deal with the attitudes of men. This makes sense given the theory of patriarchy: Heidi Hartmann's (1976) classic formulation argued that women are kept out of good jobs by a *collusion among men*—as husbands, employers, legislators, and workers. Such a "cartel" or "gentlemen's agreement" is seen as benefiting men as a group at the expense of women as a group.

This essay will first review official government data from the Republic of China on women's earnings as a percentage of men's earnings in Taiwan, and also will provide some comparative data from the United States. Hypotheses will then be formulated to account for (1) stability or change in Taiwanese men's attitudes toward gender pay equality, as measured in two surveys in Taipei conducted twenty-eight years apart, in 1963 and in 1991, and (2) why, in both the 1963 and the 1991 samples, some men favored, while others opposed, equal pay for equal work for men and women. Following the description of the methods and data I will present the findings and discuss their implications.

Gender Wage Differences in Taiwan and the United States

In the United States the Equal Pay Act Amendments to the Fair Labor Standards Act became law in 1963. This act "prohibits employers from discriminating on the basis of sex in setting wages for work requiring equal skill, effort and responsibility and performed under similar working conditions in the same establishment. However, wage differentials based on seniority, merit systems, incentive pay systems, or any factor other than sex are permissible" (Koziara 1987: 379). By the mid-1980s American women "working full-time earn on average about 40 percent less than men who work full-time" (Koziara 1987: 395). This gap narrowed by

An earlier version of this chapter appeared as "Gender and Pay in Taiwan," *International Journal of Comparative Sociology* 39, no. 1 (1988): 115–37. Used with permission.

1990 but women working full-time still earned 29 percent less than men (U.S. Department of Commerce, Census Bureau 1991, table 24). Mean-wage differences between American men and women in litigated equal-pay cases are about 15 percent (Cooper and Barrett 1984).

The earliest available data for Taiwan indicate that in 1973 women on average earned 54.5 percent of men's wages in manufacturing and 71.3 percent in service industry jobs (Cheng and Hsiung 1993). Kenneth Gannicott (1986) reported that women in Taiwan earned only 64 percent of men's earnings in 1982. When he decomposed these gross salary differentials, he found that "Even in the absence of any discrimination, women would still earn only about 85 percent of the male salary. This is because women as a group are far less endowed with productivity-enhancing characteristics" (Gannicott 1986: 724). But he stressed that "men in Taiwan receive a constant premium over the female salary, even for approximately equal work for equal productivities" (Gannicott 1986: 725; for a similar finding in the United States, see Treiman, Hartmann, and Roos 1984). The wage rate of women in Taiwan's Export Processing Zones is set 10 percent to 20 percent lower than that of males employed in similar work (Fitting 1982: 737). Lucie Cheng and Ping-chun Hsiung (1993: 48) found that the ratio of average wages for women compared to that for men in Taiwan in 1988 varied by occupational level—from only 48 percent of men's wages among production workers to 62 percent in clerical work and a high of 80 percent in managerial and administrative occupations.

For 1991, the data in Table 8.1 indicate that average monthly earnings of women as a percentage of men's earnings in Taiwan varied from a low of 60.1 percent among salaried (that is, white collar) employees in manufacturing to a high of 85.3 percent for nonsupervisory personnel in financial and other business service industry jobs.

The focus of organizers of the women's movement in Taiwan, beginning in the 1980s, was mainly on equal pay and work opportunities and shared household responsibilities between men and women (Lee 1991: 219). But the official data summarized here show that the goal of equal pay for equal work for women and men is still far from the reality in Taiwan. There was no law in the Republic of China as of 1994 that requires employers to give equal pay for equal work, but the Council of Labor Affairs has a draft law with provisions for equal pay for equal work and fines for employers with more than thirty employees who discriminate against women when determining salaries, granting promotions, and offering benefits. The draft will have to be deliberated upon by the cabinet and then ratified by the legislature (Chan 1994a: 4).

Hypotheses

Two comparable samples of Taiwanese men living in the city of Taipei, one in 1963, the second in 1991, were asked the identical question about their attitudes toward equal pay for men and women doing the same jobs in the same workplace. Since the analysis of the data will be conducted at two levels, two types of hypoth-

Table 8.1

Average Monthly Earnings of Women as a Percentage of Men's Earnings, by Industry and Status, Taiwan 1991

Industry	Status	Women's Earnings as % of Men's
Manufacturing	All employees	60.6
	Salaried[a]	60.1
	Wage[b]	63.4
Commerce	All employees	70.9
	Supervisors, technical	74.7
	Nonsupervisory	77.2
Services: financial, insurance, real estate, business	All employees	69.7
	Supervisors, technical	66.5
	Nonsupervisory	85.3
Community, social and personal services	All employees	69.2
	Supervisors, technical	64.9
	Nonsupervisory	73.8

Source: Directorate General of Budget, Accounting and Statistics, Republic of China, *Hsin-tsu yu sheng-ch'an-li t'ung-chi nien-pao* 1992 (Yearbook of Earnings and Productivity Statistics, Taiwan Area, Republic of China 1992), Taipei, 1993.

[a]Salaried employees (*chih yuan*) are white collar.
[b]Wage workers (*kung jen*) are blue collar, manual workers.

eses are called for. The first level is the aggregate distribution of attitudes toward equal pay in 1963 as compared with 1991. Any hypothesis at this level should offer an explanation of whether the distribution of Taiwanese males' views on equal pay is expected to change significantly (and in what direction), or not, over the three-decade period. The major change in Taiwanese society during the period, of course, is the massive and rapid economic development, industrialization, and social change on the island. The average annual growth rate in GNP per capita was 8.1 percent from 1963 to 1972, and 6.6 percent from 1973 to 1987 (Council for Economic Planning and Development, hereafter CEPD 1988). Between 1963 and 1989 the labor force in the primary sector (agriculture, and so forth) declined from 49.4 percent to 12.9 percent, while the secondary sector (manufacturing) grew from 21.3 percent to 42.2 percent and the tertiary sector (services, and so on) expanded from 29.3 percent to 44.9 percent (CEPD 1989; Lee 1991).

Unfortunately, theory and research on the influence of socioeconomic development on attitudes toward gender pay equality suggest conflicting hypotheses. On the one hand, modernization theory claimed that the spread of egalitarian, achievement-oriented norms would enlarge women's power by undermining patriarchal control (Inkeles and Smith 1974). Industrialization would bring opportunities for women to find paid employment outside the home, and their integration into the modern labor market (Rosen 1982) should lead to gender pay equality.

Beginning with Esther Boserup (1970) this view was challenged, and the argument that development is actually detrimental to women's status has gained support. Women's integration into the development process has worsened their subordination (Clark 1993). Studies of the development of Western industrialized societies have found that, despite the rapid increase in women's labor force participation, sex segregation in the workplace has been widespread, with women being allocated disproportionately to jobs characterized by low pay (Blau 1984; Acker 1989). What makes the attitudes of men especially relevant to the question of equal pay for equal work is that unequal pay for women may be the result not primarily of their human capital assets but of the structure of labor markets within societies dominated by patriarchal social values. The effects of female marginalization should be especially strong in Confucian societies such as Taiwan (Greenhalgh 1985).

Given these conflicting theoretical expectations, the first hypothesis cannot be proposed with a high degree of confidence:

H1: The proportion of males who favor equal pay for equal work by women will be positively related to Taiwan's level of socioeconomic development; therefore, there will be a significantly higher level of support by men for equal pay for women in 1991 than in 1963.

The second level of analysis is that of the individual respondent. Here, hypotheses must attempt to explain why some Taiwanese men in 1963, and in 1991, favored, while others opposed, equal pay for men and women doing the same jobs in the same workplace. We propose specific hypotheses that may explain men's orientations toward pay. The causal variables are drawn from three domains: objective status, subjective life chances, and kinship. We are especially interested in whether the same variables explain men's attitudes toward pay equality in both 1963 and 1991, or the constellation of causes changed over the twenty-eight-year period.

The first of the objective status factors is *age*. Assuming that older men have more conservative attitudes on the issue of equal pay for equal work, I hypothesize:

H2: Favoring equal pay for equal work for both sexes will be negatively related to age: The younger the respondent, the more likely that he will support equal pay for men and women.

Higher levels of formal education expose an individual to more modern ideas and values; therefore, the hypothesis:

H3: Favoring equal pay for equal work will be positively related to educational attainment.

The effect of education on *women's* attitudes toward pay equity should be even greater than among men. Though we lack Taiwanese women's responses to the equal-pay question, we know there is a high correlation between the educational levels of husbands and wives (r = .78 in the 1963 sample, and r = .75 in the 1991 sample). When a man with more education has a wife who is also relatively highly educated, her views on equal pay may reinforce his positive views, or prod his undecided or negative views in a more pro–equal pay direction. Thus:

H4: Favoring equal pay for equal work will be positively related to the education of the respondent's wife.

Other things being equal, the issue of equal pay may be only abstract or theoretical when a man's wife is not in the paid labor force. When she is working, however, equal pay for her can mean the difference between more and less income, which will affect total household income. Therefore, we hypothesize:

H5: Favoring equal pay for equal work will be positively related to wife's labor-force participation.

Size of workplace—the number of people who are employed at one's place of work—is associated with the degree of bureaucratization of work procedures and rewards (Weber 1968: 956–1005). Larger scale work organizations, more formally bureaucratic, are more likely to institutionalize steps leading toward equal pay for men and women performing the same jobs. Therefore:

H6: Favoring equal pay for equal work will be positively related to the size of one's workplace organization.

Susan Tiano (1987:218) states that "[W]hile capitalist development may provide jobs for women, because its *modus operandi* is the extraction of surplus value to accumulate capital, it jeopardizes women's well being." Employment and ownership status affect one's views on equal pay. Labor costs affect the owners of business firms most centrally. Even if manual and nonmanual employees are indifferent to, or in favor of, equal pay for men and women, bringing women's pay up to the level of men's will affect owners of business firms by adding labor costs, which will cut into their profits. Because this is against the interests of owners of firms, I hypothesize:

H7: Favoring equal pay for equal work will be negatively related to employment-ownership status; that is, owners of firms will be more opposed to equal pay than self-employed people with no employees, and the latter will be more opposed to equal pay than employees.

In addition to the foregoing objective status factors, other, more subjective elements that can be conceptualized as *perceived life chances* are also hypothesized to influence views on gender pay equality. Three measures of perceived life chances will be tested. First, the higher an individual thinks that children of his social class can go in the educational system, the more one sees the educational system as being open. Among Taiwanese who think of themselves as working class, for example, those who believe that children from the working class can compete not only for a high-school but also for a college education see more equal educational opportunity than those who think only a lower level of education is possible. Thus, the hypothesis:

H8: Favoring equal pay for equal work will be positively related to the perceived educational opportunities for children in one's social class.

Hypothesis 8 does not focus on educational opportunities by the *gender* of the children. A stronger hypothesis asserts that the aspirations one has for one's daughter(s)' education should be even more consequential for one's beliefs concerning gender pay equality. To be sure, a man may have high educational aspirations for his daughter(s) for motives other than gender pay equality—such as that higher education can enhance daughters' marriage prospects. However, as more Taiwanese women work both before and after marriage, men who have higher educational aspirations for their daughters are expected to be more likely to favor equal pay for equal work. Those who think their daughters need, for example, no more than the compulsory level of education are hypothesized to be more accepting of lesser pay for women.

H9: Favoring equal pay for equal work will be positively related to the educational aspirations one has for one's daughters.

Having asked respondents how much education they thought was possible for their children and desirable for their daughters, they were asked what they thought about the importance of education for one's standing in the community (Tumin 1961: 89). Can a person expect to have his opinions count in community affairs if he is not well educated? They were asked: "Some people think that one has to have at least a high school education to have his opinions respected by other members of society. Do you agree or disagree?" Those who agree are affirming that education is a requirement for community influence because one's opinions will not be respected if one has not received at least a high school education. The Taiwanese who agree with this view shall be called, here, *elitists*. Whether they favor or deplore this existential situation, they are elitists in the sense that they describe the situation in Taiwan as one in which everyone's opinions do *not* carry equal weight. In contrast, those who disagree with the statement are giving the more democratic view that one does not need considerable education to be listened to and respected in the community. For our purposes, let's call these Taiwanese *egalitarians*: Their perception is that people's opinions are taken seriously regardless of how much education they have. If egalitarianism undermines patriarchal control and enlarges women's power, men with egalitarian views are expected to be more supportive than elitists for gender pay equality.

H10: Favoring equal pay for equal work for both sexes is more likely to occur among Taiwanese who are egalitarians than among those who are elitists.

I also hypothesize that the degree to which a man is involved in the *kinship system* —especially its more traditional aspects of behavior, norms, and beliefs—will affect his views on equal pay for equal work. In the Chinese/Taiwanese context, a high rate of social interaction with extended kin involves what Candace West and Don H. Zimmerman (1987) call "doing gender," that is, playing roles that reinforce traditional gender distinctions and practices. Subscribing to traditional beliefs—for example, that elderly parents should live with their married *son* (not daughter), that people should bear their elderly parents' expenses, and that it is still important for a family to have a *male heir* to "transmit the lineage"—are all hypothesized to predispose a man to the belief that it is "natural for men and women in the same job *not* to receive equal pay." Thus, favoring equal pay for equal work will be negatively related to:

H11: frequency of interaction with extended kin;

H12: the belief that elderly parents should live with their married son(s);

H13: the belief that one should bear the expenses of taking care of one's elderly parents;

H14: the belief that it is important to have a male heir.

The 1963 and 1991 Taipei Surveys

In 1963, I conducted a survey to study social stratification, class and mobility, work, family and kinship, and attitudes toward social issues in Taipei, Taiwan. In the sampling, the universe was defined as male Taiwanese (Minnan, Hakka) household heads between the ages of twenty and sixty-nine, living in Taipei city. Resources limited the intended sample to 500, so mainlander Chinese and Taiwanese women were excluded from the sample; their inclusion would have necessitated controls for gender and ethnicity in any statistical analysis, and this would have quickly led to running out of cases. If "patriarchy" is a general cause of wage discrimination against women, it is defensible to study a sample of males in order to find out why some men oppose, whereas others favor, gender pay equality.

Taipei in 1963 was divided into ten administrative districts (ch'ü), which were subdivided into 447 *li*, and the *li* into 7,391 *lin* (neighborhoods). The stages of the systematic, multistage area sampling were, accordingly: (1) a selection of every eighth *li* in the city after starting with a random number; (2) within the fifty-six sample *li*, a selection of every third *lin*; (3) within the 317 sample *lin*, a selection of every fifth Taiwanese household whose head was male and between twenty and sixty-nine years old. The sampling stages were carried out in the ten district offices (*ch'ü kung so*) where registers are kept for all households. Interviews were completed with 507 respondents.

The 1991 survey used the same interview schedule questions and the same sampling design, but given the twenty-eight-year time lapse, no attempt was made to reinterview the same individuals. Between 1963 and 1991, the size of Taipei's population had grown from 1,027,648 to 2,719,659 and its area had expanded by administrative incorporation of adjacent units from 67 to 272 square kilometers. The percentage of the Taipei population that was Taiwanese rather than mainlander Chinese had risen from 61.7 to 73.1. Taipei municipality by 1991 was divided into 12 *ch'ü*, 440 *li*, and 9,818 *lin*; each *ch'ü* had between 18 and 56 *li*. The study stratified *ch'ü* into those with fewer than thirty *li*, from each of which two sample *li* were chosen, and those with thirty or more *li*, from each of which three sample *li* were drawn. The target sample N for each *ch'ü* was proportionate to the estimated number of Taiwanese households in all of Taipei who lived in that *ch'ü*. Every *nth* household in the sample *li* that had a male Taiwanese head between twenty and sixty-nine years old was selected for the sample. This sampling interval varied across *li* due to variations in the proportion of Taiwanese households. The 545 people interviewed were living in 431 of the 749 sample *lin* in the 34 sample *li*. In both 1963 and 1991, interviews were conducted in respondents' homes by students from National Taiwan University and other local universities.

Having comparable survey data spanning twenty-eight years—a generation—is of great value in the testing of theories about long-run processes of social change.

Variables Included in the Analysis

The dependent variable, gender pay, is measured by responses to the question asked in both the 1963 and the 1991 Taipei surveys: "Here are two opinions about men's and women's wages (*kung tsu*). First, where men and women are working in the same workplace doing the same job, there should not be any wage differences between them. Second, even where men and women are working in the same workplace doing the same job, it is natural that there should be a difference in their wages. Which opinion do you agree with?" For the logistic regression analysis the second response: "It is natural that there should be a wage difference," is coded 0; the response that "there should not be any wage difference" between men and women is coded 1.

By asking Taiwanese men what they thought about pay equality for men and women doing the *same job* in the *same organization*, we sought to remove two important causes of the gross gender pay gap: job segregation by gender and the different gender pay distribution across firms. The remaining opposition to equal pay for women, holding down the constant job and firm, is presumably based on some combination of (1) beliefs that there are differences in productivity-related human capital endowments between the sexes—such as that women work fewer years than men—and (2) a residual factor of "pure discrimination" against women. The independent variables are operationalized as follows:

Objective Status Variables. *Age* is the respondent's age in five categories from twenty to twenty-nine to sixty to sixty-nine years of age. *Respondent's education* is coded in nine categories from 0 years of formal education to 13 or more years. *Wife's education* is coded in the same way. *Wife's labor-force participation* is coded 1 if she was not employed and 2 if she was employed at the time of the interview. *Size of workplace* is the number of people employed at the respondent's place of work, coded in seven categories from 1 person to 101 or more persons. *Ownership status* is the respondent's status as (1) manual or nonmanual employee, (2) self-employed, no employees, (3) employer with one or more employees.

Subjective Life-Chances Variables. *Educational opportunity* is the three-item Guttman scale based on responses to the question, "For people of your social class, is it possible for your children to complete...level of education?" In the 1963 interviews the three levels of educational attainment were six years of school, high school, and university. In the 1991 interviews the three levels were high school, junior college (*chuan k'o-hsüeh*), and university. *Daughter's education* is the level of education the respondent thinks is desirable for his daughter(s), coded in four categories from only primary school to university or higher. *Man's opinion* is based on responses to the question "Some people think one has to have at least a high school education to have their opinions respected by others in society." The three response categories are: (1) disagree, indicating the egalitarian view that respect for one's opinions does not depend on having at least a high school education; (2) undecided; and (3) agree, indicating an elitist view that only people with higher education can expect their opinions to be respected.

Kinship Variables. *Frequency of interaction with kin* is the total number of times during the year prior to the interview that the respondent recalls attending gatherings with extended kin (*ch'in-ch'i*) on such ceremonial occasions as weddings, funerals, birthdays, childbirth, ancestor worship, New Year's and *pai-pai* festivals. Frequency is coded in four categories from (1) 0–2 times to (4) 9 or more times. *Live with son* is based on the question: "After your son(s) are married, do you expect to live with them in a large household?" We refer to "son(s)" because if a Taiwanese has more than one married son, he may live for a certain time with the firstborn, then another, in a rotating pattern, instead of residing with one of the sons permanently. Responses to this question are coded: (1) I don't expect to live with married son(s); (2) to some extent I expect to; and (3) I very much expect to. The next kinship variable, *bear parents' expenses*, is based on the question: "If you don't plan to live with your married son(s), do you expect them to bear a large portion of your living expenses?" Responses are coded in five categories from (1) definitely not, to (5) they must bear my expenses. *Male heir* is a three-category response to the question "Based on the present situation, should a family have a male heir to transmit the lineage?" The responses are coded: (1) not necessary to have a male heir; (2) it's better if there is a male heir; and (3) there should certainly be a male heir.

Results

Table 8.2 indicates that in 1963 more than two-thirds of the male respondents agreed with the "modern" view of "equal pay for equal work," 28.6 percent took the more traditional position that men and women should get different pay, and 4 percent were undecided. Frankly I was surprised that in 1963 *so many* Taipei men opted for gender equality in pay. But I was even more surprised to see that, after twenty-eight years of development, there was no significant increase in the view that men and women should get the same pay for the same work (tau c = .05). It is as if Taiwanese attitudes in this area had reached a plateau of relative moderniza-tion by 1963, above which they have not moved in the subsequent three decades. Thus, in 1991 there continued to be one-quarter of the sample who rejected the idea of equal pay for equal work.

In both 1963 and 1991, interviewers recorded the comments some respondents made to clarify their support for or opposition to equal pay for equal work. The overall impression one gets from these "reasons" is that basically the same repertory of arguments was being drawn upon in 1991 as had been used in 1963. No radically new justifications for why women should (or should not) get the same pay for the same work were put forth, again, despite all the profound changes that had occurred in Taiwan since the early 1960s. Let's quote some of the given reasons.

In both 1963 and 1991, the most common reason given by the respondents for why men should be paid more than women in the same job can be summarized as *society puts the main obligation to support the whole family on men, not on women.* Comments such as "women can rely on their husbands for their main living ex-penses" and "women only work for extra money" were typical here. A second common justification for unequal pay can be summarized as *in manual jobs, women can never match men in physical strength and endurance*: for example, "a man's work is heavier."

A third type of reason for opposing equal pay, in both 1963 and 1991, was that *women can't devote themselves to work as totally as men do.* As one 1991 respon-dent put it: "I approve of equality of men and women. But in fact, women can't do extra work at night; they have to go home on time in order to take care of their family, and it's dangerous for them to go home late at night after work." Others said: "When a woman gets married and has children, her 'equal pay for equal work' can't last" and that "women have more social intercourse and appointments than men."

Women's lesser efficiency, ability, and intelligence on the job were all a fourth type of reason advanced for their lower pay. One respondent even articulated a view that economists would call the lesser human capital–investment women on the average have: "Men and women have a different number of working years."

Other miscellaneous reasons why women should not be paid as much as men were: "Pay women less because they squander more money on clothes than men"; "a woman gets more pay if she has a baby, but men don't, so women unfairly get

Table 8.2

Taiwanese Men's Attitudes Toward Equal Pay for Women, Taipei Samples, 1963 and 1991

When men and women do the same job in the same workplace, do you think:

	1963	1991	Total
Women should get less pay	28.6	24.2	26.3
Undecided	3.8	2.8	3.3
Should be no difference in men's and women's pay	67.6	73.1	70.4
	100.0	100.1	100.0
N	507	545	1042
	(ns) tau c = .05		

more"; "many job conditions of men and women are too dissimilar." A summary of the thinking expressed in the several types of reasons reviewed in this essay was given by a 1991 respondent when he said: "Women can't do the same work as men. The sexes are different."

The majority of respondents in both 1963 and 1991 positioned themselves as in favor of equal pay. The main types of reasons for this view were as follows. First, pay should be based on various universalistic achievement grounds other than gender—education, intelligence, ability, skill and efficiency, effort, seniority. If women are equal to men in these respects, these men believe they should receive the same pay in the same jobs. (It should be noted that some of these same reasons were used by men who *opposed* equal pay: For them it was clear women are not equal in skill, efficiency, and so on, and therefore they do not deserve the same pay.) One 1991 respondent who favored equal pay for women went on to qualify his ideas: "But women have a lot of limitations. We should not simply make a law that there should be 'equal pay for equal work.'" In contrast to this, another 1991 respondent backed up his conviction that there should be equal pay for women with this articulate gloss: "We must move away from the shadow of feudal society and seek justice."

Note that the reasons given by some of these male Taiwanese who oppose equal pay for equal work by women take for granted the very things feminists have questioned. For example, on the average, women's human capital–productivity is lower than men's because women have higher absenteeism from work and more interruptions in their work history. But the reason for this is that child care and other household responsibilities fall disproportionately on women.

On the face of it, the hypothesis that gender pay equality is part of a modernized mind-set and will become a more common attitude as economic development and modern social change occur is not supported in the Taipei case. Equal pay for equal work is, to be sure, the attitude of more than two-thirds of the sample, but this attitude has not spread more widely among the Taiwanese *despite* the changes since 1963 in education and other modernizing factors that are supposedly conducive to a belief in equal pay for equal work. In rejecting hypothesis 1, it should be noted that its opposite hypothesis, that women's position *worsens* during development, is also not supported: The respondents are not significantly *more* opposed to equal pay in 1991 than they had been in 1963. Let's now turn to the remaining hypotheses that attempt to explain individual support for versus opposition to equal pay for men and women.

At the bivariate level, not all of the independent variables are significantly correlated with attitudes toward pay in both 1963 and 1991, but all of the significant relationships are in the hypothesized direction. Age, ownership status, elitism, and involvement in the kinship system have negative relationships with support for equal pay, whereas respondent's and wife's education, educational opportunities for children and for daughters, and size of workplace have significant positive relationships with equal pay for women.

To explore the effects of each independent variable on pay equality when other variables are held constant, logistic regression analysis is used. Table 8.3A presents the analysis for the 1963 Taipei sample. The dichotomized dependent variable is first regressed on the objective status variables; then the subjective life-chances variables are added to the causal model, and finally the third block of independent variables—the kinship domain—is entered into the model. At the beginning, all thirteen independent variables are used in both the 1963 and 1991 samples' analysis, regardless of whether the zero-order correlation was significant or not. Because respondent's education and wife's education are highly collinear we estimate two alternative equations, one with respondent's education, omitting wife's, and the second with wife's education, omitting respondent's education.

Consider first the unstandardized logistic coefficients for the two alternative sets of objective-status variables. In both alternatives, size of workplace has the hypothesized positive effect on equal pay; respondents in 1963 who worked in organizations with more personnel were significantly more likely to favor equal pay for men and women than those Taiwanese who worked alone or with only a few other people. In model 1A, respondent's education has the expected significant positive net effect on equal pay, but wife's education has no significant effect in model 1B when the other objective status variables are held constant. In neither models 1A nor 1B do age, wife's labor-force participation, or ownership status have a significant net influence on the log odds of favoring equal pay. The measure of goodness of fit of each model is the X^2 for the −2 log likelihood; specifically, the difference between this value for the model with only the intercept and that for the model with all the covariates. The log likelihood ratio $(L_a - L_b / L_a)$ indicates the *degree of improvement* of fit of the model with the covariates compared to that for the model without any covariates.

Table 8.3A

Logistic Coefficients for Regression of Attitudes Toward "Equal Pay for Equal Work" on Selected Independent Variables, Taipei Taiwanese Males, 1963

Independent Variable	Model 1A	Model 1B	Model 2	Model 2A	Model 3	Model 3A
Age	−.180	−.184	−.183	−.230		
Education	.139**	.114*	.171**	.023		
Wife's education.		100				
Wife's labor-force participation	−.270	−.245	−.149	−.260		
Size of workplace	.135*	.151*	.112	.102		
Ownership status	.101	.129	.030	.081		
Educational opportunities		.058		.144		
Daughter's education		.072		.172	.269**	
Man's opinion		−.244	−.272*	−.315*	−.390**	
Frequency with kin					−.215	−.288**
Live with married son				−.242	−.443**	
Bear parents' expenses				−.042		
Male heir					−.227	
Intercept	.469	.633	.796	.757	2.872	2.548
Log Likelihood Ratio[1]	.046	.037	.056	.043	.078	.066
N	391	390	370	479	339	428

* = p < .05; ** = p < .01.
[1] L_a-L_b/L_a, where L_a is the likelihood of the model with only the intercept and L_b is the likelihood of the fitted model.

The log likelihood ratio is higher for model 1A (.046) than for model 1B (.037). Model 1A, with both respondent's education and size of workplace significant, fits the data somewhat better than model 1B, in which wife's education is not significant and size of workplace is the only significant objective-status variable. Henceforth in the 1963 analysis we shall use model 1A rather than model 1B.[1]

When the subjective life-chances variables are added to the objective status variables, only the respondent's education has a significant net effect. None of the three life-chances variables exerts any significant net effect. This conclusion can be modified, however. Starting with the full set of covariates in model 2, one non-significant covariate was dropped at a time, using the criterion of the highest p-value, or the covariate farthest from the .05 level of significance. Covariates continued to be dropped until an equation was reached in which each "surviving" covariate had a significant net effect. This yielded model 2A, in which respondent's education has a significant positive net effect, and the elitism of a "man's opinion" has a significant negative net effect on pay equity. In other words, Taiwanese men in 1963 who favored equal pay were more likely to have had more education and to have been egalitarians (who believe a man's opinion is respected regardless of how much education he has). The irony here, of course, is that Taiwanese men with less education are more likely to be *elitists* who, in effect, report that *their* opinions are *not* respected because of their lower education; both these factors predispose them to oppose equal pay for men and women.

The next step in the 1963 analysis is to add the four kinship variables to the two earlier blocks of covariates. Model 3 examines the combined effects of objective status, subjective life chances and kinship involvement on attitudes toward equal pay for men and women. In the full version of model 3, only one of the twelve covariates—the elitism of a man's opinion—has a significant effect net of the other variables. As before, elitists are more likely than egalitarians to oppose equal pay for equal work for men and women.

We again deleted one nonsignificant covariate at a time until a model was reached in which each of the remaining independent variables had a significant net effect. This yielded the more satisfactory model 3A, in which three other variables in addition to "man's opinion" have significant net effects. The more education one hopes his daughter(s) can get, the more likely one is to favor equal pay for men and women. The more frequently a man attends ceremonial gatherings with extended kin, and the greater his expectation of living with his married son(s) in his older years, the more likely he is to think it is "natural" for women to be paid less than men. All four of these significant effects support the hypotheses, and together model 3A provides the most parsimonious best fit with the 1963 data (log likelihood ratio = .066).[2]

Consider now Table 8.3B, which presents the same analysis for the 1991 Taipei sample. The collinearity between the education of respondents and that of their wives again requires us to estimate separate models 1A and 1B for the objective-status variables. There is little difference between the results of models 1A and 1B.[3] Ownership status is the only variable with a significant impact on attitudes toward equal pay, net of age, respondent's (or wife's) education, wife's labor-force participation, and size of workplace. As hypothesized, Taiwanese who are employers are more opposed to equal pay for women than are the self-employed with no employees and employees. Despite the much higher level of wives' labor-force participation in the 1991 than in the 1963 sample, this variable has no significant net effect on men's attitudes toward women's pay.

When the subjective life chances are added to the objective status variables, in model 2, ownership status continues to have a significant negative effect; net of this, the educational opportunities variable has a significant positive effect. This means that the more opportunities one perceives for the educational attainment of children of one's social class, the more likely that one favors equal pay for men and women. Controlling for these variables, none of the other status or life-chances

Table 8.3B

**Logistic Coefficients for Regression of Attitudes Toward
"Equal Pay for Equal Work" on Selected Independent Variables,
Taipei Taiwanese Males, 1991**

Independent Variable	Model 1A	Model 1B	Model 2	Model 2A	Model 3	Model 3A
Age	−.212	−.189	−.180	−.231*		
Education	.019	−.024		−.111		
Wife's education	.026					
Wife's labor-force participation	−.035	−.046	.020		.005	
Size of workplace	−.095	.096	−.109	−.126*	−.139*	−.159**
Ownership status	−.127*	−.125*	−.142*	−.136*	−.174**	−.140*
Educational opportunities		.637*	.726**	.653*	.647*	
Daughter's education		.166		.110		
Man's opinion	.183	.318*				
Frequency with kin		.058				
Live with married son		−.620**	−.441**			
Bear parents' expenses		−.040				
Male heir		−.246	−.333*			
Intercept	2.365	2.287	−.293	.535	1.757	1.776
Log Likelihood Ratio[1]	.018	.017	.031	.036	.095	.071
N	448	449	403	468	385	451

* = $p < .05$; ** = $p < .01$.
[1] $L_a - L_b / L_a$, where L_a is the likelihood of the model with only the intercept and L_b is the likelihood of the fitted model.

variables at first appears to exert any significant net effect. But once again, dropping one nonsignificant covariate at a time yields a model (2A) in which not only ownership status and educational opportunities, but also age and size of workplace have a significant net effect. As hypothesized, older Taiwanese are more likely to oppose equal pay for men and women, but contrary to the size of workplace hypothesis, the more people who work at the respondent's workplace, the *less* likely he is to favor equal pay for equal work. We shall return to this unexpected finding later.

In model 3, the kinship variables are added to the model. At least one covariate from each of the three domains has a significant net effect on pay attitudes. Three variables have significant negative net effects: size of workplace, ownership status, and the expectation that one will live with married sons each increase the log odds that one opposes equal pay for men and women. Controlling for these effects, educational opportunities, as before, have a significant positive effect, but, surprisingly, the elitism/man's opinion variable has a positive effect, rather than the hypothesized negative effect. In other words, controlling for the other variables in model 3, it is elitists, who believe a person's opinion isn't respected unless he has at least a high school education, not egalitarians, who are more likely to favor equal pay for equal work. How robust is this apparent reversal of signs for the elitism variable—from a significant negative effect in 1963 to a significant positive effect in 1991?

Because model 3 has a number of nonsignificant variables, it is not parsimonious. When one nonsignificant variable at a time is dropped until a model is reached in which all surviving variables have significant net effects, we arrive at model 3A. As in model 3, size of workplace, ownership status, and live with married son continue to have significant negative effects, and educational opportunities have a significant positive effect on attitudes toward equal pay. Apart from this, there are two differences in model 3A compared to model 3. The elitism/man's-opinion variable becomes nonsignificant and is replaced by the kinship variable, male heir, which has the hypothesized negative effect on pay attitudes. The apparent reversal of signs for elitism can be dismissed from further consideration. The fit of model 3A, assessed by the log likelihood ratio of the fitted model to the model with only the intercept, is .071.

Discussion

In summary, the level of support by Taipei men for women's equal pay for equal work did not change significantly between 1963 and 1991, despite the rapid economic development and societal modernization that occurred. The situation was not that men's support for equal pay was absolutely low in 1963, and remained low in 1991; rather, two-thirds of the Taiwanese men in the survey already expressed support for equal pay as early as 1963. What is surprising, therefore, is that this level of support did not increase to a significantly higher level three decades later. The fact that an actual earnings gap continues between men and women in similar industries and job statuses in Taiwan was documented in Table 8.1. As has been shown for the United States, the Taiwan findings suggest that there is an enduring gender gap in wages that is not rapidly eroding, contrary to neoclassical economic theory. Furthermore, a substantial portion of this gap in the United States cannot be explained by gender differences in skills, experience, and effort, but instead is tied to the devaluation of work done by women (Paula England 1992). The same is probably true in Taiwan, but more research on this point is needed. McCormack (1981: 18) has suggested that instead of eliminating patriarchy, the development process may simply modernize it. Gender-based differences in pay, net of skills, experience, and effort would be an example of a "modernized form of patriarchy."

The second main finding is that although the *level* of men's support for equal pay did not significantly change between 1963 and 1991, the *causes* of this support did change in a number of ways. The study started with a common set of hypothesized independent variables in the domains of objective status, subjective life chances, and kinship. Yet the results of logistic regression analyses—the best fitting and most parsimonious models—have only one independent variable significant in both 1963 and 1991: Expecting to live with married son(s) in a three-generation household increased the odds of a man's opposition to equal pay for equal work. Apart from this one common causal effect, the causes of attitudes toward pay differ as between 1963 and 1991:

Causes of Men's Attitudes Toward Equal Pay for Women:
(sign indicating direction of effect)

Best model in 1963		Best model in 1991	
Daughter's education	+	Size of workplace	−
Elitism/man's opinion	−	Ownership status	−
Interaction with kin	−	Educational opportunities	+
Live w/ married son(s)	−	Live w/ married son(s)	−
		Male heir	−

In 1963 the characteristics of men who agreed it was "natural" for women to get less pay than men were: they did not think it was desirable for their daughter(s) to get much education; they were elitists in that they saw people's opinions not being respected if they didn't have at least a high school education; they interacted frequently with their extended kin; and they looked forward in their later years to coresidence with their married son(s) in a patrilineal extended household. Taiwanese who favored equal pay for women had the opposite characteristics.

Those who opposed equal pay for women in 1991 had a highly different profile. They worked in large-size organizations; they were business owners who employed others; they perceived educational opportunities for children of people in their social class as restricted; they expected to live with their married son(s); and they held to the traditional Chinese patrilineal preference for a male heir, a son who would "transmit the lineage."

Among these variables with significant net effects, all but one have effects in the hypothesized direction. Owners of firms with employees are more opposed to equal pay for women than are the self-employed and those who work as employees. This is consistent with the neoclassical economic explanation that "employers with 'tastes for discrimination' against women will hire women workers only at a wage discount that is sufficiently large to compensate them for the disutility of employing women" and "even if employers themselves have no tastes for discrimination against women, profit-maximizing behavior by employers may result in sex discrimination" (Blau 1984: 118).

Perceiving greater educational opportunities for the children of people in one's social class is hypothesized to make a man more favorable to equal pay for women because such a view of education indicates a more expansive sense of social possibilities, which in turn has an "elective affinity" with support for expanding women's pay to the level of men's. By the same token, men who have high expectations for their daughters' education may see it as socially inconsistent for their daughters, and other women, to be paid less than men when they enter the labor force, and this may be the reason they are more likely to favor equal pay for equal work.

In the final or best model, the elitism of a man's opinion has the hypothesized negative effect on attitudes toward equal pay only in the 1963 sample. The theoretical link suggested is that Taiwanese who are elitists in the sense that they think people's opinions are taken seriously only if they are the opinions of the educated extend their elitism to the question of women's wages, and come down on the side of unequal wages for women. Egalitarians on the subject of respect for the opinions of the less educated, on the other hand, favor equal pay for women because this is consistent with their egalitarianism.

As for the kinship variables, our hypotheses are clearly confirmed. One may prefer high rates of social contact with extended kin (as contrasted with a more exclusively nuclear family orientation, or freedom from kin ties so that one can pursue friendships and personal interests). One may for economic reasons depend on living with married son(s) rather than a more self-reliant pattern in later life. And one may cling to the traditional Chinese core element of the kinship system—the necessity of having a male heir to transmit the patrilineage. Whatever the causes and reasons Taiwanese men hold these "traditional" kinship views, the study's findings suggest that the *consequence* of this is that it makes a man believe it is "natural" that women should receive less pay for the same work. In other words, whatever the intrinsic value of extended kinship ties and traditional kinship beliefs, *to have them is to be more likely to oppose equal pay for equal work.* Recall that the one variable with a significant net effect in both 1963 and 1991 is the expectation of living with one's married son(s). Implicit in this may well be this reasoning: "Because my economic situation in old age will not permit my wife and me to live by ourselves, I must depend on living with my married son. This is an added burden he faces, from which my married daughter(s) are relieved. Doesn't it make sense, therefore, to think that even if my daughter (and Taiwanese women in general) works, *she doesn't need the same level of pay as my sons* (and men in general)?"

This finding comes as no surprise to feminist writers who explain gender pay inequality on the basis of the combined effect of patriarchy and capitalism. Capitalism, surely a dominant force in Taiwan, used preexisting patriarchal relations—systems of male domination—to accelerate its capital accumulation. Women's oppression originates in the household, the primary locus of patriarchal relations that assign women largely to reproductive roles. This patriarchal division of labor benefits capitalism, for women's unpaid domestic labor and childrearing activities reproduce the labor force at minimal cost. Even though Taiwanese women now have fewer children than in the past, their historical reproductive role continues to condition the terms of their participation in paid production. Considered subsidiary wage earners whose primary responsibility is to husband and home, they are relegated to insecure, poorly paid positions seen as extensions of their reproductive roles. Their childrearing duties and ambivalence about their role as wage earn-ers cause them to function as a surplus labor reserve, to be drawn into or expelled from the workforce according to the system's labor needs. Their primary role as mother and wife, in the view of men, is then used by men to justify their receiving less pay for the same jobs.

The one variable whose significant effect is in the opposite direction than that hypothesized is size of workplace. Drawing upon Weberian thinking, I argued that larger organizations in Taiwan, as elsewhere, are more bureaucratized, and, as such, institutionalize more universalistic rules concerning reward systems. Bureaucratic organizations in theory do not differentiate pay on the basis of gender. But the facts in the Taiwan data are otherwise. When size of firm is significant—in 1991—its effect is negative, not positive. Employees in larger organizations are more opposed to equal pay for equal work than those in smaller organizations. One can only speculate which of many possible explanations may account for this unex-pected finding. It may be that bureaucratization in the relatively few large organi-zations in Taiwan has not yet proceeded to the point of equalizing pay for men and women. Official data for 1991, as seen in Table 8.1, though not broken down by size of firm, continue to show women's earnings to lag behind men's. Alterna-tively, it may be that Taiwanese men working in larger organizations perceive women in similar jobs catching up with them in pay and react negatively.

When the foregoing significant independent variables were held constant, sev-eral other hypothesized causes of gender pay attitudes were found to have no sig-nificant additional net effect. Our data suggest that in neither the 1963 nor the 1991 Taipei samples did a man's age, education, or his wife's education and labor-force participation exert any significant effect. These negative findings are impor-tant, for they identify what apparently does *not* shape men's ideas concerning women's pay. Older and less educated Taiwanese are not significantly more op-posed to equal pay than their younger and more educated counterparts. And though the wives of the respondents were in general significantly more educated and more engaged in paid work in 1991 than in 1963, neither of these changes had any significant net effect on men's thinking about women's pay.

It is clear that the minority of Taiwanese male respondents who oppose equal pay for women use somewhat circular arguments. Women's lower human-capital investment (fewer years of work experience, less on-the-job training, and so forth) is "explained" on the basis of their patriarchally defined greater responsibility for children and home activities. Though some women may seek jobs that do not require long training periods because they do not want lifelong involvement in the labor force, many other women face employers who engage in *statistical discrimi-nation* (Blau 1984). Women are seen by employers as *on average* less committed to uninterrupted employment in the firm than men. Therefore, *all* or *most* women hired by firms with an internal labor market are assigned to segregated jobs for which there is little investment in on-the-job training, as women are seen as too risky for such investment in training by the firm. The latter then produces the deficit in human capital that causes women to earn less than men. As Taiwanese women become more fully and continuously involved in the labor force, however, these circular arguments will be harder to sustain.

This does not mean that the elimination of the female/male pay gap in Taiwan is just a matter of time. To be sure, much of this pay gap is due to occupational segregation by gender. But even if it were possible to eliminate all occupational segregation, this would not eliminate the gender pay gap. Francine D. Blau (1984) contends that reducing segregation might lead to even more discounting of female wages, as women would be moving more into traditionally "male" jobs. That would arouse stronger discriminatory tastes on the part of males. Previous research has shown that average occupational earnings vary inversely with the proportion of women in the occupation (Treiman and Terrell 1975). Therefore, men facing the entry of more women into "their" occupations run the risk of either reduced pay— as employers equalize pay by lowering men's, rather than raising women's pay— or, even worse, loss of their jobs altogether, as women are substituted for men.

Conclusion

By asking Taiwanese men what they thought about pay equality for women doing the *same jobs* in the *same organizations* as men, we tried to remove two important sources of the gross gender pay gap: job segregation by gender and the different gender distributions across firms in different market sectors of the economy. The remaining actual gender pay differential in Taiwan and the resistance against equal pay for women by between one-third and one-quarter of Taiwanese men in 1963 and 1991 are both a function of (1) real and perceived differences in productivity-related human capital endowments of men and women in the same jobs and the same firms, and (2) the residual factor of "pure discrimination" against women. These two sets of factors, of course, are not analytically independent; some of the human capital investment/productivity differences between men and women are themselves the product of earlier discrimination against women.

Notes

1. All the equations in Table 8.3A were run using the wife's education rather than the respondent's education. Her education was never significant net of the variables already shown to be significant in Table 8.3A, and the best model is identical to model 3A in Table 8.3A.

2. An alternative model, not shown, finds age to have a significant negative effect, along with the negative effect of man's opinion, frequency of interaction with kin, and expectation of living with one's married son. But this model has a lower log likelihood ratio (.060) than model 3A, and when age is added to model 3A, its effect is nonsignificant net of the effect of man's opinion, daughter's education, interaction with kin, and live with married son. Thus model 3A has the best fit.

3. Using models with wife's education rather than respondent's education in 1991 did not change any of the results shown in Table 8.3B. Neither the wife's nor the respondent's education ever had a significant effect on attitudes toward gender pay, net of the other

variables. In the interests of space, therefore, only the equations with respondent's education are shown for models 2, 2A, 3, and 3A in Table 8.3B.

References

Acker, Joan. 1989. *Doing Comparable Worth: Gender, Class, and Pay Equity*. Philadelphia: Temple University Press.

Blau, Francine D. 1984. "Occupational Segregation and Labor Market Discrimination." In *Sex Segregation in the Workplace: Trends, Explanations, Remedies*, ed. Barbara F. Reskin, 117–43. Washington, DC: National Academy Press.

Boserup, Esther. 1970. *Women's Role in Economic Development*. New York: St. Martin's Press.

Chan, Venny. 1994a. "Proposed Law Promises Equality in the Workplace." *Free China Journal* (March 25).

———. 1994b. "Women's Rights Advocates March Against Sexual Harassment Tolerance." *Free China Journal* (May 27).

Cheng, Lucie, and Ping-chun Hsiung. 1993. "Women, Export-Oriented Growth, and the State: The Case of Taiwan." *Taiwan: A Radical Quarterly in Social Sciences* 14: 39–76.

Clark, Alice W. 1993. *Gender and Political Economy: Explorations of South Asian Systems*. New York: Oxford University Press.

Cooper, Elizabeth A., and Gerald V. Barrett. 1984. "Equal Pay and Gender: Implications of Court Cases for Personnel Practices." *Academy of Management Review* 9: 84–94.

Council for Economic Planning and Development, Republic of China. 1988, 1989. *Taiwan Statistical Data Book*. Taipei.

England, Paula. 1992. *Comparable Worth: Theories and Evidence*. New York: Aldine de Gruyter.

Fitting, George. 1982. "Export Processing Zones in Taiwan and the People's Republic of China." *Asian Survey* 22, no. 8 (August): 732–44.

Gannicott, Kenneth. 1986. "Women, Wages, and Discrimination: Some Evidence from Taiwan." *Economic Development and Cultural Change* 34, no. 4: 721–31.

Greenhalgh, Susan. 1985. "Sexual Stratification: The Other Side of 'Growth with Equity' in East Asia." *Population and Development Review* 11, no. 2: 265–314.

Hartmann, Heidi. 1976. "Capitalism, Patriarchy and Job Segregation by Sex." In *Women and the Workplace: The Implications of Occupational Segregation*, ed. Martha Blaxall and Barbara Reagan, 137–69. Chicago: University of Chicago Press.

Inkeles, A., and D.H. Smith. 1974. *Becoming Modern*. Cambridge: Harvard University Press.

Koziara, Karen S. 1987. "Women and Work: The Evolving Policy." In *Working Women: Past, Present, Future*, ed. Karen S. Koziara et al., 374–408. Washington, DC: Bureau of National Affairs.

Lee, Bih-hearn. 1991. "State and Socio-Economic Development in Taiwan, 1950–1989: The Transition from Early Industrialization to Postindustrialism." Ph.D. dissertation, Temple University.

McCormack, T. 1981. "Development with Equity for Women." In *Women and World Change: Equity Issues in Development*, ed. N. Black and A.B. Cottrell, 15–30. Beverly Hills, CA: Sage.

Rosen, Bernard. 1982. *The Industrial Connection: Achievement and the Family in Developing Societies*. Chicago: Aldine.

Tiano, Susan. 1987. "Gender, Work, and World Capitalism." In *Analyzing Gender: A Handbook of Social Science Research*, ed. Beth B. Hess and Myra Marx Ferree. Newbury Park, CA: Sage.

Treiman, Donald J., and Kermit Terrell. 1975. "Women, Work and Wages: Trends in the Female Occupational Structure Since 1940." In *Social Indicator Models*, ed. Kenneth C. Land and Seymour Spillerman, 157–99. New York: Russell Sage Foundation.

Treiman, Donald J., Heidi I. Hartmann, and Patricia A. Roos. 1984. "Assessing Pay Discrimination Using National Data." In *Comparable Worth and Wage Discrimination*, ed. Helen Resnick, 137–54. Philadelphia: Temple University Press.

Tumin, Melvin M. 1961. *Social Class and Social Change in Puerto Rico.* Princeton: Princeton University Press.

U.S. Department of Commerce, Census Bureau. 1991. *Money Income of Households, Families and Persons in the United States: 1990.* Current Population Report, Consumer Income, Series P-60, no. 174. Washington, DC: U.S. Government Printing Office.

Weber, Max. 1968. *Economy and Society*, ed. Guenther Roth and Claus Wittich. Berkeley: University of California Press.

West, Candace, and Don H. Zimmerman. 1987. "Doing Gender." *Gender and Society* 1, no. 2: 125–51.

9

Carousing and Masculinity

The Cultural Production of Gender in Taiwan

Avron Boretz

For many, perhaps most men in Taiwan, an evening of entertainment in the company of friends or associates entails a set of behaviors, interactions, and self-representations that, while they may vary slightly from place to place—from south to north, foothills village to urban downtown—are nevertheless remarkably stable in composition across Taiwanese cultural space.[1] I first propose that there are seven elements that frame this activity as a particular field of social practice and cultural production (and in rough order of necessity): eating, drinking, sexual play, singing, betel nut chewing, gambling, and smoking. These elements are the constituent features of reciprocal entertaining, or *ying-ch'ou* in Taiwan. Although I touch upon all of these elements in the course of this essay, my analysis here will focus on two of these activities, namely drinking and singing, and on the production and performance of gendered identity—specifically, male identity—that attends each in turn.

Carousing and Masculinity

Ying-ch'ou is a term so plainly idiomatic that most Chinese references simply gloss over its common, familiar usage as "social intercourse in general." Starting with classical usage, *ying* often lends to a phrase with the sense "responsively/ actively attend to." *Ch'ou* appears early in the Chinese written record, although it is missing from extant archives of oracle bone and bronze-vessel inscriptions. The term first appeared, most likely, in the late Spring and Autumn period (770–476 B.C.E.) or in the early Warring States period (475–221 B.C.E.), although in reference to feasting rituals that date back to the early Chou dynasty (1027–771 B.C.E.). *Ch'ou* refers specifically to the third round of drinking during a formal gathering or feast. Following this protocol, a host (in the superior position) poured the first round (*hsien*) for his guests, leaving his own cup unfilled until the guest(s) reciprocated in the second round (*tsu*). For the third, or *ch'ou*, round, the host filled his own cup and then entreated his guests to join him in continuous drinking.

Breaking down the ritual to its constituent parts, the first two rounds are a comple-

171

mentary pair comprising initiation and completion. The priority of the host's invitation formalizes the hierarchical relation between host and guest. By serving his guests and leaving his own cup unfilled, however, the host qualifies his role qua host: that is, although he takes the uppermost position, he gives freely of his wine and hospitality (incurring, of course, the obligation to reciprocate).[2] The third round brings the ritual to completion (although the second round "completes" the exchange, it does not fully encompass the relationship thus established, and thus, a third, "exiting" or "returning" round is required) and initiates informal sociality. Anyone, host or guest, may invite or entreat anyone else to drink from this point on.

Whether or not to respond to an offer or toast then becomes a matter of situational judgment rather than ritual obligation. This allows those who can't hold their liquor to excuse themselves, but it also signals an opportunity for the remaining guests to engage in competitive drink-play. The *ch'ou* round, which marks the transition from formal ritual to informal sociality, is reproduced in the requirement that a host first serve his guests and await a reciprocating toast before spontaneous, mutual toasting can begin. What follows the initial toasts is by no means a free-for-all; rather, as anyone who has participated in a banquet in China or Taiwan can attest, drinking after the first round continues to follow protocol. However, the choice of whom to toast, and when to do so, follows implicit rules rather than explicit ritual prescription, and is contingent on the relative status of the participants. One set of protocols, however, obtains throughout any banquet or carousing session: The host urges his guests to drink (*chu ch'uan k'o*), guests respectfully toast their host (*k'o ching chu*), and guests urge each other to drink (*k'o hsiang ch'uan;* see Kuo 1990 [1989]: 235). This protocol still characterizes most feasting and other social drinking wherever variants of Han Chinese culture have taken hold, including Taiwan.

In the compound *ying-ch'ou,* then, *ying* and *ch'ou* can be understood as near-equivalents, the compound yielding a reinforced sense of "attending to and responding to" according to conventional social expectation and the protocols of hierarchy. In this sense, the dictionary glosses are accurate, if uninformative. In both ancient and modern usage, the compound *ying-ch'ou* characterizes practices that marry the symmetry of reciprocal gifting and feasting with the asymmetry of social and political hierarchy. *Ying-ch'ou* may refer to social interaction in the abstract, but in everyday conversation it most commonly refers to a particular field of social practice, namely the cycles of gifting and feasting through which informal social networks are produced. Such networks—those "based on personal, particularistic bonds and taking the form of a network of variable dyadic relations" (DeGlopper 1995: 38)—have been described most extensively in recent ethnographic literature on *"kuan-hsi* networks" in the People's Republic of China (Huang 1998: 143ff.; Kipnis 1997; Yan 1996; Yang 1994) and Taiwan (DeGlopper 1995; Weller 1987).[3]

Ying-ch'ou here comprises one domain within the process of configuring hierarchical relations of power among men in public social space. By extension, then, we can posit that *ying-ch'ou* in its various manifestations is a field of representation upon which relations of domination are enacted, contested or negotiated, and reproduced.[4] Indeed, in both interviews and casual conversations, many of my informants have suggested that "carousing" and related practices are indispensably part of the process of making and affirming both emotional and political connections, competing for status, and—within their local and extended social groups as well as in the more abstract sense of a shared cultural logic—confirming themselves as men.

The sorts of reciprocity that characterize *ying-ch'ou* serve to reproduce *particular* sorts of hierarchical relationships. In the cases I deal with here, the hierarchy is neither fixed nor explicitly denoted, but rather fluid and negotiable. Competition is implicit in these acts of greeting, entertaining, contest, and struggle—whether formal, as in the mutual greeting and testing of boundaries and skill by temple procession troupes, or mundane, as in negotiating or acknowledging relative status in competitive drinking. This competitive ethos underlies the creative negotiation that takes place amid these rituals. As simultaneous private and public contests are waged for position and "face" (*mien-tzu*), the danger of conflict both within and between groups simmers perpetually just below boiling point. Alcohol can severely exacerbate the mood, especially when a preexisting personal or political vendetta is added to the mix, and the party sometimes ends violently, even tragically. Fortunately, however, conflicts, if and when they do arise, are usually resolved peacefully, often recognized and avoided before they are able to rise to the surface. I have left aside episodes of open conflict and violence and focused instead on actions and events that more closely conform to the expectations and experience of "average" actors and "normal" events.

The drinking and feasting practices of the ancient Chinese nobility are reproduced, in a fashion, in the rounds of reciprocal feasting and entertaining that dominate social and political life for most men in Taiwan. The most significant parallel is the ritual ambiguity of the *ch'ou* stage. In dispensing with the formalities of hierarchical obligation and reciprocity embodied in the first part of the drinking ritual, "real" obligation and reciprocity—and the corresponding positions of individual actors—can be meaningfully enacted. It is in the liminal space of drunken play—that is to say, "carousing"—that the characteristic qualities of Taiwanese manhood are produced. Here the internal moral quality of "righteous honor" (*i*) is materialized (actualized as *i-ch'i*) in an enactment of prowess that calls up the collective representations of an epic world of myth. True righteousness is manifested not in the mechanical reproduction of rules in ritual, but rather in the spontaneous evocation of a righteous spirit that displays a mastery of social propriety and a *sense*—that is, a deeply intuitive understanding and consequent embodiment—of righteousness or other markers of masculine character (cf. Bourdieu 1977:10–15).

Although *ying-ch'ou* may involve everything from intimate gatherings to large, public events, carousing is the affair of small groups out on the town. By "carousing" I refer specifically to what Taiwanese men often call *chhit-tho,* roughly equivalent to the Mandarin *wan-shua* or *yu-wan* (to play, enjoy recreation).[5] The form of recreation called *chhit-tho* in this context is associated, significantly, in many people's imaginations with a set of masculine archetypes in Taiwan, including both the knight-errant swordsman and the gun-toting gangster. Though drawing on many sources, from Chinese classical outlaw literature to postwar Japanese media representations of the *yakuza* and Hong Kong gangster movies, the gangster archetype in Taiwan is generally understood to be a man from the economic margins who is loyal to the death (to his sworn brothers); for whom "face" and honor are everything; and whose survival and position rest squarely on mastery of the games of competitive reciprocity. There are at least two primary, and somewhat contradictory, types of gangster as described/imagined in popular media. One type is a loyal organization man driven to climb the "corporate ladder" (gang hierarchy) through cultivating relationships and playing his scripted role: displays of honor and prowess that instill fear and inspire respect. His ambition is to one day become a wealthy, powerful "big brother" or godfather, who, despite the social marginality of the criminal, is yet a successful, respected man, a husband and father, as well as patriarch of his fictive lineage. In this he lays legitimate claim to the fulfillment of his filial duty to bring honor to his lineage, just as any man who achieves power and reputation.

The knight-errant type, on the other hand, is a freelancer who operates outside the institutions of patriarchy and lives free of the economic, moral, and behavioral constraints of both official and domestic authority. Whether they are aristocratic, carefree wanderers like the poet Li Po or the Seven Worthies of the Bamboo Grove, martial heroes like Wu Sung, or modern free-agent assassins like Chow Yun-fat's "John" in *The Killer,* they all find inspiration in drinking and fellowship.[6]

In Taiwan, where resistance to external coercion is intrinsic to the island's historical identity, the most popular representation of the knight-errant myth is a wandering, socially alienated loner filled with impossible desire and driven by frustration to act beyond the law. As evoked in many Taiwanese films, television serials, and pop songs about life on the "rivers and lakes," as well as dramatized confessions and biographies of famous gangsters, an outlaw either fades away in anguished loneliness or goes out in a blaze of violent glory. He is generous but ruthless, fearless but driven by inner demons, obsessed with revenge and private justice. The outlaw of martial arts legend and pop song is an outcast.[7] Strong, melancholy, independent, women are drawn to him, yet he resists temptation, maintaining a strict boundary of self, retaining possession of his body and emotions.

The myth of the gangster (anti-)hero serves as an important part of the Taiwanese masculine imagination.[8] It is not, however, its totality. Rather, the myth comes to life for most men when carousing with their "brothers of the path"; singing songs full of wanderers' angst; drinking and gambling without regard to win and loss; showing loyalty and honor through generosity and standing with friends in case of threat; defending family honor; and displaying the proper balance of social dominance, sexual desire, and emotional control in his relations with women.

Manhood here is thus constituted out of contradictory qualities: As sons, beholden to their fathers (including fictive fathers, those who stand in positions of power and authority) and elder brothers (including fictive brothers), Taiwanese men are expected to unquestioningly accept their subordination to their elders' authority and the collective interest. The desire to empower themselves must be repressed until such time as the responsibilities of fatherhood and family leadership fall upon their shoulders. Then, and only then, can they wear the mantle of authority and enjoy the advantages of power due to all legitimate representatives of the social order. But young men, if they have any prospect at all of emerging as men of position and prestige, must endure a long wait during which the central marker of their social subjectivity is that of subjection and obedience. The frustration this engenders cannot be expressed openly without directly challenging those who currently own the claim to authority. The knight-errant or outlaw, then, belongs to a mythology of resistance and rebellion that represents desires that could not otherwise be expressed. The archetypes of this mythology include both the man of prowess, the mature, gifted, and skilled strategist or warrior; and the mischievous, capricious, rebellious male child who confounds, embarrasses, and upturns the social (patriarchal, for example) order by manifesting his individual desire openly and to excess.[9] Competitive, capricious, even violent action fulfills the desire, so clearly represented in myth, to transcend, if not to overtly break the bonds of filial obligation.

Both of these collective representations—one of self-mastery and dominance, one of self-indulgence and rebelliousness—are frequently performed by one and the same social actor during a single carousing event. For instance, Ah-lang, an office worker in Taichung and part of a group of high-school classmates who had become sworn brothers (all engaged in legitimate professions and with no connection to the underworld or illegal activity), seemed to particularly enjoy going beyond the limits of propriety in his interactions with hostesses. On several occasions I saw him almost get bounced from the premises of four or five different karaoke (or "KTV") clubs when, either really drunk or feigning sloppy intoxication, he would inappropriately and repeatedly grope a hostess. Yet even in this state of infantile indulgence, he was also the first to notice when others were losing control. He would intervene if things got too dangerous. If an exchange of words with another group began to escalate, for instance, Ah-lang would step in to calm the storm. If one of his friends was too drunk to drive, he would hide that friend's car or scooter keys and offer him a ride home. Some might consider this intervention a mode of "feminine" behavior—ke-pho or p'o-p'o ma-ma-teh, literally "acting like an old housewife." But as the eldest among (sworn) brothers, Ah-lang was obligated and expected to take control in these situations. His friends did indeed respect and respond to his claim of seniority, while overlooking or tolerating his sophomoric tendencies.

This changing of roles is perfectly understandable and perceived as normal at the level of practice, even if the roles or qualities performed seem logically or structurally incompatible. This case manifests the dialectic between symmetrical and complementary elements of subjectivity. Thus when drunk and in the company of friends who are in control of the situation, Ah-lang could act playfully aggressive toward females. Ah-lang played out his own sexual insecurities through the combative sexual symmetry between men and women, but safely within the idiom of what is understood by all to be a complementary, interdependent relationship between male customers and female hostesses. Later on, if and when his "younger brothers" lost control, the protective isolation from public (including family) consequences disappeared, and Ah-lang could move quickly into the role (again, complementary relative to his brothers) of protector and authority figure. Ah-lang's behaviors, appearing in sequence and under particular circumstances, did not entail any sort of contradiction, did not fix a permanent identity in their minds, nor did one behavior negate or de-legitimize the other.

Carousing is usually a matter of public social play, and, accordingly, happens at one or another public venue.[10] In Taiwan, as in many of the cosmopolitan, urbanized cultures of East Asia, entertainment is a big and highly visible business that constitutes an important aspect of, and in some cases is one of, the main creative engines of popular culture. The variety, scale, and creative design of entertainment establishments are dizzying, but here I am concerned with a certain subset of these establishments, namely, those whose main business is to satisfy the needs of small groups of carousing men. Generally these establishments are enclosed spaces like karaoke clubs, piano bars, teahouses, and restaurants. The public nature of the activity fosters a certain social permeability: In chance encounters new bonds and connections can be spontaneously created or redefined, thus changing the composition, size, and reach of the in-group over the course of even a single evening. The public nature of carousing also offers the opportunity for conspicuous performances—of social savvy, intelligence, loyalty, "righteousness," for example—that serve to create or enhance a position within the group and a reputation beyond it. Yet reciprocal entertaining and the carousing that accompanies it is almost invariably a practice of small groups. Carousing creates intimacy within the group and fosters a strong, if temporary, resistance to the intrusions of uninvited others.

An evening of carousing typically involves visits to several venues, with a fairly predictable though generally unplanned pattern of movement among the various types of establishment. For groups of friends and associates who meet regularly, there is often a default meeting location, often a restaurant. Many evenings of carousing begin unplanned at the default location where, more so than later in the evening, the composition of the group is flexible and roles—especially those of host and guests—remain ambiguous.

After a few rounds of drinks and food—during which even casual drop-ins from other tables are greeted with a full glass and a pair of chopsticks—the party begins to take shape. The decision to move on depends, in part, on the hour and the group's stage of intoxication. If the conditions are right—that is, if there is a critical mass with the will, energy, time, and cash to continue—the conversation turns to choosing the next location. Whether it turns out to be a nightclub, piano bar, or someplace else, it is nearly certain that there will be some form of public singing, probably in the form of karaoke. This form of entertainment, in which the partygoers perform for each other rather than being serenaded by professional musicians sets modern carousing apart from past practice. Yet the long tradition of courtesan performers continues in the form of senior hostesses, who are expected to possess both superior looks and skills and to perform a karaoke song or two for wealthy (and favored) customers and important guests.

I limit my descriptions in the following pages to some of the individuals and groups I encountered or worked with during several periods of field research in Taiwan, varying in duration from between three months to two years, between 1988 and 2000. I describe, in distilled form, observations during participation in carousing sessions in the cities of Taichung and Taitung. I describe specific actions and utterances of actors for whom carousing requires a major investment of time and labor. I cannot say with certainty what motivates each of these individuals to engage in carousing activity. It is fair to suggest, however, that for most it is not a matter of uncontrollable compulsion (although that may figure into the equation for some) but, rather, a combination of individual calculation (vis-à-vis social networking and self-construction) and collective (often unquestioned or unarticulated) expectation that impels them to participate.

My observations are mostly culled from visits to two kinds of establishment: upmarket KTV clubs in Taichung that are frequented mostly by middle-class urban businessmen, and more "proletarian" karaoke bars in Taitung whose clients range from off-duty soldiers (mostly draftees from the local air force base) to hometown gangsters. The most innovative and spectacular exponents of the "classier" style of nightclubs and bars, including KTV parlors, are in Taichung, from which many of the fads and fashions of Taiwanese popular culture seem to emanate.[11]

A Brief History of Taiwanese KTV

The streets and alleys that branch off Taipei's Lin-sen North Road are brightly lit by the neon signs of nightclubs, restaurants, hostess bars, massage parlors, barbershops, coffee shops, and guest houses. For much of the twentieth century until the mid-1980s, this area was the entertainment district favored by foreigners—first the Japanese colonials, who cut and paved the street that later became Chung-shan North Road; then the U.S. military (at the north end of the area around Shuang-ch'eng Street, near the U.S. military headquarters and the American Officers' Club), and later still, Western and (more frequently) Japanese businessmen and tourists.

Karaoke—now the sine qua non of entertainment establishments in Japan, Taiwan, Hong Kong, mainland China, and expatriate Chinese communities from Southeast Asia to North America—made its first, modest appearance in Taiwan in a few bars in the Lin-sen North Road area sometime in the early 1980s. Taiwanese cultural and linguistic affinity with Japan was particularly strong in this area, especially in the 1970s and 1980s, when the area thrived on Japanese tourism and Japanese business connections. Indeed, at the time, Japanese was the second language of many of the area's proprietors, bar hostesses, prostitutes, and street merchants.

Since its first appearance on the island sometime during the 1980s, karaoke has become a ubiquitous feature of *ying-ch'ou* and carousing in Taiwan. Karaoke, particularly the "follow the bouncing ball" video machine that has become the hallmark of modern karaoke technology (KTV)—has brought about important changes in carousing behavior. Karaoke literally automates the entertainment, putting control of the performance into the hands of the audience (in the form of a remote control console) and turns the guests into auto- (self-) entertainers. Nevertheless, despite changes in aesthetics, there is a notable continuity in the "poetics" of carousing from the pre-karaoke days to the present. Modern-day carousing consists of modes of interaction and self-presentation that were a large part of Ch'ing-era practice, and carousing most likely has been developing since the medieval period in China. Musical performances and drinking games were essential features of the literati carousing tradition, for instance. More recently (and locally), customers who frequented the P'ei-t'ou district's nightclubs and brothels in the 1940s and 1950s often sang along with the itinerant musicians who stopped in on their nightly circuits.

What keeps karaoke clubs in Taiwan in business is their provision of the proper sort of space and amenities that meet the basic requirements of Taiwanese-style entertaining. Like the wine shop depicted in medieval Chinese poems and knight-errant novels, the bars, dancehalls, nightclubs, and teahouses in post–World War II, pre-karaoke Taiwan also provided wine, women, and song to their clientele. These elements were necessary for the rituals of status competition, the negotiation of power among cohorts, and the presentation of the self that was and is the real provenance of these establishments.[12]

The karaoke machine itself is a Japanese conception, a product of local Japanese popular culture. Popular legend has it that the first karaoke was "hacked" together in a small bar in the Japanese port city of Kobe in the 1970s. At the time, such small bars in Japan (and Taiwan) that were too small for a full band often featured a single pianist or guitarist who would entertain the guests with currently popular songs and requests; patrons would often sing along. When the owner of this particular Kobe bar found himself without a musician for one week, he patched together pop music tapes through the bar's sound system (which included an inexpensive mixer used by the guitarist), filtered out the voice track, and thus created the world's first "empty orchestra."

The earliest karaoke machines were little more than cheap, solid-state boom boxes with a simple, built-in two-channel mixer. Not long after the introduction of the audio-only technology, the wide popularity of MTV-style music videos (in both tape and laser disc formats) led to the development of video karaoke, which provides both atmospheric visual narrative and follow-the-bouncing-ball-style song lyrics.

Although the association of drinking, singing, and showing off in front of friends may be close to a cultural universal, karaoke was a by-product of the popular culture that thrived during the Japanese "bubble economy" of the 1980s. The first karaoke bars to open in Taipei followed the Japanese model—after all, they were installed primarily to attract Japanese customers. Once planted in Taiwanese cultural soil, however, Japanese karaoke began to undergo a process of localization. By the mid-1980s karaoke clubs featuring large rooms, dance floors, and modest light shows were popping up along Lin-sen North Road. By 1988, Taiwan's karaoke clubs had evolved from sparse, simple, cozy Japanese-style hole-in-the-wall clubs to large, lavishly decorated nightclubs with gaudy, neoclassical façades and modern, cosmopolitan interiors. They had also spread well beyond the entertainment districts of the urban centers and tourist resorts to smaller cities and market towns throughout the island.

The true indigenization of karaoke, however, began with a Taiwanese adaptation of the Japanese "karaoke box," which in Taiwan became the now-ubiquitous KTV. The name "KTV" is derived from "MTV," or "movie TV," a generic term borrowed, of course, from the American cable-TV purveyor of rock music videos. In the early 1980s, video parlors with private viewing rooms sprung up in towns and cities all across Taiwan. Most featured small, private viewing rooms (*paohsiang-shih*) decorated with sofas, coffee tables, television, and a VCR or laserdisc player, and quickly became popular with privacy-starved young couples.[13] Immensely popular in their time, by 1990 the MTV phenomenon in Taiwan had almost completely succumbed to U.S. government pressure to curb copyright piracy. The "something-TV" term stuck, however, and thus the term's application to any commercial establishment adopting the private, enclosed-viewing-room concept. MTV gave way to HTV ("hotel TV," or love hotels, with tiny bed-and-porno-movie-equipped cubicles) and KTV. Accompanying the foreign-exchange–fueled stock market boom of 1987, Taiwan experienced an explosion of karaoke/KTV clubs during the late 1980s.

Most KTV clubs in Taiwan have since followed a single architectural formula: Each sports a complex of video-karaoke rooms that can accommodate from four to as many as twenty guests and hostesses, with a computer-controlled selector box in each room.[14] This arrangement of space—private rooms for high-status or high-paying customers branching off a single, large hall for common guests—has a long cultural history.[15] The way space is divided in a karaoke club, and the kinds of activity that take place within this divided space most closely resembles teahouses, tearooms, and wine shops of an earlier era.[16] The tenacity of this architectural mode and its correlation with certain cultural forms and modes of social behavior implies, if not entails, the operation of a higher-level cultural process.[17]

At their most innocent, karaoke clubs are spaces for conventional expressions of comradeship and courtship. There are certainly many "family-oriented" karaoke clubs, as well as establishments that do not explicitly serve or exploit the sexual libido of their customers. However, such establishments occupy a small niche, and, until quite recently, represented an insignificant fraction of the Taiwanese KTV industry.[18] At the other end of the spectrum, some KTV parlors are little more than brothels that provide a place for customers to ritually drink and croon before heading off with their hostess companions to the nearest hotel or guest house.

Most karaoke clubs in Taiwan (and, increasingly, in the PRC as well), however, fall somewhere in between G-rated family entertainment centers and commercial sex establishments. Moreover, as primary sites of male-centered carousing, these clubs are not simply purveyors of sex as a directly exchangeable commodity. Rather, karaoke clubs and similar entertainment establishments in Taiwan function as part of a more complex cultural process, in which sex (most often as the anticipation or aura of sex) is one signifier among many comprising the symbolic matrix through which status, honor, and manhood are presented and contested. Each of the elements of successful entertainment, alone and in combination, provides a public, actional context for the expression and production of male subjectivity. In turn, these actional contexts are predicated on a particular ethos of masculine identity and behavior.

On the Town

What, then, makes drinking and karaoke singing essential to modern-day carousing? I will show that there is an operational logic that links particular forms of carousing practice to general cultural models and desired outcomes that make up the production of male subjectivities and men's identities.

Competitive drinking in the Taiwanese mode, then, is both a performance and a trial: a performance of both physical and moral prowess, on the one hand, and a test or trial through which an individual measures and judges his own capacities, social intelligence, and "fortune," on the other. How an individual comes to be in possession of good fortune or praiseworthy characteristics is always a topic of debate; it may be due to good *feng-shui* or a reward for past deeds or devotion to a deity (Sangren 2000), but no matter what the perceived cause, success in any endeavor or activity that involves risk and competition assigns particular moral attributes to particular individuals as well as revealing the operation and structure of the sociocosmic forces themselves. Even when attributed to the possession of inborn qualities, it is believed that particular cosmic forces (with or without karmic causation or moral purpose) have come together to produce the manifest social effect. Such a metaphysical underpinning, moreover, provides a firm ideological foundation for the system of relative social prestige, as well as for the ranking of any individual within the social grid at any particular juncture.

What struck me first when I was initially invited to participate in nights of carousing in Taiwan was the absolutes of gender and age divisions. A carousing group is almost always exclusively made up of men who, more often than not, are close in age, social position, and economic status. Groups are fluid: Participants filter in and out of them on both a given evening or occasion to occasion. Once a group is constituted on a given evening, it may move from place to place. Most party locales provide the company of female hostesses as part of their service; yet the women generally do not become part of the carousing party. If the group does move on *en masse,* it is only (and usually all) the men who move. Women, of course, are necessary participants in carousing and in hostess clubs; for instance, they do have some measure of choice (which expands with their status and seniority within the establishment) about when and with whom to join in singing and drinking. But their participation is nevertheless limited by their primary role, which is to create an atmosphere of sexual possibility through which customers individually experience a desired sense of their own masculinity and define themselves, through shared enjoyment but also a sense of shared threat, as collectively male.

Social drinking among Taiwanese men, of whatever class and occupation, is driven by a symmetrical competition of appetite and capacity. Yet as descriptions of public feasting in Taiwan and China establish, and my own observations affirm, feasts and carousing sessions are critical moments in the reproduction of the status hierarchy, as well as a prime opportunity for an individual to establish his position or to reposition himself on the hierarchy. Such public self-presentations are also rife with social danger, and relative status can be gained or lost. The symmetry of competition rests upon the complementarity of social relations. One's identity and social position are under constant self-review, whereas the underlying power matrix reproduces whatever status an individual may occupy at a given juncture. Drinking performance is thus important for both the individual construction of masculine selfhood and the collective production of male subjectivity.

The act of men drinking together in Taiwan brings to the fore a specific set of expectations and behaviors. The enjoyment of drinking for Taiwanese men includes the pleasure of intoxication and the experience of camaraderie. However, the dominant expectation is not a pleasant physical sensation, but, rather, the trial of appetite, capacity, and social ability.

The competitive ethos of drinking is hardly disguised. The outward form of Taiwanese drinking practice consists, in large measure, of elements of traditional Chinese "alcohol culture" (*chiu wen-hua*) along with aspects of Japanese "alcohol culture." Drinking "protocols" (*chiu ling*) and "regulations of the goblet" (*shang cheng*) that describe drinking games and drinking etiquette date at least to the T'ang dynasty (Kuo 1990 [1989]: 185), and possibly are even more ancient (Huang 1999: 71–73). The language of these protocols, borrowed from or, perhaps later adopted into, popular discourse, mirrors the rhetoric of military and political combat: Drinking requires both courage (*chiu tan*) and capacity (*chiu liang*); one participates in a "drinking battle" (*chiu chan*), drinks as a penalty/punishment (*fa chiu*); and engages in "alcohol duels" (*tou chiu* or, more commonly in Taiwan, *p'in chiu*). Social drinking opens up a space for ordinary men in the midst of their everyday lives to perform as mythical warriors, knights-errant, and other heroes of popular tradition. Embodying such collective representations through *ying-ch'ou* practice, men can and do experience and express a self full of such readily identifiable masculine qualities. Carousing in Taiwan must be understood (in part) as a proving ground for masculine identity, a prosaic practice bound by a poetic mythos of courage, valor, and prowess.

To illustrate, I recount here the events of a typical evening of carousing in Taichung in the fall of 1989, and two extraordinary, but representative, carousing sessions in Taitung about two years later. In Taichung, I often was invited to join a group of friends who had been high-school classmates and later had become sworn brothers; Ah-lang, who appeared at the beginning of this chapter, was the eldest among them. At that time, they were all either white-collar workers or entrepreneurs in their mid-twenties.

On this particular evening we met at about seven-thirty at the Pirate Ship (Hai-tao ch'uan), a beer-house built in the shape of an eighteenth-century European sailing vessel. The owner's son belonged to this group, so the restaurant was a frequent starting place for an evening of carousing. By nine P.M., the table was crowded with plates of seafood and beer mugs in various states of emptiness. Cigarettes and betel nuts (pin-lang, pin-ng), offered around in turn by each individual, punctuated the rounds of eating and drinking. There was no formal ritual of host filling the guests' cups; rather, waiters brought full mugs of beer to the table. But the ritual principles of reciprocity and sociality were carefully observed as every gulp of beer, preferably at least a half-mug at a time, came in response to the urging of one or another of the group: Sometimes someone toasted a particular friend, sometimes another exhorted the group to drink as one. As drinking came to predominate over eating, a few rounds of drinking games (hua ch'üan) began.[19]

This sort of drinking in a spirit of friendly competition among comrades or business associates can be seen at any restaurant table just about anywhere at any time of day throughout China and Taiwan. When drinking with friends one affirms the mutual bond by drinking with abandon; to do otherwise would be to imply that present company are not "true friends."[20] Drinking on cue without hesitation conveys a shared pleasure of intoxication. Moreover, continuing to acknowledge a host or guest, even when enduring the discomfort of too much alcohol, affirms the importance of the relationship. A refusal to drink is a rejection, a slight. Among friends, and when women are present, such behavior is often met with mock collective indignation, derision, and a "fine" of "drinking penalty wine" (ho fa-chiu/ lim hoat-chiu). In a situation where the participants are not all familiars, or where existing tensions have been dissolved by intoxication, such slights, perceived or intended, can and often do induce angry, even violent responses.

Back to the Pirate Ship: At about ten o'clock, the suggestion was made that we retire to another location. A number of alternatives were mentioned—we decided to check out the Pyramid Club, a new KTV parlor just down the block. In this case, there was no need to drive. We ambled across one side street, up the stairs, and through the faux-bronze door. We told the Pyramid's hostess who greeted us that we were all shareholders of the Pirate Ship, a restaurant that, of course, she knew well. One member of the group asked directly for assistant manager so-and-so. Our credentials were good enough to put us at the top of the waiting list, and soon we were led from the atrium, through a lowly lit, black marble central bar area, to a private room opening onto a second-floor balcony. The room was typical of this sort of establishment: a carpeted space about twelve by twenty feet, a large-screen TV at one end, plush leather sofas on three sides, a low glass tea table in the center. The entire wall dividing the room from the corridor was made of frosted glass etched with half-clad female figures in a style that vaguely evoked classical Rome or nineteenth-century Paris. We took our seats, close enough to reach for proffered cigarettes and betel nuts, and far enough apart to accommodate the young female "drinking partners" (*p'ei-chiu, phoe-chiu*) who arrived a few minutes later.

Busboys appeared periodically to wipe up the tables, serve drinks and food; my friends addressed them (according to modern KTV custom) as *shao-yeh* (which has about the same connotation as the French *garçon*) in imitation of customers in late imperial teahouses and wine shops. The order for a bottle of Hennessey XO cognac was given indirectly, however. This was done through a young woman who arrived before the others, exchanging business cards with each of us in turn. The woman who performs this greeting and intermediary role is an "assistant manager" (*fu-li*). Assistant managers tend to be a bit older, more experienced, and sometimes better educated than those working as "drinking partners." The management lends face to the customers by sending in a high-status hostess to greet the customers, while the *fu-li* can assess the guests for the establishment and, in some cases, for herself. Thus low-status males are provided basic amenities, while the higher-priced and more specialized transactions (the drinks and hostesses) are handled, discreetly, by a female intermediary. This protocol is observed more strictly in places with high-class pretensions, but the pattern obtains pretty much across the whole spectrum of clubs.

The cognac arrived, and the assistant manager poured and toasted each of us in turn. After our glasses were refilled, two more women arrived. The women took their seats by two of the revelers, and invited them to drink. When conversation ran out, the drinking games began. The men challenged each other, as they had done earlier at the beer hall, but here the main interaction was between the men and the women. Soon the songbooks came out and musical numbers were chosen—perusing the song lists and choosing songs together with a "drinking partner" creates an opportunity for intimacy, or at least the illusion of intimacy.

Generally the men try to maintain a show of reserve and sobriety—demonstrated, in part, by superior skill in the drinking games. As the evening wears on, those less skilled or on a losing skid end up drinking more and more "penalty wine" and have to work harder to maintain the appearance of holding their liquor. On this occasion, every round of brandy was "bottoms up," and after a few rounds (on top of all the beer consumed an hour or so earlier), most of the group were already in their cups.

After an hour or so, we decided that this was not to be the final event of the evening. Once the decision was made to move on, friends began competing for the honor of paying the bill. Everyone in the group had a credit card (far less common in 1989 Taiwan than they are now)—although everyone seemed to know who does or does not really have the money to pay that month.

After the bill was paid, we were escorted to the door by our "assistant manager" and three of the hostesses. After the good-byes, we stopped at the stand of a sausage vendor who was parked just outside to take advantage of the KTV traffic. These sausage vendors often sport a bowl and dice, and customers can play for a freebie. Ah-lang said he was feeling lucky that evening and offered to treat us all— figuring that he could win a few rounds (he won two, and paid for the rest). As we gathered around to watch the action, others offered up cigarettes and betel nuts.

The group was going mobile now. We decided to go to the "God of Wealth Club." Motorcycles were left behind and we piled into three cars. Following Ah-hien, we sped through the backstreets of Taichung Harbor Road area, finally pulling up at the God of Wealth Club. We parked on a side street and walked around the corner to the entrance.

This club is a place that some from the group frequented often, so there was no need to ask for such-and-such a manager. Two hostesses who knew some of the group led us to one of the choice rooms, right by the piano bar. We were joined almost immediately by five or six young women, all in various stages of intoxication—it was already well into the evening, and they had all been through a high number of a few tables already. That is part of the strategy—the last table of the night will have a better chance at seduction. The women working in these clubs are not directly selling sexual favors for cash. In fact, that would completely undermine the pretext of the ritual—that the customer will attract and, if sufficiently endowed with male potency, seduce one or more of the courtesans. The challenge of the game and the uncertainty of the outcome provides a stage upon which one can perform one's masculinity. One pays direct attention here primarily to one's friends, sworn brothers, comrades—a man among men, it would be unmanly to allow oneself to be overly distracted by the feminine charms of the "drinking partners." Such behavior is subject to derision—in putting one's own sexual desire above male solidarity (*chung ssu ch'ing yu*) one is displaying a pathetic weakness (such a display is derided as weak and unmasculine perhaps because it is thought to derive from a man's infantile attachment to his mother). At the same time, the women engage the men in a sexual banter, joking suggestively about each man's sexual prowess. As closing time neared, this drinking session ended like many others—at least one from the group offered to drive a couple of the women back to their dormitory. We all said good-night, and a few of us headed off to get a midnight snack and sober up.

The evening was not yet over, however. On the way to get something to eat, one group member suggested going to a twenty-four-hour teahouse in the downtown area, a place where diehards—the after-hours crowd—can hang out. Here the smoking, betel nuts chewing, and drinking continued—alcohol along with the tea—and of course, here, too there were women to keep us company and provide the aura of sexual promise. Here, the women were a bit older, less elegantly dressed, and, perhaps given the lateness of the hour, less than enthusiastic about the arrival of yet another group of half-drunk carousers. In this establishment the women were euphemistically called "tea masters" (*ch'a i shih*); one from the group suggested that they are easier to seduce than the higher-class drinking partners.

Although it was a Taiwanese-style (that is, hybrid Chinese/Japanese) teahouse equipped with the proper tables, tatami rooms, and all the utensils and equipment necessary for brewing and serving tea, we ordered rice wine and continued to drink, accompanied by three or four "tea masters." After a few half-hearted attempts at conversation, the men and women began to play drinking games. After a few rounds, as the company became even more tired and drunk, the men started to chafe and argue among themselves, and one went off to get sick in the bathroom. The women didn't appear to be surprised by any of this, and one by one slipped off to join another party. One, an older hostess, remained, and took control of the table. When it became clear that the men were not going to order any more wine or food and were about at the end of their evening, she called in a busboy for hot towels, then convinced the men to order some expensive tea to "undo the alcohol" (*chieh chiu,* sober up). After preparing and serving the tea, she herded the group to the exit (after prodding one of the crew to help his semiconscious comrade to his feet). Later a few of the group would go off alone or in pairs to a brothel; the others would head home to sleep it off.

Typically, the next day, members of the group will get together again at the Pirate Ship and discuss the charms of the various women involved in the previous evening's revelry. At some point one group member who had taken his leave at the God of Wealth Club may insinuate a successful seduction of one of the hostesses. Although I have no reliable data on the sexual relationships between hostesses and customers, "seduction" is achieved far less frequently than claimed or implied in the next day's recounting (based on my observations of several groups of carousing men over several years). Conversely, when occasionally one of the group did become involved in a steady sexual relationship with a hostess, the group tended *not* to talk about it. Rather, it would be obvious when a particular hostess began to treat that group member with special affection and to keep her distance from the other men, or when the couple began to exhibit signs of "domesticity" in public. If the hostess was an assistant manager at one of the more expensive clubs, the relationship could enhance the man's status, assuming he was able to meet his social and financial obligations as the girl's sponsor. These obligations can include paying for frequent parties at the club. As credit is often extended to regular customers, such relationships often end when a customer overextends himself. Losing his credit (and credibility), a customer who cannot pay his bar tab loses face, but also causes "his" hostess to lose face and prestige in the club.[21]

In Taitung, carousing sessions turned out to be highly different from those I had observed and experienced in Taichung. This was due, partly, to the nature of my fieldwork and partly to differences between the socioeconomic environments of the two cities. In Taitung, the carousing groups I joined tended to consist of working-class men, often engaged in marginal professions that occasionally included illegal activities, most commonly (but not exclusively) gambling. Most of my Taichung friends and informants would have been uncomfortable venturing into the Taitung clubs. These clubs were far less lavish, partly because Taitung, at least in the early 1990s, was still an economic backwater and could not support "high-class joints" of the sort common in the larger cities.[22] The clientele in these clubs was mixed: Taitung hosts one of the larger air force bases in Taiwan, and soldiers on furlough were (until recently) one of the main sources of revenue for the nightclubs, teahouses, and massage parlors of the downtown area. But these clubs were also frequent hangouts of various local "brotherhoods."

At the temple festival celebrations and the seedy downtown nightclubs, the drinks of choice were usually beer or Shaohsing wine rather than XO brandy or imported scotch. The hostesses in the working-class clubs of Taitung were often teenage girls from aboriginal villages or unmarried mothers forced into this line of work by economic necessity. Others were virtual bond slaves, paying off gambling and business debts—their own or, more often, those of an unlucky parent or male sibling. Consequently, there were often more explicit negotiations of payment for sexual favors here than in the high-class clubs. When treating an important guest, especially a high-ranking potential business partner (often with some status, or at least connections to the upper echelons of one or another gang), the host also would usually provide him with the company of a prostitute after the drinking was done. Conversely, the sexual innuendo in conversation and physical interaction between the men and hostesses tended to be more subdued than in the big-city clubs.

Neither the competitive drinking games nor the offering of cigarettes and betel nuts vary much from place to place in Taiwan. Nor does there seem to be much local variation in the choice of karaoke songs, although ethnic origin (native-Hokkien-speaking or not, for instance) and educational background do influence the choice of song that a participant performs. But one practice that distinguishes Taitung men from their compatriots to the west is their preference for a more "primitive" style of betel nuts chewing. In most of Taiwan, the betel nuts are cut open lengthwise and stuffed with a red lime compound that includes herbal medicine, pepper, and other substances. In Taitung, however, most prefer the larger (cheaper) betel nuts, which are prepared by simply being wrapped in leaves smeared with pure, white lime. A bit of the stem is often left on to show freshness, and removed (by biting) just before being chewed. When treating guests from Taipei, Kaohsiung, and other cities to the west, Taitung hosts often profess their preference for the rougher, plainer, stronger, and presumably more masculine white lime betel nuts, while politely providing their guests with the more expensive tender, red lime (in this context, foreign, weaker, feminine) betel nuts. In part, Taitung men derive their particular form of manhood by representing themselves as hardier, rougher, and tougher than their more "civilized" and urbane but weaker comrades from the other side of the mountains. Most people in western Taiwan, if they think about Taitung at all, imagine it as wild, distant, mountainous, full of matrilineal aboriginal tribes whose women are supposed to be particularly beautiful while the men are weak and childlike. It is against this feminized version of the frontier that men in Taitung—particularly those of Han Chinese ethnicity—present these very same qualities of wildness and primitiveness as masculine and heroic. For them, Taitung's backwardness is at once an embarrassment and a point of pride, the source of an innate toughness and manliness lacking in their more "civilized" compatriots to the west. This tension between what is imagined as the outside world's contempt and a local mythos of toughness gives carousing, not to mention everyday conversation in Taitung, a special flavor.

The competitive nature of the drinking here was fiercer than anything I observed in Taichung. On many occasions I witnessed evening-long business negotiations that involved constant competitive drinking. At one session hosted by Ah-peng, a local gambling operator and temple devotee, a "big brother" (that is, a high-ranking gangster) from Taipei was the guest of honor.[23] Ah-peng was so intent on giving face to his guest that he didn't even excuse himself and step outside to vomit—he simply puked into a spittoon and, barely missing a beat, joined the next toast. Far from an exhibition of physical weakness or social subservience, this was very much a demonstration of the real spirit of *i-ch'i*. By putting his moral obligation to put his guest above his own physical misery—and doing it in such a casual, unhesitating way—Ah-peng acted heroically, giving face to his guest but confirming both his own and Taitung men's reputation for stamina, fearlessness, and—not at all least—hospitality.

Although carousing sessions in Taitung (and elsewhere) are sometimes planned, usually they are spontaneous get-togethers and celebrations that begin in late afternoon or early evening. In Taitung, where I have been doing research on temple procession troupes (*chen-t'ou*) since 1988, I have often been invited by temple devotees and their associates or sworn brothers for rounds of carousing.[24] Twice a month (at the new and full moon), and after every festival or major temple ritual, for instance, the "troops" are "rewarded" (*k'ao-chün, kho-kun*). These sacrifices also include offerings to specific deities, for example, the god of wealth (for businesses in particular) or the local god of the soil. For those temples devoted to martial deities in particular, the propitiatory sacrifice focuses on spirit generals of the five camps (*wu-ying shen-chiang*) and their ghostly minions, known as "soldiers of heaven" (*t'ien ping*). As in most Taiwanese temple rituals, the offerings consist of raw and cooked food, fruits, alcohol, cigarettes, betel nuts, and other items. Once the spirit soldiers have partaken of their share and have been sent off with a gift of spirit money, the devotees themselves feast on the "leftovers," the food of which the spirit soldiers partook only the invisible essence, leaving the material substance. Because the devotees—particularly the men of the temple— are understood to be "soldiers" of the deity as well, they are rewarded, too. Here they start the ritual as sacrificers and conclude as receivers. The participants are expected to indulge their appetites and enjoy themselves without reservation, and the mood is open and raucous. Drinking goes on throughout the meal, and continues even after everyone has (over)eaten. Some then retire to another table, or, in cooler weather, to a side room of the temple to play cards, dominoes, or mah-jongg. At this point, if one or another of the men is in an especially good mood or has had a good month, he may propose moving the party to another location. The carousing party (usually in smaller groups, divided by cohort)[25] then moves off in cars and on scooters, leaving the women, children, and a few of the older men at the temple to continue their gambling and cleaning up.

On one warm Taitung evening in mid-1991 at the Chung-ho Temple, the instigator of the carousing party was Ah-liong, a core temple member, who was also a member of the cohort, all of whom were then in their early thirties. His mother had been the beneficiary of one of the patron deity's first local miracles in the early 1950s, and family and temple history had become inextricably interwoven. Several of the carved deity images that graced his home shrine had been "divided off" from the temple's altars. Among them was a figure of Ta-yeh. Ta-yeh is better known to students of Taiwanese folk religion as the taller of the two demon-bailiffs Ch'i-yeh and Pa-yeh who serve the City God and other magistrate-deities. In mainland China, these two are called Hei Pai Wu-ch'ang ("Black and White Demon-bailiffs"). *Wu-ch'ang* (literally, "constantly in flux") is an anchor of the Ten Infernal Generals (*shih chia chiang/sip-ka-chiong*) procession troupe. Ah-liong, who lived in a small row-house down the street in one of the city's more run-down neighborhoods, had played the tall, lanky Ta-yeh for several years. A gang member while a teenager, Ah-liong had turned over a new leaf after returning from military service. With a growing family and a widowed mother to support, he had had his tattoos surgically removed so that he could take a steady job as a prison guard in nearby Taiyuan. Unfortunately, his pay was barely enough to keep the family fed and clothed, and little if anything was left over for hosting *ying-ch'ou* activities. However, Ah-liong was naturally generous and deeply conscious of his obligations as a core temple devotee. Loath to accept the low status to which his financial situation relegated him, he often went to great lengths to present himself as a man of means and connections.

One way he did this was to host parties at establishments where one or another acquaintance was working in some mid-level position, using the connection to establish enough credit for a night or two of carousing with his friends. Nightlife spots come and go, but Taitung is not a big city, and Ah-liong's reputation often preceded him. Through his temple connections and position as a low-level law-enforcement officer, however, he had managed to get most of his past debts forgiven or deferred. On this particular night, he was feeling flush, and offered to take his friends out on a carousing spree.

Starting at a basement karaoke club (no private rooms) near the Taitung railway station, the group occupied two small, round tables, leaving two or three seats at each open for hostesses or friends who might drop in from other parties. We ordered two bottles of Shaohsing wine and some snacks. A few unenthusiastic hostesses joined the group, two at a time, for a few minutes each. One of the temple group, Ah-hung, took the microphone and sang a couple of slow ballads with a wonderfully deep bass. His performance drew attention all across the room, and he was loudly applauded; a "big brother" at another table toasted him once for each song. A while later, Ah-liong went to sing his own current favorite, "Red Light Pier" (Ang-teng Be-thau), a song of love and regret with a tango beat; only our group paid attention this time. After a few more rounds of drinking and singing, Ah-liong suggested moving on. He negotiated the bill (later I learned he had some trouble extending his credit, and had to get help from others in the group, much to their annoyance), and we then headed back up to street level.

From here, we rode to a place A-liong wanted to "introduce" to us, a new "shrimp-fishing pool" (*tiao hsia ch'ang*) an acquaintance of his had opened nearby. Like many such places, quite popular for a time in the late 1980s and early 1990s, the pool was a concrete basin built in an open lot under a temporary corrugated aluminum roof. On one side of the pool, next to a single propane-fueled burner stood two or three racks of vegetables, and nearby were a beer cooler and a few glass tanks of fish and shrimp displayed for eating purposes. A few bottles of black-market liquor and packs of domestic and foreign cigarettes were displayed on a shelf behind the cashier's counter. No one was much in the mood to fish for shrimp, so we ordered two-dozen tiger prawns from the tank and barbequed self-service–style on one of several hibachis scattered around the "picnic area" next to the pool.

After we had eaten, the owner came over and joined us for a round of beer; he thanked Ah-liong for coming, and encouraged us all to drop in whenever we had some leisure time, proclaiming the myriad joys of shrimp fishing and letting us in on his shrimp-pool business philosophy: reasonable cost, guaranteed catches, biggest and freshest shrimp in town, and a clean, family atmosphere. Later on Ah-hung confided to me that he thought Ah-liong took us there primarily because he could treat us on the cheap. Business was slow, and the owner was anxious to add to his customer base. This, of course, was a one-time event, unless Ah-liong could keep the new customers coming.

Six members of the group now remained. Having talked himself into the mood for more carousing, Ah-liong invited the owner to join us at a newly opened teashop. The Azure Shores Teashop and KTV was about two kilometers away, on the other side of town. Ah-liong and the others rode their scooters, and I drove. The club was in one of the typical, older storefront buildings near downtown; long and narrow, the reception area consisted of a small sofa along one side and a counter that ran halfway along the facing wall. At the far end of the room was a small, wood-veneered door with a small, one-way mirrored pane right at eye level. Beyond the door was a corridor that led to four or five small, partitioned karaoke rooms.

We were seated in one of the rooms near the front and ordered Shaohsing wine, a dish of dried sour plums (to reduce the potency of the alcohol), and two packs of 555 brand filter cigarettes. Four hostesses joined us almost immediately (obviously business was not booming) and introduced themselves in the standard fashion, toasting each of us in turn and, with a studied awkwardness showing that they were probably new to this business and still "in training," asked how we would like to be addressed. After small talk, I asked the girls about their respective home-towns and learned that they were all aborigine girls in their teens and twenties, primarily Amis, from towns and villages between Taitung and Hualien. Most had been in the city for only a month or two. Most spoke little Taiwanese other than a few epithets and jokes they had picked up from the mama-san and customers.

One of the hostesses in our cubicle that night was an Amis girl from Hualien who had just arrived a few days earlier, "introduced" by a relative. It was her birthday and she had already been celebrating. Ah-liong joked suggestively with her, but after a few rounds of wine, she stopped talking to him and sat sullenly by herself at the end of the sofa. After a few minutes, she turned back to the group and began toasting everyone in turn, tossing down a full glass of wine at every round. Ah-liong, apparently feeling attacked by her cold-shoulder protest and drinking challenge, leaned over, put a microphone in her lap, and insisted that she sing a love-duet with him. This was the last straw for her. Thoroughly drunk and angry, she threw down the microphone (breaking it and probably incurring a deduction from her pay) and stormed out of the room, pointing and cursing at Ah-liong as she left. Two of the girls, apologizing, followed her out. Ah-liong stood up, curs-ing and motioning for us to leave. Before we could make a move, the mama-san knocked and entered; two tough-looking male employees waited outside the door.

The mama-san, a plump woman in her mid- or late forties, her hair permed, wearing a lime-green, gauzy dress and white high-heels, apologized to the group, looking at each of us in turn. She criticized the girl, calling her *hoan,* the conde-scending Taiwanese epithet for aborigines. She offered to pay the hostess fees for the girl and buy us another bottle of Shaohsing. After a few tense moments, Ah-liong relaxed and the conversation turned to joking and making light of the inci-dent. The mama-san then called in one of the male employees, who offered cigarettes and betel nuts all around while the other one went off for the wine. We took our seats again, and the mama-san personally opened the bottle, poured the drinks, and toasted Ah-liong, then each of us in turn.

When we had finished about half the bottle, Ah-liong politely but coolly thanked the mama-san and indicated that we had business elsewhere. A waiter brought in the bill; Ah-liong looked it over with a frown, and quickly disputed two of the hostess fees. He had lost face; not finishing the wine was a partial rejection of the mama-san's compensation. Implying that the bill was padded was retaliation. But the mama-san, having already lost plenty on this group, was in no mood to back off. The argument went on for several minutes; in the end, Ah-liong assented. With obvious irritation, he emptied his pockets and paid the bill. It had been a thor-oughly unsatisfying and unsuccessful episode for Ah-liong: slighted and embar-rassed by the girl, he had expected far more in compensation (a stronger show of respect and a free pass for the evening). The final blow, however, was the frustra-tion in his own inability to resolve the situation in a way that maintained either his "face" or his male pride.

By now it was after midnight. We left the Azure Shores and headed back in the direction of the temple, where some of the group had left their scooters. On the way, Ah-liong, unwilling to let the evening end on a sour note, decided to drop by the house of a friend he called Ah-kien. We pulled into a small alley behind one of the older temples in the north-central area of town. At the time, the neighborhood was still dotted with one-story Japanese-era wood-and-stucco houses. We stopped in front of a door near the corner of the alley and Ah-liong knocked and called for Ah-kien. Ah-kien came to the door, apparently not unhappy to have visitors drop by unannounced in the middle of the night. The others went on after a quick greeting, but Ah-liong and I were persuaded by Ah-kien to stick around for some tea. We shed our shoes and entered a small living room furnished with rattan chairs, a carved teak tea table, and a small altar. Ah-kien boiled water in an adjustable electric kettle popular at the time among tea aficionados. He added some tea from the open canister on the table, explaining that this was high-altitude spring tea from a private stock of "competition tea" given to him by a tea-plantation owner in Nantou. After a round or two, we struck up a conversation about spirit mediums and martial arts, shared interests of all present. Ah-kien, I learned, was a "wanderer," a low-level gangster from Huwei in central Taiwan who had slipped across the mountains to Taitung a few years before to escape one of the periodic, highly publicized police "sweeps." After things cooled down, he decided to stay in Taitung, although he frequently returned to Huwei and his work involved connections in both places.

Soft-spoken and serious, Ah-kien, who was in his mid-thirties at the time, felt that the younger "brothers" joining the "dark way" (*hei tao,* that is, the underworld) today didn't understand the code of honor and reciprocity that defined the "way" in "dark way." He explained:

> In the old days, a lot of vendettas began as slights or misunderstandings during drinking sessions in nightclubs. Things might get bad if there was tension between the followers of rival "big brothers," and sometimes people ended up in the hospital. There was always retribution, but it was in proportion—you got one of ours, we get one of yours. And for things to get violent, it had to be really bad, like refusing to acknowledge a toast or invitation to drink not just once, but three times; I mean, nowadays, these gangs of kids go after some innocent bystander and cut off his arm because they don't like the way he looked at them. They have no concept of honor [*i-ch'i*]. I don't bother going to the nightclubs much anymore; I prefer drinking at home. But sometimes, of course, I have to go for *ying-ch'ou.* My wife doesn't mind, she knows I won't act irresponsibly [*pu hui luan lai*] and my friends are righteous men, even if we're all of the rivers and lakes [*chiang-hu shang teh*].

Conclusion: Wine, Women, and (especially) Song

Up to this point, I have stressed the importance of drinking performance, the force of competition that drives such performance, and, most important, the social efficacy built into the drinking ritual. On the latter point, for instance, we can see the self-mortifying act of reciprocating toasts to the point of misery as a sacrifice that establishes a hierarchical bond (the sacrificer in the subordinate position). Indeed, the "challenge" to drink takes a highly specific form of ritual: with the right hand raising one's glass tipped in the direction of the one challenged, and making eye contact. In responding, one raises one's glass in return, touching the bottom of the glass (unless one intends to demonstrate or make a claim to social superiority) with the fingers of the left hand. The "challenge" is called "a respectful offering" (ching/ʻ k'eng), recalling the fact that both host and guest—both superior and subordinate—reciprocally toast one another. Relative position in this transaction is enacted in the timing of the toast and the attitude of the response. The act of offering merely establishes or confirms a connection, the nature of which is exterior to the toast itself.

The competitive challenge entailed by social drinking in both Chinese and Taiwanese traditions is quite explicit. Engaging in a round of drinking games is sometimes called a "drinking battle"; and as noted above, matching someone drink for drink is called "dueling" with alcohol. This symbolic violence is intrinsic to the process of producing the social hierarchy in Taiwan. There is no "thrill of victory" in such a match; both the victor and the vanquished experience the agony of alcohol poisoning. Rather, victory and defeat become part of a personal narrative and social reputation. Even a poor drinker willing to engage in alcohol duels for the sake of face or honor is admired, if ultimately pitied. Symbolic capital, therefore, accrues not only to the winner but to anyone demonstrating sufficient bravado. Capacity and endurance surely figure into the equation, but risk-taking entails courage, a moral rather than physical capacity. Such bravado is considered a mark of masculinity.

The threat inherent in the challenge to drink, however, does not operate only at the level of social discourse. Refusing to answer a challenge risks not only disgrace, but, on occasion, even violent retribution. Not to drain one's glass when challenged is to rebuff a prestation or deny a relationship. Such behavior is considered both "unrighteous" (pu chiang i, bo kang-gi), an indirect slight to the one inviting the toast, and by extension, unmanly, thus reducing as well one's reputation—and thus the fact—of prowess.

What, then, of karaoke? How are drinking and singing integrated within the whole of carousing practice? My findings suggest that karaoke singing in Taiwan, unlike drinking, is not at all a competitive performance.[26] Everyone takes a turn—experiencing the vulnerability of the spotlight, the individual sense of contributing one's due, and the sense of collectivity that subsumes this individual vulnerability to the protective support of the group. In Taiwan, karaoke singers, encouraged and, one might say, nurtured in the presence of their fellow carousers, seem remarkably un-self-conscious, especially when compared to Americans in similar situations of potential public embarrassment.

Singing, moreover, is a "performance" only in the most general sense; it is not primarily for providing entertainment or demonstrating talent. Rather, the enjoyment of public singing, for both the performer and fellow participants, derives, in large measure, from the social mutuality entailed in the act. As each singer takes the microphone, he enters a space of emotion, drawn in some measure from the sentiments of the song, drawing his fellow carousers in as he sings. This effect is, of course, enhanced by a talented singer, but talent is largely beside the point. The singer demonstrates trust in the group, putting aside his own sense of vulnerability.

Singing is thus a shared enjoyment. Whether or not an individual actually enjoys singing is also beside the point: There is a public expectation that everyone wants to sing, and that the singing is both a personal pleasure and a prestation offered to the group. The singer professes trust in his comrades by his willingness to expose his own emotional vulnerability. Not to sing is to withhold oneself, to demonstrate a lack of trust in one's fellows, thus withdrawing from the group. While there are certainly many other, equally important reasons that karaoke singing has become so essential to carousing in Taiwan, I suggest that the practice of social relations in Taiwanese society requires just such an experience of emotional solidarity, one that transcends, even as it legitimizes the calculations and symmetrical competition inherent in the game of *ying-ch'ou*.

Ying-ch'ou activities are essential as fields of productive action for men engaged in transacting business, political power, or personal prestige. Carousing, in particular, creates a space in which men can enact themselves as both cultural subjects and individual actors within their social milieu. Success in these endeavors—not simply drinking and seduction, but in the way one uses one's capacity for drink and sex to one's social advantage—is a mark of being a real man, a "Man of Prowess," in Taiwanese society. The particular forms of sociality and reciprocity played out here are gendered—masculine—although they depend directly and ineluctably on the labor of (particular "kinds" of) women.

In her study of "corporate masculinity" in Japan, Anne Allison describes styles of "ritualistic male behavior" prominently involving "alcohol, women, and sexual play" that serve to create "bonds of fellowship" among men of all classes and backgrounds (Allison 1994: espec. 151–67). The subjectivities created and enacted in the world of Japanese corporate-sponsored nightlife ultimately produce a particular kind of male ethos wherein the embodiment of masculinity entails "being a male who can pay a female to service him" (Allison 1994: 204). The reification of this ethos in carousing on the company tab both reifies the Japanese corporate hierarchy (where superiority and inferiority are universally imagined in gendered terms) and serves to reproduce it.

In Taiwan, too, carousing practice binds individual desire to the service of reproducing structures of domination, including corporate and political institutions. Moreover, carousing in Taiwan bears more than a superficial resemblance to Japanese corporate nightlife practice: the ubiquity of alcohol, sexually available hostesses, drinking games and "alcohol battles," and karaoke, to name only the most obvious common features. At a higher level of abstraction, however, comparison yields as many differences as commonalities. Subtle differences (as in the example of economic organization, above) reveal important cultural particularities that cannot be ignored. For instance, the institutional organizations reflected in and served by the practice of carousing are quite different in Japan and Taiwan. Japan's economy has long been dominated by large corporations whose economic and social reach has had a profound influence on culture, including concepts and practices that produce gendered identities throughout the society (both within and beyond the corporate workplace). Unlike Japan, however, social and economic development in postwar Taiwan favored smaller, family-scale enterprises rather than mega-corporations. One result of this convergence of this small-enterprise-oriented mode of economic development and the localist tendency in Taiwanese social organization is that the entertainment economy came to depend on mostly (at least through the early 1990s) smaller local groups of consociates than on corporate expense accounts. Clearly, the cultural, historical, and economic distance between Japan and Taiwan, despite the impact of the pre-1945 Japanese colonial presence and continued cultural and economic cross-flows, is considerable.

Nevertheless, Allison's description of "corporate masculinity" in contemporary Japan sheds important light on carousing practice in Taiwan: Entertainment that involves social interaction in public venues in Taiwan is central to the reproduction of the structures and ethos of a web of ideologies of dominators—in particular, by serving as a forum for the production and amplification of both individual identities and interpersonal relationships consistent with the patrilineal social structure and the patriarchal ideology that defines the limits of meaningful action and subjectivity within that social structure. Ritual competition establishes and amplifies both individual identities within cohorts, and the hierarchical structure and behavioral norms of the cohort itself.

In Taiwanese society, this process of cultural production has, and continues to be, articulated in the idiom of the potent male—the man of social, sexual, and economic prowess. As a nexus of social production, then, *ying-ch'ou* is also by implication (if my hypothesis is sustainable) a ground for the production, performance, and refinement of individual subjectivity. Individuals realize themselves as social subjects by signifying in culturally recognizable modes, in this case, the collective narratives of manhood that include (but are not limited to) the myths of knights-errant and gangsters. These performances, in turn, recapitulate conventional structures and expectations.

Camaraderie can be both egalitarian and stratified: Moral qualities of character, such as selflessness and generosity, bear no intrinsic relation to hierarchy. Yet the communicative performance of such qualities depends entirely on the collective agreement of an individual's place on the social grid. Who provides the cigarettes and betel nuts to whom, who lights whose cigarette, who elicits immediate response and an empty cup when toasting, who gets how much of the group's attention when singing, and who gets the attention, and, perhaps, the sexual favors of the working girls (and who pays for this and the drinking and singing bill) are all part of a process of negotiation, production, and domination—directly of the women and subordinate men; and indirectly, of all those traditionally dominated within the patrilineally modeled social institutions of Taiwanese society, even the fun ones.

Notes

1. This essay is the indirect outcome of fieldwork undertaken for a variety of research projects during numerous stays in Taiwan between 1987 and 2000. While working on the ritual construction of masculinity in Taiwanese temple communities (1988–91) and a cultural history of Taitung province (1996–2000), I found that my informants' social lives, both within and beyond the temple groups, were very much focused on, and with, carousing or nightlife. These activities, therefore, soon became an important part of my interaction with my informants, the more so when I sensed that the rapport between me and my informants often improved significantly both during and after my participation with them in drinking and singing. Fortunately, at the time I was younger, stronger, and had a good tolerance for alcohol. Had it been otherwise, I doubt this essay could have been written.

2. Here it may be instructive to consider other uses of *ch'ou*. In classical texts, *ch'ou* may signify superiors rewarding inferiors, as in *ch'ou-lao*, a lord rewarding the efforts of his retainers. Or it may indicate inferiors' supplication of superiors in recompense for favors (by gods: *ch'ou-shen*; by gods or nonsupernatural superiors: *ch'ou-yüan*)—with the implication that the supplicant will receive, or has received, some benefit in return. These usages articulate a field of social interaction that 1) is based on an asynchronous exchange of gifts or favors; and 2) constitutes social relationships as a hierarchy. Here it might be objected that the terms most often used to refer to entertainments among friends and associates—*ch'ou-tsuo* and *ying-ch'ou*—carry no implication of hierarchy, only reciprocity. Nevertheless, both etymological analysis and ethnographic evidence support the argument that hosted, reciprocal entertainment in Taiwan entails competition for status, even among recognized social equals and members of the same in-group. Both codified rules of etiquette and the spontaneous acts and expressions that define modes of speech and action during these sessions strongly suggest that status competition is one, if not the primary, pretext for *ying-ch'ou*.

3. Although the terms *kuan-hsi* and *kuan-hsi-hsueh* are not as widely used in Taiwan as in the PRC, many of my informants regularly used the terms *jen-ch'ing* (human feeling), *kan-ch'ing* (emotional bonds/connections), and *i-ch'i* (righteousness, mostly referring to generosity and selflessness—or the lack thereof—in relations with peers and inferiors) when explaining *ying-ch'ou* and its attendant activities to me and to each other. As elements of both daily discourse and emic terms of analysis, their use of these terms suggests that both the practices and discourse described here have a clear affinity, if not a direct historical link, with similar practices in the People's Republic of China and elsewhere.

4. Carousing in Taiwan is by no means limited to the category of male, heterosexual, twenty-to-fifty year-olds with plenty of disposable income. Nevertheless, modes of social performance comprising carousing are clearly premised upon collective assumptions about—and practice directed toward the production of—normative gender identity and difference in Taiwanese culture. The range of meanings and the particulars of practice certainly differ from group to group. Yengling Antonia Chao (1996) points out, for instance, that social groups outside the mainstream tend to articulate identity by indulging in certain social practices invented by and associated with the dominant social group (that is, young and middle-aged heterosexual adult males). Even as they work to create new modes of action and relationship, marginal subcultures not only reproduce patterns of hierarchical difference, but locate power in exactly those cultural representations of gender and sexuality generally associated with the dominant group.

5. This is a special usage, of course, as *chhit-tho* in everyday conversation refers to recreation of all sorts. One is actually most likely to hear the term when taking leave at the house of a friend or acquaintance: *u-ieng lai chhit-tho* corresponds to the Mandarin *yu k'ung lai wan*, "Feel free to drop by to wile away the hours whenever you have spare time."

6. Although knights-errant and martial heroes may represent or evoke the desire of young men to be free of patriarchal domination (both within the family and in the society at large),

there are characters in Chinese mythology that more unambiguously embody the vexed relationships between fathers and sons and, by extension, the paradox immanent in the process of reproducing patriarchal power—the insubordinate "trickster" Sun Wu-k'ung immediately springs to mind. See, for instance, Sangren (2000), especially chapters 2 and 8.

7. The inspirational theme of the "self-made" man runs through nearly all mythobiographies of successful men published in Taiwan, Hong Kong, the PRC, and overseas Chinese (*hua-ch'iao*) communities in Southeast Asia. It is, perhaps, a cliché that those who have made it to the top of any enterprise ultimately seek social legitimacy, but the stories of successful gangsters are essentially stories of successful businessmen, whereas those who fail to make it up the ladder have few choices for fame and reputation. This is at least one of the attractions of the outlaw myth for those limited by failure or structural alienation from the legitimate path to success.

8. From the "Biographies of Knights-Errant" and "Biographies of the Assassins" in the *Shih chi* (The Historical Records) to the *Shui hu chuan* (Water Margin) to nineteenth-century swordsman novels to Chin Yung and the Hong Kong gangster film genre, there is a long history of knight-errant and outlaw mythology. Since the end of martial law in Taiwan, an extensive popular literature of dramatized biographies and confessions of well-known criminals has appeared. See, for instance, Ch'en 1986, Chang 1996, and Shen 1988.

9. In Taiwan, low-level gangsters revealingly refer to themselves as *lung-ch'u* (*langtzu*), prodigal sons; and as *chhit-tho-lang*, "players, idlers."

10. Although private houses are frequently used as sites for *ying-ch'ou* activity in rural communities, most *ying-ch'ou* activity here takes place in the open courtyard or in the "public interior" (*t'ang/thhng* or *t'ing/tian*), clearly distinguished from the private, domestic interior, which is off-limits to all but kin and the most intimate friends during public events.

11. This is particularly true in Taichung, the City of Subcultures, as one informant described his hometown. Taichung has a reputation for many innovations of Taiwanese popular culture (the Kansai region, which includes Kobe, the birthplace of karaoke, has a similar reputation in Japan). The ubiquitous barbershop brothel, "bubble tea" (tea with tapioca), and beer pubs (*p'i-chiu wu*) as architecturally conspicuous as the wildest Las Vegas imaginings, are all considered to have originated there. Over the last decade, Taichung has grown at a faster pace than either Taipei or Kaohsiung, due (as the popular wisdom declares and city boosters proclaim) to the greater availability of space, climate, centralized location, and excellent transportation infrastructure. Service businesses have thrived, and following the city's reputation for creativity, many new forms and variations have appeared, particularly in the area of the "special professions" (*t'eh-chung hang-yeh*), that is, the sex trade. Indeed, in the summer of 2000 the manager of a large KTV in Taichung's newest entertainment district (in the southwestern quadrant of the city) proudly claimed that "Taichung boasts more hostess clubs [*chiu-tien*] than any other city in Southeast Asia."

12. A self partly constituted, of course, through the negotiation of position within the relations of dominance, but also a self striving to demonstrate independent agency—upon which an individual's perceived measure of prowess and potency within the patriarchy paradoxically depends.

13. The cubicle was not an MTV video-parlor innovation, however; dimly lit "tea parlors" with high-backed booths offered some measure of privacy to young couples on a date in Taipei's Hsi-men-ting entertainment district, whereas in southern Taiwan many such "tea parlors" and "fruit ice" parlors were actually working-class versions of the hostess club, *chiu-chia*.

14. In Taipei, many clubs are housed within existing structures, occupying one or more floors of a multiuse building, for instance. In central and southern cities, however, KTVs and nightclubs are more usually built from the ground up; they are freestanding, multistory structures. Many are decorated according to one or another exotic theme that could be nothing but houses of entertainment.

15. Not all clubs are KTVs, however: In Taichung, for instance, "piano bars" were the height of chic in the early 1990s, and the barroom-style karaoke bar persists as the most

common form in less urbanized areas of Taiwan. However, even the piano bars have karaoke equipment, and even the barroom-style joints usually have private rooms as well. The great variety of such karaoke-based establishments throughout East and Southeast Asia calls for a further refinement of karaoke taxonomy. My primary concern here, however, is not with the phenomenon of karaoke itself—rather, my focus here is what happens in the interior spaces where karaoke now provides the pretext for certain kinds of action and representation.

16. As late as 1992, in the smaller towns of southern and eastern Taiwan one could still find "tearooms" (*ch'a-shih, te-sit*) and "wine shops" (*chiu-chia, chiu-ka*), and even registered brothels (*chi-nü-hu*), which, unlike teahouses, belonged unambiguously to the category of "special business" (*t'e-chung ying-yeh, tek-chiong ieng-ip*), that is, the sex trade.

17. The first karaoke bars in Taiwan were just that: bars with primitive karaoke machines. Early on, even larger clubs that provided private rooms usually had only one karaoke machine. Customers would leave their private room and enter the main, central bar when one's turn to sing came along. This provided occasion for both performing in front of, and being toasted by, an audience of both familiars and strangers. Even after the private enclosure–style KTV replaced the open-space karaoke bar, many clubs still retained a central open space where either a piano player or big-screen karaoke kept single customers and waiting groups entertained.

18. In the early 1990s, however, many more "family-oriented" karaoke clubs opened to serve the increasing demand—partly fed by a social backlash against the ubiquity of the sex business—for "pure and simple" (*tan-ch'un*) entertainment.

19. These range from the simple and ubiquitous "rock, paper, scissors" hand-games to long, complex tongue twisters. The loser, or the one who trips over his words, must drink penalty wine, which, of course, leads to slower reflexes, impaired speech function, and more penalties.

20. The association between drinking and camaraderie is aptly illustrated by the Chinese idiom "When drinking with a true friend, even a thousand rounds aren't enough."

21. This link among economic, social, and sexual prowess, as well as the mutuality of the status-producing value of the relationship between hostesses/courtesans and customers within their separate, but intersecting social milieu, is hardly unique to Taiwan or to the contemporary period (see, for instance, Hershatter 1997 and Mann 1997 for accounts of the social world and culture of the entertainment and sex trade in Republican-era Shanghai and late imperial China, respectively). My examples here, rather, highlight the distinction between two modes of representation that comprise part of the dialectic of gender performance and identity that gives carousing its productive function: The recounting of sexual exploits is part of a sometimes-evaluative, sometimes-creative discourse that precedes and follows carousing events; whereas the set of public acts and attitudes, both verbal and nonverbal, expressed in the case of an ongoing sexual relationship, are demonstrative (or "performative," to use more familiar jargon).

22. This has since changed, as the development of Taitung's nightlife paralleled a dramatic economic expansion in the mid- and late 1990s.

23. I wasn't privy to exactly what was at stake that evening, although Ah-peng clearly was making a pitch for some kind of financial cooperation with the Taipei group. Toward the end of that long night, a very drunk, thin, middle-aged man whom I had not seen before, and who had remained rather quiet throughout the negotiations, explained to me, sotto voce, that he was an accountant at such-and-such a bank and worked for the operation by laundering money in such-and-such a way, earning a commission from each batch of funds.

24. These occasionally included gamblers and a few gangsters of a more professional stripe.

25. I was invited more often by those my age or a little younger, but after the 1991 Yüan-hsiao procession, at which point I had gotten to know the temple leaders better, I was also asked sometimes to partake in the drinking parties of the cohorts who were then in their mid-forties. It was in this group, for whom carousing was an essential feature of their economic lives, that I saw the most intense competition in drinking.

26. Here I am speaking of singing as a leisure activity; the karaoke-singing competitions often sponsored by restaurants, clubs, and organizations belong to a separate category of activity.

References

Allison, Anne. 1994. *Nightwork: Sexuality, Pleasure, and Corporate Masculinity in a Tokyo Hostess Club.* Chicago: University of Chicago Press.

Bateson, Gregory. 1972. *Steps to an Ecology of Mind: Collected Essays in Anthropology, Psychiatry, Evolution, and Epistemology.* San Francisco: Chandler.

Bourdieu, Pierre. 1977. *Outline of a Theory of Practice.* Cambridge: Cambridge University Press.

Chang Chenyue. 1994. *Taiwan hou-shan feng-t'u chih* (Gazetteer of the Customs of the Territory Beyond the Mountains). Taipei: Tai-yüan.

Chang Ch'iao. 1996. *Mo-tai liu-mang: I ko Taiwan hsiung-ti teh chi-ch'ing na-han* (Fin de Siècle Hoodlum: A Taiwanese Gangster's Call to Arms). Taipei: Jih-chen.

Chao Yengling (Antonia). 1996. "Embodying the Invisible: Body Politics in Constructing Contemporary Taiwanese Lesbian Identities." Ph.D. dissertation, Cornell University.

Ch'en Chen-feng. 1986. *Chu-lien pang hsing-shuai shih-mo* (Rise and Fall of the Bamboo Union Gang). Taipei: Tien-yüan.

DeGlopper, Donald. 1995. *Lukang: Commerce and Community in a Chinese City.* Albany: State University of New York Press.

Hershatter, Gail. 1997. *Dangerous Pleasures: Prostitution and Modernity in Twentieth-Century Shanghai.* Berkeley: University of California Press.

Huang Ch'ing-lien. 1999. *Chiu yü Chung-kuo wen-hua* (Alcohol and Chinese Culture). Taipei: Wen-hua chien-she wei-yüan-hui.

Huang Kuang-kuo. 1988. *Chung-kuo jen teh ch'üan-li you-hsi* (Chinese Power Games). Taipei: Chü-liu.

Huang Shou-ch'eng. 1984. *Tung-pu ts'ai-feng lu* (Account of Travels in Eastern [Taiwan]). Taipei: Wen-hua chien-she wei-yüan-hui.

Huang, Shu-min. 1998. *The Spiral Road: Change in a Chinese Village Through the Eyes of a Communist Party Leader.* Boulder: Westview Press.

Hyde, Lewis. 1983. *The Gift: Imagination and the Erotic Life of Property.* New York: Vintage Books.

Kipnis, Andrew B. 1997. *Producing Guanxi: Sentiment, Self, and Subculture in a North China Village.* Durham: Duke University Press.

Kung P'eng-ch'eng. 1987. *Ta hsia* (The Great Knight-errant). Taipei: Jin Kuan.

Kuo Pan-hsi. 1990 [1989]. *Chung-kuo yin-chiu hsi-ssu* (Chinese Drinking Customs). Taipei: Wen-chin.

Li Tsung-wu. *Hou hei hsüeh* (The Arts of Thick [skin] and Black [heart]). Undated paperback, no publication data.

Lin Chien-ch'eng. 1997. "Chien-yü wang Lai Shuang-hsi ti ku-shih" (The Story of Lai Shuang-hsi, the "Bonito King"). *Taitung wen-hsien* 5: 117–20.

Mann, Susan. 1997. *Precious Records: Women in China's Long Eighteenth Century.* Stanford: Stanford University Press.

Meng Hsiang-han. 1997. *Taitung hsien shih: K'ai-t'uo p'ien* (History of Taitung: Pioneering). Taitung, Taiwan: Taiwan hsien cheng-fu.

Sangren, Paul Steven. 2000. *Chinese Sociologics: An Anthropological Account of the Role of Alienation in Social Reproduction.* London; New Brunswick, NJ: Athlone.

Shen Tsui (pseudonym). 1988. *Ch'ing pang hung-men* (The Green Gang and the Hung Society). Taipei: T'ung-hsüeh.

Weller, Robert P. 1987. *Unities and Diversities in Chinese Religion.* Seattle: University of Washington Press.

Yan, Yunxiang. 1996. *The Flow of Gifts: Reciprocity and Social Networks in a Chinese Village.* Stanford: Stanford University Press.

Yang, Mayfair. 1994. *Gifts, Favors, and Banquets: The Art of Social Relationships in China.* Ithaca: Cornell University Press.

10

The Blue Whirlwind Strikes Below the Belt

Male Sexuality, Gender Politics, and the Viagra Craze in Taiwan

Paul E. Festa

Since hitting the U.S. market in March 1998, the drug Viagra has been a hot and highly controversial media topic in Taiwan. Affectionately dubbed the "little blue demon," Viagra has sold briskly (if expensively) on the local black market, been widely exchanged through relationship networks and among friends, and established its largest niche among Taiwanese men in their thirties. From political campaigns and sex education to everyday language, the "blue whirlwind" has left no stone unturned. One year later, on March 19, 1999, the first "legal batch" of Viagra arrived at Chiang Kai-shek International Airport, where Pfizer-Taiwan met its shipment with an armored car and a police escort.[1] A week later, Pfizer distributed the 50,000, 50-milligram tablets to anxiously awaiting hospitals and "Viagra clinics" throughout the island for retail distribution.[2] Worth more than its weight in gold, the precious pills were stored in specially prepared safes or locked in vaults with supplies of morphine.[3] No doubt all involved were aware that the largest pharmaceutical heist ever had been pulled off that November (1998) in the Philippines, where more than a dozen men wearing police uniforms and carrying AK-17s held up a medical drug warehouse and made off with several tens of newly arrived cases of Viagra.[4]

Viagra is the first noninvasive medical treatment for erectile dysfunction. Together with the new antidepressants such as Prozac, it is what pharmaceutical companies call a "lifestyle drug." Lifestyle drugs do much more than treat life-limiting conditions. Through media images and marketing strategies, they promise to make life happier, healthier, and more comfortable. Pfizer's marketing slogan for Viagra typifies this imagery—"Viagra: A Healthy Part of Life"[5]—as does the company's current mission statement, "Life Is Our Life's Work."[6] In the way that they "improve" and alter bodies, lifestyle drugs create a powerful and palpable "truth effect" transformative also of identities. Ning Ying-pin, a Taiwan-based professor of philosophy, makes this point in a study of Viagra in Taiwan: "If I use Prozac, it is not so much because I have some illness or physical condition but rather because I am a 'certain' kind of person who leads a 'certain' kind of lifestyle."[7] Ning predicts that lifestyle drugs will continue to flourish owing to the tremendous market potential they represent for the commercialized pharmaceutical industry in an expanding global economy.[8]

To be sure, the "blue whirlwind" in Taiwan has been far more than a matter of heightening awareness of, and treating, erectile dysfunction. A highly publicized and politicized discourse on sexuality has been whipped up in which a diversity of voices has participated. As many scholars have shown since Michel Foucault, sexuality is a dense nodal point for competing power relations, and discourses of sexuality play a crucial role in efforts both to regulate and reform the political, economic, and social orders.[9] In Taiwan, medical professionals, Pfizer-Taiwan, politicians, Chinese medicine experts, women, as well as "enlightened" men, have all been prominent voices in the Viagra craze, and debates have almost invariably been concerned with redefining gender relations and norms of sexuality. This cacophony of voices reveals with certainty perhaps only one thing—gender and sexuality are, as anthropologists Micaela di Leonardo and Roger Lancaster put it, neither "given phenomena 'over there,' impervious to human agency," nor "precultural drives anchored 'inside us,' beyond the reach of social influences."[10]

The nexus of divergent forces converging in the Viagra craze constitutes a unique context for examining the dynamics of gender politics and issues concerning (especially male) sexuality in Taiwan. As we will see, media representations of and popular discourses on Viagra have been remarkably manifold and multiperspectival. But despite the breadth of viewpoints—and the sharply critical positions most of them assume—a common thread does emerge in the taken-for-granted assumption of a set of sexual norms, namely heterosexuality, connubiality, and the primacy of intimacy over pleasure.[11] These "straight" norms are consistently, if often subtly, reaffirmed and naturalized even when the object of criticism is the masculinist narrative that most commonly animates them—to wit, men are innately promiscuous; male sexuality is inherently profuse and proceeds from men's bodies; and women desire love more than sex.[12] Punctuating this narrative is an admonitory pedagogy according to which Viagra must be domesticated or "tamed,"[13] lest men indulge their reactionary proclivity to dominate and harm women sexually, thereby buttressing the authoritative position masculinity occupies and subverting the progress of the women's movement toward gender equality.[14] But this seemingly progressive pedagogy conceals the ambiguities in male sexuality and ultimately recapitulates what anthropologist Deniz Kandiyoti calls "the enduring façade of male privilege."[15]

The only scholarly analysis of the Viagra phenomenon in Taiwan that I have seen focuses on "marginal" groups who might venture to appropriate Viagra in subversive ways. In an incisive critique, Ning Ying-pin calls for a progressive "life politics" through the "abuse" of Viagra in the pursuit of "deviant" lifestyles, especially by women, homosexuals, and masturbators.[16] Ning maintains that "health risks" and "moral infamy" are inexorably associated with "modern sex drugs," so that the decision to use them entails critical self-reflection and constitutes an agentive lifestyle choice intimately connected to personal identity and self-realization. He therefore argues that the array of social stigma associated with Viagra "will attract people looking for pleasure in risk and deviance" and could even cultivate deviant identities in users otherwise lacking such inclinations.[17] For Ning, then, the use of Viagra always smacks of "abuse," and is therefore the basis for a progressive "politics of difference" characterized by deviance from established norms.[18] But if difference is fashioned as the only legitimate basis for identity politics, then self-reflection and the potential for change are possible only among the marginal or oppressed. A politics of difference thus has the paradoxical effect of holding up an already hypostasized normative culture and, as cultural studies scholar George Yudice puts it, "keeping in place in our imaginary an ever greater monolith of power."[19] As a corollary, it tends to preclude critical analysis of the ambiguities and contradictions within the dominant culture. Without denying its significance, I wish to distinguish my approach from a politics of difference by attending to the complex dynamics of the Viagra craze at the very core of mainstream culture.

My objective is to explore the Viagra craze from divergent perspectives, illuminating the variety of understandings, identities, and practices *within* mainstream culture and *in relation to* normalizing discourses and practices. In particular, I focus on the confrontation between existing norms of sexuality and the various critical voices and local appropriations of Viagra. In addressing the question of why disciplinary incursions have failed to regulate the use of Viagra in particular and male sexual behavior in general, I aim to highlight the open and contested nature of male sexuality, while taking into account the dominant ideology's inevitable, yet indeterminate, impact on people's lives.

My analysis of the Viagra craze is based primarily on data gathered from media clips, including news coverage, editorials, periodical articles, and promotional pamphlets. I also make frequent reference to information obtained and observations made during a seven-month period of preliminary field research on male friendship and masculinity conducted in Taipei between August 1998 and March 1999. I divide my analysis into four main parts: (1) the received cultural context, (2) normative and critical voices, (3) local appropriations, and (4) the effect of Viagra's legal entry on the Taiwanese market.

Cultural Context

Following sociologists Laura Mamo and Jennifer Fishman's insightful analysis, Pfizer employs two key rhetorical devices in marketing Viagra as a lifestyle drug: "nature" and "control."[20] It seeks to impart the message that Viagra enables men to regain "control" over the "natural" sexual functioning of their bodies. The Viagra consumer pamphlet in the United States is sprinkled with open quotations such as, "I used to worry about impotence all the time. But with Viagra I don't think about it at all. I'm back in control again."[21] The pamphlet emphasizes that Viagra is neither a hormone nor an aphrodisiac, but rather an efficient drug that provides a medical cure for erectile dysfunction, thereby allowing nature to "take its course" within limits controllable by men.[22] By ignoring possible psychogenic causes or emotional factors, Pfizer appeals to the assumption that male sexuality is naturally forthcoming, unproblematic, and manageable (by the superior faculty of reason).[23] In other words, a key marketing objective adopted by Pfizer is to frame Viagra within the terms of a long-standing "modernist" trope that emphasizes the confident resumption of control by mind over body and man over nature.[24]

In Taiwan, Viagra has been quickly absorbed by a highly elastic indigenous discourse of male sexuality that subsumes the modernist idiom of "control" and "nature" into a language of energy conservation, endurance, and performance enhancement. In Chinese, Viagra is rendered as *wei-er-kang*, literally "powerful and strong," unambiguously associating it with Chinese virility stimulants (*chuang-yang-yao*) and herbal aphrodisiacs (*ch'un-yao*).[25] As Chinese medicine texts, sex manuals, and dictionaries all indicate—and as my interviews with Chinese medicine experts in both Taipei and Peking confirmed—*chuang-yang-yao* and *ch'un-yao* closely overlap in meaning.[26] Moreover, *chuang-yang-yao* and *ch'un-yao* exhaust the indigenous vocabulary for Chinese male impotence (*yang-wei*) remedies. Consequently, but for medical neologisms, there exists no native nomenclature for Viagra that does not directly imply the stimulation of virility or sexual desire, and therefore also the classical Chinese "art of the bedchamber" (*fang-chung-shu*) that informs the meaning of these two terms.[27]

The Chinese art of the bedchamber, which was taught in ancient "bedchamber manuals" (*fang-chung-shu*) and transmitted down through most of the imperial era in literary, religious, and medical sources, is a notoriously rich repository of creative methods to enhance men's bedroom performance, placing special emphasis on intercourse techniques and boosting endurance (*ch'ih-chiu nai-chan*). Wang I-chia, a widely popular scholar-author in Taiwan, in a critical analysis of gender and sexuality in traditional Chinese culture, has recently reinterpreted the art of the bedchamber based on 155 "notebook literature" (*pi-chi hsiao-shuo*) anecdotes from the Ming and Ch'ing periods (1368–1911). He points out a fixation in these stories on techniques by which men could hold back their sexual fluids and please women through intercourse and also on men's felt need to moderate carnal desire and sexual activity.[28] Wang argues that at play in these stories is the basic Chinese tenet of "extract and replenish" (*ts'ai-pu*), or in this context "extract [female] Yin in order to replenish [male] Yang" (*ts'ai-yin pu-yang*).[29] According to Chinese medical philosophy, a proper balance of yin and yang, or female and male essence, respectively, is essential for good health and long life. However, this complementary system of circulating vitalities of the body, believed to be a microcosm of the universal principles of Chinese cosmology, results in tremendous anxiety for men owing to the common belief, traceable back at least to the late classical period, that women are endowed with an infinite font of the life-giving force (*yin-*

ch'i) while men's supply (*yang-ch'i*) is limited.[30] By pleasing women through intercourse, men could most effectively extract and absorb the female life-force in order to replenish their own vital energy, and in turn preserve it by retaining their sexual fluids and moderating sexual desire. Wang thus concludes that Chinese men's elaborate preoccupation with pleasing women had selfish corporeal motives, namely to improve their own health and live a longer life, making the act of pleasing and dominating women two sides of a single coin.

Wang's emphasis on the dynamic of "extract and replenish" resonates strongly with my fieldwork discoveries in Taiwan. The discourse on Chinese medicine, the abundance of virility concoctions available at Chinese pharmacies (especially on Taipei's Ti-hua Street), and my conversations with Taiwanese all confirm that the notion of "extract and replenish" remains a potent part of Taiwanese popular culture.[31] The men among whom I have been conducting field research delight in teaching me about the intricacies of their culture of "replenishment." I have learned from my informant-friends that linkages between bodily health, sexuality, and male domination are still made by the Taiwanese, a fact also evident from the poignant challenges to this system of ideas articulated in the gender politics of the women's movement and by other critical voices.[32] Viagra has been assimilated into this local cultural idiom and been hotly pursued by Taiwanese men excited by the prospects of prolonging their erections.

Ning rejects conceiving of Viagra within the terms of traditional virility stimulants, on the grounds that the indigenous categories of China's sex culture are inadequate for a proper understanding of the drug.[33] He maintains that Viagra is a "sex drug" that, much like other modern drugs, people take as a form of "body management" in order to negotiate the problems, possibilities, and especially "risks" of modern society.[34] Unlike traditional potency medicines, according to Ning, Viagra has "reflexively modernized" by entering "the public realm of rational discourse," where moral value, social consensus, gender relations, individual freedom, and sexuality are all taken up and brought to bear on the decision to use the drug.[35] For Ning, then, "free discussion" in "open society" would seem to offer a guarantee that the meanings and values associated with Viagra will be more of the user's making, and therefore presumably more rational and progressive than culturally or structurally determined.

But as critics have pointed out, the notions of "free discussion" and "open society" are problematic, as they discount the distorting effect of ideology which is quite capable of presenting organized compliance as freedom and openness.[36] Moreover, Ning's invocation of Ulrich Beck's formulations of "reflexive modernization" and "risk society" seem to suggest a "precultural" realm of discourse and practice (including "body management") where rationality and progress, defined in part vis-à-vis "tradition," reflexively obtain.[37] As Scott Lash and Jonathan Urry argue, however, Beck belongs to the Western Enlightenment tradition that privileges "rationality, order and progress,"[38] giving short shrift to the "irrationality" in modernization,[39] to "separate expressive interests," and to the role of "tradition" as something other than that which is to be modernized and superseded.[40]

Ning's attention to body management is important, especially given the emphasis in modern consumer culture on maintaining, primping and preening, and displaying our bodies.[41] Nevertheless, I find the notion of "reflexive modernization" to be teleological and remain skeptical of its tendency to occlude the impact of inherited traditions on modern consciousness and practices. It also obscures the fact that traditional medicine is fully capable of being mobilized, or even modernized, for the purpose of "body management." Based on my research evidence, Taiwanese generally appear to be well aware of, and influenced in one way or another by, local ideas about virility stimulants and aphrodisiacs. And this indigenous tradition in fact facilitates, rather than obstructs, the instantaneous acceptance of Viagra, despite the fact that the drug hails from a very different medical tradition.[42] The ready assimilation of Viagra into native categories underscores the reported statistic that the otherwise unlikely demographic group of healthy Taiwanese men in their thirties has constituted the "little blue demon's" largest consumer group.[43]

To speak of traditions and inheritance, however, does not mean that the world was changeless before the modern era, but rather that, as anthropologist Matthew Gutmann puts it, "tradition and past customs provide questions and characterizations that confront every generation anew."[44] Borrowing from Antonio Gramsci, Gutmann develops the idea of *contradictory consciousness* in order to explain that people share both "a consciousness inherited from the past—and from the experts—that is largely and uncritically accepted, and another, implicit consciousness that unites individuals with others in the practical transformation of the world."[45] I take the notion to imply that certain contradictions (such as that between culture and necessity, and between values and norms), when they arise, are not resolved, per se, but rather are negotiated so as to shape decisions and events in specific but unpredictable ways. Viewed in this light, contradictory consciousness enables reflection, improvisation, and the construction of difference just as it constitutes a common framework of meanings by which individuals and diverse groups communicate and interact. This concept is therefore quite useful for thinking about the conflictual status of Viagra as a "sex drug" pursued to negotiate practical circumstances and personal lifestyles and as a signifier embedded within the universe of inherited meanings and concepts associated with Chinese sexual culture and medical cosmology. In a May 1998 survey, more than 50 percent of men and women claimed to believe thoroughly in Viagra's efficacy, while 47 percent of those from this group in their thirties and forties also expressed a strong readiness to use traditional potency concoctions (*shih-pu, yao-pu fang-shih*) to enhance sexual performance.[46] If contradictory consciousness works well as a descriptive category, it nonetheless remains a complicated matter to ascertain exactly how historic, systemic, practical, and bodily facets of gender constructions and sexuality piece together and interact within the specific time-space of different political, economic, and social fields.

Normative and Critical Voices

Popular and efficacious, Viagra has threatened to overtake the indigenous virility stimulant market of herbal tonics and animal-part concoctions that has long been dominated by traditional Chinese medicine. An article in the *Economist*, targeting traditional Chinese medicine's use of animal parts, touts Viagra's impressive clinical trials and its bright environmentalist prospects for eradicating "crimes against nature" in Asia—"tigers, rhinos and civets might thus have some pressure lifted from them."[47]

In response to this animal rights critique, which has also been made by Taiwanese animal rights groups, the Chinese medicine industry has played up its advances in biotechnology as well as its own "reflexively modernized" critique of animal-part concoctions: "As for the use of animal parts, such as seahorses, lizards, and deer antlers, not only are they not especially 'replenishing' but they oftentimes induce 'internal heat' (*shang-huo*), therefore we rarely use them today."[48] Chinese medicine experts have also been engaged in a strident campaign to debunk the "Viagra myth," declaring Viagra a harmful pseudo-aphrodisiac that offers only a superficial cure for "modern impotence" caused by the hurry and decadence of a contemporary urban lifestyle.[49] Many herbal specialists have stepped forward to inveigh against Taiwanese men who risk bodily harm and general well-being by imagining that Viagra is a virility stimulant or aphrodisiac. They insist that only men who lack sexual desire due to work pressures, poor eating habits, excessive drinking, or depression might benefit from Viagra.[50]

Chinese medicine experts repeatedly explain that by compartmentalizing the body Western medicine treats impotence as an isolated illness rather than a matter of overall bodily strength and spiritual well-being. In other words, Chinese medicine targets root causes, while Viagra treats only the symptom. The following admonition of one expert is illustrative: "There is a definite limit to men's vital energy. Taking a drug that gives free reign to sexual desires will lead to a diminution of the life-giving force, producing complications and doing permanent harm to the body— carnal excess is a sure invitation to injury."[51] A doctor of Chinese medicine recently published an article in the Health and Medicine section of the *China Times* announcing with alarm that Viagra users have been complaining of a lack of vital energy: "It's like having a gun without any bullets."[52] He rehearses the notion of "extract and replenish" described above and prescribes a list of foods for men to incorporate into their daily diets in order to strengthen their bodies and boost virility. If the Chinese medicine industry's critique of Viagra indicts a modern urban lifestyle of excess and overindulgence,[53] it has at the same time reinforced the inherited discourse of virility and bodily health and the corresponding mores of Chinese sexual culture centering on masculinist norms.

Standing to benefit from the significant inroads of Western medicine, Taiwan's modern medical profession has been the chief exponent of Viagra, assuming responsibility for defining norms of usage and designing programs to educate and discipline the public. Especially during the early stages of the Viagra craze, however, there seems to have been little coordination among Taiwanese doctors, who flooded the media with careless and contradictory statements. For example, in reporting the results of Pfizer's clinical trials, a Taiwanese urologist explained that a "positive outcome" was defined as "the stimulation of sexual desire" (*tz'u-chi hsing-yü*),[54] even though the normative medical discourse (including Pfizer) goes to considerable lengths to debunk the notion that Viagra is an aphrodisiac.

Doctors have also grappled with disparate terminologies. The native term for male impotence, *yang-wei*, unambiguously invokes the traditional framework of cultural meanings described above.[55] The neologism most commonly used by local urologists has been "sexual dysfunction" (*hsing kung-neng chang-ai*). If this term already lacks an accurate indigenous referent, Pfizer-Taiwan has further complicated matters by introducing yet another new term: "erectile dysfunction" (*po-chi kung-neng chang-ai*). Definitions have also been a problem for the medical profession.[56] The following definition of impotence has recently appeared on Pfizer-Taiwan's new Web site: "The inability to achieve or maintain an erection sufficient for satisfactory sexual performance." If this description of impotence is painstakingly vague, a prominent Taiwanese urologist had already gone on record, back in August 1998, with a mercilessly specific definition: a man is "impotent" if "more than half the time he fails [during sexual intercourse] to satisfy a woman" or if "he is unable to sustain an erection for at least two minutes."[57] Although rife with ambiguity, these faltering efforts to establish a definition of the impotent male manage, willy-nilly, to disseminate a normative mode of sexual behavior, to wit, heterosexual intercourse centering on male performance.

The modern medical profession, however, is not a monolith. Feeling threatened by Viagra's purely organic approach to a problem commonly thought of as psychosomatic in origin, psychiatrists in Taiwan have drawn on statistics from a survey of heterosexual women in the United States to undermine the increasing fixation on genital intercourse brought on by the Viagra craze: "41 percent obtain sexual gratification from oral sex, 23.5 percent from masturbation, and only 20 percent from sexual intercourse."[58] Taiwanese psychologists have expressed doubt that women need men who are "powerful and strong."[59] One psychiatrist directly attacked the implicit connection created by Viagra between the male erection and a fulfilling sex life as an illusion that suppresses the voices of women and leaves them unsatisfied. His corrective to the Viagra myth is: "Love is the best aphrodisiac."[60] Ironically, if urologists and psychiatrists both defend viewpoints not discordant with sexual norms, their public clash over Viagra sends mixed messages that at once heighten the drug's mystique and betray the contradictions and ambiguities that cut through mainstream norms of culture and behavior.

Once the Department of Health approved Viagra in January 1999,[61] medical professionals scrambled to secure a piece of the pie. The intervening months before the little blue pill hit the market saw the birth of "Viagra clinics" around the island.[62] The ostensible purpose of these clinics was to conduct "sexual happiness checkups" (*hsing/hsing-fu t'i-chien*) in order to determine who should and should not use Viagra. At US$60 an exam, hospitals, clinics, private practitioners, and all sorts of doctors moved quickly to get involved. A family physician from the pediatrics department at Taipei Medical Hospital, where one Viagra clinic was opened, put it this way: "Taiwanese are inveterate pill-poppers and are not aware of the potential harm to their bodies. Doctors must raise the checks against this practice, otherwise serious health complications from Viagra will strike Taiwan."[63] Urologists sharply protested the proliferation of Viagra clinics: "Too many people are misled, believing they can show up, register, and walk away with Viagra. This sends a bad message. Any doctor who discovers a case of impotence can make an evaluation. There's no need for special clinics. Even foreign doctors have found this phenomenon objectionable."[64] But outside Viagra clinics lines were weaving their way down sidewalks. Most men preferred to pay US$60 for a "sexual happiness checkup" instead of the $250 to $600 charged by urologists for a comprehensive examination.

In retaliation, urologists launched a vehement campaign to stem the Viagra craze, spearheaded by threatening reports of fatalities allegedly caused by Viagra: "Last year in the United States, Viagra caused more than a hundred deaths . . . and not all victims had a history of heart disease."[65] They even adopted a critique by psychologists that they themselves had refuted in an earlier public debate: "Normal people who take Viagra to enhance sexual performance not only risk addiction but also, paradoxically, castration, discovering one day that they cannot function sexually without the drug."[66] The U.S. experience was once again invoked: "60–70 percent of Viagra users in America are dependent on the drug and can't make love without it. These men have turned into 'sex machines'—eight times in one night [super-]men [*i-yeh pa-tz'u lang*]. For them, making love is a mere formality and involves no intimacy. Women are not only turned off, but fear the adverse consequences of men's insatiable sexual desire."[67] Despite these poignant efforts to demystify the "little blue demon," a survey showed that more than 50 percent of the male population in Taiwan desired to try Viagra, and 34 percent of this total were fully aware of the harmful side effects.[68]

In early March 1999, still before Viagra formally hit the market, a group of urologists from six hospitals teamed up and published a "Viagra IQ test," the purpose of which was not medical evaluation (as with the clinics) but to "teach the public proper knowledge about Viagra" so as "to temper over-inflated expectations."[69] At the same time, doctors also formed "Viagra clubs."[70] These were "couple's clinics" of a sort for male users and their female sex partners designed to promote proper understanding of Viagra. Pfizer liked this concept and came forward with funding, as long as the clubs incorporated a "heterosexual educational credit program" where classes would be taught to couples by urologists, psychologists, family practitioners, gynecologists, and obstetricians, as well as social workers. The objective of the classes would be twofold: to make the sex life of "man and wife" more satisfying and to prevent Viagra from being "misused." Incentives would revolve around course credits: "The more credits earned, the more Viagra a couple could obtain."[71] A public meeting to promote the "Viagra clubs" was billed as "how to make Viagra an effective prescription for marital happiness."[72]

The Viagra clubs marked the formalization of Pfizer's involvement in sex education in Taiwan. At a public forum on Viagra also convened in March by the "New Women's Federation," a group of legislators, doctors, feminists, and scholars determined that sex education, especially for youth, should be reformed to make equal rights between men and women its underlying premise.[73] The group called upon Pfizer to reinvest a portion of its local profits in sex education and to provide guidance in implementing the new program, casting in sharp relief how commercial success translates into sociocultural power. Ning Ying-pin remarks that Viagra has been an impetus toward sexual liberation in Taiwan by opening up sex to "rational discourse," a necessary first step, he maintains, for shedding sexual taboos.[74] He also notes that many youths have even invoked Viagra as the basis for challenging education authorities on matters concerning sex.[75] That Viagra has spawned public discussion on sex is of course true; however, the merger between capital and sex education consummated by the Viagra craze should give us pause, especially about the unfolding meanings and implications of so-called rational discourse.

Women have constituted a salient alternative voice in the heterogeneous critique of the Viagra craze. In recent years, the women's movement has spurred a progressive "new man" (hsin-hao nan-jen) discourse that challenges patriarchal ideology and calls for Taiwanese men to share household responsibilities, overcome their fear of intimacy (wei-chü ch'in-mi), and reflect on their inner selves.[76] This discourse portrays Taiwanese men as pathetically oppressed by traditional norms and expectations—especially a competitive obsession with success, social status, and power, so much so that they are unable to cultivate meaningful interpersonal relationships with members of either sex. The "new man" discourse sympathetically reaches out to men, inviting them to return home after a hard day at work and discover intimacy, contentment, and themselves through a modern family lifestyle together with a caring wife and children.

A blizzard of Taiwanese media coverage, editorials, and periodical articles have invoked these "new man" values in attacking Viagra, with the voices of concerned women being most pronounced.[77] Many women fear that Viagra merely encourages men to fetishize their erections and endurance as preconditions for a fulfilling sex life. They view Viagra as an obstacle in their campaign to make Taiwanese men more open, intimate, and communicative and sensitive to their needs, protesting that Viagra has relegated their sexual role to that of necessary adjunct, with their own satisfaction entirely contingent on men's. Feminist groups have criticized the state for approving Viagra so easily, without regard for its adverse consequences to women—and yet the abortion pill RU-486 remains ensnarled in bureaucratic red tape with no sign of approval forthcoming.[78] For many women, the Viagra craze reveals that traditional sexual norms still prevail in Taiwan—men are masters, "bad" women are their toys, and "good" women, such as their wives, sisters, and mothers, have no sexuality, remaining fated only to mind the home, endure men's infidelity, and perpetuate the patriline.[79] This critical discourse of women has at times revealed an uncritical affirmation of gender stereotypes, which has also been echoed within the medical profession, as the following comment by a urologist exemplifies: "At present there are two types of lines in Taiwan: women lining up at movie theaters to see *Titanic*, and men lining up at pharmacies to buy Viagra."[80] Some women have responded by calling for the inversion of this stereo-type, overturning any misconception that there is a unified "women's voice." One week after Viagra hit the market, Huang Hsiu-chin, a woman, published a feature article in the Family section of the *China Times* that went so far as to castigate Asian women, arguing that if they were more sexually assertive and active, men would be relieved of sexual pressures and anxieties and not feel the need for Viagra.[81]

Interestingly, the "new man" discourse seems also to have cultivated in some men an "enlightened" critique of male domination as accentuated in the Viagra craze. In an editorial article, one man contributed the following essay on power, emperors, and Viagra:

In the male subconscious, sex equals power. In ancient times, emperors spared no cost to obtain secret methods to bolster virility. In the present, men have rushed to Viagra to enhance their sexual capability. To put it bluntly, the Viagra craze is nothing more than men's desire to satisfy their subconscious will to power. It reveals that the emperor's dream of the past remains very much alive in the male psyche today. Owing to this dream, we have wars and massacres. What the "little blue pill" reflects is not merely a passing whirlwind, but the fact that wars and massacres will continue to plague the world. I am thirty years old. Presently, I do not need the "little blue pill." If one day I become impotent, I'll make use of my own two hands as a substitute for Viagra and embrace my partner more often.[82]

Local Appropriations

The resilience of the Viagra craze in the face of the tempest of criticism points our inquiry well beyond the obvious issue of erectile dysfunction and its cure. More-over, the evidence shows that the blue whirlwind has had as much to do with the indigenous male concern with sexual performance, bodily health, and domination as with the ways in which Viagra has been incorporated into the political, eco-nomic, and social aspects of everyday life in Taiwan. At least since hitting the U.S. market, Viagra has been widely available on the local black market and through various channels of the island's vast and vibrant informal economy, including ille-gal vendors on the Web.[83] Despite the stiff penalties for trafficking an illegal drug in Taiwan, the lucrative black market for Viagra emboldened some vendors to place newspaper advertisements for the drug, guaranteeing a genuine product im-ported from the United States.[84] Pharmacists have obtained Viagra through the Web and overseas connections, and smuggling rings backed by criminal gangs have maintained a steady underground supply of the drug. An efficient and surreptitious island-wide delivery system, door-to-door and C.O.D., is known to have been (and likely still is) in effect.[85] Demand has consistently outpaced supply, producing a formidable if unstable black-market price, ranging anywhere from US$30 to US$160 per pill. As far back as June 1998, several medical clinics were found to be openly selling Viagra, and in Taichung, a few were impudent enough even to post open advertisements on their front doors.[86]

Pricey, illegal, and potent, Viagra combines just the right ingredients to flourish within Taiwanese male culture. The "little blue pill" has thrived not only as an end, something to be acquired and used, but also as a means of activating and reproducing friendships and connections, the most enduring characteristics of Taiwanese male culture. The appeal of Viagra resides in its efficacy as both a use-value and an exchange-value. The Viagra craze has even inspired the adaptation of a popular ditty: "as a gift or for personal use, Viagra's ideal" (wei-erh-kang sung-li tzu-yung liang hsiang-i).[87]

At least for the time being, Viagra has surpassed foreign cigarettes and alcohol as the gift of choice to bring home from a trip abroad. A man from Chiayi brandished at a banquet a thirty-five-pill bottle of Viagra that he had brought back from the United States, and friends snatched up every last tablet.[88] Several members of Tainan's elite police corps returned from an overseas tour with a special gift for family and friends, the "aphrodisiac Viagra."[89] The policemen were praised in the media as being "rational" (li-hsing) for bringing back only moderate amounts of the illegal drug for prestations.[90] Members of other tour groups have been chastised for smuggling in cases to sell for a profit. Some Taiwanese travel agents are now even offering Viagra as part of their package deals to the United States, promising well-connected tour guides, touted for their "magical power," who will lead tourists to reliable suppliers.[91]

A company in Hsinchu Science Park wanted to make a special gesture of good faith on the mid-autumn festival to clients who weathered a tough year of economic recession.[92] Instead of the conventional gift of mooncakes, this firm decided on two, 100–milligram tablets of Viagra per client. Viagra was deemed to be not only a more potent offering than mooncakes but also a more practical one, "since it could be discreetly slipped to higher management officials not permitted by their companies to accept gifts."[93] Viagra also became a "pack it" staple on Taiwanese men's pleasure junkets (mai-ch'ün) to overseas destinations. A legislator from Chiayi led a tour group to China, bringing along with him fifty Viagra tablets to distribute among his charges.[94] The group made it only as far as Hong Kong when the representative phoned home to friends with the news that all the Viagra was gone. One informant-friend of mine belongs to a golfing club and a bottle of Viagra is standard equipment on their regular excursions to Hainan Island and Kunming.

For a time, my informant-friends incorporated Viagra into their KTV hostess bar routine. Following a round (three hours) of singing and carousing, one man would distribute the Viagra for the next stop at the love hotel. Ning Ying-pin suggests, and my own fieldwork conversations affirm, that extramarital sex is the preferred context in which nonimpotent men use Viagra, exposing the disciplinary design in the preoccupation of normative discourses on Viagra with sexual relations between husband and wife.[95] With few exceptions, my informant-friends regularly pursue extramarital sex and several of them are involved in long-term affairs. Jui-shan Ch'ang, in a study of popular reportage on extramarital affairs in Taiwan, notes that the media has labeled affairs a "new epidemic."[96] She found in her study that even wives are increasingly engaging in affairs, leading her to speculate that more and more Taiwanese women "construe sexual activity as part of lifestyle and identity rather than an enactment of familial or marital commitments."[97] Ch'ang shows how extramarital affairs dialectically engage issues of cultural inheritance, modernization, the body, gender relations, and sexuality. The Viagra craze has worked to intensify these issues and, given that sexual performance is often the paramount concern of extramarital affairs,[98] to up the ante of what is at stake in them sexually for both men and women. Subversive of social and familial norms, extramarital affairs betray the tensions and contradictions at the core of mainstream society and dominant ideology.

Taiwanese politicians have also capitalized on the "little blue pill." An assemblywoman from Taichung boosted her rapport by offering fifty Viagra pills to her male colleagues during a meeting. No takers came forward while they convened, but she was inundated with private requests after the meeting and the tablets quickly disappeared, commenting afterward, "I discovered that middle-class Taiwanese males have a particularly strong interest in Viagra."[99] A giant 1,000–milligram styrofoam Viagra tablet, along with a genuine bottle of the pills, was presented publicly on national television as a retirement gift to the former chief secretary of the Legislative Yüan.[100] Accompanying the offering was a couplet: "Viagra: powerful and strong, fierce and blissful."[101] Many local politicians have reportedly given away Viagra to their electorate instead of the more common practice of giving tea, believing that the "little blue pill" would instill a stronger sense of gratitude in voters.[102] The Ministry of Justice declared Viagra, but not tea, a flagrant quid pro quo, promising to target the practice in its campaign to clean up election bribery.[103]

The Market Effect

As the late March official sales date neared, the blue whirlwind reached a crescendo. In the one week between the arrival of the first batch and the official release date, attention shifted to prices and the whereabouts of the "little blue demon."[104] Pfizer repeatedly declared the total number of orders a "trade secret."[105] Moreover, the company claimed that the first batch would be limited to fifty thousand 50–milligram pills due to production problems at its Australian plant, generating panic among both patients and doctors.[106] Fearful of angry mobs, doctors pleaded with Pfizer to delay the release date until another batch could be brought in.

Pfizer may have been finessing supply and demand, perhaps in order to realize a target price high enough to sustain profits but also low enough to capture sales from the black market. Almost daily for a week, a chart appeared in newspapers tracking the whereabouts of 65 percent of the initial batch as well as anticipated prices. Additional supplies soon arrived and the price stabilized at around US$11.00 per 50–milligram pill, less than half the going black-market price and two dollars more than the U.S. price.[107]

With Viagra's formal appearance on the market, the blue whirlwind seems to have somewhat subsided.[108] Sales are still brisk, on average 3,000 pills per day, though surveys have shown that an "acceptable number" of these are probably being used as intended—to help impotent men overcome erectile dysfunction.[109] However, health-care providers seem to have obtained only limited control over Viagra's use and distribution. Statistics have shown that only a small percentage of men are returning to doctors after an initial visit, indicating that the drug is being bought and sold at local pharmacies without prescriptions, a common though nonetheless illegal practice in Taiwan.[110]

Viagra's gradual fall from the media spotlight in the weeks following its formal introduction on the market may be an indication that "the little blue demon" is no longer being so hotly pursued as an aphrodisiac, an enhancer of sexual performance, or a gift within the Taiwanese male culture of friendship and connections. Although my informant-friends still delight in recounting their Viagra episodes, most of them now admit that it never did much for them and believe that it may be harmful to their bodies. Viagra nonetheless retains a symbolic value eagerly exploited by Taiwan's all-pervasive consumer culture. For example, Xenical has been promoted as a companion "blue whirlwind" to Viagra in Taiwan. Xenical is an appetite-suppressant diet pill, also blue, which is translated as *jang-ni-k'u* (literally, "Make You Cool").[111] A new popular slogan goes, "Three Meals a Day Take 'Make You Cool,' For a Midnight Snack Pop Viagra" (*san-ts'an ch'ih jang-ni-k'u, hsiao-yeh ch'ih wei-erh-kang*).[112] For Father's Day in Taiwan in 1999, many restaurants and bakeries came out with "Viagra Meals" and "Viagra Cakes."[113] A Taipei assemblyman, Ch'en Yung-teh, held a press conference at which he publicly sliced into one of these cakes and found a 100-milligram Viagra pill, promising that guilty vendors would be prosecuted and fined.[114]

The market effect may have gone far to quell the Viagra craze, but it did so not by means of normalization. What happened resembles more what Georg Simmel calls a leveling process engendered by the market and the money form.[115] In entering the market, where value is defined in terms of universal monetary equivalents, Viagra was "downgraded" from a symbolically potent use and exchange value within Taiwanese male culture to a legally available medical commodity unambiguously attached to the mechanisms of capitalism. In the end, the market effect likely depleted Viagra of its protean significance and multifarious appropriations among many Taiwanese men. Nevertheless, commercial interests continue to fetishize the "little blue demon"—much as normalization efforts did, though this time by hitching its mystique to commodities that circulate within the marketplace.

Conclusion

In a discussion on Viagra while conducting fieldwork, an informant-friend remarked that "things" (*tung-hsi*) from all over the world come to Taiwan, and after they arrive "we" always change them a little to make them distinctively Taiwanese. In a different conversation, another informant-friend explained to me that Taiwanese are susceptible to the capricious "craze" phenomenon owing to the absence of a historically rooted culture like that of (mainland) China. To fill the void, he continued, Taiwanese rush *en masse* to acquire "new things" in the marketplace as the very essence of Taiwaneseness has become rooted in collective participation in these short-lived commercial trends. These two observations crystallize the notion of contradictory consciousness, showing how an inherited (but no less living) sense of culture is *posited* as people unite and divide in the practical transformation of the world.

In the gender politics of the Viagra craze, which illustrates well this dynamic, the Taiwanese culture of enhancement drugs has animated, and been animated by, the heterogeneous efforts by different groups to challenge and redefine existing norms of sexuality in the context of changing social situations. The inherited culture of virility stimulants and aphrodisiacs constitutes a potent universe of codes that has variously mediated normative discourses seeking to construct Viagra as a biotechnically modern cure for erectile dysfunction. If different critical voices have tended to reaffirm the "straight" discourse on Viagra usage, they have also in the process paradoxically revived and legitimized the idea of enhancement drugs,[116] contributing in no small measure to the vigor of the Viagra craze.

Viagra has had many incarnations in Taiwan, namely as impotence medicine, enhancement drug, prestation, marketing prop, and symbol of male domination. Whereas Ning Ying-pin focused on the subversive potentiality borne of the decision to use a stigmatized modern sex drug, I have chosen to emphasize the multiple and indeterminate possibilities inherent in Viagra's double career as a sex drug and an overdetermined sign. Taiwanese men and women have appropriated Viagra to a wide range of practical and symbolic purposes in the course of negotiating the particular circumstances of their individual and collective lives. And Viagra never acquires one meaning entirely independently of its other meanings, which would indicate that the reflexive process in the decision to use the drug leads to outcomes for gender and sexuality that remain open and contingent. My analysis of the Viagra craze thus calls into question a teleological rationalist interpretation of the impact of Viagra as a "modern sex drug." The product of a multiplicity of voices and competing forces, the "blue whirlwind" in Taiwan is the archetypal example of the transformative power of global capitalism that is nonetheless indeterminate, multifocal, and ultimately local.

In the end, then, it seems that normative efforts to stem the Viagra craze failed for three main reasons. First, Viagra became readily assimilated within inherited ideas that link bodily health, sexual performance, and male domination. Second, by articulating that which they sought to suppress, normative and critical discourses went far to reinforce the Taiwanese culture of enhancement drugs, thereby producing in the process many of their own stumbling blocks. And third, Viagra became absorbed within the entrenched and widely reticulating networks of Taiwanese male culture, including the island's vast and vibrant informal economy. Although I stop short of drawing any tidy or totalizing conclusions, I do so in order to foreground the complexity of the Viagra craze and the fact that its ramifications and range of implications for gender relations and sexuality are still being worked out.

Notes

Earlier versions of this paper were presented at the regional conference of the Association for Asian Studies (Hobart and William Smith Colleges, 1999), the North American Taiwan Studies Conference (Harvard University, 2000), and the regional conference of the Association for Asian Studies (Sophia University, Tokyo, 2000). I thank the discussants, Shen Hsiu-hua and Ichiro Numazaki, as well as the participants for many useful comments and questions. Special thanks to Haiyan Lee, who read and commented on this paper.

1. Huang T'ing-yü, "Wei-erh-kang lai le! tsuei ch'ih san-yüeh 26 jih shang-shih" (Viagra's Here! March 26th It Hits the Market, at the Latest), *Chungkuo shih-pao*, March 20, 1999. *All* newspaper articles cited without a page number were accessed online at that newspaper's Web site. Articles from *Chungkuo shih-pao*, *Chung-shih wan-pao*, and *Kung-shang shih-pao* can be found at www.chinatimes.com; and those from the *Taipei Times* can be found at www.taipeitimes.com.

2. See Yang Mei-chen, "Ting-huo-liang yi ta 50 wan k'o" (Orders Reach· 500,000 Pills), *Tzu-yu shih-pao*, March 21, 1999: 7; and Cheng I, "Wei-erh-kang yu hai hun-yin?" (Will Viagra Harm Marriages?), *Chung-shih wan-pao*, April 4, 1999: 13.

3. See Sheng Chu-ling, "So hao 'hsiao-wan-tzu'" (Lock Up the "Little Blue Pill"), *Tzu-yu shih-pao*, March 21, 1999: 7; and idem, "Wei-erh-kang ch'iang-shou-huo yi-yüan cheng ping-huan tseng" (Viagra's in High Demand, Hospitals Do Battle, Patients on the Rise), *Tzu-yu shih-pao*, March 16, 1999: 8.

4. Ma Ting, *Lan-ssu ching-ling: Wei-ko pao-kao* (The Blue Spirit: Viagra) (Canton: Chuhai ch'u-pan-she, 1998), 136.

5. See www.viagra.com.

6. See www.pfizer.com.

7. Ning Ying-pin, "Wei-erh-kang lun-shu ti fen-hsi: hsien-tai yung-yao yü shen-t'i kuan-li" (On Viagra: Modern Drug Use and Body Management), *Taiwan she-hui yen-chiu chi-k'an*, no. 33 (March 1999): 240. I engage aspects of Ning's sharp and provocative analysis throughout this essay (see below).

8. Ibid., 240–41.

9. See Joseph Bristow, *Sexuality* (London: Routledge, 1997); Micaela di Leonardo and Roger N. Lancaster, "Introduction: Embodied Meanings, Carnal Practices," in *The Gender/Sexuality Reader: Culture, History, Political Economy*, ed. di Leonardo and Lancaster (New York: Routledge, 1997); and Michel Foucault, *The History of Sexuality* (New York: Vintage, 1980).

10. di Leonardo and Lancaster, "Introduction," 1.

11. See Shih Yü-ch'i, "Wo yao kao-ch'ao pu-pi chih-chiu" (I Want a Climax—Not a

Marathon), *Tzu-yu shih-pao*, March 16, 1999: 44; Wang Hao-wei, *Taiwan ch'a-fu-jen* (Taiwanese Men) (Taipei: Lien-ho wen-hsüeh, 1998); Chang Li-wen, "Lai yi-k'o yeh-yeh-yeh k'uang—Taiwan lang-hsing ti mi-ssu" (Pop One Pill and Go All Night—A Taiwanese Male Fantasy), *Chungkuo shih-pao*, March 29, 1999: 8; and Cheng I, "Wei-erh-kang yu hai hun-yin?" (Will Viagra Harm Marriages?), *Chung-shih wan-pao*, April 4, 1999: 13.

12. Ibid.

13. Ning, "Wei-erh-kang lun-shu ti fen-hsi," 247.

14. For example, see Chang Li-wen, "Wei-erh-kang hsien-hsiang fu-nü t'uan-t'i, yi-hsüeh-chieh tan-hsin ch'ung-chi liang-hsing p'ing-ch'üan" (The Viagra Phenomenon—Women and Doctors Worry About Impact on Sexual Equality), *Chungkuo shih-pao*, March 20, 1999.

15. Deniz Kandiyoti, "The Paradoxes of Masculinity: Some Thoughts on Segregated Societies," in *Dislocating Masculinity: Comparative Ethnographies*, ed. A. Cornwall and N. Lindisfarne (London: Routledge, 1994), 212.

16. Ning, "Wei-erh-kang lun-shu ti fen-hsi."

17. Ibid.

18. See P'eng Huei-hsien, "Lan-yung teh an-ch'üan-kan" (The Sense of Safety in Abuse), *Chungkuo shih-pao*, July 11, 1999. P'eng maintains that a sense of safety in abusive or extreme behavior (such as Viagra-assisted carnal indulgence, binge eating and popping diet pills, embezzlement under the safe umbrella of state-business relations) has become a popular trend in Taiwan. While acknowledging the "breathing space" created by this sensibility, P'eng is generally sharply critical of it. He argues that it weakens critical consciousness and fosters fatalism and social apathy. He fears that if permitted to spread unabated, the sense of safety in abuse (*lan-yung an-ch'üan-kan*) could become highly destructive, jeopardizing everything from individual health to national security.

19. George Yudice, "What's a Straight White Man to Do?" in *Constructing Masculinity*, ed. M. Berger, B. Wallis, and S. Watson (New York: Routledge, 1995), 280.

20. Laura Mamo and Jennifer Fishman, "Potency in All the Right Places: Viagra as a Technology of the Gendered Body," *Body & Society* 7, no. 4 (2001): 13–35.

21. The consumer pamphlet may be found on-line at Pfizer's official Viagra Web site—www.viagra.com.

22. Mamo and Fishman, "Potency."

23. See Victor J. Seidler, *Unreasonable Men: Masculinity and Social Theory* (London: Routledge, 1994). Seidler critically examines the gendered basis of the parallel dichotomies—reason:emotion::culture:nature::masculinity:femininity—and how they have permeated and influenced social theory and the Western episteme.

24. Mamo and Fishman, "Potency."

25. In mainland China, Viagra is translated differently as *wei-ko*, or "great brother."

26. For example, in Liang Shih-ch'iu's *Far East Chinese-English Dictionary*, "chuang-yang-chi" is defined straightforwardly as "an aphrodisiac." In conversations with my informant-friends in Taipei, I learned that, when pressed, Taiwanese can make a distinction between the stimulation of virility and desire. However, within the context of Chinese medical cosmology, where no sharp division between mind and body is drawn, there is ultimately little significance in the distinction. The Chinese medicine experts with whom I spoke told me in no uncertain terms that there is no difference between Chinese aphrodisiacs and virility stimulants.

27. Ning also notes that in China's sexual culture there are no appropriate categories for understanding Viagra, a modern impotence medicine, so he coins a new term, "sex drug." Although traditional virility stimulants are also sex drugs, Ning emphasizes the "modern significance" of Viagra (more below). Even today, five years after Viagra was formally introduced in Taiwan, the media still uses the term for traditional virility stimulant, *chuang-yang-yao*, when referring to Viagra as well as newer impotence drugs, such as Levitra; see

P'an Hsün, "Shih-liu fen-chung chiu fa hsiung-wei Ouchou hsin chuang-yang-yao Li-wei-t'a tsai Mei shang-shih" (Virile in Sixteen Minutes, Europe's New Virility Stimulant Levitra Hits the American Market), *Chungkuo shih-pao*, August 21, 2003.

28. Wang I-chia, *Hsing-ssu ti t'u-p'u* (An Atlas of Sex in China) (Taipei: Yeh-o ch'u-pan-she, 1995), 175–209. Wang claims that his critical interpretation revises the conventional argument that the baroque sexual practices and norms of the Chinese art of the bedchamber were a means by which Chinese men sought to take advantage of their power and status both to obtain personal pleasure and to invert their relative weakness of reproductive ability (*sheng-chih neng-li*) vis-à-vis women. As with much recent Western scholarship on the Chinese art of the bedchamber, Wang's interpretation also debunks influential studies, such as those by Western sinologists, who romanticize this classic corpus as a Chinese *ars erotica*; see also Charlotte Furth, "Rethinking Van Gulik: Sexuality and Reproduction in Traditional Chinese Medicine," in *Engendering China: Women, Culture, and the State*, ed. C. Gilmartin, G. Hershatter, L. Rofel, and T. White (Cambridge: Harvard University Press, 1994), 125–46, and Judith Farquhar, *Appetites: Food and Sex in Post-Socialist China* (Durham: Duke University Press, 2002), 243–84.

A graduate of National Taiwan University's Department of Medicine, Wang chose to forgo a career as a doctor and become a writer (much like the eminent May Fourth intellectual Lu Hsün). In 1979, he and his wife, Yen Man-li, established their own publishing company, Wild Goose (*Yeh-o ch'u-pan-she*), which is dedicated to the publication of their own writings. Wild Goose publications shun mundane affairs and aim to expand the intellectual horizons of readers (especially those whom they refer to as "domestic geese") by introducing them to fresh ideas and perspectives that might transform them into "wild geese." Wild Goose maintains a Web site where Wang and his wife publish essays and a newsletter and offer visitors a discussion forum. Between the two of them, they have published more than twenty books (with Wang writing most of them), as well as numerous articles and essays. Wang's writings are very highly regarded. For example, seven of Wang's books, including *An Atlas of Sex in China*, appear on a reading list prepared by Kaohsiung City's designated "high school sex education teaching and resource center," whose objective is to develop curricula that teach and promote gender equality. Wang has a large, almost cultlike, following among high-school and college students, and in on-line forum discussions students have lavished praise on his writings and claimed to have been formatively influenced by his ideas.

29. Furth, "Rethinking Van Gulik."

30. Ibid.; see also Hugh Shapiro, "The Puzzle of Spermatorrhea in Republican China," *Positions: East Asia Cultures Critique* 6, no. 3 (1998): 551–96. Interestingly, based on a bedchamber story from sometime during the Sui and T'ang dynasties (581–907), Charlotte Furth concludes, "bedchamber manuals did not claim that the primordial vitality of yin essence, as embodied in females, was an inexhaustible reservoir available to nourish the male"; see Furth, "Rethinking Van Gulik," 134.

31. See Ts'ai Wen-t'ing, "Lao-tz'u-tsung ti 'Wei-erh-kang'? Sheng-wu k'o-chi tsai chen chung-yao 'hsiung-feng'" (Ancient Viagras?: Biotech Breathes New Life into Chinese Herbal Aphrodisiacs), *Kuang-hua* (Sinorama) 23, no. 8 (1998): 35–47; and Hsieh Ying-hua, "Tsung jih-ch'ang yin-shih tseng-ch'iang hsing huo-li" (Strengthen Sexual Activity Through Your Diet), *Chungkuo shih-pao*, October 7, 1999.

32. See Tseng Wei-chen, "Ch'üan-li, huang-ti, Wei-erh-kang" (Power, Emperor, Viagra), *Tzu-yu shih-pao*, March 31, 1999: 15; and Chuang Po-lin, "Yao-ch'ien hai-ssu jen ti ku-shih" (The Story of a Deadly Prescription), *Tzu-yu shih-pao*, March 13, 1999: 15.

33. Ning. "Wei-erh-kang lun-shu ti fen-hsi."

34. Ibid.

35. Ibid.

36. See Chris Rojek, *Decentring Leisure: Rethinking Leisure Theory* (London: Sage, 1995), 67–69.

37. Ning, "Wei-erh-kang lun-shu ti fen-hsi"; see also Ulrich Beck, *Risk Society*, trans. Mark Ritter (London: Sage, 1992). Beck's thesis, to put it baldly, is that the more clearly modern risk situations, produced ultimately by scientific experts, enter public conscious-ness, the greater the degree of reflexivity induced among lay people. This dynamic, which Beck describes as one between tradition and modernity or experts and lay people, is the generative basis for modern transformation (Beck, *Risk Society*, 155–63).

38. Ning emphasizes, for example, that body management practices (such as taking Viagra to masturbate or to use with a mistress) are about "controlling one's own body," which would align with Beck's modernist or Enlightenment sensibility (Ning, "Wei-erh-kang lun-shu ti fen-hsi," 251).

39. See P'eng, "Lan-yung ti an-ch'üan-kan."

40. Rojek, *Decentring Leisure*, 153. Although difficult to reconcile with Beck's "risk society" paradigm, the progressive role of separate or deviant (irrational?) interests is cen-tral to Ning's inspired thesis of Viagra's liberatory and transformative potential.

41. Lin Ch'i-po, "Chieh-k'ai chin-ku shen-t'i ti fu-ma—body power" (Nymphs, Babes, and Hunks Pioneer New Body Codes), *Kuang-hua* (Sinorama) 24 (August 1999): 8.

42. At a conference where I presented an earlier version of this paper, a young Taiwan-ese student commented that his friends back home were very excited about Viagra and had all tried it for recreational purposes. As if to provide a justification for his friends, he pro-ceeded to lecture me on popular Taiwanese conceptions of traditional virility stimulants. He also related that his friends now expected him to return to Taiwan with a supply of Viagra.

43. Shih Yen-fei, "Mai Wei-erh-kang ch'ing-chuang-nien pi-li tsui kao" (Young Adults Are Biggest Buyers of Viagra), *Chungkuo shih-pao*, May 16, 1998.

44. Matthew C. Gutmann, *The Meanings of Macho: Being a Man in Mexico City* (Ber-keley: University of California Press, 1996), 15.

45. Ibid.

46. When asked to state the causes of sexual dysfunction, men and women both named work pressures and poor health as the number one and two causes, respectively (Shih Yen-fei).

47. "Why Rhinos Recommend Viagra," *Economist*, May 30, 1998: 80.

48. See Ts'ai Wen-t'ing, "Tao-ti Wei-erh-kang tsai T'ai yu tuo-ta shih-ch'ang?" (Just How Big Is the Viagra Market in Taiwan?), *Chungkuo shih-pao*, August 3, 1998; idem, "Chung-yao chuang-yang liao-fa hsiang hsi-yao Wei-erh-kang t'iao-chan" (Chinese Impo-tence Remedies Challenge Viagra), *Chungkuo shih-pao*, August 4, 1998; idem, "Tung-fang Wei-erh-kang—'tung ch'ung hsia ts'ao'" (Eastern Viagra—*C. sinensis*), *Chungkuo shih-pao*, March 17, 1999: 12. I noticed an abundance of animal parts and concoctions thereof on display in nearly all the traditional Chinese medicine shops that I visited in Taipei as well as in other places throughout China.

49. Ibid.

50. See Ts'ai, "Tao-ti Wei-erh-kang tsai T'ai yu tuo-ta shih-ch'ang?" and "Chung-yao chuang-yang liao-fa hsiang hsi-yao Wei-erh-kang t'iao-chan."

51. Ts'ai, "Tao-ti Wei-erh-kang tsai T'ai yu tuo-ta shih-ch'ang?"

52. Hsieh Ying-hua, "Tsung jih-ch'ang yin-shih tseng-ch'iang hsing huo-li"; see also Ts'ai, "Tung-fang Wei-erh-kang—'tung ch'ung hsia ts'ao.'"

53. See P'eng, "Lan-yung ti an-ch'üan-kan."

54. Ts'ai, "Tao-ti Wei-erh-kang tsai T'ai yu tuo-ta shih-ch'ang?"

55. See Wang Hao-wei, *Taiwan ch'a-fu-jen.*

56. By July 1998, the debate over whether or not Viagra should be covered by Taiwan's social medicine insurance program was already underway. Detractors had the upper hand in the argument at that time, largely because of the absence of a sound clinical definition of impotence; see Shih Yen-fei, "Wei-erh-kang chien-pao kei-fu? Yen-t'ao-hui yi-chien liang-chi" (Health Insurance Coverage for Viagra? Opinions Divided), *Chungkuo shih-pao*, July

7, 1998 and Chang Li-wen, "Chien-pao ching-hsiang pu-kei-fu Wei-erh-kang" (Leaning toward No Insurance Coverage for Viagra), *Chungkuo shih-pao*, September 22, 1998.

57. Ts'ai, "Tao-ti Wei-erh-kang tsai T'ai yu tuo-ta shih-ch'ang?"

58. Chang Li-wen, "I-shih: Wei-erh-kang wu-fa tseng-chin nü-hsing hsing man-tzu" (Doctor Says: Viagra Can't Raise Women's Sexual Satisfaction), *Chungkuo shih-pao*, September 28, 1998.

59. Ibid.

60. Ts'ai, "Tao-ti Wei-erh-kang tsai T'ai yu tuo-ta shih-ch'ang?"

61. Governments throughout the world have approved Viagra with unprecedented speed and ease. In 1998 alone, Pfizer released Viagra in more than forty countries. In Japan, where drug approval typically takes years, Viagra was approved for marketing (January 1, 1999) only six months after Pfizer first filed its application with the government; see "Ending on a Blue Note," *Asiaweek*, February 12, 1999: 43.

62. See "Lan-ssu hsiao-wan-tzu hua-pu-tao liang-ch'ien pien chih 'hsing-pu-hsing'" (For Less Than NT $2000, Find Out if Viagra's for You), *Chungkuo shih-pao*, January 5, 1999; Yang P'ei-chün, "Wei-erh-kang men-chen pa-hsün lao-weng ts'e hsiung-feng" (Eighty-Year-Old Man Gets Masculinity Test at Viagra Clinic), *Chungkuo shih-pao*, January 5, 1999; and Chang Li-wen, "Wei-erh-kang yüeh-ti shang-shih yü-yüeh wu-men" (Viagra Hits the Market at Month End—All Doors Closed for Advanced Orders), *Chungkuo shih-pao*, March 8, 1999.

63. Yang, "Wei-erh-kang men-chen pa-hsün lao-weng ts'e hsiung-feng."

64. Chang, "Wei-erh-kang yüeh-ti shang-shih yü-yüeh wu-men."

65. Chang, "Pu-p'a fu-tsuo-yung Taiwan chih-shao wan-jen ch'ih-kuo" (Showing No Fear of Side Effects, at Least Ten Thousand Taiwanese Have Tried [Viagra]), *Chungkuo shih-pao*, March 20, 1999.

66. Ibid.

67. Yang Mei-chen, "Wei-erh-kang yung-fa i-shih k'ai-pan shou-k'o" (Viagra Usage—Doctors Hold Classes), *Tzu-yu shih-pao*, March 24, 1999: 8; see also Chang Li-wen, "I-yeh chi-tu yu ch'ün-feng huei chiao fü-hsü Wei-erh-kang" (Repetitive Sex—Some Wives Regret Telling Their Husbands about Viagra), *Chungkuo shih-pao*, March 8, 1999.

68. Chang, "Pu-p'a fu-tsuo-yung Taiwan chih-shao wan-jen ch'ih-kuo."

69. Chang, "Ch'ien-chin 'hsing' fu-tao—IQ ta-ts'e-yen" (Improve Sex on Treasure Island—The Viagra IQ Test), *Chungkuo shih-pao*, March 8, 1999.

70. Wu Ching-kuei, "'Yin-chin Wei-erh-kang—ling-lei ti-lei ku kung-t'ing-huei ts'e-chi" (Import Viagra—An Alternative Minefield), *Tzu-yu shih-pao*, March 23, 1999: 15, Yang, "Wei-erh-kang yung-fa i-shih k'ai-pan shou-k'o."

71. Yang, "Wei-erh-kang yung-fa i-shih k'ai-pan shou-k'o."

72. Wu, "Yin-chin Wei-erh-kang."

73. Ibid.; Chang, "Wei-erh-kang hsien-hsiang fu-nü t'uen-t'i, yi-hsüeh-chieh tan-hsin ch'ung-chi liang-hsing p'ing-ch'üan."

74. Ning, "Wei-erh-kang lun-shu ti fen-hsi," 233–34.

75. Ibid.

76. Ts'ao Yu-fang (Taiwanese), *Nan-jen chen ming-k'u* (Men Have It Tough) (Peking: Hsin-shih-chieh ch'u-pan-she, 1999), *passim*; Hsieh Shu-fen, "Hsin-hao nan-jen—huei chia ti lu hai hen ch'ang" (At a Male's Pace: New Men Adapt to Changing Gender Roles), *Kuang-hua* (Sinorama), no. 3 (1999): 205–13.

77. For example, see Teng Ch'ao-chung, "Pieh jang ni ti nan-jen luan ch'ih Wei-erh-kang" (Don't Let Your Man Abuse Viagra), *Chia-t'ing yüeh-k'an* (Family Monthly), no. 270 (March 1999): 124–25; Huang Shu-ying, "Wei-erh-kang pei niu-ch'ü luan-yung" (Viagra Gets Abused), *Tzu-yu shih-pao*, March 23, 1999; Hsü Nan-ch'in, "Wei-erh-kang ta 'chü' ju ch'in pu-teng-yü nü-jen hsing fu" (Viagra's Great Invasion Doesn't Mean Sexual Bliss for Women), *Shih-pao chou-k'an*, no. 1100 (March 28–April 3, 1999): 104–6; Chang Li-wen,

"Lai i-k'o yeh-yeh-yeh k'uang—Taiwan lang-hsing ti mi-ssu"; and Cheng I.

78. Lin Ch'un-hua, "Chen-so wei-fa fan-shou Wei-erh-kang" (Clinics Illegally Sell Viagra), *Chungkuo shih-pao*, June 24, 1998; Hsü, "Wei-erh-kang ta 'chü' ju ch'in pu-teng-yü nü-jen hsing fu."

79. Hsü, "Wei-erh-kang ta 'chü' ju ch'in pu-teng-yü nü-jen hsing fu."

80. Chang, "I-shih: Wei-erh-kang wu-fa tseng-chin nü-hsing hsing man-tzu."

81. Huang Hsiu-chin, "Han ya-tzu tsen-neng yung yü ai ho?" (Can Dry Ducklings Swim in the Sea of Love Forever?), *Chungkuo shih-pao*, April 2, 1999.

82. Tseng, "Ch'üen-li, huang-ti, Wei-erh-kang."

83. For example, see Chang Li-wen, "Chung-shih yao-chü yao-fang san-ch'eng-liu wei-kuei" (Taichung—Thirty-six Percent of Pharmacies Violate Regulations), *Chungkuo shih-pao*, August 24, 1999; and Chang Li-wen, "Pu-hsiao yao-shang pan-hsing 5–7 nien" (Unscrupulous Drug Merchants Get Five to Seven Years), *Chungkuo shih-pao*, July 4, 1999.

84. Hsiao Ch'eng-hsün, "Tso-ssu Wei-erh-kang hei-shih sheng-hsing" (Viagra Gets Smuggled In—Black Market Prospers), *Chungkuo shih-pao*, June 26, 1998.

85. Ibid.; Chang, "Pu-hsiao yao-shang p'an-hsing 5–7 nien."

86. Lin, "Chen-so wei-fa fan-shou Wei-erh-kang."

87. Ts'ai Ch'ang-keng, "Wei-erh-kang: sung li chiao-i liang-hsiang i" (As a Gift or for Personal Use, Viagra's Ideal), *Chungkuo shih-pao*, August 17, 1998; see also Lu Chün-wei, "Sung li, chiu sung Wei-erh-kang" (Need a Gift?—Give Viagra), *Tzu-yu shih-pao*, March 24, 1999: 8.

88. Ts'ai, "Wei-erh-kang."

89. Ch'en I-chih, "Ch'u-kuo tsuei-chia k'uei-tseng li-wu—Wei-erh-kang" (Most Valued Gift to Bring Home from Abroad: Viagra), *Chungkuo shih-pao*, September 4, 1998.

90. Ibid.

91. Ts'ai, "Wei-erh-kang."

92. Ch'en Ai-chu, "Hsinchu k'o-hsüeh yuan-ch'ü ch'ang-shang chung-ch'iu sung-li Wei-erh-kang" (Viagra Is Mid-Autumn Festival Gift of Choice for Hsinchu Science Park Firm), *Chungkuo shih-pao*, October 3, 1998.

93. Ibid.

94. Ts'ai, "Wei-erh-kang."

95. Ning, "Wei-erh-kang lun-shu ti fen-hsi," 244–45; see also Chang, "Lai i-k'o yeh-yeh-yeh k'uang—Taiwan lang-hsing ti mi-ssu."

96. Ch'ang Jui-shan, "Scripting Extramarital Affairs: Marital Mores, Gender Politics, and Infidelity in Taiwan," *Modern China* 25, no. 1 (1999): 69–99.

97. Ibid., 69–72. In her sociological investigation of extramarital sex in China, Li Yin-ho found a starkly more conservative situation, owing, she argues, to the persistence of harsh social and legal sanctions rather than to individual desires; Li Yin-ho, *Hsing hun-yin: tung-fang yü hsi-fang* (Sex and Marriage: East Versus West) (Sian: Shan-hsi shih-fan ta-hsüeh ch'u-pan-she, 1999), 171–92.

98. Both Ch'ang and Ning make this point.

99. Lin Ch'ün-hua, "Nü-yi-yüan sung Wei-erh-kang 'kung-pu-ying-ch'iu'" (Female Legislator Dishes Out Viagra: "Demand Exceeds Supply"), *Chungkuo shih-pao*, September 10, 1998.

100. Lu, "Sung li, chiu sung Wei-erh-kang"; Chang Li-wen, "Sheng i-huei kung-k'ai sung Wei-erh-kang" (Legislative Assembly Makes Public Offering of Viagra), *Chungkuo shih-pao*, July 17, 1998.

101. Chang, "Sheng i-huei kung-k'ai sung Wei-erh-kang."

102. Ts'ai, "Wei-erh-kang"; Yang Shu-huang, "Nan-t'ou wen-hsüan Wei-erh-kang hou-hsüan-jen yang-ming" (Viagra as Campaign Propaganda in Nantou—Candidate Achieves Notoriety), *Chungkuo shih-pao*, November 9, 1998.

103. Ts'ai, "Wei-erh-kang."

104. Sheng Chu-ling, "Wei-erh-kang 22 jih shang-shih shou-chia ti-yü ssu-pai-yüan" (Viagra Hits the Market on the 22nd—Price Drops Below NT $400), *Tzu-yu shih-pao*, March 13, 1999: 1; Wu Huei-fen, "Mei-k'o 350 yüan Wei-erh-kang chiang-chia lo!" (NT$350—Viagra Price Is Down!), *Chung-shih wan-pao*, March 25, 1999: 3; Yang Mei-chen and Sheng Chu-ling, "Wei-erh-kang k'ai-mai lao-ping-hao lo-t'ou" (Viagra Hits the Market—Chronic Sufferers Rejoice), *Tzu-yu shih-pao*, March 25, 1999: 9.

105. Chang, "Wei-erh-kang yü-ti shang-shih yü-yüeh wu-men."

106. Sheng, "Wei-erh-kang 22 jih shang-shih shou-chia ti-yü ssu-pai-yüan."

107. Wu, "Mei-k'o 350 yüen Wei-erh-kang chiang-chia lo!"

108. Wu Huei-fen, "Shang-shih man-yüeh Wei-erh-kang man-yi-tu hsia-chiang" (After a Month, Viagra's Satisfaction Rate Declines), *Chung-shih wan-pao*, April 20, 1999.

109. Wu Huei-fen, "Wei-erh-kang shang-shih-hou i-ssu ch'ih-ssu 4 jen" (Four Alleged Viagra-Related Deaths Reported), *Chung-shih wan-pao*, September 14, 1999.

110. Ibid.; see also Chang, "Chang-shih yao-chü yao-fang san-ch'eng-liu wei-kui."

111. Lin Wen-ch'ün, "Chien-fei hsin yao 'jang-ni-k'u' sheng-shih chih-chui Wei-erh-kang" (New Diet Pill "Make You Cool"—Prestige Approaches Viagra), *Chung-shih wan-pao*, July 4, 1999; Wu Huei-fen, "Lan-ssu hsüan-feng jang-ni-k'u yu-jen han san-ts'an ch'ih" (The New Blue Whirlwind—"Make You Cool"—Three Times a Day with Meals), *Chung-shih wan-pao*, August 9, 1999; Chang Han-ch'ing, "Jang-ni-k'u shou-shen li-wei yeh feng-k'uang" ("Make You Cool" Diet Pill—Legislators Also Mad for It), *Chung-shih wan-pao*, August 9, 1999.

112. Wu, "Lan-ssu hsüan-feng jang-ni-k'u yu-jen han san-ts'an ch'ih."

113. Ch'eng Chin-lan, "Wei-erh-kang tan-kao ch'iang-shou kuan-yüan ch'u-fa" (Viagra Cakes Selling Like "Hot Cakes"—Official Breaks Law), *Chung-shih wan-pao*, August 7, 1999; Ch'en Hsiu-ling, "Tan-kao t'ien-chia Wei-erh-kang tsuei-kao fa 12 wan" (Viagra Cakes—Maximum Fine NT$120,000), *Chungkuo shih-pao*, August 8, 1999; Lin Ching-jung, "Wei-erh-kang tan-kao mai-pu-te" (Viagra Cakes Illegal), *Chungkuo shih-pao*, August 6, 1999.

114. Cheng, "Wei-erh-kang tan-kao ch'iang-shou kuan-yüan ch'u-fa."

115. Georg Simmel, "Money in Modern Culture," *Theory, Culture, & Society*, no. 8, (1991): 17–31.

116. See Jack Hitt, "The Second Sexual Revolution," *New York Times*, February 20, 2000.

Part III

Feminisms and Cultural Critique

11

Transcribing Feminism

Taiwanese Women's Experiences

Hwei-syin Lu

"If a Westerner asks me whether I'm a feminist, my answer will be yes. But if a Chinese asks me the same question, I'll say no. Western people make a clear distinction between feminists and nonfeminists, while a Chinese woman will hesitate to label herself as a feminist lest her family, marriage, and human relationships break."

This quoted remark was addressed to me by a female psychological consultant of a women's group, the Taipei Women's Development Center, which aimed at helping widows or women who encountered marital problems to achieve economic and emotional independence. The consultant, who was in her mid-thirties, single, and had received her master's degree in cinema studies in America, often encouraged members of this group to live on their own. Once I asked her about her view of feminism (*nü-hsing chu-i*, literally meaning "the doctrine of women") and whether she is a feminist. She responded in an equivocal way, as the above quote shows. Then she added, "The notion of *nü-hsing chu-i* has already been distorted in Taiwan. People ridiculed feminists by saying that the latter simply hate men and fail to communicate with men. Spiritually I'm a feminist, but I don't like to be called feminist."

Her viewpoint echoed many other voices I heard when conducting my dissertation research on three women's self-growth groups in Taipei in 1987–89. Although the establishment of these groups was in one way or another influenced by the Awakening, the first feminist group to introduce feminist ideas to Taiwan, many members from these groups avoided identifying themselves as feminists. They equated feminism with being antimen or antifamily, both of which in their cognition were questionable. These women, mostly middle class, often emphasized that both genders are equally important, and that women should cooperate or negotiate with, rather than oppose, men. Quite a few of these women criticized Taiwanese feminists as too aggressive or arrogant, implying that they lacked gentleness, consideration for others, and compassion, all of which are valued as Chinese women's gender attributes. And these attributes are associated with women's domestic roles and identities.

Given the foregoing, can we conclude that these Taiwanese women are yet to raise their female consciousness and to be liberated from the Chinese family that is notably patriarchal? For a Western feminist who views the family as an institution that confines and subordinates women to the service of men, this inference may be rational. Yet as an indigenous anthropologist, I will argue that this view reflects Western ethnocentrism and ignores the native meaning of femaleness and maleness, the primary interests of Chinese women, and viable ways of searching for gender equality in the Chinese cultural setting. When a Taiwanese woman says she dislikes the term *nü-hsing chu-i*, this does not necessarily mean that she is an antifeminist, as we can tell from the female consultant's comments above. It is only that they feel the concept of *nü-hsing chu-i* is not reflective of their experience or practical enough to help them resolve problems in their daily lives. Many Taiwanese women disagree with the notion of *nü-hsing chu-i* not because of what they perceive as feminist goals but because of feminist methods and manners, and the terms of feminist arguments. These methods, manners, and arguments may conflict with their ideas of "what it is to be a Chinese woman."

I am not drawing a fundamental contrast between Chinese women and their Western counterparts. In fact, they share similar experiences with regard to many facts of gender inequality originating from patriarchy. However, the way that women cope with these inequalities and the strategies they take can vary culturally, as many scholars have noted (Babb 1984; Nader 1986). Thus, in this chapter I am concerned with how and to what extent the idea of Western feminism can be transcribed in Taiwan. I examine Taiwanese women's feminist experience as reflected in their marriage and family. I postulate that the sociocultural principle of "positionality," on the one hand, confines Chinese women to relationally defined domestic roles, and, on the other hand, allows them to select one role in preference to another and to maneuver between domestic and public arenas in searching for interests and power.

By "positionality" I mean that human relationships in Chinese society are regulated in a hierarchical order. The order is represented by the Confucian Three Bonds (*san kang*), which dictates three metaphorical sets of relations (emperor : subject :: father : son :: husband : wife) and Five Human Relationships (*wu lun*) (emperor to subject, father to son, husband to wife, older brother to younger brother, and friends to one another). Based on the rules of *san kang* and *wu lun*, the Chinese are allotted different positions, or roles, and the duties prescribed to those positions. These rules undergird Chinese ideas of social personhood (Tu 1976). With regard to gender in the family, although the notion of positionality implies male dominance, it also crosscuts gender by subordinating some men to other men (e.g., sons to fathers), some women to other women (e.g., daughters-in-law to mothers-in-law), and some men to some women (e.g., sons to mothers). Tani Barlow (1985) thus remarked that the supremacy of the Chinese patrilineal family never nurtures a male/female opposition. Instead, she illuminates:

Kinship discourses and clan regulations positioned all Chinese inside the "natural" hierarchies of *jia* (family), *zu* (lineage), and a myriad of pseudo-femalist instructions. . . . Inside the multitude of hierarchical, architectonic, designated places, gender existed neither as *place*, nor, as in the bourgeois West, *essence*, nor as a *symbolic* expression of fecundity or fertility. Gender was rather a single axis among many. (Barlow 1985: 1–2, emphases in original)

This passage shows that the social identities of both Chinese men and women are bound up with their domestic identities, although more so for women. The biological fact of gender does not determine a person's social positions in Chinese society. It is a person's position in the web of relationships that defines how she/he acts toward others.

In other words, we can say that "woman" (*nü*) in Chinese society is never a unitary category but, as Barlow (1989) noted, a framework for women of different kinship roles, such as sisters, mothers, wives, and daughters. The differentiation of women into these subcategories highlights the association of women with domesticity and marriage. The differentiation leads Chinese gender relationships and female status to be multiple, depending on which role a Chinese woman takes.

In this chapter, I show that in the modernizing Taiwanese society, where many women's problems have emerged as important social issues, a fundamental opposition between women and men is lacking. Unlike Western feminists who view the two genders as essentially antagonistic to each other (Alcoff 1988; Daly 1978; Rich 1976), Taiwanese women's criticism of men is generally limited to a single category of men—mostly the kin category of "husband"—rather than a generic category of Man. Accordingly, Taiwanese women search for autonomy and power through their various domestic positions. In doing so, they often engage themselves in a dialectical relationship with men, who may dominate, patronize, negotiate with, or be challenged by, women. Their concern with the principle of "positionality" characterizes Taiwanese women's feminist practices and bears on Taiwanese women's ambivalence toward Western feminism.

Women's Self-Growth Groups: Background

The women I study in this chapter are members of three women's self-growth groups in Taipei, Taiwan. These groups were among grassroots women's groups that were founded in the mid- and late 1980s, under the influence of the political process of democratization and the introduction of Western feminism. Their goals were to expand women's sphere of activities and interests from the domestic to the public sphere, or to resolve economic and psychological problems caused by divorce, the husband's death, or marital troubles. They were all women's voluntary or self-support groups: the first group, the New Environmental Homemakers' Association, was composed of housewives; the second and the third groups, the Taipei Women's Development Center and the Warm Life Association, were composed of divorced women, widows, and women who had encountered familial and marital adversity. Membership in all these groups was open to the wider society without discrimination against any women. Although most members were middle class, some were socioeconomically disadvantaged. Their age ranged largely from the late twenties to the early forties. Most members had a high school education or above.

Women in these groups constantly reflected upon their domestic roles, concerns, relationships, and problems. They represented many Taiwanese women's efforts to have better control of their lives, and to support each other through widowhood and postdivorce life. Many women regarded self-growth groups as a medium for them to "find their own sky" (*tien k'ung*), metaphorically referring to their search for freedom. These women's groups functioned as a medium for them to gain resources or support in order to gain autonomy and power in playing domestic roles. Unlike many tradition-oriented women's groups that taught women to be better housewives, women in these groups were mainly concerned with personal change, attempting to redefine and counteract the patriarchal definition of their roles as submissive, caring, and self-sacrificing (Cheng 1928).

In women's interactions among these three groups, they often drew upon notions of "self-consciousness," "self-autonomy," "independence," and "growth," all of which had been reiterated in the texts of the *Awakening* magazine published by the feminist group Awakening, and in its members' public discourse. While borrowing the Western notion of self, women of the three groups nurtured their sense of individuality within or in relation to the Taiwanese cultural context. In the following sections, I will describe three facts that show how the cultural notion of "positionality" has shaped or mediated the self-development of many Taiwanese women. First, many of the women in the groups that I studied tended to highly value their maternal roles, based on which they enhanced their power and status in both the family and the wider society. Second, in order to defend their legitimate positions, especially as mothers in the family, many of these women were reluctant to divorce even though their marital relationships had deteriorated. However, they also developed strategies to lead their own lives. Third, many of them divorced under the support of their natal families, which further patronized them in their post-divorce lives. The resurgence of their identities as daughters characterizes the way they achieved independence and adapted to the cultural principle of "positionality."

Mothers' Interests and Power

Among the three groups in this study, maternal identities and power were best represented in the women of the New Environmental Homemakers' Association (NEHA). Founded in January, 1987, by a volunteer group of housewives, their motive is to "unite people to promote environmental protection, ecological protection, public health and safety, and the quality of life." Its membership rapidly increased to 400 in less than two years. Most members belonged to the middle or upper-middle class; they were mostly college-educated and in their early thirties or forties.

Assuming mothers' identities, NEHA members told the public that the best reason to protect the environment was to protect the health of our children and offspring. While promoting ideas and measures to help reduce garbage in local communities, recreational areas, and schools, members broadly defined the "environment" to include schools and homes. At the association's weekly lectures, the topic of children's education drew the biggest audiences. These educated middle-class housewives demonstrated that they took major responsibility for their children's daily needs—including their intellectual, moral, and psychological development—until their children were in their teens. Lacking other help in child rearing, they were the main caregivers, companions, and even tutors for their children.

Women in the NEHA often shared child-rearing experiences and studied skills for nurturing children. The ideas and skills that these women learned were influenced by contemporary Western culture, mainly American, because these middle-class women had received American-oriented educations themselves. Aiming to be loving and knowledgeable mothers—as defined in terms of American motherhood (Ehrenreich and English 1978)—NEHA core members deliberately carried out various acts. For example, they published a "Children's Safety Booklet," perhaps the first guidebook ever published in Taiwan regarding methods of protecting children from sexual harassment and malicious strangers. The booklet is a translation of the American book, *It's OK to Say No!* (Lenett and Crane 1985), and is supplemented with precaution against local problems. Given that sexual harassment of women and child abuse have become important issues in recent years in Taiwan, this booklet achieved a circulation of 100,000 in just a few months. Using this book as a medium, the NEHA recruited people to organize the "365 Parents' Alliance," which aims to improve the quality of children's education at home and in school ("365" means that they will work for this goal every day of the year). The group soon had 400 members, mainly mothers.

The establishment of this alliance provided women with a legitimate public space in which they could harness their maternal power as mothers. For example, the alliance mailed questionnaires about educational matters to parents and teachers. According to the results of these surveys, it made suggestions for reforms to the government; based on many women's arguments that their children did not get enough sleep, the alliance influenced the Department of Education to cancel early-morning self-study sessions. The members named their alliance the "Mothers' Military Mission" when they launched a campaign to strengthen the functions of Parents' Committees in supervising the school system. The term "military mission" registered both women's claim to parental authority and what society felt was its license for women to take aggressive social action in the interests of the children. Conversely, the mission represented a social expansion of women's maternal power.

The "365 Parents' Alliance" represents a new form of female social power that was previously nonexistent but is in line with traditional parental authority in Chinese society. Norma Diamond (1973) observed in the early 1970s that many middle-class housewives in Taipei were isolated and confined to nuclear family responsibilities that included supervising their children's schoolwork. She noted that by failing to capitalize on their own education for self-development, these housewives were relegated to second-class roles of serving others in the family—a situation of "one step forward, two steps back." In the late 1980s, during the period covered by this study, many urban housewives continued to assume the duty of childrearing, yet they were neither isolated nor powerless. Rather, they searched for outside resources and aid in child rearing, and they tried to be better-informed mothers. These mothers made motherhood "prestigious and attractive," as is the case in mainland China (Honig and Hershatter 1988). Moreover, by establishing the NEHA and the "365 Parents' Alliance," many women gained a base from which they could shape their own views on mothering, and exercise maternal power in the social realm.

The Alliance also helped increase women's maternal power in the domestic arena. Educated housewives' newly learned expertise in child rearing contributed to their greater influence in families. New expertise equipped these housewives with special skills—which their husbands may have lacked—in directing their children's intellectual and psychological development. While conducting this study, I heard many women claim that they understood and cared for their children better than their husbands did, and that they often disagreed with their husbands on methods. Some women even viewed themselves as parenting instructors to their husbands.

When discussing parenting, women of the NEHA tended to associate the attributes "gentle" and "elastic" with mothers who responded to their children's emotional needs. In contrast, they associated the attributes "strict" and "stiff" with fathers who were not expressive toward their children. To a certain degree this contrast reflects continuance of the traditional notion of "strict father and benevolent mother" (yen fu tz'u mu). Capitalizing on the oppositional nature of mother-child and father-child ties, many Taiwan women now consider themselves and their children as constituting—in several NEHA members' words—a "little circle." Sometimes the "circle" might exclude their husbands; at other times women purported to incorporate their husbands into this domain of influence. The NEHA members who have spoken on the issue see themselves as central agents in mediating father-child relations. For these women, such a mediating role was unique, irreplaceable, and indispensable to maintaining a family. Moreover, in either excluding or incorporating their husbands, women's control of mother-child ties eclipsed male control of the family.

To summarize, NEHA members promoted vivid images of "mother caregiver" and "mother educator" in social contexts such as environmental protection and educational reform. They possessed a positive public image that was likely better than that of any other contemporary grassroots women's group in Taiwan. NEHA women earned this good reputation not as individuals, but as loving and capable mothers. These middle-class housewives' participation in public affairs extended their maternal power to the wider society. They deliberately emphasized housewives' moral values—especially as mothers—to bolster their social prestige. Furthermore, they were concerned with honing their ability to have greater control in childrearing, thus enhancing their domestic power in order to compete with patriarchal authority.

The Defense of Domestic Identities

We now turn to the other two women's groups (the Taipei Women's Development Center and the Warm Life Association) to observe the reinforcing of maternal identities and power in the wake of marital or familial collapse. While many women who sought help from these two groups played down the importance of conjugal relations or marriage, their maternal roles increased in importance and reshaped their perception of the family in time of crises. Maternal identity motivated many of these women to search for independence—economically and emotionally—and to create mother-centered families.

The Taipei Women's Development Center (TWDC) was set up in 1984 by the Taiwanese Christian Presbyterian Church as an institution for social work. Its major task was to help women who were divorced or widowed, or whose husbands were disabled, mentally deranged, or missing, by offering job training, employment guidance, and psychological counseling. These women were organized into a section called the Love Alliance (*ai lien hui*), which emphasized using "sisterly" love (*chieh-mei-ai*) to support each other through difficulties. Its membership ranged from seventy to ninety each year. Insofar as the TWDC's help with regard to job placement was limited by the small job market for these women, this Alliance concentrated more on providing moral support for members. Its activities were comprised of "Heart Talk Time" (*t'an hsin shih-chien: tan* is to talk; *hsin* is heart, mind, emotions; *shih-chien* is time), which gave women the opportunity to share feelings and experiences; lectures covering topics such as single-parenting, home management, and women's health; visits to the families of new members; and recreation, such as calisthenics and hiking.

Among these activities, "Heart Talk Time" was the most effective in encouraging women to be independent through female bonds. Lasting two hours, it was held once a month on a weekday night; it was a mixture of moral exhortation, women's stories, and narration of personal problems. Attendees numbered less than twenty. Quite often core members led and directed the conversation, emphasizing ideas of self-help and self-determination. They used either Christian beliefs or the Chinese work ethic of "eating bitterness and enduring hard work" (*ch'ih k'u nai lao*)—or a combination of both—to nurture the spiritual strength needed to combat the difficulties of divorce or widowhood and afterward achieve independence.

The Warm Life Association (WLA) also featured intimate communication and dealt with similar women's issues. It was primarily a discussion group for divorced women, women on the verge of divorce, and, occasionally, widows. Formerly the "Give-a-Hand Club," which was organized in 1984 by several divorced women in order to support each other during post-divorce difficulties, the WLA was established in 1986 on the basis of a broader membership. By 1989, a total of nearly four hundred women had attended this group. For these divorced women and widows, the phrase "Warm Life" was associated with their regaining the confidence and courage to lead peaceful and beautiful lives.

The major activity of the WLA was a two-part meeting held each Monday night; each meeting lasted from two to three hours. The first part consisted of a lecture given by senior WLA members and outside speakers. Topics focused on post-divorce adjustment, single-parenting, contemporary marital crises, coping strategies, and the problems of Chinese women. The second part of the meeting, designated "Garbage-Pouring Time" or "Heart Talk Time," was similar to the TWDC's "Heart Talk Time." By "garbage-pouring" the WLA members meant letting go of all negative emotions such as resentment, grief, loneliness, and bewilderment. As compared to the TWDC's members, the WLA women were more vocal about their troubles. One reason was that the WLA women were generally younger than the TWDC women; the former were in the age range of their late twenties to forty while the latter were between the ages of thirty and their early fifties. In addition, the socioeconomic situation of WLA members was better than that of TWDC members. Most WLA members had salaried jobs or their own business, while many of the TWDC members were wage laborers or had to go through job training in order to enter the job market. As a consequence, the majority of WLA members were pragmatic in counting their losses while the TWDC Love Alliance members tended to resort to spiritual/religious salvation to achieve self-autonomy.

Despite these differences, women in the TWDC and the WLA showed similar tendencies in drawing upon maternal roles to safeguard their interests, to refrain from divorce for the purpose of protecting their social identities, and to downplay the importance of remarriage in the case of divorced women. "Heart Talk Time" proceeded in similar fashion in both the WLA and TWDC, although the former's audiences were much larger and more heterogeneous than the latter's. In both cases, senior members initiated talks with lectures or storytelling about themselves; newcomers then presented their own problems, which were highly emotional and charged with tears and anger. They received sympathy and suggestions from the other women in the audience. All of the women engaged in commenting on family systems, on men, on gender relations, and on social stereotypes of women in order to clarify their problems and devise solutions for themselves.

In the "Heart Talks" of both groups—particularly the WLA—the problems of married women centered mostly on their husbands' extramarital affairs (wai-yü: wai means "the outside"; yü means "an encounter or meeting"). The issue of men's wai-yü has been widely discussed in Taiwan's mass media. Generally speaking, experiences of and responses to their husbands' wai-yü by TWDC and WLA women were representative of those of many middle-class women in the wider society. Many women in these two groups agonized over, accused, analyzed, and constantly reconstructed their views of men's *wai-yü* in reference to their own gender roles. For example, they resented their husbands' affairs, stating: "I take care of the children. I manage the household well. I do everything for the family. I am a good woman. How could he do this to me?" What struck the wives about their husbands' affairs appeared to be humiliation or injustice against them. No woman explicitly made romantic love (*ai-ch'ing*) her main focus, as one woman furiously said, "He has a good time with another woman outside, while I work to death at home. What kind of thing am I?" She meant that her devotion to her family was worthless because her husband did not reciprocate her commitment by being loyal to her.

In criticizing their husbands, many women defended themselves as being "good women" (*hao nü-jen*) in order to maintain their marriage and familial identities. Although in anguish, some women reacted strongly when asked whether they would consider divorce: "Why should I? I have done nothing wrong." This statement of self-defense also reflected an age-old moral view that, for her husband to divorce her, a woman must be unvirtuous, incapable of performing her domestic roles, or immoral in her behavior. Intertwined with their moral concern was their claim of legitimacy (*ming-fen: ming* is "name, title"; and *fen* is "social position") through their marital status and positions as wives and mothers. The notion of *ming-fen* was frequently used by a married Taiwanese woman as a weapon to put her husband's mistress in her place. For example, one woman in a troubled marriage said in one of the Heart Talk Times, "I won't let that woman intrude on my family. She'll never have *ming-fen*. My heart for my husband is dead. But I have *ming-fen*. I have children. I still have a family." Words of comfort for these women also reinforced the same thought.

In a situation like the above case, the role of mother constituted a powerful base from which many TWDC and WLA women asserted their legitimate positions in the family. Their attachment to their children outweighed their attachment to their husbands. Moreover, they used their mother-child ties as a form of moral capital in confronting or negotiating with their husbands, and even with "the third party." For example, one woman told her husband's lover. "I tolerate you and my husband because I want to give my children an intact family. Just think about a mother's heart. Don't push my husband to marry you for your personal interests. Don't ruin my family." A statement like this marked the marginal nature of "the third party" in the marriage system, under which a married woman intentionally created symbolic opposition between herself and the third party—such as legitimate/illegitimate, self-sacrificing/selfish, responsible/irresponsible, creator of the family/ruiner of the family—in order to show her superiority, both morally and in social status. This symbolic opposition, intentionally constructed, favors married women as mothers. The traditional idea that Chinese marriage is a lifelong commitment made in order to perpetuate the family offers women structural incentives to claim their legitimate positions as mothers/wives. However, the married women's statements cited above also revealed that the family they perceived and valued was mother-centered rather than male-centered.

The senior members of both the TWDC and WLA tended to support the decision of their still-married members to refrain from divorce, even though some of these senior members had planned their own divorces. The reasons given included that the children would be hurt, that children needed their mother, and that not every woman was able to endure post-divorce problems such as financial difficulties, social pressure, and loneliness. Aside from a few cases in which husbands severely abused their wives or completely neglected their responsibility to support the family, most marriages, said these women, were workable. Their reservations about advising women to divorce were perhaps a product of the cultural expectation that a married couple should be "united for one hundred years" (*pai nien hao ho*), that the goal of marriage is to perpetuate the family. To a troubled couple, a Chinese idiom advises that "a married couple [when they have friction] should be advised to unite rather than separate" (*fu ch'i ch'uan ho pu ch'uan li*).

In most cases, the senior members encouraged married women to find out what went wrong in their marriages and to remedy it. On the other hand, they advised women to ignore their husbands, or mothers-in-law, who caused conjugal friction, and to go out more often to expand their social circles. For example, senior members encouraged the other women, saying, "We should take care of ourselves. Don't suppress yourself just because you want to satisfy others," "Rearrange your life in good order, come out of the house, enlarge your life." They often suggested that married women lead (*kuo*) their own lives in both the economic and social senses. For example, they taught their troubled members to "grasp the [couple's] money tightly" and hoard their "private money" (*ssu-fang ch'ien*) behind their husbands' back or to look for a job. They were concerned with saving women's personal finances, in case they someday needed money to support themselves. The married women were also encouraged to participate in social activities, such as those in the TWDC or WLA, including to make their own friends and learn new things, and, in doing so, to mitigate marital tensions in the domestic sphere.

"Leading one's own life" may also be a protest by women against their husbands' infidelity, in that it allows them to distance themselves from the physical domain of the family. Some women in these two groups considered it a strategy to warn their husbands that they were not as controllable as men think. They had abrogated their overwhelming concern of caring for their husbands and explored their own social lives. In a few cases, women proceeded to catch their husbands in adultery, either through their own efforts or by hiring an investigation agency. They then used this evidence to coerce their husbands into ending the affairs, threatening to file a suit against their husbands or "the third party."

What made these women believe that their marriages could be saved was a generally shared view among both married and divorced women in the TWDC and WLA that men did not mean to cause a divorce by taking a mistress. Taiwanese men have always been said to "step on two boats," a metaphor illustrating that men want to keep both their wives and their lovers. Men, women in the TWDC and WLA often said, needed their wives to take care of their children, and they were also afraid that their children would suffer from "broken families." The women also acknowledged that family ideals restrained men from divorcing as well. If a man's affair leads him to divorce, he risks social criticism for being self-indulgent, irresponsible, immoral, and unconscientious. Thus, these women described men's affairs as "wild bites," or "a snack aside from a regular meal." In expressing it this way, they referred to the nature of desires for extramarital affairs as greedy, abnormal, and illegitimate, insofar as the word *wai* means "the outside."

Women in the TWDC and WLA tried to minimize the consequences of their husbands' philandering by diagnosing it and despising it. The women's groups provided them with opportunities to collectively denigrate men's affairs outside marriage as "immature," "sick," and "transient." In doing so, they not only found an emotional outlet for their rancor but also developed a sense of the moral superiority of women in characterizing men's behavior as morally and psychologically defective. Sometimes they pitied men for their "failure to resist temptations because of their animal-like nature," to use some women's words. Such a humanistic view was influenced by the cultural expectation that women be considerate and benevolent wives and mothers.

Group therapy in the TWDC and WLA for married women who suffered from their husbands' affairs stressed exploring one's own social life and recruiting economic resources within marriage. Making divorce a second choice, many women defended their legitimate positions as wives/mothers to safeguard their living situations and to maintain their social identities. Although appearing to compromise themselves with gender inequality in the case of their husbands' affairs, they strategically took the conjugal family as a stronghold to maneuver between family and society. Ironically, their tendency to nurture individual interests outside the family was grounded in their association with domestic identities.

The next section describes how divorced women in the TWDC and WLA repudiated the importance of marriage and the conjugal family in their pursuit of independence and autonomy. Many of them even resisted remarriage or downplayed its importance. I will also show that their continual dedication to maternal roles and their close ties with their natal families highlight these women's practice of the cultural principle of positionality—their "repositioning" among different domestic positions.

Post-divorce Independence and Gender Repositioning

In the TWDC and WLA, the problems of divorced women were often cast in terms of outcast misery, social discrimination, economic pressure, concern about children in the custody of ex-husbands, and the burden of being a single parent. These women in general had been socialized to view divorce as a stigma. They felt abandoned by their ex-husbands. The social stereotype held by the general public that divorced women are not virtuous or good enough to maintain their marriages also alienated them from their usual social relationships. Most of these women also had to cope with financial distress after divorce, particularly in the case of single parents. Taiwanese Civil Law lacks means of enforcement of the payment of alimony and child support by the ex-husband. Some women lose custody of their children because, according to Taiwanese law, the husband retains custody unless he agrees to cede it to the wife, or unless the wife appeals to a court for custody. In such cases women thus worried that their children would be mistreated or neglected by their ex-husbands' parents or sister who took care of the children.

To console and encourage these divorced women who came to the TWDC or WLA for help, the senior members drew upon the notion of self-help that primarily referred to the pursuit of economic independence. They talked about their own stories of how they endured—thus transcended—hardship and worked diligently to stand on their own. In both groups, the success of a few senior members in their struggle for independence was taken as a model for the other women. Their stories were told and retold, either by themselves or by others, so as to become virtually inscribed in the meeting's moral texts. Although the job market in Taiwan was not favorable to the divorced women of this study, who were mostly in their thirties or early forties, for many senior members most of the difficulties were surmountable. Many of them did blue-collar work and insurance sales, later being promoted to professional or managerial positions.

Many divorced women regarded the search for self-sufficiency as a remedy for post-divorce depression and low self-esteem, and as a means of reconstructing their gender identity. They gained a sense of fulfillment and freedom from economic independence. Moreover, they showed society that they were not weak individuals who had to rely on men. Some members even proudly pointed out that their businesses had surpassed that of their ex-husbands.

Although wifely identity had been discarded, maternal identity was a motive for many of these women to search for post-divorce independence. In the cases of single parents, they felt obliged to raise their children. For those women whose ex-husbands refused them rights to visit their children, maternal identity was no less important. For example, they received comfort from other women who stated, "Your children will come back to you sooner or later. Their hearts are with their mothers by nature. At present you should work hard to save your money. Otherwise, how will you show your children in the future that you are reliable and capable mothers?" Moreover, the mother's role provided women in the TWDC and WLA with leverage to redress injustices or improve their social status. The injustices are social stereotypes that view widows as symbols of "bad luck" and divorced women as incapable or not virtuous enough to manage their marriages.

In the TWDC's bulletin, members who became successful in standing on their own were praised as devoted mothers. The image of these mothers was that they worked hard to raise their children in the hope of sending them to college. In a sense, they are no different from traditional Chinese widows who conformed to the cultural ideal of a virtuous mother as devoted and sacrificing (Mann 1987), and who expected to be repaid and glorified by their children's achievements. However, contemporary Taiwan women's devotion to motherhood carries implications of defending themselves against social discrimination. For example, one woman renounced the social view of widows and divorced women as dejected with this statement: "We want to let society know that we are doing very well. We still hold a positive attitude toward rearing our children."

By committing themselves to their children, many of these female single parents dismissed the idea of remarriage. On the one hand, they feared that they might be deprived of the freedom to be in control of their lives if they remarried. In many of these women's experiences, within marriage they were often expected to be like an "old female servant" (lao-ma-tzu) who served the family and the husband's needs. On the other hand, strong mother-child bonds made remarriage less attractive to many women. They had worked to obtain a satisfactory companionate relationship with their children.

Many of these women's commitment to motherhood was reinforced by mutual support. In the TWDC and WLA, issues concerning single-parenting and children's education were often raised in lectures. Both groups held recreational activities— such as camping, games, dinner parties, and Christmas and New Year's parties— for members and their children. A social network was established among some members through get-togethers of single-parent households. Members sometimes helped to take care of or tutor each other's children.

In the course of this study, very few WLA members had remarried. Some women had boyfriends or were open in searching for sexual partners and the possibility of a second marriage. Nevertheless, like others, they claimed that marriage was no longer important to them. Some women pointed out that they would not consider remarriage until they had reached age fifty, at a time when their children would have grown up. According to them, their remarriage would be geared toward having a companion in their old age. In contrast to their first marriages—aimed at fulfilling women's relationally defined roles as wives, daughters-in-law, and mothers—their remarriage would serve to fulfill their personal needs, highlighting their self-consciousness.

One may wonder to what extent these women were able to achieve economic independence, given that Taiwanese women, like American women (Newman 1986), tended to be financially deprived after they were divorced. However, I suspect that in Taiwan, divorced women's economic pressure may be less insofar as many of them get support from their natal families (niang chia). My study shows that in many cases women's niang chia was crucial as a source of support and shelter for them through the divorce crisis. In contemporary practice, the affection that the niang chia in traditional society might show to a married daughter during marital hardship is brought into full play. Many widows' and divorced women's ties with their niang chia were more solid than those of married women. They lived with their parents or close to them. They were emotionally devoted to their *niang chia* who supported them. Their parents might help them with childcare or living subsidies.

On the other hand, as filial and devoted daughters, many of these women had helped to take care of elderly parents, manage households, and mediate familial relationships. For women who were economically well off, their great economic contribution to their natal families put them in a particular position of authority to monitor their *niang chia*'s domestic affairs. In other words, they were no longer the "spilled water" (a Chinese folk metaphor that means "no return," referring to the fact that women are married out and belong to another patrilineal family) that they would have been in traditional society. They not only reincorporated themselves into their natal families but also achieved high domestic status—as daughters rather than as wives.

In studying women's domestic status in African societies, Karen Sacks (1979) differentiated women's roles as "sisters" from their roles as "wives." Even when "wives" are subordinate, she notes, "sisters" can be very powerful within their kinship networks. Here I adopt her view to address the fact that contemporary Taiwanese women have different statuses as wives and sisters. I see a woman's status as varying according to the particular relations in which she is involved. As Naomi Quinn emphasizes, we should "treat women's status as a composite of many different variables, often causally independent from one another" (1977:183). While many Taiwanese women encounter constraints or oppression as wives, they gain autonomy and power as sisters and daughters. Their high status in their *niang chia*, which is also emotionally gratifying, contributes to many women's lack of motivation to remarry.

Many Taiwanese widows' and divorced women's attachment to their *niang chia* was evidenced in their appreciation of the TWDC and the WLA as commensurate with their *niang chia*. The TWDC and WLA filled the role of the *niang chia* in providing women with emotional support. Many women expressed their gratitude to these two groups, saying that without the groups' support, they would not have been able to come out of the shadows of broken families and to become independent. Members further used the kinship term *chieh mei* ("sisters") to emphasize their intimacy with each other. Especially for those women whose *niang chia* did not give them support, these two groups took the place of their own *niang chia*. By ascribing the image of *niang chia* to the two groups, members deliberately refuted the formal system of patriarchy that neglected their affections and feelings. Furthermore, it also revealed that being socially discriminated against, these Taiwanese widows and divorced women searched for a new socially acceptable position in relation to the family—as daughters. They endeavored to "reposition" themselves from wives to daughters within the same set of culturally ascribed roles.

The solutions for marital problems and the independence sought by women in the TWDC and WLA involved a reconstruction of gender identity. By self-growth they referred to expanding their spheres of activities in order to reject male control, and to developing autonomous motherhood. While wifely roles were degraded or ignored, many women turned to emphasizing their identities as mothers and daughters. Although they had achieved a rising consciousness of personal well-being, their occupation with familial roles seemed to somewhat constrain them. Along with the NEHA women, what did the TWDC and the WLA women tell us about the changing roles and experiences of Taiwanese women? And what are the implications of their "repositioning" with respect to feminism?

Indigenous Practice of Feminism

To summarize, the NEHA, whose membership consisted primarily of middle- and upper-middle class housewives, couched its goal of promoting environmental protection in the issue of improving the welfare of the family and their offspring. Members' social participation through this group aimed to enhance their maternal power both at home and in society. By comparison, the widows and divorced women of the TWDC and WLA were alienated from society, victims of the traditional view that they were symbols of "bad luck," or "immorality." By sharing their experiences of suffering, these women supported each other through difficulties. Despite a few women's attacks on patriarchy, the majority of the women in all three groups drew upon the principle of "self-help" or "self-support" without opposing men or politicizing their goals.

Given that these three women's self-growth groups fell short of political legitimacy and authority, they might be viewed as marginal social groups that reinforced women's secondary position in the patriarchal system. In particular, sisterhood in the TWDC and WLA was based primarily upon women's common concerns about "repositioning" themselves within individual families, and thus conforming to domestic role expectations. Does this fact reflect what many early feminist anthropologists (e.g., Sanday 1973; Lamphere 1974; Rosaldo 1974) have argued, that female solidarity is an indication of female subordination, no matter what power women may have? Does female solidarity in the present study arise only with the permission of male authority structures (Lamphere 1974)?

These views are restricted to one structural perspective of gender relationships and overlook the practices that female solidarity groups may create and generate by coping with female "positionalities." I see Taiwanese women's maneuvering between different domestic positions—repositioning, as I call it—as strategic practices to better their interests and positions. These women are actors who move across contexts to accrue the resources—economic, social, or ideological—available to them, as many anthropologists have argued in other case studies (Lederman 1990; Meigs 1990; Quinn 1977). By contexts, I mean role-related contexts. When the wife's role subsides, the mother's role often takes on greater prominence; so does the daughter's role. In shifting positions, Taiwanese women are searching for greater control over their lives in order to overcome the effects of patriarchal constraints.

I posit that these strategic practices are dialectical, rather than subordinate to the patriarchal system. Although the patriarchal structure confines Taiwanese women in some contexts, it, ironically, also leaves them room to maneuver for power and autonomy in other contexts. Whether the patriarchal structure restricts or empowers women depends on the particular positions women take and how they fulfill those positions. As has been described, Taiwanese women observe the culturally codified principle of "positionality" in various ways to meet their own needs. In many cases, the principle of "positionality" ceases to be a social mechanism of coercion. Rather, it is used by individual women to display their values, to negotiate with men according to gender role differences, and to ensure their power as mothers by exploiting social and economic resources. In other situations, women claimed their moral superiority to men by denigrating their husbands' affairs and thereby safeguarded their "legitimate" wife/mother roles.

Therefore, the idea of "positionality" can be viewed as being much like Bourdieu's notion of "cultivated disposition" that allows for an infinity of practices and confrontational strategies for adapting to endlessly changing situations (1977: 15–16). To say that Taiwanese women are required to fulfill certain domestic roles is one thing. How they perform these roles as well as the meanings and purposes of their performance are another. Indeed, many married women engaged in developing their interests and personal space outside the home—"leading one's own life," as they called it. Furthermore, among the members of the three women's groups I studied, the degree to which they identified with their diverse domestic roles might vary. While maternal roles were generally emphasized and accorded a high value, the wifely role could be poorly performed. More than a few women showed little concern about their husbands or their conjugal relations. Their observance of wifely roles could be considered a "symbolic compliance" with the social role in such a way as to make "the *impression* of compliance without its substance" (Scott 1985: 26, emphasis in original). This reluctant compliance was intended to avoid conjugal tensions in the domestic domain and to enable women to move smoothly toward other domains of activities.

This brings us to the next issue: that the structural imperative of "positionality" is not only fulfilled in various manners but also practiced in such a way as to undermine male-dominant ideologies. This points to the separation, tension, and dialectics between the hegemonic or rule-governed structures and the everyday practices of individuals (Bourdieu 1977; Certeau 1984; Collier and Yanagisako 1989; Ortner 1984). My focus below is on how the cultural principle of "positionality" is transformed by female agents; as Sherry Ortner acknowledged, "the system may be changed by practice" (1984: 154).

Michel de Certeau defines oppositional practices as subversions of the dominant powers "by a style of social exchange, a style of technical invention, and a style of moral resistance—that is, by an economy of the 'gift' . . . by an aesthetic of 'moves,' 'triumphs,' or 'strikes'... and by an ethic of tenacity" (1980: 4). In the Taiwanese case, women's oppositional practices take various forms. For example, married Taiwanese women insisted upon male reciprocity in loyalty and respect in exchange for their fulfillment of roles as wife and mother. They used a principle of conjugal reciprocity, similar to Certeau's "economy of the gift," in deciding the extent to which they conformed to domestic role requirements, and the extent to which they were dedicated to conjugal relations. Many women in this study no longer represented their domestic image as self-sacrificing and submissive as traditional women did. Rather, they were, or came to be, volitional and pragmatic in protecting their own interests. Even though many of these women identified their interests with those of their husbands and the patriarchal family, they were more concerned about recruiting financial resources for themselves. This fact is similar to what Bourdieu observes about Algerian Kabyle society, in which women "are less sensitive to symbolic profits [political interests of the lineage] and freer to pursue material profits" (1977: 62).

Some of these Taiwanese women's oppositional practices involved the manipulation of one's own power in a legitimate space—in this case, women's power from their positions as mothers and married women. In other situations, mainly those of the divorced women and widows, women resorted to the ethics of tenacity—endurance of hardships and hard work in achieving economic independence—to resist patriarchal control. They claimed victory in becoming independent, and gained a compensation for the loss of family and personal dignity as a result of marriage failure. They reconstructed women's subjectivities by further imposing a certain degree of gender segregation, such as the deemphasis of conjugal relations.

One question remains to be addressed: Why are these Taiwanese women's oppositional practices to patriarchal hegemony unable to mobilize women toward a wider political agenda? My answer is that Taiwanese women's overall concern with positionality makes it difficult for them to organize themselves as a unitary or unified category. Their efforts to "position" themselves within a web of relationships lead to their ambivalence toward Western feminism. Because this web of relationships always includes their intimate male kin—their fathers and brothers—their criticism of men is primarily directed toward their husbands, rather than toward all men. It is this feature, I maintain, that makes Taiwanese women's feminist experiences differ from those of Western feminism.

In addition to the notion of social positionality, the Chinese ideological construct of gender complementarity also explains why Chinese gender relations are not immanently oppositional. The notion of gender complementarity derives from the philosophical concept of yin/yang complementarity. Yang and yin, dating back 3,000 years, represent the duality of universal order, principles, and forces (Riencourt 1958; Gernet 1982; Granet 1973). They are represented by pairs such as heaven and earth, day and night, sun and moon, male and female. Although yang is generally considered positive, powerful, strong, and male, while yin is negative, tender, fragile, and female, yang and yin are also viewed as interdependent and constituting "two complementary facets of the totality" in which there is cooperation and alternation (Riencourt 1958: 81).

According to the classic *I ching* (Book of Changes) of 3000 B.C.E., yin/yang complementarity underlies the relation between a husband and wife, which *I ching* defines as the primordial form of human relationships. The idea of complementarity in marriage is exemplified in the different roles and attributes assigned to each gender. The classic *Li chi* (Book of Rites) of the same era dictates a division of labor in which men are charged with the extradomestic sphere while women are charged with the domestic sphere. The notion of complementarity also shapes the Chinese cultural definition of gender attributes, in which women's gentleness and docility are seen as complementary to men's strength and indomitability.

The notion of gender complementarity combines with the notion of positionality in shaping Chinese women's gender roles and behavior. We have seen that women in this study did not confront men by denying female attributes. Rather, they bolstered and celebrated their attributes of care, love, and compassion, which were associated with maternal roles. They searched for power and interests on a par with men mainly through their domestic positions. As a reflection of this, the self-growth groups in this study seem to have been organized on the basis of the problems and concerns of a particular set of female roles—mothers, wives, and daughters.

I contend that many Taiwanese women reject the sex/gender antagonism that Western feminists uphold, in defending their "positionalities" rather than the male-dominant structure. Examples are found in the indigenous feminist discourse that reveals the cultural influence of women's positionalities. For instance, the housewives in the NEHA, in alliance with the Awakening Foundation, campaigned against pornography in the mass media, asserting that pornography would have negative effects on their children. Their appeal from the mother's perspective turned out to be a powerful statement in the public forum. In the Awakening Foundation's protest against the judicial system's ignoring of child prostitution, the women resorted to the emotional appeal that child prostitutes are "our sisters" and "our daughters" who need to be rescued. As such, the indigenous feminist discourse is supported by the Taiwanese women's claims to their positional rights—that daughters' and sisters' well-being should be protected by other family members.

Tani Barlow criticizes many Western scholars' preoccupation with the Western notion of individuality, thereby their seeing Chinese women as not yet liberated from the family. She argues:

> There is no essential "Woman in the Chinese family" waiting to be released from bondage. The female person Han familism constructs is not a Woman. Chinese women were in the past and continue to be constructed in multiple ways under specific given conditions and normalized practices. One of the most powerful of those normalizing practices is precisely power-as-relation—the notion that one is oneself not in abstract and autonomous Being but through systems of reciprocal, unequal, hierarchical exchange. (Barlow 1989: 325)

Barlow maintains that Confucian tradition produced many positions from which Chinese women "spoke, maneuvered, resisted power, oppressed others" (1989: 325) and Chinese women in kin and fictive kin networks use strategies of power, including maternal control of mother-child ties.

Barlow's insights into Chinese women's embeddedness in the family system support my argument that the way women search for power and autonomy is culturally specific. Chinese women's feminist experiences are different from Western women's. Because of the primacy of the family institution in Chinese society, Chinese women are concerned primarily with recruiting power resources to their various domestic positions. Their notion of power is what Barlow calls "power-as-relation." Although many of the women in this study verbally objected to being defined relationally to men and the family, I suggest that they nevertheless meant to have autonomy and authority over practices in fulfilling domestic roles—in controlling how and which role to play at which time, at their discretion. Their sense of "self," as often emphasized in the term "self-growth," was intertwined with their reconstruction of domestic identities. As Irving A. Hallowell argues, the self is also a cultural product, "the field of behavior that is appropriate for the activities of *particular* selves in *their* world of culturally defined objects is not by any means precisely coordinate with any absolute polarity of subjectivity-objectivity that is definable" (1955: 84, emphases in original). What he means is that human self-awareness is always mediated by, and comes to interact with, cultural ideas and patterns, which do not exist as "objects" to individual subjects. For the Taiwanese women of this study, the creation of self resides in their manipulation of the principle of positionality by which they map their subjective will and interests onto some of these socially defined positions.

Conclusion

In this chapter, I have examined how Taiwanese women constructed and reconstructed their domestic identities and power relationships in the family. I have focused on how ideas of Western feminism are interpreted and practiced by members of three women's self-growth groups in Taipei, Taiwan. I argue that Taiwanese women's perceptions of gender politics lack an oppositional dichotomy between the two sexes, in contrast to the perception of Western feminist thoughts. Western women are often caught up in the issue of what the "essentialized" woman can do to defeat those cultural assumptions that subordinate and marginalize women and yet ironically constitute the very basis of female solidarity (Alcoff 1988). To Taiwanese women there is no such issue of essentialism in their struggle to resist male control. With regard to the family, women are concerned about how to increase their interests and power through maneuvering between different domestic positions. "Positionality" as a sociocultural principle defining human relationships in Chinese society shapes women's experiences in their search for autonomy and gender equality.

This study has attempted to echo the increasing concern among many scholars who note that women's challenges to male dominance can take different forms and pathways in light of different sociocultural configurations. Feminism is essentially indigenous and can be expressed in richly varied ways across cultures.

References

Alcoff, Linda. 1988. "Cultural Feminism Versus Post-structuralism: The Identity Crisis in Feminist Theory." In *Feminist Theory in Practice and Process*, ed. Micheline R. Malson, Jean F. O'Barr, Sarah Westphalwihl, and Mary Wyer, 295–326. Chicago: University of Chicago Press.

Babb, Lawrence A. 1984. "Indigenous Feminism in a Modern Hindu Sect." *Signs* 9, no. 3: 399–416.

Barlow, Tani. 1985. "The Place of Women in Ding Ling's World: Feminism and the Concept of Gender in Modern China." Ph.D. dissertation, University of California, Davis.

———. 1989. "Asian Perspective." *Gender and History* 1, no. 3: 318–29.

———. 1994. "Theorizing Woman: Funu, Guojia, Jiating." In *Body, Subject, and Power in China*, ed. Angela Zito and Tani Barlow, 25–52. Chicago: University of Chicago Press.

Beauvoir, Simone de. 1952. *The Second Sex*. New York: Vintage Books.

———. 1958. *The Long March*. New York: World.

Bourdieu, Pierre. 1977. *Outline of a Theory of Practice*, trans. Richard Nice. London: Cambridge University Press.

Certeau, Michel de. 1980. "On the Oppositional Practices of Everyday Life." *Social Text* 3: 3–43.

———. 1984. *The Practice of Everyday Life*. Berkeley: University of California Press.

Cheng Tung-yuan. 1928. *Chung-kuo fu-nü sheng-huo-shih* (The History of Chinese Women). Shanghai: Commercial Press.

Collier, Jane F., and S.J. Yanagisako. 1989. "Theory in Anthropology since Feminist Practice." *Critique of Anthropology* 9, no. 2: 27–37.

Daly, Mary. 1978. *Gyn/Ecology*. Boston: Beacon Press.

Diamond, Norma. 1973. "The Middle Class Family Model in Taiwan: Women's Place is in the Home." *Asian Survey* 13: 853–72.

Ehrenreich, Barbara, and Deirdre English. 1978. *For Her Own Good: 150 Years of the Experts' Advice to Women*. New York: Anchor Press.

Gernet, Jacques. 1982. *A History of Chinese Civilization*. Cambridge: Cambridge University Press.

Granet, Marcel. 1973. "Right and Left in China." In *Right and Left: Essays on Dual Symbolic Classification*, ed. Rodney Needham, 43–58. Chicago: University of Chicago Press.

Hallowell, A. Irving. 1955. "The Self and Its Behavior Environment." In *Culture and Experience*, ed. Hallowell, 75–110. Philadelphia: University of Pennsylvania Press.

Honig, Emily, and Gail Hershatter. 1988. *Personal Voices: Chinese Women in the 1980s*. Stanford: Stanford University Press.

Irigaray, Luce. 1985. *The Sex Which Is Not One*. Ithaca: Cornell University Press.

Kristeva, Julia. 1976. "China, Women and the Symbolic. An Interview by Josette Feral." *Sub-Stance* 13: 9–18.

Ku, Yen-lin, and Jui-Hsiung Wang. 1987. "Ts'ung ch'u-fang tao chieh-t'ou: Wo-guo fu-nü hsin-hsing t'uan-t'i k'ua ch'u hsing-li-cheng" (From the Kitchen to the Street. The New Way for New Women's Groups in Taiwan). *China Times Daily News*, March 9.

Lamphere, Louis. 1974. "Strategies, Cooperation and Conflict Among Women in Domestic Groups." In *Woman, Culture and Society*, ed. M.Z. Rosaldo and L. Lamphere, 97–112. Stanford: Stanford University Press.

Lederman, Rena. 1990. "Contested Order: Gender and Society in the Southern New Guinea Highlands." In *Beyond the Second Sex: Essays in the Anthropology of Women*, ed. Peggy Sanday and Ruth Goodenough, 43–74. Philadelphia: University of Pennsylvania Press.

Lenett, Robin, and Bob Crane. 1985. *It's OK to Say No! A Parent/Child Manual for the Protection of Children*. New York: Tom Doherty Associates.

Mann, Susan. 1987. "Widows in the Kinship, Class, and Community Structures of Qing Dynasty China." *Journal of Asian Studies* 46, no. 1: 37–56.

Meigs, Anna. 1990. "Multiple Gender Ideologies and Statuses." In Sanday and Goodenough, eds., *Beyond the Second Sex*, 99–112.

Nader, Laura. 1986. "The Subordination of Women in Comparative Perspective." *Urban Anthropology* 15, no. 3–4: 377–97.

Newman, Katherine S. 1986. "Symbolic Dialects and Generations of Women: Variation in the Meaning of Post-Divorce Downward Mobility." *American Ethnologist* 13, no. 2: 230–52.

Ortner, Sherry B. 1984. "Theory in Anthropology Since the Sixties." *Comparative Studies in Society and History* 26, no. 1: 126–66.

Quinn, Naomi. 1977. "Anthropological Studies on Women's Status." *Annual Review of Anthropology* 6: 181–225.

Rich, Adrienne. 1976. *Of Woman Born*. New York: Norton.

Riencourt, Amaury de. 1958. *The Soul of China*. New York: Coward-McCann.

Rosaldo, Michelle Z. 1974. "Woman, Culture, and Society: A Theoretical Overview." In Rosaldo and Lamphere, eds., *Woman, Culture, and Society*, 17–42.

Sacks, Karen. 1979. *Sisters and Wives: The Past and Future of Sexual Equality.* Westport, CT: Greenwood Press.

Sanday, Peggy R. 1973. "Toward a Theory of Status of Women." *American Anthropologist* 75: 1682–1700.

Scott, James C. 1985. *Weapons of the Weak: Everyday Forms of Peasant Resistance*. New Haven: Yale University Press.

Tu, Wei-ming. 1976. *Centrality and Commonality: An Essay on Chung-yung*. Honolulu: University Press of Hawaii.

12

Lu Hsiu-lien and the Origins of Taiwanese Feminism, 1944–1977

Murray A. Rubinstein

Lu (Annette) Hsiu-lien is one of the pioneers of feminism and women's liberation on Taiwan. But she is more than that. She is an articulate and, at times, brilliant writer and public speaker and a savvy and effective politician. And she has been, from the beginning of her involvement in the public sphere, a person capable of analyzing situations and political environments, defining issues, developing philosophies, and, finally, laying out social and political agendas that address the problems Taiwan faces.

This chapter charts the first stages of Lu Hsiu-lien's multifaceted career and follows her as she moves from her role as student to her role as government worker and founder of Taiwan's feminist movement. In the process, I show how she transforms—or recreates—herself, and then plays those roles and provides the ideas, tactics, and strategies that are appropriate to the new social and political environments confronting herself and her movement.

One basic objective serves as leitmotiv and informs the parallel and intersecting narratives found within the text. Lu was one of the pioneers of feminism and women's liberation on Taiwan. Her work as a feminist is at the core of her career.[1] Thus the objective is to examine her life within the context of the history of women in China and on Taiwan and also within the contexts of both the contemporary (Second Wave) women's movement in the West and the worldwide feminist movement.[2]

Providing the structure of this essay is role theory. This construct was first introduced and developed in English literature by William Shakespeare. In his masterful and not-so-comic comedy, *As You Like It*, the Bard has his most interesting character, the exiled duke, spell out Shakespeare's own view of the different roles an individual plays over the course of a lifetime. This viewpoint is contained in the famous and oft-quoted soliloquy that begins with the words, "all the world's a stage and all the men and women merely players. They have their exits and their entrances and one man, in his time, plays many parts."[3] Role theory, a useful body of literature that exists in the border zone between sociology and psychology, takes its lead—its basic rationale—from that famous speech.[4]

Role theory provides us with a useful descriptive device for laying out the basic contours of this and the later phases of a long career, a means to allow us to analyze each of these specific roles or role sets, and, finally, a framework within which we can see the unfolding of the leitmotiv that informs, and at key moments highlights and propels, the narrative thrust of the chapter.[5]

Lu as Daughter, as Sister, and as Student, 1944–1971

This first section examines Lu Hsiu-lien's youth and education on Taiwan and in the United States. Her life—and her perceptions of the society in which she grew up— is presented not as an isolated phenomenon but within the larger context of development in Taiwan in the years from 1944 until 1971.

Lu Hsiu-lien was born in the northwestern Taiwanese city of T'aoyüan in 1944— the final year the island was part of the Japanese empire. She was born on June 6— D-Day. Perhaps it was a symbol or portent that a person born on the day that the liberation of Nazi-controlled Europe began would become a symbol of and a worker for the liberation of Taiwanese women and for the liberation of the Taiwanese (here meaning both Minnan and Hakka ethnic Chinese) who settled Taiwan during the Ch'ing dynasty, but who would, after August 1945, become subjects of a harsh mainlander regime under the Nationalist Party (Kuomintang, KMT).

She has no recollections of the Japanese occupation itself, but learned from her family and others that the Japanese often viewed both the Minnan- and Hakka-speaking Han-Chinese with contempt. "The Japanese," she notes, "had looked down on the Chinese, calling them Si-na—something like Chink in English—and left them feeling humiliated and angry." She adds that, "People who lived during that period also felt frustrated because they didn't have their own country."[6]

Lu was born into a family of small merchants in T'aoyüan, a small city near the Taiwan Strait that is now the site of the Chiang Kaishek International Airport. As she notes in her as yet unpublished English-language biography, her clan was originally from Honan but had migrated to Taiwan two hundred and sixty years earlier. They are a major clan in the T'aoyüan area and number in the thousands. While the clan, composed mostly of those involved in agriculture, was large, it was also rather poor. Lu's grandfather was a farmer.

Lu's father also began his working life as a farmer, renting a small plot of land and raising vegetables. One of her early memories is of her beloved older brother— eight years her senior and an important figure in her life—picking vegetables and taking them to the market before he went to school. By the time she was able to remember more details of her life, Lu's father had been able to buy a strategically located plot of land in T'aoyüan and was running a store in the front of that house where he sold dried fish. Taiwan's economy had suffered during the war and the early years of the Retrocession and many families could not afford meat. Thus, dried fish was added to the rice, providing both flavor and much-needed protein. The business did well and, with partners, Ms. Lu's father was able to expand his business to two other towns in T'aoyüan county.[7]

Later her father became one of many merchants supplying the needs of local farmers, obtaining sweet potatoes and other agricultural products and selling them to farmers in the region to feed their pigs. He obtained these products from farmers in the coastal plain to the south and thus often traveled by train to that region. When he could not do so, his wife took over these responsibilities, taking Lu with her on occasion. He proved to have a talent for business, as did his wife and another of his daughters, Lu's second sister, and the firm grew to what Lu described as mid-sized. Certainly the family lived a comfortable though not luxurious life, with each family member possessing a deeply entrenched work ethic and an abiding sense of family loyalty—and affection.[8]

The family home and the neighborhood in which it was located left indelible impressions on her. It was, as I have noted, in a busy area. An alley to the rear of the house was rather infamous in the town. It was here that the city's red-light district was located. Many women helped their families to survive by providing them with a portion of their income from prostitution. With this money in hand, male members of these families were able to attend school.[9] Relatives of Lu worked in these brothels and their mothers would visit them when they could, stopping off at the Lu family's house while in the area.[10] It is apparent that Lu Hsiu-lien grew up with vivid images of the subordination and powerlessness of women in rural and small-city Taiwan.

Her parents were rebellious in their own way, Lu notes, for they married for love and not through an arranged marriage. Both had been adopted into families and were supposed to marry siblings in these families, but they found each other, revolted against the system, and shocked many of their relatives. Perhaps because of this, relations were sometimes strained between Lu's parents and the older generation.[11] Here was a streak of unconventionality and rebelliousness that Lu would inherit, though only later in life did she learn her parents' dark and scandalous secret.[12] There is another ironic element in this story. In the 1980s, Lu's elder brother, now a successful attorney in the area, built an ancestral hall for his clan. Thus, this member of an unconventional family has upheld and maintained classic traditions. What Lu's narrative shows us is that the past and the present—the traditional and the modern—are never far away from each other, at least in this one coastal area of western Taiwan.

Family tradition—in the form of the practice of adopting out (and adopting in) children—almost became a factor in Lu Hsiu-lien's life. On two occasions during her early life, she came close to sharing the fate of her parents in being adopted to families that were better off than her birth family. When she was two she was almost given out to a business associate of her father and his wife. The couple were childless and knowing this, her father, in jest, said that they could have her, for he already had two daughters. They took him seriously, not catching—or wanting to catch—the joking tone of his voice, and obtained the services of a broker. Lu's mother agreed to the plan as well. Only the quick action of her older siblings saved her, for they snatched her away and hid her with an aunt. The couple now saw how much her brothers and sisters loved her and discontinued the adoption process.[13]

On a second occasion she was about to be adopted by a local doctor who had taken a liking to her. Her mother approved of the plan once again, believing, according to Lu, that she was providing her daughter with a better life. However, the doctor decided to adopt the child of his brother. When commenting upon this episode, Lu notes that she was thankful to have been spared the possibility of growing up spoiled like the woman who had been adopted.[14]

During her second and third years of life, her homeland experienced the Retrocession: it was returned to the then-legitimate government that controlled the Chinese mainland, a regime dominated by the KMT. It is sad to note that all too many of the military and civilian personnel who came to Taiwan in 1945 were both rapacious and vicious. These officials also made it clear from the beginning that they looked upon the Taiwanese as suspect—as tainted by the long years of Japanese control.[15] This is how they rationalized their actions over the next two years. They saw the island as ripe for the picking and began to systematically strip away those industrial resources that the Japanese had helped the Taiwanese develop. To make matters worse, some of the soldiers, ill trained and from the hinterland, felt they had the right to any woman they wanted.

As result of this treatment the Taiwanese quickly learned to hate both the mainlander civilian officials and the military, much as the vast majority of the Chinese population on the western shore of the Taiwan Strait hated and feared the Nationalist regime.

The resistance to these policies—this general treatment of Taiwan as occupied territory—may have been inevitable and any small incident had the potential to ignite a general uprising. That precipitating incident took place in Taipei in February 1947, when soldiers beat up a woman who was illegally selling cigarettes. The soldiers display of what had become rather commonplace brutality served as the spark needed for revolt. People on many parts of the island attacked KMT troops, civilian officials, and the families of newly arrived mainlander emigrants. Within a week of the outbreak of this February 28 Incident, the mainlanders were on the defensive. The government officials bought time by negotiating with Taiwanese leaders, holding out the promise of major reforms and a redress of grievances. These officials had no real wish to negotiate in good faith, however, and when troop reinforcements arrived, the general in charge unleashed them to quell the revolt. Thousands were killed and many thousands more were arrested.[16] Some never returned to their families and thus may be added to the number liquidated. Many intellectuals and leaders of Taiwanese society were targeted and eliminated as potential or actual leaders of resistance. To those who lived through it, February 28 is still clearly remembered as a "Taiwanese holocaust."[17]

Lu discussed this painful period in her English-language essay on women's liberation prepared for the Hong Kong conference on Taiwan (a conference convened by the Taiwan Studies Group and the University of Hong Kong), which is part of her unpublished English-language autobiography, and in other articles. In her essay on women's liberation, she sums up these years: "Taiwan began to be dominated by the KMT in 1945 after Japan surrendered its colony. A brutal massacre was executed to suppress the Taiwanese uprising that took place on February 28, 1947, against the KMT's corruption, pillage, and economic depression. Two years later, Generalissimo Chiang Kaishek fled to Taiwan where he established the martial law regime."[18]

Once he had consolidated his power on Taiwan, Chiang tried to rectify the situation on the island—now one of the few parts of China his regime held—so that he would not face a totally alienated populace. Economic conditions slowly improved and institutions such as temples and churches were again allowed to function, although under the watchful eye of the government.[19]

In the early 1950s, with U.S. support for the KMT regime secured, the leaders speeded up the process of reform of the governmental and political sectors.[20] The first years the transplanted regime introduced these policies were considered the most painful for the Taiwanese, but the situation was even more painful for many of the new arrivals.[21] These same years saw the full force of government authority fall upon corrupt officials and ineffective military personnel as the regime set about cleaning house in earnest.[22]

This rigid control of the society and the individuals who made it up had a dramatic effect on Taiwan. According to Lu: "As a result [of the occupation] various previously taboo topics surfaced. Anyone who dared express [an] unorthodox idea or to discuss sensitive taboo subjects was considered a dissident. Dissidents were subjected to political harassment, arrest, torture, incarceration and even execution." She continues—and one can feel the cold fury with which she wrote these words:

> Until July 15, 1987, when the decree of martial law was lifted, fundamental rights such as freedom of expression, freedom of assembly, and freedom of the press were infringed upon. Orthodoxy was deeply engraved by control of thought starting in childhood. Thought control was pervasive in the schools as everywhere else in society. An unverified estimate is that over the thirty-eight years of martial law, hundreds of persons had been executed and thousands jailed for political reasons, with a total of six thousand years of imprisonment. In a word, to advocate something different from orthodoxy was to start a journey toward the dark jail.[23]

One must add, however, that these first years as well as subsequent years were notable for the government's attempt to introduce local self-government within the carefully defined confines of a one-party state.[24]

These first years of KMT rule were also marked by the introduction of major economic and social reforms. Taiwan's leaders, with the help of American advisers, were able to build upon the infrastructure developed by the Japanese during their five decades of rule. Land reform, industrial reorganization, and the development of a reinvigorated private sector all took place during the period from 1949 to 1959.[25] In all, the government's concentration upon heavy industry and the opening up of certain sectors to entrepreneurs resulted in what Thomas Gold, a perceptive observer of the Taiwan scene, terms, "an explosive release of latent productive forces on the island."[26]

But the economic development of the 1950s was not solely a story of triumph. By the late 1950s and early 1960s, side effects of the changes had begun to appear. The government's concentration on certain types of industries had created imbalances, and there were calls for major readjustments in the economy.[27] The KMT leadership needed to decide just how to free the economy of its reliance upon high rates of domestic consumption. Such decisions would be made in the early 1960s. The U.S. role in this economic miracle was readily apparent. By the early 1950s, the U.S. government had decided not only to defend Chiang's regime but also to bankroll it.

Important social and cultural changes were also apparent and many of these changes were better managed than the initial phase of economic restructuring. For example, the government was intent upon improving education for the masses. It had first introduced such changes in the early 1950s, building upon the educational facilities the Japanese had developed. The foundation for an effective system of education for the entire populace was now in place.[29]

During these first years and during the early years of Nationalist consolidation, Lu Hsiu-lien attended primary school and then the first phase of high school, what in the United States might be called middle school or junior high school. Recalling this period, Lu suggests that, while she was aware of this prejudice against females, she suffered relatively little from it and was raised as if she were a boy. A fortuneteller had told her parents she was the third son and this colored their thinking about her. Perhaps romanticizing a bit, she has noted that her father and her beloved older brother treated her as the intelligent and inquisitive human being that she was and as if she were a male child—a member of the privileged sex, not the unprivileged one—and she was never told of the limits a female would face in Taiwanese society. One can also see that in her family women did assume far-ranging responsibilities for the family welfare, and this ingrained sense of family semi-equality was an important factor in her childhood. Her father, an intelligent but self-made and very much self-educated man, strongly encouraged her by reading to her about politics and world affairs, expecting that she would do well in school. Her older brother also treated her more as an equal and never as, to use her words, "a weak girl." He would invite her to join him on hikes in the countryside near T'aoyüan, expecting on such hikes that she carry her own weight and not be given any special preference based on her sex.[30]

Such treatment—such "sex-role blindness"—had its effect. When Lu first entered school and had to list her sex, she listed male, so unaware was she of her true sex and of the expectations that a strongly patriarchal society had of members of that second sex. This mode of childrearing served her well, she believed, for she was told she could be all that she wanted to be. In January 1995, looking back on these years, she considered this experience the root of her decision to enter the confrontational and male-dominated arena of Taiwanese politics.[31]

Her father and her brother encouraged her and prepared her well, and her mother seemed determined to give her an opportunity that had not been made available to her older sisters. School gave the young girl further opportunities to shine and to demonstrate that her family's confidence was well placed. She did well in her class work and was soon called upon to tutor other students. During a one-week absence of her teacher, she took over his duties. As a result of this willingness to help others and this ability to lead and teach her peers, she was usually elected class president. On one occasion, in what was described as a mock election, she was chosen as county superintendent by the students of the school.

Once when she was in sixth grade, her teacher asked her to assist with the task of class ranking. What she discovered was corruption in the system—the teacher often ranked students not on the basis of ability but on the basis of class and economic status and on the basis of the fact that he received fees for helping to tutor certain students. She felt that the practice was wrong and led the students on a sort of sit-down strike. Her teacher responded by striking her. What she had said spread, and the teacher retaliated by calling her a liar. She reacted by refusing to go to school, staying out until her brother negotiated a settlement.[32] The many painful lessons learned from this experience were ultimately useful to one who would live a life engaged in social action.

When the time came to attend the next level, high school, Lu's family, now in better economic health, was able to help her. She received a high grade on the entry examinations and her family was able to send her to the most prestigious school open to women, the Taipei First Girls' School. She now began a difficult period, one that entailed sacrifice from Lu and her immediate family. Taipei was an hour away by train and Ms. Lu was forced to wake early, at 5:30 A.M., to prepare herself and then take the 6:00 A.M. train to the capital. Her mother would wake before her, prepare a breakfast and then pack a lunch in one of the metal boxes one still sees school children carry, and which were made famous in the Ang Li film *Eat, Drink, Man, Woman*. This was an important time in the relationship between mother and daughter—a time of affection and bonding—and it had its impact upon decisions that Lu had to make later. The trip was long and she often had to stand. She learned how to cope—discovering that she could budget her time and she could study even while standing up. Once she reached Taipei she had a twenty-minute walk to the school. On rainy days she took the bus. The school day ended at 5:00 P.M., when she would begin the long trek back. She reached T'aoyüan and the family home at 7:00 P.M.

The years in middle school, from the time Lu was twelve until she was fourteen, were productive but she discovered she possessed certain limitations that prevented her from excelling as she had in primary school. A person's standing was based on how well one did in all facets of school life, athletics included. Here she failed as a self-described nonathletic and uncoordinated child. She realized later that her problems in this regard may have been because of a thyroid condition. But she was a good student and this served her well as she adjusted to her new environment. Another problem she faced and dealt with was the reality of her upbringing both as a Taiwanese and as a girl from a small town. Many of her fellow students were of mainlander background and from comfortable urban families. However, she discovered that these city kids wanted to know more about her and her life and she was able to make friends and to adjust to the social environment as well as to the rigors of the daily commute.[33]

While she may not have done as well as she wanted to do, it was clear that she was now on a fast track. She was following in the footsteps of her favorite brother, the one who watched over her even as he competed with her. And, as she would demonstrate over the course of the 1960s, in Taipei she found an educational/ intellectual environment equal to her talents and her ambitions.

The social transformation through which Taiwan was passing had its painful aspects. Large segments of the populace experienced a deep sense of dislocation during the late 1940s and the 1950s.[34] Taiwan was an arena of social conflict and a laboratory of socioeconomic change.[35] Taiwan's society was perhaps unique in that those who dominated the government were themselves a newly arrived émigré population; the conqueror was also the political refugee. Those who now controlled the island were experiencing the same sense of dislocation and disorientation that any displaced people would feel. The mainlanders who came to the island during these years talked of the difficulties of adjustment and of the populace's open hostility.[36] Taiwan was part of China but it was not *their* China. The Taiwanese themselves also felt disorientation and unhappiness brought on by the brutalization and exploitation visited upon them by those who supposedly were their liberators. The two groups, mainlanders and Taiwanese, had little love for each other, and this simply added to the spreading sense of social confusion.

The social crisis had a powerful, and sometimes tragic, effect upon those who experienced it. But this crisis did open them to new religious experiences, alternatives that Western missionaries were happy to provide, and conversions among mainlanders and among Taiwanese increased as a complex Protestant community took shape.

Lu Hsiu-lien has given us another way to view the society that evolved as she grew to womanhood in the 1950s and 1960s. Before I move the narrative forward, I will use Lu Hsiu-lien's own observations, written in the 1970s, to suggest the nature of the observations and insights she presented to the Taiwanese public.

During the early 1970s, as Lu Hsiu-lien began to involve herself ever deeper in the women's movements, she began to study Western feminist theory. Then, drawing upon the theories and models she had read, she began to analyze her own society on Taiwan as viewed through the lens of this Western feminist theory. And it was then, in the years immediately following her return to Taiwan after her studies in the United States—and her exposure to Western feminism—that she began to analyze her own society, but now as one who was conscious of and sensitive to the patriarchal and chauvinistic nature of Taiwanese society. In these essays and books written during the years she was helping to mold the first wave of Taiwanese feminism, Lu reflected on the decades of rapid socioeconomic change that she had lived through when she began to discuss issues related to the suppression of women.

The first few articles she wrote soon became a flood of books—more than nineteen as of 1977—in which she analyzed and critiqued her society. One of a number of seminal works she wrote during this period—and one I consider central to her efforts as an activist—is *Hsin nü-hsing chu-yi* (New Feminism). In 1973 she published the first edition of what would be her most comprehensive book, *New Feminism*. In this important and censored work she spelled out her own carefully wrought and deeply critical analysis of male-dominated Chinese/Taiwanese society.[37] Now in its fifth edition, it remains a landmark work. In the paragraphs that follow, I use this book and other relevant articles she has written to detail Lu's critique of the Taiwan in which she grew up.

Surveying Taiwan's long history of invasions and dominations, Lu found one constant—that males were in control and that women played subservient roles. The two major nations that controlled Taiwan were at their core Confucian in culture. Confucianism was, in her view, a philosophy that made women into second-class citizens at best and into little more than chattel at worst. Confucianism, she argues, contains a subideology of gender hierarchy and domination and women were enculturated in ways that gave them little choice but to accept this ideology. The core ideas that provided the framework for this systematic process of suppression and subordination are encapsulated under the headings of the Three Obediences and the Four Virtues. The Three Obediences required that a woman obey the father before marriage, obey the husband after marriage, and answer to the son after the death of her husband. The Four Virtues included attention to criteria that women had to meet to be "virtuous": morality, skill in handicrafts, appearance, and propriety in speech. These very traditional "virtues" and the custom of the binding of the feet led to what Lu termed "the Three-Way Bondage of Women." These were to bind the head by cultivating the belief that a woman's ignorance was a virtue, to bind the waist by condemning women for infidelity while encouraging men's practice of sex and romance outside the confines of marriage, and to bind the feet, making such feet a standard of beauty with heavily erotic overtones.

Although the constitution of the Republic of China (ROC) contained clauses that addressed the equality of the sexes, Lu argues that the laws of the nation were written in such a way as to undercut the language of that progressive-seeming document. Rather than implement gender equality in law, the government wrote legislation that continued to permit the legal and social subservience and subjugation of women. She demonstrates this by discussing the law on marital property, which, she argues, served to limit a woman's basic personal and economic rights. The key assumptions of this law are, she suggests, as follows:

1. the husband's obligation is to support and the wife's duty to render services;
2. proper gender roles are defined by female servitude at home and male employment outside the household;
3. the wife's household service is worth no more than her own support;
4. every wife needs a guardian, for which purpose the husband is the most suited.

What she demonstrates here is that this law infringes upon the economic capacity
of a woman when she marries and prevents her from gaining any measure of economic and personal independence.[38]

In practical terms, this meant that a woman was limited in what she could hope
to do in many realms of society. In the evolving quasi-democratic representative
politics of Taiwan, women could and did play only a limited role until and even
after the consciousness-raising effort of the 1970s. In the economic sphere, women
found limited opportunities and salaries much below those available for men. And
in the realm of education, the gateway to economic and political success and status
in a strongly education-oriented society, women, while making gains, by the early
1970s, were being confronted by male backlash and a government that was ready-
ing itself to severely limit women's opportunities for higher education.[39] The contemporary American debate over "family values" resonates in one's mind when
one reads of this retrogressive policy the ROC state was planning to implement to
ensure that women continued to play the roles they were expected and enculturated
to play.

Now let us return to our two-layered narrative thread—the national and the
personal. The ROC changed rapidly over the course of the 1960s and early 1970s,
as the nation moved from the status of a less-developed country (LDC) to a newly
industrialized country (NIC), from an agricultural society to an industrial society.
Other problems grew out of the political transformations and crises accompanying
these economic and social changes.

As we have seen, during the 1950s, Taiwan's financial situation had stabilized
and the economy had been able to develop. But the government still dominated the
economy and directly controlled and ran a number of key industries and industrial
concerns. This practice ran counter to the views of many foreign experts working
in Taiwan, such as officials from the U.S. Agency for International Development,
who believed that the major sectors of the economy would do better if placed in
private hands. Furthermore, the country's inordinately large defense establishment
drew off an estimated 80 percent of the government's annual budget. Finally, Taiwan was still predominantly a producer of agricultural products and the health of
the Taiwanese economy was still overly dependent upon its ability to export large
quantities of high quality agricultural products.[40]

The 1960s and 1970s witnessed a dramatic shift from the earlier patterns we
have discussed. The government's role in the economy declined and the conditions under which goods were produced changed, as did those goods themselves.[41]
The most visible change was the U.S. decision first to reduce and then to end its
annual infusions of direct economic aid. While military help would continue well

into the 1970s, other forms of aid had ceased by 1965. The U.S. advisers realized one simple fact: The Taiwanese were now able to develop on their own.[42]

The actions taken by the government set the stage for future development. Over the course of the 1960s, government investment in infrastructure projects increased and major improvements in transportation and in the production of hydroelectric power were soon in evidence. Tax-free and duty-free industrial processing zones were expanded and new ones were set up in areas such as Taichung. The government also offered foreign firms tax incentives and introduced other liberal policies for inducing foreign investment. It could offer such investors large numbers of well-trained workers who could be paid half the amount received by a worker in Hong Kong and one-quarter what the typical Japanese worker received. The fact that labor unions were tools of the government made much of this possible. Furthermore, private firms were given a freer hand than they had before.[43] Meanwhile, the government began staffing its ranks with increasing numbers of well-educated, modern-thinking technocrats.[44]

The rapid economic development that began during these years affected all aspects of life in Taiwan. The need for a well-trained workforce—for managers, skilled workers, and technical personnel such as engineers—forced the government to develop the educational system and create modern elementary schools, secondary schools, and colleges and universities. It also forced the government to expand the range and increase the size of the research facility of the Academia Sinica at Nankang in Taipei.

The government has also been willing to allow its students to receive advanced degrees in the West. Although this has resulted in a brain drain, a sufficient number of these graduate students and new Ph.D.s do return to meet their society's needs.[45] One of those who would benefit from this opening to the West and this opportunity to receive graduate degrees in American universities was Lu Hsiu-lien. We now return to our examination of her life.

During the 1960s, Lu was able to continue her education. She remained at the excellent school to which she had been admitted after sixth grade, attending high school there. As she matured, she found that she grew more and more comfortable in this challenging academic environment. By the time she reached the upper grades, she was winning prizes and gaining attention for her writing. She was also demonstrating leadership, as she had done in primary school. People saw her as a strong and effective leader. One also gets the impression that she was self-conscious and naïve in matters of the flesh and the heart, and this continued into her college years. The segregation of the sexes and the still rather puritanical Taiwan of those years—before MTV and videotapes—probably account for this as does the influence of her somewhat conservative, traditional, and controlling parents. I read this as a subtext in her own comments in the unpublished autobiography.

What she also found in high school were a number of female role models. One was the school's principal, Chiang Hsüeh-chu. And, interestingly, one of the things that made this woman attractive to the students—and a figure of myth—was a rumored romance with the philosopher, language reformer, and educator Hu Shih. She remained unmarried and went on to be influential in the special sphere open to her and to other educated women in this male-dominated society. Let me be clear here: she was not seen as a positive role model by the majority of newly educated women. However, in Lu's opinion, the life of Chiang Hsüeh-chu presented an alternative to the life pattern most would follow. Although it followed a path that ran counter to the one typical of marriage and family that most women on Taiwan were expected to follow, some women were nevertheless willing to embrace it.[46]

In her final year of high school in 1962, Lu Hsiu-lien took the unified entrance exam, the test that determines university placement. Her older brother had survived the process, gained entrance to National Taiwan University (T'aita) Law School, and graduated college. By the time Lu took her exams, her brother was already working for the government. He advised her and provided her with ways to think about and study for the exam. She took his advice and though she thought she had not done well enough—72 percent—she discovered that she had placed first among those who wanted to enter the undergraduate school of law at T'aita. Her years at the prestigious high school had ended well.[47] Thus, she was following in the footsteps of her brother. This relationship of older brother and younger sister was proving to be a major one in her life. Her brother provided her with the kind of advice and support her less-educated father could not.[48]

Once in the university, she did not let up. She continued to push herself in a school dominated by men. Rather than slack off and enjoy college as a break before entering a profession—as men so often did in Taiwan and Japan, societies with exam-driven, highly competitive educational systems—she kept pressing ahead, knowing intuitively, as did her peers in the United States, that a woman had to be best even to be considered equal. And she succeeded in reaching her goal— she graduated first in her class.[49]

This did not mean there were no frustrations and painful moments along the way. She had to learn to deal with men in a man's world and this sometimes proved difficult. She had to come to grips with relationships with men and this proved a slow process—she had to be ready to be less self-conscious. Here her autobiography is almost painful to read as Lu reflects honestly on her vulnerability in this facet of life.[50]

The most difficult problem was one she never overcame—passing the exam for a judgeship. She took it a number of times and failed each time. Her brother had passed and she wanted to follow him in this as well. The problem came down to something simple and basic—penmanship. This exam, in some odd way, became a sort of eight-legged essay, and both presentation and content were all important. But Lu did not write well —again possibly the result of the undiagnosed thyroid problem—and thus never made it through. She felt disappointed and frustrated—she had never met with this type of failure before—but suggests that she was better for it.[51]

Lu Hsiu-lien's success at school convinced her to apply for the Li Foundation

Scholarship, a scholarship that guaranteed a graduate education abroad. She had already made plans to go abroad, to visit Europe. In Europe she hoped to meet a bright and able man she had known from a distance but had never met in person. She had been carrying on a "relationship by mail." That relationship had moved so far along that the man's family had already checked her out and had approved of her even before they first set eyes upon each other. He was in France, studying law and she hoped to meet him there.[52]

As this planning was going on, tragedy struck. Lu Hsiu-lien's father died of cancer. He was fifty-five, a relatively young man, but had been suffering for some time until the end came. The death was a painful loss to the family and for Lu it meant the loss of an ally.[53]

With the period of mourning behind her, Lu planned for a trip to Europe even as she waited to hear about the Li scholarship. She received a short-term grant to study criminology in the Netherlands having majored in criminal law at T'aita. This grant gave her the chance to meet her special friend. She knew she was third in line for the Li scholarship, but thought she had little chance, only to find out two weeks before she left for Europe that it had come through. She had already applied and been accepted to the M.A. program in comparative law at the University of Illinois. She had been forced to delay her attendance and thus the period that she had to reply had come and gone. She was able to communicate with the school to inform them she could attend. The school authorities then informed her that she should come to the Urbana-Champaign campus to pursue her degree. She wrote her "friend" in Europe about her plans to visit Europe as a part of her longer sojourn to the West and then prepared for the trip. The last weeks at home were difficult as Lu had to face a mother who was reluctant to let her go, and who used various emotional weapons to break down her daughter's will. An aunt who opposed Lu's move hid her mother for a few days in an attempt to put more pressure on Lu, and this threw the whole family into a panic. However, this tactic did not work. Lu Hsiu-lien would not budge or sacrifice her chance for advanced education. She was an ambitious woman, as she admits in her sometimes too-honest autobiography, but at that moment she did not know just what her ambition might cost her. The battle was won and Lu Hsiu-lien set off for the West.[54]

She flew to Illinois in 1969 and returned after her graduation in 1971. The years in the West—in the United States and in Europe—were important ones for her and she learned much about the world, about the other people to whom she became close, and about herself. But, as is so often the case in life, such lessons were learned at a high price—at the cost of pain and suffering to herself and to others.

Setting off in 1969, Lu flew from Taipei to Tokyo, spending a few days in Japan with some friends. The Japanese socioeconomic miracle confronted her and she was impressed by what she saw, thrilled that an East Asian people could make such progress. She then flew to the United States and settled in at Urbana-Champaign. She lived with other Taiwanese students in rather sparse conditions. She quickly decided to live in the dorm and spare herself the student poverty she saw that first day. This was more comfortable, and enabled her to adjust and begin her studies with little trouble.

The education she received at the university was a useful one. She found comparative law a pragmatic subject to study, given her interests, and she was able to get a sense of the way the basic legal systems functioned. She admits that she did not at that point really gain a deep understanding of the American judicial system, but feels that what she did learn permitted her to see the Taiwanese system in a different light. She gives her readers the impression that the perspectives she was able to gain served her well when she returned to Taiwan.[55]

Of far greater value were the other lessons she learned. One was in the realm of Taiwanese politics. The University of Illinois was a place where many Taiwanese students had decided to study. There had evolved a political/national consciousness and a student solidarity of sorts, for the United States provided the freedom lacking on Taiwan. There were spies, however, so there were limits to the freedom within the group, but much could be said and discussed, nevertheless.

The early 1970s were crisis-ridden years for Taiwan, and the core crisis in 1970–71, as well as the ouster of the ROC from the United Nations and the Nixon visit to the People's Republic of China (PRC) were all in the diplomatic realm. The Tiao-yü-t'ai episode—the Japanese government's attempt to press its claim to a few small islands north of Taiwan—set things off, and that crisis spurred the students to action at the university. There were consequences, for the KMT was against the students' actions, but there were valuable lessons for all concerned. The interaction with different types of Taiwanese was valuable to Lu, who made friends—as well as enemies.[56]

Lu also matured as a person through what became the end of her long-distance romance. She found that she had greatly disappointed her friend (although he had become her beau in both their minds, despite their never having met face to face) when she told him she was going to the University of Illinois. She still wanted to meet with him, get to know him, and see where things would go. They arranged to meet in December in New York, where her friend was planning to visit. They were then to spend time together visiting the Washington, D.C. area and one of Lu's pen pals.

Simply put, the trip was a disaster. She had built up such high hopes of this god she was to meet that a single flaw—his lack of height—was enough to burst the bubble. She tried to hide her feelings but things went from bad to worse. The relationship that seemed so promising fell apart before it could begin as something more than an exaggerated pen-pal romance. Today the equivalent would be a relationship on e-mail or America On-line. Perhaps it was doomed from the start. These two educated and intelligent people realized things were not going well and tried to make amends, analyzing what had gone wrong. And six months later, while on a trip to Europe with two American friends—an unforgettable adventure (and education) in and of itself—the two star-crossed individuals saw each other, each realizing again that they were not made for each other. I see this unconsummated relationship as an important moment in Lu Hsiu-lien's life. If I read her words correctly, she realizes once again that her only partner is her own ambition—that she is not capable of sharing what she is.[57] And after the bitterness and the pain that took place in the aftermath of those grim December days—days whose description evoked in me the feelings I had when reading in Waugh's *Brideshead Revisited* of the end of Charles Ryder's love affair with Julia Flyte—Lu Hsiu-lien knew more about who she was as a woman and as a person, and knew what path she had to follow.

In the late spring of 1971, Lu Hsiu-lien returned to Taiwan to a future that was bright, but as yet unclear, the wiser, even if sadder, for her exciting and sometimes painful years in the West.

Lu Hsiu-lien, Taiwan's First Waves of Protest, and the Evolution of Taiwanese Feminism

We now shift to the period from mid-1971 to mid-1977. It was a time of intense political conflict and transformation on Taiwan. During this period, Lu organizes the Taiwanese feminist movement. How she defines and initiates the movement, how she works for it to take root, how she copes with the difficulties she and the movement encounter, and how she fits this struggle for women's rights into the larger process of social change then taking place are examined.

Sociopolitical Transformation and Diplomatic/Political Crisis in the Republic of China 1971–1977

Taiwan's rapid industrial development also produced an urban revolution. This could be seen in the 1960s, and the trend accelerated during the 1970s. Such cities as Taipei in the north and Kaohsiung in the south became world-class cities boasting commercial centers and industrial facilities.[58] Smaller cities—such as Taichung in central Taiwan; Tainan, the acknowledged cultural capital of Taiwanese Taiwan; and Keelung and Hualien along Taiwan's beautiful and forbidding eastern coast— all experienced impressive growth and by the late 1970s were fast becoming centers of trade and industry. As the agricultural sector became less important,[59] many people moved to the suburbs and to the inner-city neighborhoods of the urban centers closest to their home villages. It has been demonstrated that Tainan and Kaohsiung in the south have developed in this fashion.[60] Similar growth patterns can be seen in Taipei in the development of a host of urban villages in the newer parts of the city.

This economic revolution also created a religious renaissance. Minnan people, Hakka, and mainlanders all returned in droves to the orthodox religious centers, the temples of the major folk gods, and the shrines of the I-kuan-tao (the Way of unity) and other heterodox sects. Festivals mattered once again; Chinese religion was again a vibrant and exciting element in people's lives. The people felt blessed by their new prosperity, and, as Chinese have done so often in the past, wanted to thank those gods they felt were responsible for helping them to obtain the new wealth.

The transformed economy and the resulting changes in the distribution of wealth, the spread of education, the development of the major cities, the return to traditional religion, and the rise of a new middle class all had their effect on the political realm. The KMT had engineered an economic miracle that in turn had produced a well-educated and increasingly comfortable middle class that, by the 1960s and early 1970s, was becoming uncomfortable with the rigid and undemocratic regime led by the old Generalissimo Chiang and run on a day-to-day level by his son and eventual successor, Chiang Ching-kuo. When this middle-class discomfort reached a critical mass, a new political era began.

The starting point of this political change was Taiwan's problems with the outside world. In the years from 1971 to 1977 Taiwan faced a number of diplomatic crises that created problems at home for the KMT-dominated regime.[61] And it was also during this period that Chiang Ching-kuo came to power, in real, if not formal, terms. With this power firmly in his grasp, this astute political animal—with a surprisingly approachable public persona—was able to define, in outline, the directions, the policies, and the programs that would transform Taiwan's political system and ensure his party's continuing viability and survival.

This series of failures in the diplomatic sphere set in motion a series of precedent-shattering events on Taiwan. Middle-class intellectuals and students, enjoying new status and wealth, now began to feel dissatisfied with the frozen political process and the many restrictions on freedom of expression. And the regime, once seemingly respected in the world community, was now regularly losing face. The result was a brief period of political activism highlighted by challenges to the regime in its legislative organs and by actions taken in the streets.

On the political front, newcomers such as Kang Ning-hsiang, and Huang Hsin-chieh began the loosely knit political faction that would become known as the *tangwai* (opposition). In the streets, a series of demonstrations and open demands for political change were held, led by college professors. The government was not yet ready to allow such open dialogue and by 1973 it began to arrest the leaders of the new political movement and fire those professors who openly criticized the regime.[62]

Chiang Ching-kuo, now the president, was forced to deal with this confrontation and open challenge to his regime. His first response was harsh, but fit the political realities and the political contexts of the day. The iron fist had to be used to warn the opposition, but the velvet glove that hid it also had to be used to show the opposition and those members of the educated middle class still reserving judgment that he could learn the lessons of open dissent.

In the next few years he began what can be seen as a process of Taiwanization. There was a precedent for the moves that he took. In 1969 the KMT had initiated a rapid turnover of party executives at the county and municipal levels. In increasing numbers, Taiwanese were appointed to these local committee posts. Even at higher levels such as central party headquarters, more Taiwanese (Minnan and Hakka) were being rewarded with very visible posts.[63]

There were other reforms as well, reforms that opened the way for even higher levels of Taiwanese participation. Again at the urging of Chiang Ching-kuo, the government planned to expand its popular base, increasing the number of seats open to election by the Taiwanese in its major representative organs, the National Assembly and the Legislative Yüan.[64] The administration committed itself to be more accessible and open and there were to be new attempts to curb corruption. Next, the government was to provide career planning and seek closer contact with the new generation. Finally, it would address social welfare issues and problems faced by workers and peasants.[65]

These reforms demonstrate that the KMT under its new leader was attempting to deal with the dissatisfaction expressed in the demonstrations of the early 1970s. However, to respond by reform did not mean to concede to demands for a totally open political system with room for contending parties. Seeing the regime's attempt to reform itself and open its ranks to Taiwanese, the *tangwai* thought that it could push things farther, and in 1975 and 1976 attempted to contest elections and demand even more changes in the basic political structure. Again Chiang responded to the challenge by taking off the velvet glove, and 1976 saw a return to the policy of arrests and repression. The new president—Chiang's father had died in 1975 and been buried in grand ceremonial fashion, presided over by the Baptist minister, Chou Lien-hua—demonstrated once again that he was willing to play the role of good cop–bad cop, but now as the nation's formal leader and not just the man behind the throne.

These social and political changes created the environment in which Lu Hsiu-lien learned to operate and in which she helped to create a feminist consciousness and founded the women's movement.

Lu Hsiu-lien and the Origins of Taiwanese Feminism

The Taiwan to which Lu Hsiu-lien returned late in the spring of 1971 was a place different from the one she had left just a few years earlier. She would soon discover the new national mood and enter battles that suited and took advantage of the disturbed temper of the times.

That was not her plan when she first arrived home, however. She had hoped when she returned that her stay would be brief. She had been admitted to the Ph.D. program at the University of Washington in Seattle and hoped to begin in the fall. But her mother put enormous pressure on her, and she came to the conclusion that as a person in her twenties she had done little in the real world. Her mother also told her that Ph.D. also meant "push husband down." This pithy expression summed up her belief that the advanced degree would be seen as yet another barrier to her daughter's marriage. The decision not to pursue the Ph.D. transformed Lu Hsiu-lien's life and—it is a bit dramatic but fair to say—the lives of thousands of Taiwanese women as well.[66]

She felt she was qualified to work for the government and applied, finding two interesting possibilities. The first was to serve with the Department of Investigation of the Ministry of Justice. She was interviewed in Hsintien, south of Taipei, and seemed to do well. However, the job involved internal security—FBI-type covert activity directed against Taiwanese dissidents who were based in the West. She was offered a job and told her brother about the position. Already an established lawyer and a budding anti-KMT figure himself, he asked why she would want to take such a position, for, in his words, "That's like working for the king of hell." His words and arguments had their effect. She looked elsewhere, soon finding a place in the Law and Regulations Committee (or Commission on Laws and Regulations) of the Executive Yüan. Her superior was a man she had met while traveling in Rome, Dr. Cheng, a man who like herself had studied abroad and received a Ph.D. from the University of Vienna. She spent four years here and learned how the bureaucracy of the ROC functioned. In her autobiography, she gives a generally favorable portrait of her office and its work but without masking its flaws. There were a host of difficult cases: some of the decisions made by her superiors were made for political reasons and did not do justice to the matter at hand. But here were individuals with strong moral fiber and some, such as her superior, Dr. Cheng, resigned rather than compromise on matters of principle. What she saw, she suggests, gave her hope that trained and dedicated people were coming into the system.[67] This fundamental respect for the basic organs of government and for the possibility that the system could function well lies at the heart of her role as pragmatic reformer. She appears to suggest that based on this experience she is a person who is not willing to totally overthrow the system, but is willing to make those changes that might work better and thus serve the people of Taiwan better.

This was her day job, for about thirty-five hours a week, and it helped support her and her other activities. She was given two afternoons to do some teaching at the Min-ch'üan Girls Technical School. This was an institution that she feels had a great impact on the women of the island. It served as a major training center for professional women who would make up the backbone of many of the city's—and the island's—smaller firms as well as its major corporations. The Technical School gave women the business skills necessary to go from school to the Taipei workplace and thus served a role similar to that of community colleges or private two-year business schools.[68]

But what of the feminist movement? First, the movement was very much a product of Lu Hsiu-lien's efforts, though, given the nature of her support, it would seem other women and men were ready to begin the struggle for gender equality but needed a leader and a spokesperson. She was there at the right moment, in the right place, with the right motivation, and with an underlying ambition that allowed her to seize the moment. This first phase of her involvement in the movement—from 1971 to 1977—can be broken down into three subphases, each with its own dynamics and its own set of challenges and problems. She suggested what these phases were in her English-language autobiography, working through each subphase in a narrative framework. She also discussed her work in a cross-sectional fashion in her article on women's liberation, the paper presented at the Hong Kong conference, setting up a number of categories and then fitting the various activities she had helped organize into each of these. Finally, in both her autobiography and her article, she discussed the response to the movement on the part of the people of Taiwan and the government. The following discussion employs an eclectic approach, using both narrative and cross-sectional analysis, to lay out the development of the movement and then present the reactions and the responses to this initial stage of the feminist movement on Taiwan.

Let us begin with the origins of the movement and then trace its evolution, subphase by subphase. It would seem that her entry into this movement, or, more accurately, her creation of it came about almost by chance and is the classic providence in the fall of a sparrow that the Bard's Hamlet talks about. In 1971, a debate was raging about the issue of higher education for women. The examinations for higher education were objective, and the names of the students were unknown to those grading the actual examination papers. By that time, women had become the majority of students who passed the rigorous examination in a number of subject areas. These included literature and history. Those who administered the exam, educators as well as officials in the Ministry of Education, found this alarming and felt that a reserve quota had to be instituted for men. The issue was not women's use of their education, but men's failure—or unwillingness—to enter certain fields. The quotas were a means of ensuring the continuing role of men in such fields—and by implication their continuing dominance of such fields. Lu Hsiu-lien and others saw this as an attempt to maintain what might be termed male hegemony. Lu was so enraged by what she read that she submitted a long article to the *Lien-ho pao* (United Daily), one of the nation's leading newspapers. The paper was considered conservative and thus Lu was surprised when they decided to publish it in eight installments. The article raised its own firestorm of controversy. And it also gave Lu a number of supporters who urged her to continue her efforts. A young man and his fiancée were among those who volunteered and invested in a feminist coffee shop that she set up.[69]

The articles yielded other results. Lu Hsiu-lien was asked to lecture at the T'aita Law School on Woman's Day—March 8, 1972. Twenty-three years later, on March 8, 1995, she made a formal announcement of her candidacy for president—with the full pomp and ceremony such an act required. That initial speech was not well attended, though Lu's brother and his daughters were there to ask questions. This became the first of many such speeches she was asked to give during this initial phase of what became the Taiwanese feminist movement.[70]

The embryonic movement was pushed forward by a rather terrible—and all too common—crime. A Taiwanese man, Chung Chao-mao, studying at the University of California, San Diego, killed his wife, Tang Ming-yu. The arranged marriage had been a disaster from the start and the attractive young woman rebelled against her stodgy and unattractive husband. The couple fought, he murdered her, and then flew back to Taiwan. He received a seven-year sentence. The press played up the case with a chauvinist slant—the man, a brilliant and talented student, dealt with his unfaithful wife in a brutal but morally acceptable manner—divorce Taiwan style. And he was treated as a hero. Lu Hsiu-lien's brother handled the wife's civil suit initiated to clear her name and thus she learned more about the case. Her response was to write another article, "Which Is More Important, Life or Chastity?" which was published in the *China Daily*. This second article, also considered important, struck a nerve. Many women now rallied behind Lu. One of them was Li Yüan-chen, a professor of literature at Tamkang University, feminist author, and, as of 1989, a leader of the Taiwanese feminist movement.[71]

The next few years saw Lu become ever more involved in the movement and she branched out in a number of directions. I suggest that, as she did, Western feminism and the women's liberation movement served as her models and blueprints for action. She had learned about women's liberation while at Illinois but only in a superficial way. However, student that she was, she seems to have read widely enough to present a coherent picture in her book, *Feminism*, and other works.[72] She was also practical and wise enough—and knew enough about her own culture—to go about things quietly and on a relatively small scale. Still, as she admits in her autobiography and in her articles, she was naïve about some things and this hurt her and the movement during this formative period.

A first step was "consciousness-raising." Lectures were given and debates were held, even as a steady stream of articles was produced. University campuses and many nongovernmental organizations were the sites of the lectures and debates. Television and radio were also used to publicize the new movement. The newspapers covered these events as well, giving them much-needed publicity.[73]

The movement also needed a foundation of strong organizations. Here Lu met with failure, at least at first. She attempted to found the Association for the Promotion of Women. However, she chose as a coworker, Su Chih-kuan, who was a pioneer of family planning and thus deemed suspect by an inherently chauvinist state. Permission to found the group was denied and this initial effort came to little.[74] When she attempted to set up a second such organization, she was more cautious and worked to demonstrate the nonthreatening nature of the group. She thus organized the Taiwan branch of the Business and Professional Women's Clubs and did so with the support of KMT-related women. This effort did succeed.[75] However, it seemed to develop a life of its own and became a social club of sorts for high level and high income women. Many of those closest to Lu could not afford the dinners and the style of activities that had evolved, so they dropped out. And when Lu attempted to become the leader of the organization she had helped to found, the government began to attack her.

The Pioneer Coffee Shop was another such organization that helped promote the feminist movement. The financial backing from one of her earliest supporters proved crucial in this. With NT$50,000, the shop was set up and the young man managed it for a few years. However, it ran into a variety of problems such as location, and, moreover, it catered to students, individuals who did not spend enough money in the shop to allow it to prosper or even make its own way. The couple who had run the coffee shop in the first few years moved to America and were not heard from again. A number of managers took over the reins but had no success either.[76]

The second subphase of the movement, or at least of Lu's direct participation in it, began in April 1974, in a most dramatic and life-threatening fashion. Lu decided to go for the yearly medical checkup that was covered under her health plan. At its conclusion, the physician noticed that Lu's thyroid was abnormal—it was swollen. Medicine, rather than immediate surgery, was prescribed and she took the medicine as directed from April through May. However the lump got bigger and she was losing weight, even as she ate heartily because of ravenous hunger, and she felt tired and slept poorly. Those who were close to her noticed the problem and the continued growth of the lump. Her older brother was worried and strongly suggested—ordered is the word she used—that she go to see the doctor again. The physician provided a decidedly chauvinist rationale for his failure to operate in April—he thought the resulting scar would hurt her chances of getting married.

Now, however, there was no choice. The doctor realized just how difficult a case it was and transferred her to the National Taiwan University Hospital. Lu did not know how serious the problem was, and thus she put the report in her drawer at work. Only when her sister told her she was going to take her to the hospital did she look at that report and become aware of the fact that she had thyroid cancer. Even then, perhaps because she was in a state of emotional shock, she was slow to take action. Only on the insistence of her brother did she consult another thyroid specialist—this one in her home town of T'aoyüan. He recommended that he operate on her at the Tri-Services Medical Hospital, a major facility located only a few blocks from T'aita in Taipei. She entered the hospital a few days early for the various workups and on a Monday in early May had half of her thyroid removed. There was some danger of damage to the vocal chords but the surgeon was a skillful and precise man and did his work well.

She spent the next three weeks in the hospital and then returned home to T'aoyüan to continue her recuperation. And when the ordeal was over she felt that she had been given a second life because of the efforts of her family and her doctor.[77]

The surgery and the struggle of the previous years had taken their toll and Lu was now ready for another trip to the West. She returned to work and soon thereafter began planning for a trip and applying for the visa. However, the visa was not easily obtained. She was informed that there were records of her meetings with various overseas Taiwanese who had connections to World United Formosans for Independence (WUFI) and other organizations. At this juncture it was suggested that she join the KMT as a way of speeding the process of visa approval. She did this and was a member for about six months. It was the right move at the time for it provided the document she needed to escape the island and the pressures of her job and her feminist-related activity, though she would find in the following years that many in the emerging opposition were suspicious of her, even though a number of them had done much the same thing in joining the party. She suggests that they had made the decision, as she had, to act pragmatically for a limited set of gains and had not joined because of any commitment to or love for the ruling party. She does differentiate the way she left the KMT from the way well-known Democratic Progressive Party (DPP) members left the party. She did so quietly and without fanfare during the period she was safely away from Taiwan with visa well in hand. However, these other key figures did so publicly and as a response to the failure of local KMT organizations to nominate them for office.[78]

The time she spent in the West proved more difficult than she thought it would be on a number of fronts. While she records that the ostensible reason for the trip was to involve herself in activities in the United States, Japan, and Korea under a grant from the Asia Foundation, she suggests that there were numerous other rationales and agendas that prompted her decision. One was simply to take a break and leave the work of the movement to others now that the initial steps had been taken. Another was to make contact with Taiwanese groups in the West, not as an agent but as one interested in the same issues they were. There was yet another reason. She was compelled to participate in KMT-run "summer camps" for party members who were located abroad. Such a gamut of reasons produced a journey that must have been difficult to live through, and, given the evidence I have examined, also must have proved even more difficult to talk about and write about.

At each stop in this journey, the path was strewn with unexpected obstacles. At one point, while on the East Coast, she met with members of the overseas Taiwanese community and participated in a multiday summer camp. Rather than receive a warm welcome and a nod of appreciation for the work she had done in raising women's consciousness, it seems that she encountered criticism for beginning the movement in the first place and thus providing a wedge that destroyed the unity of the people of the island. She was also taken to task for working for the Executive Yüan and for being a member of the KMT. Because of these links and because of the furious reaction that had greeted Taiwanese feminism—a movement she loudly defended at these meetings—she was accused of being a party spy who was in the United States to cause turmoil. WUFI leaders, she suggests, saw her as the enemy and tried to destroy this camp. Certainly, her account of the emotional pain she suffered during these days and the fact that she left before the formal end of the camp program show they had partially achieved their objective.[79]

That same summer she attended another conference, this one held at New York University and run by the World Taiwanese Association. Here too, anti-KMT politics and discussions of independence were the order of the day. Not all agreed, however. One well-known figure spoke heresy of reunification with the mainland and suffered the fate of the outsider, even though this individual—a Taiwanese woman named Lin Pi-yu—espoused left-leaning and radical political views that were one element in the overseas Taiwanese community's well-known ideology. Even this woman's brother was disappointed in her for stating her unpopular views. Lu learned that the overseas community was harsh to its own as well as to those from Taiwan who gave the illusion of kowtowing to the ruling party and she suggests—if I read the subtext properly—that she felt less alone than before and more secure in her evolving dislike of the Taiwanese stateside community as it existed in the mid-1970s.[80]

As a government employee, Lu had yet another obligation, to meet with KMT members in the United States at a summer conference in California similar to the one she had gone to on the East Coast. The KMT knew how to do things in a grand manner and their meeting was held in the lush and beautiful surroundings that one finds at Lake Tahoe in the summer. Here she met with and talked to a man who described himself as a diplomat but who turned out to be a member of the Department of Investigation. They had an honest conversation and he admitted who he was. As a result, she gave him material on what she had been doing and saying that was controversial enough to meet the needs of the man's superiors but not inflammatory enough to be damning or to put her in danger.[81] This was the workable compromise Lu had negotiated with this agent from the king of hell, whose family, she suggests, was held captive on Taiwan while he did the dirty work of shadowing those of whom the government was suspicious. Here was the White Terror in action, though mitigated by an unwilling actor clearly caught in the middle.

Japan and Korea were the last two stops on her itinerary. In Japan she met a number of distinguished WUFI leaders who were in exile in the nation that had occupied Taiwan for fifty years and had created the infrastructure that provided the foundation for the oft-touted KMT-directed economic miracle. She was also able to meet with a number of feminist leaders, thus fulfilling the basic objective of her grant. From Japan she went to Korea. Here, too, she met a number of leading feminists and also gathered information and data on the status of Korea's women. She came away unimpressed with what she had seen in the Hermit Kingdom.[82]

Whatever the difficulties encountered, Lu Hsiu-lien could count the trip as a useful one. She had met with a variety of Taiwanese communities. She had met with leaders of women's organizations and she had gathered data that enabled her to develop a comparative perspective on women's issues and on the state of feminist activity in East Asia and the United States. And she also seems to have come back revitalized and ready for new battles in the struggle for women's rights.

With her return to health and with her challenging and sometimes traumatic trip abroad behind her, Lu was ready to begin a new, and, in some ways, more productive phase of the feminist movement. Her first step was quite dramatic. She left her position with the Executive Yüan in order to devote all her time to the development of the feminist movement. She still had economic resources because the Asia Foundation had provided a grant that allowed her to study and write about feminist

theory and to begin to develop new modes of action that were concrete and pragmatic expressions of these theories.

Kaohsiung became the new center of effort and the place where theory became
action. Lu made contact with a doctor involved in social action named Luo Fu-
yeh. She began by making speeches on women's rights, thus preparing the community for more defined steps that were to be implemented. A new organization
was then established. This was the Women's Service Center. Here a Women's Protection Hotline was set up. Its purpose was to "console and assist rape victims and
battered women." Many volunteers were recruited, and Lu went down south once
a month to advise these volunteers and chart their progress. Given both the complex nature and the scope of the problems of domestic violence in the area, Lu
realized she could not work alone or without health professionals, social workers,
and psychologists. Many professionals in these fields joined her as the effort gained
publicity and the calls kept coming in. The program proved to be important because, as a result of its operation, the problems experienced by thousands of women
were brought to light. Of equal importance to the fact that light was shone on this
hidden area of Taiwanese life, the women who contacted the hotline were given
valuable information about what options they had. A similar hotline was also set
up in Taipei after a swirl of controversy created by two rather original activities Lu
organized. The first of these was a cooking contest in which only men could participate. The second was a "tea and conversation" session designed to get housewives out of their kitchens. Role reversal was the hook here. Admission was charged,
and the funds collected and the attention garnered proved valuable in setting the
stage for a second hotline, a hotline in the national capital and the nerve center of
the island.[83]

In her autobiography, Lu gives the reader some sense of the cases that the hotline
worked on. In one instance, a poorly dressed women who smelled of a pig farm
came in. She proceeded to give a description of abuse by her husband that included abnormal acts. Her only refuge was the pig shed and that explained why
she smelled the way she did. The daughter of generations of farmers knew what
that world was like—and what it smelled like—and was able to zero in on the
problems this woman faced. Another woman came accompanied by her mother.
She was covered with bruises and described receiving beatings at the hands of her
mainlander husband, a retired soldier who worked as a street cleaner. In yet a third
case, a woman from Hsinchu found that her husband's family had simply written
her out of the family records after she moved to Taipei to escape abuse at the hands
of her husband and her mother-in-law. There were, Lu suggests, thousands of similar
cases, cases that demonstrated abuse was not centered in any one area or any one
social class or occupational group.[84]

A related organization, a women's reference center, was set up in Taipei in the
year that followed. The center became the base for a systematic survey of housewives in the city.[85] Another step taken was a survey of women and women's problems. This survey was conducted by high school student volunteers. The information

collected was the type of hard data needed to make policy and to convince the state and its citizens that real problems did exist and they had to be recognized and dealt with. The responses showed that many women were dissatisfied with their husbands and their married lives but felt that they had few options. On the basis of analyses of these surveys, seminars were set up to serve as forums for the discussion of issues of marriage and sex on the island. In the mid-1970s, 10,000 people participated in such seminars.[86]

Yet another important enterprise established during this third subphase, and one that proved successful in a number of ways, was the Pioneer Press. This press published Lu's growing body of works as well as related works on women's issues. Three women, Wang Chung-ping, an activist in the women's movement, Shih Shu-ching, a writer with an American husband, and Lu Hsiu-lien herself, each put up funds for the press and each played a role in its management. The details of the establishment of the press as well as its business operations were very involved and they led Lu into a number of battles and controversies. Lu spells these out in detail in her narrative.[87] What is of greatest significance is that Lu and the feminist movement she was working to create now had their own press. Over the course of the next few years, a number of important books were produced, some of them works of great controversy.

Among the key works published were *Their Tears, Their Sweat, and Their Blood*, a book depicting the lives of rural women, industrial working class women, and prostitutes. The government took direct action against this book, banning it, and claiming that it was intended to promote social disorder by displaying the negative side of Taiwanese life.

A second book was also controversial, *What Made Them Famous?* This was a direct attack on social standards of excellence created by a male society. A number of women from various walks of life were profiled and the criteria upon which they were judged to be famous or noteworthy were challenged. One of the women was Ho Hsiu-tze, a famous prostitute-turned-madam. In the article, based upon an interview with Wang Chung-ping, this famous—or notorious—woman presented many reasons to justify her business as an alternative means of making a living in a hypercritical male society. Lu argues that Ho seems to have been less exploitative than the typical madam—or tried to present herself that way—and resembled a Taiwanese version of Polly Adler, the author of the famous tome *A House Is Not a Home*. Needless to say, the article created yet another firestorm of criticism. After the controversy had subsided, Lu published this single, long article, along with letters that were critical of it and its subject, under the title "The Ho Hsiu-tze Incident," and gave it away to those who published the book of essays on the concept of fame. This demonstrates that the press was becoming a powerful weapon in the arsenal of the Taiwanese feminist movement and the books that were published were stirring things up, as they were intended to do.[88]

The foregoing outlines the scope of the movement and the nature of its evolution over the course of the 1970s. There is a darker side to all this and a hidden narrative that only began coming to light after martial law and heavy press censorship ended with the arrival of democratization in the late 1980s. I refer to the harassment of Lu Hsiu-lien and her movement, which gradually wore down Lu and some of her coworkers. An outline narrative of this harassment can be found in the English-language article on women's liberation, in the most recent edition of *Feminism*, and in the as-yet unpublished autobiography.

The harassment took many forms and was the work of two different opponents, one disorganized and the other all-too-well organized. The first opponent was the general public, or, to be more exact, many members of the male populace who felt threatened by the attempt of the women's movement to gain gender equality or at least recognition of the existence of widespread inequality. They felt the movement was a form of Western cultural pollution, an attack on the traditional hegemony and traditional sets of power relationships, and an attack on traditional values.[89] Lu herself was criticized as one who adopted dangerous Western ideas and who as an unmarried woman was suspected of being, to use Lu's words, "abnormal."[90] I assume that this word was used rather than the harsher and more loaded term "gay." Lu was also subjected to a barrage of hate mail, which she discusses in her manuscript and describes as "filthy." Her response was both original and effective. She collected these letters, most of which were unsigned, and used photocopies of the most flagrant of them as exhibits in the front section of her book *The Pioneering Footsteps*. She suggests that this unusual tactic was effective because "No one dared to write to insult her again."[91]

The government would use its power to regulate clubs and public organizations to make things difficult for those attempting to found new societies and agencies designed to help women come together to discuss their problems. Lu's attempt to start a new organization in 1972 demonstrates how the authorities made Lu and her coworkers jump through all the necessary hoops only to be denied the permits they needed. In 1975, many assumed that Taipei, given its role in Taiwan's life, was the logical place for the first hotline. Yet, the web of regulations was so thick that it was decided to take the path of least resistance and establish the hotline in Kaohsiung, where a social service group open to serving as the home of the hotline had already been set up. These are but two examples of the way formal procedure could become a tool in the government's arsenal.

A more insidious form of harassment was the use of intelligence agencies to monitor and spy on the individuals involved in the work of the feminist movement. Spies, in place by 1972, were infiltrating the movement in a variety of ways. The most famous of these individuals was Lai Chun-ming, a man who eventually served as one of the managers of the coffee shop. He was considered a friend and confidante, at least at first. When his true role was revealed, Lu was hurt to the core, and, even seventeen years later, as she edited the interviews that would make up her autobiography, her pain over this singular act of betrayal came through.[92]

Yet another agent infiltrated both the hotline operation and other related organizations that feminists had begun in 1976. He used his position as a manager to seduce young women and sabotage the work itself in various ways.[93] There were other individuals Lu believed were agents but she had little factual proof.

The fear of infiltration, ongoing conflict with the authorities over issues of censorship and the issuing of permits, and the hostility of many men and women to the feminist cause all took their toll. By 1977, Lu Hsiu-lien was exhausted and ready to pull back for a while and renew herself. She wanted to go abroad to study again and got her wish. With the help Chen (Chang) Fu-mei, another famous alumnus of the T'aita Law School who had gone on to Harvard for her graduate studies, Lu Hsiu-lien was admitted to the great university in the other Cambridge to study for another master's degree in law.[94]

Conclusion

In this chapter, we have traced the role played by a rather singular woman in the formation of Taiwanese feminism. We have set this woman's life and this evolution of a social movement against the backdrop of Taiwan's dramatic and sometimes spectacular socioeconomic development and sometimes halting movement toward a viable form of democracy. And what we have witnessed in examining these early stages of Lu's life and career has been her ability to assume seemingly different roles, even as she remained true to herself and to those constituencies that she saw, and continues to this day to see, as her own.

In 1996, as this chapter was being written, she remained concerned and devoted to the women of her nation for whom she helped to construct a viable feminist movement. After 1977, she expanded the scope and range of her activities. She played a major role in the Meilitao movement of the late 1970s, was arrested, and had to serve almost five years in prison. When she was released, she went to Harvard for more study and contemplation and renewed her energies, even as Taiwan changed hands and became Lee Teng-hui's island, not Chiang Ching-kuo's. She returned to Taiwan in 1988 and began to play a number of roles in politics as a spokesperson for different causes. And because she was seen as a prominent figure, she was asked to serve as a member of the National Consultative Assembly, a body that began the process of constitutional change on Taiwan. In the months that followed she involved herself in the Taiwan reentry in the United Nations issue, and, with that as her central issue, was elected to the Legislative Yüan in 1992. She continued to push the government on that crucial issue going so far as to establish a lobbying group in New York. And in 1993, 1994, and 1995 Lu and her coworkers lobbied in the halls of the United Nations itself for the cause of Taiwan's reentry. She took the most dramatic action of her career in the spring of 1995 when she announced her candidacy for the presidency of Taiwan. She was the first woman to do so, and though her efforts were not successful, she helped make such a candidacy a viable option for the other women active in Taiwan's more open and more democratic political arena.

Thus, since 1977, Lu Hsiu-lien has begun to speak in an ever louder and more influential voice for the Taiwanese majority—male and female—which had too often been mistreated by the mainlander minority government that held the political power and the forces—and the guns—to maintain that sometimes oppressive and sometimes misused power.

I suggested in my introduction that role theory would serve as the core device in structuring this chapter. I would argue that I have indeed used that set of constructs, but without setting up an overly elaborate or heavy-handed theoretical construct. Let me recapitulate what I discussed in a long footnote. Role theory (or a least the form of role theory I feel most useful and most descriptive of the realities I have observed) stresses that each person has a core role—and this core role encapsulates that individual's fundamental character traits. Role theorists further develop the notion that each of the other roles a person plays at different stages in his or her life grows out of that core role as branches grow out of the sturdy trunk of a tree. This metaphor holds true in Lu Hsiu-lien's case: We have seen what she was early on and seen her develop and mature while at the same time remaining true to the basic values she absorbed and adopted as child, adolescent, and young adult. These include a high regard for family and community, a respect and abiding love for her parents, a sense of gender equality that was dampened in some measure by a growing sense of the reality of the position and status of women in Taiwanese life, a deep commitment to the women of Taiwan, a deep sense of her destiny as a public actor, and a powerful sense of ambition that would force her to forgo (at considerable emotional cost) the more mundane—and conditioned—pleasures of life, such as deeply felt intimacy with a member of the opposite sex. I would suggest that the roles she evolves—which she comes to assume in rather seamless fashion—one after another in the distinct stages that make up her life stem from the core personality/character that I have described.

How do we sum up these first phases in the life of this rather extraordinary woman? We can suggest that during these years she became an important model for women on Taiwan. A generation of women have now seen what Lu has founded and how she built upon that base and used it to involve herself in a number of related sociopolitical movements. That same generation has seen what she has done and learned much from her life, her actions, and her words. Today some members of the new generation of Taiwanese women view her as a bit old and dowdy—as a bit too much a persona from an earlier decade and a different stage in the struggle for women's liberation. Hearing such words spoken in the past, I have said, in Lu Hsiu-lien's defense, and can only repeat now that, without her—and without the core of women and men she worked with—there would be neither recognition of the need to create a gender-equal and gender-neutral Taiwan nor the opportunity to actually do so.

Notes

1. First, I thank Lu Hsiu-lien and her friend, the head of the New York office of the Taiwan International Alliance, Margie Joy Walden, for giving me material for use in writing the chapter. I am grateful to Lu for taking time out of her busy schedule to grant me an interview. Margie and I have crossed swords on occasion, but I regard her as a friend and a teacher. She helped me on this chapter and on another major project, offering wise critiques as well.

Thanks are due to two China scholars: Catherine Farris, a major contributor to feminist anthropology and to the study of gender on Taiwan, and Angela Zito of Barnard's Department of Religion and a student of both late Ch'ing ritual and the practice of footbinding in China.

I also thank Susan Mann, whose bibliographical essay on the new literature on women in Chinese history and on the integration of feminism as well as her essay in *Engendering China* were very useful to me in gaining a sense of the research in an evolving subfield. See Susan Mann, "Learned Women in the Eighteenth Century," in *Engendering China: Women, Culture, and the State*, ed. Christina K. Gilmartin, Gail Hershatter, Lisa Rofel, and Tyrene White, 27–46 (Cambridge: Harvard University Press, 1994).

Discussions with Vena Talwar Oldenburg, a colleague at Baruch, and an important contributor to the study of women's history in India, and with Carol Berkin, a student of colonial America and of feminism in the United States, have also proved useful as I attempted to get a grounding in what is an extensive, complex, and often controversial body of literature.

I also thank Chou Bih-er for her friendship and the gift of knowledge on the role of women in Taiwanese society and politics.

2. In an attempt to do justice to this core aspect of her life and work, and with the help and guidance of a number of friends and colleagues, I have begun to study the literature on modern feminism and women's liberation. What follows is a rather spare list of the works I consulted and feel are valuable for those attempting to develop a foundation for the deeper study of feminist history and theory. On history, see Flora Davis, *Moving the Mountain: The Women's Movement in America Since 1960* (New York: Simon and Schuster, 1991). This is a clear, insightful, and very well-written work of popular history that has the added virtue of containing a good basic bibliography. For a second work that combines history and theory, see David Bouchier, *The Feminist Challenge: The Movement for Women's Liberation in Britain and the United States* (London: Macmillan, 1983). Bouchier is a sociologist who recognizes, as I do, the inherent difficulties present when a man writes about a topic related to feminist history or theory. His is a sensitive and comprehensive work that provides readers with the added information and insights afforded by a scholar who is willing to construct a work of comparative history/theory. For a useful overview of feminist theory as seen from the perspective of a powerful and articulate African-American feminist scholar, see Bell Hooks, *Feminist Theory: From Margin to Center* (Boston: South End Press, 1984). Recent works on the later stages of the women's movement include Suzanne Gordon, *Prisoners of Men's Dreams: Striking Out for a New Feminine Future* (Boston: Little, Brown, 1991), Judith Levine, *My Enemy, My Love: Man-hating and Ambivalence in Women's Lives* (New York: Doubleday, 1992), and Naomi Wolf, *Fire with Fire: The New Female Power and How It Will Change the 21st Century* (New York: Random House, 1993). A major monograph on women in politics in Taiwan is Chou Bih-er, Cal Clark, and Janet Clark, *Women in Taiwan Politics: Overcoming Barriers to Women's Participation in a Modernizing Society* (Boulder, CO: Lynne Rienner Publishers, 1990).

3. William Shakespeare, *As You Like It* (New York: Bartleby.com, 2000) (www.bartleby.com/70/index20.html).

4. Role theory (or at least the form of role theory I feel is most useful and most descriptive of the realities I have observed) stresses that each person has a core role—and that this core role encapsulates that individual's fundamental character traits. Role theorists further develop the notion that each of the other roles a person plays at different stages in his or her life grows out of that core role as branches grow out of the sturdy trunk of a tree.

5. The basic work on role theory is Michael Banton, *Roles: An Introduction to the Study of Social Relations* (New York: Basic Books, 1965).

6. In writing this essay I made use of a manuscript by Lu Hsiu-lien, based upon interviews conducted with her by Linda Arrigo. I will refer to it as Lu, "Autobiography." I have also made use of excerpts of a longer manuscript. These are found in Lu Hsiu-lien et al., "Imprisonment to Empowerment: One Woman's Story of the Struggle for Democracy," section 1. Early years (outline for a film with excerpts from Annette Lu's autobiography undated). This typescript lays out the narrative line for a biographical documentary on Lu Hsiu-lien and contains vivid images and impressions of key stages in her life. I refer to it and cite it throughout this chapter. Copies of this document, as well as other documents—position papers, speeches, news releases, and so forth—were made available to me by Margie Joy Walden, head of the New York office of the Taiwan International Alliance.

7. Lu et al., "Imprisonment to Empowerment," section 1. See also Lu, Family Background in "Autobiography," 2.

8. Interview with Lu Hsiu-lien, New York, January 25, 1995. See also Lu, "Autobiography," 8–9.

9. See Margery Wolf, *Women and the Family in Rural Taiwan* (Stanford: Stanford University Press, 1972).

10. Lu et al., "Imprisonment to Empowerment." See also Lu, "Autobiography."

11. This practice of adoption can be found in some parts of China and in Japan as well. See Arthur P. Wolf and Huang Chieh-shang, *Marriage and Adoption in China 1845–1945* (Stanford: Stanford University Press, 1980).

12. Lu et al., "Imprisonment to Empowerment." See also Lu, "Autobiography," 2.

13. Lu et al., "Imprisonment to Empowerment." See also Lu, "Autobiography," 4.

14. Lu et al., "Imprisonment to Empowerment." See also Lu, "Autobiography," 4–5.

15. This rationale is a subtext in Lai Tse-han, Ramon H. Myers, and Wei Wou, *A Tragic Beginning: The Taiwan Uprising of February 28, 1947* (Stanford: Stanford University Press, 1991).

16. A conservative estimate of Taiwanese deaths is 5,000, but other estimates range as high as 20,000. On the February 28 Incident, see Lai, Myers, and Wou, *A Tragic Beginning*; and George Kerr, *Formosa Betrayed* (Boston: Houghton Mifflin, 1965), 254–329. See also Douglas Mendel, *The Politics of Taiwanese Nationalism* (Berkeley: University of California Press, 1970), 27–15. For a personal account see Peng Ming-min, *A Taste of Freedom* (Taipei: Taiwan Publishing Company, 1994), 64–72. See also Thomas Gold, *State and Society in the Taiwan Miracle* (Armonk, NY: M.E. Sharpe, 1986), 51. In interviews, informants recounting their memories of this event described it as a holocaust. The Presbyterian Church in Taiwan remains concerned with the 2–28 Incident. For example, see *Taiwan Church News*, no. 1879 (March 6, 1988), 9.

17. One final comment is in order here. This once-forbidden topic is now widely discussed and written about in Taiwan. Since 1987, when many of the restrictions on freedom of the press were lifted, I, like many other students of Taiwan's history, have been able to obtain a new library on 2–28, and each year I return to add new books to the collection. The newest effort is the publication of volumes of documents by the Institute of Modern History/Academia Sinica.

18. A year later, in 1948, Nationalists admitted that the bureaucrats and military men had gone too far. Some attempts were made to clean up the worst corruption. By that time, conditions had so deteriorated on the mainland that many in the KMT government had

moved their families and their wealth to Taiwan or to safe havens in the West. Lu Hsiu-lien gave her own view of these events and their impact on Taiwan in a paper presented at a conference in Hong Kong in the summer of 1988. The paper, subsequently published in the conference proceedings and, later, in a reader on modern Taiwan, is the best English-language introduction to the feminist movement in the Republic of China. I make use of it in this and later sections of my chapter. See Lu Hsiu-lien, "Women's Liberation Under Martial Law," in *Taiwan: Economy, Society and History*, ed. E.K.Y. Chen, Jack Williams, and Joseph Wong (Hong Kong: Centre of Asian Studies, University of Hong Kong, 1991), 339–54 (reprinted as Hsiu-lien Annette Lu, "Women's Liberation: The Taiwanese Experience," in Murray A. Rubinstein, ed. *The Other Taiwan* [Armonk, NY: M.E. Sharpe, 1994]). I cite the article in its final version in this chapter. See also Lu, "Autobiography," 4 and 10, for a discussion of personal incidents in her life and in the life of her family relating to 2–28.

19. Gold, *Taiwan Miracle*, 52–55.

20. The Communist threat was the most commonly stated rationale for the actions that were taken. In the name of security, the secret police, led by Chiang's son, Chiang Ching-kuo, the future president, rounded up and punished suspected political activists and those it defined as Communists. This new period of terror was described at some length by a British journalist, H. Maclear Bate, who was on the island in 1950 and who was a vociferous advocate and loyal friend of the Nationalist regime. In his useful, if neglected book, he showed that the younger Chiang built and ran a powerful force that paralleled similar organizations on the mainland, which he ran with ruthless efficiency—the kind of efficiency that, when exercised in the economic and managerial sphere, had helped to make Shanghai a model city on the mainland in the years of postwar chaos. The rationale for this action was that there were, during these early years, numerous reports of Communist plots. Such plots had to be suppressed and for that reason the agents and conspirators involved in them were summarily executed. In the view of the Taiwanese, Bate suggested, the period was a reign of terror.

21. The pace of terror and repression—and of KMT house cleaning—slowed down after the United States declared its intention to defend the regime and it became obvious that the Republic of China on Taiwan would survive. What is clear from Bate's account and that of other observers, such as Ralph Clough and George Kerr, is that many of the economic reforms were possible because the government had clarified what it would do to dissenters. Repression and reform were linked in these early and difficult years. See H. Maclear Bate, *Report From Formosa* (New York: Dutton, 1952), 64–78. See also Ralph N. Clough, *Island China* (Cambridge: Harvard University Press, 1978), 47–60; and Kerr, *Formosa Betrayed*, 417–33.

22. The graft and bribery of the KMT on the mainland had been legendary and together with hyperinflation had done much to break the Nationalist hold on the country. The U.S. advisers stressed that there would be no aid without wide-scale reforms. Chiang could no longer turn a deaf ear to such suggestions and his regime, while still harsh, was at least rid of corruption.

23. Lu, "Women's Liberation," 290.

24. In 1950, counties and cities began to elect officials such as mayors, municipal councils, and magistrates, and 1951 saw the establishment of the Provincial Assembly. Indirect elections were the rule for this body until 1959, but after that year the people were allowed to elect their provincial assemblymen directly. This was a means of opening the political process to the Taiwanese majority and thereby, perhaps, making them feel that they had a stake in the continued existence of the KMT regime. Today one can see that politics at the provincial level are vigorous and competitive given the built-in constraints of the system. Clough, *Island China*, 55. Arthur J. Lerman, *Taiwan's Politics: The Provincial Assemblyman's World* (Lanham, MD: Rowman and Littlefield, 1981).

25. Although the Nationalist state dominated most industries and introduced large-scale programs that improved the infrastructure, certain sectors were opened to private capitalists. The milling industry and the textile industry were two. At first mainlander insiders were the only ones able to take advantage of this move to capitalism, but by the mid-1950s Taiwanese entrepreneurs also benefited. One such group formed the Tainan Textile Corporation. Those Taiwanese landowners who had been forced to surrender their lands when land reforms were introduced also became beneficiaries of the government's attempt to create a viable mixed economy. They had been paid for the land they gave up and often used these funds as start-up capital. Thus a member of the Panchiao-based branch of the powerful Lin family became head of the Taiwan Cement Corporation. When he gave up the post he was succeeded by a member of another major landlord family, C.F. Ku. On economic development see: Samuel Ho, *Economic Development of Taiwan* (New Haven: Yale University Press, 1978), 70–92; Neil H. Jacoby, *U.S. Aid to Taiwan* (New York: Praeger, 1966); Gold, *Taiwan Miracle*, 65–67; Lin Jingyuan, "The 1949–53 Land Reform," in *The Taiwan Experience, 1950–1980*, ed. James C. Hsiung, 140–44 (New York: Praeger, 1981); and K.T. Li, *The Experience of Dynamic Economic Growth on Taiwan* (Taipei: Me Ya Publications, 1976), 379–92.

26. Gold, *Taiwan Miracle*, 71.

27. The agricultural export economy that existed under the Japanese had lost its major markets abroad and the Taiwanese domestic market was simply too small to absorb the necessary amount of produce or industrial goods. Dramatic economic progress had indeed been made; industrial production had increased markedly as had agricultural production, but important decisions lay ahead. This aspect of the Taiwan miracle is based upon Thomas Gold's analysis (Gold, *Taiwan Miracle*, 74–90). See also K.T. Li's account of the process in his *Experience of Dynamic Growth*, 302–52, 359–78. Li succeeded Yin as "economic tsar" and his essays on the development of Taiwan, collected in his book, provide important insights into various aspects of Taiwanese development.

28. The U.S. role in this economic miracle was readily apparent. By the early 1950s, the U.S. government had decided not only to defend Chiang's regime, but also to bankroll it. Americans helped in other ways as well, providing outright relief in the form of agricultural supplies and clothing, as well as military assistance and training. Furthermore, the colleges and universities on the island benefited from the presence of Fulbright Lecturers who committed themselves to one- or two-year terms as instructors. The scale of the American commitment was enormous, given the size of the island and its population, and the results, which could be seen as early as 1960, were equally impressive. See Jacoby, *U.S. Aid to Taiwan*, 103–49; Ho, *Economic History*, 147–85. On the educational exchange, see Chang P'eng-yuan, "Sino-American Scholarly Relations as Seen from Taiwan, 1949–1979," *American Asian Review* 1, no. 3 (Fall 1983): 46–86.

29. Thus, National Taiwan University (T'aita) was established on the campus of the former Taihoku Imperial University that had operated there. The same is true of other campuses such as those of the Taiwan Normal University, in Taipei, and Cheng Ch'eng-kung University, the university in Tainan named after the Ming loyalist and Taiwanese hero the Dutch called Koxinga.

30. Lu discussed her own lack of awareness of being a girl in her unpublished memoir. See Lu et al., "Imprisonment to Empowerment." See also Lu, "Autobiography," 10.

31. Lu, "Women's Liberation," p. 290.

32. See Lu et al., "Imprisonment to Empowerment."

33. Ibid.; see also Lu, "Autobiography," high school years, 1–2.

34. Bate, *Report From Formosa*, 79–93, 150–70.

35. Peng, *A Taste of Freedom*, 72–105.

36. These comments are based on both formal and informal talks with mainlanders on Taiwan and in the United States. Those interviewed included academics, businessmen, technocrats, and clergy. These interviews and conversations occurred between 1979 and 1986.

37. I discussed this book and its various editions with Lu. I have concluded from that discussion and an examination of the text that the fourth edition of the book published in 1986 contains essentially the basic discussion of issues of feminism that is found in the first edition. Furthermore, after further examining this material and examining the 1988 article that was subsequently republished in *The Other Taiwan*, I have concluded that these chapters have been summarized in the English article on feminism. See Lu Hsiu-lien, *Hsin Nü-hsing chu-yi* (New Feminism) (Taipei: Pioneer Press, 2000), and Lu, "Women's Liberation," 290.

38. Lu, "Women's Liberation," 291.

39. Ibid., 291–92.

40. On this development in the 1950s see Li, *The Experience*, 117–19, 164–70, 309–10, 316–22.

41. Li's *The Experience* is also important for an examination of the Taiwan miracle.

42. Jacoby described the way the Nationalist government dealt with the U.S. decision in the following terms: "The government acted in many ways to further improve the climate for private investment, to promote exports, and to seek capital and credit from the World Bank, the Export Import Bank, and other countries. It dispatched trade missions to Latin America and Africa and eased controls of foreign trade and payments" (Jacoby, *U.S. Aid*, p. 230). See also Li, *The Experience*, 216–25.

43. Ho, *Economic History*, 121–46. See also Li, *The Experience*, 146–57, 212–13, 265–68, 330–39.

44. If one measures development in terms of growth of a nation's gross national product, then Taiwan's progress has indeed been impressive. Taiwan's rate of increase from the 1960s into the early 1990s averaged over 8 percent. After 1965, Taiwan built upon the base of economic stability it had created in the previous fifteen years and began to develop at an ever more accelerated rate. Li, *The Experience*, 238–46, 268–70, 454–67. Ho, *Economic Development*, 186–223.

45. The "brain drain" is examined by Li in *The Experience*, 247–60.

46. Lu, "Autobiography," high school years, 1–3.

47. Ibid., 6.

48. Marc Cohen, *Taiwan at the Crossroads* (Washington, DC: Asia Resource Center, 1988), is a powerful and useful book. Though opinionated, it is direct and clear in its biases, and very much in the muckraking tradition. Thus I see it as a useful corrective to more formal and scholarly—and ostensibly "objective"—works by those of us in the academy.

49. DPP UN Conference Presentation (conference held at UN Plaza Hotel, January 25, 1995). This was a DPP attempt to lobby for Taiwan's admission to the United Nations. Annette Lu was the spearhead of the movement.

50. Lu, "Autobiography," college years, 1–6.

51. Ibid., 6–7.

52. Ibid., 9, 13–14.

53. Ibid., 10–13.

54. Ibid., 16–19.

55. Lu, "Autobiography," arrival in Champaign, 5–7.

56. Ibid., 1–5.

57. Lu, "Autobiography," college years, 16–20.

58. Lu, "Autobiography," topics, 7–11.

59. Li, *The Experience*, 352–58.

60. Agriculture remains important, however. See Li, *The Experience*, 409–12, 419–30.

61. Ibid., 261–64.

62. The best account of this period remains Mab Huang, "Intellectual Ferment for Po-

litical Reforms in Taiwan, 1971–1973," *Michigan Papers in Chinese Studies*, no. 28 (1976). For a liberal/radical critique of the period, which is better as journalism than as formal political analysis see Cohen, *Taiwan at the Crossroads*, 32. See also Clough, *Island China*, 60–63.

63. Hung-Mao Tien, *The Great Transition: Political and Social Change in the Republic of China* (Stanford: Hoover Institution Press, 1989), 69.

64. Huang, "Intellectual Ferment," 81. On the complex structure of the government of the Republic of China see "Central and Local Government," in *Republic of China, 1986* (Taipei, 1986), 125–42. This is a basic guide to the republic published for the government. It contains a wealth of useful information but, of course, does not present an objective picture of conditions on the island.

65. Huang, "Intellectual Ferment," 81–101.

66. Lu, "Autobiography," start of the feminist movement.

67. Ibid.; "Autobiography," return to Taiwan, 8–15. See also Cohen, *Taiwan at the Crossroads*.

68. Lu, "Autobiography," start of the feminist movement, 4–5.

69. Ibid.; 2; Lu Hsiu-lien, interview, January 25, 1995. See also the account in Lu, "Women's Liberation," 293.

70. Lu, "Autobiography," start of the feminist movement, 2.

71. Ibid., 3–4; Lu, "Women's Liberation," 293.

72. She describes the origins of this work in her manuscript. See Lu, "Autobiography," start of the feminist movement, 6–7.

73. Ibid.; Lu, "Women's Liberation," 293.

74. Lu, "Autobiography," start of the feminist movement, 10–11; Lu, "Women's Liberation," 293.

75. Lu, "Autobiography," start of the feminist movement, 13; Lu, "Women's Liberation," 293.

76. Lu, "Autobiography," start of the feminist movement, 12; Lu, "Women's Liberation," 293.

77. Lu, "Autobiography," start of the feminist movement, 16–19.

78. Lu, "Autobiography," summer camp and encounters with the world, 1–2.

79. Ibid., 2–4.

80. Ibid., 5.

81. Ibid., 6.

82. Ibid., 7.

83. Lu, meeting with Lee Tae-jung; idem, "Autobiography," start of the feminist movement, 2–3; idem, "Women's Liberation," 294.

84. Lu, "Autobiography," feminist movement continued, 4.

85. Ibid., 13; Lu, "Women's Liberation," 294.

86. Lu, "Autobiography," meeting with the Feminist Movement continued, 3.

87. Lu, "Autobiography," meeting with Lee Tae-jung and starting of the feminist movement, 3–5.

88. Lu, "Autobiography," feminist movement continued, 1–2.

89. Lu, "Women's Liberation," 294; idem, "Autobiography," start of the feminist movement, 7.

90. Ibid.

91. Lu, "Women's Liberation," 294.

92. Lu, "Autobiography," start of the feminist movement, 14.

93. Lu, "Autobiography," feminist movement continued, 6–7.

94. Lu, "Autobiography," study at Harvard, 1.

13

The Story of Power and Desire

A Brighter Summer Day

Yu-hsiu Liu

[It is dark. Suddenly a lamp is turned on. It sheds meager light—on what? On the lamp itself, a lamp that attracts attention because, to the audience, it is both familiar and defamiliarized. It is defamiliarized by being put on the screen, the screen of a nostalgia film, a reconstructed past.

The lamp is simply a naked bulb—a reminder and an epitome of the years impoverished by the horrendous war and the ensuing upheavals. It is a hint, suggesting to the viewer that the story that unfolds subsequently in the film is illuminated by the light of retrospection and criticism. The following article, which forms the first part of a paper entitled "A Myth(ology) Mythologizing Its Own Closure: A Brighter Summer Day,"[1] is devoted to analyzing the story illuminated and made visible by the light. The regions, at the intervals and on the vast margins, which remain purposefully in the dark, and also their relations with the told story, are discussed in the second part of the paper (which is not included below). It is found that the film's effort at self-scrutiny has not arrived at any valid self-criticism. Instead, the film plunges into an unlimited indulgence in, or an unending study of, its own structure. The "structurality" of the film becomes the theme of the film. Thus, the patriarchal system based on the recurrent murder of the unfaithful woman is consolidated again, this time by way of dismissing her murder as "something less important than the film's structure."]

The Tragedy of Father–Son Love and Hatred

Edward Yang's film, *A Brighter Summer Day* (1991), tells the story of power and desire. First, let us talk about power.

The movie's profound theme is unanimously acknowledged by the critics of the film. For instance, Liu Ta-jen, a culture critic, pointed out that the young gangster characters in the film were trying to establish a new world and a new moral view.[2] Chang Ta-ch'ün, a writer, commented on the film's "national implication,"[3] while Huang Chien-yeh, a film critic, stated that film director Edward Yang was attempting to "transform individual experience into a national fable."[4] What is the ambitious view this "national fable" attempts to propound? In brief, it is to reform patriarchy, to eliminate the ruthlessness of the patriarchal figure, and to establish a nation of brotherly love, a nation based on equality and mutual trust among men.

The father-son relationship is depicted from a number of perspectives. First, it is presented as one between state bureaucracy and individuals. The bureaucratic apparatus includes the Garrison Command [a unit of the martial law security administration—eds.], the government department in which the father of the protagonist Hsiao Ssu works, the youth detention office under the police bureau, and the disciplinary office at the middle school, as well as the school infirmary, and so on. A striking similarity among these bureaucratic agencies is that they all treat individuals with aloofness, indifference, and distrust. The individuals who deal with them, on the other hand, are either cunning and deceitful, such as Slippery and Leaf, or cold, distrustful, and rebellious in the form of outcast sons such as Hsiao Ssu, the father of Hsiao Ssu, Honey, and others. The film launches a barrage of criticism against this type of father: the bureaucrat is coarse, lacking in any sense of feeling, and profoundly unjust. He is the primary cause of the tragedies that befall the victims, including Hsiao Ssu, who is gradually driven to self-destruction.

The second type of father-son relationship is depicted in that between Shantung—the head of the Soldiers' Village gang—and his subordinates.[5] The followers of Shantung are servile toward him, but they treat each other and especially outsiders with great cruelty and coarseness. Such a master-subordinate relationship in the private and individual realms is a replica or parallel of the first type of father-son relationship. These two types of father-son relationships are presented in the movie as antagonistic and evil, and are contrasted with two positive relationships, as well as with an ideal model of society.

The third type of father-son relationship is seen in the one between Hsiao Ssu and his father.[6] Based on blood ties, this, as Liu Ta-jen points out, is an ideal relationship without the usual generation gap.[7] Huang Chien-yeh notes: "In the 'new cinema,'[8] it is rare to see such a cordial and loving father-son relation since the majority of the 'new cinema' films suggest that the generation gap between father and son cannot be breached. *A Brighter Summer Day* depicts a positive father-son relationship that is rarely seen in other films."[9] The phrases "rare to see" and "rarely seen" demonstrate Huang's emphasis on highlighting the director's intention. Chang Ta-chün observes: "Edward Yang purposefully characterizes the father as a brother of his children, thus making it possible to romanticize the father-son relationship."[10] This creates the possibility of formulating a romantic dream of brotherhood built on the basis of equality and trust.

The fourth type of father-son relationship is the one between the Park gang leader Honey and members of the gang. In Honey we find a winning broadness and romanticism. He is quite different from the cunning crook Shantung. The two gangs of these leaders also have different features: the Soldiers' Village gang forces its subordinates to obey the master while the Park gang emphasizes the spontaneous bonds of brotherhood. The relationship between Honey and Hsiao Ssu, one of the focal points of the movie, is characterized as open-minded, generous, equal, and based on mutual trust, a replica of the warm relationship between Hsiao Ssu and his father at home. The apparent intent of the movie is to use these two types of positive relationships as the new principle and paragon of the new morality. This seems in line with Liu Ta-jen's comment about the film, when he argues that the youngsters aim at establishing a "new morality."[11]

This "new morality" is extremely idealistic, and by no means an easy task to present in a cogent fashion to the audience. The artistic method adopted in the film is the typical form of tragedy: to reveal an ideal, a universal idea, through the failure of individuals. The disloyalty of the heroine, Light, results in a deadly fight between Hsiao Ssu and his pal, Horse—brothers are turned into enemies. As a result, Hsiao Ssu decides to sink further into the swamp by stealing his mother's jewelry to exchange for spending money. His father mistakenly blames his second son for the theft and in a rage beats him up—the "brother-like father" has been transformed into a ruthless father. The tragic mixes with the sublime and produces a strong longing for the dream of the brotherly state.

In contrast, the movie's fault-filled and patriarchal world is one in which the deserted and outcast sons suffer; the majority of the offspring of the military and the middle- and lower-ranking officials all belong to gangs. Even Hsiao Ssu's father becomes a son, too, when confronting the aloof and indifferent bureaucratic organization; he appears at times frustrated and at other times rebellious.

The sons' world is also abnormal and sick. Tanks roll side by side with cars and buses; people constantly ask when they will be able to return to the mainland or whether it will be possible for them to return at all. "Returning" refers to a normal world of order and joy. The concepts "yet to return" and "impossible to return" refer to their present state: a world of desertion, betrayal, distrust, and darkness. (The movie employs a tightly woven, economical style that presents the lives of the non-Taiwanese population who followed the Kuomintang [KMT, or Nationalist party] government to Taiwan after 1949, as well as the activities of Hsiao Ssu and his pals in the dark at night school, as a kind of powerful and cogent universal metaphor.)

The problems of this abnormal world are seen in depictions of: law-abiding civilians arbitrarily interrogated by Garrison Command officers; student baseball bats confiscated by the disciplinary officers of the middle school (out of fear that the bats would be used as weapons); students operating under enormous academic pressure prone to nearsightedness, both physically and mentally; the youngsters' habitual use of foul language and remarks referring directly to sexual organs, such as "Great dick!" and "Fuck your mom's cunt!"; women such as Light and Green constantly fooling around with men; men getting into fights over women, and so on.

The father-son relationships and the fights between the brothers depicted in the film shall be analyzed from the perspective of the theories of Sigmund Freud and René Girard.

Freud argues that patriarchy, the inevitable mode of human civilization, confronts a structural and intrinsic crisis, namely, the Oedipus complex.[12] The effective operation of patriarchy depends on the smooth resolution of this complex, which itself stems from patriarchy. But just what is the Oedipus complex? Freud contends in *The Ego and the Id:*

> At a very early age the little boy develops an object cathexis for his mother . . . the boy deals with his father by identifying himself with him. For a time these two relationships proceed side by side, until the boy's sexual wishes in regard to his mother become more intense and his father is perceived as an obstacle to them; from this the Oedipus complex originates. His identification with his father then takes on a hostile coloring and changes into a wish to get rid of his father in order to take his place with his mother.[13]

In *The Interpretation of Dreams,* Freud states that like Oedipus of the ancient Greek tragedy, we [i.e., men—eds.] have a desire to kill our fathers and marry our mothers. "It is the fate of all of us, perhaps, to direct our first sexual impulse toward our mother and our first hatred and our first murderous wish against our father."[14] In other words, the son "by fate" hates his father because of love for his mother and even develops an urge to kill the father in order to gain possession of his position.

The Oedipus complex directly threatens the viability of patriarchy. Therefore, a safety measure must develop within the patriarchal system to resolve the problems presented by the complex. The mechanism resolving the complex, according to Freud, is the "castration complex." Culture hints to the little child in various subtle ways that if he misbehaves, something terrible might be done to the organ he is so proud of (i.e., the penis). Out of narcissism,

> the child's ego turns away from the Oedipus complex. . . . The object-cathexes are given up and replaced by identifications. The authority of the father or the parents is introjected into the ego, and there it forms the nucleus of the super-ego, which takes over the severity of the father and perpetuates his prohibition against incest, and so secures the ego from the return of the libidinal object-cathexis. The libidinal trends belonging to the Oedipus complex are in part desexualized and sublimated, . . . and in part inhibited in their aim and changed into impulses of affection.[15]

Of the two components of the Oedipus complex—sexual wishes toward the mother and hatred against the father—Freudian theory emphasizes the former. Girard, however, attempts to shift the focus. He tries to modify Freud's theory by suggesting that the father-son relationship and other similar relationships (for instance, the uncle-nephew relationship carried over from matriarchal society) are under the same threat; that is, the subtle imitation, competition, and antagonism between master and subordinate, model and disciple. The son (the disciple) naturally identifies with the father (the model). The former identifies with the latter in every way, including his desire; thus, both compete for one and the same object. The patriarchal system has laid out ways of resolving such conflicts; it allows the father to forestall the son's possible crimes or usurpation by incriminating and punishing him in advance. For instance, in the Oedipus myth the gods had predicted prior to Oedipus's birth that he would kill his father and marry his mother. In other words, even before the son is capable of killing the father and marrying the mother, culture has already predicted and condemned his guilt. Guilt, according to Girard, is transformed as the superego in Freudian theory. The superego is in reality a continuation of the son's identification with his father; as a result of this identification, the son once again accepts the laws and orders of his father (or society) after he has passed through the Oedipus complex, which is itself a form of identification with the father.[16]

Freud attempts to pinpoint the Oedipus complex, that is, the desire of the son toward the mother, as the central point of his theory of psychoanalysis. Girard, in contrast, believes that the son's love for the mother results from his imitation of the father and thus the son's identification with and imitation of his father should be seen as the key phenomenon. The argument between Freud and his follower, Girard, is itself a reflection of the love-hate tragedy going on between father and son. It is clear that Freudian theory positions the father figure in the center as if he is thundering: "You hate me out of some untold conspiracy . . . all because you love your mother!" Girard, however, stands on the side of the son, and feeling unfairly accused, he retaliates: "I am innocent. I merely followed suit."

A Brighter Summer Day depicts exactly the same kind of father-son tragedy, a tragedy whose central themes are desire and identification. The son tries to identify with the father and wants everything the father possesses, including light/knowledge (the large flashlight Hsiao Ssu steals); power/weapon (the sword left by an unknown Japanese general, and the handgun of Horse's father); head/status (Hsiao Ssu wantonly puts on the school doctor's hat and poses in a ready-to-shoot position just as Honey dons a navy uniform); the sexual organ of the father (large flashlight, handgun, gentlemen's hat, navy cap); and woman (Light, whom all the main male characters desire).

Confronted with the supposedly inappropriate acts the sons committed in imitation of the father, the various father figures issue their punishments: the director of the school disciplinary office accuses Hsiao Ssu of fighting with a baseball bat and confiscates it; suspected of cheating on an examination, Hsiao Ssu is severely punished; the school doctor (who obviously considers Hsiao Ssu's attraction to Light as a threat to his protection of the girl) admonishes Hsiao Ssu in a highly authoritarian tone; the school nurse (an extension of the school doctor's authority) also joins in scolding Hsiao Ssu; the Garrison Command imprisons and interrogates Hsiao Ssu's father for unknown reasons; Hsiao Ssu's father mistakenly believes that his second son stole his mother's jewelry and beats him up; and so on.

The father's uncompromising stand and his decision to punish the son to avert even more trouble bring out the son's feelings of guilt. This can be seen in the tension and frustration that Hsiao Ssu's father endures in his confrontation with the Garrison Command. This sense of guilt drives him to rely even more thoroughly on the laws and orders of the father figure. On the one hand, he holds high the banner of "state organization" (itself an agent of the father figure), and he begins to doubt his wife's suggestion to leave the corrupt civil service system and seek out new vistas; on the other, he draws on his fatherly authority to subject his second son to severe punishment. The same is true with respect to Hsiao Ssu. Aware of his own misbehavior, he confesses to Honey; after receiving Honey's forgiveness and understanding, he proclaims himself Honey's heir. Hsiao Ssu thus becomes the guardian of the laws of the father on his own behalf and on behalf of Honey and he will strive to punish the disloyal Horse and the unfaithful Light.

All of this is quite consistent with the Freudian theory of the emergence of the superego. Girard, however, holds a different view, namely, that unjust punishment and impure violence produce "mimetic rivalry" and that the vicious cycle of using violence to deal with violence causes a collapse in the norms governing the ties between old and young, thereby transforming everyone into "twins of violence."[17] It is just such chaos that occurs in *A Brighter Summer Day*. After dealing with the intrusive school doctor and school nurse, and outraged by his own father's unjust arrest at the hands of the Garrison Command, Hsiao Ssu abandons his usually courteous manner and begins to curse others: "Fuck your mother's cunt! Who the hell do you think you are? The Garrison Command?" Soon afterward, face to face with the unfair and vicious director of the school disciplinary office, Hsiao Ssu swings his baseball bat (was it not previously confiscated?) and smashes the light—to extinguish the (sham) light/truth of the father figure. And at the same time, fights between and within the two gangs become even more frenzied.

In short, *A Brighter Summer Day* contains elements of Freudian theory, with its emphasis on the authority of the father and the identification of the son, and of Girard's notion that the traditional father/son relationship is threatened by mimetic violence. Thus, the film presents a world of chaos brought on by the collapse of patriarchal order.

The Theory and Phenomenon of the Femme Fatale

We discussed above the struggle for power between father and son and among brothers. The following section is devoted to exploring the other dimension of the Oedipus complex, that of desire and the various problems and phenomena it creates.

It is not hard for the viewer of this film to notice that behind the heroic theme of the male struggle for power there is a concomitant theme, less boisterous, yet persistent and profound. Closer observation shows that this subdued theme is, in reality, the skeleton of the entire structure.

This is the theme of the disloyalty of woman. The disloyalty of Light brings about a cluster of events. Hsiao Ssu happens to see one of his night school classmates, Slippery, flirting with a girl. Rumors about the identity of the young lady spread quickly; some say that it is Green, the flirt in the movie, and others claim that it is Light, the girlfriend of the Park gang's runaway leader, Honey. Annoyed by all of this talk, Slippery attempts to avenge himself on Hsiao Ssu. While Slippery ends up being expelled from school, Hsiao Ssu is also punished. Light, it turns out, was not only fooling around with Slippery but also with another of Hsiao Ssu's classmates named Tiger, who was also attracted to her. Next, Hsiao Ssu himself falls in love with Light. Everyone, it seems, falls into a kind of collective infatuation with Light, and eventually she becomes something of a destructive force among the gangs. The destructive force functions as follows. First, Honey engages himself in a duel with Red Hair, the leader of the Soldiers' Village gang, and ends up killing him. As a consequence, Honey has to run away and take cover. The new head of the Soldiers' Village gang, Shantung, exploits Slippery's infatuation with Light and lures him into selling out the Park gang and joining up with the Soldiers' Village gang by offering to "back him up." Honey returns to deal with the matter but gets killed by Shantung; the Park gang then takes revenge and kills Shantung. Light now falls under the "custody" of Hsiao Ssu because Honey, before being killed, has nodded assent to Hsiao Ssu's love for her. Light then starts to flirt with the young school doctor, thus arousing hostility between the doctor and Hsiao Ssu. Irritated, Hsiao Ssu takes out his anger on his elders and wantonly destroys public property, all of which causes him to be expelled from school. In the meantime, Light tries to get her mother a job as a housekeeper for the family of another of Hsiao Ssu's classmates, Horse; this leads Horse to take Light as his girlfriend. Angered, Hsiao Ssu is determined to kill Horse; however, Light happens by and enrages Hsiao Ssu, who then kills her and in so doing destroys himself.

All these events show Light as a femme fatale. But what makes Light, or any woman, a femme fatale?

Let us return to Freud's theory of the castration complex. Both boys and girls experience the castration complex. The key moment occurs when the boy or girl lays eyes on the sexual organ of a sibling or playmate of the opposite sex. The boy then realizes that the threat of castration is not a sham, that it can actualize. He consequently develops "horror of the mutilated creature or triumphant contempt for her," which may "permanently determine the boy's relations to women." As for girls, "they notice the penis of a brother or playmate, strikingly visible and of large proportions, at once recognize it as the superior counterpart of their own small and inconspicuous organ [i.e., the clitoris], and from that time forward fall a victim to envy for the penis."[18] After becoming aware of "the wound to her narcissism," a woman develops, "like a scar, a sense of inferiority" and "begins to share the contempt felt by men for a sex which is the lesser in so important a respect."[19]

The inferiority of women serves a powerful functionality (and it is this powerful—too conspicuously powerful—functionality that makes us feel that perhaps society plans and produces this inferiority of women to advance its social function). Once an individual woman attains the collective "knowledge" and realizes that as a woman she belongs to the sex inferior to men, she will, in resignation, abandon the active, aggressive posture she previously shared with boys and for the rest of her life maintain a passive role. Thus, she has accomplished development toward "normal femininity." Women who fail to undergo such a change suffer from what is called "masculinity complex."[20]

This theory very likely results from reversing cause and effect. However, it helps to "explain" how women exist in the patriarchal power system. The female characters in *A Brighter Summer Day*, we find, are certainly treated that way. Freudian theory and a work like *A Brighter Summer Day* are apparently orthodox products of patriarchy; the theory, the film, and the underlying power system form close relations and function to support each other. The following discussion based on Freudian theory aims to expose these complex relations.

Passivity and lack of personal initiative are the main features characterizing Light. These characteristics result from intrinsic as well as extrinsic factors. In Light, the mutual reinforcement of femininity and the feminine situation forms a vicious circle and contributes to her extreme dependence on men.

From the bits and pieces of information provided in the film, we can tell that Light's father was a military man who was killed on the mainland (or perhaps he remained behind?). Light, along with her mother, followed her uncle to Taiwan where the mother works as a housekeeper. But because of asthma the mother sometimes loses her job and has no choice but to go to the Soldiers' Village where her brother resides, taking Light with her. The scene in the film where Light dares not accept the bowl of rice offered by her aunt is the epitome of the suffering and difficulties she experiences in her life. Growing up in such an unstable and unreliable environment, Light has developed her femininity to an extreme: in her, desire and the sense of insecurity are inextricably interwoven. For her, as with all other women, men represent security; however, unlike other women who feel secure with one man (previously their father, then their husband, and later their son), Light never experiences this particular sense of security. Thus, in her perpetual pursuit for an adequate sense of security, she keeps moving from one man to another, causing the men to fight over her. For instance, after begging Hsiao Ssu to protect her and getting his promise, she then, in a manner blending flirtation and pitifulness, goes to the school doctor, who treats her ill mother without receiving pay, and in this way arouses antagonism between Hsiao Ssu and the young school doctor. Horse also mentions that Light has real problems with her sense of security. He asks Hsiao Ssu: "Did she mention Honey to you when you were together, claiming that you did not provide her with a sufficient sense of security?" The word "you" in the phrase "you did not provide her with a sufficient sense of security" does not simply refer to Hsiao Ssu or a particular person, but to any man with whom she had been associated.

Light never stops pursuing men and relying on them, even when she has the opportunity to become independent. For instance, after a screen test, she fails to follow up with the film studio, thus losing an opportunity to become an actress. Her preference is to rely on the school doctor to meet her mother's medical costs.

Intentional or not, this gives her the opportunity to get close to and flirt with the doctor. By relying on the doctor, she tries to kill two birds with one stone—satisfying both her desire and her need for security.

Because of her complete lack of security and the unsettledness of her desire, Light becomes the embodiment of pure femininity: she is extremely weak and fragile, lacking any will power. Because of this—because of the weakness of her ego, or, more strictly speaking, because the lack of ego becomes her "ego"—she emerges as the exact opposite of the masculinity evidenced in men, and in this way she becomes a mystery in the eye of men. Her power, if she has any, resides in her pure lack of power. This is a very strange kind of power—a pure negativity or destructiveness. To herself, to the men associated with her, to patriarchy, she becomes the consummate source of trouble, disaster, and fatality.

Light represents the wanton woman, while Hsiao Ssu's mother represents the virtuous woman. Yet, these two women are two sides of the same coin of femininity; they share the fundamental characteristics of femininity; that is, passivity and subordination. Hsiao Ssu's mother is obviously more intelligent and courageous than her husband, but she devotes herself wholeheartedly to him while ignoring her own professional life (after having children, she resigns from her teaching position and does not return to work until later in life when she has to make family ends meet).

Even Hsiao Ssu's brilliant second elder sister is no exception. She talks a lot about religion and morality, but we are never allowed to forget that she is a woman because we are constantly reminded of her spiritual dependence. Her sublime thoughts do not come from within but from the pastor heading her congregation. She is also restricted by her role as the good daughter and sister who devotes all her actions and efforts to the well-being of her parents and brothers.

Light does not believe in men naïvely (she says: "Many men tell me that they love me, but once I get into trouble, they are nowhere to be found"). Likewise, Hsiao Ssu's mother well knows her husband's inflexibility and is upset by his lack of tenderness. However, all these women intuitively rely on men, indicating that in addition to extrinsic factors, deep down it is the peculiar form of their desire that leads women to depend on men and turns them into the willing lesser sex, just as Freud described. After they lose their independence as a result of both extrinsic and intrinsic factors, their desire and dependence mingle together. This submergence of desire in passivity becomes a typical feature of the traditional woman.

Details in this film consistently demonstrate, moreover, the victory of the male over the female organ in a fashion completely consistent with Freudian theory. "Great dick!" is the expression a gang member uses when he wants to pay a compliment to a pal, and "Fuck your mother's cunt!" when they want to curse at someone. In the midst of persuading Hsiao Ssu, the father suddenly shifts to Cantonese and says: "Without the male organ, you will be in trouble!" The shopkeeper of the ice cream store who contemplates suicide after being deserted by her lover kneels down and begs the gangsters to lend her their Samurai sword (the male organ). The scene in which Light shoots a gun is especially impressive. She just lifts up the gun owned by Horse's father and playfully shoots at Hsiao Ssu (who, fortunately, does not get hurt). Livid with fear and anger, Horse rushes over and slaps her. The scene is a subtle depiction of women's ignorance about guns (the male organ/power) and their unintentional usurpation. Subsequently, Light makes her mother work as a maid for Horse and his parents. The mother and the daughter then move into the house of Horse's family. This shows that Light accepts Horse's punishment, and that consequently she becomes submissive toward the punisher, the owner of the gun (the male organ) and the executor of the father's law. In all, *A Brighter Summer Day* reveals the superiority of the male organ. Moreover, women's admiration of men is basically an admiration of the male organ—not only the male physical organ (the penis) but also the male organ as the symbol of patriarchal power (the phallus). This notion is again fully consistent with Freud's views.

Based on his theory of the superiority of the male organ, Freud attempts to comment on the moral character of mature women. Women not only become passive because of their lack of a male organ, they are also deprived morally. The boy, for fear of losing the male organ, interjects the authority and severity of the father and in this way forms his superego.[21] Thus, the boy learns to control his instinctual impulses, and this "institution of conscience and morality" represents "the victory of the race over the individual."[22] Thus prepared, the boy is now ready to "find a place in the cultural community."[23] The case with girls is different. "In girls the motive for the demolition of the Oedipus complex is lacking" because "castration has already had its effect." In consequence, "their superego is never so inexorable, so impersonal, so independent of its emotional origins as we require it to be in men." This disadvantage, according to Freud, can sufficiently explain the character traits of women—"that they show less sense of justice than men, that they are less ready to submit to the great exigencies of life, that they are more often influenced in their judgments by feelings of affection or hostility."[24]

In moral terms, women are the inferior sex. They are different and do not follow the superego as men do. The woman thus pulls along a long shadow, a "dark continent"[25] to the male rationality. After degrading and condemning women, both Freud[26] and the film admit that they know little about women. The film simply depicts Light as the symbol representing the dark world about which men are ignorant (in the film, persistent night is used to produce strong symbolism). Light is a mystery to men. All of these men probe and struggle in darkness but none is able truly to understand or take control. Light mentions that she has often tried to persuade Honey that "This world will not change simply because of you." Honey would blame her for discouraging him, which provoked constant fights between the two. Similarly, Light tells Hsiao Ssu not to try to change her: "I, like this world, will not be changed by you."

These remarks of Light deserve special attention. She uses generalized and conceptualized language as if she is stating certain universally accepted concepts and as if she is quoting certain cultural themes to depict herself: "I, as a woman, am like this world, which will never be changed by you." Such a statement indicates that culture views women as a symbol of the objective world men feel is at odds with them everywhere. Or, culture itself, we may say, identifies women with the dark world men are unable to understand or control. Men thus hold women accountable for their misfortunes wrought by the dark forces. In the film, it is precisely on hearing what Light has said that Hsiao Ssu, infuriated beyond control, suddenly draws the sword out of the sheath and kills her. That Light is named "Light" is an irony intended to satirize men who want so much to understand and control her.

The Problem of Desire and Sexual Ethics

In considering desire, if it can be said that the problem for women is that they mix a yearning for security with desire, then for men desire is submerged in or even replaced by the lust for power.

The theories of Sigmund Freud and René Girard that were discussed above illustrate the following points: patriarchy puts the father figure (paragon, authority) in a position of prestige and allows him to possess all the power and good things; the son (disciple, subordinate), in imitating the father out of admiration and identification, develops a desire to mimic the father and wants to possess everything owned by him. The existing cultural mechanism tends to make the father interpret the son's imitation of him as evidence of usurpation on the son's part, so he forestalls this by punishing the son; thus, violence and tension penetrate deep into the father-son relationship, which is the fundamental relationship of patriarchy. The son reacts in two possible ways. One is to obey and assimilate the laws of the father into his own superego and thus become a "normal" son and heir. The other reaction is to meet violence with violence and to become the treacherous or even patricidal son, thereby throwing the patriarchal system into chaos until the father reclaims his dominant position or the son becomes the new father.

Within such a system, women are defined as belonging to the father. They are objects buried among the father's many possessions. Deprived of independent status, women do not form the other sex. They become "the lesser," as Freud says, or what Jacques Lacan describes as "not all."[27] Because women are degraded and objectified, and also because an unending power struggle is going on among men, women become one of the objects over which men fight. Desire is replaced by the operation and percussion of power. Girard has richly outlined these symptoms. He is anxious to clear up the entanglement formed around desire, and in so doing he, harboring the frustration and anger of the son, focuses conspicuously on the power struggle between father and son. Freud, by comparison, was in the position of the father and thus had the luxury of meditating on issues concerning sexuality and sexual desire. This difference between Girard and Freud is rather intriguing. We might say that by combining the theories of the two we can conveniently resolve the double myth of the father-son and the man-woman relationships.

Fighting over women as one of the dimensions of the struggle for power among men is a pervasive theme of *A Brighter Summer Day*. This is made perfectly clear when the gang members engage in fierce fights over Light. Another example comes when Hsiao Ssu lets out his anger by cursing the nurse (a representative of the power system): "Fuck your mother's cunt! Who the hell do you think you are? The Garrison Command?!" The audience is undoubtedly left with the impression that the movie is full of filthy language, and, moreover, they might also feel that remarks blatantly referring to sexual organs convey meanings directly related to violence. Such an impression certainly illustrates the close connection between desire and power. The filthy language displays the state of mind of the son whose sexual desire has been stimulated in a fashion that Freud depicts in his theory of the Oedipus complex. For example, "Fuck your mother's cunt!" illustrates both the state of power struggle, with one side saying to the other that "I am your father" and "My status is above yours," and the state in which desire is stimulated and seeks to be satisfied. An expression like "Fuck your mother!" places the user of the expression on rival—therefore "equal"—terms with the opponent. Power struggle levels all sides involved by turning them into "twins of violence," just as Girard points out. In addition, narcissistic aggression in states of power struggle reveals regression to what Lacan calls the mirror relation or the imaginary relation in which "the ego is the other, and the other is me."[28] The "you" referred to in the expression "Fuck your mother!" is in reality the ego, the me. Seen this way, the slang reveals a definite incestuous wish and is thus consistent with Freud's theory. Hsiao Ssu's inclusion of "Garrison Command" in his string of curses further hints that the curser (son) wants to challenge the authoritative organization (father). The fact that Hsiao Ssu combines "fuck your mother" and "Garrison Command" just proves what both Freud and Girard have stated: the overlap between fighting for women and fighting for power. The persistent incestuous wish, though repressed and therefore unconscious, fuels the dual fight by providing the latter with inexhaustible psychic energy.

In accordance with the axiom of "the imitation of desire," the strength of Hsiao Ssu's desire for Light increases, just as with other male characters in the film, in proportion to the clarity of his awareness that he should stay away from her, for the simple reason that she is the gang leader's woman. From the very beginning, the love the male characters show for her stems from what Girard terms the "mimetic rivalry," and is penetrated by lust for power, by violence. What they are fighting for is, therefore, not the simple, enjoyable love between a man and a woman or the satisfaction of both parties. Instead, it is a fight to assert control and gain possessions. Time and again, Hsiao Ssu tells Light that he will "protect" her. The word "protect" actually means "possess." When later he learns that his pal Horse is also involved with Light, he becomes so outraged that he is determined to kill him. This incident indicates that possessiveness is the essence of his love for Light.

The reason a man loves a woman is because she is the woman, or the same type of woman, loved by his father and his brothers. Loving her means, therefore, fighting other men for the sole possession of her. This is perhaps the ultimate truth about men's love/desire. In this truth, we have found the symbiosis of the possessor and the possessed while failing to discover the *jouissance* that the woman, or anyone, is said to be able to enjoy.[29]

In this way, culture grants active power to men while demanding that they pay a high price—that is, love/desire and its satisfaction. This point is vividly depicted in the scene in which Hsiao Ssu kills Light. Hsiao Ssu takes a sword (?) and stabs Light. She closes her eyes in pain (?) while holding onto Hsiao Ssu who continues to stab her. The sword is not revealed on the screen but the viewers can see clearly the percussion each stab causes until there is a moan and Light collapses. The audience is immediately aware that the entire scene demonstrates a sexual climax! The moral dubiousness of the scene is as astonishing as its artistic excellence.

Hsiao Ssu resorts to "punishing her" (a necessary means to gain exclusive control and possession over a woman) as a surrogate for "loving her," and in the same vein substitutes "making love" with "stabbing her to death." Or perhaps it can be said that Hsiao Ssu loves by way of proving that he possesses power/penis (i.e., having the male spirit and daring to kill with a weapon), and that he attempts to prove once and for all that he possesses power/penis by way of killing off his own love/desire along with its object. In this way, he has become a man with "the gun" and is qualified to enter the patriarchal system that is symbolized by the male organ. Killing Light (killing women) is a ritual marking Hsiao Ssu's entry to manhood.

A male is qualified to enter the macrocultural system only if he possesses the ability to punish woman. This is a point that deserves further discussion, for it appears in many forms in various patriarchal cultural structures. Clytemnestra in the *Oresteia* and P'an Chin-lien in *Shui hu chüan* (The Water Margin) are just two examples of women killed in this way. Hsiao Ssu is, in fact, modeled on Wu Sung and Shih Hsiu.[30] Thanks to the relentless precision and coherence of Edward Yang's style, the story of Hsiao Ssu has the power to expose the hidden connection in the aforementioned phenomenon: Wu Ta and Wu Sung, Yang Hsiung and Shih Hsiu, respectively, are actually one person. The man who loves a woman deeply and the one who kills her are actually one and the same. To put it another way, the processes of loving a woman and then of killing her are actually an inevitable development of the same cultural mechanism. Such a cultural mechanism makes men's love for women appear in the end as a dire form of terror. If a man truly loves a woman and allows her to gain freedom and power—"she," a woman, the symbol and embodiment of the dark world antagonistic to men—he will surely end up killing her to terminate the shame and injustice brought about by her. Time and again, the patriarchal culture admonishes and reiterates stories such as those about Wu Ta, Yang Hsiung, and Hsiao Ssu.

The portrayal of Light, the source of trouble and misfortune, is also quite thought-provoking. She is presented in the film as the most innocent and pitiful of all the characters. In this sense, *A Brighter Summer Day* is a description of the fate of weak and fragile women. However, this does not mean that the film in any way calls for thorough cultural reform. Light does indeed deserve our sympathy. The fate of women like Light forms a mystery with a logic, a raison d'être, of its own, so that Light, and also Green, can with good reason avoid self-examination and instead blame Hsiao Ssu as selfish, conceited, and arrogant. The movie makes all this very clear. And yet the movie makes it even clearer that no matter how innocent and pitiful, women are the source of misfortune, that until they are safely controlled the world will remain in chaos, and that killing Light, though necessary, is a tragic move that could have been prevented. And the way to prevent it is the central message the film attempts to convey. At the police bureau, Horse cries out with great regret: "He [Hsiao Ssu] was my only friend." And the young school doctor, on learning of the murder of Light, holds fast to his virtuous wife-to-be. Such arrangements have a moral purpose, which is to tell men, first, you should never fool around with your pal's woman and you should make every effort to maintain the chastity of every woman possessed by every man as well as friendships among men. In this, it is clear that the consolidation of men (also of society) depends on the chastity of women. And second, the primary criterion for choosing a woman is to determine whether she is chaste, as all other factors are secondary.

Viewed from the perspective of consolidation among men, the killing of Light by Hsiao Ssu is a heroic act. Through his crime and suffering he has reclaimed the rod that guards the entire cultural system—the knife with which one kills the unfaithful woman and the law that monitors, harnesses, and punishes women. In this way, the movie redelineates the blueprint of the patriarchal system in which men shoulder the responsibility of controlling women (as well as children). The family of Hsiao Ssu, with his father as the master of the household, is typical of this kind of patriarchal system, in which the father is tough and strict, the mother kind and benevolent, and the siblings all take care of one another. Most important, the female members of the family (Hsiao Ssu's mother and his two elder sisters) are all paragons of women who protect and care for sons and brothers.

A brief, tranquil scene in the film describes the succession of generations in the traditional family. In the vast courtyard of the school doctor's house, the old doctor (the school doctor's father) points at a tea-flower tree and says to his would-be daughter-in-law that the unblemished white flower has traditionally been the Chinese people's favorite because it is "noble and graceful," and that "it always reminds me of your late grandfather (meaning his own deceased father)." The white tea flower symbolizes the united race, ancestry, and the chastity of the daughter-in-law. This brief scene economically depicts the entire realm of the patriarchal lineage, family, and society. It tells us that the family has to rely on the pure woman who marries into the family to serve the holy function of continuing the generation line, and that such a family itself is the basic unit of the entire nation.

Such a woman is the necessary choice of man. She shoulders indispensable responsibilities. In real life, however, she is boring and uninteresting, just like the school doctor's wife-to-be who speaks not a word and is always timid, rigid, with neither desire nor interests—a sample of Freud's normal mature woman, a woman who is both "rigid"[31] and "frigid."[32] Light actually warns the school doctor: "There is no feeling between the two of you. She does not suit you."

The patriarchal culture sets up all kinds of hurdles so that women cannot influence men by manipulating their desire: on the one hand, it bestows power on men; on the other, it blocks the avenue by which men satisfy their desire for women. (As for women, desire is precisely what they must be deprived of since this is the surest guarantee of their chastity.) It is not hard to imagine that men who are forced (?) to take hold of power are generally dissatisfied with the situation in which they are placed, either consciously or unconsciously. Men therefore resort to their imagination to build up an all-satisfying dream—this is a woman chaste and wild, who cannot only passionately meet her man's desire but also remain faithful to him. In *A Brighter Summer Day* we indeed find refracted the portrayal of such a dream woman. Cat, a chum of Hsiao Ssu, finds a package in the attic of his house (which is a relic of the Japanese rulers) containing a small samurai sword and the picture of a Japanese girl, and he begins to ponder: "It appears that the small sword was hers and might have been used to commit suicide to maintain her purity!" Hsiao Ssu takes the picture home and inserts it into his diary and gazes at it whenever he is alone. It is with the help of the contrast between Light and this dream woman that the film can embody in Hsiao Ssu a motive and an impetus strong enough for him to give Light the punishing stabs—with the sword that Hsiao Ssu's *ko-erh-men*[33] imagines to have been used by a passionate chaste woman to kill herself! Thus, the sword Hsiao Ssu uses to kill Light becomes a powerful symbol of the patriarchal ideology, an embodiment of the vast system propped up by the fundamental, dichotomous pair—the chaste woman as the basis of stability versus the unfaithful woman, the femme fatale, as the source of misfortune and chaos.

Notes

1. Liu 1993, 1–38.
2. "An Allegory of Innocence and Power," 45.
3. Ibid., 55.
4. Ibid., 57.
5. The Kuomintang (KMT, the ruling party in Taiwan since 1949) settled the families of the soldiers it took to Taiwan in the so-called Soldiers' Villages. Such villages were usually isolated from the activities of the outside world. The head of the Soldiers' Village gang in the movie is nicknamed "Shantung"; this indicates that his parents (very probably his father only, because the old residence law—which was in force until 1992—acknowledged only the site of the father's ancestral home) came from the province of that name on the east coast of China.
6. Hsiao Ssu, literally "little number four," means "the fourth child in the family." This nickname of the film's protagonist is connected with the film's central concerns about family values and about the family as the component unit of society.
7. "An Allegory of Innocence and Power," 50.
8. Films of the "new cinema" are, strictly speaking, products of the New Taiwanese Cinema Movement (1982–86). Thematically, the new cinema concentrates on problems concerning the urbanization and modernization of Taiwan; technically, they are character-

ized by long camera shots, nonprofessional actors, and on-location shooting. Hou Hsiao-hsien and Edward Yang were the leading directors of the movement. *A Brighter Summer Day* belongs, strictly speaking, to what is called the Post–New Taiwanese Cinema Movement, which is a continuation and modification of the earlier movement. (For a detailed account, see Chen 1992.)

9. "An Allegory of Innocence and Power," 50.

10. Ibid.

11. *A Brighter Summer Day*, a nostalgia film attempting to reconstruct the sociopolitical panorama of the 1960s, reminds us of what Lévi-Strauss calls a *bricolage*, a product of the mythopoeic activity that "builds up structured sets . . . by using the remains and debris of events . . . , fossilized evidence of the history of an individual or society" (Lévi-Strauss 1966, 21–22). In the movie, the name "Honey," which retains the English pronunciation, is "fossilized evidence of the history of society" par excellence. To the characters in the movie as well as the local audience, who well know the economic and cultural influences of the United States in the post–World War II era, "honey" is an *American* word that means the sweet, nutritious, natural food offered by some benevolent power, and that is also used as a term of endearment for a loved one and to refer to the good things in life. In fact, honey, Lévi-Strauss points out in *From Honey to Ashes*, is used transculturally as a metaphor that represents benevolence and harmony (1973, 15–48). The name "Honey" in the film functions (1) to express the longing for a world characterized by harmony and benevolence, (2) to imply that such a world is something transcendental, granted by some benevolent mystical power, and (3) to indicate that such an ideal—that is, the brotherly state—is a product of Western influences. Thus located between nature and culture, the native and the imported, honey, with its English pronunciation, becomes a powerful symbol, a sign of recovery from the set of signs or "fossilized evidence" of the history of a society. All of this helps make Honey, the absent leader of the Park gang, the convincing "Holy Spirit" of the trinity of the film (i.e., Honey + Hsiao Ssu's father + Hsiao Ssu).

12. In Freud's account, patriarchy was the inevitable destination toward which prehistoric human society evolved, matriarchy being merely a transitory stage in the process. See Freud 1939, 81–84; 1913, 100–161.

13. Freud 1923, 31–32.

14. Freud 1900, 262.

15. Freud 1924, 176–77.

16. Girard 1977, 169–92.

17. Ibid., 67–88.

18. Freud 1925, 252.

19. Ibid., 253.

20. Freud 1933, 112–35.

21. Freud 1924, 176.

22. Freud 1925, 257.

23. Freud 1931, 229.

24. Freud 1925, 257–58.

25. This is the epithet Freud uses to describe the female psyche (see Freud 1926, 212).

26. For a detailed account of the complaints Freud made about the obscurity of the female psyche, see the Editor's Note in Freud 1925, 243–44.

27. "There is no such thing as The woman since of her essence, she is not all." This means that "when any speaking being whatever lines up under the banner of women it is by being constituted as not all that they are placed within the phallic function" (Lacan 1982, 144).

28. Lacan 1991, 96. See also "The Mirror Stage as Formative of the Function of the I" (Lacan 1977, 1–7).

29. According to Lacan, women, and also certain male mystics, are able to enjoy a *jouissance* that is "beyond the phallus" (Lacan 1982, 145–47).

30. These are two famous characters in *Shui hu chüan.* They are also the protagonists of many Chinese operas. Wu Sung kills P'an Chin-lien, the adulterous and murderous wife of Wu Sung's crippled elder brother, Wu Ta. Shih Hsiu is the guardian of the male law and the male interest; he kills the adulterous wife of his friend, Yang Hsiung.

31. Freud 1933, 134.

32. Ibid., 133.

33. In the film, the gangsters call themselves *ko-erh-men* (buddies), which is the informal form of *hsiung-ti-men* or *ko-ko-ti-ti-men* (brothers).

References

"An Allegory of Innocence and Power." 1991. In *Edward Yang,* ed. Golden Horse Award Film Committee, 44–57.

Chen, Robert. 1992. "Cultural-Historical Experience of the New Taiwanese Cinema," Ph.D. dissertation, School of Cinema-TV, University of Southern California.

Freud, Sigmund. 1974. *Standard Edition of the Complete Psychological Works of Sigmund Freud (SE).* Trans. and ed. James Strachey. London: Hogarth Press and the Institution of Psychoanalysis.

———. 1900. *The Interpretation of Dreams.* Vol. 4.

———. 1913. *Totem and Taboo.* Vol. 13.

———. 1923. *The Ego and the Id.* Vol. 19.

———. 1924. *The Dissolution of the Oedipus Complex.* Vol. 19.

———. 1925. *Some Psychical Consequences of the Anatomical Distinction Between the Sexes.* Vol. 19.

———. 1926. *The Question of Lay Analysis.* Vol. 20.

———. 1931. *Female Sexuality.* Vol. 21.

———. 1933. *Femininity.* Vol. 22.

———. 1939. *Moses and Monotheism: Three Essays.* Vol. 23.

Girard, René. 1977. *Violence and the Sacred.* Baltimore: Johns Hopkins University Press.

Golden Horse Award Film Committee, ed. 1991. *Edward Yang.* Taipei: China Times Press.

Lacan, Jacques. 1977. *Ecrits.* Trans. Alan Sheridan. New York: Norton.

———. 1982. "God and the Jouissance of The Woman." *Feminine Sexuality.* Ed. Juliet Mitchell and Jacqueline Rose; trans. Jacqueline Rose. London: Macmillan.

———. 1991. *The Seminar of Jacques Lacan.* Book II, ed. Jacques-Alain Miller; trans. Sylvana Tomaselli. New York: Norton.

Lévi-Strauss, Claude. 1966. *The Savage Mind.* Chicago: University of Chicago Press.

———. 1973. *From Honey to Ashes.* Trans. John and Doreen Weightman. New York: Harper and Row.

Liu (Huang) Yu-hsiu. 1993. "A Myth(ology) Mythologizing Its Own Closure: *A Brighter Summer Day." Taiwan: A Radical Quarterly in Social Studies* 14:1–38.

14

Between Bosses and Workers

The Dilemma of a Keen Observer and a Vocal Feminist

Ping-chun Hsiung

This chapter analyzes the challenges and opportunities I encountered when I conducted fieldwork in Taiwan's satellite factories in the summer of 1989 and the beginning of 1990. Methodologically, this chapter centers on the issues of negotiating entry, maintaining access, and resolving conflicts and tensions. My discussion derives from, and seeks to contribute to, the recent feminist debate appraising the power relations between researchers and informants. My analysis also must be seen in the context of earlier accounts of fieldwork in Asia, with special emphasis on those focusing on the Chinese communities in Asian countries. I first situate my own fieldwork experiences at the point where my personal trajectory as a Chinese woman intersects with my previous knowledge of the research topic. My dilemmas in fieldwork arise from a number of contradictions: between my roles as a participant and as an observer, between my status as an insider (as an indigenous woman) and as an outsider (a feminist), and between my vocal feminism and my role as a keen observer. My discussion of the dilemmas inherent in feminist fieldwork takes into account all these contradictions. My experience as a participant-observer in a setting where the power structure is openly constructed and contested along class and gender lines provides invaluable insights for my analysis of patriarchal capitalist control in Taiwanese society. At the same time, however, my critical attitude toward capitalist practices puts me in direct conflict with the very phenomena I set out to study. From the beginning, therefore, I found myself in constant negotiation with the system itself and with the agents of that system–the bosses–on whom I depended for gaining entry, and sustaining access, to the satellite factories.

My indigenous status gave me many advantages. Knowing the language, the ecological environment, and the cultural norms and practices in Taiwan put me on par with my Chinese colleagues. Unlike foreigners, I did not need to rely on a translator or research assistant.[1] As a native speaker, I was able to overhear simultaneous con-

Originally published in *Feminist Dilemmas in Fieldwork,* ed. Diane L. Wolf. Copyright 1996 by Westview Press, a division of Perseus Books Group. Reprinted by permission of Westview Press, a member of Perseus Books, L.L.C.

versation on the shop floor and to engage in daily spontaneous dialogue with others on a variety of topics. From the first days of my fieldwork, familiarity with the ecological environment allowed me to get on a motorcycle (the most common transportation in Taiwan) in order to explore small factories in the midst of the rice fields and in dark alleys. My familiarity with Chinese culture and Taiwanese society provided the broader context I needed to interpret interactional relationships experienced at the micro level. On the negative side, however, my insider status as an indigenous woman rendered me subject to patriarchal control in the field.

I entered the field as a researcher influenced by Western feminist scholarship, as well as being an outsider who viewed existing class and gender inequalities with a critical eye. Together with what I learned as an insider, this outside perspective enabled me to use my fieldwork experience to deconstruct the formation and mechanism of the power dynamics in the satellite factories. I have also come to challenge the dichotomous portrayal of the power relations between female ethnographers and female subjects, recently articulated in many discussions of feminist methodology (Patai 1991; Stacey 1991: Acker et al. 1983). I argue that in the fieldwork setting, the power relationship is more complex. In my view, it is simplistic to assume that the only power relationship is that which exists between the researcher and the researched—the powerful and the powerless, respectively. To overemphasize a binary power relationship is to overlook the patriarchal context in which both the (female) feminist ethnographer and her female informants are caught and situated. It also fails to take into account the potential power possessed by individual agents of the patriarchal system. In order to contextualize feminist fieldwork, I propose that we think in terms of a multidimensional power relationship, of which the patriarchal/capitalist system, individual agents of the system, female informants, and female feminist researchers are all key constituents.

I was involved in my own fieldwork as an indigenous feminist researcher in a specific setting. Nonetheless, it is valuable to compare my experience with the reports of female researchers who entered and observed Asian societies as foreigners. A number of these foreign researchers of an earlier era provided valuable records of obstacles they encountered. Thus Mary Sheridan and Jane Salaff (Kung, Arrigo, and Salaff 1984) and Linda Arrigo (1984) discovered, to their dismay, that the formal interview, a standard method of data collection in the West, fails to provide the same high-quality data when used in Asia. Lydia Kung (Kung, Arrigo, and Salaff 1984) and Mary Sheridan (1984) also found it frustrating that although certain personal information that is usually not revealed openly in Western society is public knowledge in Chinese communities, other information is virtually inaccessible to outsiders. Moreover, several of these scholars were fully aware of, and readily acknowledged, their outsider status. Sheridan and Salaff (1984: 3), for example, discussed the ways in which their background, as Western-trained social scientists who "matured in the individual-centered humanism of Western civilization," affected their research. Although feminist scholars have only recently begun to reflect on, and analyze, their experiences in the field, these earlier accounts can provide useful information as we try to develop more comprehensive research methods. Less useful are fieldwork accounts that overly emphasize the positive aspects of the research procedure.[2] Thus Kung tells us that she "obtained an introduction to the management, explained my research project, and received permission to carry out informal interviews in the plant during working hours" (Kung, Arrigo, and Salaff 1984: 98) but does not inform us how entry was negotiated, on what terms it was granted, how continuing access was sustained, and how potential tension was resolved.

By employing ethnographic data, my approach departs from mainstream sociology, where the deductive approach is practiced as a dominant mode of investigation. Being aware of the strength and limitations of quantitative as well as qualitative approaches, I was deeply concerned about the indiscriminate employment of statistical models by some of my colleagues. My concern echoes what Chen Yiyun calls "a Westernization of sociology in China," where the widespread use of computers has led many researchers to develop an addiction to positivism. According to Chen, Chinese researchers often adopt concepts and questionnaires originally designed for sociological enquiry in the West, without properly considering the highly different social, cultural, and political contexts in which they were developed. And "Certain foreign colleagues are even more ingenious: if they can get hold of a floppy disk of data, they can stuff China's numbers into a theoretical framework, and thus complete a 'sinological' treatise" (Chen 1994: 70).

By discussing the embedded contradiction between the roles of a keen observer and a vocal feminist, I hope to shed light on some critical methodological issues that feminists need to address. At the same time, a pressing task is to question the applicability to Sinology of statistical models developed by Western social scientists. When sociology as a discipline was first introduced to China in the 1930s, it was pursued as knowledge deeply grounded in social realities. Leading scholars of the time, such as Fei Hsiao-t'ung, relied primarily on fieldwork data to disentangle the unique social fabric of Chinese society.[3] Before sociology begins using shallow terminology and detaches from the social reality of Chinese society, it is essential that sociology once again becomes deeply rooted in the knowledge of the people and their environment. Comprehensive and systematic fieldwork accounts are essential in the development of the research methods and the feminist scholarship appropriate to indigenous societies.

Entering Where Others, and I, Left Off

In my last years of graduate study, I became interested in the work, marriage, and family experiences of Taiwan's first cohort of factory girls. Studies have documented that once married, most of them are forced to resign (Kung 1983; Lu 1986). A few reports have indicated the existence of a large number of married women in the small factories (Niehoff 1987; Stites 1982, 1985). My hunch then was that Taiwan's first cohort of factory girls might have moved to factories in their own neighborhoods or worked at home for these small factories on a piecework basis.

My hunch was supported by what I had witnessed in the mid-1970s as a junior high schoolteacher in a fishing village in central Taiwan. On my regular visits to my students' families, I saw that toys, plastic flowers, and Christmas ornaments were all made by my female students, their aunts, and their mothers. "These are for the Americans," I was told.

Although factories with fewer than thirty workers composed up to 89 percent of Taiwan's manufacturing industry throughout the 1970s and 1980s, scholars, until recently, have failed to recognize the uniqueness and significance of these small factories in Taiwan's economic development. Most studies of that development have focused on large corporations in the export processing zones (EPZ). The failure to recognize the role of these small factories evidences an intellectual bias in which the path and pattern of Western industrialization are held as norms in studying Third World economic development. Such negligence could be partially logistical, in that it is much easier to gather data on large factories in the EPZs than to do research on the numerous small factories scattered throughout local communities.[4] Before entering the field, I found that the existing literature told me nothing about the operational mechanisms and labor politics of Taiwan's satellite factory system.[5] Knowledge of the effects of Taiwan's economic development on women has been based mainly on studies of young single women working in large factories (Arrigo 1980; Diamond 1979; Kung 1976, 1983).[6] Except in a few cases, the experiences and lives of married women who work outside of the EPZs have been left out, despite the fact that, since the 1970s, the rate of increase in their participation in the labor force has been higher than that for single women (Gallin 1984a, 1984b; Hu 1982, 1984).[7]

Because so little was known at the time, I wanted to take an inside look at what was going on in the factories. Participant-observation seemed to be the best approach for my groundbreaking task as I felt it would give me the depth and insight I was looking for. Before my departure from the United States to Taiwan, I was warned about the tensions between management and workers and how these tensions might create difficulties for me if I intended to cover both sides of the story. Covering both could become disastrous, I was told. It was suggested that I study either the management's or the workers' side of the story. I thought I would focus on the workers if I had to choose between the two.

In the summer of 1989, I set out to explore Taiwan's "economic miracle," which was created by small-scale and family-centered satellite factories and constructed by women through their paid and unpaid labor. I ended up spending three months in the factories. I worked in six factories and visited about thirty others during my first field trip. In December 1989 and January 1990, I revisited the factories and talked to the people I had met on my first trip.

In the field, I was seen, treated, and approached as an insider and outsider simultaneously. From the standpoint of factory workers, my outsider status came from what I do (studying in the United States), whereas my insider status came from who I am (an indigenous woman). On a personal level, I found it was easy to get on a friendly footing with factory workers due to our shared experiences. During a break, an owner's mother, a widow in her mid-seventies, told me what types of odd jobs she had taken in order to raise her children. When she described how hard it was to make straw hats at night under oil lights, I understood what she said, because when I was a child, my family once lived in a remote mountain village where there was no electricity or running water. I told her that I did my homework by candlelight and that my sister and I used to carry water from a mountain spring an hour away from our home. On one conversation, several male factory owners and I ended up talking about the games we used to play in the rice fields after school.

My coworkers' curiosity about my life and experiences in the United States allowed them to relate to me as both an insider and an outsider. The fact that I had been making extra efforts to get rice from Chinese grocery stores in Monterey Park, California, brought comments such as: "We never realized it could be an issue" and "I could never live without rice." My coworkers were surprised but delighted to learn that, rather than beefsteak, my favorite dish was bitter melon, a popular vegetable in Taiwan but available only in a few Chinese grocery stores in the United States. During a conversation, I told a coworker in her early sixties that, being away from home, I once dreamed of a bitter melon dish, "but because I was too excited, I woke up before I had a chance to taste it in my dream." The few times I was invited to her home after that, she made sure that there was bitter melon on the table. When she and I went to their garden patch in the middle of a rice field to pick some herbs and dig out some sweet potatoes for a special soup I had not had since my family left that mountain village, I felt as if I had come home at last.

Working in the factory was for me like experiencing a life from which I had just escaped by a small margin. Throughout those years, it became clear to me that my continuing advancement in higher education has less to do with my school performance than with my father, who treasures his daughters as much as his sons, and my mother, who believes that her daughters are inferior to no one's sons. By the time I was accepted to the university, many of my girlfriends from elementary school were married. As I moved on to various stages of my life, I have never stopped wondering what would have happened if the girl sitting next to me in fifth grade had been given the same opportunity as her brothers or I got, and what has happened to the female students I taught in the fishing village. When my coworkers told me stories about their work experiences and family lives, I felt as though it was my students or childhood girlfriends who were telling me what had happened to them since my departure.

Between Bosses and Workers: A Multidimensional Power Relationship

After I was in the field, I realized that covering both sides of the story was the only way to go. With factory sizes that ranged from three to thirty workers, it was virtually impossible to gain access to workers without the consent of their bosses. Interacting with the bosses not only served my data-collection purposes by giving me access to the workers, but hearing them talk about the operational struggles of their firms also gave me additional insight into the structural constraints experienced by Third World reporters. Even if it would not have been logistically problematic, I soon realized that an exclusive focus on factory workers would have left me with an incomplete understanding.

My entry was granted by male factory owners partly because of the national (Third World) identity they perceived us to share. Almost all the factory owners complained about the problems that they have experienced due to the fluctuations of the global market. They readily pointed out the ways in which increasing competition, unstable demand, and fluctuating foreign-exchange rates affect their daily operations at the factory level. Beating the odds brought them a pride that has been missing among many Chinese people ever since the Opium War in the mid-nineteenth century. One owner believed that if he granted me entry, the major role of satellite factory entrepreneurs in constructing Taiwan's economic miracle, and the hard work their success entailed, might finally be recognized by the Taiwanese state and by the international community. Another owner saw himself as someone who was helping a compatriot to become internationally successful on her own terms. The connections and ties that I was able to establish with these factory owners should not be overly romanticized, however. My goodwill in establishing reciprocal relationships with them in the field put me in a vulnerable position that was subject to engulfment and potential exploitation. Throughout my fieldwork, I constantly struggled to gain as much autonomy as I could under the circumstances.

When I first met Mr. Li, the owner of a factory that assembled wooden jewelry boxes, I told him I would like to understand the production and operational mechanisms of Taiwan's satellite factory system. He was highly enthusiastic about my project and promised to help me out by introducing me to all the satellite factories that did subcontracting work for him. In exchange, I offered to help in his factory. During the first two days, he took me with him whenever he went on routine visits to his satellite factories; I ended up visiting seven factories over those two days. Between visits, I spent most of my time working on the shop floor with other workers. It didn't take long for Mr. Li to realize that it wouldn't hurt to have an extra pair of hands around, even with my not-so-impressive productivity. As time went by, Mr. Li took me out less and less. My role as a worker (participant) gradually took over my identity as a researcher (observer). I didn't really mind this shift. Even though the work was physically taxing, it gave me firsthand experience of factory work. I also gained opportunities to interact with other workers and learn what was happening on the shop floor. I would arrive at the factory in the morning and work all day long. Usually I didn't stay for the evening work but left around five or six o'clock at night, and then went home to write my field notes until three or four o'clock in the morning.[8] By the end of the second week, I felt that the overtime was taking its toll on me, physically and with regard to my research.

The prospect of possible exploitation didn't really dawn on me until my first request to move on to another satellite factory was rejected by Mr. Li, who said, "There isn't anything interesting there. You can learn everything here, at Ta-yu." It was only after I told him firmly that I had to complete my observations in at least one satellite factory of each type in the chain of jewelry-box production that Mr. Li reluctantly introduced me to one of his satellite factories.[9] In his introduction, he referred to me as a woman who "just came back from the States and wants to understand how things work in your factory. . . . No, you don't have to pay her. She works for free. She takes notes every now and then. . . . It will just be a matter of five to ten minutes. . . . All you need to do is to buy her a lunch box" (that is, buy me lunch). Similar concern over my free labor took a different form in another factory. After working at Wei-der for a week, I was told that the owner had said he would not talk to me unless I agreed to work in his factory for more than a month.

My free labor was an issue not only among factory bosses. Different groups of workers also competed for my labor. One woman worker in her early sixties told me during a lunch break that I should not help a group of "outsiders," the subcontracting workers.[10] An insider herself, she explained:

> We are paid daily. The outsiders are paid piece-rate. When you help them to assemble the drawers, you aren't helping us in the factory. The work they are doing is not part of our job any longer. It has been subcontracted out. Besides, those women are young. They earn much more than I do.

Apparently, given the labor-intensive and physically taxing work, even an extra pair of inexperienced hands could save the workers some sweat.

Competition over my labor demonstrates only one aspect of the power struggle I experienced in doing fieldwork in Taiwan's satellite factory system. My efforts to cover the perspectives of both factory bosses and workers ran up against my political concerns over the workers' welfare. Such embedded contradictions intensified the pressures I felt about the hierarchical power relationship between the factory bosses and myself, a female feminist researcher originally from Taiwan.

I still remember vividly the grinding uneasiness I felt when a factory owner insisted on taking me to a factory right after telling me that the driver, who often had me accompany him on his daily delivery trips, was in the hospital after a severe car accident. The owner ignored my concern for the driver and my immediate desire to visit him in the hospital. "Don't worry. He won't die," he said. On another occasion, comments I made that encouraged the restless workers to organize and confront the owner were reported to the owner. Although I was not thrown out of the factory, a possibility that had caused as much anxiety to me as to the workers at the scene, the owner made it known that such involvement on my part was inappropriate.[11]

These incidents illustrate the multidimensional axes of tension and of power relations in the factories: Bosses are pitted against the researcher and the workers, whereas the workers confront the researcher as well as one another. The terms of my access to the shop floor and to the workers were largely determined by the imbalance in the power relationships between the factory owners and myself. Furthermore, my trip in the winter of 1989–90 was rendered less than satisfactory due to the dominating presence of their husbands when I visited the women workers at home. I had initially planned to conduct in-depth interviews with the married female workers whom I had met the preceding summer. As it turned out, when I arrived at the women's homes, I was often greeted by their husbands, who proceeded to dominate the conversation, even though many of the women had been highly articulate when I had talked with them in the factories.

The Dilemma of a Keen Observer and a Vocal Feminist

On the shop floor, as men and women routinely interacted with one another, I encountered multidimensional power relationships structured around the patriarchal system, involving the Chinese women workers and myself. Consequently, I was forced to juggle two modes of self-presentation every day. In order to hear what the factory owners would normally say to the workers, and to see how wives could quietly disarm their bossy husbands, I complied with the observer principle of doing nothing to disturb the setting. On occasion, however, I found myself openly expressing my feminist beliefs and political position simply for the sake of my own sanity. The superior power position attributed to female feminist researchers in recent discussions of feminist methodology does not speak to my own fieldwork experiences. I thus find myself calling into question the dichotomous conceptualization of the power relationship said to pertain between female feminist researchers and their informants. Looking back, I am also struck by the fact that I constantly had to renegotiate the terms of my fieldwork with the agents—mostly men—of the very system I had set out to study. This process of negotiation gave me firsthand experience of patriarchal and capitalist control in Taiwanese society.

Doing fieldwork in overwhelmingly gender-defined and structured social settings presented me with real challenges. On the shop floor, I did my best to be a keen observer, so that the setting would not be turned into an instance of "savage social therapy," which Marie-Françoise Chanfrault-Duchet and D. Patai describe as occurring in interview situations (Patai 1991: 148). In order to capture and understand how workers in general, and female workers in particular, are perceived by their bosses, I had to subdue my feminist inclinations and the political beliefs that had brought me to the field in the first place. Instead of jumping to a quick conclusion, I calmly asked a male factory owner to explain why he believed that female home-workers were "petty minded." With women workers, I was especially careful not to be self-righteous or to make others uncomfortable. At lunch, I followed my female coworkers in the setting up of a folding table in the corner upon which the women and I were to eat after all the men had taken the main dining table in the center of the kitchen. I didn't think I should say anything when a fight between the children of my coworkers Ah-chu and Ah-hsia inspired comments such as: "Your kid and my kid always get into fights. This is simply because they are both boys. If one of them were a little girl, I bet they would not have fought."

In retrospect, I see that my compliance with the role of uninvolved observer served two functions. By giving priority to the voices and actions of the people in the setting, it allowed incidents to unfold and events to take their full course. It also prevented me from imposing my feminist ideology on others. My efforts to be an impartial observer ran into difficulties, however. In my fieldwork, I was surrounded by, and subjected to, various forms of everyday sexism—daily norms and practices that were overtly oppressive toward women or that covertly perpetuated gender inequality. Posters for pornographic movies decked the electric poles in the streets, the walls of apartment buildings, and bulletin boards, side by side with advertisements for aphrodisiacs and surgical cures for impotence. Seminaked women danced erotically in flower carts at weddings, during festivals, and even at funerals.[12] On my visits to factories I was sometimes greeted with whistles and such remarks as "what a pretty woman" from male workers on the shop floor. Conversations there usually started with such questions as, "Are you married?" "How many kids do you have?" and "How long have you been married?" (in exactly that order). Although such personal questions are not out of place in the Chinese context, information about my personal background enabled others to judge me in accordance with indigenous norms and practices.[13]

Comments such as "She is lucky to be married. Most men don't want to marry women with too much education" were exchanged among the male managers. My female coworkers, on the other hand, believed that I should get a permanent, keep my skin pale, and wear skirts more often. On several occasions the women expressed their sincere concern over my childless status. Their comments ranged from simple curiosity, "Isn't it strange not having kids?" to female propriety, "It isn't very nice not giving his family descendants," to an opinionated moralism, "He is the only son of his parents, isn't he? Then you have to have at least one son for his family." The comments not only indicated the cultural norms to which every Chinese woman is expected to conform, but they reminded me of my ambiguous insider/outsider status and occasionally generated alienated feelings and discomfort on my part.

On the shop floor, I was overwhelmed by the pervasiveness of men's social control over women. Remarks such as "You women always complain" and "You [women] don't know what you're talking about" were made daily in conversations to trivialize or ridicule women. I didn't anticipate that staying with my parents rather than my in-laws while I worked on the project would cause raised eyebrows.[14] One of my coworkers asked me specifically if I had "gone back" to my in-laws right after I arrived in Taiwan. When I told her in a matter-of-fact way that I had gone straight from the airport to my parents' home, I saw envy and amazement in her eyes. It was only later that I learned that this woman's in-laws had granted her only three visits to her parents since her marriage fourteen years earlier. Nonetheless, she said that she could not comprehend how my parents could have allowed this. In her opinion, my parents had failed to teach me how to be a proper daughter-in-law.

My outsider status did give me a certain immunity when I inadvertently violated some of the patriarchal norms and practices. On the other hand, it did not give me the power or privilege to escape from the most overt form of patriarchal control, namely, sexual harassment. My gender took precedence over my academic credentials, for example, when a man who was supposed to help me get entry to a factory turned a factory tour into an incident of sexual harassment. He began by asking me what an American man would say to initiate a date. My indifferent response to his inquiry did not keep him from posing questions about how to talk to attractive women in English. When I refused his invitation for a date, he verbally insulted me: "What other fun can you have on Saturday afternoon when your husband is not around?" This incident demonstrates how easily individual women are perceived as, and turned into, sexual objects. Indeed, jokes or remarks that refer to Chinese women purely as sexual objects are part of everyday reality. A woman who showed up at work sleepy was teased as having had "too much of a good time last night." A manager offering a job to a deliveryman was heard to say: "Why don't you come and work for me? I'll make you a supervisor and get a pretty woman to be your assistant." In response, the driver said: "No, it won't work. That would deplete my vitality."

The pervasive degradation of women in the satellite factory system made it impossible for me, a female Chinese feminist, to confine myself totally to the observer role. At a banquet celebrating the newborn baby of a female worker, a man who was introduced to me as a lawyer joined my table. My coworkers made remarks such as "Mr. Wong is a big-time lawyer"; "Mr. Li [owner of the factory] and our factory really rely on him"; or "He makes big money." Mr. Wong looked extremely narcissistic in his three-piece suit, especially in contrast to me and my coworkers as we all wore the usual yellowish T-shirts. What happened next was one of the few instances where my action interrupted the course of an event that could have gone in other directions.

After several drinks, he moved next to me and started telling those at the table pornographic jokes.[15] Although others around the table (maybe a total of five to six men and two women) were simply smiling and nodding, I found both the jokes and the scene offensive. I told Mr. Wong that he should stop making jokes that were degrading to women. "They are just jokes," Mr. Wong replied, "Don't be so serious." "I don't find jokes that are degrading to women funny," I said. Mr. Wong was a little bit uncomfortable being confronted, but offered to tell a "really good one" anyway. Before I had a chance to say anything, he started the joke by saying, "We are all adults. You, Dr. Hsiung, I assume you are no longer adolescent." At this point, I took my glass and rose from my seat. "I'm moving to another table," I protested. "Don't take things so seriously. It's just a joke," Mr. Wong defended himself. "I'll leave if you continue," I said. I stood there and didn't want to put up with it any more. After a few awkward seconds he said, "All right! All right! I'll leave." He bowed stiffly and left our table. He looked embarrassed.

On another occasion, I made comments about the unequal relationship between men and women when, on our way to a factory, my male coworker was jokingly trying to talk another factory owner into taking a mistress. After my comments, they looked a bit uneasy and changed the subject.

The incidents I have described illustrate the extent to which I was part of everyday gender politics while doing my fieldwork. My observer role demanded that I either pretend not to hear the sexist jokes or, adopting the customary code of silence, simply smile and say nothing, as Chinese women are expected to do. Whenever I was provoked to define and defend myself, I inevitably interrupted the action and so had an effect on the course of events.

Discussion and Conclusion

Recent discussion of feminist methodology and epistemology raises questions concerning the unequal power relations between the researcher and the researched. The debate focuses on the intrusion and intervention of the researcher into the lives of the informants, the appropriation of the informants' private emotions/stories by the researcher, and the dominant position of the researcher in presentation and representation of the researched (Patai 1991; Stacey 1991; Acker et al. 1991). My examination of the multiple axes of power relations in the field and the contradiction between my roles as a keen observer and a vocal feminist illustrate that the power relations are much more complex. The processes of gaining entry, sustaining access, and resolving tension involve negotiation among the patriarchal/capitalist system, the agents of the system, and the female feminist researcher. The conceptualization of a binary-power relationship between female ethnographers and their informants does not leave sufficient room to explore how power structures are constructed and contested through everyday interaction between men and women.

The issues I raised in this chapter center around the logical contradictions that arise when an indigenous feminist does fieldwork in an active way, as a participant-observer. Nevertheless, they bear a strong resemblance to the difficulties mentioned in recent accounts of fieldwork by several First World feminists. For example, although I myself did not require the prior approval of government officials before entering the field, the sense of powerlessness I felt while doing my fieldwork corresponds closely with that experienced by Margery Wolf during her 1980 field trip in the People's Republic of China (1985). In her chapter "Speaking Bitterness," Wolf discusses at length her experience of lost autonomy and her lack of independent access to Chinese women during her field trip in the People's Republic of China. I can very much relate to the pressures that made Wolf create a false identity that conformed to the norms of the Chinese communities she studied, but conceal what was really going on in her personal life (1992). As for Dorinne Kondo, although I did not go through the pains-taking process that transformed her from a Japanese American into a "culturally competent" Japanese woman (1990), I was made fully aware of the gender as-criptions that I had unwittingly violated.

All in all, these recent accounts suggest that, although doing fieldwork in Asian societies poses different challenges to indigenous and First World feminists, the conflict between acute observation and feminist involvement represents an em-bedded contradiction that all feminist researchers need to confront.

Notes

An earlier version of this chapter was presented at the American Sociological Association annual meeting in Miami in 1993. I appreciate Rita Gallin's supportive ears at the conference. Natalie Beasoleil, Francesca Bray, Shelley Feldman, Bonnie Fox, Charles Harris, Roxana Ng, Aysan Sev'er, and Diane Wolf have read various drafts of this chapter. I especially thank Diane Wolf for her useful comments and Francesca Bray, Shelley Feldman, and Roxana Ng for their encouragement and suggestions. I thank Liza McCoy and Joan Campbell for edito-rial assistance. In particular, I appreciate Joan Campbell's meticulous work.

1. The assistance of indigenous translators and research assistants is freely acknowl-edged in many accounts by First World researchers who have done fieldwork in Asia. Such helpers engage in a variety of tasks: doing simple translation, introducing the re-searcher to the local community, identifying potential informants, and even acting as the interpreter of local norms and practices. Nonetheless, few researchers have systemati-cally analyzed how using an indigenous translator or assistant affected their research project. Bernard Gallin's accounts on the roles of his translator are a rare exception (B. Gallin 1966: appendix I).

2. Particularly in the earlier era, fieldwork accounts tended to focus on the steps taken by researchers or factors presented in the field that eventually helped the success of their fieldwork. A typical example is Kung's account of her fieldwork project on young female factory workers in Taiwan. Kung states that her presence should not have disturbed the setting "because other anthropologists have lived in the area" (Kung, Arrigo, and Salaff 1984: 97). According to Kung, her talks with female factory workers while they were work-ing did not present any problems because the conversation "relieves the monotony" of factory jobs. She also came to the conclusion that her high educational background "prob-ably heightened their (the female workers') curiosity and increased their willingness to talk" (Kung, Arrigo, and Salaff 1984: 99).

3. For a discussion of this early period of development, see Gary G. Hamilton and Wang Zheng, "Introduction: Fei Xiaotong and the Beginnings of a Chinese Sociology," in Fei 1992.

4. The first systematic attempts to examine Taiwan's small factories have been carried out independently by Cheng (1992), Hsiung (1991), and Shieh (1992).

5. I use this term to conceptualize Taiwan's small-scale, family-centered, and export-oriented factories. These factories are connected through subcontracting arrangements (Hsiung 1991).

6. For example, Arrigo studies an electric factory with several hundred female workers (Arrigo 1980). Kung did fieldwork at "one of Taiwan's largest factories," which employed some 4,000 female workers (Kung, Arrigo, Salaff 1984: 98). Diamond studied a textile plant employing about four hundred workers. Around 80 percent of them were young women (Diamond 1979).

7. In 1984, about 43 percent of the labor force in manufacturing industries was made

up of women. From 1967 to 1988, the growth of female labor force participation among young single women was 22 percent, whereas it was 65 percent for married women (Hsiung 1991: 197).

8. The typical working schedule of the peak season in the satellite factory is:

Monday, 8:00 A.M.–12:00 noon, 1:00–5:00 P.M., 5:30 P.M.–9:00 P.M.
Tuesday, 8:00 A.M.–12:00 noon, 1:00–5:00 P.M., 5:30 P.M.–9:00 P.M.
Wednesday, 8:00 A.M.–12:00 noon, 1:00–6:00 P.M.
Thursday, 8:00 A.M.–12:00 noon, 1:00–5:00 P.M., 5:30 P.M.–9:00 P.M.
Friday, 8:00 A.M.–12:00 noon, 1:00–5:00 P.M., 5:30 P.M.–9:00 P.M.
Saturday, 8:00 A.M.–12:00 noon, 1:00–6:00 P.M.
Sunday, 8:00 A.M.–12:00 noon, 1:00–6:00 P.M. (every other week)

9. I eventually worked in six factories: one box body factory, one hardware factory, one glasses factory, one painting factory, and two assembly factories.

10. "Insiders" and "outsiders" are terms used in Taiwan's satellite factory system to differentiate two groups of workers. The former term refers to workers hired by a factory on daily wages. They work in the factory on a monthly basis and are usually its main labor force. The "outsiders," on the other hand, are subcontract workers. With four to ten members, each outsider group specializes in one specific semiskilled task, such as screwing the door to the boxes, pasting down the flannel, or assembling the drawer. A factory owner subcontracts a particular task to each outsider group. These outsiders are therefore constantly on the move from one factory to another.

11. Because of the lack of institutional support, labor politics in Taiwan's satellite factory system have been clandestine rather than confrontational. Only one such incident happened during the period of my fieldwork. In my dissertation I provide a detailed account of this incident. I also discuss the implications of such occurrences for our overall understanding of labor politics in the satellite factory system (Hsiung 1991).

12. Although the commercialization of the female body is not a new development, the collective consumption of the female body by the hiring of seminaked women dancers at weddings and religious festivals is a recent phenomenon (Chang 1993).

13. Hill Gates describes the differences between the Chinese and American ways of personal interaction. "Where we (the Americans) make small talk about the weather or current events, for example, they (the Chinese) inquire if a new acquaintance has brothers and sisters, or ask the amount of her salary" (Gates 1987: 5–6). The main function of more-personalized small talk is to expand or enhance personal networks. Inquiries about personal matters, such as birthplace, school graduated from, or work experiences, are made to initiate/search for any possible connection.

14. The patrilineal and patrilocal norms call for a woman, upon marriage, to move into the household of her parents-in-law. The norms are incorporated into legal codes that give a Chinese husband the right to divorce his wife if she refuses to comply with this practice of patrilocal residence.

15. Telling pornographic jokes is a common occurrence at banquets in Taiwan. Men compete for attention and entertain other diners, both men and women, with exotic and often offensive jokes. These jokes usually boast of masculinity by demeaning women. Recently, the implications of pornographic jokes for gender stratification and, especially, for gender politics in the workplace have been heatedly debated in Taiwan. Some argue that such pornographic joking is a form of sexual harassment (Hsia-hung-mao 1993; Wu 1993); others stress the similarity between "joking relationships" and "patriarchal relationships." Pornographic joking, in this interpretation, is simply another indirect way for men to assert their power over women (Huang 1993). But others encourage Chinese women to counter pornographic jokes with jokes that are equally demeaning to women, in my view (Hsin-liang-hsing 1993; Lin 1993).

References

Acker, J.; K. Barry; and J. Esseveld. 1983. "Objectivity and Truth: Problems in Doing Feminist Research." *Women's Studies International Forum* 6, no. 4: 423–435.

Arrigo, L.G. 1980. "The Industrial Work Force of Young Women in Taiwan." *Bulletin of Concerned Asian Scholars* 12: 25–34.

Chang, S.C. 1993. "The Gender Questions in Folk Religion of Taiwan: Public Display of Naked Female Body in 'Electronic-Flower-Card.'" Paper presented at the Conference of Gender Issues in Contemporary Chinese Societies, Miami Beach, Florida.

Chen, Y. 1994. "Out of Traditional Halls of Academe: Exploring New Avenues for Research on Women." In *Engendering China: Women, Culture, and the State*, ed. C.K. Gilmartin et al., 69–79. Cambridge: Harvard University Press.

Cheng, J.C. 1992. *The Economic Structure and Social Characteristics of Taiwan's Small and Medium Size Factories*. Taipei: Lang-chin.

Diamond, N. 1979. "Women and Industry in Taiwan." *Modern China* 1, no. 1: 3–45.

Fei, Hsiao-t'ung. 1992. *From the Soil: The Foundations of Chinese Society: A Translation of Fei Xiaotong's Xiangtu Zhongguo*. Trans. Gary G. Hamilton and Wang Zheng. Berkeley: University of California Press.

Gallin, B. 1966. *Hsin Hsing, Taiwan: A Chinese Village in Change*. Berkeley: University of California Press.

Gallin, R.C. 1984a. "The Impact of Development on Women's Work and Status: A Case Study from Taiwan." East Lansing: Michigan State University, Women in International Development Publication Series, Working Paper no. 9.

———. 1984b. "Rural Industrialization and Chinese Women: A Case Study from Taiwan." East Lansing: Michigan State University, Women in International Development Publication Series, Working Paper no. 47.

Gates, H. 1987. *Chinese Working-Class Lives: Getting By in Taiwan*. Ithaca: Cornell University Press.

Hsia-hung-mao, S. 1993. "Huang-ssu hsiao-hua pu hao-hsiao" (The Pornographic Joke Is Not Funny). *Hsin-liang-hsing, li-pao* (Gender Edition: Independent News), August 1.

Hsin-liang-hsing. 1993. "Chiang chiang huang-ssu hsiao-hua yeh pu-ts'ou?" (Let's All Make Pornographic Jokes). *Hsin-liang-hsing, li-pao* (Gender Edition: Independent News), August 1.

Hsiung, P.C. 1991. "Class, Gender, and the Satellite Factory System in Taiwan." Ph.D. dissertation, University of California, Los Angeles.

Hu, T.L. 1982. *Hsi-fu ju-men* (When a Daughter-in-Law Enters Her Husband's Family). Taipei: Shih-pao Press.

———. 1984. *My Mother-in-Law's Village: Rural Industrialization and Change in Taiwan*. Taipei: Institute of Ethnology, Academia Sinica, Monograph Series B, no. 13.

Huang, Liying. 1993. "Yu-mo hu? Erh-hsin hu? Nü-jen yü huang-ssu hsiao-hua" (Is It Humorous? Is It Disgusting?) Women and Pornographic Jokes). *Awakening* 1 (June): 24–27.

Kondo, Dorinne. 1990. *Gender, and Discourses of Identity in a Japanese Workplace*. Chicago: University of Chicago Press.

Kung, L. 1976. "Factory Work and Women in Taiwan: Changes in Self-Image and Status." *Signs* 2, no. 1: 35–58.

———. 1983. *Factory Women in Taiwan*. Ann Arbor: UMI Research Press.

Kung, L.; L.G. Arrigo; and J.W. Salaff. 1984. "Doing Fieldwork." In *Lives: Chinese Working Women*, ed. M. Sheridan and J.W. Salaff. Bloomington: Indiana University Press.

Lin, F. 1993. "Cheng-ch'ü fa-yen-ch'üan: Nü-hsing yü huang-ssu hsiao-hua" (Raising Voices:

Women and the Pornographic Joke). *Hsin-liang-hsing*, *li-pao* (Gender Edition: Independent News), August 1.

Lu, R. 1986. *T'a-men wei-shen-mo pu neng chieh-hun?* (Why Can't They Get Married?). Taipei: Wei-li Attorney Office.

Niehoff, J.D. 1987. "The Villager as Industrialist: Ideologies of Household Manufacturing in Rural Taiwan." *Modern China* 13, no. 3: 278–309.

Patai, D. 1991. "U.S. Academics and the Third World Woman: Is Ethical Research Possible?" In *Women's Words: The Feminist Practice of Oral History*, eds. S. Berger Gluck and D. Patai, 137–53. New York: Routledge.

Sheridan, M. 1984. "The Life History Method." In Sheridan and Salaff, eds., *Lives: Chinese Working Women*, 11–22.

Sheridan, M., and J.W. Salaff. 1984. "Introduction." In *Lives: Chinese Working Women*, ed. Sheridan and J.W. Salaff, 1–10. Bloomington: Indiana University Press.

Shieh, G. S. 1992. *"Boss" Island: The Subcontracting Network and Micro-Entrepreneurship in Taiwan's Development.* New York: Peter Lang.

Stacey, J. 1991. "Can There Be a Feminist Ethnography?" In Gluck and Patai, eds., *Women's Words: The Feminist Practice of Oral History*, 111–19.

Stites, R. 1982. "Small-Scale Industry in Yingge, Taiwan." *Modern China* 8, no. 2: 247–279.

———. 1985. "Industrial Work as an Entrepreneurial Strategy." *Modern China* 11, no. 2: 227–246.

Wolf, D.L. 1992. *Factory Daughters: Gender, Household Dynamics, and Rural Industrialization in Java.* Berkeley: University of California Press.

Wolf, M. 1985. *Revolution Postponed: Women in Contemporary China.* Stanford: Stanford University Press.

Wu, Z. 1993. "Shuo huang-ssu hsiao-hua tsao-ch'eng hsing-sao-jao" (Pornographic Joking Is Sexual Harassment). *Hsin-liang-hsing*, *li-pao* (Gender Edition: Independent News), August 1.

15

Feminist Art in Taiwan

Textures of Reality and Dreams

Richard C. Kagan

Traditionally, many books written on modernization and development contrast the traditional culture to the political, social, and economic changes of the contemporary society. When we read about Taiwan, there is a general introduction about shamanism and native traditions, or Confucianism and Chinese rule, or, for the more sophisticated, the colonial legacies of Japanese imperialism, which focused on native or indigenous folk art. Then there is the mad dash into the chapters on change: population growth, urbanization, political reform, economic progress, social reorganization, and gender roles. However, a chapter or discussion on cultural and artistic changes is scarce at best. The reader is left with a picture only of a Taiwan with an aesthetic and creative tradition frozen in an earlier time and seen as just an extension of Chinese culture. The Taipei government and tourist offices reserve classical Chinese opera for special events and as a "showpiece" for Western visitors. "Traditional" temples bang out their nativistic music, their ritualized prayers, and clouds of incense. Many foreign journalistic and public relations reports on Taiwan just promote cultural events and nightlife that mimic Western tastes. This includes everything from the pervasive knockoff of Western pop music, to high-class performances of Western orchestras in the Chiang Kai-shek Memorial Hall.

The denial of the existence of a modern culture, whether intentional or unintentional, results in two basic cultural negative consequences: (1) the belief that Taiwan is split between the "cultured" past of its local rituals or its Chinese traditions, and the bareness of modernization; or (2) the observer is conned into believing that there is no "culture" in Taiwan except for the dominance of Western imports.

Contrary to the above popular impressions, the reality is that there is a vibrant culture in Taiwan's artistic circles that is gaining international influence and is becoming distinctly and authentically Taiwanese. The purpose of this chapter is to provide a brief background on the traditional limitations of women's art, and to make known that the freedom for women artists occurred only after the end of martial law in 1987. My description and analysis will focus on only four women artists—three painters and one installationist. Needless to say, this selection does not provide a complete account of female talent in Taiwan. It is hoped, however, that this introduction will encourage more attention to Taiwan's women artists and incorporate their importance in forthcoming studies on this country.

The Historical Setting

During most of Chinese history, the major female artists were trained by either concubines or prostitutes. Their art was derivative of male parlor art—women in domestic positions—such as arranging flowers, playing with children, or being engaged in women's occupations such as weaving or silk production. Women learned calligraphy in order to teach their sons the arts of the mandarin or official. Male artists would paint historically important women, such as Yang Kuei-fei, the imperial consort of T'ang dynasty emperor Hsüan-tsung. There were also male-authored "pillow books" that narrated and illustrated the arts of love. In all of these works, the woman was restricted to social and sexual roles dictated by men.[1]

In the twentieth century, art, and women, began to take on new roles. For both men and women, art served the purpose of politics. Under both the Nationalists (Kuomintang, KMT) and the Communists, artists were mobilized to reflect in their artwork the principles and values of the political leadership. Under the Nationalists, the artistic themes included portraits of the great leaders of China, such as Confucius, and great patriots such as Chu Yüan. Traditional themes were also encouraged: calligraphy, plum blossoms, lions, landscapes, and historical events. The Chinese Communists opposed any type of "art for art's sake." They engineered art projects to depict model workers, model patriots, and model martyrs. The exaggeration of the feminine form in terms of their proportions and healthiness reflected the values of Soviet theories of monumentalism. A romantic vision of the Chinese revolution, the struggle against Japan, and the creation of a socialist state insinuated itself in all government-sponsored works. One well-known piece showed the Long March in the genre of Chinese landscapes, in which little figures struggled up the mountains that were brazenly colored red and jutted out through the clouds. Needless to say, the Communist Party dictated the aesthetic and the production of Chinese "art." Because of the party's policies, all art during the Cultural Revolution (1966–76) was to be left unsigned by the artist; thus there is no obvious way to determine the gender of the artist of this period. In any case, the art was not highly creative, as it was commissioned and produced under the strictures of a committee, and was used as propaganda for mass movements. The individual artist had little or no chance to develop his or her abilities.

Meanwhile, the Japanese on Taiwan had taken over control of artistic expression from 1895 to 1945. Japanese rule allowed for a few female artists to attend the Tokyo Art School. The style at that time was Impressionism. Many homey and nonutilitarian works in watercolor and oil were devoted to Taiwan's landscape, to village life, to families on a picnic or in nature, and to portraits of common people. Several well-known artists painted pictures of their wives and daughters.

After Japan's surrender in 1945, not only did Taiwan's political rulers change, but its artistic world also reflected that change. The Nationalists were prejudiced against Japanese-trained artists. Chiang Kai-shek's government was committed to retaining and enforcing traditional Chinese culture. Taiwan's native artists were seen as lackeys to the Japanese, and as unorthodox.

A brief history of the Taipei Fine Arts Museum reflects the political uses of art during Nationalist rule. Until the mid-1970s, the government supported only the fine arts of classical China. The great National Palace Museum of Art housed magnificent pieces of art that were crated and carted to Taiwan by the Nationalists just before the Communist victory in 1949. In 1976, under the guidance of the government's Central Cultural Policy, Taipei mayor Lin Yang-kang ordered the creation of the Taipei Fine Arts Museum. Seven years later, in 1983, the building was completed, and the first public exhibition was opened on December 24, 1983. The first acting director, Ms. Su Jui-p'ing, was a native of Shansi province. She received her master's degree in art history from the Chinese Cultural College in Taiwan and earned another master's degree in art history at Columbia University in New York City. She worked in the National Palace Museum for sixteen years as a calligrapher and researcher in the painting department. Her successor, Mr. Huang Kuang-nan, became the first director in 1986 and served until 1995. His areas of expertise are Chinese flower-and-bird painting, and the history of Chinese painting. Both directors promoted classic Chinese art over modern art or Taiwanese native art. During their tenure, there was never a special exhibition of Taiwanese artists, nor of female artists. The art collection emphasized the modernization of Chinese art—calligraphy, landscapes, flora, fauna, birds, and depictions of Chinese and Taiwanese history.

Women and Women's Art in Taiwan

The end of martial law in 1987 resulted in a frenzied dance of artistic expression. With the end of martial law came not only the freedom to travel abroad, but also the freedom to return home. Many Taiwanese artists returned from their self-imposed exile in Spain, France, Germany, Canada, and, of course, the United States. In the words of Victoria Lu Jung-chi, a prominent art critic and writer in Taiwan:

> The 1990s have so far seen increasingly bizarre art in a stylistic sense, and a hesitant overall sense of human development as humanity wavers back and forth on the brink of change, unable to decide where to turn.
>   In the early 1990s, together with the diversification of political views and fracture of social mores, culture displayed unprecedented diversity in Taiwan. Art promotion, formerly the exclusive territory of officialdom, was opened to participation from all sectors of society to become a diversified order. . . . artists became prime movers in artistic promotion.[2]

The end of martial law freed up the male artist from his parlor art. Many would draw women to express their views on sexual identity, or political resistance. Ho

Chun-ming, born in 1963 in Chia-yi, graduated from Taiwan's National Institute of Art. His *Costs of Desire* embraced porno-pop imagery to depict a world gone mad with lust, pain, and torture. Regarding one of his ink drawings that depicts a rather vulgar birthing process, he commented on the idea that the separation from women was fatal.

The most infamous case of politicizing the nude female was initiated by Chang Chen-yu. Then Taipei mayor Chen Shui-bian appointed the maverick painter Chang Chen-yu to the position of director of the Taipei Fine Arts Museum. His tenure term lasted for only nine months, from September 1995 to June 1996. Chang, born in 1957 to a Hakka family in Taichung, studied art in Taiwan's National Normal University and at the State University of New York (1987). Artistically he is best known for his nudes. Intellectually, he is a neo-Marxist. After years of hiding his thoughts under martial law, he stated his manifesto in the late 1990s without apology or fear from arrest, detention, or torture:

> I have the responsibility to make the art world involved in justice. Art must be spontaneous and not be ruled by colonial and cultural hegemonists. If our society is run by these forces, then we will live in a bad eco-system and not survive. My nudes are not painted for an artistic reason. I do not put clothes on my young female images. Clothes indicate social status and class meaning. A nude represents everyone's state of mind. And most of my nudes are teenagers because this is the most curious stage of life. (Interview with the artist, Taipei, 1998)

Of course, he was attacked by the politicians who stressed Taiwan's links with tradition. The city council, composed of pro-mainlander parties, insisted that Chang should resign. He did, and his published works were withdrawn from the museum's bookshop.

Meanwhile, on the wall in Mayor Chen's living room was a four-by-three-foot painting by Chang Chen-yu entitled *Under Martial Law*. Clearly revealing the style of his mentor, Balthus, Chang portrays a naked teenager kneeling over two open books—a small Western book tucked inside a large, traditionally bound Chinese text. A red imperial or colonial chair obstructs the view of her body between her knees and her stomach. The chair represents the dictator whose absent presence still threatens the vulnerable areas of her naked body. The young woman is reading a small "unauthorized" book that she can hide in the larger text on the Chinese classics. She reads in an awkward kneeling position, with one leg half-raised, and the other receiving the force of gravity on her kneecap. Her off-balanced position displays the fact that she cannot really stand up for her own views, and yet she is willing to engage in a subversive activity in order to develop her own identity. Chang's allegory is almost as direct as his oral ideological testimony. The colonial chair represents the mainlander government that has colonized Taiwan; the nude body represents all Taiwanese who have been forced to succumb to the Chinese educational and cultural system; the red color of the chair represents Chinese chauvinism. The title, *Under Martial Law*, refers not only to the legal tyranny from 1947–87, but, more important, to the spiritual and emotional subjugation under mainlander rule.

Both Ho's and Chang's works are utilitarian, using the female body to express their respective ideologies and commitment. Although similar in function to Chinese traditional art, their art can be viewed as revolutionary because it breaks the pattern of viewing women just for the consumer tastes of men. Women are no longer a utensil to promote the male world. The art of these two artists opens up the workhouses that kept female artists reproducing classical styles of calligraphy and nature painting.

In the last twelve years Taiwan's female artists have displayed a diverse group of identities. Initially, many eschewed the utilitarianism of direct political commentary. Their collective experience made them wary of being used by yet another powerful institution. Some women did engage in explicit sexual identity searches; others took up the issues concerning pornography; and others returned to the traditional images but with a luxurious or modernistic flair that openly challenged the way of the traditional masters. Women artists in Taiwan are just getting acquainted with their art forms, their relationships to the history of Taiwan, the history of the feminist movement, and the history of the international art scene. The term "feminist" is preferable to the term "female" or "woman" because the latter terms are still closely identified with traditional Chinese gender roles. Being a "feminist" artist is not necessarily a statement of a specific style, but is a statement of a sense of separation from Chinese tradition. While "feminist" suggests a struggle against standard norms, "female" or "woman" is just a taxonomic term that places the artist within the Chinese body politic.

What will follow is only an introduction to four different female artists. It is neither an attempt to create an organizing frame of reference nor an attempt to channel them into a narrow definition of female art. Many other artists could have been chosen. But these four signify for me that part of feminist art that attempts to express deep, personal feelings of freedom. Gender becomes the focus, but not necessarily in the scatological and porno-pop manner of self-indulgence by male artists to shock the viewer. The consumer is "seduced" by the subtlety, the sense of feeling, and the invitation to enjoy the textures of reality and dreams.

Four Artists

Yan Ming-huy

The earliest expressions of feminist art occurred in the late 1980s and were derivative from Western modern themes. Yan Ming-huy was born in 1956 in Pu-tze, Taiwan, and studied at the State University of New York, Albany. She "was the first female artist in Taiwan to express an explicitly feminist creative consciousness."[3] Yan's *Three Apples*, completed in 1988, depict two large Washington Delicious apples with a slice of apple with an exposed seedpod squeezed between

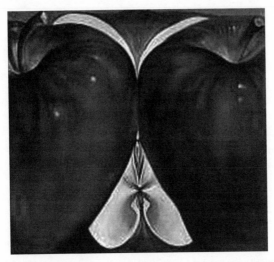

Yan Ming-Huy, "Three Apples," 1998. Oil on canvas. (Used with permission of the artist)

them. Georgia O'Keefe's legacy is easily discernable in the magnification of the fruit's eroticism. The large, formal symbol of a red Delicious apple is associated with Western ideas, the natural world, and a gateway of oral pleasure. The close-up of the apples' redness juxtaposed to the seedpod and its obvious vaginal form creates a subliminal message. But this message is not broadcast to an eager carnal audience. The painting is just the result of an observation of an apple. It may symbolize Eve, seduction, or sensuality, but it is not a piece of propaganda that has a direct message. Its meaning is multilayered. Its message must be interpreted by the viewer. Yan's feminist art emphasizes the natural environment—its texture and its double entendres.

Chen Hsin-wan

Chen Hsin-wan, born in Taichung in 1951, allied her paintings with the spontaneity of dance movements. Her 1992 painting *In Search of Life* co-opts a calligraphic style of ink on paper to break from the rigid structural traditions of the brush stroke in order to create an aesthetic statement for freedom. The brush strokes' natural flow suggests that the ink is controlled by a spontaneous pull of gravity. There is a grace and serenity in the narrow descending strokes that remind one of antennae seeking contact with and explanation of the world. The energy of the painting derives from a sense of the traditional Wu-wei (i.e., the doctrine of "inaction") of Chinese Taoist expressionism. There is no outlined or premeditated form. This painting engages in pure expression liberated from formalized figures, and is designed to promote a personal search without any external authority.

Chen Hsin-wan, "In Search for Life," 1992. Ink on paper, each 140 x 70 cm. Collection of Taipei Fine Arts Museum. (Used with permission of the artist)

Chen's drip method engages the viewer into thinking about the natural flow of life. It reminds one of Helen Frankenthaler's method of soaking the paper and dripping the ink. This style enforces the conclusion that the artist does not control his or her own creation. Chen's style is a statement against the political, social, and economic controls that seem to confront and possibly subjugate the Taiwanese citizen caught up in the tentacles of rapid modernization. It is a call for each person to find his or her personal energy and movement and to roam free.

Wu Mali

Wu Mali, born in 1957 in Taipei, graduated in 1986 from the National Academy of Arts in Düsseldorf. She became known at first for her translations of German Dadaist texts. Rather than attacking the icons directly, Ms. Wu employs allegorical and symbolic expressions to break down the original meanings of words or traditions to mock or satirize Taiwan's plunge into capitalism. Her 1991 installation *Prosperity Car* showrooms a car painted entirely in gold made out of two large geometric blocks, representing the cab of the car, and placed on four tires with gold hubcaps. On the hood of the car is a red bow like the teased-up wrapping tape on a present. The installation of a boxy car is a parody on Taiwan's hyper-industrialization. The car is hollow, yet covered with opaque gold paint so that a driver or passenger, if any, cannot be seen. There is no place to enter, and no hinged and functioning doors. The irony is that in China the color gold represents permanency and wealth. The "Made in Taiwan" label has made Taiwan wealthy, but to what end? There is a complete dislocation with the natural, with the organic, and with life itself.

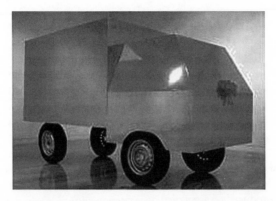

Wu Mali, "Prosperity Car," 1991. Installation mixed media. (Used with permission of the artist)

The attachment of the red bow to the hood of the model car reminds one of the kiss of Bishop Lamourette. This cleric, with the burlesque stagelike name of "a passing infatuation," was a deputy in the National Assembly during the terror of the French Revolution. At the height of the legalistic denunciations, he called upon all the deputies and officials, including the king, to kiss each other in order to show signs of affection and love for one another. After the kissing, the Assembly began to devour its own with the use of the guillotine. This historical event could match any Dadaist history. Ms. Wu's Dadaism is expressed in the presentation of a wrapping commonly used to be the flourish on a present. This bow is attached to the cold inanimate vehicle without a driver and without any visible drive shaft to give it motion. It is a useless hunk of ersatz gold, which cannot nurture life and whose presence seems to substitute for the gods of old. It says, "Worship me with your sacrifice of your life for wealth. Make me into a gift for your civilization, then go out and put your head under the guillotine of the Taiwan Miracle."

Ms. Wu's return to Taiwan was filled with social protest and political activism. She combined the artistic and social criticism of her mentor, Joseph Beuys. Beuys was the most famous post–World War II conceptualist German artist. Ms. Wu studied in Düsseldorf in the 1980s and associated herself with Beuys's Zeit Geist (Time Spirit) school. On the one hand, Beuys condemned Germany's genocidal policies prior to and during the war. On the other hand, he was not openly propagandistic. His method and message were to find simple artifacts and then find paradisiacal and arcane references to the real world. He would surround his work with vast areas of space in order to isolate the object from reality, and thus examine it in a pure state. His artifacts would usually be broken or withered objects. These would be products that were no longer useful, and their role in the art would often be inscrutable. Often there would be writings that were either unintelligible or indecipherable.

Beuys's indelible contribution to Ms. Wu's work is apparent in the way she isolates the car in a full corner of the museum. Her motorless car on a museum floor, kissed by a bouquet that will fade in the sun or be covered by the dust from the polluted air, highlights its bizarre value in our motorized society.

Ms. Wu's studies abroad coincided propitiously with the advent of installation art. Experimentation with new forms of art, which included crossing over into various other forms of media, was fueled by strong political and social iconoclasm. The primary target was the art world itself; the new artists wanted to reject its commodification of art. They did not want their art or self-images to be directly marketable, nor demeaned with a "for sale" sign. Their resentment toward the art dealers and the elite art institutions was manifested in the impermanence of their installations. Their momentary art was set up with materials or in a manner that could not be reproduced or displayed on someone's living-room wall. This art had no investment value. It would only wither or become soiled with age. It was too big, too bulky, and, with mixed-media arrangements, too loud or unwieldy to be packaged, moved, or arranged in a storage area or hung decoratively in someone's living space.

This type of art best reflected the pluralistic, temporary, and experimental existence of modern society. This form of art became the darling of many who sought to connect issues of ethnicity, gender, and access with the compelling political questions of modernization and individual integrity. Installing a room filled with music and images, or a corridor filled with videos and apparitions, forced the observer to relate the experience to his or her own life. The installation provided the viewer with a mixture of reality of being there and of texture—walking through or around the constructed art form; and of dreams—seeking to understand the work in a nonrational way. And, finally, once the exhibit was over, the opportunity to experience the event was gone forever.

It may be premature to conclude that installation art can find support from Taiwan's cultural tradition. Without supportive quantitative documentation, it may be far afield to suggest that the shamanistic tradition of public sacred theater, the popularity of Taiwanese puppet shows and folk opera, and the open-air fairs of traditional Taiwanese cults and performances will make the histrionic and installation art acceptable and appreciated.

Ms. Wu's 1997 installation called *Epitaph* creates a room: two walls with written messages border a large video screen at the end of the hallway. The screen has images of the ocean churning on rocks. We are once again looking at the artistic artifact through the space of a corridor with a vision of endless sky and ocean at the far end. The title, *Epitaph*, refers to the February 28, 1947, massacre of Taiwanese by Nationalist government troops. The ocean video was made at Keelung Harbor—the site where many corpses were dumped into the ocean waters. The purpose of the "Epitaph" is to provide condolence to the female victims. Ms. Wu's walled calligraphy calls upon us to think of the women who died and suffered. On one wall we are asked to empathize and identify with the suffering of the women in a man's world: "Her sorrow has always been our sorrow." On the other wall is a

Wu Mali, "Epitaph," 1997. Installation video, sandblasted glass. (Used with permission of the artist)

short inscription: "His/tory has been revised—the rioter may become the hero/ How about her story?" Like her German mentor, she calls on us to find meanings within ourselves and not in the dogma of outside authorities. We are left to engage with the installation as though it were a shrine—the rhythms of nature at a distance further displace us from the present by electronic technology. We are in a timeless tomb, and we leave it, carrying only our emotional reactions to the induced dreams. No one would want to take the piece home and put it in the corridor to our own bedroom.[4]

Chiu Tse-yan

Chiu Tse-yan was born in Ping-tung, Taiwan, in 1961 and graduated from National Taiwan Normal University in 1984. She has developed a surrealist probe into the flesh of Taiwan's beastly economic and political body. Utilizing charcoal drawings that are illuminated at strategic points by an intense spotlight, she connects herself to the Zen tradition of using black, gray, and brown. There are no erotic reds or distancing blues—no heat and no depth. The mysticism of these Zen paintings induce an emotional quality that is subdued, and rejects the emotional impact for the world of the irrational or surreal.

Chiu's "Dreamland of Night Walk" was shown in 1993 in an exhibition entitled *Animals and Their Souls* at the Taiwan Gallery. The drawing appears three-dimensional: The somber chalk-white moonlike landscape reveals a deep hole in the shape of an off-centered cross. Inside this excavation is a partially obscured egg formation. And above the massive hole a wolf is leaping into the air. Behind the muzzle, in the dark sky, a bright light shimmers.

Although neither expressing the traditional values of feminist art in terms of sexual identity nor of political protest, Chiu's work deserves due recognition for qualities that have been developed by women who are trying to reach new levels of

Chiu Tse-yan, "Dreamland of Night Walk," 1993. Charcoal on paper. (Used with permission of the artist)

understanding about themselves and their society—the eerie abyss, the elliptical shape of the egg contrasted to the rough edges of the sunken cross, the absence of human beings. Chiu complements the Taiwanese feminist approach to gender by blurring gender roles. What is the meaning of the juxtaposition of the leaping wolf over the partially submerged egg? Why is the hole shaped like a sunken yet misshaped cross? The work's use of organic, natural forms with its use of gray clearly marks it in the category of feminist texts that favors components of organic and symbolic naturalism. Chiu's art expresses dreams of silence and of wonder, encouraging the viewer to look inside oneself. Its cold, dark presentation creates a quiet mysticism that is nurturing, and is not a call to action.

Conclusion

Art provides a pattern to consciousness. It is out of the mind's repository that all things are created. What appears almost incredible is the rapidity and ingenuity with which Taiwan's artists react to their life experiences. Although they never seem to be at a loss to create innovative artistic products, it is obvious that they have not yet fully discovered their own voice. The female artists of the nineties primarily received their training from Chinese male artists in studios that still featured the classics of Chinese traditions or abroad in Europe and the Americas. The new, younger female artists will have studied from their female mentors. They will produce a very different type of Taiwanese art—one that will become more distant from both traditional China and the West. As we come to appreciate, discuss, and recognize Taiwanese female artists' interpretations of the changing realities of life, we too will expand our sensitivities and perceptions about historical memory, the reality of change, and of the appreciation for the future. Their art will soon contribute to visions of ourselves, and to new patterns of consciousness. The artistic creations and expressions of the next generation of Taiwanese female artists will register on our own emotional compasses. We will hold onto their visions as our own. Their freedom to follow the paths to their own discoveries will become inextricably related to our own freedoms to interpret and communicate the aesthetic value of our own experiences. A true Taiwanese art will become part of the internationalism of artistic expression that we can all appreciate and draw upon for our own depictions of reality and our own source of dreams.

Notes

1. See Liao Wen, "Tumultuous History of China's Feminist Values and Art." *Chinese Contemporary Art* online magazine, 1998; available at www.chinese-art.com/volume1issue2.

2. "New Art, New Tribes." In *The Contemporary Art of Taiwan* (Sydney, NSW: G+B Arts International, 1995), 74.

3. Victoria Y. Lu, "Striving for a Cultural Identity in the Maze of Power Struggles: A Brief Introduction to the Development of Contemporary Art of Taiwan." In *Inside Out: New Chinese Art*, ed. Ming-Lu Kao (Berkeley: University of California Press for the San Francisco Museum of Art, 1998), 170.

4. Correspondence with Wu Mali.

Conclusion

16

Women's Liberation Under "East Asian Modernity" in China and Taiwan

Historical, Cultural, and Comparative Perspectives

Catherine S.P. Farris

Introduction: What Is "Women's Liberation"?

Is the idea of women's liberation a cross-culturally valid, universal category, or, merely a concept derived from and embedded in Western political and philosophical discourses and traditions? Today in the Chinese societies of both the People's Republic of China (PRC) and the Republic of China on Taiwan (ROC) (hereafter, Taiwan), there is much discussion about the nature and significance of "women's liberation." But what does this concept mean to people in these Chinese societies? The emancipation of women is usually considered as part of the larger historical process of "modernization." I follow Stevan Harrell (1994: 166) in taking "modernity to be a set of characteristics shared to some extent by all industrial societies," and including two levels of transformation: the material and the ideational. The "material factors are perhaps determinative, or at least necessary, conditions for the emergence of the ideational changes. But in practice, they interact" (Harrell 1994: 167). Among other changes accompanying modernization, traditional views of and attitudes about women's roles also undergo transformation. While modernization is a global trend, it is not to be equated with "Westernization." Harrell points to the example of Japan as a *modernized* society that has maintained significant *cultural* distinctiveness. Tu Weiming asserts that the rise of Japan and the "four little dragons," namely South Korea, Taiwan, Hong Kong, and Singapore, "as the most dynamic region of sustained economic development since World War II raises challenging questions about tradition in modernity" (Tu 1991: 6–7). The economic success of these societies (the recent financial crisis in Asia notwithstanding), all deeply influenced by Confucian Chinese civilization, suggests to Tu that a distinctively East Asian modernity is emerging, and that mainland China need not abandon tradition wholesale in order to achieve the so-called Four Mod-

Earlier portions of this chapter appeared in "Contradictory Implications of Socialism and Capitalism under 'East Asian Modernity' in China and Taiwan," in *Democracy and the Status of Women in East Asia*, edited by Rose J. Lee and Cal Clark. Copyright 2000 by Lynn Rienner Publishers, Inc.

ernizations. Thus, the interaction of modernization and local traditions should be viewed as a dialectic or dialogic process.

Modernization began in Western countries, which historically have sought and continue to seek both economic and cultural hegemony over the underdeveloped world. As Tani Barlow (1997a: 1) points out, "Colonialism and modernity are indivisible features of the history of industrial capitalism." China is a country that was "semi-colonized" by Western European countries, the United States, and Japan in the nineteenth and first half of the twentieth centuries; so we cannot understand the process of modernization as it has occurred there without reference to colonialism's legacy. The case is somewhat different for Taiwan, which became a Japanese colony as a result of the Sino-Japanese War of 1895 and remained so until the end of World War II. In looking at Chinese societies in the PRC and Taiwan we must not lose sight of the historical meanings of women's liberation and the material circumstances of their lives. This chapter is an anthropologically informed commentary on the processes of women's liberation in the PRC and on Taiwan that is sensitive to critiques of First World readings and allows voices of Chinese women and men to inform the discourse.

Socialist Feminism and the Romance of Chinese Women's Liberation

The history of Chinese women's struggles for liberation since the nineteenth century holds a special place in the mythology of Western feminism. In fact, Rey Chow (1991) argues, Westerners discursively constructed "China" as a feminized space from which to critique the West. In the 1960s and 1970s, many Western feminists were involved in romanticizing socialism and its liberating effects on women. Socialist feminism begins with the classic work of Frederick Engels, *The Origin of the Family, Private Property, and the State*, in which he argues that the rise of private property relations, monopolized by men, reduced women's status to one of dependency within the conjugal family. For Engels, women's liberation from the patriarchal family depended on participation in wage-labor and the socialization of housework and childcare under a socialist system of ownership. Socialist feminists looked in particular to Communist China as that model society in which women had achieved true liberation; in Mao Tse-tung's words, "women hold up half the sky." As Emma Teng points out, a simplistic periodization of "traditional" and postrevolutionary China was used, as socialist feminists "attempted to use the status of women in China as a test case of the viability of socialism for women's liberation" (Teng 1996: 139). For example, Karen Sacks (1975) argues that women's housework and childcare are devalued under capitalism, which treats them as less than social adults. Full social equality for women and men can come about only when family and society are no longer separate economic spheres of society. "Production, consumption, childrearing, and economic decision making all need to take place in a single social sphere—something analogous to the Iroquois *gens* as described by Engels, or to the production brigades of China during the Great Leap

Forward" (Sacks 1975: 234). We shall see, however, that Chinese women did not necessarily experience the Great Leap Forward as liberating.

Today we know that the salutary effects of socialism on women's status must be qualified in a number of ways. In a critique of women's position in socialist societies, Maxine Molyneux argues that "while actually existing socialist states have not eradicated sexual inequality, they have promoted substantial improvements in the position of women" (1981: 167). Further improvements are hindered in part by material constraints of underdevelopment and the rural nature of most of these societies, but, more profoundly, are hindered by "the prevalence in official thinking of conservative ideologies which underlie policy on the family and women's position in it" (Molyneux 1981: 198). For women, new roles in the labor force are simply grafted on to the older roles of housewife and mother, and the burden of domestic labor falls almost completely on women's shoulders. This is the infamous "second shift," suffered by many working women in socialist and capitalist countries alike! Molyneux's characterization of socialist societies in general could well describe women's conflicting roles in the Mao years (1949–1976), which are an even greater burden in the reform era, where the modernization drive has helped to redefine the role of women in Chinese society and the meaning of "women's liberation." Whereas the Maoist vision insisted on equality between the sexes, the demands of production in the reform era, when the PRC is attempting to develop a "socialist-market" economy, relegate women to supportive roles in production, with reproduction of the labor force their main contribution to modernization. Nonetheless, many argue for real progress for women within a socialist framework. It is particularly instructive, therefore, to compare progress toward Chinese women's liberation in the PRC with transformations in Chinese women's status on capitalist Taiwan. On Taiwan, modernization processes have had a generally salutary effect on women's status, such as a rise in educational levels, greater labor force participation and thus economic independence, control over fertility, and greater power within marriage. However, cultural values about the nature of women and their proper place in society endure.

In her book on the "unfinished liberation" of Chinese women, Phyllis Andors (1983) points to scholars who argue that the family is the historical root of women's oppression; thus, the beneficial effects on women's status of economic changes will be limited, absent a fundamental change in family dynamics. Similarly, Gayle Rubin (1975) argues that the oppression of women historically is prior to the rise of capitalism (although capitalist relations make good use of women's unpaid household labor). Rubin notes that Engels also emphasized relations of sexuality; thus, she argues, a focus on kinship systems should be seen as the key to women's secondary status. She draws on the work of anthropologist Claude Lévi-Strauss who argued that human cultural complexes emerged in prehistory with the universal incest taboo, which necessitated that men "exchange" women in marriage. If this is so, then true liberation for women, Rubin concludes, will only come about with a revolution in kinship. Indeed, the Chinese kinship system, embedded in a larger apparatus of hierarchy, appears to be at the root of women's secondary status. Hill Gates shows how women and girls literally *became* commodities in the economy of early modern China (from the tenth century to the end of the nineteenth century) as the traditional tributary mode of production came into increasing conflict with what she calls the "petty capitalist mode of production." "Men could, and frequently did, exchange their female kin for money, whether in marriage, adoption, or sale into slavery or prostitution" (Gates 1989: 799). Chinese women's subordination was supported structurally and ideologically by a patrilineal system of descent, which forced women to "marry out" of their natal family and become the means through which their husband's family reproduced their descent line, and by the principle of patrilocal postmarital residence, in which women went to reside with her new husband and his family (Baker 1980).

Looking at women's status from a cross-cultural perspective, Pasternak, Ember, and Ember (1997) discuss interrelated factors that contribute to women's status in different societies. Although various indicators of women's status are not strongly associated, clusters of related traits can be used to test the predictive value of relative status, including: property control, power of women in kinship contexts, domestic authority, and control over women's marital and sexual lives (citing Whyte 1978: 66–67). The only predictors of higher status for women were female-centered kin groups (matrilineal descent reckoning), female-centered marital residence (matrilocal postmarital residence), and a low level of social complexity. Given that 67 percent of the world's societies in the ethnographic record have patrilocal residence forms, and that there are few extant societies less complex than agricultural states, the prevalence of women's lower status in most societies is not difficult to understand. Ominous for women in Chinese societies is a link between patrilineal descent reckoning, patrilocal residence patterns, and the oppression of women. "The dynamics and economics of family life in pre-industrial patrilocal societies invariably operate to women's disadvantage" (Pasternak et al. 1997: 218). Women's natal families are reluctant to invest in education for daughters, whose productive and reproductive labor will ultimately "belong" to another family. And in pre-industrial societies, the labor of sons in the fields is crucial. In addition, there is typically little in the way of public welfare institutions to support people in old age; hence, they must rely on their grown sons. In traditional Chinese societies, another social structural factor that created bias against girls was that only sons could worship their ancestors and carry on the family line. In the PRC, despite the radical transformations of collectivization in the countryside, which occurred in the 1950s, the rural agricultural economy continued to support a patriarchal social structure. Aspects of the economic reforms, begun in 1978, have actually allowed traditional practices—such as large dowries and bride price, and also female infanticide and neglect—to reemerge. In Taiwan, large extended families wherein the young were subordinated to the old and women to men have largely disappeared, but important elements of the patrilineal principle remain.

Both socialist and capitalist modernization processes in the PRC and in Taiwan have indisputably improved the status of women, while the Chinese family has adapted by playing dual roles of a refuge *from* capitalism and a refuge *for* patriarchy.

Identity Politics

Can Western scholars such as myself represent the experiences of women in China and Taiwan without distorting, exploiting, or, colonizing them? Chandra Mohanty has critiqued Western feminist scholars' focus on "the extreme nature of Chinese patriarchy" as part of a phenomenon that marginalizes "Third World women" and that represents "a means not only of understanding cultural differences but also of asserting the superiority of women's status in the West" (1991, cited in Teng 1996: 125). As a Western feminist and an anthropologist, this dilemma is one that I struggle with in my own scholarly research and writing on Chinese societies and women's experiences there.[1] Are "women's liberation," "gender equality," or "sexual harassment" culture-free categories that can be applied to any society? Or, are they categories derived from a Western, and, more specifically, an American cultural tradition, categories that we attempt to fit onto indigenous ones only with difficulty and distortion? On the other hand, is there any "culture-free" place to stand, from which to observe our own, or other, societies? For example, on Taiwan, the term for "sexual harassment," *hsing sao-jao*, clearly is a new coinage, borrowed from American English. I first heard it from a university-educated woman when I was on Taiwan in 1983. But the *lao-pai-hsing* (the common folk) had no clear idea of what it referred to. Instead, they spoke of *ch'ih tou-fu* ("eating someone's tofu") and *ch'ih ping-ch'i-ling* ("eating someone's ice-cream"), that is, to grope or ogle someone, usually a woman. Urban women on Taiwan at that time seemed to accept these behaviors, usually by strange men, as an annoying but inevitable facet of going out in public. What is the Taiwanese public's response to Western-educated intellectual women who impose this Western-derived concept of *hsing sao-jao* onto workplace relations between the sexes? We need to think more critically about the nature of culture contact and the resulting adoption and assimilation of foreign concepts into Chinese cultures on Taiwan and in the PRC. That is, we should not assume that Chinese intellectuals or the general public (two groups that might well have different ideas about these terms) mean the same thing by terms such as *hsing sao-jao* or *liang-hsing p'ing-teng* as American scholars do when they refer to "sexual harassment" or "gender equality."

A Chinese man from the PRC, upon hearing that I was a "feminist," told me that in modern Chinese society, men are disadvantaged compared to women (*nan-jen pu ju nü-jen*). He explained that, although men occupy most positions of authority in politics and business, in the home, women are the absolute authorities. I inquired sweetly, "Isn't this just the traditional division of labor *nan chu wai, nü chu nei* (man rules the outside, woman, the inside)?" "Oh, no," he explained, "because in traditional society women had only limited authority within the home, while men had ultimate authority even there. But today in the domestic realm, what women say goes!"

Although this example portrays the thinking of an educated mainland Chinese man, I would argue that he probably speaks for many men and women in Chinese society on Taiwan as well. The value system that he articulates is one of *gender complementarity*, rather than equivalence, and is one that points a fundamental difference between feminist movements in the United States and in Chinese societies. The mainstream feminist movement in the United States, previously dominated by educated, white middle-class women, has focused on *gender equality*, with the goal of a "gender-blind" society, in which ability, talent, and interest, not gender, are the basis for social roles, including occupation and leadership positions, as well as familial roles. Women of color in the United States have long criticized mainstream feminism not only for lack of attention to such factors as class, ethnicity, and sexual orientation, which may divide women, and also have criticized it for the selfish individualism they perceive behind demands for women's "rights." Where is the connection to family and community, they ask, in this vision of gender equality (e.g., Maxine Baca Zinn and Bonnie Dill 1994; Johnnetta Cole 1986)? I have no doubt that many Chinese women in Taiwan and in the PRC would echo these sentiments. Further, in Taiwan, to the extent that the public perceives the women's movement as influenced by and "buying into" the Western vision of gender equality and individual rights, it will continue to meet opposition from some men and women and to be dismissed as a vulgar Western import, as a form of "cultural imperialism," that Chinese culture can do without. Nonetheless, in both Chinese societies, some form of women's liberation is considered legitimate. On Taiwan, some women's organizations work willingly within the status quo, while others continually challenge it. In the PRC, despite the lack of social activism, a semi-autonomous women's studies movement (*fu-nü-hsüeh*) calls for a feminism "with Chinese characteristics," at the same time that they are eager to "link the rails" with an international women's movement (Zheng 1997).

As foreign scholars, we must collaborate with native scholars and lay people to develop explanations of women in Chinese societies that are designed for consumption by the English-speaking world. We must also strive to keep in touch with native scholarship and popular writings *in Chinese* that address issues relevant to our research. To avoid reproducing structures of cultural hegemony, we should seek a dialogue with Chinese people in the PRC and on Taiwan that will result in increased intercultural understanding. I agree with Cole that, "Even when there is evidence of female oppression among women of diverse backgrounds, it is important to listen to the individual assessment which each woman makes of her own condition, rather than assume that a synonymous experience of female oppression exists among all women" (1986: 5).

Are these two Chinese societies truly comparable? Kuang-hua Hsieh and Robert Burgess (1994) point out the paucity of comparative studies on women's status in the PRC and on Taiwan. At the same time, there is a real sense in which we are comparing "apples and oranges," as the cliché goes, or, more appropriately, perhaps, "apples and watermelons," in terms of the relative size of these two societies. Whatever one may wish to argue is or should be Taiwan's political status in the world today, historically at least it was merely a province of China. To compare a society of 21 million with one of 1.3 billion is full of misleading possibilities. If our only interest is in the question, "Does the status of women improve more under a socialist political economy or under a capitalist one?" then it would be more accurate to compare the PRC with India, the world's largest democracy and a free market economy in the early stages of industrialization, and a country with a history similar to China's as an ancient civilization with a large, impoverished, and poorly educated rural population. Here the relative status of rural and urban women in the PRC compares favorably in many ways to the status of women in India under an enduring legacy of patriarchy.[2] However, here we are interested in comparing the relative strength of similar cultural forms—derived from Chinese civilization—in interaction with radically different political economies, issues of scale notwithstanding.

In the sections below, I begin with a brief summary of the extent to which sustained contact between China and Western countries in the nineteenth and early twentieth centuries acted as a catalyst for the transformation of women's status and roles, as the "liberation of women" came to be associated with a modern state that the Chinese yearned to establish. This is followed by a discussion of the Republican period (1912–1949), with attention to contrasts between the policies and the rhetoric of the Kuomintang (KMT, Nationalist Party)-led government and the young Chinese Communist Party (CCP). I will also briefly review the progress of women in colonial Taiwan during the first half of the twentieth century. We then turn to a contrast between the radical Maoist period (1949–76) in the PRC and the take-off stage of industrial development on Taiwan (1949–75). Finally, I contrast the PRC during the ongoing reform era, begun by Teng Hsiao-p'ing in 1978, and Taiwan as a newly industrializing country (NIC) and a newly emerging democracy. It is necessary to compare the policies and actions of the CCP and the KMT toward women, as the latter's policies were transplanted to Taiwan in the postwar period. Yet Taiwan's history diverged from that of the mainland in 1895 and its progress toward modernization therefore—at least for the first half of the twentieth century—was primarily a result of the colonial influence of Japan, a newly industrialized Asian power, and not the Western powers. There are many enduring cultural values about the nature of women and their proper places in society that the PRC and ROC regimes share. But there are also important differences, which are contingent upon their separate lines of historical and social development. Finally, we consider the question, is there a "Chinese woman," whose liberation we in the West can once again attempt to measure?

Historical Perspectives: Women and the Birth of "Modern China"

Reform and Rebellion in the Ch'ing Dynasty

There is some evidence that prehistoric Chinese society was matrifocal; however, many archaeologists dispute this (Pearson and Underhill 1987). As far back as the historical record goes, China has been an agrarian society with patrilineal and patriarchal extended families as the core unit. However, the "myth" of matriarchy plays key symbolic roles today. In the PRC, it fits in with the Marxist view of historical progress, as derived from the nineteenth century anthropologist Lewis Henry Morgan, in which matriarchy preceded patriarchy in historical evolution. And in Taiwan, some feminist writers draw on the "golden age" of Chinese matriarchy as a vision of the future more than of the past (e.g., Jen 1978). Regardless of an imagined past, both on Taiwan and in the PRC today a patriarchal social structure remains dominant. Judith Stacey (1983) argues that "patriarchal-socialism" continues to limit women's options in the PRC, while Rita Gallin (1984: 398) asserts that on Taiwan there is a convenient "marriage of patriarchal ideology and contemporary capitalism." Our saga begins in the mid-nineteenth century, when the Ch'ing (Manchu) dynasty was in deep decline after the Opium Wars with Great Britain and other Western powers. What was the reaction of Western colonialists to Confucian patriarchal China?

When Europeans, particularly the British, began the forcible opening up of China in the nineteenth century, many were appalled at the apparent low status of Chinese women. Western representations of Chinese women as "other" go back to this period, when Western missionary women and men saw it as one of their civilizing duties to free Chinese girls and women from the bonds of Confucian patriarchy; female subordination to them was starkly indexed by practices such as footbinding, concubinage, arranged marriages, female infanticide, and the buying and selling of girls and women. Teng (1996: 121) notes that nineteenth-century missionaries in China who concerned themselves with Chinese women's lives emphasized "their victimization and weakness," and pointed to Confucian ideology as the basis of female subordination, inscribed in classical precepts such as the "three obediences and four virtues" (*san ts'ung ssu teh*). But while nineteenth-century Westerners saw women as an oppressed class, Barlow (1994) argues that prior to the imposition of Western colonialism in China, there was no essentialized category of "women" (*funü*). Rather, women were signified by their relationships within the family, as daughter, sister, wife, mother, and so on. Waltner, however, suggests that, "there is ample evidence that some thinkers in premodern China conceptualized gender as a semi-autonomous category, linked to roles but on occasion transcending them" (1996: 423). Whatever the native system of personhood might have been, it is clear that Chinese reformers during the Ch'ing Restoration period (1860–1898) were challenged by categories derived from the West. As these Chinese searched for an elusive modernity, China's weakness in the face of Western military and technological superiority came to be inscribed onto the bodies of Chinese women, so that their weakness and subordination became a metaphor for China's, and to progress to modern nationhood meant to strengthen women's status.

One of the earliest indigenous calls for the liberation of Chinese women occurred as part of the Taiping Rebellion in the 1850s. Its leader, Hung Hsiu-ch'üan, was a scholar who had failed the government examinations twice, and, having been exposed to Protestant fundamentalism in a missionary school, fell ill and had visions that he was the younger brother of Jesus Christ. He believed that he had been sent by God to rescue China from both Westerners and Manchus and to establish a "Heavenly Kingdom of Great Peace," the *T'ai-p'ing T'ien-kuo*. Kazuko Ono (1989) notes that as part of his revolutionary message he called for the collectivization of land equally distributed to all people, men and women alike. Great numbers of the downtrodden, including many women, flocked to his banner. Separate women's military camps were set up and women contributed to the cause as soldiers or as laborers. Footbinding was outlawed, love matches, rather than the traditional arranged marriages, were common, and adultery was forbidden for both women and men (Hung himself, however, was exempted from this provision and had many concubines). Although the Taiping rebels finally fell in 1864, Ono asserts that it was "the starting point for the next one hundred years of revolution in China against imperialism and traditional society" and that the emancipation of women began here, in a rural revolution.

During the Ch'ing Restoration and the Hundred Days' Reform Movement of 1898, Chinese reformers such as K'ang Yu-wei and Liang Ch'i-ch'ao called for the emancipation of women, encouraging antifootbinding societies, the education of girls, and so on. These Chinese nationalists came to inscribe onto the bodies of Chinese women and girls the backwardness of China compared to the West. How could a country such as China, in which females have such an inferior position, compete with the modernizing and industrializing Western countries? Liang Ch'i-ch'ao argued for women's education on the grounds that they would no longer be "parasites," living off the labor of others, and, if educated, they could teach their children the rudiments of learning before the age of ten. He also admired the Western habit of drilling women in calisthenics, because it would produce healthier babies (Ono 1989: 26–27). Reformers like Liang understood the emancipation of women, "not as something derived from rights women intrinsically possessed as human beings," but as something to enrich the nation and strengthen the military (Ono 1989: 28). Similarly, K'ang Yu-wei, the leading adviser to the emperor during the Hundred Days' Reform, created an antifootbinding society as early as 1883, and wrote a memorial to the emperor in 1898 to outlaw the practice because "it weakens the race hereditarily" and "it invites the slander of those other nations known as 'barbarians'" (cited in Ono 1989: 33). Women's liberation had become a trope of modernity, and the urgency of reform and revitalization of the nation would only become more pressing in the decades preceding and following the overthrow of the monarchy in 1911.

At the beginning of the twentieth century and after the failure of the Hundred Days' Reform, many Chinese intellectuals and members of the elite class, men and women alike, despaired of a reformed monarchy and looked instead to either a Western-style liberal democracy, or, more radically, a socialist society. By this time, women's liberation and the nationalist enterprise were inextricably linked. Liang Ch'i-ch'ao argued that "in order to secure the liberation of the nation and the people, women first . . . had to begin by gaining their own independence" (Ono 1989: 57). The woman who did so most famously was Ch'iu Chin (1875–1907), who abandoned her husband from an arranged marriage—and her two children— and went to Japan to study. Once there she joined several revolutionary organizations of overseas Chinese that had been established by Sun Yat-sen and were dedicated to overthrowing the Ch'ing dynasty. She also advocated the liberation of Chinese women. Returning to Shanghai, China, in 1907, she began publication of *Chung-kuo nü-pao* (Chinese Women's Newspaper) to promote women's education. Next she became a teacher at a girls' school in Chekiang province, keeping in touch with local secret societies and preparing for an armed revolt. The plans for the revolt leaked out and she was captured and executed on July 25, 1907, at the age of thirty-two (Ono 1989: 59–63). After Ch'iu Chin died, other women anarchists organized the Society for the Reinstatement of Women's Rights, which attacked the bourgeois women's movement and the family as the root of women's oppression. As the 1911 Revolution approached, women formed their own army units to take part, or participated in medical units and the like (Ono 1989: 73–80). After the fall of the monarchy and the establishment of the Republic of China in 1912, these women activists and loyal nationalists expected to be rewarded with enfranchisement and equal rights. They were, however, to be cruelly disappointed.

Women's Rights and Republican Politics

At first, Sun Yat-sen, the "father of the Chinese revolution," recognized the call for women's rights as appropriate, but after the north-south compromise, which made the northern warlord Yüan Shih-k'ai president instead of Sun, his advocacy of gender equality became tepid. In the provisional constitution, as Ono (1989: 82) notes, women's rights were not specifically mentioned. Surely Ch'iu Chin and other women nationalists had not spilled their blood alongside their male compatriots only to be denied equal treatment under the new Republic. Women's rights' advocates stormed the parliament in Nanking where women's suffrage was being debated, caused a ruckus, broke windows, pushed around the guards. In these actions, they were greatly influenced by the radical women's suffrage movement in England, which was agitating for the vote at the same time, and when the British suffragettes heard about the Chinese women's actions, they sent a congratulatory telegram. The actions of the Chinese women were in vain, however. When Sun's Revolutionary Alliance merged with other, more conservative parties to form the Nationalist Party, two items were expunged from the party platform: Sun's "people's livelihood" (often seen as too socialist) and equal rights for men and women. To his credit, Sun delivered a speech in which he stressed that eventually gender equality would have to be legally recognized "if the civilization of the nation was to progress" (Ono 1989: 87–88). However, by this time, Sun's diminished authority could not carry the day. Christina Gilmartin (1993: 311) points out that most of the women who were active in the 1911 Revolution withdrew from politics shortly after that, either to raise children or because of their disenchantment with party politics after the KMT betrayal. Only a few of these women found their way back into politics with the outbreak of student protests in 1919, during the famous May Fourth movement.

When the Chinese public discovered that the Allies had betrayed China after World War I, by secretly granting Japan the right to its illegally seized territory in the former German concession in Shantung province, students in Peking marched on T'ien-an-men Square to protest the Versailles treaty. This event marks the beginning of the modern student movement in China, and greatly increased political activities and nationalistic feelings all over the country in urban areas. During the so-called May Fourth era that followed, Chinese intellectuals desperately sought solutions to perceived Chinese weakness in the face of the Western onslaught. Tu Weiming (1991) sees "the May Fourth intellectual dilemma" as an "intertwining of nationalism (patriotism) and iconoclasm (antitraditionalism)," which, he argues, is evoked in the current debates over the opening to the West during the reform era in the PRC, which began in 1978. During the May Fourth era, the Confucian moral order was attacked, including customs of arranged marriages, concubinage, prostitution, footbinding, and the double moral standard for men and women. The May Fourth generation advocated the education of women and their participation in public life (Spence 1990: 310–19). In 1924, as part of an alliance between the Nationalist Party and the young Chinese Communist Party, the Central Women's Department was established. Resolutions were passed declaring equal rights for men and women in law, economy, education, and society. However, as Margery Wolf points out, "the demands being made by students and urban intellectuals of the May Fourth era [such as enfranchisement and equal educational opportunities] were realistic for students and urban intellectuals, but they were hopelessly irrelevant to the lives of rural or working class women" (1985: 13).

When the KMT-CCP alliance ended in 1927, the Women's Department was reorganized under the conservative Nationalists. Women's roles were defined as service to the country, to national development, and to the anti-Japanese and anti-Communist fronts. As Croll notes, "The Guomindang Party never ceased to talk about revolution and emancipation, it simply redefined the terms," as "emancipation included the often contradictory demands for a return to the virtues of traditional femininity and new opportunities for professional employment" (1978: 153). During the New Life movement in the early 1930s, for example, "Chinese women were urged to cultivate the 'four virtues' . . . and were told not to be hoodwinked into blindly following feminist ideas" (Spence 1990: 416). Nonetheless, the Nationalist government was concerned about modernizing China and took steps to elevate women's status in the legal code. In Olga Lang's classic work on the changing Chinese family in the early twentieth century, based on research carried out in the mid-1930s, she discussed the new Civil Code for family law that was established in 1931 (Lang 1946: 115–17). The code outlawed arranged marriages and concubinage, males and females were to inherit equally, and divorce was to be available to both women and men. A clear patrilineal principle remained in part; custody of children was automatically given to the father, as they "belonged" to the father's family. Adultery was made an offense equally punishable for men and women, which, on paper at least, did away with the sexual double standard. Because of the limited reach of the KMT government, however, the provisions of the new Civil Code were not widely promulgated.

Despite the new Civil Code, change was slow as old values and practices continued to constrain women's lives. For example, Lang notes that most marriages were still arranged. Some changes in traditional family practices took place in urban areas, mostly in the form of compromises between tradition and the new laws. Parents asked the consent of their children before arranging their marriage, or, children would choose a mate and ask the parents' approval. Surprisingly, Lang found that among those she interviewed, "modern marriages," that is, not arranged, were more often made by working-class industrial workers in Shanghai than by the middle class, whereas the elite maintained strict control over their children's marriage arrangements, no doubt because of the importance of dowry and bride price for this class. Traditional marriage practices continued unchanged among peasants in the countryside—most of whom had never even heard of "modern marriages"—until the Communist victory in 1949 (Lang 1946: 122–25). When the Nationalists lost the civil war in 1949 and retreated to Taiwan, they took with them Republican policies and values about the roles of women in society; this will be discussed in the section below on women on Taiwan.

After the promulgation of the new Civil Code, leading Republican feminists declared that, on the basis of these new constitutional gains, women were emancipated. However, these conservative women leaders feared that women of most classes were not ready for new legal rights; in particular, they were concerned that if marriage and divorce were made easy, "that those without the appropriate education would confuse liberty and license" (Croll 1978: 157). Thus, a new ideal of womanhood was proclaimed, which Croll has dubbed the "feminine mystique" (after Betty Friedan's book) in which the traditional "virtuous wife and good mother" (*hsien-ch'i liang-mu*) roles were glorified. Women were to be educated in order to improve their standards of housekeeping and to better raise their children. As part of the New Life movement's Women's Department, chaired by Soong Mei-ling (Madame Chiang Kaishek), women from the upper classes were encouraged to participate in women's organizations for the improvement of society. At the same time, expanding educational and economic opportunities gave rise to new groups of educated professional and career women, as well as working class women.

Under the impetus of the modernization processes, the roles of women in the urban and periurban areas began to change in the first decades of the twentieth century. Working class women, many of rural background, were an important part of the urban workforce, particularly in the textile mills. Footbinding came to be viewed as unsuitable for a modern labor force and was attacked. As women joined the workforce in large numbers, educational opportunities were also opening up for them. Some women from the elite class were active in the 1911 Revolution and by the time of the Nationalist Revolution of 1925–27, working class and peasant women were active in trade unions, peasant unions, and even the army (Lang 1946: 103–7). However, Croll (1978) notes that the KMT government strongly discouraged women's organizations from becoming politically active, while in schools, outspoken girl "agitators" were attacked as Communists and expelled.

As the economy expanded in the 1930s and 1940s, Croll notes, urban, educated women joined the workforce in increasing numbers, as teachers, clerks, nurses, or professional people such as doctors, lawyers, and journalists. Meanwhile, peasant men and women from the countryside began streaming into the treaty port cities to work in the new factories and swell the ranks of the urban proletariat. Rural and working class women also worked as household servants, wet nurses, peddlers, and entertainers or prostitutes. In particular, as Hershatter (1997) details in her book on prostitution in twentieth-century Shanghai, there was a sharp increase in "modern" forms of prostitution during the Republican era, including work in teahouses, massage parlors, dance halls, bathhouses, and beauty shops. The courtesan system, staffed by déclassé elite women and patronized by elite men, was slowly supplanted by modern "sex work," pursued either full or part time by a large percentage of urban women from all social classes and backgrounds. After the invasion of China by Japan in 1937 and the outbreak of full-scale hostilities, inflation and unemployment rose in the cities and the rural economy deteriorated further. Croll notes that women workers were the first to lose their jobs in the cities, while in the countryside, desperate conditions led to an increase in buying and selling of women and girls. Economic distress also contributed to the rise in prostitution. As Hershatter points out, prostitutes were increasingly portrayed in public discourse both as victims and as embodiments of social dangers, through sexually transmitted diseases (STDs) and the like. The dangers of prostitution became discursively linked with the health of the Chinese "body politic."

All three groups of women in Republican China, educated professional, peasant, and urban working class women "faced increasing discrimination in employment, and conflicting ideologies, traditional, modern, and Western" conflicts, which were particularly apparent in their family lives (Croll 1978: 168). Thus, as Lang shows (noted above), most rural people had never even heard of the marriage and divorce provisions of the new Civil Code, and the traditional subordination of old to young and women to men continued unabated. Working class women in the cities did not necessarily view factory work as liberating, and most indicated a preference for the housewife role. Some factory women did see factory work as an outlet from traditional familial constraints, citing a variety of family problems, such as maltreatment by stepmothers, quarrels with sisters-in-law, husbands, or parents-in-law. However, they also experienced discrimination and maltreatment in the factories and tended to return home once the domestic situation improved (Croll 1978: 174–75).

As the Japanese troops penetrated farther and farther into north China, the Nationalist government could no longer suppress patriotic political movements, including the participation of women. Madame Chiang helped the government mobilize women for the anti-Japanese war as the KMT grudgingly made a second "United Front" with the Chinese Communists, temporarily calling off their civil war to fight the invaders. While the KMT's policy toward women continued to circumscribe their public activities within traditional bounds (with a modern flair), the CCP had been busy organizing rural and working class urban women and men for a much more radical vision of China's future.

Women's Rights and the Early Chinese Communist Party

Gilmartin argues that despite "a radical program on gender transformation," the founders of the Chinese Communist Party, all men, "reproduced and reinscribed central aspects of the existing gender system from the larger society within their own revolutionary party organization" (Gilmartin 1993: 299). The CCP's gender ideology was a synthesis from various sources, most important, May Fourth feminism and the Marxist critique of the family as articulated by Engels, while also including anarchist elements (Gilmartin 1993: 300). After the establishment of the CCP in 1921, the party promoted women's emancipation as part of the socialist transformation of society. Ch'en Tu-hsiu, a founding member of the CCP, had played a key role during the May Fourth era in promoting women's emancipation through his writings in the influential journal *New Youth* and later through the Communist periodical *Labor and Women*. Female Communist Party members were active organizing women workers in the cities and, later, peasant women in the countryside. However, as Gilmartin points out, from the beginning, women had difficulty gaining formal political status and leadership roles in the party except in the women's program, and tended to be influential only as long as they were attached to powerful men within the party hierarchy. Despite their rhetoric of gender equality, many of the male CCP members apparently retained some traditional expectations of gender roles. For example, most male party members assumed that their wives would continue to perform domestic chores and childcare, and expected them to cater to and defer to the men's personal and political activities. These CCP women also contributed to the reproduction of traditional gender roles by gravitating to the roles of organizers and managers within the party structure, at the same time continuing to fulfill the traditional "virtuous wife and good mother" roles within the home. Thus, while the founding fathers of the CCP "were eager to do away with the most brutal forms of gender oppression . . . they were not willing to relinquish decision-making power" (Gilmartin 1993: 322). After the establishment of the Communist state in 1949, a power hierarchy dominated by men continued, while women were relegated to an informal power system through marriage to high-level leaders; the result of which would lead to considerable resentment against women in politics (Gilmartin 1993: 323).

After the KMT's betrayal of the CCP in the First United Front of 1927, in which thousands of party activists—including many women—were slain by the Nationalist Army in conjunction with the infamous underworld Green Gang, the CCP was forced underground and into the rural hinterland. During the Kiangsi Soviet years (1931–34) and later, during the Yen-an period (1934–49), the party leadership wrestled with how to mobilize and emancipate women peasants. Andors (1983: 19–23) reports that the Marriage Law of the Kiangsi Soviet attacked the Confucian patriarchal family by, among other things, granting women freedom of marriage and divorce. When long-oppressed women seized on the divorce option in particular, this engendered sharp resistance from male peasants and also from mothers-in-law. The party began to rethink the route to women's liberation. During the Japanese and civil war years, the main task of the CCP women's movement was to support the army; in the fields, women replaced men who had been recruited and also organized sewing groups to make uniforms and so on. Women's liberation was increasingly portrayed as part of the larger class struggle, and not separate from it (see also Wolf 1985: 14–16). However, "the issue of political rights . . . was kept alive by a group of Western-educated women who had come to Yanan from the urban areas" (Andors 1983: 24). The conflict between party policy and feminism came to a head with the publication of the writer Ting Ling's article, "Thoughts on March 8," that is, International Women's Day, which pointed out contradictory demands on women made by the party. They had to participate in production and also manage household and childcare responsibilities. For this criticism, Ting Ling was struggled against in the 1942 Rectification movement and her feminist viewpoint was declared "outdated and its implications detrimental to revolutionary mobilization" (Andors 1983: 25). The almost all-male leadership of the CCP would discover, when they became China's rulers, that compromises had to be made regarding socialist principles of women's liberation, in order to maintain and solidify their grip on power and to initiate and sustain economic development. Before turning to an examination of the progress of women's liberation in the early days of the PRC and the ROC on Taiwan, I will briefly discuss changes in women's status in colonial Taiwan.

Women and Colonial Modernity on Taiwan (1895–1945)

Although there has been considerable material about colonial Taiwan published by Japanese scholars in Japanese, or, less frequently, in English, it has only been in the past decade that Chinese scholars on Taiwan have explored this historical period. In the early days of KMT rule on Taiwan, no history of "Taiwan" was allowed to be taught in the schools, where education—in the newly mandated "national language" (*kuo-yü*, that is, Mandarin) emphasized the glories of Chinese civilization on the mainland. As Edwin Winckler points out, "the state's main objective was resinicizing the Taiwanese" (1994: 30). Only after the lifting of martial law in 1987 has public discussion of the modern history of Taiwan been allowed. Gold (1996: 1108) notes that an important new trend in cultural circles is "the emergence of a nativist school and the exploration and definition of a Taiwanese identity" through art forms and historical research, and this includes gender studies. Scholars at the Institute of Modern History of the Academia Sinica launched a new journal in 1993, *Research on Women in Modern Chinese History* (Chin-tai Chung-kuo fu-nü shih yen-chiu), which includes new research on women in Japanese-occupied Taiwan. In addition, there have been conference papers and at least one book published in Chinese on aspects of women's lives during this period (Yang 1993).

Japan joined the world's "colonial club"—the first non-Western and Asian nation to do so—when it defeated the Chinese on the Korean mainland in the Sino-Japanese War of 1895. By the treaty of Shimonoseki, Japan gained Taiwan (or Formosa) and a number of outlying islands as a colony. After putting down local resistance by the Chinese and the aboriginal population, the Japanese proceeded to turn Taiwan into a profitable colony as part of its expanding empire. Many of these policies had beneficial effects on the status of women. Transportation and communication systems were built and agricultural research was undertaken; modern processing industries for raw materials were developed. While business profits went to Japan, taxes remained on Taiwan where they were spent on infrastructure and administration. Yu Chien-ming notes that a tight police network was established throughout the island and police were involved in public security, justice, public health, the economy, and education (1996: 11). Chen Ching-chih discusses the Japanese policy of eventual assimilation and points out that the colonial authorities argued this could only occur after the "three major evil customs" on Taiwan—namely, opium-smoking, queue wearing, and footbinding—were eliminated (1994: 33). Most Japanese administrators advocated a gradualist approach to the transformation of Taiwanese customs that they believed were detrimental to the development of the colony.

Improvements in health care and education greatly benefited the populace. Modern hygienic standards were introduced and many contagious diseases were brought under control (Yu 1996). By the 1920s, six years of primary school education—in the Japanese language—was available to urban residents, including girls, although they did not attend in numbers as great as their brothers did. Eventually, middle schools and vocational high schools were open to the Taiwanese so they could be trained as teachers, medical personnel, low-level administrators, and so on. Patricia Tsurumi (1977) estimates that by 1930, 27 percent of the population was literate in Japanese. Women from the middle and upper classes were able to receive education and many joined the workforce as elementary-school teachers, secretaries, nurses, midwives, and in other feminine-type occupations. For example,

Yu Chien-ming (1996) notes that the professionalization of midwifery was part of the public health and educational policies of the Japanese for Taiwan. Furthermore, by the 1920s, children of the elite class, both men and women, could travel to Japan for university education. In Japan, they were exposed to mainland Chinese students and to the great debates of the day over modernization in Asia and the relative value of liberal Western-style democracy, socialism, anarchism, and other Western political philosophies.

For the majority of Taiwan's people, who remained in rural areas, traditional Chinese customs and practices regarding marriage and family, religion, and so on, were generally left undisturbed by the colonial authorities, as long as they did not affect public security or health. Among the rural elite, the large joint families such as those described by Myron Cohen (1976) continued to organize the lives of all family members, and, no doubt, traditional practices of arranged marriages, patrilocal postmarital residence, and the subordination of children to parents and of wives to husbands and to mothers-in-law, continued. Margery Wolf's (1972) descriptions of rural women's lives in Taiwan of the 1950s and 1960s suggest considerable continuity with traditional practices, which regulated and circumscribed the lives of girls and women. This is not to say that social changes did not occur in the rural areas of Taiwan under the Japanese. Arthur Wolf and Chieh-shan Huang (1980) show how the "minor marriage" form (i.e., when a girl is adopted as a baby or small child by her future husband's family), which was quite prevalent in Taiwan in the early twentieth century, gradually declined and disappeared by the 1930s. The decline is attributed to factors such as the growing influence of modernized transportation systems and opportunities in the nonfarm sector, which gave young women as well as men more economic independence from the family. This in turn allowed the couple to rebel against parental authority and refuse an essentially "brother-sister" marriage that many of them found repugnant. However, we still have little information on how Japanese colonial policies affected the lives of rural and working class people in Taiwan.

Recall that the liberation of women became a trope of modernity in the discourse of late Ch'ing dynasty reformers and among May Fourth intellectuals. Hsin-yi Lu asserts that "woman" was "an encompassing sign which signifies the emergence of modernity, as well as the ambivalent colonial mentality, in colonial Taiwan" (1997: 1). Taiwanese students in Japan established a journal, *Taiwan Youth*, in 1920, the mission statement of which "expressed anxiety toward the global modernization inspired by pan-European and Indian nationalist movements" (Lu 1997: 5). The journal called on Taiwanese youth to "wake up" and catch the trend of global transformation, including gender egalitarianism and labor movements. In the journal, the status of women was portrayed as equivalent to Taiwan's backward situation compared to other nations, a theme echoing that of the earlier mainland Chinese intellectuals. According to Lu, some Taiwanese intellectuals accepted a radical view of gender equality including the abolition of the gendered division of labor within the family, while others supported the notion prevalent in Meiji

Restoration Japan that women's domestic roles should be consolidated to strengthen the nation. These positions are similar to those of the Chinese Communists and Nationalists on the mainland, respectively. *Taiwan Youth*, with a new name, moved to Taipei in 1927. On Taiwan, contributors gave speeches and held study meetings all over the island, crucially participating in various social movements: labor, peasant, nationalist, as well as women's emancipation. Writers called for the education of women and their participation in politics, critiqued arranged marriages, polygamy, and the dowry system; one writer called for the establishment of an egalitarian "mutually responsible family." Lu concludes that, contrary to previous readings of the activities of Taiwanese elites during the 1920s and 1930s as anticolonial resistance and a strategy to consolidate a national consciousness, many of these colonial elites had a more problematic relationship with colonialism. They were anxious to participate in global modernity, and women's issues were one new way of thinking that they had to deal with. However, this polyvocal nature of the discourse on women and colonial modernity was soon to be stifled when the KMT regime came to town in 1945.

Women's Status and Economic Development in the Early Postwar Years

In the years between the two World Wars, both the Chinese Communist Party and the KMT made commitments to women's liberation, but backed away from these commitments in practice. After the establishment of the PRC in 1949, China enacted more dramatic reforms concerning women's roles than had the Nationalist government, but again actual social change was less than originally intended. On Taiwan, rapid industrialization significantly altered women's roles, without necessarily "liberating" them from the Confucian patriarchal family, while the terms of Taiwan's incorporation into the world capitalist economy unevenly exploited women beyond class exploitation. I turn first to a discussion of women's lives in the countryside and cities of Mao's China, and then contrast this with Taiwan during the take-off stage of industrialization.

Women in the PRC during the Maoist Era (1949–1976)

After the Communist victory in 1949, the CCP moved to "remold" the populace into citizens of a socialist society. Along with the Agrarian Reform Law, a Marriage Reform Law was promulgated (similar to the Civil Code of 1931 under the Nationalists), which outlawed arranged marriages and concubinage and allowed women to initiate divorce. The continuing power of the patriarchal family in the Chinese countryside was evident during attempts at education of the population concerning the new Marriage Law and the rights of women. At the time, the biggest threat to the peasant farmers was the new divorce law, because it threatened the labor upon which peasant farmers depended, namely, their wives. Men could not support a government that potentially took from them the wives upon whom they depended for productive and reproductive labor. Older women—mothers-in-law—were also against the new divorce law, as it would remove from them a source of household labor. After an initial surge in divorces, the party backed away from implementing this portion of the Marriage Law (Andors 1983: 33–35).

During the 1950s, the CCP also moved to stamp out prostitution, whose historical vestiges were viewed as remnants of feudalism and colonialism and whose modern forms they saw as the scourge of capitalism. According to Hershatter, brothels were first regulated, then made illegal; next, prostitutes were rounded up and put in "labor training institutes." In these institutions, STDs and other health problems of these former prostitutes were corrected; they were taught job skills and were reunited with their families, or given help in finding husbands. In 1958, the PRC declared that it had eradicated prostitution from China, and that this symbolized China's emergence "as a strong, healthy, and modern nation." Hershatter argues, however, that only "publicly visible" prostitution in fact disappeared from China, and that there is ample evidence that forms of prostitution continued in clandestine ways, including work units that supplied women to visiting party officials and even to foreign guests (1997: 304–6).

Under Mao's leadership in the 1950s, the party concentrated on economic development and socialist transformation. Few distinctions were made with regard to gender when ascribing positions for labor. All women were encouraged to leave the home and participate in production as members of the labor force. The aim of this socialist model was to increase economic development as well as aid in the liberation of women. Thus, the government gave "the woman problem" much attention, launching various campaigns to change the patriarchal ideology that had survived for centuries. However, the government was once again confronted with contradictory goals of women's liberation versus the political loyalty of male peasants who had supported the revolution. Norma Diamond (1975a) notes that when women in the rural areas began to criticize male oppression within the family during "speak bitterness" campaigns, the women were persuaded to desist. Other campaigns urged the rural population to understand that women were as good workers as were men. From this period, photographs of women engaged in such "manly" work as electrical repairs on high wires were disseminated to the West, and we heard of "iron girl brigades," composed of young women who could work a field just as well as a man could (Davin 1975). Obviously, the standard of gender equality was based on a masculine one. Croll (1995) argues that women's liberation was defined *solely* in terms of labor force participation; women were to embrace identities as workers first, and as women second. Croll also points out that the Maoist phrase "women hold up half of heaven" (commonly translated as "half the sky") rhetorically placed women in an untenable position symbolically, because in the Taoist cosmological system of yin/yang dualism, woman was associated with earth and man with heaven. During the Mao years, Croll asserts the disparity between government rhetoric about the liberation of women and their lived experiences of continuing patriarchy created an intellectual and emotional rupture for women that rendered them mute.

During the Great Leap Forward, giant communes in the countryside organized the lives of the rural residents completely; communal kitchens and nurseries were established so all adult women could take part in labor full time. Workers were paid not in money but in "work points," based on a system that calculated both the difficulty of a particular task and the strength and ability of the individual worker; women were regularly given fewer work points than were men. Diamond notes that the lowest level of the commune—the production team—coincided with all or part of a village, and males related through patrilineal ties administered these new "work units," so in important ways patrilineal lineages continued to organize the lives of rural people. Gao Xiaoxian (1994) points out that rural-to-urban migration was strictly controlled and contributed to the continued insular nature of rural areas. Patrilineal descent reckoning and patrilocal residence continued to be the norm in the countryside. However, based on her fieldwork, Diamond (1975a) offers several examples of women who married matrilocally, and who were much more active in local politics than most women; this supports the assertion of Pasternak et al. (1997) that matrilocal residence is beneficial for women. After the failure of the Great Leap Forward and gradual decollectivization, rural women once again faced the double burden of housework and agricultural production (Gao 1994: 83–84). For many young married women, household help came from the mother-in-law, who might be too old or infirm to take part in farm work. Diamond argues that this changed the balance of power between these generations of women, but not between men and women. She concludes that the authority of patrilineal lineages during collectivization allowed the reproduction of "the feudal-patriarchal ideology" (1975a: 374).

After the debacle of the Great Leap Forward's agricultural policies, which killed an estimated 30 million people from starvation or opportunistic diseases, the ultra-Maoists who had advocated putting "politics in command" were in temporary disgrace. Mao himself had resigned from some official posts and had retreated to Shanghai. Pragmatists like Teng Hsiao-p'ing were in control and decollectivization of the countryside began. Croll (1995: 82) notes that during the early 1960s, some discussion was permitted of the gap between the rhetoric of women's emancipation and their lived experience of continued inequality. The official Women's Federation magazine, *Chung-kuo fu-nü* (Women of China), editorialized that "women's reproductive functions and the traditional definition of women's roles meant that they would continue for some time to face difficulties if they wanted to enter production and at the same time continue to be women," and women were encouraged to look into their own individual experiences. *Chung-kuo fu-nü* invited readers to write in and discuss two questions: "What do women live for?" and "What should be the criteria for selecting a husband?" Some responded that a "warm and enjoyable small family" was most important while others mentioned the importance of an adequate material standard of living, provided by a husband. Still other readers criticized these views as narrow and neglectful of the greater social good. The editors of *Chung-kuo fu-nü* had hoped that this discussion would be the beginning of a wide-ranging forum on women's lives and experiences, but the Cultural Revolution (1966–1976) intervened. Articles that emphasized "the purpose and importance of work and political study for women" now appeared (Croll 1995: 84). In the Women's Federation, much of the political study focused on criticism of the forum initiated by *Chung-kuo fu-nü* on "the problem of women." During the Cultural Revolution, publication of *Chung-kuo fu-nü* was suspended and the Women's Federation disbanded.

Mao launched the Great Proletarian Cultural Revolution to root out "revisionism" and "people taking the capitalist road," by energizing the youth of China to attack authority figures in the party, government, and ultimately even in the military. During this period, most distinctions between the sexes were deliberately suppressed. Both men and women dressed in dull "Mao suits," sported Mao buttons, and would not be caught dead without their pocket size "Little Red Book," *Quotations from Chairman Mao*. Romance, fashion, and personal adornment were all looked down upon as "bourgeois" and one was supposed to choose a mate based on good socialist ideological principles. Ironically, as Gail Hershatter points out, this androgynous clothing was "read" by Western tourists in the 1970s "as a sign of women's liberation, only to learn in the 1980s that many Chinese regarded the androgynous dress and silence about desire of the Cultural Revolution as instances of state suppression" (1996: 87). Despite the continuation of a covert masculine standard for both sexes, women workers became pervasive throughout the labor force, and even moved into some positions of authority in management, and, less often, in politics (Andors 1983: ch. 5). In the post-Mao era, the twice-purged Teng reemerged in 1978—this time as paramount leader—and initiated major economic policy shifts. These new economic policies have had both positive and negative consequences for women's lives. I turn now to a comparative look at women's statuses and roles during the first three decades of KMT rule on Taiwan. Taiwan's gender system operates within the context of many cultural values and beliefs about women's place that are the same as those of the PRC. However, the historical context and political realities of Taiwan have resulted in sometimes very different strategies for emancipation.

Women in the "Economic Miracle" of Taiwan

The Chinese on Taiwan and the KMT regime are justifiably proud of their "economic miracle" (Gold 1986), wherein Taiwan emerged as a newly industrializing country by 1975 and remains relatively unscathed by the recent Asian financial crisis of 1997. Rubinstein (1994) points out that the ROC government had considerable economic and military aid from the United States, with which it was allied during the Cold War. However, in fairness to the KMT, he goes on, many of the leaders were determined not to make the same disastrous economic policy mistakes that they had on the mainland. After firmly establishing authoritarian control, the KMT initiated a successful "land to the tiller" program that made many tenant farmers landowners for the first time. The KMT stimulated industrial development through a policy of primary import substitution and promoted domestic savings. U.S. economic aid was critical in the 1950s, as Taiwan was able to build up its industrial sector, primarily in manufacturing, to a self-sustaining level by the 1960s. Industry now began to disperse to the countryside to gain access to cheap labor and raw materials; special export processing zones were established for foreign investors, attracted by Taiwan's political stability and cheap and elastic labor supply, many of whom were young, unmarried women. In the decade from 1965 to 1975, Taiwan pursued a successful policy of export-oriented manufacturing and the transformation from a primarily agriculturally based economy to an industrially based one was accomplished (Galenson 1979). Along with other features of industrial modernization, women's status has rose as they began to achieve near equal levels of education with men and access to the job market. However, many women, particularly unmarried daughters and young wives, found themselves still subordinated to the patriarchal family and now exploited by capitalism as workers in the new global assembly line.

When the KMT took control of Taiwan from the Japanese, it introduced Republican Chinese policies and values toward the place of women in society (Chiang and Ku 1985). In a continuation of ROC policy on the mainland, women's status was declared to be equal to that of men while their roles were seen to be complementary; the urban middle- and upper-class women were expected to contribute to the stability and prosperity of Taiwanese society in their capacities as wives, mothers, and volunteer workers. Meanwhile, working class women contributed crucially to their family's income through factory or service work, including unpaid labor in family businesses. Some of them worked as illegal prostitutes, or as licensed ones, especially in the brothels that the military set up for soldiers. During the Vietnam War era, many prostitutes on Taiwan also serviced U.S. military personnel who were stationed on the island or who visited on leave.

For rural women during the early stages of industrialization, according to Margery Wolf's (1972) account, most traditional practices such as arranged marriages and patrilocal residence remained. She coined the phrase "the uterine family" to refer to a family consisting of a married woman and her children and bound together by ties of affection and loyalty, established informally within the patrilineal family for whom it was her duty to reproduce. Rural women whom Wolf studied from 1959 to 1968 were also adept at creating another informal institution, the "women's community," which successfully kept the errant behavior of husbands and mothers-in-law within bounds through gossip and the threat of loss of face. Changes in the form of factory employment opportunities and "free choice" marriage were just beginning in the rural communities studied by Margery Wolf and her anthropologist husband, Arthur, in the 1960s. By 1965, young women and girl graduates of elementary and junior high school were encouraged by government rhetoric to enter the workforce, helping to fuel economic expansion (Galenson 1979; Gallin 1984). By this time, few farm families depended primarily on agriculture for income, and many families strategically deployed unmarried children, particularly their daughters, to work in one of the new factories. These girls, directly out of elementary or lower middle school, either commuted from the family farm or lived in dormitories provided by the factory. They remitted their wages to the family head who gave them an allowance, usually spent on consumer goods, and used the rest for other expenses, including the further education of a son, education not thought necessary for a daughter who would marry out of the family (Kung 1994, 1984; Gallin 1984; Arrigo 1984).

Although these rural daughters were exploited by their natal families and by the emerging world capitalist system, they slowly gained increased independence and self-esteem through participation in the wider society. Their economic contribution encouraged their families to value them more, and delayed marriage meant that they were more mature and had more influence over marriage arrangements than their mothers' generation did. Ming-cheng Chang (1980) examined the family backgrounds and changing lifestyles of women born between 1940 and 1959 and found that from the oldest to the youngest age cohort, women's educational level, work outside the home, self-arranged marriage, and premarital sex had all risen steadily. Women who lived away from home before marriage (in factory dorms, or with friends or relatives) were most likely to control their own money, exercise free choice in marriage, and engage in premarital sex. Obviously, the complete subordination of the younger generation to the older was changing dramatically.

Rising educational levels and increased labor force participation of women on Taiwan are part of a dynamic in which fertility rates have declined and the spousal bond has been strengthened at the expense of the parent-child bond. In 1968, universal public education was expanded from six to nine years. In 1965, 26 percent of the labor force was illiterate; in 1984 this figure was 5.8 percent for men and 13.4 percent for women (Liu 1983). Of those born after World War II, educational levels are similar for women and men; in urban areas this level is about ten years. Beginning in 1966, family planning was actively promoted by the government and the total fertility rate declined from 7.0 in 1951 to 2.5 in 1980 (Liu 1983: 3). However, in these years many people still desired to continue having children until they had a son. Lolagene Coombs (1980: 311) found that the perceived benefits of having children—particularly expectations of care in old age and living with a son after marriage—outweighed the perceived costs.

By the 1970s, Taiwan's society had become quite urbanized and nuclear family residence more common than previously, although patrilocal residence was still the norm (Li 1984). With the rise of "free choice" marriages, the conjugal bond is more important than before, but important emotional and often financial ties to the husband's family remain. Working women often depend on their mothers-in-law for childcare, while care given by the elder generation tends to reproduce traditional gender roles in the next generation. Gallin (1984) and Diamond (1975b) assert that a generational power shift from the mother-in-law to the daughter-in-law has not upset the subordinate relation of women vis-à-vis men. Hu T'ai-li (1985) disagrees, arguing that women have enhanced their status through participation in the labor market and that increased dowries and closer ties to their natal families are reflections of this enhanced status. In her view, the power of the male head of the family has also decreased.

Women, especially those who had children, were discouraged from divorcing, no matter how unhappy, because of laws that automatically awarded custody to the father and because they had little control over marital assets. Some men, particularly of the upper class, continued in modern form the traditional practice of concubinage—although outlawed—with women whom they set up as "little wives" (hsiao lao-p'o). As long as these men fulfilled their financial obligation to the wife and children, she was not supposed to complain. In addition to "little wives," men from all walks of life are known to visit prostitutes. Many people in Taiwan see prostitution as inevitable, and argue for its regulation rather than criminalization. As in the United States until the "sexual revolution" of the 1960s, in Chinese society on Taiwan, there are "good" girls and "bad" girls. For the former, a strict code of premarital virginity and postmarital chastity was enjoined.

By the 1970s, economic prosperity had contributed to the growth of a new urban middle class and government rhetoric once again valorized "the virtuous wife and good mother" roles, as the proper sphere of women. Diamond (1973, 1975b) has characterized this era as a "variation on feminine mystique" for middle-class urban women in Taiwan, aptly invoking Betty Friedan's critique of the position of middle-class women in the United States during the "Ozzie and Harriet" years of the 1950s.[3] Indeed, I shall argue below that one of the effects of modernization on women's roles and status in all societies is obligatory passage through the "feminine mystique" era. Linda Arrigo (1991), using a Marxist framework, analyzes the decade of the 1970s on Taiwan as a period in which, for middle-class women, sex role differences—the woman as homemaker and the man as breadwinner—are "mystified." Working class women might have aspired to the dependent status of homemaker, but they also contributed much needed labor to the family. The newly bourgeois culture of urban Taiwan in the 1970s also witnessed the beginning of an activist women's movement, led by a Harvard-trained scholar, Annette Lu Hsiu-lien. She wrote the first feminist book on Taiwan, New Feminism, which criticized gender inequalities in educational levels, the feminization of low-status, low-paying jobs, a sexual double standard, and the continued denigration of women within a Confucian value system (Lu 1986). At the same time, she emphasized that women need not lose their femininity in order to be liberated. I think that Lu was sensitive to the probable reaction of her society to feminist issues when she returned from study in the United States in the early 1970s and began public activities, which led to the modern women's movement. Thus, while Lu has been criticized by some Taiwanese women's leaders for extolling traditional feminine attributes in her book, we can also read this as an attempt to fore-stall arguments that women's activities, moving from the inside realm to the out-side, that is, the public sphere, would defeminize them. Lu herself explains that she set aside some issues that were not urgent and that were too sensitive, such as sexual freedom and homosexuality, and "from the strategic point of view, she [i.e., Lu] also appeared to be moderate with regard to the validity of marriage and the feminine nature of women, so that objections could be decreased" (Lu 1994: 298).

Lu Hsiu-lien also felt it necessary to address the objection to feminism as a Western import. She does not deny that Taiwanese feminists were influenced by this, as many of them studied in the United States or read Simone de Beauvoir's *The Second Sex* and Betty Freidan's *Feminine Mystique*, which had been trans-lated by an overseas Taiwanese feminist, Yang Mei-hui, in the early 1970s. But Lu also drew on the thought of Sun Yat-sen to argue for the universal necessity of a movement for women's liberation. Applying Sun's notion that "a doctrine is a kind of thought, of belief, and of power," she defined feminism as:

> a *thought* that emerged from the demand of society along with the tide of history; a *belief* that the prosperity and harmony of androgynous society shall be founded on the basis of substantial equality between men and women; and a *power* that will abolish the traditional prejudice against women, reconstruct a new and sen-sible value system, create independence and dignity for women, and foster the realization of true equality of sexes. (Lu 1994: 297; emphases added)

During the 1970s, Lu and her associates gave a series of lectures, debates, and writings on gender equality, opened a bookstore and publishing house to promote feminist writings, established telephone hotlines for victims of rape and abuse, and organized activities such as a men's cooking class and a workshop on "women outside of the kitchen." Although the activities of these early feminists generated much interest and controversy, it was also a very dangerous undertaking in the years of martial law on Taiwan. Lu had to be very cautious about advocating for women's liberation in such a hostile climate, especially since she was also in-volved in the activities of the *Tang-wai* ("outside the party-party"), the unofficial opposition to the KMT.

In a memoir of the times, Lu discusses the systematic harassment she experi-enced at the hands of government agents (Lu 1994). She was one of the leaders of the *Mei-li-tao* ("beautiful island," that is, Formosa) group that organized protests over the cancellation of local elections in 1979, after the government panicked in the wake of its "derecognition" by the Carter administration in the United States. She and her comrades were arrested after riots broke out in the wake of police oppression; they were tried and convicted in a military court for sedition and all received long prison terms. Lu was released in 1986 on medical grounds and was allowed to go to the United States for treatment. Thus, at the end of the 1970s, Taiwan had emerged on the world stage with a distinctive Asian modernity, similar to South Korea's and Singapore's, combining impressive economic growth with political repression under a strict authoritarian regime. In the next section, I turn to a comparison of women's liberation in the PRC under Teng's economic reforms and in Taiwan under the democratization process.

Recent Changes: Trends and Countertrends in the PRC and on Taiwan

Recent economic and social changes in the PRC and on Taiwan suggest an ironic countertrend in women's liberation. Under the leadership of Teng Hsiao-p'ing and his successors since 1978, the PRC has "opened the door" to Western science and technology (while trying vainly to keep out "spiritual pollution") and has begun market reforms that are integrating the PRC into the global economy. The results of these sweeping reforms for the status of women have been quite mixed. In many ways, the economic reforms have brought regression for women; in the countryside, patriarchal norms and treatment of women are resurgent, while in the urban areas, job discrimination against women is blatant. Women (and men) do nevertheless have more economic opportunities; rising prosperity has benefited many regions of the country, and there is far less government interference in people's daily lives. On Taiwan, agitation for democratic change in the 1970s and 1980s resulted in the lifting of martial law (1987) and a raucous multiparty democracy emerged in the 1990s. With continued capitalist industrialization, women have benefited from broader and more equal educational and employment opportunities. At the same time, women's groups have been key players in the development of a civil society, which has contributed to and benefited from the democratization process. In this section, I review these recent trends in the PRC, discussing changes in the countryside and in the cities separately, then turn to recent changes in Taiwan, before concluding with a comparative analysis.

Economic Reforms in the PRC and the Status of Women in the Countryside

Under the rural reforms, known as the "agricultural production responsibility system," individual farm families now contract with the commune to work a particular piece of land or to manage a rural enterprise. Anything produced over quota may be consumed by the farm household, or sold on the free market (Spence 1990: 700–701). This reform has resulted in sharply increased yields and rising prosperity in many areas of the country, especially on the southeast coast and near large urban centers. However, in the hinterland and other remote areas, many populated by ethnic minorities, the reforms have been less beneficial and the government is concerned about growing regional disparities in income. The gutting of the commune structure (the brigades and production teams remain but with diminished responsibilities) and its replacement with a household-based economy once again has reinforced the traditional value of child labor, and, in particular, the value of sons. The commune structure offered some old age security for childless people; today adult sons have resumed the primary responsibility to care for old parents (although by law both sons and daughters bear this responsibility). Daughters also contribute to the household economy by helping their mothers with domestic chores or sideline production, or by engaging in wage labor in rural enterprises, while others migrate to urban areas to engage in seasonal labor, to work in factories, or to serve as "nannies" for a growing middle class of two-career couples. Hershatter (1997) reports that many rural migrant women may also engage in prostitution, either full time or part time, to supplement their low wages. Gao (1994) argues that the rural reforms have opened up many new opportunities for women and that social modernization is leading to individual modernization. She notes that in comparison with the past, many more peasant families today are accepting of women working outside the home, that most young people believe in free choice marriage (with the parents' consent!), and that couples should have only two children (ideally, one boy and one girl). In her view, "The awakening of women's self-consciousness has been an intrinsic driving force in the changes in women's status. Its effects should not be underestimated" (1994: 89).

Other scholars paint a more mixed picture of women's status in the countryside. Croll (1995: 127–28) points out that more than 75 percent of rural women are still engaged in agriculture, fisheries, or forestry. For many women, this is an added burden to their domestic work, which, in addition to housekeeping, might include sideline or household-based commodity production. In addition, many rural men have migrated to the cities for work, leaving millions of women as heads of households in "half-side families," and they are often poorer than their neighbors. Increased demands for child labor have also resulted in pulling daughters out of school, in earlier marriage age, and in increases in bride price, as well as in reports of the selling and abduction of young women. Gao also points to continuing problems for rural women, such as their lower labor force participation than men, poor working conditions, low wages and low-skilled work in rural enterprises, and exploitation in the special economic zones. She also mentions the extra burden for women of housework, problems with interrupted education, and the continued practice of patrilineal inheritance and patrilocal residence (1994: 90–95).

Gender inequalities in educational access for rural girls have been exacerbated by the reforms. With the breakdown of the commune system and increase in school fees, girls are more likely to be kept out of school than boys. They help with domestic chores and care of younger siblings, or even help their mothers do piecework in areas where household enterprises have developed (Judd 1994). In Margery Wolf's (1985: 124) sample, the illiteracy rate of women between the ages of eighteen and thirty-nine years is ten times that of men, and 31 percent of women in this age group could not read. Gao (1994: 94–95) reports that in 1988, 83 percent of the school-age children who were not enrolled in school were girls, while 70 percent of the 3 million who left school were girls. One out of every 4.5 rural women is illiterate. Yet modernization of agriculture requires literate farmers who can read about new technologies, and education is a prime force in individual modernization. Gao emphasizes that the government and the Women's Federation must concentrate on improving rural women's levels of education in order to aid in women's liberation.

In rural China today, the patrilineal principle of descent remains strong and patrilocal postmarital residence is still the norm in many localities. This resurgent patrilineality may be connected with ancestor worship. Wolf (1985: 141) reported that in three of the six sites she visited, ancestor worship continued, either openly or surreptitiously; by the 1990s, this practice had become even more open. According to Wolf, mothers and go-betweens conduct marriage arrangements and the couple has "veto" power, itself a significant compromise with tradition but certainly not in keeping with Marriage Laws that grant free choice to children. "Romantic love" is viewed as a Western concept unimportant to most rural Chinese; couples get to know each other during a dating period after the engagement is finalized. The age at marriage has been set by law to regulate birth rates. The trend toward later marriages as compared with the pre-1949 period (i.e., in one's twenties) has benefited daughters' status in the family as they contribute to their natal family's income through work in factories and the like. More mature daughters therefore have greater say in their marriage and other family decisions (Wolf 1985, ch. 6). Despite the retrogressive emphasis on sons as carriers of the patriline and parents' support in old age, Greenhalgh and Li (1995: 616) note in their study of demographic trends in Shansi province that cultural attitudes toward daughters are shifting. Many people desire to have a daughter (in addition to at least one son) for emotional support in old age; this has coincided with "the growing emotional distance between older parents and the culturally preferred caregivers, their sons and daughters-in-law."

In a nation of over 1 billion people, population control is of urgent concern to the government. Because of the implementation of the "one child per family" policy, fertility rates have fallen throughout the country. However, the rate has decreased much more slowly in rural than in urban areas, as rural women are pressured by the husband and his family to bear at least one son. Beginning in the 1980s, the Western press reported instances of coercive family planning, including forced abortions, female infanticide, or selective neglect (e.g., a shorter period of nursing for girls), as well as out-adoption of daughters, underreported births, and falsified birth control records. Most distressing is the rise of sex-selective abortions among people who have access to this technology (summarized in Greenhalgh and Li 1995: 609–10). Incredibly, this seems to be occurring on Taiwan as well, with enough frequency to skew the sex ratio (Selya 1995, cited in Gold 1996). In the reform era, there has also been an increase in crime in the countryside, including the abduction and selling of women and girls into prostitution or as wives for peasants, many of whom view these women as legitimate purchases. After a forced pregnancy, many of these women are too humiliated to return home even if they have the opportunity to do so. Other forms of violence against women that began to receive public attention in the 1980s include rape and wife battering (Honig and Hershatter 1988: ch. 8).

In terms of local political leadership, women cadres are usually confined to "women's work" (this was also true during the years of Mao's leadership), such as enforcing the government's birth control policy, supervising preschool education, promoting political study, and acting as domestic mediators. For example, Ellen Judd notes that, in the Shantung provincial villages that she studied, the women cadres focused on improving the income-generating capacity of local women, primarily through the development of household enterprises (1994: 221–22). In some of these villages, the head of the women's committee was not even included in the formal structure of local governance—the village committee. Wolf (1985) argues that many women have experienced a rise in self-esteem through new responsibilities that take them beyond their traditionally narrow familial concerns, although Judd is less optimistic about this. She sees rural women as agents in their own lives, but as constrained in many ways by patriarchy, which is neither "essentially or even primarily based in a family or domestic context . . . [rather it is] one strand in a wider complex of hierarchical relations in China" (Judd 1994: 213). Nonetheless, most women in the countryside of China, both young and old, agree that women are infinitely better off now than they were in preliberation times. Whether they are better off now than they were during the Mao years, or would be if they lived under a capitalist system, are issues more difficult to untangle.

Status of Women in Urban Areas

Women's status in urban China differs in a number of ways from that of their rural sisters. Here, the one-child-per-family policy has been largely successful, because of factors such as crowded living conditions, old age pensions, various incentives, for example, access to better jobs, the higher education of women, and more exposure to the party line of gender equality. Whyte and Parish point out that influences promoting fertility decline in urban China are similar to those in other developing countries, although the rapid rate of decline is affected by the particular nature of urban institutions in the PRC (1984: 165–67). Although marriage practices in urban areas still follow the patrilineal descent rule, in contrast to the rural pattern, mate selection is more likely to be by the couple. However, it is difficult to meet prospective mates, as little cross-sex contact is allowed in school and Western-style dating is seen as scandalous. Instead, friends are often used as "go-betweens." Parents still have a say in children's marriages, and if they strongly disapprove of a proposed match, it is usually broken off. Arranged marriages still occur. For example, elite urban families have been known to forge alliances through their children's marriage (Wolf 1985: ch. 6). The majority of urban households show a nuclear family pattern. In Whyte's and Parish's sample, based on data collected from 1972 to 1978, 68 percent of families were nuclear, while 24 percent were patrilineal extended families of the stem (three generations) or joint type (two or more married sons). They point out that this pattern is not greatly different from that in prewar urban areas of China, where, for example, nuclear families accounted for from 48 percent to 61 percent of urban residents. Elite groups, especially government officials, are more likely to reside in extended families.

Looking at educational access, clearly, levels for men and women are more equal than in the countryside. Whyte and Parish (1984: 199) note that the gender gap in education has been closing, a trend that began under the Nationalists, with men on average having about 8.5 years of education and women, 8 years. More recently, Croll (1995) reports that as of 1990, females made up 45 percent of primary school enrollment, 44 percent of junior middle school, 39 percent of senior middle school, and 34 percent of college and university enrollment.[4] Clearly, fewer women than men go to senior high school and college. As is true in Taiwan today, urban men in the PRC do not want to marry women more educated than themselves and women are perhaps responding to the marriage market. It is also true that college-educated women have been experiencing much more difficulty than their male peers have in finding employment and this factor may also influence their striving for educational opportunities.

In terms of employment, the new economic reforms have been a mixed blessing for women. Many factories and other work units are often hesitant to hire women, as they must by law provide pregnancy leave and childcare facilities, which are costly. Moreover, with the government's move to shut down unprofitable state enterprises, women are often the first ones laid off, or the ones who find it more difficult to get a job in the first place (Rai 1994). Many state enterprises openly discriminate against hiring women, or, in the case of those already employed, strongly encourage them to take years of maternity leave. Whyte and Parish (1984) point out that while the percentage of women in the workforce is extraordinarily high, even by standards of developed countries (in their sample, over 90 percent of women ages twenty to thirty-nine were employed), sex segregation in the workplace with women occupying mostly low-wage, dead-end jobs is quite common. Urban women in China must also contend with the "second shift," that is, responsibility for childcare and housekeeping on top of full-time employment. This limits overtime work and career advancement, and women's salary levels rise more slowly than men's. Women are often seen as, and view themselves as, less committed to work than men are. Many retire early (at age fifty) so a child can take over their job. Older women may work in "neighborhood workshops," which are dead-end jobs with low wages and no benefits. Nonetheless, urban women derive self-esteem from working for wages and agree with their rural counterparts that women in the PRC today have come a long way since preliberation times (Wolf 1985: ch. 3).

According to Hershatter, some women, of various educational levels and both rural and urban backgrounds, are also turning to prostitution, either to supplement a low-wage job or as a lucrative career in itself (1997: 327–50). Prostitutes may be farmers who work part time, service personnel, factory workers, entrepreneurs, and also students, teachers, and engineers. Profitable networks have grown up around the trade, including corrupt police and underworld gangs. Treated as a reappearance of something that had once disappeared in China, many Chinese people view prostitution as a price to be paid for opening up to the West. While it first flourished in hotels and bars that catered to foreigners, especially *hua-ch'iao* (overseas Chinese), by the 1980s, a domestic clientele had also emerged among those who had acquired wealth or official privilege. The government's response was similar to the campaign of the 1950s, which supposedly eradicated prostitution: incarceration and reeducation. But this response is clearly not working; those unlucky enough to get caught, usually inexperienced country girls, are soon back on the streets again. The official line is that pre-1949 prostitutes were forced into the work by dire circumstances, while reform-era prostitutes work by choice, especially in the pursuit of money. The proliferation of prostitution in the late twentieth century is part of a public discussion on "what kind of modernity China should seek" (Hershatter 1997: 327).

Return of the Feminine Mystique?

In the reform era, the idea of women's liberation has clearly taken a backseat to the "four modernizations" (in agriculture, industry, science and technology, and defense) that the PRC has made its goal. A biologically based model of sex differences and a perceived "natural" division of labor have been reasserted. In the context of socialist modernization where a mixed socialist-market economy is developing, an inevitable result is growing unemployment. If the workforce must be reduced it seems more appropriate for women to be the ones to return home. Or, if skilled women remain in the workforce, they occupy support positions and are clear about the fact that the home front is their most important duty.[5] This sounds a lot like the feminine mystique "with Chinese characteristics."

As Lisa Rofel notes:

> Ideas about biology have become central. Biology is inescapable and determines capabilities. This has replaced the emphasis on social explanations for women's oppression prevalent in the Maoist era. . . . This production of knowledge that biology is inescapable is tied to the notion that individuals should engage in those activities for which they have the most biological talent. This has meant that women are becoming more strongly tied to domesticity and motherhood. Women's activities in the home are no longer condemned as feudal social arrangements. Rather, they are said to be a natural expression of the female self. (Rofel 1994: 244)

Western feminists may claim that this is not in women's interests, Rofel notes, but one should first appreciate that this generation has come of age during a time when the state has determined their feminism, through the official Women's Federation in particular. Rather than looking at Chinese women's choices through the lens of Western feminist standards, she argues that, "These women who embrace motherhood and reject productivity are voicing their resistance to the state and attempting to wrest from it some measure of control over the definition of their bodies. If the state is increasingly ordering work and work life, women workers have thrown up motherhood and family life as barricades" (Rofel 1994: 245). Rather than view their choice as uninformed, or, simply a product of "mystification," we—Western feminists—must learn to respect the autonomy and integrity of those choices. However, not all native observers are as sanguine about such choices. Gao Xiaoxian (1994) mentions the phenomenon of Ta-chiu Village in Tientsin, an area of heavy industry, where all women were sent home "to do full-time housework to compensate for lack of service industries." She argues that this is not in women's best interests as it simply "repeats the historical pattern of women sacrificing individual development in exchange for men's realization of their greater social value" (Gao 1994: 92).

This shift in the cultural definition of gender equality recalls Joan Scott's (1994) deconstruction of the "equality versus difference" debate in U.S. feminism today. The meaning of equality is often associated with sameness or identity ("men and women are alike") but it really entails the suppression of or irrelevance of difference ("men and women should be treated the same under the law"). The "difference" proponents emphasize "natural" differences between the sexes, which therefore necessitate different treatment (e.g., protective legislation for women workers). But this emphasis on the difference between men and women obscures the differences *among* women, based on factors such as class, ethnicity, sexual orientation, and the like. In the history of China since the founding of the PRC, we can see a definite shift in official ideology, rhetoric, and policy from a focus on equality in the Maoist era, to one of difference in the post-Mao reform era. And as in the case of Western feminist movements, the equality position in the PRC implicitly accepted the masculine as norm, so the formulation should read, not "men and women are alike" but "women are like men." In the reform era, a turn to difference is in part a return to traditional Chinese values about the complementarity of the gender system: "men rule the outside, women rule the inside," but in a contemporary political and economic context. As Scott argues in the case of U.S. society, in the "equality argument" differences *among* women are thereby obscured. In the Chinese case, important differences such as between generations (the mother-in-law versus the daughter-in-law), urban versus rural, differing educational levels, and so on, are obscured by the "difference" argument. For example, while economic reforms have led to greater job opportunities for many rural women, the situation is arguably worse for urban workers.

These efforts to biologize women's roles in Chinese society have not gone unchallenged. Throughout the 1980s, Honig and Hershatter collected articles and books from the Chinese press, which articulated a "full-fledged debate about gender roles" (1988: v). And since the 1980s, vigorous women's studies movements have flourished, led by the Women's Federation after a decade of dormancy during the Cultural Revolution, but also featuring semi-autonomous nongovernmental women's organizations active in scholarship and popular writing (Gilmartin et al. 1994; Li and Zhang 1994; Wan 1988). Tani Barlow (1997b: 506–7) has explored the debates on the question of women's subjectivity that have emerged in post-Mao China. In the late 1970s, the Women's Federation began documenting Chinese women's gains under communism, thereby reviving *fu-nü*, the Maoist revolutionary women subject. This discourse provided a critical opening for historians of women's history, especially the influential Li Xiaojiang, to set into circulation a counter-identity to which they referred as *nü-hsing* (essential woman). Li was the first to argue that Maoist policies denaturalized women's bodies during the Cultural Revolution; her solution was to create an essentialized Woman who is the deficient other of Man. These theorists argued that women must recapture their femininity from state control, which obliterated it. Thus, in rejecting the state definition of them as workers first, women second, many women appear to be responding to this call for an essentialized woman. Barlow points out that the essentializing message of Li and her associates is contended by other voices in the emerging field of women's studies, such as Lacanian psychoanalysis. However, for women working in low-paying, dead-end jobs and coming home to the second shift, it is not difficult to see how "essential woman" might exert a powerful pull. Alternatively, as Hershatter (1997) shows, some women may subvert the gender order by simultaneously becoming a rich man's mistress *and* keeping a handsome young man on the side. Wang Zheng notes that the power to define women has shifted from the state to market forces, as commercial interests have found in femininity a lucrative commodity (1997: 138). In this light, Li Xiaojiang's writings may turn out to be, as Barlow remarks, "nothing less than the ideological justification for a form of national womanhood that is handmaiden to economic boom and frontier capitalism" (1997b: 536).

In the PRC, although academic "women's studies" flourishes, there is no "women's movement" of activists marching in the streets to demand equality, as there is in Western countries and also in Chinese society on Taiwan (Farris 1990; Ku 1989). This should not surprise us. As Jane Record and Wilson Record point out, "In a pluralist state [such as the United States] the interests of individuals and intermediate groups—such as women's movements—have independent value. In a totalistic state [such as the PRC] . . . the interests of the collectivity . . . have overriding importance" (Record and Record 1976: 405). In socialist states, women's liberation is officially viewed as inseparable from the socialist transformation of society as a whole. To agitate for a separate women's movement, therefore, is ideologically incorrect. Thus, women's organizations in China can go only so far in challenging the official position on women. Since 1990, the women's movement in China has become much more transnational in outlook, while retaining an insistence upon the indigenous historical and cultural background of Chinese women. As Zheng notes, this transnational Chinese feminism was accelerated by the United Nations' Fourth World Conference on Women, held in Peking in 1995.

While ideological controls were temporarily tightened shortly before and during the conference, the net result was positive for the women's movement. The government signed the Platform for Action and the Peking Declaration, and the media declared that these two documents voice the aspirations of women all over the world (Zheng 1997: 146). These documents have created legitimacy for expanding Chinese women's activism and for "connecting the rails" or merging with international women's movements. Increasingly, women activists in the PRC and on Taiwan see women's liberation as a global struggle, in which, however, local issues and interpretations play a crucial role.

Can Capitalism and Democracy in Taiwan Liberate Women?

The modern movement for women's liberation on Taiwan is part of the development of a civil society that both contributed to and is allowed to flourish in the more open political atmosphere since the twilight of President Chiang Ching-kuo's rule. Gold notes that "women have been especially active in the creation and consolidation of civil society" (1996: 1113). In the 1980s on Taiwan a plurality of public discourses began to flourish; social activism of women's groups, religious groups, environmental groups, and others began to agitate for reform (Gold 1996; Tu 1996; Winckler 1994). Taiwan began a slow transformation from one-party authoritarian rule to more democratic rule; martial law was lifted (1987), opposition political parties legalized, and multiparty elections held. Unlike their mothers who came of age in the 1960s and 1970s, young women in Taiwan today are staying in the workforce after marriage or the birth of children. In 1960 only 25 percent of women over the age of fifteen were in the workforce; in 1970 this rate had risen to 30.2 percent (Galenson 1979). By 1990, 45 percent of all women were in the workforce and this rate has remained stable since then. For the generation that came of age in the 1980s, education levels are in many cases much higher than those of their parents (e.g., elementary school level of the parents versus college training of their children). Fertility levels are lower and women are increasingly seeking meaningful social roles in addition to the traditional familial ones. The women's movement on Taiwan is now entering its fourth decade and roles and statuses of women have clearly been transformed in the modernization process (Ku 1989). However, certain patriarchal values and practices remain.

Marriage and Family

During the decade of industrial expansion, Taiwan passed early through the demographic transition. A successful family planning program reduced population growth and today women have an average of 1.86 children. In fact, since 1984, the birth rate has fallen below the replacement level, prompting the government to urge people to marry earlier and to have two children (Gold 1996: 1092). Furthermore, the aging population of Taiwan has the potential to create a crisis in elder care. Traditionally, adult children, preferably sons, took responsibility for the care of elderly parents as part of the obligations of *hsiao* (filial piety). The government encouraged this as a way to save money on universal medical care and a social security program; only in 1980 did the government promulgate the Welfare Law for the Aged (Gold 1996: 1092). As the age structure of the population changes, however, there is an increasing burden on the younger working population. This can have a significant impact on women's roles in particular, for it is usually the daughter-in-law who is responsible for the day-to-day care of an aged parent-in-law who lives with the son. This increases the "double burden" on the woman, who is now being encouraged by government rhetoric to have more children at the same time that she is encouraged to participate in the workforce part time or full time. Many women of childbearing age are very interested in maintaining a lowered fertility rate. However, for those in the generations that came of age in the prewar period or shortly thereafter, sons are more valued than daughters and in-laws often pressure their daughters-in-law to keep trying until they give birth to a son. In my interviews and discussions with parents of preschool children conducted in 1990, many of these people, who are mostly in their thirties, indicated that a two-child family was the ideal whether or not they had at least one son; women, however, were more adamant about it than were their husbands (Farris 1993).

Although there have been many changes in relations among family members in the postwar years, there is also continuity with traditional Chinese values regarding masculinity and femininity. Notably, the ideal of a "virtuous wife and good mother" is still relevant to many women, and, even among those who work, social mores still dictate that they take primary responsibility for housework and childcare. For unmarried children, "although the role of parents in controlling mate choice has decreased, they still exercise considerable influence over marriage and even dating, although in consultation with children" (Gold 1996: 1096). For the newly married couple, although nuclear family residence in urban areas is now quite common, this is not the nuclear family as Westerners know it. Rather, it is the "new nuclear family" (*hsin ho-hsin chia-t'ing*), which is still dominated by patrilineal principles. Daughters are still viewed as "marrying out" of their natal families; sons are responsible for parents in old age, and only sons expect to inherit (Chen Yi-ping 1994). Postmarital residence is often near the husband's parents, and, regardless, the new couple often relies on his parents for economic support and childcare. Some women are beginning to assert the right to maintain strong ties with their natal families (*niang-chia*). Tsui Yi-lan (1985) has shown that, after marriage, highly educated urban women use their greater economic independence to help their natal families financially. Many of the mothers of preschoolers whom I interviewed told me that they would prefer to have their mothers rather than their mothers-in-law serve as babysitters. Thus, various tensions within the family are evident as women assume new roles in the larger society. Many men resent challenges to their traditional prerogatives of domination in the public domain and also resent challenges to a sexual double standard. This contributes to domestic discord and a slowly rising divorce rate. Indeed, Gold (1996: 1097) reports that "Taiwan has the dubious distinction of having the highest divorce rate in Asia . . . [and] most take place by mutual consent, with adultery the prime cause." Given the long history of concubinage in Chinese society, it goes without saying which spouse is usually accused of adultery.

Education and the Law

As part of the process of modernization accompanying industrialization on Taiwan, the social and juridical status of women has also improved. In 1968, compulsory education was extended from six to nine years and today educational levels in the cities are comparable for men and women. Island-wide, almost all elementary graduates go on to junior high school and the illiteracy rate is only 6 percent (Gold 1996: 1097). In senior high school, however, for which students must take joint entrance exams, there are fewer girls than boys attending. A sex-based quota system is used and girls are disadvantaged here (Hsieh 1997). Other sex-discriminatory issues in education include practices such as gender bias in curricular materials and "tracking" of students into sex-stereotypic fields; for example, girls are encouraged to study humanities and fine arts and boys to study natural sciences and computers (summarized in Hsieh 1997). Tu Weiming, however, asserts that "women have . . . overshadowed their male counterparts in most academic disciplines at the best universities for years . . . [and] it seems inevitable that Taiwanese education, from primary school to college, will be in the hands of female intellectuals" (Tu 1996: 1135–36). Somehow I doubt that my Chinese colleagues who study gender and education issues in Taiwan have as optimistic a view of things, and I suspect that Tu is reacting much as the mainland gentleman whom I quoted in the introduction as asserting that today "men are disadvantaged compared to women." They see gender equality as a zero-sum game; if women's status rises, men's must fall!

Women now have nearly equal rights under law, although these rights are not always realized in practice. For example, the legal code stipulates equal inheritance for sons and daughters, but many people are either unaware of this law or choose to ignore it and continue the practice of dowry as the only claim a daughter has on her father's estate. In December 1996, the Chinese Association for Human Rights released an annual report that surveys various indicators, and women's rights receives the lowest scores (Huang 1997). Only in marital and family rights have women's positions improved in the five years since these annual reviews were begun. In 1994, the Council of Grand Justice ruled that the article of the civil code granting the husband the right to the couple's property and to custody of children (in cases of divorce) was unconstitutional. In 1996, the code was amended so that "married couples can now own their assets separately

. . . [and] upon divorce, the father is no longer guaranteed the right to custody" (Huang 1997: 5–6). Indeed, as I pointed out in an analysis of the "social discourse on women's roles" (Farris 1990), the fact that husbands still controlled the joint property and were automatically awarded custody of children discouraged many women from seeking a divorce despite an unhappy marriage. Although the legal code has now changed, it will be interesting to see the extent to which women are still pressured by their husband's family, or even their own, to let him take custody of the children—especially a son—whom many people still believe "belong" to the husband's lineage.

A segment of the women's movement, led by the only openly "feminist" organization, the Awakening Group (Fu-nü hsin-chih; literally, "the awakening of women") has been active in promoting changes in public policy and legislation to give women equal rights under the law. Ku Yenlin (1996) has analyzed the processes by which the feminist movement effected changes in two areas: the legalization of abortion and equal employment opportunity. She argues that the language of the Eugenic Healthcare Act of 1984, which legalized abortion, "continued to reflect the concerns of a patriarchal state to reproduce the labor market and to reduce population growth as a threat to national security and development." Feminist concerns, such as control over one's own body, were absent from the document, and thus "could not act as a catalyst to raise women's collective awareness of their subordination" (ibid.: 4). Although abortion is now legal, patriarchal constraints remain; a woman must obtain the consent of her husband or legal guardian to have an abortion. In contrast, the fight for equal employment opportunity— especially the outlawing of the de facto rule that women must quit their jobs after marriage or the birth of their first child—because it came after the lifting of martial law, "was more successful in touting the feminist agenda and in rallying women to the cause" (ibid.). Other areas in which Taiwan's feminists urge legal change include sexual harassment on the job and spousal abuse.

I am leaving out an extended discussion of women in politics because of time and space constraints, not because I think it unimportant. Both in the PRC and on Taiwan, women are largely, but not wholly, absent from higher decision-making processes. Taiwan has a "reserved seat" system guaranteeing that women make up at least 10 percent of elected officials (see Chou, Clark, and Clark 1990 and Arrigo's 1993 critique of it). In practice, as many complain, this has acted as a ceiling on the number of women in office and many women's rights leaders are eager to abolish it.[6] However, Rose J. Lee (1997) points out that since the 1980s, women elected to both the National Assembly and the Legislative Yuan have exceeded the quota (18–19 percent and 13–14 percent, respectively). In comparing Taiwan women's relative success in formal politics to Korean women's lack of success, Lee argues that in the early stages of industrialization and democracy, a quota system can be beneficial to women. The issue on Taiwan is whether or not it is still necessary. In 1999, the Democratic Progressive Party (DPP) passed a resolution authorizing a quota of one-fourth women candidates for all seats for public office and in the 2001 elections for the Legislative Yüan, fully 33 percent (75 out of a total of 225 seats) of those elected were women. In what for some people was probably a quixotic gesture, the head of the Warm Life Association (mentioned below), Shih Chi-ching, declared herself a candidate in the 1996 presidential elections. "The purpose of my campaigning," she said, "was to generate publicity and educate women" (cited in Huang 1997: 7). Also in 1996, the founder of the modern women's movement on Taiwan, Annette Lu was elected head of T'ao-yüen county, the second-largest county in Taiwan. In 2000 she made history when she ran for vice-president on Chen Shui-bian's DPP ticket. Together they were elected as the first successful opposition party in Chinese history and took executive power from the KMT in a peaceful democratic transition. Lu is one of the few female politicians in an Asian society who has achieved power on her own, that is, not by virtue of her relationship with a powerful man (as did, for example, Indira Gandhi, Benazir Bhutto, and Corazon Aquino). However, her never-married status and radical credentials, I would argue, make her less than an ideal role model for a new generation of women leaders. Obviously, the issue of political power for women in a Communist regime such as the PRC would have very different dimensions, but a comparison with Taiwan would be valuable. For example, among the much-touted village level elections in the PRC, what percentage of candidates and elected officials were women? Gilmartin (1993) has documented how a patriarchal gender system that was inscribed on the "body politic" of the CCP in the 1920s continues to the present. Croll reports that women in the PRC make up only 13 percent of party membership and only 7 percent of cadres at all administrative levels (1995: 132). These figures suggest that politics is still largely a man's world in the PRC; in this area women on Taiwan are clearly ahead of their mainland sisters.

Workforce Participation of Women

In the 1990s on Taiwan, women's domain is not only in the home; women, including married women with small children, are in the workforce in large numbers (45 percent of all women). For women between the ages of twenty-five and twenty-nine, this figure is 66 percent, while some 70 percent of all college graduates are in the workforce (Hwang 1977; Gold 1996). Business management and administration remain a largely male domain, arenas that many people, including some women, view as not "suitable" (*pu ho-shih*) for women. Men are still considered the main providers for their families, and women's work in the labor force is seen as supplemental household income. The division of labor in the workplace mirrors traditional roles, for example, women are preschool and elementary school teachers, nurses, secretaries, clerks, unskilled or semiskilled factory workers, farmers, or unpaid help in family businesses. As on the mainland, they may also be full-time sex workers or supplement low-paying jobs, such as restaurant work, with part-time prostitution.[7] There are, however, more employment options for women on

Taiwan than for those in the PRC. Chou Bih-er (1994) has analyzed changing patterns of women's employment on Taiwan from 1966 to 1986. She indicates that women workers are well integrated *horizontally* into all areas of the economy, including manufacturing, commerce, and service industries. However, in terms of vertical *integration*, "although women workers have made significant gains in commerce and service industries at all levels, including employer class in commerce, the majority of women are still located in the lower end of the production relationship. . . . Sex segregation at the level of ownership of the means of production remains the biggest obstacle in the way of gender equality" (Chou 1994: 352).

Workplace gender inequality is being challenged by two women's groups in particular, Pink Collar Solidarity and the Taipei Association for the Promotion of Women's Rights, both of which are involved in promoting gender equality in the workplace (Hwang 1997). They have agitated for an end to the "single and no pregnancy rule," which, although outlawed (see above), is still practiced by many employers, and for an end to other forms of discrimination such as lower pay, restricted opportunities for promotion, and sexual harassment. These women's rights activists attribute the unfriendly working environment to traditional Chinese concepts about women's roles in society. Given the sex-segregated workforce and continued limits on opportunities for women to break through the "glass ceiling," combined with traditional expectations of responsibility for the household, how are we to interpret the phenomenal success of the book *Nü ch'iang-jen* (The Strong Woman), by Chu Hsiu-chuan (published in 1984), about a high school graduate who fails the college entrance exam but goes on to make it big in business? Sung Mei-hua argues that the term "strong woman," which has entered popular discourse, "has come to signify a new gender role for women, marked by talent, assertiveness, and economic independence" (1994: 276). While some women undoubtedly identify with the "strong woman" image, I suspect that many more have read the book as catharsis. In a similar way, millions of American women (as well as women in the PRC and on Taiwan) devoured the saccharine novel, *The Bridges of Madison County* (Waller 1996), with no intention of having an adulterous affair. Anru Lee (personal communication) suggests that readers of different socioeconomic classes may come away from *Nü ch'iang-jen* with varied interpretations, for example, working class women may see the book as a tale of upward mobility, rather than primarily the story of a successful woman.

Rural Women's Lives

In rural areas and small towns of Taiwan, although traditional values and customs regarding women remain strong in many ways, here, too, modernization has had a significant impact. Young women typically have a junior high school education and often work in rural industries. Because they contribute to the family purse, they usually have more say in family decision making than did their mothers' generation. Although parents still have an important role in marriage decisions, rural couples may certainly veto any choice to which they will not agree. According to Gallin, many married women work in family businesses, often without wages, and they resent this; "they felt their husbands were withholding a resource which, they believed, gave a woman a degree of control over her life and a measure of self-respect" (1991: 14). Anru Lee has documented some of the gender contradictions of industrial development on Taiwan for women in small towns (1996, and in this volume). She shows how young women who work in a family-owned textile factory are exploited by capital and by patriarchy. Because of family strategies for survival in the declining textile industry, these daughters are often discouraged from going on to higher education. Instead, they are encouraged to work long hours for the family firm, while all the family pride is placed in brothers. Nonetheless, the woman Lee interviewed eventually returned to school, hoping to find a job that she will really like. In addition to the familial exploitation of young women, this example shows intergenerational tensions in the family, as parents' authority is increasingly challenged. Gallin (1986) argues that it is the older generation of rural women—those who are now mothers-in-law—who have seen their status in the family decline relative to their mothers. These older women usually have little or no education; they are primarily responsible for housework and farm work and perhaps care of their grandchildren, while their daughters-in-law work for wages. Social mores no longer sanction the complete domination of daughters-in-law and the traditional closeness of mothers with their adult sons is often lost as husbands establish closer and more equal relations with their wives. In short, an increase in status and power within the family for young women, to some extent, has been at the expense of the older generation of women. This is undoubtedly true in the PRC as well. Although rural areas and small towns are rapidly disappearing on Taiwan, there is still need for more research on their gendered dimensions.

The Women's Movement

While some leaders of the Taiwanese women's movement espouse values of gender equality, in the sense in which mainstream white feminists in the United States argue (e.g., sexual liberation from a double standard), other women's leaders—scholars and activists—perceive this as a misguided attempt by Western-educated Chinese women to impose a foreign value system on Taiwan's society. It should not be surprising to learn that many women activists in Taiwan refuse the self-label "feminist" (*nü-ch'üan-chu-i-che* or *nü-hsing-chu-i-che*), which is associated in the popular mind with Western values and also sometimes with sexual license. Some women's studies scholars on Taiwan are concerned with locating indigenous sources for a "women's consciousness," such as nineteenth-century antifootbinding societies, or, the May Fourth movement. Other scholars focus on modern women's organizations, such as the Warm Life Association (Wan ch'ing fü-nu hsieh-huei), an advocacy group for widows and divorcees, which may not directly promote gender equality, but nonetheless acts to empower women (Lu 1991 and in this volume). Nonetheless, the women's movement and its sympathizers have introduced into Taiwan concepts and values originating in Western feminist movements, including equal opportunity in education and work, and freedom from abuse and harassment.

The modern women's movement on Taiwan is now beginning its fourth decade and is by no means a unified institution. Advocates range from conservative "work within the status quo" people to those considered radical in Taiwan society, such as Ho Ch'ün-jui (Josephine Ho), whose recent articles on Taiwan on "sexual liberation" (*hsing chieh-fang*) have, as the cliché goes, ignited a storm of controversy. In a public demonstration against sexual harassment in 1994, Ho carried a sign reading: "I don't want sexual harassment; I want sexual climax!" (*hsing kao-ch'ao*, literally "sexual high tide"). In an equally controversial book she authored in 1993, *The Unruly Woman: Feminism and Sexual Emancipation* (Hao-shuang nü-jen, nü-hsing chu-i yü hsing chieh-fang), Josephine Ho advocates sexual liberation of Chinese women, an end to the cult of virginity for unmarried women, and for married women, an end to a lifetime of frigid love to one, probably unfaithful, man, followed by enforced celibacy in widowhood or divorce. Needless to say, Ho's "pushing the edge of the envelope" for public discourse on women's roles has been met with strong conservative reaction. Men are, of course, threatened by this challenge to their traditional sexual license. For example, unlike the PRC, which—before the reform era—had done much to eliminate public prostitution, the ROC government on Taiwan actually licensed brothels in major cities (underage prostitution is illegal, however) and for military personnel until 1992. Probably many young men lose their virginity during compulsory military service. In Taipei and Kaohsiung, the two largest cities, a few hundred licensed prostitutes continue to operate, as do hundreds of thousands of illegal ones.[8] Feminists in Taiwan are divided about whether prostitution is inherently oppressive to women or merely a legitimate and sometimes lucrative form of labor in which they may voluntarily choose to engage. Among married men, visits to prostitutes or even the practice of keeping a "little wife" are still condoned, although this attitude seems to be changing.

Whereas some feminists, such as Ho, advocate sexual liberation for women, others want to enforce a puritanical code of sexual morality on women *and* men. But Ho's advocacy of sexual liberation also threatens women; especially the woman who has devoted herself to being a "virtuous wife and good mother." For her, the "new woman" (*hsin nü-hsing*) in Taiwan's society, that is, the educated career woman, is a real threat to her marriage and to her self-image. Calls for sexual liberation only reinforce the fear that many women feel toward the "new woman." However, Ho's writings have opened up new spaces for public discourse on sexuality, including (in her words) "sexual minorities," by which, I believe, she means anyone whose sexual practices do not conform to the married, heterosexual ideal. There is also a gay liberation movement active on Taiwan (Tan 1997) in which gay men and lesbians ironically are referred to as *t'ung-chih-men* (comrades), a usage originating in Hong Kong and obviously poking fun at the Communist Chinese term, which was introduced to replace and obviate hierarchical titles.

Conclusions

Mainstream Western feminists have pointed to women's labor force participation and familial roles as particularly important sites for the struggle over gender equality. Socialist feminists in particular draw on the work of Engels to argue that economic independence through paid work, along with public childcare and an end to kinship structures that subordinate females to male descent groups, are necessary prerequisites for the true liberation of women. In the context of the Chinese societies in the PRC and on Taiwan, these assertions generate a number of questions. First, how have modernization processes of socialism versus capitalism affected progress toward women's liberation? Are there distinct models of modernization based on different modes of production or different cultural contexts? Is there an East Asian model of modernity, and, if so, can women be liberated within it? Do Chinese women themselves see "liberation" in the same light that Western feminists do?

Consider first the issue of paid labor. Women in the PRC clearly participate in the labor force in higher numbers than do women on Taiwan (70 percent versus 45 percent; see Hsieh and Burgess 1994), and there is some evidence that this contributes to greater equality in terms of marital role attitudes, if not behavior. Hsieh and Burgess (1994) found that college students in the PRC expressed more egalitarian attitudes toward the importance of the wife's career and role alterations between husband and wife (e.g., the woman having a higher education level); whereas college students on Taiwan had more egalitarian attitudes toward institutionalized equality, such as legal rights to family property or responsibility for family finances. Unsurprisingly, in both societies, male students expressed more traditional attitudes than did female students. This high labor force participation of women in the PRC is associated with the government's call for economic development, and, as Whyte and Parish (1984) note, is clearly higher than in other developing and even developed countries; only advanced socialist countries come close. But does participation in paid labor allow women more independence and autonomy? We have seen that both on Taiwan and in the PRC, women are usually relegated to low-paying, often menial jobs, although this statement is more accurate about the PRC than Taiwan. In both societies women have the second shift to do when they return home. However, because of the relative lack of consumer goods and services in the PRC, housework is considerably more onerous there than on more economically advanced Taiwan. To the extent that women who make an economic contribution to the family, either as unmarried daughters or wives and mothers, have more power within the family, women in the PRC with their higher labor force participation seem to be in better shape to achieve equality than are their sisters on Taiwan.

Contradictory trends for women in the current reform era in the PRC make generalizations difficult. Urban women are increasingly becoming marginalized within the reform policies, while rural women have more employment opportunities than before but also more responsibilities in farm work and domestic labor. In the cities of Taiwan, many women and men still feel that women's most important job is the household and childcare; if they work outside the home, their earnings are viewed as supplemental. Career women are frustrated by subtle and not-so-subtle discrimination in the workplace and by the familiar demands of the second shift. Comparing groups of college students in the PRC and on Taiwan, Hsieh and Burgess hypothesized that marital attitudes would be more egalitarian in the PRC, and were surprised to find that this was not so for all measures. They speculate that a "regressive trend in gender equality in post-Mao China may have occurred," while on Taiwan, due to "increasing contacts with Western societies and their egalitarian ideology during the past decade, the people in Taiwan may have advanced further in their views" (Hsieh and Burgess 1994: 417).

I agree that Western feminist ideas have influenced the women's movement on Taiwan, but this may also be seen as the expected outcome of modernization processes that open up spaces in which to challenge traditional values and practices. And the regression noted by Hsieh and Burgess as well as by many other scholars (e.g., Rofel 1994) regarding women's liberation in the PRC seems to me to be largely an effect of changing economic circumstances as the PRC is pulled inexorably into the world capitalist system. In that process, women become surplus labor, pulled into or pushed out of the workforce as the needs of capital dictate. Recent economic changes in the PRC as they affect women's status resemble Taiwan in its early stages of industrialization in the 1960s and support the claim that modernization has similar effects in diverse societies. We would also expect the PRC to resemble East European countries, which are also attempting to integrate into the global economy. These countries have a similar history of official rhetoric concerning the necessity of liberating women, which would suggest that their current trajectories will differ somewhat from a society like Taiwan's, which has evolved from a state capitalist system under authoritarian rule to a free market democracy.

In the PRC, the Maoist state discourse, which denied femaleness to women, has been followed predictably in the reform era by a reactionary emphasis on "essential woman." This fits neatly with the "frontier capitalism" brought about by the state's new economic policies. Thus, there is anecdotal evidence to suggest that the feminine mystique is just around the corner for increasingly prosperous urban families, and this is combined with a regressive trend toward a sexual double standard. At the 1997 Association for Asian Studies meeting, participants in panels on gender issues in the PRC mentioned the emergence of a new class of businessmen whose status was enhanced if he could afford a stay-at-home wife *and* a mistress on the side! Faced with increasing discrimination in the workplace (or the difficulty of finding employment in the first place), we should not be surprised to learn that many women prefer to make home and family life their first priority. The commodification of women is evidenced in a robust beauty industry, the widespread sex trade, and traffic in women and girls. For those women in the PRC who do wish to have a career outside of sex work, I predict an uphill battle. Insofar as Taiwan's economy is more advanced, women should have more success in the workplace, although, as we have seen, they also face such issues as discrimination and harassment.

In light of the move to a "socialist-market" economy in the PRC, it may be too late to usefully compare the status of Chinese women under socialism versus capitalism. Even though socialism as an economic system has been shown to produce less overall prosperity than capitalist economies do, this should not negate the real advances that Chinese women in the PRC have made since 1949. Whether or not they would have made similar progress under KMT-led policies in a state capitalist system, we shall never know.

Turning now to the Confucian patriarchal family and its modern transformation, both in the PRC and on Taiwan, I see enduring cultural values about men and women and their places in society. While there are clear differences between rural and urban populations in both societies, the patrilineal principle, hierarchical relations between the generations, and the duties of filial piety still have a strong, although diminished, hold on the individual's imagination. There is some evidence that the hegemonic model of patrilineal and patrilocal family structure in the countryside of the PRC is challenged in practice. Judd (1986) has described the continuing ties between a married woman and her natal family, which include "dual residence" (especially during the first year of marriage), frequent visiting, and emotional and financial help when possible. It is clear from the comparative ethnographic record and from specific research in Chinese societies that the patrilineal-patrilocal family structure is disadvantageous to women. Judd argues that the solution previously encouraged by the government, uxorilocal (that is, matrilocal) residence, is simply not viable. With smaller families, sometimes consisting of only one son, parents are unwilling to allow their sons to marry into the wife's family; in addition, the son's labor and assistance in old age is critical. However, informally, many rural families have found other solutions to the patrilocal trap, such as intravillage marriage, or marriage between people from neighboring villages, so that a woman may have continuing ties to her natal family. Judd also notes that the revised Marriage Law of 1981 makes daughters as well as sons responsible for the care of elderly parents. Together, these trends suggest that Chinese rural women as agents of change creatively manipulate a structural system that is biased against them.

On Taiwan, modernization processes have resulted in urbanization, smaller families, more nuclear family patterns, an end to the complete domination of the younger generation by the older, and a strengthening of the spousal tie at the expense of the parent-child one. Yet here also, enduring family ties and patrilineal principles remain. Women on Taiwan have been more successful in a legal sense in realizing equality with men in the family (e.g., concerning inheritance and child custody), although these legal victories have not always been realized in practice. Yet, despite evidence of their continued subordination within the family, most women on Taiwan do not see it as a source of oppression from which they need to be liberated. In looking at women, work, and family on Taiwan, Skoggard (1998: 4) ponders an issue that many First World feminists have trouble accepting, "Why [do] Third World women remain loyal to the family and endure such hardship?" He argues that because of the corporate nature of family property in Taiwan's society, both women and men have a stake in it; in addition, "under capitalism, the family becomes a site of resistance to the alienation of capitalist social relations" (Skoggard 1998: 4). The family as a refuge for women is also a point made by many women of color in the United States, as Cole (1986) points out; these women argue that classism and racism in American society are more fundamental problems for them than is patriarchy. Feminism for Chinese women does not necessarily mean liberation from the family, as it does for many second-wave feminists in the West. Anthropologist Aihwa Ong agrees:

> By giving up our accustomed ways of looking at non-western women, we may begin to understand better. We may come to accept their living according to their own cultural interpretations of a changing world, and not simply acted upon by inherited traditions and modernization projects. They may not seek our goal of secularized autonomy, nor renounce the bonds of family and community. (Ong 1994: 379)

Although both men and women seek some autonomy from the Confucian patriarchal family of the past, they probably do not seek independence in the Western sense. Chinese on both sides of the Taiwan strait are still deeply attached to family, and both these Chinese societies continue to be "sociocentric" rather than "egocentric," in emphasizing interconnectedness among people, and the rights and obligations that adhere to specific social roles (Hsu 1985). As has been emphasized in many places, the Western, in some ways peculiarly American, focus on individual rights and personal autonomy remains largely outside the value system of Chinese societies.

And now to the questions of a distinctive "East Asian modernity" and women's liberation within it. Beginning in the nineteenth century, women's emancipation from the Confucian patriarchal family was used as a trope of imagined modernity, both for Chinese reformers and revolutionaries on the mainland and for Taiwanese intellectuals of colonial Taiwan. In the twentieth century, the Chinese Communist Party and the Nationalist Party envisioned dramatically different paths to women's liberation. For both parties, the emancipation of women was not the central concern, rather, it was to be an index of modern nationhood. Both the bourgeois and the Communist visions of gender equality were, of course, imported from the West. Does this mean it is largely irrelevant for Chinese women? I think not. Problems of female infanticide and neglect, wife beating, forced prostitution, and denial of equal educational and employment opportunities are truly global women's issues and are perceived by the international community as violations of human rights. Recognition of these problems and solutions to them must come largely from women and men within their own communities. Other issues dear to the hearts of Western feminists, such as sexual liberation and freedom from family constraints, may not be relevant to most Chinese women. Again, the issues and the solutions must be generated locally. I will leave the question of an "East Asian modernity" to more qualified scholars. However, I agree with Gao (1994: 90) that, "the immediate goal of modernization is to develop the economy, not to improve women's status" and that modernization has both positive and negative effects for women. We have seen this to be true for both socialist and capitalist modernization in these Chinese societies.

While the progress of women's liberation on Taiwan may seem much more familiar to a North American audience than is the process in the PRC, there are significant differences. We should not assume that, just because Taiwan is a newly industrialized society, the quest for modernity has the same goals or outcomes as that in Western societies in general and U.S. society in particular. In conclusion, I believe that we—Western scholars—must be sensitive to the need to be self-reflexive about our formulations of "women's liberation," and to avoid making the intellectual error that Aihwa Ong (1994) warns against: participating in the neocolonial enterprise of constructing a "nonfeminist other" as a foil for our own yearnings. The process of women's liberation from Chinese patriarchy is taking different forms in the PRC and on Taiwan and cannot be expected to have the same outcomes in both places. To the extent that the battle is waged against a similar set of values, beliefs, and customs, we can expect the solutions to look similar. To the extent that these Chinese societies have distinct modern histories, we might see diverging outcomes. In either case, we should not make the assumption that the evolution of women's liberation in either Chinese society will resemble that of our own.

Notes

This chapter originated as an invited lecture, entitled "Women's Liberation in China and Taiwan: Historical, Cultural, and Comparative Perspectives," presented at the University of Northern Iowa (UNI) History Department, Phi Alpha Theta colloquium series, and was cosponsored by the UNI Women's Studies program. Some of this material is drawn from an unpublished paper coauthored with Heather Dolphin (Dolphin and Farris, undated). A much-revised version of this paper was presented at the Second Annual Conference on the History and Culture of Taiwan, organized by the Research Group for Taiwanese History and Culture, sponsored by the Department of East Asian Languages and Literatures, Columbia University, August 28–31, 1997, in New York, and again at the symposium "Social and Political Change in Postwar Taiwan," sponsored by the Joint Center for East Asian Studies, Washington University and the University of Missouri—St. Louis, with the Chiang Ching-kuo Foundation, October 16–18, 1997. The paper was also presented at the Graduate Institute of Sociology at Tsing-hua University in Hsinchu, Taiwan, in April 1999. I am grateful for participant comments at these forums. In particular, I thank Anru Lee, Cal Clark, Murray Rubinstein, Alan Wachman, Charles Jones, Douglas Fix, and Chou Bih-er for their input, while reserving responsibility for all errors. Special thanks to Hsin-yi Lu for allowing me to cite her unpublished conference paper (revised version in this volume). Earlier portions of this chapter appeared as "Contradictory Implications of Socialism and Capitalism Under 'East Asian Modernity' in China and Taiwan," in *Democracy and the Status of Women in East Asia*, ed. Rose J. Lee and Cal Clark (Boulder: Lynne Rienner, 2000).

1. I do wonder, however, why it is that I, as a Western female scholar, feel compelled to state my various subject positions (read: biases), while most Western male scholars do not feel this urge.

2. See, for example, Nandita Gandhi and Nandita Shah (1993) who discuss the many problems that the Indian women's movement faces as it confronts issues like illiteracy and myriad forms of violence against women, including dowry deaths and female infanticide.

3. As noted above in the section on women in Republican politics, Elisabeth Croll (1978) also used this term to describe the policies of the KMT toward women in the 1920s and 1930s on the mainland. I believe it is more accurately used for the postwar period of the ROC on Taiwan, where rising prosperity made a middle-class life of leisured dependency possible for a much larger percentage of the population.

4. I am leaving out here Croll's figures on vocational and technical high school enrollments; the high schools mentioned are on the "college track."

5. See, for example, the series of translation articles on employment and education of Chinese women in Rosen (1987, 1988).

6. See, for example, the interviews with four women leaders in the *Free China Review* (Underwood 1994).

7. In the past decade, there has been an increasing number of female sex workers from the PRC. They were either brought to Taiwan believing legitimate work or marriage awaited them, or came willingly to work the trade. Many feminists in Taiwan are ambivalent about highlighting the exploitation of these women, as nationalistic sentiment wars with feelings of sisterhood.

8. Prostitution was made illegal in Taipei in 1999, but because of protests from legal sex workers, a grace period was extended until 2000, by then-mayor Chen Shui-bian. In 2001, Mayor Ma Ying-cheou of the KMT, who followed Chen in office, made the mistake of declaring that in a few months he would wipe out the illegal prostitution remaining in Taipei. This has not happened yet!

References

Andors, Phyllis. 1983. *The Unfinished Liberation of Chinese Women, 1949–1980.* Bloomington: Indiana University Press.

Arrigo, Linda. 1993. "Review of *Women in Taiwan Politics* (Chou, Clark, and Clark) and *The Chosen Women in Korean Politics* (Soh Chung-Hee)." *Bulletin of Concerned Asian Scholars* 25, no. 1: 70–80.

———. 1991. "The Dimensions of Gender Ideology Among Young Working Women in Taiwan." Paper presented at SUNY Conversations in the Disciplines: Gender and Industrialization in Asia. State University of New York, Purchase, May 3–4.

———. 1984. "Taiwan Electronics Workers." In *Lives: Chinese Working Women*, ed. M. Sheridan and J. Salaff, 123–44. Bloomington: Indiana University Press.

Baku, Hugh D. 1980. *Chinese Family and Kinship.* New York: Columbia University Press.

Barlow, Tani. 1997a. "Introduction: On 'Colonial Modernity'." In *Formations of Colonial Modernity in East Asia*, ed. Barlow, 1–20. Durham: Duke University Press.

———. 1997b. "Women at the Close of the Maoist Era in the Polemics of Li Xiaojiang and Her Associates." In *The Politics of Culture in the Shadow of Capital*, ed. Lisa Lowe and David Lloyd, 506–44. Durham: Duke University Press.

————. 1994. "Theorizing Woman: Funu, Guojia, Jiating." In *Body, Subject, and Power in China*, ed. Angela Zito and Tani Barlow, 25–52 . Chicago: University of Chicago Press.

Chang, Ming-cheng. 1980. "The Modernization of Taiwan and Behavioral Tendencies of Women in Young Adulthood" (in Chinese). *Bulletin of the Institute of Economics* 11, no. 10: 209–26. Nankang, Taiwan: Academia Sinica.

Chen, Ching-chih. 1994. "The Japanese Ideal and Ideas of Assimilation in Taiwan, 1895–1945." In *Unbound Taiwan: Closeups from a Distance*, ed. Marshall Johnson and Fred Y.L. Chiu, 31–48. Chicago: Center for East Asian Studies, University of Chicago.

Chen, Yi-ping. 1994. "Hsin 'ho-hsin chia-t'ing'" (The New "Nuclear Family"). *Bulletin of the Women's Research Program* 32, no. 6: 14–15. Population Studies Center, Women's Research Program, National Taiwan University (ROC).

Chiang, Lan-hun Nora, and Ku Yenlin. 1985. *Past and Current Status of Women in Taiwan*. Women's Research Program, Population Studies Center, National Taiwan University (ROC).

Chou, Bih-er. 1994. "Changing Patterns of Women's Employment in Taiwan, 1966–1986." In Rubinstein, ed., *The Other Taiwan, 1945 to the Present*, 305–29.

Chou, Bih-er, Cal Clark, and Janet Clark. 1990. *Women in Taiwan Politics: Overcoming Barriers to Women's Participation in a Modernizing Society*. Boulder: Lynne Rienner.

Chow, Rey. 1991. *Woman and Chinese Modernity: The Politics of Reading Between West and East*. Minneapolis: University of Minnesota Press.

Cohen, Myron. 1976. *House United, House Divided: The Chinese Family in Taiwan*. New York: Columbia University Press.

Cole, Johnnetta, ed. 1986. *All American Women: Lines That Divide, Ties That Bind*. New York: Free Press.

Coombs, Lolagene. 1980. "Economic Factors in Fertility Decisions: The Role of Costs and Benefits." Institute of Economics, *Academia Economic Papers* 8, no. 2: 89–122. Nankang, Academia Sinica.

Croll, Elisabeth. 1995. *Changing Identities of Chinese Women: Rhetoric, Experience and Self-Perception in Twentieth-Century China*. London: Hong Kong University Press, Zed Books.

————. 1978. "'The Feminine Mystique': Guomindang China." In *Feminism and Socialism in China*, ed. Croll, ch. 4. London: Routledge and Kegan Paul.

Davin, Delia. 1975. "The Women's Movement in the People's Republic of China: A Survey." In *Women Cross-Culturally*, ed. Ruby Rohrlic-Leavitt, 457–69. The Hague: Mouton.

Diamond, Norma. 1975a. "Collectivization, Kinship, and the Status of Rural Women in China." In Reiter, ed., *Toward an Anthropology of Women*, 372–98.

————. 1975b. "Women Under Kuomintang Rule: Variations on the Feminine Mystique." *Modern China* 1, no. 1: 3–45.

————. 1973. "The Status of Women in Taiwan: One Step Forward, Two Steps Back." In *Women in China*, ed. Marilyn Young, 211–42. Ann Arbor: Center for Chinese Studies, University of Michigan.

Dolphin, Heather, and Catherine Farris. Undated. "'This Job Is Not Suitable for a Girl!': Factors Contributing to Diversity in Career Choices Among Chinese Women Studying International Trade in Guangxi Province."

Farris, Catherine S., and Marshall Johnson, eds. 1996. "Gender in the *Wai* (Outer) World." *Taiwan Studies* 1, no. 4 (Winter).

————. 1990. "The Social Discourse on Women's Roles in Taiwan: A Textual Analysis." In *Michigan Discussions in Anthropology*, special issue on Gender Transformations (Spring 1990): 89–105. Reprinted in Rubinstein, ed., *The Other Taiwan: 1945 to the Present*.

————. 1993. "Women, Work, and Childcare in Taiwan: Changing Family Dynamics in a Chinese Society." *American Asian Review* 11, no. 3 (Fall 1993): 501–18.

Galenson, Walter. 1979. *Economic Growth and Structural Change in Taiwan*. Ithaca: Cornell University Press.

Gallin, Rita. 1991. "State, Gender, and the Organization of Business in Rural Taiwan." In

Trajectories of Patriarchy and Development, ed. Valentine Moghadam. Oxford: Clarendon.

———. 1986. "Mothers-in-law and Daughters-in-law: Intergenerational Relations Within the Chinese Family in Taiwan." *Journal of Cross-cultural Gerontology* 1: 31–49.

——— . 1984. "Women, the Family, and the Political Economy of Taiwan." *Journal of Peasant Studies* 12, no. 1: 76–92.

Gandhi, Nandita, and Nandita Shah. 1993. *The Issue at Stake: Theory and Practice in the Contemporary Women's Movement in India*. New Delhi: Kali for Women.

Gao, Xiaoxian. 1994. "Chinese Modernization and Changes in the Social Status of Rural Women." In Gilmartin et al., eds., *Engendering China*, 80–100.

Gates, Hill. 1989. "The Commoditization of Chinese Women." *Signs* 14, no. 4: 799–832.

Gilmartin, Christina. 1993. "Gender in the Formation of a Communist Body Politic." *Modern China* 19, no. 3 (July): 299–329.

Gilmartin, Christina; Gail Hershatter; Lisel Rofel; and Tyrene White, eds. 1994. *Engendering China: Women, Culture, and the State*. Cambridge: Harvard University Press.

Gold, Thomas B. 1996. "Taiwan Society at the *Fin de Siècle*." *China Quarterly*, no. 148 (December): 1091–114.

———. 1986. *State and Society in the Taiwan Miracle*. Armonk, NY: M.E. Sharpe.

Greenhalgh, Susan, and Jiali Li. 1995. "Engendering Reproductive Policy and Practice in Peasant China: For a Feminist Demography of Reproduction." *Signs* 20, no. 3: 601–41.

Harrell, Stevan. 1994. "Playing in the Valley: A Metonym of Modernization in Taiwan." In Harrell and Huang, eds., *Cultural Change in Postwar Taiwan*, 161–83.

Harrell, Stevan, and Huang Chun-chieh, eds. 1994. *Cultural Change in Postwar Taiwan*. Boulder, CO: Westview Press.

Hershatter, Gail. 1997. *Dangerous Pleasures: Prostitution in Twentieth-Century Shanghai*. Berkeley: University of California Press.

———. 1996. "Sexing Modern China." In *Remapping China: Fissures in Historical Terrain*, ed. Hershatter, Emily Honig, Jonathan Lipman, and Randall Stross, 77–93. Stanford: Stanford University Press.

Ho, Ch'ün-jui (Josephine Ho). 1993. *Hao-shuang nü-jen, nü-hsing chu-i yü hsing chieh-fang* (The Unruly Woman: Feminism and Sexual Emancipation). Taipei: Shih-pao.

Honig, Emily, and Gail Hershatter. 1988. *Personal Voices: Chinese Women in the 1980s*. Stanford: Stanford University Press.

Hsieh, Hsiao-chin. 1997. "Gender Differences in Educational Opportunity in Taiwan: Two Taipei Junior High Schools." *Taiwan Studies* 1, no. 4 (Winter 1995–96): 6–43.

Hsieh, Kuang-hua, and Robert Burgess. 1994. "Marital Role Attitudes and Expected Role Behaviors of College Youth in Mainland China and Taiwan." *Journal of Family Issues* 15, no. 3 (September): 403–23.

Hsu, Francis. 1985. "The Self in Cross-cultural Perspective." In *Culture and Self: Asian and Western Perspectives*, ed. Anthony Marsella, George DeVos, and Francis Hsu, 24–55. New York: Tavistock.

Hu, T'ai-li. 1985. "The Influence of Taiwan's Rural Industrialization on Women's Status" (in Chinese). *Proceedings of the Conference on the Role of Women in the National Development Process in Taiwan* 2: 337–56. Taipei: National Taiwan University, Population Studies Center.

Huang, Anita. 1997. "Women Wronged." *Free China Review* (February): 4–11.

Hwang, Jim. 1997. "Glass Ceilings, Transparent Walls." *Free China Review* (February): 12–17.

Jen Ta-jung. 1978. "Verification of a Matriarchal System in Ancient China" (in Chinese). In *Chung-kuo fu nu shih lun chi* (Collected Essays on the History of Chinese Women), ed. Pao Chia-lin, 1–10. Taipei: Mutong.

Judd, Ellen. 1994. *Gender and Power in Rural North China.* Stanford: Stanford University Press.

———. 1986. *"Niangjia:* Chinese Women and Their Natal Families." *Journal of Asian Studies* 48, no. 3: 525–44.

Ku, Yenlin. 1996. "Interaction Between the Women's Movement and Policy Formation." In Farris and Johnson eds., *Taiwan Studies,* 1996, 44–72.

———. 1989. "The Feminist's Movement in Taiwan, 1972–1987." *Bulletin of Concerned Asian Scholars* 21, no. 1.

Kung, Lydia. 1994 [1973]. *Factory Women in Taiwan.* New York: Columbia University Press.

———. 1984. "Taiwan Garment Workers." In Sheridan and Salaff, eds., *Lives: Chinese Working Women,* 109–22.

Lang, Olga. 1946. *Chinese Family and Society.* New Haven: Yale University Press. Reprinted, Hamden, CT: Archon Books, 1968.

Lee, Anru. 1996. "A Tale of Two Sisters: Gender in Taiwan's Small-Scale Industry." In *Anthropology for a Small Planet: Culture and Community in Global Perspective,* ed. Anthony Marcus, 67–79. St. James, NY: Brandywine Press.

Lee, Rose J. 1997. "Democratization, Electoral Systems, and Women's Representation: A Comparative Study of Women's Legislative Participation in South Korea and Taiwan." *Pacific Focus* 11, no. 1 (Spring): 67–89.

Li, Tung-ming. 1984. "The Study of Newly Married Couples' Family Planning Knowledge, Attitudes, and Practices" (in Chinese). *Kung-kung wei-sheng* (Public Health): 384–400. Taipei: Taiwan Provincial Public Health Institute.

Li, Xiaojiang, and Xiaodan Zhang. 1994. "Creating a Space for Women: Women's Studies in China in the 1980s." *Signs* 20, no. 1 (Autumn):137–51.

Liu, Paul. 1983. "Trends in Female Labor Force Participation in Taiwan: The Transition Towards Higher Technological Activities." *Academia Economic Papers* 11, no. 1: 293–323. Nankang: Academia Sinica, Institute of Economics.

Lu, Annette Hsiu-lien. 1994. "Women's Liberation: The Taiwanese Experience." In Rubinstein, ed., *The Other Taiwan,* 289–304.

———. 2000 [1974]. *Hsin nü-hsing-chu-i* (New Feminism). Taipei: Pioneer Press.

Lu, Hsin-yi. 1997. "Colonial Modernity and Its Gendered Aspect, Constructing 'New Women' in Colonial Taiwan." Paper presented at the second annual Conference on the History and Culture of Taiwan, Columbia University, New York, August.

Lu, Hwei-syin. 1991. "Women's Self-growth Groups and Empowerment of the 'Uterine Family' in Taiwan." *Bulletin of the Institute of Ethnology,* Academia Sinica 71: 29–62.

Mohanty, Chandra Talpade. 1991 "Under Western Eyes: Feminist Scholarship and Colonial Discourses." *Boundary* 2, 12 (3)/13 (1): 333–58.

Molyneux, Maxine. 1981 "Women in Socialist Societies: Problems of Theory and Practice." In *Of Marriage and the Market: Women's Subordination in International Perspectives,* ed. Kate Young, Carol Wolkowitz, and Roslyn McCullagh, 167–201. London: CSE Books.

Ong, Aihwa. 1994 [1988]. "Colonialism and Modernity: Feminist Re-presentations of Women in Non-Western Societies." *Inscriptions* 3, no. 4: 79–93. Reprinted in *Theorizing Feminism: Parallel Trends in the Humanities and Social Sciences,* ed. Anne Herrmann and Abigal Stewart, 372–81. Boulder: Westview Press.

Ono, Kazuko. 1989. *Chinese Women in a Century of Revolution, 1850–1950.* Ed. Joshua Fogel. Stanford: Stanford University Press.

Pasternak, Burton; Carol Ember; and Melvin Ember. 1997. *Sex, Gender, and Kinship: A Cross-Cultural Perspective.* Upper Saddle River, NJ: Prentice-Hall.

Pearson, R., and A. Underhill. 1987. "The Chinese Neolithic: Recent Trends in Research." *American Anthropologist* 89, no. 4: 807–22.

Rai, Shirin M. 1994. "Modernization and Gender: Education and Employment in Post-Mao China." *Gender and Education* 6, no. 2: 119–29.

Record, Jane, and Wilson Record. 1976."Totalist and Pluralist Views of Women's Liberation: Some Reflections on the Chinese and American Settings." *Social Problems* 23, no. 4 (April): 402–14.

Reiter, Ranya R. 1975. *Toward an Anthropology of Women.* New York and London: Monthly Review Press.

Rofel, Lisa. 1994. "Liberation Nostalgia and a Yearning for Modernity," In Gilmartin et al., eds., *Engendering China,* 226–49.

Rosen, Stanley, ed. 1987. "Chinese Women." *Chinese Sociology and Anthropology* 19, no. 1 (Fall).

———. 1988. "Chinese Women." *Chinese Sociology and Anthropology* 20, no. 2 (Spring).

Rubin, Gayle. 1975. "The Traffic in Women: Notes on the 'Political Economy' of Sex." In Reiter, ed., *Toward an Anthropology of Women,* 157–210.

Rubinstein, Murray A., ed. 1994. *The Other Taiwan: 1945 to the Present.* Armonk, NY: M.E. Sharpe.

Sacks, Karen. 1975. "Engels Revisited: Women, the Organization of Production, and Private Property." In Reiter, ed., *Toward an Anthropology of Women,* 211–34.

Scott, Joan W. 1994 [1988]. "Deconstructing Equality Versus Difference: Or, The Uses of Poststructuralist Theory for Feminism." *Feminist Studies* 14, no. 1: 33–50. Reprinted in Herrmann and Stewart, eds., *Theorizing Feminism,* 358–71.

Selva, Roger M. 1995. *Taipei.* New York: John Wiley.

Sheridan, Mary, and Janet Salaff, eds. 1984. *Lives: Chinese Working Women.* Bloomington: Indiana University Press.

Skoggard, Ian. 1998. "Women's Work and Family Property in Taiwan's Postwar Development."

Spence, Jonathan D. 1990. *The Search for Modern China.* New York: Norton.

Stacey, Judith. 1983. *Patriarchy and Socialist Revolution in China.* Berkeley: University of California Press.

Sung, Mei-hwa. 1994. "Feminist Consciousness in the Contemporary Fiction of Taiwan." In Harrell and Huang, eds., *Cultural Change in Postwar Taiwan,* 275–93.

Tan, Chong-kee. 1997 "The Rise of Lesbian Discourse in Contemporary Taiwan." Paper presented at the second annual Conference on the History and Culture of Taiwan, Columbia University, New York, August.

Teng, Jinhua Emma. 1996. "The Construction of the 'Traditional Chinese Woman' in the Western Academy: A Critical Review." *Signs* 22, no. 1: 115–51.

Tsui, Yi-lan, Elaine. 1985. *Are Married Daughters 'Spilled Water'? A Study of Working Women in Urban Taiwan.* Women's Research Program, monograph 4, National Taiwan University, Population Studies Center, Taipei.

Tsurumi, E. Patricia. 1977. *Japanese Colonial Education in Taiwan.* Cambridge: Harvard University Press.

Tu, Weiming. 1996. "Cultural Identity and the Politics of Recognition in Contemporary Taiwan." *China Quarterly,* no. 148: 1115–40.

———. 1991. "Cultural China: The Periphery as the Center." *Daedalus: Journal of the American Academy of Arts and Sciences* 120, no. 2 (Spring): 1–32.

Underwood, Laurie. 1994. "Women in Office." *Free China Review* (May): 38–43.

Waller, Robert. 1996. *The Bridges of Madison County.* New York: Warner Books.

Waltner, Ann. 1996. "Recent Scholarship on Chinese Women." *Signs* 21, no. 2 (Winter): 410–28.

Wan, Shanping. 1988. "The Emergence of Women's Studies in China." *Women's Studies International Forum* 11, no. 5: 455–64.

Whyte, Martin K. 1978. *The Status of Women in Preindustrial Societies.* Princeton, N.J.: Princeton University Press.

Whyte, Martin K., and William Parish. 1984. *Urban Life in Contemporary China*. Chicago: University of Chicago Press.

Winckler, Edwin. 1994. "Cultural Policy on Postwar Taiwan." In Harrell and Huang, eds., *Cultural Change in Postwar Taiwan*, 22–46.

Wolf, Arthur, and Chieh-shan Huang. 1980. *Marriage and Adoption in China, 1845–1945*. Stanford: Stanford University Press.

Wolf, Margery. 1985. *Revolution Postponed: Women in Contemporary China*. Stanford: Stanford University Press.

———. 1972. *Women and the Family in Rural Taiwan*. Stanford: Stanford University Press.

Yang, Tsui. 1993. *Women's Liberation Movement in Taiwan Under Japanese Occupation* (in Chinese). Taipei: Shih-pao.

Yu, Chien-ming. 1996. "Midwives During the Japanese Occupation." In Farris and Johnson, eds., *Taiwan Studies*, 1996, 6–48.

Zheng, Wang. 1997. "Maoism, Feminism, and the U.N. Conference on Women: Women's Studies Research in Contemporary China." *Journal of Women's History* 8, no. 4 (Winter): 126–52.

Zinn, Maxine Baca, and Bonnie Thornton Dill. 1994. *Women of Color in U.S. Society*. Philadelphia: Temple University Press.

About the Editors and Contributors

The Editors

Catherine Farris is a linguistic anthropologist who received the Ph.D. from the University of Washington and has taught at the Universities of Michigan, Northern Iowa, St. Edward's, and Tsing Hua University in Taiwan. She has been doing research on Taiwan since 1983 and has written numerous articles that cover topics including gender development in childhood, the nuances of male-female sociolinguistic interaction, and Taiwanese feminism as reflected in popular media. She now lives in Austin, Texas, where she is an independent trainer and consultant on cross-cultural communication, global diversity and greater China. For the 2004-2005 academic year, Catherine will be visiting Senior Lecturer at the University of Texas, Department of Asian Studies.

Anru Lee did her Ph.D. work at the Graduate Center of the City University of New York. She is now a member of the Department of Anthropology at John Jay College of Criminal Justice, City University of New York. She is the author of *In the Name of Harmony and Prosperity: Labor and Gender Politics in Taiwan's Economic Restructuring* (SUNY Press, 2004).

Murray A. Rubinstein received his Ph.D. in history at New York University and has spent his academic career as a member of the History Department of Baruch College of the City University of New York. He is now chair of the Asian/Asian-American Studies Program at Baruch. He has written two monographs and edited four books on Christianity in China and Taiwan.

The Contributors

Susan Mann is currently a member of the Department of History at the University of California, Davis, and was president of the Association for Asian Studies (1999–2000). She specializes in the history of late Imperial China and is regarded as one of the pioneers of the study of Chinese women's history.

Ping-chen Hsiung did her Ph.D. on the history of late imperial China at Brown University. She is a member of the Institute of Modern History at the Academia

Sinica in Taiwan. She has also taught in major universities in the United States. Her research and writing focuses upon the history of childhood and on the history of health care in imperial China. She has also helped redefine the nature of the high-school history curriculum on Taiwan.

Emma Teng did her doctoral work in Chinese literature at Harvard University. She is now a member of the history faculty of the Massachusetts Institute of Technology, specializing in Asian-American literature and Chinese literature. Her main area of research is Chinese colonial travel literature and the colonization of Taiwan. She has published a book on the history of Taiwan's international relations and articles on Chinese women's studies, gender in Asian-American literature, and Chinese travel literature.

Sue Gronewold teaches Asian history and women's studies in the History Department of Kean University in New Jersey. Her research interests focus on women in twentieth-century China and on cultural encounters between Chinese and Western women. Her book, *Beautiful Merchandise: Prostitution in China 1860–1937*, was published by Haworth Press (1982). She is revising for publication her 1996 Columbia University dissertation, "Encountering Hope: The Door of Hope Mission in Shanghai and Taipei 1900–1976."

Hsin-yi Lu obtained her Ph.D. in anthropology at the University of Washington. She is assistant professor in social and behavioral sciences at the University of Southern Maine at Lewiston-Auburn, where she teaches cultural anthropology and global studies. She is the author of *The Politics of Locality: Making a Nation of Communities in Taiwan* (Routledge, 2002).

Fang-chih Irene Yang did her Ph.D in speech communication at the University of Illinois at Urbana-Champaign and most recently joined the faculty in the Department of English of National Dong-Hwa University in Hualien, Taiwan. She has published articles and given conference papers on issues related to media, feminism, and Taiwanese educational opportunities.

Robert M. Marsh, a professor of sociology at Brown University, is a prominent scholar of social change on Taiwan. His most recent book is *The Great Transformation: Social Change in Taipei Since the 1960s* (M.E. Sharpe, 1996). His current research focuses on social capital, organizational participation, and trust in Taiwan.

Avron Boretz received his Ph.D. in anthropology from Cornell University. He is a member of the faculty in the Department of Asian Studies and the Center for East Asian Studies at the University of Texas at Austin. He has done extensive research on religious groups and martial arts troupes in southeastern Taiwan and on gender relations on Taiwan and has published articles in a number of recent edited volumes both in Taiwan and in the United States.

Paul E. Festa is a Ph.D. candidate in anthropology at Cornell University and is currently completing a doctoral dissertation on friendship, masculinity, and the nation in Taiwan. He is the author of "Mahjong Politics in Contemporary China: Civility, Chineseness, and Mass Culture," in *Positions: East Asia Cultures Critique* (forthcoming).

Hwei-syin Lu has a Ph.D. in anthropology from the University of Illinois at Urbana-Champaign. She was a member of the Institute of Ethnology, Academia Sinica, for many years, doing research and writing important articles about issues concerning women on Taiwan. She is currently on the faculty of the Institute of Religion and Culture at Tzu Chi University in Hualien, Taiwan.

Yu-hsiu Liu is a professor of English in the Department of Foreign Languages and Literatures at National Taiwan University. She is an influential figure on gender issues and grassroots organization empowerment in Taiwan.

Ping-chun Hsiung did her Ph.D. in sociology at the University of California, Los Angeles, and teaches sociology at the Scarborough College/University of Toronto. She does research on women in the workplace, feminism, and related topics. She has written *Living Rooms as Factories: Class, Gender, and the Satellite Factory System in Taiwan* (Temple University Press, 1996). She also co-edited, with Maria Jaschok and Cecilia N. Milwertz, *Chinese Women Organizing: Cadres, Feminists, Muslims, Queers* (Berg Publishers, 2002).

Richard C. Kagan is a member of the history faculty at Hamline University in St. Paul, Minnesota. He has written and edited numerous books and articles on religion and society in Taiwan, China, and Southeast Asia.

Index